W9-AEA-212

A HOMERIC DICTIONARY

FOR SCHOOLS AND COLLEGES

Based Upon the German of

GEORG AUTENRIETH

Translated by

ROBERT P. KEEP

Revised by

ISAAC FLAGG

NORMAN: UNIVERSITY OF OKLAHOMA PRESS

International Standard Book Number: 0–8061–0394–9

 Manufactured in the U.S.A. First printing of the new edition, 1958; second printing, 1961; third printing, 1966; fourth printing, 1969; fifth printing, 1972.

PREFACE

More than eighty years have elapsed since Georg Autenrieth's *A Homeric Dictionary* was first made available in English. It has since become an almost indispensable tool for thousands of students who have undertaken the reading of the *Iliad* and the *Odyssey* of Homer. This long record of usefulness and the continuing high esteem in which it is held by classical scholars provide ample justification for the present edition.

Professor Charles H. Reeves of the University of Oklahoma speaks of it as "far and away the handiest and most helpful of all the aids to the reading of Homeric Greek that have yet appeared." As the translator wrote in his preface to the first American edition, "The editor's own experience leads him to believe that a pupil with this dictionary in his hands will easily read two pages of Homer in the time which, with a large lexicon, would be required for one page. The dictionary also supplies, in good degree, the place of a commentary, and will be found equally full upon all parts of the two poems." I can only add that two decades of teaching Greek to preparatory students have confirmed all of the excellence that others have attributed to Autenrieth's work.

While *A Homeric Dictionary* needs no dedication at this late date, I should like to think that this particular edition of it might be dedicated to the earnest young students of Greek at Thomas Jefferson School, St. Louis, of this year and years past, whose unflagging interest in Homer has been one of the rewarding experiences of my career as a teacher.

ROBIN MCCOY

Thomas Jefferson School
St. Louis, Missouri
January 2, 1958

Corrections from Previous Printings

Line References

	Is	Should Be
ἀάατος	Φ 81	Φ 91
ἀπολήγει	Z 146	Z 149
ἀργεστής	X 334	Φ 334
ἐξαίσιος	O 577	O 598
ἰθύς	Z 69	Z 79
πῖαρ	A 550	Λ 550
πιστόω	Z 283	Z 233

Additional Line References

Word	*Line*	*Definition*
ἄατος	X 218	see ἆτος
ἄκλαυτος	X 386, λ 54	(1) unwept (2) δ 494, tearless
ἀπείρητος	P 41	unskillful, β 170; untried, P 41
δῆρις	P 158	rivalry, ω 515; battle, P 158
κλαυθμός	Ω 717	weeping, esp. in lament for the dead, ρ 8

Alphabetical Order

παίων follows παιήων

Additional Definitions

ἤλεκτρον : amber (in plural, pieces of amber), ο 460, σ 296; an alloy of gold and silver, δ 73.

EXPLANATION OF REFERENCES.

References are made to the several books of the Iliad and the Odyssey respectively, according to the usage of the ancient commentators, by the large and small letters of the Greek alphabet. Thus A 10 signifies Iliad, Bk. I., line 10; and ω 8 signifies Odyssey, Bk. XXIV., line 8; or, in detail:

A	Iliad	I.	Odyssey	α	N	Iliad	XIII.	Odyssey	ν
B	"	II.	"	β	Ξ	"	XIV.	"	ξ
Γ	"	III.	"	γ	O	"	XV.	"	ο
Δ	"	IV.	"	δ	Π	"	XVI.	"	π
E	"	V.	"	ε	P	"	XVII.	"	ρ
Z	"	VI.	"	ζ	Σ	"	XVIII.	"	σ
H	"	VII.	"	η	T	"	XIX.	"	τ
Θ	"	VIII.	"	ϑ	Υ	"	XX.	"	υ
I	"	IX.	"	ι	Φ	"	XXI.	"	φ
K	"	X.	"	κ	X	"	XXII.	"	χ
Λ	"	XI.	"	λ	Ψ	"	XXIII.	"	ψ
M	"	XII.	"	μ	Ω	"	XXIV.	"	ω

The character † designates Homeric *ἅπαξ λεγόμενα*.

Two references connected by the word *and* designate *δὶς λεγόμενα*.

Il. or Od. affixed to a definition denotes that the word defined occurs only in the Iliad or only in the Odyssey.

The references in general are to be understood as explanatory, and not as exhaustive: they are uniformly made to the small Teubner edition of the Iliad and Odyssey, edited by Dindorf.

To aid the eye, the first word of each article, or, if that chance not to occur in Homer, the first Homeric form, is printed in full-faced type.

The characters ϝ and *j* represent the semi-vowel spirants *v* (*w*) and *y*.

LIST OF ABBREVIATIONS.

acc.	signifies	accusative.
act.	"	active.
adj.	"	adjective.
adv.	"	adverb.
aor.	"	aorist.
cf.	"	confer, compare.
cogn.	"	cognate.
coll.	"	collective.
coll. forms	"	collateral forms.
comm.	"	commonly; common gender.
comp.	"	comparative.
compd.	"	compound.
conj.	"	conjunction.
constr.	"	construction.
dat.	"	dative.
dep.	"	deponent.
d., du.	"	dual.
epith.	"	epithet.
esp.	"	especially.
euphem.	"	euphemistically.
exc.	"	except.
fem.	"	feminine.
follg.	"	following.
foreg.	"	foregoing.
freq.	"	frequent.
fut.	"	future.
gen.	"	genitive.
imp.	"	imperative.
indic.	"	indicative.
inf.	"	infinitive.
instr.	"	instrumental.
intrans.	"	intransitive.
ipf.	"	imperfect.
irreg.	"	irregular.
iter.	"	iterative.
κ. τ. λ.	"	καὶ τὰ λοιπά, etc.
lit.	"	literally.
masc., msc.	"	masculine.
met.	"	metaphorical.
mid.	signifies	middle.
nom.	"	nominative.
neut., ntr.	"	neuter.
opp.	"	opposed to.
opt.	"	optative.
orig.	"	originally.
part.	"	participle.
pass.	"	passive.
pf., perf.	"	perfect.
pers.	"	person, personal.
plupf.	"	pluperfect.
pl.	"	plural.
pr., pres.	"	present.
prob.	"	probably.
q. v.	"	quod vide, see.
red.	"	reduplicated.
reg.	"	regular.
sc.	"	scilicet, supply.
signif.	"	signification.
sing., s., sg.	"	singular.
sq., sqq.	"	sequens, sequentia.
subj.	"	subject, subjunctive.
subst.	"	substantive.
sup.	"	superlative.
sync.	"	syncopated.
trans.	"	transitive.
verb.	"	verbal adjective.
v.	"	vide, see.
vid. sub voc.	"	see under.
v. l.	"	varia lectio, different reading.
w.	"	with.
in tmesi, tm., tmesis	"	separation of preposition from verb in a compound.
in arsi	"	in the arsis (the unaccented syl. of the ft.).
1, 2, 3	"	adjectives of one, two, or three terminations.

INDEX OF ILLUSTRATIONS.

PLATES, AT END OF THE VOLUME.

* Plates II., IV., and V. have been added by the translator.

INDEX OF OBJECTS ILLUSTRATED BY EACH CUT.

(The number of the cut comes first, then the page, then the words that the cut illustrates.)

THE CHIEF PECULIARITIES

OF THE

HOMERIC DIALECT.

IN GENERAL.

A. VOWELS.

1. **η** is regularly found when, in Attic, **ᾱ** only would be admissible, e. g. *ἀγορή*, *ὁμοίη*, *πειρήσομαι*.
2. Similarly, **ει** is sometimes found for **ε**, **ου** for **ο**, e. g. *ξεῖνος*, *χρύσειος*, *πουλύς*, *μοῦνος*.
3. More rarely **οι** is found for **ο**, **αι** for **α**, **η** for **ε**, e. g. *πνοιή*, *αἰετός*, *τιθήμενος*.
4. By what is called metathesis quantitatis, **αο** becomes **εω** (for *ᾰω*). Similarly, we have *ἕως* and *εἷος*, *ἀπερείσιος* and *ἀπειρέσιος* **κ. τ. λ.**

B. CONTRACTION OF VOWELS.

1. Contraction, when it occurs, follows the ordinary rules, except that **εο** and **εου** form **ευ**, e. g. *θάρσευς*, *βάλλευ*.
2. But the contraction often does not take place, e. g. *ἀέκων*; and a few unusual contractions occur, e. g. *ἱρός* (*ἱερός*), *βώσας* (*βοήσας*), *ἐυρρεῖος* instead of *ἐυρρέους* from *ἐυρρέ-εος*.
3. Two vowels which do not form a diphthong are often blended in pronunciation (synizesis), e. g. *'Ατρειδέω*, *δὴ αὖ*, *ἐπεὶ οὐ*, *ἢ οὐ*.

C. HIATUS.

Hiatus is allowed:

1. After the vowels **ι** and **υ**.
2. When the two words are separated by cæsura or a mark of punctuation.
3. When the final (preceding) vowel is long and in thesis.
4. When the final (preceding) vowel, though naturally long, stands in arsis and has been shortened before the following short vowel.
5. When the final vowel of the preceding word has been lost by elision, e. g.:

    1. *παιδὶ ὄπασσεν*, — ⏑ ⏑ | — ⏑.
    2. *'Ολύμπιε, οὖ νύ τ' 'Οδυσσεύς*, ⏑ | — ⏑ ⏑ | — ⏑ ⏑ | — —.
    3. *ἀντιθέῳ 'Οδυσῆι*, — ⏑ ⏑ | — ⏑ ⏑ | — ⏑.
    4. *πλάγχθη ἐπεί*, — ⏑ ⏑ | —.
    5. *ἄλγε' ἔδωκεν*, — ⏑ ⏑ | — ⏑.

Remark.—Many apparent cases of hiatus result from the loss of a digamma or other consonant, e. g. **τὸν δ' ἠμείβετ' ἔπειτα Ϝᾶναξ ανδρῶν 'Αγαμέμνων.**

D. ELISION.

Elision is much more frequent than in prose. **α, ε, ι, ο** are elided in declension and conjugation; **αι** in the endings *μαι*, *σαι*, *ται*, *σθαι*; **οι** in *μοι*; **ι** in *ὅτι*.

E. APOCOPE.

Before a consonant, the final short vowel of ἄρα, and of the preps. ἀνά, παρά, κατά, may be cut off (apocope).

Remark.—The accent in this case recedes to the first syllable, and the consonant (now final) is assimilated to the following consonant, e. g. κὰδ δύναμιν, κάλλιπε, ἂμ πεδίον.

F. CONSONANT-CHANGES.

1. Single consonants, esp. **λ, μ, ν, ρ,** and **σ,** at the beginning of a word, after a vowel, are frequently doubled, e. g. ἔλλαβον, τόσσος. So also a short final vowel before a follg. liquid is often lengthened by doubling (in pronunciation, though not in writing) the liquid, e. g. ἐνὶ μεγάροισι.
2. Metathesis of vowel and liquid is common, e. g. κραδίη and καρδίη, θάρσος and θράσος.

DECLENSION.

G. SPECIAL CASE-ENDINGS.

1. The termination **φι(ν)** serves for the ending of the gen. and dat. sing. and pl., e. g. ἐξ εὐνῆ-φι, βίη-φι, ὀστεόφι θίς, σὺν ἵπποισιν καὶ ὄχεσφι.
2. The three local suffixes θι, θεν, δε answer the questions where? whence? whither? e. g. οἴκοθι, οὐρανόθεν, ὅνδε δόμονδε.

H. FIRST DECLENSION.

1. For **ᾱ** we find always **η,** e. g. θύρη, νεηνίης, except θεά.
2. The nom. sing. of some masculines in **-ης** is shortened to **-ᾰ,** e. g. ἱππότα, νεφεληγερέτα.
3. The gen. sing. of masculines ends in **-ᾱο** or **-εω,** e. g. Ἀτρείδαο and Ἀτρείδεω.
4. The gen. pl. of masculines ends in **-άων** or **-έων** (rarely contracted, as in Attic, into **-ῶν**), e. g. θεάων, ναυτέων, παρειῶν.
5. The dat. pl. ends in **-ῃσι** or **-ῃς,** rarely in **-αις,** e. g. πύλῃσι, σχίζῃς, but θεαῖς.

I. SECOND DECLENSION.

1. The gen. sing. has retained the old ending in **-ιο,** which, added to the stem, gives the termination **-οιο.** Rarely occurs the termination **-οο**—more commonly the Attic ending **-ου.**
2. The gen. and dat. dual end in **-οιιν.**
3. The dat. pl. ends in **-οισι** or **-οις.**

K. THIRD DECLENSION.

1. The gen. and dat. dual end in **-οιιν,** e. g. ποδοῖιν.
2. Dat. pl. **-σι, -σσι,** usually joined to a consonant stem by a connecting vowel **ε,** e. g. πόδ-ε-σσιν and ποσσί, βελέεσσι, βέλεσσι, βέλεσι.
3. Stems ending in **-σ** are generally uncontracted in declension, but **-εος** often contracts into **-ευς.**
4. Words in **-ις** generally retain the **ι** in all their cases, e. g. μάντις, μάντιος.

   Remark.—For the various forms of πόλις, vid. sub voc. in Lex.
5. Stems in **-ευ** generally lengthen **ε** to **η** in compensation for the omitted **υ** (Ϝ), e. g. βασιλῆος, βασιλῆι. But proper names may retain the **ε,** e. g. Τυδέα.

L. ADJECTIVES.

1. The feminine of adjs. of the 1st and 2d declensions is always formed in **η**, e. g. *ὁμοίη, αἰσχρή*, exc. *δῖα*.
2. The Attic rule, that compd. adjs. have only two terminations, is not strictly observed, and, vice versâ, some adjs. which in Attic have three terminations have only two in Homer.
3. Adjs. in **-υς** are often of only two terminations, and often change the fem. **-εια** to **-εα** or **-εη.** For the various declensional forms of *πολύς*, vid. sub voc. in Lex.
4. The comp. and superl. endings **-ίων** and **-ιστος** are much more extensively used in the Homeric than in the Attic dialect.

M. PRONOUNS.

1. For special forms of pers. prons., vid. sub vocc. *ἐγώ, νῶι, ἡμεῖς. σύ, σφῶι, ὑμεῖς. οὗ, σφωέ, σφέων.*
2. **ὁ, ἡ, τό,** in Homer, is dem. pron. In nom. pl. the forms **τοί** and **ταί** occur by the side of **οἱ** and **αἱ.** The forms beginning with **τ** have often relative signif., vid. sub voc. in Lex. *τοίσδεσσι* and *τοίσδεσι* are forms of *ὅδε*. *κεῖνος* is another form for *ἐκεῖνος*.
3. For peculiar forms of rel. pron., as well as for demonstr. meaning of some of these forms, vid. sub voc. *ὅς*.
4. For peculiar forms of interrog., indef., and indef. rel. prons., vid. sub vocc. *τίς, τις*, and *ὅστις*.

CONJUGATION.

N. AUGMENT AND REDUPLICATION.

1. The augment may be omitted; in this case the accent is thrown back as far as possible toward the beginning of the word. Monosyllabic forms with a long vowel take the circumflex, e. g. *λῦσε* (*ἔλυσε*), *βῆ* (*ἔβη*).
2. The 2d aor. act. and midd. is often formed in Homer by a reduplication. The only examples of a similar formation in Attic are *ἤγαγον, ἤνεγκον* (*ην-ενεκ-ο-ν*), and *εἶπον* (*εϝεϝεπον*). Among the examples of reduplicated aorists may be mentioned: *ἐπέφραδον* (*φράζω*), *ἐκέκλετο* and *κέκλετο* (*κέλομαι*), *πεφιδέσθαι* (*φείδομαι*), *πεπίθομεν* (*πείθω*), *πεπύθοιτο* (*πυνθάνομαι*), *ἀμπεπαλών* (*ἀναπάλλω*). Examples of a very peculiar reduplication are *ἐνίπ-απ-ον* (*ἐνίπτω*) and *ἐρύκ-ακ-ον* (*ἐρύκω*). Here the last consonant of the stem is repeated after a connecting **α.**
3. There are a few examples of a reduplicated fut. of similar formation with the reduplicated aor., e. g. *πεφιδήσομαι, πεπιθήσω.*

O. ENDINGS.

1. The older endings of the sing. number *μι, σθα, σι*, are common in Homer *ἐθέλωμι* (subj.), *ἐθέλησι* (also written *ἐθέλῃσι*).
2. The ending of the 3d pers. dual in the historical tenses is **-τον** as well as **-την** in the act., **-σθον** as well as **-σθην** in the midd., voice. In 1st pers. pl., **μεσθα** is used for **μεθα,** and **μεσθον** for 1st pers. dual.
3. The 2d sing. midd. and pass. often loses **σ** and remains uncontracted, e. g. *ἔχηαι, βάλλεο, ἔπλεο* (also *ἔπλευ*), *ὠδύσαο.* In perf. midd., *βέβληαι* occurs for *βέβλησαι*.

3. In the 2d aor. sub. act., to meet the requirements of the verse, the mood sign is sometimes shortened and the stem-vowel lengthened. Thus arise such forms as θείω, θείῃς, and θήῃς; στήῃς, γνώω, δώῃσι, and δώῃ. Sometimes the α of the stem is weakened to ε, and this again protracted to ει. Thus arise the forms στέωμεν and στείομεν (=στῶμεν), βείομεν (=βῶμεν).
4. For peculiar Homeric forms from the verbs ἵστημι, τίθημι, ἵημι, δίδωμι, εἶμι, εἰμί, οἶδα, ἧμαι, and κεῖμαι, vid. sub vocc. in Lex.

A.

A-: in composition—(1) 'privative,' see ἀν-. —(2) 'copulative,' originally σα, contains an idea of union, as in ἅπᾱς (πᾶς), ἀολλής (Ϝείλλω). —(3) 'prothetic,' a simple euphonic prefix, as in ἄποινα (ποινή), ἀστήρ (Eng. 'star').

ἆ: interjection expressive of pity or horror, freq. w. voc. of δειλός, e. g. ἆ δειλώ, *Ah! wretched pair!* P 443, Λ 816, ξ 361.

ἀ-ᾰᾱτος (ἀϜάω): of doubtful meaning. —(1) *inviolable* (if α privative), νυν μοι ὄμοσσον ἀάᾱτον Στυγὸς ὕδωρ, Ξ 271; cf. Στυγὸς ὕδωρ, ὅς τε μέγιστος | ὅρκος δεινότατός τε πέλει μακάρεσσι θεοῖσιν, O 37 f.—(2) *baleful* (if α copulative), or *mad*, of the suitors' contest with the bow, φ 81 (echoed by Odysseus, χ 5). —Signif. (2) may be assumed in Ξ instead of (1), representing the Styx as baleful to him who swears falsely in its name.

ἀ-ᾱγής, ές (Ϝάγνῡμι): *unbreakable*, λ 575.†

ἄ-απτος: *unapproachable, invincible.*

ἀά-σχετος: lengthened form of ἄσχετος.

ἀάω (ἀϜάω), aor. ἄασε, ἆσε, 2 sing. ἆσας, mid. ἀᾶται, aor. ἀασάμην, -ατο, ἄσατο, pass. aor. ἀάσθην, -ης, -η, part. -είς: I. act., *bring to grief*, Θ 237; esp. of the mind, *delude, befool, befuddle*, ὃ δ' ἐπεὶ φρένας ἄασεν οἴνῳ, φ 297; pass., T 136, φ 301; μέγα, Π 685; πολλόν, T 113. —II. mid., *commit folly, be infatuated, deceive oneself*, T 95; causative, '*beguile*,' (Ἄτη), ἣ πάντας ἀᾶται, T 91, 129.

ἀβακέω, aor. ἀβάκησαν: word of doubtful meaning, *be unaware, suspect nothing*, δ 249.†

Ἄβαντες: a tribe in Euboea, B 536.

Ἀβαρβαρέη: a Trojan fountain-nymph, Z 22.

Ἄβᾱς: son of the dream-reader Eurydamas, slain by Diomed, E 148.

Ἄβιοι: a fabulous tribe of the North, δικαιότατοι ἀνθρώπων, N 6.

Ἄβληρος: a Trojan, Z 32.

ἀ-βλής, ῆτος (βάλλω): *unsped*, i. e. 'new,' 'fresh,' of an arrow, Δ 117.†

ἄ-βλητος (βάλλω): *not hit*, Δ 540.†

ἀ-βληχρός (α prothetic, μαλακός): *soft, feeble, gentle*, χείρ, τείχεα, θάνατος, E 337, Θ 178, λ 135.

ἄ-βρομος (βρέμω): *loud-roaring, clamorous*, N 41.†

ἀβροτάζω (ἀβροτεῖν, ἀμβροτεῖν, ἀμαρτεῖν): aor. subj. ἀβροτάξομεν, *miss*, w. gen., K 65.†

ἄ-βροτος (=ἄμβροτος): *divine*, νὺξ ἀβρότη, Ξ 78.†

Ἄβῡδος: *Abȳdus*, a town on the southern shore of the Hellespont, B 836.—**Ἀβῡδόθεν**: *from Abȳdus*, Δ 500. —**Ἀβῡδόθι**: *in Abȳdus*, P 584.

ἀγα-: an old adv., later ἄγαν, employed only as a prefix, *greatly, strongly, highly.*

ἀγάασθαι, ἀγάασθε: see ἄγαμαι.

ἀγαγεῖν, ἄγαγον: see ἄγω.

ἀγάζομαι: see ἄγαμαι.

ἀγαθός: *good.*—Hence (1) of persons, 'valiant,' 'brave,' ἢ κακὸς ἢ ἀγαθός, P 632; 'skilful,' ἰητῆρ' ἀγαθώ, B 732, freq. w. acc. of specification or an adv., βοήν, πύξ. —Often 'noble' (cf. optimates), opp. χέρηες, ο 324. —(2) of things, 'excellent,' 'useful,' etc.; ἀγαθόν τε κακόν τε, 'blessing and curse,' δ 237; ἀγαθοῖσι γεραίρειν, 'honor with choice portions,' ξ 441; ἀγαθὰ φρονεῖν, 'wish one well,' α 43; 'be pure-minded,' Ζ 162; εἰς ἀγαθόν or ἀγαθὰ εἰπεῖν, 'speak with friendly intent;' εἰς ἀγ. πείθεσθαι, 'follow good counsel.'

'Αγάθων: son of Priam, Ω 249.

ἀγαίομαι=(ἄγαμαι): 'view with indignation,' ἀγαιομένου κακὰ ἔργα, υ 16†; cf. β 67.

ἀγα-κλεής, gen. ἀγακλῆος (κλέος): *highly renowned.*

'Αγακλέης: a Myrmidon, Π 571.

ἀγα-κλειτός: *highly renowned, famous,* epith. of men, of a Nereid, Σ 45, and of hecatombs.

ἀγα-κλυτός=ἀγακλεής, ἀγακλειτός.

ἀγάλλομαι: *take delight* or *pride in* (τινί); ἀγαλλόμενα πτερύγεσσιν, 'on exultant wings,' Β 462; met. of ships, 'revelling in the fair breeze' (Διὸς οὔρῳ), ε 176.

ἄγαλμα (ἀγάλλομαι): anything in which one takes *delight* or *pride*, a 'treasure,' Δ 144; applied to votive offerings, γ 274; a sacrificial victim, γ 438; horses, δ 602; personal adornments, σ 300.

ἄγαμαι (ἄγη), fut. ἀγάσσεσθαι, aor. ἠγασάμην, ἠγασσάμην (also unaugmented), and from parallel form **ἀγάομαι**, ἀγάασθε, ἀγάασθαι, ipf. ἠγάασθε. The form ἄγαμαι only in signif. 1:—(1) *admire, wonder at, be amazed,* θαυμάζειν οὔτ' ἀγάασθαι, π 203.—(2) in bad sense, *be indignant at,* w. acc. β 67, w. dat. θ 565; *be vexed,* Ψ 639; with κότῳ, Ξ 111; hence *envy, begrudge,* with inf. ε 129, esp. of envy of the gods, δ 181.

'Αγαμεμνονέη: fem. poss. adj. from 'Αγαμέμνων, ἄλοχος, γ 264.

'Αγαμεμνονίδης: *son of Agamemnon,* Orestes, α 30.

'Αγαμέμνων: *Agamemnon,* son of Atreus and grandson of Tantalus; his wife, Clytaemnestra, Α 113 f.; his children, Orestes, Chrysothemis, Laodice, and Iphianassa, cf. Β 104, Ι 287. King of Mycēnae, likewise ruler over 'many islands and all Argos,' Β 108. His wealth in ships, Β 576, 610–614. Epithets, δῖος, κρείων, εὐρυκρείων, ἄναξ ἀνδρῶν, ποιμὴν λαῶν. His stature, Γ 166, 178, Β 477–483; ἀριστεῖα, 'exploits,' Λ 91–661; honor accorded to him, Ψ 887; sceptre, Β 104; his return from Troy, γ 143 ff., 156, 193 ff., 234 f.; his death at the hands of Aegisthus and Clytaemnestra, his wife, γ 248 ff., δ 91, 512–537, 584, λ 387–463, ω 20–97.

'Αγαμήδη (cf. Μήδεια): *Agamēde,* daughter of Augēas, granddaughter of the Sun-god, Λ 740.

ἄ-γαμος: *unmarried,* Γ 40†.

ἀγά-ννιφος ([σ]νίφω): *snowy,* 'snow-capped,' epith. of Mt. Olympus. (Il.)

ἀγανός (cf. γάννυμαι): *pleasant, gentle, kindly;* ἔπεα, δῶρα, βασιλεύς (opp. χαλεπός), β 230; εὐχωλαι, Ι 499, ν 357; οἷς ἀγανοῖς βελέεσσι, 'with his (her) gentle shafts,' describing a (natural) sudden, painless death dealt by Apollo upon men, by Artemis upon women, γ 280.

ἀγανο-φροσύνη: *gentle-mindedness, kindliness,* λ 203; cf. β 230.

ἀγανό-φρων: *gentle-minded,* Υ 467†.

ἀγάομαι: see ἄγαμαι.

ἀγαπάζω (=ἀγαπάω) and -ομαι: *receive lovingly* (τινά), π 17, η 33; 'espouse the cause of,' Ω 464.

ἀγαπάω: *welcome affectionately,* ψ 214; 'be content,' φ 289.

ἀγαπ-ήνωρ: *loving manliness, manly.*

'Αγαπήνωρ: 'Αγκαίοιο πάϊς, Β 609, king of the Arcadians, a vassal of Agamemnon, to whom he brought the equipment of sixty ships.

ἀγαπητός (ἀγαπάω): *beloved,* always with παῖς, *son,* which is implied in β 365.

ἀγά-ρροος ([σ]ρέω): *strong-flowing,* 'Ελλήσποντος, Β 845.

'Αγασθένης (σθένος): son of Augēas, king in Elis, Β 624.

ἀγά-στονος (στένω): *moaning,* epith. of Amphitrite (i. e. the Sea), μ 97†.

'Αγάστροφος: a Trojan, Λ 338.

'Αγαύη: a Nereid, Σ 42.

ἀγαυός (ἄγαμαι): *wondrous;* hence, *illustrious, high-born,* epith. of honor applied to rulers and nations; freq. to the suitors; to the noble πομπῆες, ν 71; to Tithōnus, ε 1; and thrice to Persephone.

ἀγγελίη: *tidings, message, report:* ἀγγ. πατρός, 'news of my father,' α 408, cf. β 30; 'command,' ε 150, η 263; ἀγγ. ἐλθόντα, 'on a mission,'

Λ 140; in Γ 206 gen. of cause or purpose, according to some authorities, but see ἀγγελίης.

ἀγγελίης: *messenger;* assumed as nom. masc. by Aristarchus in Γ 206, Ν 252, Ο 640, Δ 384, Λ 140.

ἀγγέλλω, fut. ἀγγελέω, aor. ἤγγειλα, inf. Ο 159: *report, announce* (τί, also τινά); w. inf. 'bid,' π 350, Θ 517.

ἄγγελος: *messenger;* common phrase, ἦλθέ τινι, Λ 715; Ὄσσα Διὸς ἄγγελος, Β 94; also of birds, ο 526.

ἄγγος, εος: *pail* or *bowl,* for milk, wine, etc., and for provisions, β 289.

ἄγε, ἄγετε, imp. of ἄγω, used as interjection: *quick! come!* Freq. ἀλλ' ἄγε, ἄγε δή, and foll. by subj. or imp. ἄγε often w. pl., e. g. παῖδες ἐμοί, ἄγε κτλ., Τ 475. See also εἰ δ' ἄγε.

ἀγείρω, aor. ἤγειρα, pass. pf. ἀγήγερμαι, aor. ἠγέρθην, 3 pl. ἄγερθεν, mid. 2 aor. ἀγερόμην, inf. ἀγερέσθαι (accented ἀγέρεσθαι by ancient grammarians), part. ἀγρόμενος: *collect, call together, assemble;* pass. and aor. mid. *gather together;* ἐς φρένα θυμὸς ἀγέρθη, 'consciousness' ('presence of mind,' Δ 152), 'was restored.'

ἀγελαῖος (ἀγέλη): *of the herd, herding,* βοῦς, βόες.

Ἀγέλᾱος (ἄγω, λαός): (1) a Trojan, son of Phradmon, Θ 257.—(2) a Greek, Λ 302.—(3) a suitor, son of Damastor, Ἀγέλεως, χ 131, 247.

ἀγελείη (ἄγω, λεία): *booty-bringing,* 'the forayer,' epith. of Athena; cf. ληῖτις.

ἀγέλη (ἄγω): *herd* of cattle, but *drove* of horses, Τ 281; ἀγέληφι, 'with the herd.' Π 487.

ἀγεληδόν: *in herds,* Π 160†.

ἀγέμεν = ἄγειν.

ἄγεν = ἐάγησαν, from ἄγνῡμι.

ἀ-γέραστος (γέρας): *without a gift.*

ἀγέρωχος: (if from ἐρωή) *impetuous, mighty in combat;* anciently interpreted as if from γέρας, 'gifted.'

ἄγη: *astonishment;* ἄγη μ' ἔχει = ἄγαμαι, Φ 221.

ἀγηγέραθ' (ατο); see ἀγείρω.

ἀγ-ηνορίη: v i r t u s, *manliness, valor;* said in reproach, Χ 457, and still more so, Ι 700, 'pride.'

ἀγ-ήνωρ (ἄγα, ἀνήρ): *very manly, valorous;* hence, 'bold,' 'proud,' in both good and bad sense; freq. w. θῡμός.

Ἀγήνωρ: son of the Trojan Antenor and Theano, Λ 59.

ἀ-γήραος, ἀ-γήρως (γῆρας): *ageless, unfading,* always with ἀθάνατος.

ἀγητός (ἄγαμαι): *wondrous, magnificent;* with εἶδος as acc. of specification, but in agreement w. εἶδος, Χ 370.

ἀγῑνέω (ἄγω), inf. -έμεναι, ipf. ἠγίνεον and ἠγίνευν, Σ 493; iter. ἀγίνεσκον, *lead, conduct, bring;* of a bride, Σ 492; 'haul' wood, Ω 784.

ἀγκάζομαι (ἀγκάς): *take in the arms;* νεκρὸν ἀπὸ χθονὸς ἀγκάζοντο, 'lifted from the ground,' Ρ 722†.

Ἀγκαῖος: (1) son of Lycurgus, chief of the Arcadians, Β 609.—(2) a wrestler from Pleuron, vanquished by Nestor, Ψ 635.

ἀγκαλίς, only ἐν ἀγκαλίδεσσι: *in the arms.*

ἀγκάς, adv.: *into* or *in the arms,* with ἔχε, ἐλάζετο, etc.

ἄγκιστρον: *fish-hook.* (Od.)

ἀγ-κλῑνας: see ἀνακλίνω.

ἀγκοίνη: *bent arm;* ἐν ἀγκοίνῃσιν ἰαύειν, 'to rest in one's embrace.'

ἄγκος, only pl. ἄγκεα: *winding vales, gorges.*

ἀγ-κρεμάσᾱσα: see ἀνακρεμάννῡμι.

ἀγκυλο-μήτης, εω (μῆτις): *crooked in counsel,* epith. of Κρόνος.

ἀγκύλος: *bending, curved,* epith. of bow and of chariot.

ἀγκυλό-τοξος (τόξον): armed *with the bent bow.*

ἀγκυλο-χείλης (χεῖλος): *with crooked beak.*

ἀγκών: *elbow;* τείχεος, 'corner' of the wall, Π 702.

ἀγλαΐζομαι (ἀγλαός): *glory in,* fut. inf. ἀγλαϊεῖσθαι, Κ 331†.

ἀγλαΐη: *splendor, brilliancy;* of Penelope's 'dazzling beauty,' σ 180; 'display,' 'fine show,' ρ 244, 310.

Ἀγλαΐη: wife of Charops, and mother of Nireus, ὃς κάλλιστος ἀνὴρ ὑπὸ Ἴλιον ἦλθεν, Β 672.

ἀγλαό-καρπος: *with shining fruit;* of orchard trees, η 115.

ἀγλαός (root γαλ-): *splendid, shining, bright;* epith. of pellucid water, golden gifts, etc.; met. 'illustrious,' 'famous,' υἱός, δ 188; 'stately,' Τ 385; in reproach κέραι ἀγλαέ, 'brilliant with the bow,' Λ 385.

ἀ-γνοέω, sync. aor. iter ἀγνώσασκε

(for αγνοήσασκε), ψ 95; from ἀγνοιέω, only aor. ind. ἠγνοίησεν, subj. ἀγνοιῇσι, ω 218, part. ἀγνοιήσᾶσα, υ 15: *fail to recognize.*

ἁγνός: *holy, pure.*

ἄγνῡμι (Ϝάγνῡμι), fut. ἄξω, aor. ἔαξα, ἦξα, inf. ἆξαι, pass. pr. part. ἀγνυμενάων, aor. ἐάγην (ἐάγην, Λ 559), Ϝάγη, Ϝάγεν (= ἐάγησαν): *break, shiver, shatter;* rather of crushing and destroying than of rending asunder (ῥήγνῡμι); of the ships pelted and smashed by the Laestrȳgons, κ 123.

ἀ-γνώς: *unknown,* ε 79†.

ἀγνώσασκε: see ἀγνοέω.

ἄ-γνωστος: *unrecognized, unrecognizable.* (Od.)

ἀγ-ξηρᾱ́νῃ: see ἀναξηραίνω.

ἄ-γονος: *unborn,* Γ 40†.

ἀγοράομαι (ἀγορή), pres. ᾱ̓γοράασθε, Β 337, ipf. ἠγοράασθε, ἠγορόωντο, aor. only 3 sing. ἀγορήσατο: *hold assembly,* Δ 1, *harangue.*

ἀγορεύω (ἀγορή), fut. ἀγορεύσω, aor. ind. only ἀγόρευσεν, Θ 29, inf. and imp. more common: *harangue,* strictly with reference to form and manner of speaking; then generally, *speak, say, declare;* freq. with acc. ἔπεα πτερόεντα, ἀγορᾶς ἀγόρευον, 'were engaged in haranguing,' Β 788, ἣν ἀγορεύω, 'of which I speak,' β 318; often in connection with words denoting the manner of speaking, παραβλήδην, 'insinuatingly,' Δ 6, ὀνειδίζων ἀγορεύοις, 'talk insultingly of,' σ 380.

ἀγορή (ἀγείρω): (1) *assembly* of the people or army, distinguished from the βουλή or council of the chiefs. ἀγορὴν ποιεῖσθαι, τίθεσθαι, καθίζειν, ἀγορήνδε καλεῖν (through the heralds), ἐς δ' ἀγορὴν ἀγέροντο, etc.—(2) *public speech, discussion.*—(3) *place of meeting, market,* pl. θ 16. As designation of time, ἐ π ὶ δ ό ρ π ο ν ἀνὴρ ἀγορῆθεν ἀνέστη, μ 439.

ἀγορῆθεν: *from the assembly.*

ἀγορήνδε: *to the assembly.*

ἀγορητής: *haranguer, speaker.*

ἀγορητύς: *gift of speaking, eloquence,* θ 168†.

ἀγός (ἄγω): *leader, chief.*

ἀγοστός: *hand* bent for seizing; ἐν κονίῃσι πεσὼν ἕλε γαῖαν ἀγοστῷ, 'clutched the ground,' said of the warrior's dying agony, Λ 425; cf. κόνιος δεδραγμένος (δράσσομαι).

ἄγραυλος (ἀγρός, αὐλή): *lying in the field* (passing the night out-doors), βοῦς, πόριες, ποιμένες.

ἄγρει, and **ἀγρεῖτε,** υ 149, imp. from ἀγρέω (= αἱρέω), used as interjection like ἄγε: *quick! up! forward!* Used alone or with μάν, δή, νῦν, followed by imp., or inf. used as imp.

ἄγρη: *hunt, chase.* (Od.)

ἄγριος, 2 or 3 (ἀγρός): *wild,* as opp. to tame; met., *ferocious, savage.*

Ἄγριος: son of Portheus in Calydon, Ξ 117.

ἀγριό-φωνος: *rude-voiced,* of the Sintians of Lemnos, θ 294†.

ἀγρόθεν, r u r e: *from the field, country.* (Od.)

ἀγροιώτης: *rustic, peasant;* as adj., Ο 272.

ἀγρόμενος: see ἀγείρω.

ἀγρόνδε: *to the field, country,* i. e. from town.

ἀγρο-νόμος (νέμω): *inhabiting the fields, rural,* νύμφαι, ζ 106†.

ἀγρός: *field, country,* opp. to town, ἐπ' ἀγροῦ ν ό σ φ ι π ό λ η ο ς, π 383; ἐξ ἀγροῖο π ο λ ί ν δ ε, ρ 182.

ἀγρότερος (poet. parallel form to ἄγριος): *wild;* of Artemis as huntress, 'ranging the wild,' Φ 471.

ἀγρότης: *rustic,* π 218.

ἀγρώσσω (ἄγρα): *catch,* intensive; of the sea-gull 'ever catching' fish, ε 53†.

ἄγρωστις: *field-grass, grass;* identified by some with 'dog's tooth,' by others with 'panic.'

ἀγυιᾱ́ (ἄγω): *road, way, street;* σκιόωντο δὲ πᾶσαι ἀγυιαί, 'shadowy grew all the ways,' of the approach of night.

ἄγυρις (ἀγείρω): chance *gathering, company, host,* ἀνδρῶν, νεκύων, νηῶν (when drawn up on shore), Ω 141.

ἀγυρτάζω (ἀγύρτης, ἀγείρω): *collect as beggar,* τ 284†.

ἀγχέ-μαχος (ἄγχι, μάχομαι): *fighting hand to hand* (c o m i n u s).

ἄγχι: *near, hard by,* τινός. The dat., if used, generally modifies the verb of the sentence, but probably with ἄγχι in Υ 283. Of time, ἄγχι μάλ', 'in the near future,' τ 301.

ἀγχί-αλος (ἅλς): *near the sea.*

Ἀγχίαλος: (1) a Greek, slain by Hector, Ε 609.—(2) father of Mentes, and ruler of the Taphians, α 180.—(3) a noble Phaeacian, θ 112.

ἀγχι-βαθής (βάθος): *deep near the shore*, ε 413†.

ἀγχί-θεος: *near to the gods* (i. e. by relationship, descent), of the Phaeacians, ε 35; see η 56 ff.

ἀγχι-μαχητής = ἀγχέμαχος.

ἀγχί-μολος (μολεῖν): *coming near*, mostly adv. acc. with ἐλθεῖν, ἔρχεσθαι, foll. by dat.; ἐξ ἀγχιμόλοιο, Ω 352, cf. ἐγγύθεν. Implying time, ἀγχίμολον δέ μετ' αὐτόν, 'close after him,' ρ 336.

ἀγχί-νοος (νοῦς): *near*-, i. e. *ready-minded*, ν 332, cf. 'presence of mind.'

Ἀγχίσης: (1) son of Capys, father of Aenēas, E 268.—(2) father of Echepōlus, from Sicyon, Ψ 296.

Ἀγχῑσιάδης: *son of Anchīses*, (1) Aenēas, P 754.—(2) Echepolus.

ἄγχιστα: see ἄγχιστος.

ἀγχιστῖνος: *close together, one upon another*.

ἄγχιστος (sup. of ἄγχι): *nearest, most nearly, closely*, only adv. neut. sing. and pl.; met. w. ἔοικα and ἐίσκω.

ἀγχόθι = ἄγχι.

ἀγχοῦ = ἄγχι.

ἄγχω: *choke, strangle*, ipf. 'was choking,' Γ 371†.

ἄγω, fut. ἄξω, aor. ἦξα (imp. ἄξετε, inf. ἀξέμεν, ἀξέμεναι), mid. ἠξάμην (ἄξεσθε, ἄξοντο), more common 2 aor. act. ἤγαγον, subj. ἀγάγωμι, mid. ἠγαγόμην (also unaugmented): I. act., *lead, conduct, bring*, ρ 218 ('brings like to like,' ὡς is prep.), 219; βοῦν, ἵππους ὑπὸ ζυγόν, ὑφ' ἅρματα, 'put to harness'; *bring* or *carry with one*, esp. of booty and prisoners, *lead captive, carry off*, thus joined w. φέρω, E 484; hence 'transport,' 'convey,' with persons or things as subj., ναῦται, νῆες; 'remove,' νεκρόν, κόπρον; 'guide,' 'control,' Λ 721, Φ 262; esp. an army, ships, etc., B 580, 631, 557. Met. 'bring to pass,' 'occasion,' Ω 547, 'spread abroad,' κλέος, ε 311. The part. ἄγων is often added to a verb by way of amplification, α 130, B 558.—II. Mid., *take with* or *to one* what one regards as his own, Γ 72, ζ 58, prizes, captives, etc.; esp. γυναῖκα, 'lead home,' 'take to wife,' said of the bridegroom, and also of those who give in marriage, or who accompany the bride, ζ 28.

ἀγών (ἄγω): (1) *assembly*, esp. to witness games, ἵζανεν (Ἀχιλλεύς), Ψ 258, λῦτο, Ω 1, then *contest, games*, θ 259.—(2) *assemblage* or *place of assemblage*, of the ships, νεῶν ἐν ἀγῶνι (the Greek camp), Π 500; θεῖος, 'of the gods,' Σ 376, but H 298 of the 'temple-hall,' containing the statues of the gods.—(3) *place* or *scene of combat, arena*, including the space occupied by the spectators, Ψ 531.

ἀ-δαημονίη: *want of knowledge*, ω 244†.

ἀ-δαήμων: *unacquainted with*, τινός.

ἀ-δάκρῡτος: *tearless*.

Ἄδαμας: a Trojan, son of Asius, N 759, 771.

ἀ-δάμαστος (δαμάζω): *not to be prevailed over*, i. e. 'inexorable,' Ἀίδης, I 158†.

ἀδδεές: see ἀδειής.

ἀδδηκώς, ἀδδήσειε: see ἀδέω.

ἄδδην: see ἄδην.

ἀ-δειής (δέος): *fearless*; κύον ἀδδεές, 'shameless hussy.'

ἀδελφεός, ἀδελφειός: *brother*.

ἀδευκής: *odious, unpleasant*; θάνατος, πότμος, φῆμις.

ἀ-δέψητος (δέψω): *untanned*.

ἀδέω, only aor. opt. ἀδδήσειε, perf. part. ἀδδηκότες, also written ἀδη- and ἁδη-: *be satiated, feel loathing at*; καμάτῳ, ὕπνῳ, 'be overwhelmed with.'

ἄδην, ἅδην, ἄδδην: *to satiety, to excess*; ἄδην ἐλάαν κακότητος, πολέμοιο, 'until he gets enough' of trouble, etc.

ἀ-δήριτος (δῆρις): *uncontested*, P 42†.

ἀδινός: probably *thick*, esp. of things densely crowded and in motion. Hence 'throbbing' (κῆρ), 'swarming' (μέλισσαι), 'buzzing' (μυῖαι), 'flurried' (μῆλα), 'sobbing' (γόος), 'voiceful' (Σειρῆνες). Adv. with corresponding signification ἀδινόν, ἀδινά, ἀδινώτερον, 'more dolefully,' ἀδινῶς ἀνενείκατο, 'fetched a deep sigh,' T 314.

ἀδινῶς: see ἀδινός.

ἀ-δμής (δάμνημι): *untamed, unbroken*; παρθένος, 'unwedded;' cf. δάμαρ. (Od.)

ἄ-δμητος: *unbroken*, not yet brought under the yoke.

Ἄδμητος: husband of Alcestis, and

father of Eumēlus, B 713 f., Ψ 289, 391, 532.

ἄδον: see ἀνδάνω.

ἄδος, ἄδος (see ἀδέω): *satiety, disgust.*

Ἀδρήστεια: a town on the Propontis, in what was afterward Mysia, B 828.

Ἀδρήστη: a handmaid of Helen, δ 123.

Ἀδρηστίνη: *daughter of Adrastus*, Αἰγιάλεια, E 412†.

Ἄδρηστος (διδράσκω, the 'unescapable'): (1) from Argos, fugitive to Sicyon, succeeds Polybus there as king; becomes also king in Argos, harbors Tydeus, and gives him his daughter in marriage, cf. Ξ 121; his swift steed Areion, Ψ 347.—(2) son of Merops, from Percōte, founder of Adrasteia, leader of Trojan allies from thence, B 380, Λ 328.—(3) a Trojan, slain by Menelāus, Z 37, 45, 63.—(4) a Trojan slain by Patroclus, Π 694.

ἀδροτής (ἀδρός): *maturity, vigor;* ἀδροτῆτα, questionable reading in Il., see ἀνδροτής.

ἄ-δυτον (δύνω, not to be entered'): *shrine*, 'holy of holies.'

ἀεθλεύω, ἀθλεύω (ἄϝεθλον): *institute*, or *contend in, a gymnastic contest;* ἐπί τινι, 'in honor of' some one; for ἀθλέω, *toil*, Ω 734.

ἀέθλιον = ἄεθλον. Also pl. *implements of combat*, 'weapons,' φ 4, 62, 117.

ἄεθλον, ἆθλον (ἀϝεθ.): (1) *prize.*—(2) *prize-contest.*

ἄεθλος, ἆθλος: (1) *prize-contest*, distinguished from war, ἢ ἐν ἀέθλῳ | ἠὲ καὶ ἐν πολέμῳ, Π 590.—(2) *combat* (in war), Γ 126; then 'toil,' 'hardship,' esp. of the 'labors' of Heracles, imposed by Eurystheus (Εὐρυσθῆος ἀέθλοι, Θ 363).

ἀεθλο-φόρος, ἀθλοφόρος: *prize-winning;* only of horses.

ἀεί, αἰεί, αἰέν: *always, ever;* joined with ἀσκελέως, ἀσφαλές, διαμπερές, ἐμμενές, μάλα, νωλεμές, συνεχές. Also αἰεὶ ἤματα πάντα.

ἀείδω (ἀϝείδω), fut. ἀείσομαι, aor. ind. ἄεισε, imp. ἄεισον, inf. ἀεῖσαι: *sing*—I. trans., παιήονα, κλέα ἀνδρῶν, 'lays of heroes;' also w. acc. of the theme of minstrelsy, μῆνιν, A 1; Ἀχαιῶν νόστον, α 326; with ὡς, θ 514; acc. and inf., θ 516.—II. intrans., μάλ' ἀεῖσαι, 'merrily', λίγα, καλόν (adv.); met. of the bow-string, φ 411.

ἀ-εικείη (ἀϝεικής): *disfigurement*, Ω 19; ἀεικείας φαίνειν, 'exhibit unseemly behavior,' υ 308.

ἀ-εικέλιος, 2 and 3, = ἀεικής: '*ill-favored*, ζ 242; adv., ἀεικελίως: *disgracefully.*

ἀ-εικής (ἀϝεικ., ϝέϝοικα): *unseemly, disgraceful; νόος οὐδὲν ἀεικής*, 'a likely understanding,' οὔ τοι ἀεικές, etc.; μισθὸς ἀεικής, 'wretched' pay; πήρη, 'sorry' wallet, ἀεικέα ἕσσαι, 'thou art vilely clad.'

ἀ-εικίζω (ἀϝεικής), ipf. ἀείκιζεν, aor. subj. ἀεικίσσωσι, mid. ἀεικισσαίμεθα, ἀεικίσσασθαι, pass. ἀεικισθήμεναι: *disfigure, maltreat, insult.*

ἀείρω, αἴρω (ἀϝείρω), aor. ἤειρα and ἄειρα, mid. I. ἀειράμην, pass. ἀέρθην (ἀερθείς, ἀρθείς), plupf. ἄωρτο, cf. ἄρνυμαι: *raise up, lift;* freq. w. ὑψόσε; of 'swinging' the lash (μάστῑγα), of the 'carrying' capacity of ships (ἄχθος ἄειραν, γ 312), 'made him light,' T 386; mid. and pass., *rise up, lift oneself*, of dust in the air, of the balance, Θ 74, of birds 'soaring,' and of horses flinging up their heels. The part. ἀείρᾱς is added to verbs by way of amplification, α 141. Of 'bringing and offering,' Z 264, esp. mid. (out of one's store), 293, ο 106.

ἀεῖσαι: see ἀείδω.

ἀ-εκαζόμενος (ἀϝέκων): *unwillingly, reluctantly;* w. πολλά, 'much against one's will.'

ἀ-εκήλιος (ἀϝεκ.): *unwelcome*, 'woful,' ἔργα, Σ 77†.

ἀ-έκητι (ϝέκητι): *against the will of;* freq. w. θεῶν.

ἀ-έκων, ἄκων, -ουσα (ϝεκών): *unwilling, reluctant;* 'unintentionally,' Π 264, βίῃ ἀέκοντα, 'by force against my will,' O 186; σὲ βίῃ ἀέκοντος ἀπηύρα, δ 646; cf. A 430.

ἄελλα (ἄϝημι): *gust of wind, blast, squall;* of a whirlwind, Π 374.

ἀ-ελλής, ές (εἴλω): *dense;* **κονίσαλος**, Γ 13.

ἀελλό-πος (ἄελλα, πούς): *storm-footed;* of Iris, the swift messenger, cf. ποδήνεμος. (Il.)

ἀ-ελπής (ϝέλπομαι): *unhoped for*, 'beyond hope,' ε 408†.

ἀ-ελπτέω: *be hopeless; ἀϝελπτέοντες σόον εἶναι*, 'despairing of his safety,' i. e. 'recovering him safe beyond their hopes,' Η 310†.

ἀε-νάων, αἰε-νάων (ἀεί, ναω): *ever-flowing*, 'never-failing,' 'perennial,' ὕδατα, ν 109†.

ἀέξω (ἀϝέξω, 'wax'), only pres. and ipf.: *make to grow, increase, let grow up*, υἱόν, ν 360; mid. and pass., *grow, grow up; μέγα πένθος*, 'cherish'; ἔργον, 'prosper,' ξ 66; ἀέξετο ἱερὸν ἦμαρ, 'was waxing,' i. e. advancing toward the meridian, Θ 66, ι 56.

ἀ-εργίη (ϝέργον): *sloth*, ω 251†. The ῑ is a necessity of the rhythm.

ἀ-εργός: *slothful, idle, lazy.*

ἀερθείς, ἀερθέν: see ἀείρω.

ἀερσί-πος (ἀϝείρω, πούς): *high-stepping*; epith. of horses, cf. Ψ 501.

ἄεσα (ἄϝεσα), ἀέσαμεν, ἄσαμεν, ἄεσαν, inf. ἀέσαι, only aor.: *pass the night, rest*, not necessarily in sleep; νύκτα, νύκτας. (Od.)

ἀεσι-φροσύνη: *thoughtlessness*, dat. pl. 'thoughtlessly,' ο 470†.

ἀεσί-φρων (cf. φ 301 f.): *light-headed, thoughtless, silly.*

ἀζάλεος (ἄζη): *dry, withered, sere.*

'Αζεΐδης: son of Azeus, Ἄκτωρ, Β 513.

ἄζῃ, dat. from ἄζα (ἄζομαι): *dry dirt*, 'rust,' χ 184†.

ἀ-ζηχής, ές: *unceasing, incessant*; adverbial ἀζηχές.

ἄζομαι (act. ἄζω, Hesiod): *dry, grow dry*, 'season,' Δ 487†.

ἅζομαι, only pres. and ipf.: *dread, stand in awe of*; w. inf. Ζ 267, ι 478; w. μή, 'lest,' Ξ 261.

ἀηδών (ἀϝείδω, the 'songstress,' κατ' ἐξοχήν): *nightingale.* In the Homeric legend the daughter of Pandareus, wife of Zethus of Thebes, mother of Itylus, whom she slew by mistake, τ 518† ff. See Ἴτυλος.

ἀ-ηθέσσω (ἀηθής, ἦθος): *be unaccustomed to*; w. gen., Κ 493†.

ἄημι (ἄϝημι), 3 du. ἄητον, inf. ἀῆναι, ἀήμεναι, part. ἀέντες, ipf. ἄη, ἄει, pass. ἀήμενος: *blow*, of wind; (λέων) ὑόμενος καὶ ἀήμενος, 'buffeted by wind' and rain, ζ 131; met. δίχα . . . θυμὸς ἄητο, 'wavered,' Φ 386.

ἀήρ, ἠέρος: *the lower, denser atmosphere*, distinguished from αἰθήρ, 'sky'; hence 'vapor,' 'mist,' 'cloud,' esp. as means of rendering invisible, Γ 381.

ἀήσυλος = αἴσυλος, Ε 876†.

ἀήτης (ἄϝημι): *wind*, ι 139; mostly pl. w. ἀνέμοιο, Ζεφύροιο, ἀνέμων, *blast, breeze.*

ἄητο: see ἄημι.

ἄητος: word of doubtful meaning, *stormy, impetuous* (if from ἄημι); ἄητον θάρσος, Φ 395†.

ἀ-θάνατος (the ᾱ is a necessity of the dactylic rhythm): *deathless, immortal*; also as subst., opp. βροτοί, θνητοί, ἄνδρες; said of 'imperishable' possessions of the gods, δ 79, Β 447; ἀθάνατον κακόν (Charybdis), μ 118.

ἄ-θαπτος (θάπτω): *unburied.*

ἀ-θεεί (θεός), adv.: *without god; οὐκ ἀθεεὶ ὅδ' ἀνὴρ . . . ἵκει* (i. e. 'he is a godsend to us'), said in mockery, σ 353†.

ἀ-θεμίστιος (θέμις): *lawless, unrighteous, wicked; ἀθεμίστια εἰδέναι*, foster 'godless thoughts.'

ἀ-θέμιστος = ἀθεμίστιος, ι 106, cf. 112; opp. ἐναίσιμος, ρ 363.

ἀθερίζω, ipf. ἀθέριζον: *disregard, despise*; always w. neg.; opp. μεγαλίζομαι, ψ 174.

ἀ-θέσφατος (θεός, φημί, 'not to be said even by a god'): *unspeakable, indescribable, immense, prodigious* (of quality or quantity); γαῖα, θάλασσα, ὄμβρος, νύξ, and even οἶνος, σῖτος.

'Αθῆναι, 'Αθήνη (η 80): *Athens*, Β 546, 549, γ 278, 307.

'Αθηναίη, 'Αθήνη: the goddess *Athena*, ἀγελείη, 'Αλαλκομενηΐς, γλαυκῶπις, ἐρυσίπτολις, εὐπλόκαμος, ἠύκομος, λαοσσόος, ληῖτις, πολύβουλος; cf. 'Ατρυτώνη, Τριτογένεια, esp. Παλλάς. Fosters the arts, ζ 232, ψ 160, esp. domestic and feminine accomplishments, Ι 390, β 116; as a goddess of war, she protects cities ('Αλαλκομενηΐς), and is the especial patron of Odysseus.

'Αθηναῖος: *Athenian*, Β 551, etc.

'Αθήνη: see 'Αθῆναι, 'Αθηναίη.

ἀθηρη-λοιγός (ἀθήρ, λοιγός): *chaff-destroyer*, designation of a winnowing-shovel in Teiresias' prophecy to Odysseus, λ 128, ψ 275.

ἀθλεύω (= ἀθλέω): see ἀεθλεύω.

ἀθλέω (ἆθλος), only aor. part. ἀθλήσας: *wrestle, toil, labor.*

ἀθλητήρ: *fighter*, δ 164†, cf. δ 159 f.

ἆθλος: see ἄεθλος.

ἀθλοφόρος: see ἀεθλοφόρος.

'Αθόως, όω: *Athos*, Ξ 229†, the mt. terminating the promontory of Acte in Chalcidice, now Monte Santo.

ἀθρέω, only aor. ἀθρήσειε, ἀθρῆσαι: *gaze, look*, in the effort to see something, then *descry;* abs. and w. εἰς, K 11; also w. acc., M 391.

ἀθρόος, ἀθρόος, only pl.: *(all) together, in crowds;* freq. ἀθρόα πάντα.

ἄ-θῡμος: *spiritless, despondent*, κ 463†.

ἄθυρμα (ἀθύρω): *plaything, toy, trinket.*

ἀθύρω: *play, sport;* ἀθύρων, O 364†.

"Αθως: see 'Αθόως.

αἰ, αἴ: *if, if only, whether;* conjunction, used in conditional clauses, and in the expression of a wish; always with κέ, κέν (never ἄν), or γάρ, and never separated from these particles by another particle (εἰ δέ κε, never αἰ δέ κε).—I. conditional, regularly foll. by subj., rarely by opt. (H 387, ν 389). Here belongs the so-called 'interrogative' use, as πειρήσομαι αἴ κε τύχωμι, E 279.—II. optative, to express a wish, 'would that,' αἲ γάρ, or αἲ γὰρ δή w. opt., generally referring to fut. time, but sometimes of an unfulfilled wish in pres. time (H 132); foll. by inf., η 311, ω 376.

αἶα: *earth, land;* πᾶσαν ἐπ' αἶαν, 'the world over.'

Αἰαῖος, only fem. Αἰαίη: *Aeaean.*—(1) νῆσος, the home of Circe (see μ 3 f., 9), a fabulous isle, located by the Romans at Circeii, near Terracina.—(2) the goddess Circe herself, sister of Aeëtes (see κ 137).

Αἰακίδης: *descendant of Aeacus;* (1) his son, Peleus, Π 15.—(2) his grandson, Achilles, B 860.

Αἰακός: son of Zeus and Aegina, grandfather of Achilles, Φ 189.

Αἴας: *Ajax.*—(1) Τελαμώνιος, Τελαμωνιάδης, μέγας, 'the greater,' son of Telamon from Salamis, half-brother of Teucer; second only to Achilles in prowess, λ 550 f.—(2) 'Οϊλιάδης, 'Οΐλῆος ταχὺς Αἴας, μείων, 'the lesser,' Oileus' son, leader of Locrians, his death, δ 499.—The two heroes are often coupled in dual or pl., e. g. Αἴαντε δύω, θεράποντες 'Αρῆος, 'the Ajaxes.'

Αἰγαί (cf. αἰγιαλός): a town in Achaea, seat of worship of Poseidon, Θ 203.

Αἰγαίων (cf. αἰγίς): epithet of Briareus, A 404†.

αἰγανέη: a light *hunting-spear, javelin*, ι 156; thrown for amusement, B 774, δ 626; also used in war, Π 589 ff.

Αἰγείδης: *son of Aegeus*, Theseus, A 265†.

αἴγειος, αἴγεος (αἴξ): *of a goat;* 'of goat's milk,' or 'goatskin,' τυρός, ἀσκός, κυνέη.

αἴγειρος: *black poplar;* as tree in the lower world, κ 510.

αἴγεος = αἴγειος, ἀσκός, ι 196†.

Αἰγιάλεια: daughter of Adrastus, wife of Diomed, E 412†.

αἰγιαλός: *beach, strand.*

Αἰγιαλός ('Coast-land'): (1) a district in N. Peloponnesus, afterward Achaea, B 575†.—(2) a town in Paphlagonia, B 855†.

αἰγί-βοτος (βόσκω): *fed upon by goats;* as subst., *goat-pasture*, ν 246.

αἰγίλιψ: *precipitous;* πέτρη, I 15, Π 4.

Αἰγίλιψ: a district, or island, under the rule of Odysseus, B 633†.

Αἴγῑνα: an island in the Saronic gulf, still bearing its ancient name, B 562†.

Αἴγιον (cf. Αἰγιαλός): a town in Achaea, afterward the capital of the Achaean league, B 574†.

αἰγί-οχος (ἔχω): *aegis-holding*, epith. of Zeus.

αἰγίς (originally emblematic of the 'storm-cloud,' cf. ἐπαιγίζω): the *aegis*, a terrific shield borne by Zeus, or at his command by Apollo or by Athena, to excite tempests and spread dismay among men; the handiwork of Hephaestus; adorned with a hundred golden tassels, and surmounted by the Gorgon's head and other figures of horror, E 738, B 448.

Αἴγισθος: son of Thyestes, and cousin of Agamemnon. As paramour of Clytaemnestra, he murders Agamemnon, and after ruling seven years over Mycenae, is himself killed by Orestes, γ 196, δ 512 ff., λ 409.

αἴγλη: *radiance, gleam;* of daylight, ζ 45; of sun and moon; of weapons, B 458.

αἰγλήεις: *radiant, resplendent*, epith. of Olympus.

αἰγυπιός: *vulture;* with ὄρνῑς, H 59.

Αἰγύπτιος (in cases ending w. a long syllable, read w. synizesis, as Αἰγυπτ͡ίους): (1) *Egyptian;* as subst., δ 83.—(2) *Aegyptius*, an old man of Ithaca, β 15.

Αἴγυπτος: (1) *Egypt*, δ 355.—(2) Homeric name of the river Nile, δ 477; w. ποταμός, ξ 258.—Αἴγυπτόνδε, δ 483, ξ 246.

αἰδεῖο: see αἰδέομαι.

αἰδέομαι, αἴδομαι (αἰδώς), pr. imp. αἰδεῖο, ipf. αἴδετο, fut. αἰδέσ(σ)ομαι, aor. mid. ᾐδεσάμην and αἰδεσσάμην, pass. ᾐδέσθην, αἰδέσθην, 3 pl. αἴδεσθεν: *feel shame, regard*, or *mercy* (from moral or humane scruples, toward oneself or others, even toward inferiors); τινὰ, *respect, have regard for, stand abashed before*, A 23, γ 96; w. inf., *scruple, be ashamed*, from modesty, or from motives of propriety, good-taste, etc., ξ 146, σ 184; αἰδομένων, 'self-respecting' (opp. φευγόντων), E 531.

ἀίδηλος: *destructive, destroying;* 'pestilent,' E 880, χ 165.—adv. ἀιδήλως, Φ 220.

Ἀίδης, Αιδωνεύς (root ϝιδ, god of the *unseen* world), gen. Ἀίδᾱο, Ἀίδεω, Ἄιδος, dat. Ἄιδι, Ἀίδῃ, Ἀιδωνῆι, acc. Ἀίδην: *Hades;* ἐνέροισιν ἀνάσσων, Ζεὺς καταχθόνιος, κρατερὸς πυλάρτης, πελώριος, κλυτόπωλος, ἴφθῑμος, στυγερός. Freq. Ἄιδος δόμον εἴσω, ἐν δόμοις, etc.; often only Ἄιδόσδε, εἰς or ἐν Ἄιδος (sc. δόμον, δόμῳ).

αἰδοῖος (αἰδώς): (1) *modest, bashful*, ρ 578.—(2) *honored, respected*, of those who by their relationship, position, or circumstances have a claim to deference or merciful treatment, as the gods, kings, suppliants, mendicants, and the 'housekeeper' (ταμίη).—As subst. neut. pl. αἰδοῖα, 'the parts of shame,' 'privy parts,' N 568†.—Adv., αἰδοίως ἀπέπεμπον, 'with due honor,' 'fitting escort,' τ 243.

αἴδομαι: see αἰδέομαι.

Αιδος, Ἄιδόσδε: see Ἀίδης.

ἀιδρείη: *ignorance;* ἀιδρείῃσι νόοιο, i. e. 'unwittingly,' λ 262.

ἄ-ιδρις (ϝίδρις): *ignorant, unacquainted with* (τινός), *witless*, Γ 219.

αἰδώς, οῦς: *shame* (restraint), *regard, respect, mercy* (see αἰδέομαι); 'scruple,' αἰδῶ καὶ νέμεσιν, N 122 (cf. O 561), αἰδὼς | καὶ δέος, O 657; 'diffidence,' γ 14; in reproach, αἰδώς! 'for shame,' Π 422, E 787; w. acc. and inf., 'it's over bold,' γ 22; equiv. to αἰδοῖον, 'that hide thy nakedness,' B 262.

αἰεί, αἰέν: see ἀεί.

αἰει-γενέτης: *immortal, eternal.*

αἰει-νάων: see ἀε-νάων.

αἰετός: *eagle;* the 'bird of Jove,' and 'most perfect' bird of omen, Ω 310 f., Θ 247.

ἀίζηλος: *unseen;* τὸν μὲν (δράκοντα) ἀίζηλον θῆκεν θεός, 'put out of sight,' B 318† (v. l. ἀρίζηλον).

αἰζηός, αἰζήιος: *vigorous;* with ἀνήρ, and as subst. (μ 440); esp. pl., θαλεροί, ἀρηίθοοι αἴζηοί, 'lusty,' 'doughty youths.'

Αἰήτης: son of Helius and Perse, brother of Circe, holder of the golden fleece won by the Argonauts, μ 70.

αἴητος: epith. of Hephaestus, πέλωρ αἴητον, 'terrible;' 'puffing' (if from ἄημι), Σ 410†. By some thought to be the same word as ἄητος.

αἰθαλόεις, εσσα, εν (αἴθω): *smoky, sooty;* μέλαθρον, μέγαρον, B 415, χ 239; κόνις, 'grimy' dust (opp. πολιός), ω 316, Σ 23.

αἴθε: particle of wishing, 'Would that,' 'Oh, that,' more common in Homer than εἴθε. Foll. by opt., or by ὤφελον and inf.

Αἴθη: name of a mare, 'Sorrel' ('Fire-bug'), Ψ 295.

αἰθήρ: the upper air, or *sky, aether;* αἰθέρι ναίων, of Zeus, dweller in the heavens; more exactly conceived as having οὐρανός beyond it, B 458; separated from the lower ἀήρ by the clouds, as Hera in O 20 swings ἐν αἰθέρι καὶ νεφέλῃσιν.

Αἴθῑκες: a tribe dwelling near Mt. Pindus, B 744†.

Αἰθίοπες (αἴθω, the 'swarthy'), acc. ῆας: *Aethiopians*, a pious folk, loved and visited by the gods, dwelling on the borders of Oceanus, in two divisions, east and west, α 22 ff.

αἰθόμενος: *burning, blazing.*

αἴθουσα: *portico, corridor.* We distinguish two αἴθουσαι, an outer and an inner, see plate III. at end of volume.—(1) the outer (*αἰθ. αὐλῆς*, φ 390, ν 176, χ 449), on either side of the vestibule, entering the court.—(2) the inner (*αἰθ. δώματος*), leading from the court into the house; this one served as a sleeping-place for guests (γ 399, δ 297), and was roofed.

αἴθοψ (*αἴθω*): *gleaming, sparkling; χαλκός, οἶνος*; 'red,' of smoke mingled with flame, κ 152.

αἴθρη (cf. *αἰθήρ*): *clear sky, serenity.*

Αἴθρη: mother of Theseus, follows Helen as captive to Troy, Γ 144.

αἰθρη-γενέτης, αἰθρηγενής: *aether-born*, Boreas.

αἶθρος: *cold, frost.*

αἴθυια: *water-hen.*

αἴθων: *shining, tawny;* of metal (Δ 485), and of horses, cattle, eagle, and lion.

Αἴθων: (1) a name assumed by Odysseus, τ 183.—(2) name of a horse, Θ 185; see *Αἴθη*.

αἴκ': see *αἴ* (*κε*).

ἀΐκή (*ἀΐσσω*): *darting; τόξων ἀΐκάς*, 'whizzing bow-shots,' Ο 709†.

ἀικῶς (= *ἀεικῶς*): *ignominiously*, Χ 336†.

αἷμα: *blood, bloodshed, carnage;* of relationship, race (*γενεὴ καὶ αἷμα*), Ζ 211, Τ 105.

αἱμασιή: *thorn-bush; αἱμασιὰς λέγειν*, 'gather hedge-brush,' σ 359 and ω 224.

αἱματόεις, *εσσα, εν*: *bloody, bleeding;* met. *ἤματα, πόλεμος*.

Αἱμονίδης: *son of Aemon*, Laerces, Ρ 467†.

Αἱμονίδης: *son of Haemon*, Maeon, from Thebes, Δ 394†.

αἱμο-φόρυκτος (*φορύσσω*): *reeking with blood; κρέα*, υ 348†.

αἱμύλιος: *wheedling, winning*, α 56†.

αἴμων: *skilled in*, w. gen., Ε 496†.

Αἴμων: a comrade of Nestor, Δ 296†.

αἰν-αρέτης (*αἰνός, ἀρετή*), only voc. *αἰναρέτη*: *woful-valorous*, of Achilles' misdirection of his might from the battle-field to the nursing of his wrath, Π 31†.

Αἰνείας, gen. *Αἰνείαο, Αἰνείω*: *Aeneas*, son of Anchises and Aphrodite, ruler of the Dardanians, by his descent from Tros, a relative of Priam (see Υ 230–240), with whom he was at feud, Β 820, Ν 460; held in the highest honor by the Trojans, Ε 467, Λ 58; destined to rule over the Trojan race, Υ 307.

αἰνέω (*αἶνος*), fut. *αἰνήσω*, aor. *ᾔνησα*: *praise, commend, approve.*

αἰνίζομαι = *αἰνέω*, Ν 374 and θ 487.

Αἴνιος: a Paeonian, slain by Achilles, Φ 210†.

Αἰνόθεν: *from Aenus* (in Thrace), Δ 520†.

αἰνόθεν (*αἰνός*, = *ἐκ τοῦ αἰνοῦ*): adv. used for emphatic repetition, *αἰνόθεν αἰνῶς* (*direst of the dire*), Η 97†; cf. *οἰόθεν οἶος*, 39.

αἰνό-μορος (*μόρος*): *dire-fated.*

αἰνο-παθής (*πάσχω*): *dire-suffering*, 'poor sufferer,' σ 201†.

αἶνος: *praise, eulogy.*

αἰνός: *dread, dreadful, dire;* either with full force and seriousness of meaning, or colloquially and hyperbolically; *αἰνότατε Κρονίδη*, 'horrid,' Α 552 (cf. Θ 423), *αἰνῶς ἔοικας κείνῳ*, 'terribly' like him, α 208.—Adv., *αἰνότατον, αἰνά, αἰνῶς. τί νύ σ' ἔτρεφον αἰνὰ τεκοῦσα* (since I bore thee 'to sorrow'), Α 414, cf. 418, *αἰνῶς κακὰ εἵματα* ('shocking' bad clothes), ρ 24.

αἴνυμαι, only pres., and ipf. *αἴνυτο*: *take;* met. *πόθος αἴνυται*, 'I am seized with' longing, ξ 144.

αἰνῶς: see *αἰνός*.

αἴξ, *αἰγός*, dat. pl. *αἴγεσιν*: *goat.*

ἀΐξασκον: see *ἀΐσσω*.

Αἰολίδης: *son of Aeolus*, see **Κρηθεύς, Σίσυφος**.

Αἰολίη, *νῆσος*: the *Aeolian* isle, residence of Aeolus, lord of winds, κ 1 ff.

αἰόλλω (*αἰόλος*): *turn quickly; ἔνθα καὶ ἔνθα*, υ 27†.

αἰολο-θώρηξ: *with glancing cuirass.*

αἰολο-μίτρης (*μίτρη*): *with glancing belt of mail*, Ε 707.

αἰολό-πωλος: *with glancing (swift) steeds*, Γ 185†, cf. Τ 404.

αἰόλος: *quick-moving, lively;* of wasps (*μέσον*, 'at the waist'), gad-fly ('darting'), serpent ('squirming'), worms ('wriggling'); then *glancing, shimmering*, of lively (changeable) colors, esp. metallic, Ε 295, Η 222.

Αἴολος, gen. *Αἰόλοο*, κ 36, 60: (1) son of Hippotas, and lord of winds, κ 2.—(2) father of Sisyphus, Ζ 154.

Αἴπεια: a town on the Messenian gulf, I 152, 294.

αἰπεινός, αἰπήεις (εσσα), **αἰπός**: see αἰπύς.

αἰπόλιον: *herd of goats, herd.*

αἰπόλος (αἴξ, πέλομαι): *goat-herd, herder.*

Αἰπύ: a town subject to Nestor, B 592†.

αἰπύς, εῖα, ύ: *steep, towering;* of mountains, towns (here esp. the form αἰπεινός), streams with steep banks (αἰπὰ ῥέεθρα, Θ 369, Φ 9, cf. 10), a noose 'hung high,' λ 278; met. πόνος, 'arduous;' ὄλεθρος, 'utter,' etc.; αἰπύ οἱ ἐσσεῖται, he will find it 'steep,' N 317.

Αἰπύτιος: *of Aepytus,* progenitor of a royal line in Arcadia, B 604†.

αἱρέω, fut. -ήσω, aor. εἷλον, ἕλον (Ϝέλον), iter. ἕλεσκον, mid. αἱρεύμενοι, αἱρήσομαι, εἱλόμην, ἑλόμην: I. act., *take,* 'grasp,' 'seize' (freq. w. part. gen.), '*capture,*' 'overtake' in running; of receiving prizes (Ψ 779), embracing (λ 205), putting on ('donning') garments (ρ 58), 'taking up' a story at some point (θ 500); γαῖαν ὀδὰξ ἑλεῖν, 'bite the dust;' freq. of hitting in combat, and esp. euphemistic, ἕλεν, he 'slew'; met. of feelings, χόλος αἱρεῖ με, ἵμερος, δέος, etc., so ὕπνος.—II. mid., *take* as one's own, to or for oneself, *choose;* of taking food, robbing or stripping another, taking an oath from one (τινός, δ 746, τινί, X 119); also met., ἄλκιμον ἦτορ, φιλότητα ἑλέσθαι, Π 282.

Ἄ-ιρος (Ϝῖρος): Ἶρος Ἄϊρος, 'Irus un-Irused,' σ 73†, cf. 6 f.

αἴρω: see ἀείρω.

Ἄϊς: see Ἀΐδης.

αἶσα: allotted *share,* or *portion, lot, term of life, destiny;* prov. ἐν καρὸς αἴσῃ (cf. Att. ἐν οὐδενὸς μέρει); κατ' αἶσαν, 'as much as was my due,' οὐδ' ὑπὲρ αἶσαν, Z 333; ὑπὲρ Διὸς αἶσαν, P 321; ὁμῇ πεπρωμένος αἴσῃ, O 209.

Αἴσηπος: (1) son of Abarbarea and Bucolion, Z 21†.—(2) name of a river emptying into the Propontis, near Cyzicus.

ἀΐσθω (ἀϜίω, 2), only pres. and ipf. **ἄϊσθε**: *breathe out;* **θυμόν,** of giving up the ghost, Π 468 and Υ 403.

αἴσιμος (αἶσα): *destined, due, suitable, right;* αἴσιμον ἦεν, αἴσιμον ἦμαρ, day 'of destiny,' αἴσιμα εἰδέναι, 'righteous thoughts;' pers., φρένας αἴσιμη ἦσθα, ψ 14.

αἴσιος (αἶσα): *auspicious, opportune,* Ω 376†.

ἀΐσσω (ᾱ except ὑπαΐξει, Φ 126), aor. ἤϊξα (ἀΐξω, ἀῖξαι, ἀΐξᾱς), ἀΐξασκον, mid. aor. ἀΐξασθαι, pass. ἠΐχθην, ἀϊχθήτην: *speed, dart, spring;* of persons, animals, birds flying, and of inanimate things (arrows, a beam of light, 'fluttering' mane of horses); of the shades of the dead 'flitting' to and fro; freq. the part. w. another verb of motion, βῆ ἀΐξᾱσα, ἀΐξαντε πετέσθην, O 150, and conversely, ἤϊξε πέτεσθαι, 'darted away' in flight, Φ 247; often of hostile movements, ἀντίος ἀΐξᾱς, φασγάνῳ, 'with his sword,' etc.; met., of the mind, νόος ἀνέρος, O 80 (cf. πτέρον ἠὲ νόημα, η 36).

ἄ-ιστος (Ϝιδεῖν): *unseen;* οἴχετ' ἄιστος, ἄπυστος, α 242; καί κέ μ' ἄιστον ἔμβαλε πόντῳ, 'to be seen no more.'

ἀιστόω (ἄϜιστος): *put out of sight, annihilate;* ἀιστώθησαν, *vanished,* κ 259.

αἰσυητήρ: see αἰσυμνητήρ.

Αἰσυήτης: (1) father of Antenor, B 793.—(2) father of Alcathous, N 427.

αἰσυλό-εργος: *evil-doing,* v. l. for ὀβριμόεργος, E 403†.

αἴσυλος: *evil,* neut. pl. with ῥέζειν, μυθήσασθαι.

Αἰσύμηθεν: *from Aesyme,* in Thrace, Θ 304†.

αἰσυμνητής: *princely,* dat. Ω 347†, v. l. αἰσυητῆρι.

αἰσυμνήτηρ: *umpire,* θ 258†.

Αἴσυμνος: a Greek, slain by Hector, Λ 303†.

αἶσχος, εος: (1) *ugliness.*—(2) *disgrace, reproach, outrage;* αἶσχος, λώβη τε (σ 225), αἴσχεα καὶ ὀνείδεα (Γ 342), αἴσχε' ἀκούω (Z 524), αἴσχεα πόλλ' ὁρόων (α 229).

αἰσχρός, comp. neut. αἴσχιον, sup. αἴσχιστος: (1) *ugly,* B 216.—(2) *disgraceful, insulting, outrageous.*—Adv. αἰσχρῶς.

αἰσχύνω (αἶσχος), aor. ᾔσχῡνε, perf. pass. ᾐσχυμμένος: I. act., *disfigure,* then *disgrace, insult;* ἀρετήν, 'tarnish' the fame of my prowess, Ψ 571.—II.

mid., *be ashamed* of, or to do or say anything disgraceful.

Αἴσων: son of Cretheus and Tyro, father of Jason, and king in Iolcus, λ 259.

αἰτέω, fut. -ήσω, aor. part. -ήσᾱσα: *ask, demand, beg, sue for*; abs., of a mendicant, σ 49; freq. τινά τι, w. inf. Z 176, acc. and inf. (ᾐτέομεν δὲ θεὸν φῆναι τέρας), γ 173.

αἰτιάασθαι: see αἰτιάομαι.

αἰτιάομαι (αἴτιος), resolved forms constantly, inf. αἰτιάασθαι, opt. αἰτιόῳο, ῳτο, ipf. ᾐτιάασθε, ᾐτιόῳντο: *accuse*; οἷον δή νυ θεοὺς βροτοὶ αἰτιόωνται, 'how mortals do bring charges against the gods!' α 32.

αἰτίζω (stronger than αἰτέω): *beg, importune.* (Od.)

αἴτιος (αἰτίᾱ): *to blame, guilty*; οὔ τί μοι αἴτιοί εἰσιν, 'I have no fault to find with them,' A 153, so β 87.

αἰτιόωνται, αἰτιόῳο: see αἰτιάομαι.

Αἰτώλιος, Αἰτωλός: *Aetolian.*

αἰχμάζω: *wield the lance*; αἰχμὰς αἰχμάσσουσι, Δ 324†.

αἰχμή: *point* of lance, *lance, spear.*

αἰχμητής, αἰχμητα (E 197): *spearman, warrior*; freq. implying bravery, with ἀνδρῶν, Γ 49.

αἶψα: *forthwith, at once, directly*; αἶψα δ' ἔπειτα, αἶψα μάλα, αἶψα καὶ ὀτραλέως. αἶψά τε, *speedily*, in general statements, τ 221.

αἰψηρός (αἶψα): *quick(ly)*, used with the sense of the adv.; λῦσεν δ' ἀγορὴν αἰψηρήν, T 276, β 257; αἰψηρὸς δὲ κόρος, 'soon' comes, δ 103.

1. **ἀίω** (ἀϝίω), only pres. and ipf. ἄιον: (1) *hear*; abs., and w. gen. or acc. —(2) *mark, perceive*, never inconsistently with the sense of *hearing*, πληγῆς ἀίοντες, the horses hear the lash as well as feel the stroke, Λ 532.—οὐκ ἀίεις (=ἀκούεις;); or, sometimes, 'markest thou not?' 'remarkest,' O 248, α 298.

2. **ἀίω** (cf. ἄϝημι): *breathe out*; φίλον ἄιον ἦτορ, 'was (near) breathing my last,' O 252†.

αἰών, ῶνος (cf. a e v u m), m., fem. X 58: *lifetime, life.*

ἀκάκητα: *deliverer*; epith. of Hermes, Π 185 and ω 10.

ἀκαλα-ρρείτης (ἀκαλός): *gently-flowing*; epith. of Oceanus, H 422 and τ 434.

ἀ-κάμᾱς, αντος (κάμνω): *untiring.*

Ἀκάμᾱς: (1) son of Antenor and Theano, a leader of Dardanians, Ξ 478. —(2) son of Eussōrus, a leader of Thracians, Z 8.

ἀ-κάματος = ἀκάμᾱς, epith. of fire.

ἄκανθα (root ακ): *thistle*, pl. ε 328†.

Ἄκαστος: king of Dulichium, ξ 336†.

ἀκαχείατο, ἀκαχεῖν, ἀκαχήσω, ἀκαχημένος: see ἀκαχίζω.

ἀκαχίζω (root αχ), aor. ἤκαχε, ἀκαχεῖν, and ἀκάχησε, mid. ἀκαχίζομαι, pf. ἀκάχημαι, 3 pl. ἀκηχέδαται, part. also ἀκηχεμένη, αι, inf. ἀκαχῆσθαι, plup. 3 pl. ἀκαχείατο, aor. ἀκάχοντο, -οιτο: *distress, grieve*, π 432, Ψ 223; mid., *be distressed, grieve*; with causal gen. or dat., θανόντι, 'were he dead,' α 236; ἀκαχημένοι ἦτορ, 'with aching hearts'; θῡμῷ, Z 486. Cf. ἄχος, ἀχέω, ἀχεύω, ἄχνυμαι.

ἀκαχμένος (root ακ): *sharpened, pointed*; ἔγχος ἀκαχμένον ὀξέι χαλκῷ 'tipped with sharp point of bronze,' πελεκὺς ἀμφοτέρωθεν ἀκ., 'double-edged' axe, ε 235.

ἀκάχοιτο: see ἀκαχίζω.

ἀκέομαι, ἀκείομαι, ἀκειόμενος, aor. ἠκεσάμην (imp. ἄκεσσαι): *heal*; νῆας, 'repair,' ξ 383; met. of thirst ('slake'), troubles ('make good'), N 115, κ 69.

ἀ-κερσε-κόμης (κείρω, κόμη): *with unshorn hair*; Φοῖβος, Υ 39†.

ἄκεσμα (ἀκέομαι): *means of healing*, 'alleviating,' ὀδυνάων, O 394†.

Ἀκεσσάμενος: a king of Thrace, father of Periboea, Φ 142†.

ἀκεστός (ἀκέομαι): *curable*; ἀκεσταί τοι φρένες ἐσθλῶν, 'can be mended,' N 115†.

ἀκέων (cf. ἀκήν), mostly as adv. and indecl., but ἀκέουσα, ἀκέοντα, ἀκέοντε: *in silence, still, quiet(ly).*

ἀ-κήδεστος (κηδέω): *uncared-for*, i. e. of the dead, 'unburied,' Z 60; adv. ἀκηδέστως, *pitilessly.*

ἀ-κηδέω (ἀκηδής); aor. ἀκήδεσεν: *be neglectful, neglect.*

ἀ-κηδής, ές (κῆδος): *uncaring, unfeeling*, Φ 123, ρ 319; *free from care*, Ω 526; pass *neglected*, esp. 'unburied.'

ἀ-κήλητος (κηλέω): *not to be charmed*, 'proof against enchantment,' νόος, κ 329†.

ἀκήν: adv. *silent*, with ἴσαν, ἔσαν, ἀκὴν ἐγένοντο σιωπῇ, 'were hushed' in silence, π 393.

ἀ-κηράσιος = ἀκήρατος, ι 205†.

ἀ-κήρατος: *untouched, pure.*

1. ἀ-κήριος (κήρ): *unharmed.*

2. ἀ-κήριος (κῆρ): (1) *dead.*—(2) *spiritless, cowardly*; δέος, E 812.

ἀκηχέδαται, ἀκηχέαται, ἀκηχεμένη: see ἀκαχίζω.

ἀκιδνός, only comp. ἀκιδνότερος: *insignificant*; οὐδὲν ἀκιδνότερον γαῖα τρέφει ἀνθρώποιο, nothing 'more frail,' σ 130. (Od.) [(Od.)

ἄ-κῑκυς (κῖκυς): *strengthless, feeble.*

ἀ-κίχητος (κιχᾰ́νω): *unattainable*; ἀκίχητα διώκων, P 75†.

ἄ-κλαυτος (κλαίω): *unwept, tearless.*

ἀ-κλεής, ές, **ἀκληής, ἀκλειής** (κλέος), acc. sing. ἀκλεᾶ or ἀκλέᾶ, nom. pl. ἀκληεῖς: *inglorious*, adv. ἀκλεὲς αὔτως, 'all so ingloriously,' H 100.—Adv. ἀκλειῶς.

ἄ-κληρος (κλῆρος): *portionless*, λ 490†.

ἀκμή (root ακ): *edge*, in the prov. ἐπὶ ξυροῦ ἵσταται ἀκμῆς, K 173†.

ἀκμηνός (ἀκμή): *full-grown*, Ψ 191†.

ἄκμηνος: *without taste* (*of food or drink*); only in T.

ἀ-κμής, ῆτος (κάμνω): *unwearied*, only pl. (Il.)

ἀκμό-θετον (ἄκμων, τίθημι): *anvil-block.*

ἄκμων, ονος: *anvil.*

ἄκνηστις: *backbone*, κ 161†.

ἀ-κοίτης (κοίτη): *husband, consort, spouse.*

ἄ-κοιτις, acc. pl. ἀκοίτῑς: *wife, consort.*

ἄκολος: *morsel*, pl. ρ 222†.

ἀ-κομιστίη (κομίζω), ῑ from the necessity of the rhythm: *want of care*, φ 284†.

ἀκοντίζω (ἄκων), aor. ἀκόντισ(σ)α: *hurl the javelin, hurl*; δοῦρα, δουρί.

ἀκοντιστής: *javelin-thrower, javelin-hurling*, as adj. Π 328.

ἀκοντιστύς: *contest of the dart*, Ψ 622.

ἀ-κόρητος (κορέννῡμι): *insatiate*, w. gen.

ἄκος (ἀκέομαι): *cure, remedy.*

ἄ-κοσμος: *disorderly*, B 213†.

ἀκοστάω (ἀκοστή): *eat barley*; only aor. part., στατὸς ἵππος, ἀκοστήσᾱς ἐπὶ φάτνῃ, 'well fed at the grain-crib,' Z 506 and O 263.

ἀκουάζομαι: *listen* with delight, ἀοιδοῦ, 'to the bard;' δαιτὸς ἀκουάζεσθον ἐμεῖο, 'hear from me the glad call to the feast,' Δ 343.

ἀκουή: *hearing*; μετὰ πατρὸς ἀκουήν, 'to hear tidings' of father; ἕκαθεν δέ τε γίγνετ' ἀκουή, 'can be heard' afar, Π 634.

ἄ-κουρος (κοῦρος): *without male heir*, η 64†.

ἀκούω, ipf. ἤκουον, mostly ἄκουον, (mid. ἀκούετο, Δ 331), fut. ἀκούσομαι, aor. ἤκουσα, mostly ἄκουσα: *hear*; hence 'listen,' 'give ear to,' 'obey'; abs., or w. acc. of thing, gen. of person, (dat. of advantage, Π 516), sometimes gen. of thing; foll. by participle, gen., Ω 490, α 289, rarely acc. H 129; inf., Z 386; Ἀτρείδην ἀκούετε, ὡς ἦλθε (i. e. ὡς Ἀτρείδης ἦλθε), γ 193.

ἀ-κρᾰ́αντος (κραιαίνω): *unfulfilled, unaccomplished.*

ἀκρ-ᾱής, έος (ἄκρος, ἄϝημι): *sharp-blowing*, of favorable winds. (Od.)

ἄκρη (ἄκρος): *summit, promontory, cape*; κατ' ἄκρης, 'from on high'; μέγα κῦμα, ε 313 (ingens a vertice pontus); then 'from top to bottom,' 'utterly' (ὤλετο, ἑλέειν, O 557).

ἄκρηθεν: see κατάκρηθεν.

ἄ-κρητος (κεραννῡμι): *unmixed, pure.*

ἀκρίς, ίδος: *locust*, pl., Φ 12†.

ἄκρις, ιος (ἄκρος): *mountain-top*, only pl., 'heights.' (Od.)

Ἀκρισιώνη: *daughter of Acrisius*, Danaë, Ξ 319†.

ἀ-κριτό-μῡθος: *indiscriminate in speech*; Thersites, 'endless babbler,' B 246 (cf. 213, 796); of dreams, 'mazy,' τ 560.

ἄ-κριτος (κρίνω): *unseparated, undecided, confused, endless*; τύμβος (*undistinguished*, i. e. common to many dead), νείκεα, ἄχεα, μῦθοι.—Adv., ἄκριτον, 'unceasingly.'

ἀκριτό-φυλλος (φύλλον): *dense with leaves* or *foliage*, B 868†.

ἀκρο-κελαινιάω (κελαινός): only part., *with darkling surface*, Φ 249†.

ἀκρό-κομος (κόμη): *with hair* done up *at the crown of the head*, Δ 533†.

ἄκρον, subst.: *point, promontory, summit.*—Adv., see ἄκρος.

'Ακρόνεως (*ναῦς*): name of a Phaeacian, θ 111.

ἀκρό-πολις: *citadel*, only in Od. In Il., separated, ἄκρη πόλις.

ἀκρο-πόλος (πέλομαι), only dat. pl.: *lofty*.

ἀκρο-πόρος (πείρω): *with piercing point*, acc. pl., γ 463†.

ἄκρος (root ακ), sup. ἀκρότατος: *uttermost*, *topmost*, *highest*, *at the top*, *end*, *edge*, or *surface of* (s u m m u s); **πόλις** ἄκρη, ἄκρη πόλις, 'upper city' (=ἀκρόπολις); **κατ'** ἄκρης, see ἄκρη.—Adv. ἄκρον, 'along the top,' Υ 229.

'Ακταίη: a Nereid, Σ 41†.

1. **ἀκτή**: *meal*, *corn*; always with ἀλφίτου, or Δημήτερος.

2. **ἀκτή**: *shore*, esp. rocky and jutting parts, ἀπορρῶγες, προβλῆτες.

ἀ-κτήμων (κτῆμα): *without possession*, with gen.

ἀκτίς, ῖνος, only dat. pl., ἀκτῖσιν, ἀκτίνεσσι: *ray*, *beam* of the sun.

'Ακτορίδης: *descendant of Actor*, Echecles, Π 189†.

'Ακτορίς: an attendant of Penelope, ψ 228†.

'Ακτορίων: *son of Actor;* there were twins, '**Ακτορίωνε**, called also Μολίονε after their mother Molione, Λ 750.

"Ακτωρ: (1) son of Azeus, Β 513.—(2) father of Menoetius, Λ 785, Π 14.—(3) son of Phorbas, brother of Augeas, and father of the '**Ακτορίωνε**.—(4) father of Echecles.

ἄκυλος: *edible acorn*, *sweet acorn*, κ 242†.

ἀκωκή (root ακ): *point* of a weapon.

ἄκων, οντος (root ακ): *javelin*, *dart*.

ἄκων: see ἀέκων.

ἅλα-δε: *seaward*, *into the sea*; with εἰς, κ 351.

ἀλάλημαι: see ἀλάομαι.

ἀλαλητός (cf. ἀλαλάζω, and for the reduplication also ὀλολύζω, ἐλελεῦ, etc.): loud, resounding *yell*, *yelling*, *war-cry*, of a tumultuous throng; usually a triumphant outcry, but raised by the panic-stricken victims of Achilles, Φ 10; in the assembly, by a majority opposed to fighting, ω 463.

ἄλαλκε, -εῖν, -ών: see ἀλέξω.

'Αλαλκομενηίς (ἀλαλκεῖν): the *Defender*, an epithet of Athena, with which is connected the name of '**Αλαλκομεναί**, a city in Boeotia, Δ 8, Ε 908.

ἀλαλύκτημαι (cf. ἀλύω, ἀλύσκω): perf. w. pres. signification, *am bewildered*, Κ 94†.

ἀλάομαι, imp. ἀλόω, ipf. ἠλώμην, ἀλώμην, aor. ἀλήθην, pf. ἀλάλημαι, ἀλαλήμενος: *wander*, *rove*, *roam*, of adventurers, freebooters, mendicants, and homeless or lost persons. The perf. is only more intensive in meaning than the present, β 370, etc.

ἀλαός: *blind*.

ἀλαο-σκοπίη: only in the phrase, οὐδ' ἀλαοσκοπίην εἶχε, he kept no *blind* (i. e. heedless) *watch*.

ἀλαόω: *make blind*, w. gen. ὀφθαλμοῦ. (Od.)

ἀλαπαδνός, comp. **νότερος**: *easily exhausted*, *unwarlike;* σθένος οὐκ ἀλαπαδνόν, *exhaustless* strength, and freq. w. neg.

ἀλαπάζω, ipf. ἀλάπαζε, fut. -ξω, aor. ἀλάπαξα: *empty*, *drain*, esp. with πόλιν, *sack;* then of ships, men, etc., 'destroy,' 'slay.'

ἀλαστέω (ἄλαστος), only ipf. ἠλάστεον, aor. part. ἀλαστήσᾱς: *be unforgetting*, *be wroth*, Μ 163 and Ο 21.

'Αλαστορίδης: *son of Alastor*, Tros, Υ 463.

ἄ-λαστος, *ον* (λαθέσθαι): *never to be forgotten*, 'ceaseless;' ἄλος, πένθος, ἄλαστον ὀδύρομαι, ἄλαστε, 'eternal foe,' Χ 261.

'Αλάστωρ: (1) a Lycian, Ε 677.—(2) a leader of the Pylians, Δ 295.—(3) father of Tros.

ἀλαωτύς (ἀλαός): *blinding*, ι 503†.

ἀλγέω (ἄλγος), aor. subj. ἀλγήσετε, part. ἀλγήσᾱς: *feel pain*, *suffer;* met., μ 27.

ἄλγιον, ἀλγίστη: see ἀλεγεινός.

ἄλγος: *pain;* freq. met., and esp. pl., *hardship*, *troubles*, *woe;* of hunters, οἵ τε καθ' ὕλην | ἄλγεα πάσχουσιν, ι 121; often of Odysseus, πάθεν ἄλγεα θῡμῷ, etc.; πόλλ' ἄλγεα δυσμενέεσσιν, 'vexation,' ζ 184.

ἀλδαίνω (root αλ, a l o): *make to grow;* only aor. μέλε' ἤλδανε ποιμένι λᾱῶν, 'filled out' his limbs. (Od.)

ἀλδήσκω (root αλ): *grow full;* **ληίου** ἀλδήσκοντος, Ψ 599†.

ἀλέασθαι: see ἀλέομαι.

ἀλεγεινός (ἄλγος), comp. neut. ἄλγιον, sup. ἄλγιστος: *painful*, *hard*, *toilsome;* **πυγμαχίη, κῦματα, μαχλο-**

σύνη, 'fraught with trouble,' Ω 30; freq. w. inf., ἡμίονος ἀλγίστη δαμάσασθαι, Ψ 655.—Adv. ἄλγιον, used in exclamations, τῷ δ' ἄλγιον, 'so much the worse' for him!

'Αλεγηνορίδης: *son of Alegenor*, Promachus, Ξ 503†.

ἀλεγίζω (ἀλέγω), only pr. and ipf. without augment: *care for, heed*, τινός. Always with neg.; abs. οὐκ ἀλεγίζει | οὐδ' ὄθεται, Ο 106.

ἀλεγύνω (ἀλέγω): *care for, attend to*, only w. δαῖτα, δαῖτας. Said comprehensively, for 'partaking of,' 'enjoying' the meal. (Od).

ἀλέγω, only pres.: *care, care for, be concerned*, τινός (acc. Π 388); ἀλέγουσι κιοῦσαι, 'are troubled' as they go, Ι 504; usually w. neg., abs. κύνες οὐκ ἀλέγουσαι, *careless* (good-for-nothing) hussies, τ 154. In ζ 268 equiv. to ἀλεγύνω.

ἀλεείνω: parallel form of ἀλέομαι, only pres. and ipf.

1. **ἀλέη** (ἀλέομαι): *shunning, escaping, escape*, Χ 301†.

2. **ἀλέη**: *warm sunshine*, ρ 23†.

ἄλειας, ατος (ἀλέω): *flour, wheaten flour*, υ 108†.

ἀλείς: see εἴλω.

'Αλείσιον: a town in Elis, Β 617, Λ 757.

ἄλεισον: *tankard*, usually costly; χρύσεον, ἄμφωτον, χ 9.

ἀλείτης: *sinner, evil-doer*, Γ 28, υ 121.

ἄλειφαρ, ατος (ἀλείφω): *ointment, fat* or *oil;* for anointing the dead before cremation, and in γ 408 for polishing marble, 'glistening with oil.'

ἀλείφω (λίπα), aor. ἤλειψα and ἀλ., mid. ἀλειψάμην: *anoint*, usually λίπ' ἐλαίῳ, but of smearing with wax, μ 200.

'Αλεκτρυών: father of Leïtus, Ρ 602†.

'Αλέκτωρ: father-in-law of Megapenthes, δ 10†.

ἄλεν, ἀλέν: see εἴλω.

ἀλεξάμενος, -ασθαι: see ἀλέξω.

'Αλέξ-ανδρος: *Alexander*, Greek name of Paris, and perhaps a translation of that word. See Πάρις.

ἀλεξ-άνεμος: *protecting against the wind*, ξ 529†.

ἀλεξητής, ῆρος: *averter;* μάχης, stemmer of battle,' Υ 396†.

ἀλεξί-κακος: *averting ill*, Κ 20†.

ἀλέξω (root αλκ), inf. ἀλεξέμεν (αι), fut. ἀλεξήσω, red. aor. ἄλαλκε, subj. ἀλάλκῃσι, inf. ἀλαλκεῖν, -έμεναι, -έμεν, aor. opt. ἀλεξήσειε, and subj. mid. ἀλεξώμεσθα: *ward off, avert*, τί, τινί, and τινί τι, hence *defend* one against something; mid., *ward off* from, *defend* oneself.

ἀλέομαι, ἀλεύομαι (ἀλέϝομαι), aor. ἠλεύατο, ἀλεύατο, -ντο, opt. ἀλέαιτο, imp. ἄλευαι, ἀλέασθε, inf. ἀλέασθαι, part. ἀλευάμενος (subj. ἀλέϝηται, ἀλεϝώμεθα, aor. or pres.): *shun, avoid, flee from, flee;* abs., and freq. τί, rarely τινά (θεούς, 'shun their wrath,' ι 274); also w. inf.

ἄλεται: see ἅλλομαι.

ἀλετρεύω: *grind*, η 104†.

ἀλετρίς (ἀλέω): *one who grinds*, γυνή, woman 'at the mill,' υ 105†.

ἀλεύεται: see ἀλέομαι.

ἀλέω, only aor. ἄλεσσαν: *grind*, υ 109†.

ἀλεωρή (ἀλέομαι): *shunning, escape, means of shunning* or defending against, τινός.

ἄλη (ἀλάομαι): *wandering, roving, roaming.*

ἀ-ληθείη (ἀληθής): *truth.*

ἀληθείς: see ἀλάομαι.

ἀ-ληθής (λήθω): *true;* of a person, 'honest,' Μ 433, neut. sing. γ 247, elsewhere only neut. pl.

'Αλήιον, πεδίον: the *Aleïan* plain, scene of Bellerophon's wandering, in Cilicia according to the later legend, Ζ 201†. The name seems to involve a play upon ἀλᾶτο (in the same v.), cf. 'Αλύβᾶς.

ἀ-λήιος (λήιον): *without corn-land*, i. e. *without property*, cf. ἄκληρος.

ᾱ-ληκτος, ἄλληκτος (λήγω): *unceasing;* adv. -τον, *unceasingly.*

ἀλήμεναι, ἀλῆναι: see εἴλω.

ἀλήμων, ονος (ἀλάομαι): *roving, wandering, wanderer.*

ἄληται: see ἅλλομαι.

ἀλητεύω (ἀλήτης): *roam about.* (Od.)

ἀλήτης (ἀλάομαι): *vagabond, beggar.* (Od.)

'Αλθαίᾱ: wife of Oeneus in Calydon, mother of Meleager, Ι 555†.

ἄλθομαι: *be healed;* ἄλθετο χείρ, *was healing*, Ε 417†.

ἁλι-ᾱής, έος (ἅλς, ἄημι): *blowing on the sea*, of favorable, off-shore winds, δ 361†.

Ἁλίαρτος: a town in Boeotia, Β 503†.

ἀ-λίαστος (λιάζομαι): *unswerving*, hence *obstinate*, *persistent*; πόλεμος, πόνος, γόος. (Il.)

ἀλίγκιος: *like*, *resembling*.

ἁλιεύς, ῆος (ἅλς): *seaman*, *fisherman*; as adj., π 349.

Ἁλιζῶνες: a tribe of Trojan allies from Pontus.

Ἁλίη: a Nereid, Σ 40†.

Ἁλι-θέρσης: an Ithacan, the son of Mestor, and a friend of Odysseus, β 157, ρ 78. (Od.)

ἁλι-μῡρήεις, εντος (ἅλς, μύρω): *mingling with the sea*, epith. of rivers.

1. **ἅλιος** (ἅλς): *of the sea*; γέρων, Nereus (Α 556), Proteus (δ 365), θεαί, and as subst. ἅλιαι, the Nereids, ω 47.

2. **ἅλιος**: *fruitless*, *ineffectual*, *vain*, *in vain*; adv. ἅλιον.

Ἅλιος: (1) a Lycian, Ε 678.—(2) a son of Alcinous, θ 119, 370.

ἁλιο-τρεφής, έος (τρέφω): *sea-nurtured*, epith. of seals, δ 442†.

ἁλιόω (ἅλιος 2), only aor. ἀλίωσε, -ῶσαι: *render fruitless*, *baffle*, with βέλος, 'hurl in vain,' Π 737.

ἁλί-πλοος (πλέω): *sailing in the sea*, 'submerged,' acc. pl., Μ 26†.

ἁλι-πόρφυρος: *sea-purple*, *purple as the sea*. (Od.)

ἅλις (ϝάλις, cf. ἐϝάλην, εἴλω): *crowded together*; of persons, 'in throngs'; bees, 'in swarms'; corpses, 'in heaps.' Then *in plenty*, *abundantly*, *enough*; ἅλις δέ οἱ, he has carried it 'far enough' already, Ι 376; ἦ οὐχ ἅλις ὅτι (ὡς), is it not *enough* (and more than enough), etc.?

ἁλίσκομαι (ϝαλ.), pres. not in Homer, aor. ἥλω, subj. ἁλώω, opt. ἁλῴην, ἁλοίην, inf. ἁλῶναι, part. ἁλούς (ᾱλόντε, Ε 487): *be taken*, *captured*, of men, towns; met. θανάτῳ ἁλῶναι, and without θανάτῳ of being 'killed,' 'slain' (cf. αἱρέω).

ἀλιταίνω, aor. ἤλιτον (Ι 375), ἀλιτόμην, pf. part. ἀλιτήμενος: *sin against*, τινά, or τί (Ω 586); θεοῖς ἀλιτήμενος, a *transgressor* in the eyes of the gods, δ 807.

ἀλιτήμων, ονος (ἀλιταίνω): *sinning against*, *offending*.

ἀλιτρός (ἀλιταίνω): *sinner*, *offender*; δαίμοσιν, 'in the eyes of heaven;' colloquially, 'rogue,' ε 182.

Ἀλκά-θοος: son-in-law of Anchises.

Ἀλκ-άνδρη: wife of Polybus, in Egyptian Thebes, δ 126†.

Ἄλκ-ανδρος (cf. Ἀλέξανδρος): a Lycian, Ε 678.

ἄλκαρ (root αλκ): *protection*, *defence*, Ε 644 and Λ 823.

ἀλκή, ῆς (root αλκ), dat. ἀλκί, ἀλκῇ: *defence*, *defensive strength*, *valor*, *might*; common phrases, θούριδος ἀλκῆς, ἀλκὶ πεποιθώς, ἐπιειμένος ἀλκήν. Joined with βίη, μένος, σθένος, ἠνορέη. Personified, Ε 740.

Ἄλκηστις (root αλκ, she averted death from her husband by dying for him, but this legend is not mentioned by Homer): *Alcestis*, daughter of Pelias, wife of Admetus of Pherae, and mother of Eumelus, Β 715.

ἀλκί: see ἀλκή.

Ἀλκι-μέδων: son of Laerces, a leader of the Myrmidons, and charioteer of Achilles after the death of Patroclus.

Ἀλκιμίδης: *son of Alcimus*, Mentor, χ 235†.

ἄλκιμος (ἀλκή): *efficient in defence*, *valiant*, opp. δειλός, Ν 278; freq. ἄλκιμον ἦτορ, also applied as epith. of weapons.

Ἄλκιμος: (1) father of Mentor.—(2) a Myrmidon, friend of Achilles.

Ἀλκί-νοος: king of the Phaeacians in Scheria, a grandson of Poseidon, η 61 ff.

Ἀλκ-ίππη: a slave of Helen at Sparta, δ 124†.

Ἀλκ-μαίων: son of Amphiarāus and Eriphȳle, ο 248†.

Ἀλκ-μάων: a Greek, the son of Thestor, Μ 394†.

Ἀλκ-μήνη: wife of Amphitryon in Thebes, mother of Heracles by Zeus, and of Iphicles by Amphitryon.

ἀλκτήρ, ῆρος: *defender against*, *averter*.

Ἀλκυόνη: a name given to Cleopatra, daughter of Idas and Marpessa, and wife of Meleager, Ι 562.

ἀλκυών, όνος: *halcyon*, a sea-bird with plaintive note, Ι 563†.

ἀλλά (ἄλλος, cf. ceterum): *but, nay but, but yet, yet;* combined ἀλλ' ἄρα, ἀλλὰ γάρ, ἀλλ' ἤ (τοι), ἀλλά τε, ἀλλὰ καὶ ὥς, ἀλλ' οὐδ' ὥς, etc.; very freq. after a negation (when ἄλλος or ἕτερος precedes, like 'than,' Φ 275), but also used like δέ correl. to μέν, and after concessive statements, *yet*, A 281; often in appeal, *nay*, A 32, and w. imp. or hortative subj., ἀλλ' ἴομεν, esp. ἀλλ' ἄγε, ἄγετε.

ἄλλεγεν, ἀλλέξαι: see ἀναλέγω.

ἄλλῃ: *elsewhere, another way;* of place (ἄλλον ἄλλῃ, θ 516), direction (ἄλλυδις ἄλλῃ), or manner (βούλεσθαι, O 51); ὅ μοι γέρας ἔρχεται ἄλλῃ, goes 'into other hands' (than mine), A 120.

ἄλληκτος: see ἄληκτος.

ἀλλ-ήλων (ἄλλος, ἄλλος), gen. du. ἀλλήλοιιν, K 65: *each other, one another, mutually.*

ἀλλό-γνωτος: *known to others*, i. e. *foreign*, β 366†.

ἀλλοδαπός: *strange, foreign;* also subst., *stranger*.

ἀλλο-ειδής, or ἀλλο-ϊδής, only neut. pl. ἀλλοϝϝειδέ' or ἀλλοϝιδέα: *different-looking, strange-looking*, ν 194† (cf. π 181).

ἄλλο-θεν: *from elsewhere;* 'from abroad,' γ 318; ἄλλοθεν ἄλλος, 'one from one side, another from another.'

ἄλλο-θι: *elsewhere*, 'abroad;' γαίης, part. gen., 'in the world,' β 131, but with πάτρης, gen. of separation, 'far from,' ρ 318.

ἀλλό-θροος: *speaking a strange tongue.* (Od.)

ἀλλοϊδής: see ἀλλοειδής.

ἀλλοῖος: *of another sort, different;* implying inferiority, τ 265.

ἄλλομαι, aor. 2 and 3 pers. sing. ἆλσο, ἆλτο, subj. ἄληται, ἄλεται, part. ἅλμενος: *leap, spring;* met. of an arrow 'leaping' from the string, Δ 125.

ἀλλο-πρόσ-αλλος: *changing from one to another*, epith. of Ares, 'fickle god,' E 831 and 889.

ἄλλος: *other, another*, (οἱ) ἄλλοι, *the rest;* freq. in antithetical and reciprocal clauses, ἄλλος μὲν . . ἄλλος δέ, ἄλλοθεν ἄλλος, etc.; very often idiomatic and untranslatable, ἔκτοθεν ἄλλων | μνηστήρων, 'from the others, the suitors,' i. e. from the throng of suitors, α 132. Phrases: ἄλλο τόσον, as much 'more'; ἰδὼν ἐς πλησίον ἄλλον, with a look towards his next 'neighbor'; ἔξοχον ἄλλων, ἄλλο δέ τοι ἐρέω (marking a transition), similarly ἄλλ' (ἄλλο) ἐνόησε (a 'new' idea). In υ 213, ἄλλοι implies 'strangers,' i. e. other than the rightful owners; so 'untrue' (other than the true) is implied, δ 348.

ἄλλο-σε: *to another place, elsewhere*, ψ 184 and 204.

ἄλλο-τε: *at another time;* hence 'formerly,' or 'in the future' (T 200); often in reciprocal and antithetic phrases, ἄλλοτε ἄλλῳ, ἄλλοτ' ἐπ' ἄλλον, ἄλλοτε μὲν . . ἄλλοτε δέ (αὖτε), *now . . then, now . now.*

ἀλλότριος: *of* or *belonging to another, strange;* γαῖα, ἀλλότρια, 'others' goods'; ἀλλότριος φώς, 'foe-man'; γναθμοῖσι γελώων ἀλλοτρίοισιν, were laughing 'with jaws as of other men' (distorted faces), description of supernatural effects, υ 347, cf. 351 ff.

ἄ-λλοφος: see ἄλοφος.

ἀλλο-φρονέω: *be abstracted, unconscious* (Ψ 698), only pres. part.

ἄλλυδις: *to another place*, always with ἄλλος, or with ἄλλῃ, 'now in one way, now in another,' 'now this way, now that.'

ἀλ-λύεσκεν, ἀλλύουσα: see ἀναλύω.

ἄλλως: *otherwise;* freq. implying 'in vain' ('idly'), 'besides,' 'for some other reason' (ρ 577), 'as it is' (φ 87), 'better' (E 218, θ 176).

ἅλμα (ἅλλομαι): *leaping*, as a contest, game, θ 103 and 128.

ἅλμη (ἅλς): *sea-water, brine.* (Od.)

ἁλμυρός: only ἁλμυρὸν ὕδωρ, *salt* water. (Od.)

ἀ-λογέω (ἄλογος): *be disregardful*, fut., O 162 and 178.

ἁλό-θεν: *from the sea;* ἐξ ἁλόθεν, 'from out the sea,' Φ 335†.

ἀλοιάω (ἀλωή): *thresh* by treading, only ipf., γαῖαν χερσὶν ἀλοίᾱ, she *smote* the ground, I 568†.

ἀλοιφή (ἀλείφω): *ointment, grease, fat;* rubbed into a bow of horn to render it pliant, φ 179.

'Αλόπη: a town in the domain of Achilles, B 682†.

῎Αλος: a town in the domain of Achilles, B 682†.

ἁλο-σύδνη: *child of the sea;* Thetis, Υ 207; Amphitrite, δ 404.

ἄ-λοφος, ἄλλοφος (λόφος), ᾱ before λ: *without plume; κυνέη*, K 258†. (See cut under λόφος.)

ἄ-λοχος (λέχος): *wife;* epithets, μνηστή, αἰδοίη, κυδρή, κεδνή, πολύδωρος.

ἀλόω, ἀλόωνται: see ἀλάομαι.

ἅλς (cf. s a l): (1) m., *salt, grain of salt*, prov. οὐδ' ἅλα δοίης, ρ 455; pl. ἅλες, *salt* (as we say 'salts' in medicine), λ 123, ψ 270.—(2) fem., *the sea.*

ἆλσο: see ἅλλομαι.

ἄλσος, εος: *grove* (l u c u s), usually with an altar, and sacred to a divinity, B 506, ζ 321.

Ἄλτης: king of the Leleges, father of Laothoe, Φ 85.

ἆλτο: see ἅλλομαι.

Ἀλύβᾱς, αντος: feigned name of a place, with a play upon ἀλάομαι ('Wanderley'), ω 304†.

Ἀλύβη: a country near Troy, productive of silver, B 857†.

ἀλυσκάζω (stronger than ἀλύσκω), only pres. and ipf.: *skulk, seek to escape;* abs., and with acc. of thing avoided.

ἀλυσκάνω=ἀλυσκάζω, ipf., χ 330†.

ἀλύσκω (ἀλεύομαι), fut. ἀλύξω, aor. ἤλυξα and ἄλυξα: *shun, avoid, escape;* abs., and with τί, less freq. τινά, ἤλυξα ἑταίρους, 'evaded their observation,' μ 335.

ἀλύσσω (ἀλύω): *be frenzied*, of dogs after tasting blood, X 70†.

ἄ-λυτος: *not to be loosed, indissoluble.*

ἀλῡ́ω (cf. ἀλάομαι): *wander in mind, be beside oneself, distraught*, with pain, grief (Ω 12), or sometimes with joy (σ 333); ἀλῡ́ων, 'frantic with pain,' ι 398.

ἀλφάνω, only aor. ἦλφον, opt. ἄλφοι, 3 pl. ἄλφοιν, υ 383: *yield, bring; μῡρίον ὦνον*, 'an immense price,' ο 453, cf. Φ 79.

Ἀλφειός: (1) a river in Arcadia and Elis (flowing past Olympia), B 592.—(2) the river-god *Alphēüs*, γ 489.

ἀλφεσί-βοιος (ἀλφάνω, βοῦς): *earning cattle*, epith. of maidens, whose parents, when the daughter is married, receive presents of cattle from the bridegroom, Σ 593†. See ἔδνα.

ἀλφηστής (ἀλφάνω): *wage-earning, toiling;* ἄνδρες ἀλφησταί.

ἄλφιτον: *barley*, in sing. only gen. ἀλφίτου ἀκτή, *barley-meal;* pl. ἄλφιτα, *barley-groats* or *meal.*

Ἀλωεύς, ῆος (ἀλωή): father of Otus and Ephialtes, husband of Iphimēdīa, E 386.

ἀλωή: *threshing-floor* (a r e a), Υ 496; also *orchard* or *vineyard*, Σ 561. See γουνός.

ἁλώῃ, ἁλῴη, ἁλώμενος: see ἁλίσκομαι.

ἀλώμενος: see ἀλάομαι

ἁλώω: see ἁλίσκομαι.

ἄμ, ἀμ: see ἀνά.

ἅμα: (1) adv., *at once, at the same time;* ἅμα πάντες, ἅμ' ἄμφω, H 255; freq. with τὲ . . καί (B 281), or with following δέ, ἅμα μῦθος ἔην, τετέλεστο δὲ ἔργον, 'no sooner said than done,' T 242.—(2) prep. w. dat., *at the same time with, along with*, ἅμ' ἠελίῳ καταδύντι, ἅμ' ἕπεσθαι, 'attend,' 'accompany,' ἅμα πνοιῇς ἀνέμοιο, 'swift as the winds,' α 98, Π 149.

Ἀμαζόνες: the *Amazons*, a warlike community of women, dwelling on the river Thermōdon in Pontus. They invaded Lycia, also Priam's realm in Phrygia, Γ 189, Z 186.

Ἀμάθεια: a Nereid, Σ 48†.

ἄμαθος (ψάμαθος): *sand*, E 587†.

ἀμαθῡ́νω (ἄμαθος): *reduce to dust;* πόλιν δέ τε πῦρ ἀμαθῡ́νει, I 593†.

ἀμαιμάκετος: doubtful word, *unconquerable, monstrous;* epith. of the Chimaera, Z 179 and Π 329; of a floating mast, 'huge,' ξ 311.

ἀμαλδῡ́νω, aor. inf. ἀμαλδῦναι, part. -ῡ́νᾱς, pass. pr. subj. ἀμαλδῡ́νηται: *crush, efface*, τεῖχος. (Il.)

ἀμαλλο-δετήρ, ῆρος (ἄμαλλα, δέω): *binder of sheaves.* Only in Σ.

ἀμαλός: *tender*, epith. of young animals.

ἄμαξα, ἅμαξα (ἅμα, ἄξων): four-wheeled draught *wagon*, distinguished from the war-chariot (ἅρμα), which had two wheels, ι 251; also the constellation of the Great Bear (*the Wain*), Σ 487, ε 273.

ἁμαξιτός (ἅμαξα): *wagon-road*, strictly adj., sc. ὁδός, X 146†.

ἀμάρη: *canal, ditch* for irrigation, Φ 259†.

ἁμαρτάνω, fut. ἁμαρτήσομαι, aor. ἥμαρτον and ἤμβροτον: (1) *miss, fail* to *hit*, τινός, and abs., ἥμβροτες, οὐδ' ἔτυχες, Ε 287; met., 'mistake,' 'fail of,' 'lose' (just as τυχεῖν = 'get'), η 292, ι 512, φ 155; οὔ τι φίλων ἡμάρτανε δώρων, 'failed not to bring,' Ω 68.—(2) *err*, *do wrong*, ὅτε κέν τις ὑπερβήῃ καὶ ἁμάρτῃ, Ι 501; αὐτὸς ἐγὼ τόδε ἤμβροτον, 'was guilty of this oversight,' χ 154.

ἁμαρτέω: see ὁμαρτέω.

ἁμαρτῇ, ἁμαρτῆ (ἅμα, root αρ): *at once*, *together*.

ἁμαρτο-επής, ές (Ϝέπος): *erring in word*, *rash-speaking*, Ν 824†. Cf. ἀφαμαρτοεπής.

Ἀμαρυγκείδης: *son of Amaryncеus*, Diores, Β 622, Δ 517.

Ἀμαρυγκεύς, έος: ruler of the Epeians at Buprasion in Messenia, Ψ 630†.

ἁμα-τροχάω: see τροχάω.

ἁμα-τροχίη (τρέχω): *running together*, *collision* of chariots, pl., Ψ 422†.

ἀμαυρός: *shadowy*, *darkling*; εἴδωλον ἀμαυρόν, δ 824 and 835.

ἀ-μαχητί: *without contest*, Φ 437†.

ἀμάω (cf. 'mow,' which orig. means to lay in heaps), ipf. ἤμων, aor. part. ἀμήσαντες, mid. ἀμησάμενος: *mow*, *reap*, Σ 551; ἀπ' (adv.) οὔατα ἀμήσαντες, 'lopping off,' φ 300; mid. ἀμησάμενος, 'collecting,' 'scooping up' his curds, ι 247.

ἀμβαίνω, ἀμβάλλω: see ἀναβ-.

ἄμ-βατος (ἀναβαίνω): *to be ascended*, *scaled*.

ἀμ-βλήδην (ἀναβάλλω): adv., *with deep-fetched breath* (= ἀμβολάδην), *deeply*, γοόωσα, Χ 476†. According to others, *as prelude* (ἀναβάλλομαι), *at first*.

ἀμ-βολάδην (ἀναβάλλω): adv., *bubbling up*, Φ 364†.

ἀμβροσίη (ἀμβρόσιος), adj. used as subst.: *ambrosia*; the food of the gods and of their steeds; also used as ointment, for embalming, for perfume.

ἀμβρόσιος (ἄμβροτος): *ambrosial*, *divine*; epith. of anything belonging to, pertaining to, or conceived as bestowed by the gods; χαῖται, Α 529; εἶδαρ (for their steeds), Η 369, νύξ, ὕπνος.

ἄ-μβροτος (βροτός): *immortal*, *divine*; θεός, Υ 358, and like ἀμβρόσιος (αἷμα, τεύχεα, νύξ, λ 330).

ἀ-μέγαρτος (μεγαίρω): *unenviable*, *dreadful*; voc. as term of reproach, *miserable*, ρ 219.

ἀμείβω, fut. ἀμείψω, -ομαι, aor. ἠμείψατο, ἀμείψατο: I. act., *change*, *exchange*; τινός τι πρός τινα (something with one for something else), Ζ 235; ὀλίγον γόνυ γουνὸς ἀμείβων, 'only a little changing knee for knee' (in retreating slowly step by step), Λ 547; part. as subst., ἀμείβοντες, 'rafters' of a house, Ψ 712.—II. mid., *change with each other*, *answer*, *pass*; of responsive ('amoebean') singing, Α 604; 'alternating' in the dance, θ 379; θρῴσκων ἀμείβεται, 'springs alternately,' Ο 684; 'passing from house to house,' α 375; 'requiting' one with gifts, ω 285. In the sense of *answer*, very freq. the part. ἀμειβόμενος, 'in reply,' ἀμειβόμενος προσέειπεν, ἠμείβετο μύθῳ.

ἀ-μείλικτος (μειλίσσω): *unsoftened*, *harsh*, *stern*, *relentless*. (Il.)

ἀμείλιχος = ἀμείλικτος.

ἀμείνων, ον, irreg. comp. of ἀγαθός: *better*. For implied meanings, see ἀγαθός.

ἀμέλγω, only pr. and ipf.: *milk*; pass., ἀμελγόμεναι γάλα λευκόν, 'yielding,' Δ 434.

ἀ-μελέω, (μέλω), only aor. ἀμέλησα: *neglect*, *forget*; τινός, always with negation.

ἄμεναι: see ἄω.

ἀ-μενηνός (μένος): *powerless*, *feeble*, Ε 887; of the shades of the dead, νεκύων ἀμενηνὰ κάρηνα, of dreams, 'unsubstantial,' τ 562.

ἀ-μενηνόω (ἀμενηνός): *make powerless*, *ineffective*, only aor., Ν 562†.

1. **ἀ-μέρδω** (μέρος), aor. ἤμερσα, ἄμερσα, inf. ἀμέρσαι, pass. pres. ἀμέρδεαι, aor. subj. ἀμερθῇς: *deprive of one's share*, *deprive*, θ 64; pass., *be deprived of*, *forfeit*, τινός, Χ 58, φ 290.

2. **ἀ-μέρδω** (μάρμαρος), only pres. and ipf.: *dazzle*, *blind* by excess of light, Ν 340; similarly, *make lustreless*, *tarnish*, ἔντεα κάπνος ἀμέρδει, τ 18.

ἀ-μέτρητος (μετρέω): *immeasurable*, τ 512 and ψ 249.

ἀ-μετρο-επής (Ϝέπος): *of unmeasured speech*, Β 212†.

ἀμητήρ, ῆρος (ἀμάω): *reaper*, pl., Λ 67†.

ἄμητος (ἀμάω): *reaping, harvest,* metaph., T 223†.

ἀ-μηχανίη (ἀμήχανος): *helplessness, despair,* ι 295†.

ἀ-μήχανος (μηχανή, μῆχος): (1) act., *helpless, despairing,* τ 363.—(2) pass., of that with which one can do nothing, *impossible,* Ξ 262; ὄνειροι, 'inscrutable', τ 560; ἀμήχανα ἔργα, 'irreparable mischief,' Θ 130; of persons, 'impracticable,' 'unmanageable,' K 167; ἀμήχανός ἐσσι πιθέσθαι, 'it is hopeless to expect you to comply,' N 726.

Ἀμισώδαρος: a king in Caria, father of Atymnius and Maris, Π 328†.

ἀ-μιτρο-χίτωνες (μίτρη, χιτών): *without belt beneath their coat of mail* (χιτών), epith. of the Lycians, Π 419†.

ἀμιχθαλόεις, εσσα: *smoky, hazy;* epith. of Lemnos, which is a volcanic island, Ω 753†.

ἄμμε, ἄμμες, ἄμμι: see ἡμεῖς.

ἀμ-μῖξᾱς: see ἀναμίγνῡμι.

ἀ-μμορίη (μόρος): μοῖράν τ' ἀμμορίην τε, all that is 'fated and unfated,' υ 76†. Cf. ἄμμορος (2).

ἄ-μμορος (μόρος, μοῖρα): (1) *without share* or *portion,* with gen., λοετρῶν Ὠκεάνοιο, said of the constellation of the Great Bear, which in Greek latitudes never sinks below the horizon, ε 275, Σ 489.—(2) *luckless, unhappy,* Z 408, Ω 773.

ἀμνίον: *basin* for receiving the blood of sacrificial victims, γ 444†. (See cut.)

Ἀμνῑσός: the port of Cnōsus in Crete, τ 188†.

ἀ-μογητί (μογέω): *without trouble,* Λ 637†.

ἀμόθεν (ἀμός, obsolete word = εἷς, for τὶς): *from somewhere;* ἀμόθεν γε, θεά, εἰπέ, 'beginning at any point whatever,' relate, α 10†.

ἀμοιβάς, άδος (ἀμείβω): adj., *for a change,* χλαίνη, ξ 521†.

ἀμοιβή (ἀμείβω): *recompense, requital, gift in return.* (Od.)

ἀμοιβηδίς: *by turns,* Σ 506 and σ 310.

ἀμοιβός (ἀμείβω): *one who changes* place with another, ἦλθον ἀμοιβοί (as *substitutes*), N 793†.

ἀμολγός: doubtful word, always (ἐν) νυκτὸς ἀμολγῷ, in the *darkness* of night, 'at dead of night,' as an indication of time.

Ἀμοπάων: a Trojan, son of Polypaemon, slain by Teucer, Θ 276†.

ἀμός, ἀμός = ἡμέτερος.

ἄμοτον: *eagerly, vehemently;* esp. with μέμαα, κλαίω, κεχολωμένος, τανύοντο.

ἀμπ-: see ἀναπ-.

ἀμπελόεις, εσσα, εν (ἄμπελος): *full of vines, vine-clad;* of districts and towns. (Il.)

ἄμπελος, fem.: *grape-vine, vine.* (Od.)

ἀμ-πεπαλών: see ἀναπάλλω.

ἀμ-περές: always διὰ δ' ἀμπερές, see διαμπερές.

ἀμπ-έχω (ἀμφί, ἔχω): *surround, cover,* ἅλμη ἄμπεχεν ὤμους, ζ 225†.

ἀμ-πήδησε: see ἀναπηδάω.

ἀμ-πνεῦσαι, ἄμ-πνυε, ἀμ-πνύνθη, ἄμ-πνυτο: see ἀναπνέω.

ἄμπυξ, υκος (ἀμπέχω): *head-band,* worn by women, χ 469. (See cut.)

ἀμυδίς (ἅμα): Aeolic adv., *at once.* —(1) of place, *together, in a mass*, καθίζειν, κικλήσκειν, etc., πάντ' ἀμυδίς, μ 413, Μ 385.—(2) of time, *at once, immediately*, Ψ 217, ξ 305; *at the same time*, ε 467.

'Αμυδών: a city of the Paeonians, on the river Axius, in Macedonia, Β 849 and Π 288.

'Αμυθάων: son of Cretheus and Tyro, father of Bias and Melampus, λ 259†.

'Αμύκλαι: a city in Laconia, near the Eurotas, 20 stadia S.E. of Sparta, and the residence of Tyndareus, Β 584†.

ἀ-μύμων, ονος (μωμος): *blameless, excellent*, both of persons and things, ὃς δ' ἂν ἀμύμων αὐτὸς ἔῃ καὶ ἀμύμονα εἰδῇ, τ 332 (opp. ἀπηνής, 329); often to mark personal appearance or nobility of birth, and sometimes without regard to moral excellence, ἀμύμονος Αἰγίσθοιο, α 29; θεοῦ ἐς ἀμύμονα νῆσον ('faultless' isle, because it belonged to the god), μ 261.

ἀμύντωρ, ορος (ἀμύνω): *defender, protector.*

Ἀμύντωρ: son of Ormenus, father of Phoenix, Ι 448, Κ 266.

ἀμύνω, inf. ἀμῡνέμεν, -έμεναι, aor. ἤμῡνε, ἄμῡνε, opt. ἀμύναι, inf. ἀμῦναι, imp. ἄμῡνον, mid. ipf. ἀμύνετο, ἠμύνοντο, aor. opt. ἀμυναίμην: I. act., *ward off, defend;* abs., τινί, Ε 486; freq. τινί τι (dat. of interest, though we say 'from'), less often τινός τι, Δ 11; also merely τί, and τινός, ἀπό or περί τινος, of the person or thing defended, Ν 109, β 59, Ρ 182.—II. mid., *ward off* from oneself, *defend* oneself or what is one's own, with the same constructions as the act.; εἷς οἰωνὸς ἄριστος, ἀμύνεσθαι περὶ πάτρης, 'to fight in defence of our country,' Μ 243.

ἀμύσσω, ipf. ἄμυσσεν, fut. ἀμύξεις: *scratch, tear*, στήθεα χερσίν, Τ 284; met., θῡμὸν ἀμύξεις, 'shalt rend' thy soul, Α 243

ἀμφ-αγαπάζω, ipf. ἀμφαγάπαζον, mid. -όμενος: *embrace lovingly, greet warmly*, of entertaining guests, Π 192, ξ 381.

ἀμφ-αγείρομαι: *gather around*, only aor. 2, θεαὶ δέ μιν ἀμφαγέροντο, Σ 37†.

ἀμ-φαδίην (ἀμφάδιος): adv., *openly, publicly.*

ἀμ-φάδιος (ἀναφαίνω): *open, public*, 'regular,' γάμος, ζ 288.

ἀμ-φαδόν and **ἀμ-φαδά** (ἀναφαίνω): adv., *openly, publicly;* opp. κρυφηδόν, ξ 330; βαλέειν, 'in regular battle,' Η 243 (opp. λάθρῃ); ἀμφαδὰ ἔργα γένοιτο, 'be revealed,' 'come to light,' τ 391.

ἀμφ-αραβέω: only aor., τεύχεά τ' ἀμφαράβησε, *clattered about him*, Φ 408†.

ἀμ-φασίη (φάναι): *speechlessness*, w. obj. gen. ἐπέων, Ρ 695, δ 704.

ἀμφ-αφάω, part. ἀμφαφόων, -όωσα, mid. inf. -άασθαι, ipf. -όωντο: *feel about, handle*, esp. to test or examine something; τρὶς δὲ περίστειξας κοῖλον λόχον ἀμφαφόωσα (Helen walks around the Trojan horse and 'feels over' it, while the Greeks are concealed within), δ 277; of examining a necklace, χερσίν τ' ἀμφαφόωντο, ο 462.

ἀμφ-εποτᾶτο: see ἀμφιποτάομαι.

ἀμφ-έπω: see ἀμφιέπω.

ἀμφ-έρχομαι: *come about*, 'sound' or 'rise about,' of sound or savor 'stealing over' one, 'meeting the senses,' only aor. ἀμφήλυθε, ζ 122, μ 369. (Od.)

ἀμφ-έχανε: see ἀμφιχαίνω.

ἀμφ-έχυτ': see ἀμφιχέω.

ἀμφ-ήκης, ἄμφηκες (root ακ): *two-edged*, of a sword, π 80.

ἀμφ-ήλυθε: see ἀμφέρχομαι.

ἀμφ-ηρεφής, ές (ἐρέφω): *covered at both ends, close-covered, closed*, Α 45†.

ἀμφ-ήριστος (ἐρίζω): *contested on both sides, doubtful*, victory (or victor), Ψ 382†.

ἀμφί (cf. ἀμφίς, ἄμφω): *on both sides;* the distinction between ἀμφί and περί ('around') is of course not always observed; the two words are used together, ὄχθαι δ' ἀμφὶ περὶ μέγαλ' ἴαχον, 'round about,' Φ 10, but on the other hand are sometimes interchangeable, ἀμφὶ δὲ κυανέην κάπετον, περὶ δ' ἕρκος ἔλασσεν | κασσιτέρου, Σ 564; cf. Ψ 561 f.—I. adv., *on both sides* (or *ends*, or *above and below*, Ζ 115), *about, around;* here belongs the so-called use 'in tmesi,' and in many instances where the word seems to govern a subst., it is really adverbial, and the case of the subst. must be explained independently, ἀμφ' ὀβελοῖσιν ἔπειραν (ὀβ. dat. instr.), ἀμφὶ δὲ χαῖται | ὤμοις ἀΐσσονται (ὤμ. local dat.). In case of an apparent ambiguity of construction the presumption is in favor of adverbial interpretation in Homer.—II. prep., (1) w. gen., *about, concerning;* ἀμφί τινος μάχεσθαι (Π 825), ἀείδειν (θ 267).—(2) w. dat., (a) local, Β 388, Γ 328; ἤριπε δ' ἀμφ' αὐτῷ, 'over,' Δ 493; τὴν κτεῖνε ἀμφ' ἐμοί, 'near,' λ 423, Ι 470; ἀμφὶ πυρί, 'on,' etc.—(b) causal, 'for,' ἀμφί τινι ἄλγεα πάσχειν, μάχεσθαι, δικάζεσθαι, εἴρεσθαι (τ 95), 'as regards' (Η 408).—(3) w. acc., local, mostly to denote motion or extension in space, ἀμφ' ἅλα ἔλσαι 'Αχαιούς, Α 409; ἀμφὶ ἄστυ ἔρδειν ἱρά, 'around in,' Λ 706; οἱ ἀμφὶ Πρίαμον, 'Priam and his followers.'

'Αμφί-αλος: a Phaeacian, θ 114.

ἀμφί-αλος: *sea-girt.* (Od.)

'Αμφι-άρᾱος: a seer and warrior of Argos, son of Oecles, great grandson of the seer Melampus. Through the treachery of his wife Eriphȳle, who was bribed by Polynīces with the gift of a golden necklace, he was forced to meet his death by joining the expedition of the Seven against Thebes, ο 244.

ἀμφ-ιάχω: only part. with termination of perf., ἀμφιαχυῖαν, as she flew *screaming about,* Β 316†.

ἀμφι-βαίνω, perf. ἀμφιβέβηκας, -κε, subj. ἀμφιβεβήκῃ, plup. ἀμφιβεβήκει: *go* (perf. *stand*) *about* or *over, surround,* with acc. or dat.; ἠέλιος μέσον οὐρανὸν ἀμφιβεβήκει ('had reached mid-heaven in its round,' i. e. stood at the zenith), Θ 68; Τρώων νέφος ἀμφιβέβηκε | νηυσίν, Π 66; ἄχος φρένας ἀμφιβέβηκεν, 'has overwhelmed,' θ 541; met., *protect* (the figure from an animal standing over its young), ἀργυρότοξ', ὃς Χρύσην ἀμφιβέβηκας, Α 37, ι 198.

ἀμφι-βάλλω, aor. 2 part. ἀμφιβαλών, mid. fut. ἀμφιβαλεῦμαι, aor. inf. ἀμφιβαλέσθαι: I. act., *throw about, embrace;* τῷ δ' ἐγὼ ἀμφιβαλὼν θάλαμον δέμον (i. e. the chamber was built around the tree), ψ 192; ἀμφιβαλόντε ἀλλήλους, Ψ 97; κρέας, ὡς οἱ χεῖρες ἐχάνδανον ἀμφιβαλόντι (as much as his hands could hold 'in their clasp'), ρ 344; met., κράτερον μένος ἀμφιβαλόντες (cf. ἐπιέννῡμι), Ρ 742.—II. mid., *throw about oneself,* δὸς δὲ ῥάκος ἀμφιβαλέσθαι, ζ 178, χ 103.

ἀμφί-βασις: *protection,* sc. νεκροῦ, Ε 623†.

ἀμφί-βροτος: *man-protecting* (reaching from head to foot, cf. Ζ 117), ἀσπίς. (Il.) (See cut.)

3

'Αμφι-γένεια: a town subject to Nestor, Β 593†.

ἀμφι-γυήεις (γυῖον): *strong in both arms* (ambidexter), epith. of Hephaestus, usually as subst., Α 607, θ 300.

ἀμφί-γυος (γυῖον): *with limb at both ends, double-pointed,* ἔγχος. Cf. οὐρίαχος. (See cuts below.)

ἀμφι-δαίω: *kindle about,* only perf. intr. (and fig.), πόλεμος ἄστυ ἀμφιδέδηε, *blazes round,* Ζ 329†.

'Αμφι-δάμᾱς, αντος: (1) from Cythēra, Κ 268.—(2) from Opus, Ψ 87.

ἀμφί-δασυς, σεια (δασύς): *shaggy all around, thick-fringed,* epith. of the Aegis, Ο 309†.

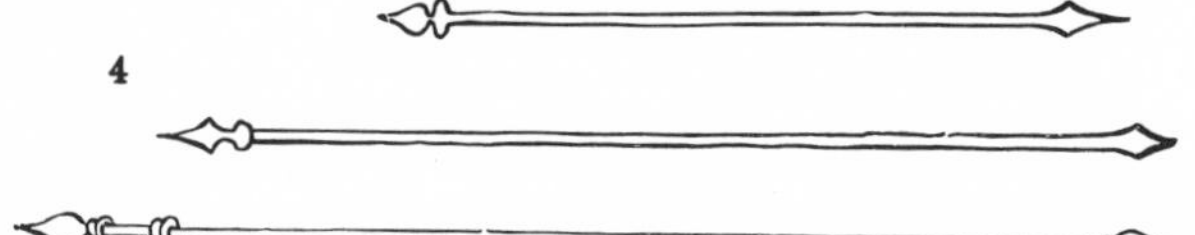
4

ἀμφι-δῑνέω: *twirl about;* only perf. pass., χεῦμα κασσιτέροιο ἀμφιδεδίνηται, a casting of tin 'is run around,' Ψ 562; of the scabbard 'enclosing' a sword, θ 405.

ἀμφι-δρυφής (δρύπτω): *with both cheeks torn* (from grief), B 700†.

ἀμφί-δρυφος (δρύπτω): *torn on both sides*, 'both torn' (from grief), παρειαί, Λ 393†.

ἀμφί-δυμος: *double*, only pl., λιμένες (on both sides of the island), δ 847†.

ἀμφι-έλισσα (Ϝελίσσω): *curved at both ends, curving*, epith. of ships. (See cut.)

ἀμφι-εννῡμι (Ϝέννῡμι), fut. ἀμφιέσω, aor. ἀμφίεσ(σ)α, mid. aor. ἀμφιέσαντο, imp. ἀμφιέσασθε, pres. and ipf. not in Homer: *put on* clothing; act., on another, ε 167; with two accusatives, ο 369; mid., on oneself, *don*, ψ 131.

ἀμφι-έπω, ἀμφ-έπω (ἕπω), only part. ἀμφιέπων and ipf.: *move round, envelop*, γάστρην τρίποδος πῦρ ἄμφεπε, Σ 348; of persons, *be busy about*, in preparing meat, attending to sacrifices, etc., ὥς οἵ γ' ἀμφίεπον τάφον Ἕκτορος, Ω 804; freq. the part. in connection with another verb, ἀμφιέποντες, *busily*.

ἀμφ-ιζάνω: *settle upon*, only ipf., Σ 25†.

ἀμφι-θαλής, ές (θάλλω): *flourishing on both sides*, epith. of a child whose father and mother are still living, X 496†.

Ἀμφι-θέη: wife of Autolycus, grandmother of Odysseus, τ 416†.

ἀμφί-θετος (τίθημι): *to be placed both ways, reversible*, φιάλη, probably with double base and bowl, Ψ 270, 616. Cf. ἀμφικύπελλον.

ἀμφι-θέω: *run about*, with acc., κ 413†.

Ἀμφι-θόη: a Nereid, Σ 42†.

ἀμφι-καλύπτω, fut. ἀμφικαλύψω, aor. ἀμφεκάλυψα, subj. ἀμφικαλύψῃ: *cover round, hide;* often τινί τι, the acc. of the thing used to cover with, καί οἱ σάκος ἀμφεκάλυψεν, Θ 331, θ 569; met., of sleep, death, feelings, ἔρως φρένας ἀμφεκάλυψε, 'engrossed my heart,' Γ 442.

ἀμφι-καρής, ές (κάρα): *double-headed;* ἀμφικαρῆ σφέλα (for the feet of two persons), v. l. for ἀμφὶ κάρη, ρ 231.

ἀμφι-κεάζω: *split* or *hew around;* τὸ μέλαν δρυὸς ἀμφικεάσσᾱς, ξ 12†.

Ἄμφι-κλος: a Trojan, slain by Achilles, Π 313†.

ἀμφί-κομος (κόμη): *surrounded by foliage, leafy*, P 677†.

ἀμφι-κύπελλον, δέπας: *double-cupped* goblet, whose base is bowl-shaped and adapted to drink from. Cf. ἀμφίθετος. (The above is the explanation of Aristotle, *Hist. An.* xix., 40; but no specimens of the form described have been found amongst antique remains or representations.)

ἀμφι-λαχαίνω: *dig about;* φυτόν, ω 242†.

Ἀμφί-λοχος: a seer of Argos, son of Amphiarāus and Eriphȳle, ο 248†.

ἀμφι-λύκη (root λυκ, lux): *with doubtful light;* νύξ, i. e., neither day nor night, twi-light of dawn, H 433†.

ἀμφι-μαίομαι, only aor. imp. ἀμφιμάσασθε: *seek about* with the hands, hence *wipe off* all over, σπόγγοισι, υ 152†.

ἀμφι-μάχομαι: *fight around* or *for;* πόλιν, I 412; νέκυος, τείχεος (as for a prize), O 391. (Il.)

Ἀμφί-μαχος: (1) son of Cteatus, a leader of the Eleans, N 203.—(2) son of Nomion, a leader of the Carians, B 870.

Ἀμφι-μέδων: a suitor of Penelope, son of Melaneus, slain by Telemachus, χ 242.

ἀμφι-μέλᾱς, αινα: *black round about*, only φρένες ἀμφιμέλαιναι, 'darkened heart,' said with reference to the effect of passion (anger, grief, warlike impulse), A 103, P 83, 573.

ἀμφι-μῡκάομαι: *bellow round;* only perf., δάπεδον δ' ἅπαν ἀμφιμέμῡκεν, 'moans round about,' i. e., echoes with the sound of the loom and the voice within, κ 227.

ἀμφι-νέμομαι, only pres. and ipf.: *dwell around*, or *dwell around in*, B 521, τ 132.

Ἀμφι-νόμη: a Nereid, Σ 44.

Ἀμφί-νομος: a suitor of Penelope, son of Nīsus, from Dūlichium, slain by Telemachus, χ 89.

ἀμφι-ξέω: *hew around about*, only aor., ψ 196†.

Ἄμφῖος: (1) a Trojan chief, son of Merops, B 830.—(2) son of Selagus, from Paesus, an ally of the Trojans, E 612.

ἀμφι-πέλομαι: *be about* one, ἀκουόντεσσι νεωτάτη ἀμφιπέληται, the newest song to 'meet their ears,' α 352†. Cf. ἀμφιέρχομαι.

ἀμφι-πένομαι, only pres. and ipf.: *work about, attend (to), tend;* of persons, esp. the sick or wounded, sometimes of things, T 278; ironically, τὸν ἴχθυες ἀμφεπένοντο, 'were at work around him,' Φ 203, Ψ 184.

ἀμφιπερί: see ἀμφί.

ἀμφι-περι-στέφω: see περιστέφω.

ἀμφι-περι-στρωφάω: see περιστρωφάω.

ἀμφι-πίπτω: *fall about*, only aor. part., γυνὴ πόσιν ἀμφιπεσοῦσα, 'falling upon (and embracing) the body' of her lifeless husband, θ 523†.

ἀμφι-πολεύω (ἀμφίπολος): *wait on, take care of,* ὄρχατον, ω 244; βίον, σ 254; ironically, υ 78.

ἀμφί-πολος (πέλομαι): *female attendant, handmaid;* ἀμφίπολος ταμίη, ἀμφίπολοι γυναῖκες, but regularly subst.; the noble dame of the heroic period is constantly attended by one or more of her maids when she appears in public, α 331; distinguished from δμωαί, χ 483 f.

ἀμφι-πονέομαι, fut. ἀμφιπονήσομαι: *labor about, attend to*, τί, τινά, Ψ 159, 681, υ 307. Cf. ἀμφιπένομαι.

ἀμφι-ποτάομαι: *flutter about*, only ipf., ἀμφεποτᾶτο τέκνα, B 315†.

ἀμφί-ρυτος (ῥέω): *sea-girt.* (Od.)

ἀμφίς (cf. ἀμφί, ἄμφω): I. adv., *on both sides, apart, in two ways;* 'with both hands' at once (Φ 162), γαῖαν καὶ οὐρανὸν ἀμφὶς ἔχουσιν (α 54), 'separately (χ 57), ἀμφὶς φράζεσθαι, 'be at variance,' B 13.—II. prep., mostly following its case, (1) w. gen., *all round, apart from, away from*, B 384; ἀμφὶς ὁδοῦ, Ψ 393.—(2) w. acc., *about, around*, ἀμφὶς ἕκαστον (ἀμφὶ Ϝέκαστον), Λ 634, ζ 266, Ξ 274.

ἀμφ-ίστημι, aor. 2 ἀμφέστην, 3 pl. ἀμφέσταν (for -έστησαν), pass. ipf. ἀμφίστατο, -σταντο: *place around*, pass. and intr., *stand around*, Σ 233, Ω 712; ἄστυ, 'beleaguer,' Λ 733.

ἀμφι-στρατάομαι: *besiege*, only ipf., ἀμφεστρατόωντο, Λ 713†.

ἀμφι-στρεφής (στρέφω): *turning all ways*, Λ 40†.

ἀμφι-τίθημι, mid. aor. 2 ἀμφέθετο, pass. aor. part. ἀμφιτεθεῖσα: *put around;* κυνέη, encircling the head, K 271; ξίφος, 'gird on,' φ 431.

Ἀμφι-τρίτη (cf. Τρίτων): *Amphitrīte*, goddess of the sea, personifying the element, κυανῶπις, ἀγάστονος, μ 60, 97; μετὰ κύμασιν Ἀμφιτρίτης, γ 91.

ἀμφι-τρομέω: *tremble for*, w. gen., δ 820†.

Ἀμφι-τρύων: king of Tiryns, husband of Alcmēna and reputed father of Heracles, E 392, γ 266.

ἀμφί-φαλος (φάλος): *double-ridged, double-crested*, of a helmet with divided crest. (Il.)

ἀμφι-φοβέω: *put to flight around* one, only aor. pass., Π 290†.

ἀμφι-φορεύς, ῆος (φέρω); for ἀμφορεύς: *two-handled vase* or *jar* for wine; also used as *urn* for ashes of the dead, ω 74. (See cuts 6 and 7.)

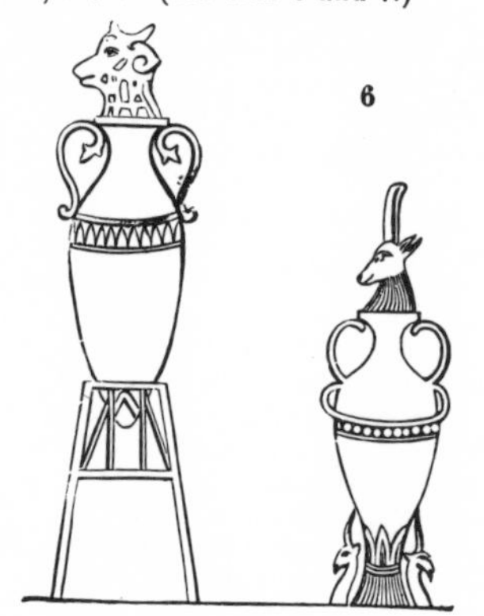
6

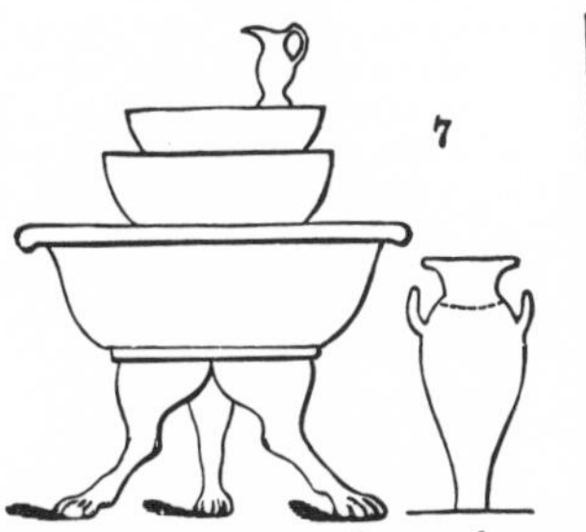

ἀμφι-χαίνω: *yawn about*, only aor. 2, ἐμὲ κὴρ ἀμφέχανε, has 'engulfed' me, Ψ 79†.

ἀμφι-χέομαι (χέω), ipf. ἀμφεχεόμην, aor. 2 ἀμφεχύμην, ἀμφέχυτο, pass. aor. ἀμφεχύθην: *pour* or *be diffused* or *shed around*, *embrace*; πάρος κόνιν ἀμφιχυθῆναι, before the dust (stirred by the feet of Ajax immediately in advance) could 'pour (rise) round' him (Odysseus), Ψ 763; ἀμφιχυθεὶς πατέρα, π 214, ἀμφεχέοντο ('thronged around') καὶ ἠσπάζοντ' Ὀδυσῆα, χ 498; metaph., of sounds (B 41), feelings (δ 716), sleep (Ξ 253).

ἀμφιχυθείς, -ῆναι: see ἀμφιχέομαι.

ἀμφί-χυτος (χέω): *poured* (spread) *around*, *demolished*, of an earthen wall, Υ 145†.

Ἀμφίων: (1) son of Iasius, and king of Orchomenus in Boeotia, λ 283.—(2) son of Zeus and Antiope, husband of Niobe, and brother of Zethus, with whom he built the walls of Thebes, λ 262.—(3) a leader of the Epeians, N 692.

ἀμφότερος (ἄμφω): *both*; sing. only neut. as adv., foll. by τέ . . καί, etc., ἀμφότερον βασιλεύς τ' ἀγαθὸς κρατερός τ' αἰχμητής, 'at once both,' etc., Γ 179, N 166, ο 78; as subst., ἀμφοτέρῃσι (sc. χερσί), E 416, κ 264.

Ἀμφότερος: a Lycian, slain by Patroclus, Π 415†.

ἀμφοτέρω-θεν: *from* or *on both sides*, *at both ends*.

ἀμφοτέρω-σε: *in both directions*.

ἀμφ-ουδίς: adv. with the sense of ἀμφ' οὔδει, *on the ground* (specifying πρὸς γῆν), ρ 237†.

ἀμ-φράσσαιτο: see ἀναφράζομαι.

ἄμφω: *both*, whether of individuals or of parties, A 363, B 124; 'the two pieces' (defined by what follows), μ 424.

ἄμφ-ωτος (οὖς): *two-eared*, *two-handled*, χ 10†.

ἀ-μώμητος (μῶμος): *irreproachable*, M 109†.

1. ἄν: modal adv., indicating a condition; essentially equivalent to κέν, and of less frequent occurrence. The use of ἄν is less exactly defined in Homer than in Attic Greek; besides the regular usages in Attic, Homer employs ἄν with the subj. in independent sentences, and κέ (rarely ἄν) with the fut. indicative. In final clauses the use of ἄν or κέ prevails, and it is not uncommon even with the opt. in conditions. On the other hand the potential opt. occurs without ἄν (κέ) oftener than in Attic. The following examples will illustrate the most important of these peculiarities of usage:—(1) ἄν w. subj. in independent sentence, οὐκ ἄν τοι χραίσμῃ κίθαρις, 'perchance the harp may avail thee not,' Γ 54, cf. A 205.—(2) ἄν w. fut. ind., αὐτὸν δ' ἂν πύματόν με κύνες . . ἐρύουσι, ἐπεί κέ τις κτλ., 'me like enough last of all will dogs drag about, after I am slain," etc., X 66.—(3) ἄν w. opt. in final clause, σὺ δέ με προΐεις . . ὄφρ' ἂν ἑλοίμην δῶρα, ω 334. — (4) ἄν w. opt. in condition, στεῦτο γὰρ εὐχόμενος νικήσεμεν, εἴπερ ἂν αὐταὶ | Μοῦσαι ἀείδοιεν, B 597.

2. ἀν-: negative prefix, the original form of the so-called α 'privative,' a still fuller form being ἀνα-, preserved in ἀνάϝεδνος. Cf. Lat. in-, Eng. 'un-.'

3. ἄν, ἀν: by apocope for ἀνά, before ν (K 298), before τ (E 167), before στόμα (ε 456); and in ἂν δέ (sc. ὤρνυντο), Γ 268, Ψ 709, 755, 812, θ 110, 115, 118.

ἀνά, by apocope ἄν (ἀν), before labials ἄμ (ἀμ): *up*, opp. κατά.—I. adv., ἄνα (with anastrophe), hortative, *up! quick!* Σ 178, σ 13; *up* there, *thereon*, μέλανες δ' ἀνὰ βότρυες ἦσαν, Σ 562; *back*, ἀνά τ' ἔδραμ' ὀπίσσω, E 599, ἀνὰ δ' ἴσχεο, 'hold up,' 'refrain,' H 110. The use with verbs 'in tmesi' is of course adverbial; likewise when a subst. occurs in a case that defines the adv. (thus showing the transition to a true preposition), ἂν δ' ἄρα Τηλέμαχος νηὸς βαῖνε (νηός local or part. gen.), β 416.—II. prep., (1) w. gen., only ἀνὰ νηὸς ἔβην, ι 177, see the remark on β 416 above.—(2) w. dat., *up* on, *upon*, A 15, O 152, ἀνά τ' ἀλλήλῃσιν ἔχονται, hold on (close up) 'to' one another, ω 8.—(3) w. acc., *up* to, *up* through, K 466, χ 132, X 452; of motion, ἀνά generally denotes *vague* direction (up and down, 'up through,' 'throughout'), ἐννῆμαρ μὲν ἀνὰ στρατὸν ᾤχετο κῆλα θεοῖο, A 53, whereas κατά rather indicates motion toward a definite point or end (A 483, 484); with the idea of motion less prominent, N 117, 270; of time, ἀνὰ νύκτα, Ξ 80; βασιλῆας ἀνὰ στόμ' ἔχων, 'bandying their names up and down,' B 250; ἀνὰ θυμὸν φρονεῖν, ὁρμαίνειν, θαμβεῖν, ὀίεσθαι, B 36, β 156, δ 638; ἀν' ἰθύν, 'straight forward,' Φ 303; following the governed word, νειὸν ἀν(ά), 'up and down' the field, ν 32.

1. ἄνα: see ἀνά, I.

2. ἄνα: see ἄναξ.

ἀνα-βαίνω, ἀμβαίνω, aor. ἀνέβην, mid. aor. ἀνεβήσετο, aor. 1 part. ἀναβησάμενοι: *go up, ascend (to)*, οὐρανόν, ὑπερώιον, etc.; φάτις ἀνθρώπους ἀνα βαίνει, 'goes abroad among' men, ζ 29; esp. *go on board* ship, *embark*, A 312 and often, ἐς Τροίην ἀναβημέναι, 'embark for Troy,' α 210; trans., aor. 1 mid., νὼ ἀναβησάμενοι, 'taking us on board their ship,' ο 475.

ἀνα-βάλλω, ἀμβάλλω: *throw up*.—I. act., *postpone*, ἄεθλον, τ 584.—II. mid., (1) 'strike up' a prelude, w. inf., φορμίζων ἀνεβάλλετο καλὸν ἀείδειν, α 155, cf. ρ 262.—(2) *postpone* for oneself, ἔργον, B 436.

ἀνα-βέβρυχεν: defective perf., *bubbles up*, P 54† (v. l. ἀναβέβροχεν).

'Ανα-βησί-νεως: a Phaeacian, θ 113†.

ἀνά-βλησις (ἀναβάλλω): *postponement*. (Il.)

ἀνα-βραχεῖν, only aor. 3 sing. ἀνέβραχε: of armor (*clanged*), T 13; of a door ('groaned'), ἠύτε ταῦρος, φ 48. Cf. βραχεῖν.

ἀνα-βρόχω, only aor. opt. ἀναβρόξειε, and aor. 2 pass. part. ἀναβροχέν: *gulp back* (again), of Charybdis, her whirlpool, μ 240, λ 586.

ἀνα-γιγνώσκω, only aor. 2 ἀνέγνων: *know* for certain, *know again, recognize*, α 216, δ 250, τ 250, N 734; πῶς κέν με ἀναγνοίη τὸν ἐόντα, 'how can she know me for that one?' (i. e. for her son), λ 144.

ἀναγκαίη (=ἀνάγκη): *necessity, constraint;* dat., *perforce*, Δ 300; ἀναγκαίηφι δαμέντες, Υ 143.

ἀναγκαῖος, η, ον (ἀνάγκη): *constraining;* μῦθος, command 'of force,' ρ 399, χρειώ, 'dire' need, Θ 57; esp. with reference to slavery, ἦμαρ ἀναγκαῖον (= δούλιον ἦμαρ), Π 836, δμῶες ἀναγκαῖοι, 'bond' servants, ω 210; πολεμισταί, warriors 'perforce,' ω 499.

ἀνάγκη: *necessity, constraint;* freq. ἀνάγκη (ἐστίν, ἦν) foll. by inf., E 633, Ω 667, κρατέρη δ' ἐπικείσετ' ἀνάγκη, 'stern necessity,' Z 458; often ἀνάγκῃ, καὶ ἀνάγκῃ, 'even against his will,' ὑπ' ἀνάγκης, 'by compulsion.'

ἀνα-γνάμπτω, only aor. act. ἀνέγναμψαν and pass. ἀνεγνάμφθη: *bend back;* of undoing a prisoner's fastenings, ξ 348.

ἀν-άγω, fut. ἀνάξω, aor. 3 ἀνήγαγον: *lead* or *bring up* or *back* (O 29); from the coast to the interior, δ 534, etc.; of 'carrying away' in general, esp. over the sea, γυναῖκ' εὐειδέ' ἀνῆγες | ἐξ ἀπίης γαίης, Γ 48, or of 'carrying home,' γ 272; mid., *put to sea* (opp. κατάγεσθαι), A 478, τ 202.

ἀνα-δέδρομε: see ἀνατρέχω.

ἀνα-δέρκομαι: *look up*, only aor., ἀνέδρακεν ὀφθαλμοῖσιν, 'opened his eyes,' Ξ 436†.

ἀνα-δέσμη (ἀναδέω): *head-band*, πλεκτή, X 469†. (See cut.)

ἀνα-δέχομαι, aor. 1 ἀνεδεξάμην, sync. aor. 2 ἀνεδέγμην: *receive*, E 619; metaph., *undergo*, ὀιζύν, ρ 563.

ἀνα-δύομαι, ἀνδύομαι (δύω), aor. 2 ἀνέδυν, opt. ἀναδύη (vulg., -δύῃ), inf. ἀναδῦναι, mid. aor. ἀνεδύσετο: (1) *emerge;* ἁλός, 'from the sea,' A 359, λίμνης, ε 337; with acc., κῦμα θαλάσσης, 'arose to the wave,' surface, A 496.—(2) *draw back;* abs., ι 377, ἐς ὅμιλον, H 217; trans., πόλεμον, 'back out of,' N 225

ἀνά-εδνος (*Ϝέδνα*, see *ἀν-*, 2): *without bridal gifts.* Cf. *ἔδνα.* (Il.)

ἀν-αείρω (=*ἀναίρω*), aor. 1 *ἀνάειρε*, inf. *ἀναεῖραι*: *lift up*, θ 298; said of wrestlers who try to 'pick each other up,' Ψ 724, 725, 729; of 'carrying off' a prize received, Ψ 614, 778.

ἀνα-θηλέω (*θάλλω*): *bloom again*, fut., A 236†.

ἀνά-θημα (*ἀνατίθημι*): only *ἀναθήματα δαιτός*, *delights, glories* of the feast (song and dance). (Od.)

ἀνα-θρώσκω: *bound up*, of a stone rolling down hill, only part., N 140†.

ἀν-αιδείη (*ἀναιδής*): *shamelessness, impudence.*

ἀν-αιδής, *ές* (*αἰδώς*): *shameless, pitiless;* applied to inanimate things (personified), *κυδοιμός*, 'ruthless,' E 593; *πέτρη*, N 139; *λᾶας*, λ 598.

ἀν-αίμων, *ονος* (*αἷμα*): *bloodless*, E 342†.

ἀν-αιμωτί (*αἷμα*): *without bloodshed.*

ἀναίνομαι, ipf. *ἀναίνετο*, aor. *ἀνήνατο*, *ἠνήνατο*, subj. *ἀνήνηται*, inf. *ἀνήνασθαι*: *deny, refuse;* in both senses w. inf., Σ 500, 450; governs both persons and things, *σὲ δ' ἀναίνεται ἠδὲ σὰ δῶρα*, I 679; opp. *ὑποδέχεσθαι*, H 93.

ἀν-αιρέω, aor. 2 part. *ἀνελών*, mid. fut. *ἀναιρήσομαι*, aor. 2 *ἀνειλόμην*, *ἀνελόμην*: *take up;* mid., for oneself, or what is one's own, N 296; 'into one's service,' *ἦ ἄρ κ' ἐθέλοις θητευέμεν, εἴ σ' ἀνελοίμην*, σ 357; in bad sense, *κούρᾱς ἀνέλοντο θύελλαι*, 'snatched away,' υ 66.

ἀν-ᾱΐσσω, aor. *ἀνήῑξα*: *dart up, spring up; πηγαί*, X 148; w. acc. of end of motion, *ἅρμα*, Ω 440. Cf. *ἀΐσσω.*

ἀν-αίτιος (*αἰτίᾱ*): *guiltless, innocent.*

ἀνα-καίω: *kindle*, only ipf. (Od.)

ἀνα-κηκίω: *gush up* or *forth*, of blood and sweat. (Il.)

ἀνα-κλΐνω, aor. *ἀνέκλῑνα*, part. *ἀνακλίνᾱς* and *ἀγκλίνᾱς*, pass. aor. part. *ἀνακλινθείς, -θεῖσα, -θέντες*: *make to lean back* or *upon; τινὰ πρός τι* (σ 103), *τόξον ποτὶ γαίῃ*, 'bracing against the ground,' Δ 113; of doors, *open* (opp. *ἐπιθεῖναι*), Θ 395, χ 156, λ 525; pass., *lean* or *sink back*, *ἀνακλινθεὶς πέσεν ὕπτιος*, ι 371; *εὗδεν ἀνακλινθεῖσα*, δ 794; in rowing, ν 78.

ἀν-ακοντίζω: *shoot up* or *forth*, of blood, E 113†.

ἀνα-κόπτω: *strike back*, 'shoot back,' of door-bolts, φ 47†.

ἀνα-κράζω, aor. *ἀνέκραγον*: *screech out* (said purposely with exaggeration) ξ 467†.

ἀνα-κρεμάννῡμι, aor. part. *ἀγκρεμάσᾱσα*: *hang up*, α 440†.

ἀνακτόριος (*ἀνάκτωρ*): *belonging to the master*, *ὕες*, ο 397†.

ἀνα-κυμβαλιάζω (*κύμβαλον*, 'cymbal'): *fell rattling over*, ipf., Π 379†.

ἀνα-λέγω, ipf. *ἄλλεγον*, aor. inf. *ἀλλέξαι*· *gather up*, *ὀστέα.* (Il.)

ἀν-αλκείη (*ἀλκή*): *want of valor;* only *ἀναλκείῃσι δαμέντες*, overcome *by their cowardice.* (Il.)

ἄν-αλκις, *ιδος*, acc. *-ιδα* (*-ιν*, γ 375): *invalorous, cowardly.*

ἄν-αλτος (root *αλ*, a l e r e): *insatiable.* (Od.)

ἀνα-λῡ́ω, ἀλλῡ́ω, part. *ἀλλῡ́ουσα*, ipf. iter. *ἀλλῡ́εσκεν*, aor. *ἀνέλῡσαν*, mid. fut. *ἀναλῡ́σεται*: *untie, unravel.* (Od.)

ἀνα-μαιμάω (cf. *μέμαα*): *rage through*, *πῦρ*, Y 490†.

ἀνα-μάσσω: *wipe off; μέγα ἔργον, ὃ σῇ κεφαλῇ ἀναμάξεις* (fig. from the custom of murderers wiping off the bloody weapon upon the head of the slain, as if to divert their guilt upon the victim himself; hence, here = 'shalt atone for with thine own life' (cf. χ 218), τ 92†.

ἀνα-μένω, aor. *ἀνέμεινα*: *await*, τ 342†.

ἀνα-μετρέω, aor. opt. *ἀναμετρήσαιμι*: *remeasure* (the way to), *Χάρυβδιν*, μ 428†.

ἀνα-μῑ́γνῡμι, ἀναμῑ́σγω, aor. part. *ἀμμίξᾱς*: *mix up* with, *mix together*, κ 235, Ω 529.

ἀνα-μιμνήσκω, aor. *ἀνέμνησας*: *remind*, *τινά τι*, γ 211†.

ἀνα-μίμνω (= *ἀναμένω*): *await;* abs., *stand fast*, Π 363. (Il.)

ἀνα-μορμῡ́ρω, ipf. iter. *ἀναμορμῡ́ρεσκε*: *seethe up*, of Charybdis, μ 238†.

ἀνα-νέομαι, ἀννέομαι: *come up again, rise*, *ἀννεῖται ἠέλιος*, κ 192†.

ἀνα-νεύω, aor. *ἀνένευσα*: *nod backwards* (a backward inclination of the head was a sign of negation, cf. ι 468, hence), *deny, refuse; καρήατι*, X 205; with inf., Π 252.

ἄν-αντα (ἄντα): *up-hill*, Ψ 116.

ἄναξ (Ϝάναξ), ακτος, voc. ἄνα (only in addressing a god, otherwise), ἄναξ, dat. pl. ἀνάκτεσι: *lord* (*king*), *master;* of gods, Ζεῦ ἄνα (Γ 351), ὕπνε ἄναξ πάντων τε θεῶν πάντων τ' ἀνθρώπων (Ξ 233), θεῶν ἀέκητι ἀνάκτων (μ 290); of men (esp. Agamemnon), ἄναξ ἀνδρῶν, and in general of any man as lord and master of his possessions, ἐγὼν οἴκοιο ἄναξ ἔσομ' ἡμετέροιο | καὶ δμώων, α 397; ἦ σύ γ' ἄνακτος | ὀφθαλμὸν ποθέεις, 'miss your master's eye,' said by the blinded Polyphemus to his ram, ι 452.

ἀνα-ξηραίνω, aor. subj. ἀγξηράνῃ: *dry up*, Φ 347†.

ἀν-οίγεσκον: see ἀνοίγνῡμι.

ἀνα-πάλλω, aor. 2 part. ἀμπεπαλών, aor mid. ἀνέπαλτο: I. act., *brandish* (drawing) *back;* ἀμπεπαλὼν ('having poised and drawn back') προΐει δολιχόσκιον ἔγχος, Γ 355, etc.—II. mid. and pass., *be flung up, leap up*, Ψ 692, 694, Θ 85, Υ 424.

ἀνα-παύω, aor. ἀνέπαυσε: *cause to leave off*, τινά τινος, Ρ 550†

ἀνα-πείρω, aor. part. ἀμπείραντες: *pierce* with spits, *spit*, Β 426†.

ἀνα-πεπταμένᾱς see ἀναπετάννῡμι.

ἀνα-πετάννῡμι, only perf. part. ἀναπεπταμένᾱς: *spread back, open*, of doors (opp. ἐπικεκλιμένᾱς), Μ 122.

ἀνα-πηδάω, aor. ἀμπήδησε: *jump up*, Λ 379†.

ἀνα-πίμπλημι, fut. ἀναπλήσω, aor. ἀνέπλησα: *fill up;* only met., πότμον βιότοιο, 'fulfil,' Δ 170, κακὸν οἶτον, Θ 34; κακὰ πολλά, 'endure to the end,' Ο 132, ε 207, 302.

ἀνα-πλέω, fut. inf. ἀναπλεύσεσθαι: *sail up;* στεινωπόν, μ 234; ἐς Τροίην (over the high seas), Λ 22.

ἀνά-πνευσις (ἀναπνέω): *recovering of breath, respite;* πολέμοιο, 'from fighting.' (Il.)

ἀνα-πνέω, aor. ἀνέπνευσα, inf. ἀμπνεῦσαι, aor. 2 imp. ἄμπνυε, pass. aor. ἀμπνύνθη, mid. aor. 2 ἄμπνῡτο: *breathe again, take breath, revive;* abs., Λ 327, 800, Ξ 436; w. gen., 'have a respite from,' κακότητος, Λ 382; πόνοιο, Ο 235.

ἀν-άποινος (ἄποινα): *without ransom*, Α 99†.

ἀνα-πρήθω: *let stream up*, only δάκρυ ἀναπρήσᾱς, 'with bursting tear,' Ι 433, β 81. Cf. πρήθω.

ἀν-άπτω, aor. ἀνῆψα, pass. perf. imp. ἀνήφθω: *fasten up, attach*, freq. of cables, μ 162; ἐκ δ' αὐτοῦ πείρατ' ἀνήφθω, 'let the rope-ends be tied to the mast itself,' μ 51; met., μῶμον, β 86.

ἀνά-πυστος (ἀναπεύθομαι): *notorious*, λ 274†.

ἀνα-ροιβδέω: see ἀναρροιβδέω.

ἀν-αρπάζω, aor. ἀνήρπαξα and ἀνήρπασα, part. ἀναρπάξᾱς: *snatch up, snatch away*, esp. of sudden gusts of wind, δ 515.

ἀνα-ρρήγνῡμι (Ϝρήγνῡμι), only aor. ἀνέρρηξα: *rend* or *burst open*, Σ 582, Υ 63; of demolishing a wall, Η 461.

ἀνα-ρριπτέω (Ϝρίπτω), **ἀνα-ρρίπτω,** ipf. ἀνερρίπτουν, aor. ἀνέρριψα: *fling up*, ἅλα πηδῷ, of vigorous rowing; without πηδῷ, κ 130. (Od.)

ἀνα-ρροιβδέω, aor. ἀνερροίβδησε: *swallow up* (again), of Charybdis. (Od.)

ἀν-άρσιος (ἀραρίσκω): *unfitting*, hence *unfriendly, hostile;* δυσμενέες καὶ ἀνάρσιοι, Ω 365.

ἄν-αρχος: *without leader*.

ἀνα-σεύω: only aor. 2 mid. ἀνέσσυτο, *rushed up*, Λ 458†.

ἀνα-σπάω, aor. mid. ἀνεσπάσατο: *pull back*, ἔγχος ἐκ χροός, Ν 574†.

ἄνασσα, ης (Ϝάναξ): *queen*, but only of goddesses, for Odysseus when he addresses Nausicaa as ἄνασσα, doubts whether she is divine or mortal, ζ 149.

ἀνάσσω (Ϝάναξ), ipf. ἄνασσε, ἤνασσε, fut. ἀνάξω, mid. aor. inf. ἀνάξασθαι: *be king, lord*, or *master of, rule over, reign*, said of both gods and men; τινός or τινί (dat. of interest), and freq. w. μετά, sometimes ἐν; abs., of Nestor, τρὶς γὰρ δή μιν φᾱσιν ἀνάξασθαι γένε' ἀνδρῶν (γένεα, acc. of time), γ 245; pass., ἀνάσσονται δ' ἐμοὶ αὐτῷ, 'by me,' δ 177.

ἀνα-σταδόν (ἵστημι): adv., *standing up*. (Il.)

ἀνα-στεναχίζω = ἀναστενάχω, ipf., Κ 9.

ἀνα-στενάχω, mid. ipf. ἀνεστενάχοντο: *fetch sighs, groan;* τινά (*bewail*), Ψ 211. (Il.)

ἀνα-στοναχίζω: v. l. for ἀναστεναχίζω.

ἀνα-στρέφω, aor. opt. ἀνστρέψειαν: *overturn*, Ψ 436; mid., *wander through* (versari), γαῖαν, ν 326.

ἀνα-στρωφάω (frequentative of ἀναστρέφω): *turn over and over*, φ 394†.

ἀνασχέμεν, ἀνάσχεο, ἀνασχέσθαι, ἀνασχόμενος, ἀνασχών: see ἀνέχω.

ἀνα-τέλλω, aor. ἀνέτειλε: *cause to spring up*, Ε 777†.

ἀνα-τίθημι, fut. ἀναθήσει: *put upon*, met., ἐλεγχείην, 'heap upon,' Χ 100†.

ἀνα-τλῆναι, inf. of aor. 2 ἀνέτλην, part. ἀνατλάς: *bear up, endure; φάρμακον*, 'withstand,' κ 327. (Od.)

ἀνα-τρέπω: only aor. 2 mid. ἀνετράπετο, *fell over backward*. (Il.)

ἀνα-τρέχω, only aor. 2 ἀνέδραμον and perf. αναδέδρομε: *run up, run back*; σμώδιγγες, 'start up,' Ψ 717.

ἄν-αυδος (αὐδή): *speechless*. (Od.)

ἀνα-φαίνω, aor. inf. ἀναφῆναι: I. act., *make to shine* or *appear, show, exhibit*; ἀμοιβηδὶς δ' ἀνέφαινον, i. e. they made the torch-wood blaze up to give light, σ 310; Ὀδυσῆα μετὰ Τρώεσσ' ἀναφῆναι, 'reveal his presence,' δ 254.—II. mid., *appear*.

ἀνα-φανδά and **ἀναφανδόν**: *openly, publicly*, 'regularly.'

ἀνα-φέρω, only aor. act. ἀνένεικα, mid. ἀνενείκατο: *bring up*; mid., *fetch* a deep sigh, Τ 314.

ἀνα-φράζομαι, aor. opt. ἀμφράσσαιτο: *remark again, recognize*, τ 391†.

ἀνα-χάζομαι, aor. part. ἀναχασσάμενος: *draw back, withdraw*; esp. in battle, 'fall back,' Ε 600; with ἄψ, ὀπίσω, τυτθόν, πολλόν.

ἀνα-χωρέω, imp. ἀναχωρείτω, fut., aor.: *go back, retreat*, Δ 305; with ἄψ, Γ 35, etc.

ἀνα-ψύχω (ψῦχος), aor. pass. ἀνέψῡχθεν (for -ησαν): *cool off, refresh*, δ 568, Κ 575.

ἁνδάνω (Ϝανδάνω, (σ)Ϝηδύς), ipf. ἑήνδανε, ἥνδανε, perf. part. ἑαδότα, aor. εὔαδε (ἔϜαδε) and ἅδε: *be acceptable, please*, τινί, often w. θυμῷ added; impers., or with a thing as subj., δίχα δέ σφισιν ἥνδανε βουλή, γ 150, τοῖσι δὲ πᾶσιν ἑαδότα μῦθον ἔειπεν, σ 422.

ἄν-διχα: *in twain, asunder*. (Il.)

ἀνδρ-άγρια (ἀνήρ, ἄγρη): *spoils taken from men, spoils* of arms, Ξ 509†.

Ἀνδρ-αιμονίδης: *son of Andraemon*, Thoas, Η 168†.

Ἀνδρ-αίμων: king of the Aetolians in Calydon, Β 638, ξ 499.

ἀνδρακάς: *man by man* (viritim), ν 14†. (v. l. ἄνδρα κάθ'.)

ἀνδρά-ποδον, dat. pl. ἀνδραπόδεσσι: *slave*, Η 475†.

ἀνδρ-αχθής, ές (ἄχθος): *man-burdening* (heavy for a man to carry), ἀνδραχθέσι χερμαδίοισιν, κ 121†.

ἀνδρεϊ-φόντης (root φεν): *man-slaying*, Ἐνῡάλιος. (Il.)

ἄνδρεσσι: see ἀνήρ.

ἀνδρό-κμητος (κάμνω): *wrought by men's hands*, Λ 371†.

ἀνδρο-κτασίη (κτείνω): *slaughter of men* in battle; *manslaughter*, Ψ 86.

Ἀνδρο-μάχη: *Andromache*, wife of Hector, daughter of Eëtion, king in Cilician Thebes, Ζ 371, 395, Χ 460.

ἀνδρόμεος, ον (ἀνήρ): *of a man* or *men, human*; αἷμα, χρώς, also ὅμῑλος, Λ 538; ψωμοί, morsels 'of human flesh,' ι 374.

ἀνδροτής, ῆτος: *manliness, manly beauty*; λιποῦσ' ἀνδροτῆτα καὶ ἥβην, Π 857, Χ 363; ἀνδροτῆτά τε καὶ μένος ἠύ, Ω 6, **where the first syllable is** shortened. See **ἀδροτής**.

ἀνδρο-φάγος (φαγεῖν): *man-eating*, of the Cyclops, κ 200†.

ἀνδρο-φόνος (root φεν): *man-slaying*; φάρμακον, 'deadly,' α 261.

ἀνδύεται: see ἀναδύομαι.

ἀν-εγείρω, aor. ἀνέγειρα, inf. ἀνεγεῖραι: *wake up*; met., ἀνέγειρα δ' ἑταίρους | μειλιχίοις ἐπέεσσι, 'roused' them from their despair, κ 172.

ἀνέγνω: see ἀναγιγνώσκω.

ἀνεδέγμεθα: see ἀναδέχομαι.

ἀνέδραμον: see ἀνατρέχω.

ἀνέεδνος: see ἀνάεδνος.

ἀν-εέργω (Ϝέργω), ipf. ἀνέεργον: *hold back, check*. (Il.)

ἄν-ειμι (εἶμι), part. ἀνιών, ipf. ἀνήιον: *go up* or *back, return*, (of the sun) *rise*; παρὰ νηὸς ἀνήιον ἐς περιωπήν (i. e. from the shore inland), κ 146; ἐκ Τροίης ἀνιόντα, κ 332; ἅμ' ἠελίῳ ἀνιόντι, Σ 136.

ἀν-είμων, ονος (εἷμα): *destitute of (bed) clothing*, γ 348†.

ἀν-είρομαι (ἔρομαι), ipf. ἀνείρετο: *inquire, ask*; τινά or τί, or with double acc., ὅ μ' ἀνείρεαι ἠδὲ μεταλλᾷς, 'what you ask me about,' Γ 177, α 231.

ἀνειρώτων: see ἀνερωτάω.

ἀν-εῖσα, defective aor., only opt. ἀνέσαιμι, part. ἀνέσαντες: *set upon,* N 657; 'bring back' to their nuptial couch, Ξ 209. (Il.)

ἀν-εκτός, όν (ἀνέχω): *endurable, υ* 83; usually with **οὐκέτι,** so the adv., οὐκέτ' ἀνεκτῶς, 'in a fashion no longer to be endured,' ι 350.

ἀνελθών: see ἀνέρχομαι.

ἀν-έλκω, only pres. and ipf.: *draw up* or *back;* **τάλαντα,** scales, M 434; mid., ἔγχος, his spear out of the body, χ 97.

ἀνελών: see ἀναιρέω.

ἄνεμος: *wind;* often in gen. w. synonymous words, ἀνέμοιο θύελλα, ἀήτης, ἀυτμή, πνοιαί, and ἶς ἀνέμοιο, O 383; Βορέῃ ἀνέμῳ, ξ 253. The other winds named by Homer are Eurus, Notus, and Zephyrus.

ἀνεμο-σκεπής, ές (σκέπας): *sheltering from the wind,* Π 224†.

ἀνεμο-τρεφής, ές (τρέφω): *wind-fed;* κῦμα, 'swollen,' O 625; ἔγχος, made of a tree 'toughened by the wind,' Λ 256.

ἀνεμώλιος (ἄνεμος): *windy,* hence *empty, useless, idle,* (*in*) *vain;* **σὺ δὲ** ταῦτ' ἀνεμώλια βάζεις, Δ 355.

Ἀνεμώρεια: a town in Phocis, B 521.

ἀνενείκατο: see ἀναφέρω.

ἀνέπαλτο: see ἀναπάλλω.

ἀν-ερείπομαι (ἐρείπω), aor. ἀνηρείψαντο: *snatch up, sweep away;* esp. of the Harpies, α 241; of the rape of Ganymede, τὸν καὶ ἀνηρείψαντο θεοὶ Διὶ οἰνοχοεύειν, Υ 234.

ἀν-έρχομαι, aor. 2 ἀνήλυθε, part. ἀνελθών: *come* (or *go*) *up* or *back, return;* σκοπιὴν ἐς παιπαλόεσσαν ἀνελθών, κ 97; ἄψ ἀναερχομένῳ, Δ 392; of a tree, φοίνῑκος νέον ἔρνος ἀνερχόμενον, 'shooting up,' ζ 163, 167. Cf. ἄνειμι.

ἀν-ερωτάω: only ipf. ἀνειρώτων (-ηρ-), *questioned repeatedly,* δ 251†.

ἀνέσαιμι, ἀνέσαντες: see ἀνεῖσα.

ἄνεσαν, ἀνέσει: see ἀνίημι.

ἀνέσσυτο: see ἀνασεύω.

ἀν-έστιος (ἑστίᾱ): *hearthless, homeless,* I 63†.

ἄνευ (ἀν-): prep., w. gen., *without;* ἄνευ θεοῦ, 'without divine aid,' β 372, O 213; ἄνευ δηΐων, 'clear of,' N 556.

ἄνευθε(ν): adv., *away, away from, without;* abs., X 300 (opp. ἐγγύθι); ἄνευθε τιθέναι τι, X 368; as prep. w. gen., ἄνευθε θεοῦ, E 185, Π 89 (cf. ἄνευ); οἶος ἄνευθ' ἄλλων, X 39.

ἁ-νέφελος (νεφέλη), ᾱ before **ν**: *cloudless,* ζ 45†.

ἀν-έχω, aor. 2 ἀνέσχον (inf. ἀνασχέμεν) and ἀνάσχεθον (inf. ἀνασχεθέειν), mid. fut. ἀνέξομαι (inf. ἀνσχήσεσθαι), aor. ἀνεσχόμην, imp. ἀνάσχεο, ἄνσχεο: I. act., *hold up* or *back* (Ψ 426), as the hands in prayer (χεῖρας ἀνασχών), or in boxing, σ 89; met., εὐδικίᾱς ἀνέχῃσι, 'upholds,' τ 111; intr., *rise* (from under water), ε 320; 'press up through,' αἰχμή, P 310.—II. mid., *hold up* oneself or something belonging to one, *keep up;* χεῖρας ἀνασχόμενοι γέλῳ ἔκθανον, σ 100, and freq. ἀνασχόμενος, of 'drawing up' to strike, Γ 362, ξ 425; of a wounded man, οὐδέ σ' ὀΐω | δηρὸν ἔτ' ἀνσχήσεσθαι, E 285; met., *endure, bear, tolerate;* abs., **τέτλαθι καὶ** ἀνάσχεο, A 586; w. acc., **τί** or **τινά,** and w. part. belonging to either subj. or obj., εἰς ἐνιαυτὸν ἐγὼ **παρὰ σοί** γ' ἀνεχοίμην | ἥμενος, δ 595.

ἀνεψιός, gen. ἀνεψιόο (sic), O 554: *sister's son, nephew,* O 422; sometimes of other relations, 'cousin,' K 519.

ἄνεῳ, nom. pl.: *speechless, silent,* ἐγένοντο, ἦσαν, etc.; adv., ἄνεω, ἣ δ' ἄνεω δὴν ἧστο, ψ 93.

ἀνήγαγον: see ἀνάγω.

ἀνήῃ: see ἀνίημι.

ἀνήιον: see ἄνειμι.

ἀν-ήκεστος (ἀκέομαι): *incurable;* χόλος, *unappeasable,* O 217.

ἀν-ηκουστέω (ἀνήκουστος, ἀκούω): *be disobedient,* w. genitive. Cf. **νηκουστέω.** (Il.)

ἀν-ήμελκτος (ἀμέλγω): *unmilked,* ι 439†.

ἀν-ήνοθεν (cf. ἄνθος), defective perf 2 with aor. meaning: *gushed up,* Λ 266†. See ἐνήνοθε.

ἀν-ήνυστος (ἀνύω): *unaccomplished;* ἀνηνύστῳ ἐπὶ ἔργῳ, 'do-nothing' business as it is, π 111†.

ἀν-ήνωρ, ορος (ἀνήρ): *unmanly,* κ 301 and 341.

ἀνήρ, gen ἀνδρός and ἀνέρος, dat. ἀνδρί and ἄνερι, acc. ἄνδρα, voc. ἄνερ, pl. nom. ἄνδρες, ἀνέρες, dat. ἀνδράσι, ἄνδρεσσι, acc. ἄνδρας, ἀνέρας, dual. ἄνδρε, ἀνέρε: *man* (vir); as distinguished from γυνή, ο 163; as *husband*, λ 327; emphatically, ἀνέρες ἔστε καὶ ἄλκιμον ἦτορ ἕλεσθε, Ε 529; frequently joined with a more specific noun, ἰητρὸς ἀνήρ, Σίντιες ἄνδρες. The distinction between ἀνήρ and ἄνθρωπος (homo) is disregarded at will, βροτοὶ ἄνδρες, πατὴρ ἀνδρῶν τε θεῶν τε, etc.

ἀν-ήροτος (ἀρόω): *unploughed.* (Od.)

ἀνήφθω: see ἀνάπτω.

ἄνθ' = ἄντα, Θ 233.

῎Ανθεια: a town in Messēne, Ι 151, 293.

᾿Ανθεμίδης: *son of Anthemion*, Simoeisius, Δ 488†.

᾿Ανθεμίων: father of Simoeisius, of Troy, Δ 473†.

ἀνθεμόεις, εντος (ἄνθος): *flowery;* λέβης, κρητήρ, 'adorned with flower-work,' γ 440, ω 275. Cf. cut No. 98.

ἀνθερεών, ῶνος: *chin;* to take by the chin in token of supplication, Α 501.

ἀνθέριξ, ικος: (beard of) *ear of grain*, pl., Υ 227†.

ἀνθέω, aor. inf. ἀνθῆσαι: *bloom*, λ 320†.

᾿Ανθηδών: a town in Boeotia, on the Eurīpus, Β 508†.

ἄνθινος, ον (ἄνθος): *of flowers; εἶδαρ ἄνθινον, flowery food*, of the fruit of the Lotus-tree, ι 84†.

ἀνθ-ίστημι: only aor. 2 ἀντέστη and ipf. mid. ἀνθίσταντο, *resisted.* (Il.)

ἄνθος, εος: *blossom, flower;* fig., ἥβης ἄνθος, Ν 484.

ἀνθρακιή (ἄνθραξ): *heap of glowing coals*, Ι 213†.

ἄνθρωπος: *man* (homo); mostly pl., as opp. to gods, ἀθανάτων τε θεῶν χαμαὶ ἐρχομένων τ' ἀνθρώπων, Ε 442; *mankind*, πάντας ἐπ' ἀνθρώπους, 'the world over,' Ω 535; joined with a more specific word, ἄνθρωπος ὁδίτης, Π 263, ν 123.

ἀνῑάζω (ἀνίη), ipf. ἀνίαζον: *torment, annoy, weary*, Ψ 721, τ 323; usually intrans., *be tormented, wearied;* θῡμῷ ἀνῑάζων, *agonized* at heart, of the mortally wounded Eurymachus, χ 87; similarly Φ 270, δ 460; often weakened colloquially, ἤδη μοι ἀνῑάζουσιν ἑταῖροι, 'are worrying' by this time, δ 598; ironically Σ 300.

ἀνῑάω (ἀνίη), fut. ἀνῑήσω, pass. **aor.** part. ἀνῑηθείς: = ἀνῑάζω, act., τινά, β 115; abs., 'be a torment,' 'nuisance,' τ 66, υ 178; pass., ἀνῑηθείς, *tired out*, 'tired to death' by the long story, γ 117, Β 291, α 133, ο 335.

ἀν-ῑδρωτί (ἱδρώς): *without sweat*, Ο 228†.

ἀνίη, ης: *torment, vexation;* ἄνευθε πόνου καὶ ἀνίης, η 192; of Scylla (abstr. for concr.), *bane*, μ 233; and so of persons, δαιτὸς ἀνίη, ρ 446 (cf. 377); ἀνίη καὶ πολὺς ὕπνος, an 'infliction,' 'weariness to the flesh,' ο 394, cf. υ 52. Cf. ἀνῑάζω. (Od.)

ἀνῑηθείς: see ἀνῑάω.

ἀν-ίημι (ἵημι), 2 sing. ἀνιεῖς, opt. ἀνιείης, part. ἀνιεῖσα, ipf. ἀνίει, fut. ἀνήσω (3 sing. ἀνέσει, σ 265), aor. ἀνῆκα, ἀνέηκα, 3 pl. ἄνεσαν, subj. ἀνήῃ, opt. ἀνείην, part. ἀνέντες, mid. pres. part. ἀνῑέμενος: *let go up, let up.*—I. act., ἀήτᾱς Ὠκεανὸς ἀνίησιν, δ 568; ὕδωρ ἀνίησι, Charybdis, μ 105; *let go*, opp. ἀλῶναι, σ 265; so of 'loosing' bonds, 'opening' doors, ὕπνος, 'forsake,' ω 440; ὀδύνη, 'release,' Ο 24; then of 'giving free rein' to one, Ε 880; hence, *incite*, τινὰ ἐπί τινι, Ε 882; abs., Ρ 705; νῦν αὖτέ με θῡμὸς ἀνῆκεν, 'impels,' 'prompts,' followed by inf., Χ 252, and often.—II. mid., κόλπον ἀνῑεμένη, letting up, i. e. 'laying bare her' bosom, Χ 80; similarly αἶγας ἀνῑεμένους, ripping up, 'flaying' for themselves, β 300.

ἀνῑηρός (ἀνίη): *vexatious, wearisome*, ρ 220, 377; comp., αὐτῷ ἀνιηρέστερον ἔσται, the *sorer* will it be for him, β 190; cf. ἄλγιον.

ἀνιπτό-πος, ποδος (ἄνιπτος, πούς): *with unwashed feet*, pl., Π 235†.

ἄ-νιπτος (νίπτω): *unwashed*, Ζ 266†.

ἀν-ίστημι, ipf. ἀνίστη, fut. ἀναστήσουσι, ἀνστήσ-, aor. 1 ἀνέστησε, opt. ἀναστήσειε, imp. ἄνστησον, part. ἀναστήσᾱς, ἀνστήσᾱσα, aor. 2 ἀνέστη, dual ἀνστήτην, 3 pl. ἀνέσταν, inf. ἀνστήμεναι, part. ἀνστάς, mid. pres. ἀνίσταμαι, ἀνιστάμενος, ipf. ἀνίστατο, fut. ἀναστήσονται, inf. ἀνστήσεσθαι: I. trans. (pres., ipf., fut., aor. 1, act.), *make to stand* or *get up*, η 163, 170; γέροντα δὲ χειρὸς ἀνίστη, took him by the hand and 'made him arise,' Ω 515, ξ 319; violently, Α 191; so of 'rousing,' Κ

32; raising the dead, Ω 756; instituting a migration, ζ 7, etc.—II. intrans. (aor. 2 and perf. act., and mid. forms), *stand up, get up;* ἐξ ἑδέων, ἐξ εὐνῆς, etc.; especially of rising to speak in the assembly, τοῖσι δ' ἀνέστη, 'to address them,' τοῖσι δ' ἀνιστάμενος μετέφη, A 58; ἀνά repeated as adverb, ἂν δ' Ὀδυσεὺς πολύμητις ἀνίστατο, Ψ 709.

ἀν-ίσχω (parallel form of ἀνέχω, q. v.): only pres. part., χεῖρας θεοῖσιν, Θ 347, O 369.

ἀν-ιχνεύω (ἴχνος): *track back*, X 192.

ἀννεῖται: see ἀνανέομαι.

ἀ-νοήμων: *unintelligent, unreflecting.* (Od.)

ἀν-οίγω, ἀνα-οίγω, ipf. ἀνέῳγε, ἀνῷγε, iter. ἀναοίγεσκον, aor. ἀνέῳξε: *open;* θύρᾱς, κληῖδα, 'shove back;' ἀπὸ χηλοῦ πῶμα, 'raise,' Π 221.

ἀν-όλεθρος: *untouched by destruction*, pl., N 761†.

ᾱ̓νομαι: see ᾱ̓νω.

ἄ-νοος: *silly, foolish;* κραδίη, Φ 441.

ἀνόπαια: doubtful word (and reading), perhaps name of a species of bird, α 320†. See ὀπαῖα.

ἀν-ορούω, only aor. ἀνόρουσεν, -σαν, part. -σᾱς: *spring up;* ἐκ θρόνων, ὕπνου, ἐς δίφρον, P 130; ἠέλιος, 'climbed swiftly up the sky,' γ 1.

ἀ-νόστιμος (νόστος): *not returning;* ἀνόστιμον ἔθηκαν, 'cut off his return,' δ 182†.

ἄ-νοστος: *without return* (cf. ἀνόστιμος), ω 528†.

ἄ-νουσος (νοῦσος): *without sickness*, ξ 255†.

ἀν-ούτατος: *unwounded*, Δ 540†. See οὐτάω.

ἀν-ουτητί: *without inflicting a wound*, X 371†. See οὐτάω.

ἀνστάς, ἀνστᾶσα, ἄνστησον, ἀνστήτην, ἀνστήσεσθαι: see ἀνίστημι.

ἀνστρέψειαν: see ἀναστρέφω.

ἀνσχεθέειν, ἄνσχεο, ἀνσχήσεσθαι: see ἀνέχω.

ἀν-σχετός (ἀνασχ-, ἀνέχω): *endurable*, with neg., β 63†.

ἄντα, ἄντ' (cf. ἀντί): adv. and prep., *opposite, over against;* ἄντα τιτύσκεσθαι, aim 'straight forward;' ἄντα ἰδὼν ἠλεύατο χάλκεον ἔγχος, N 184; ἄντα μάχεσθαι, 'with the enemy;' στῆ δ' ἄντα σχομένη, halted and 'faced' him, ζ 141; θεοῖσιν ἄντα ἐῴκει, 'in visage,' Ω 630 (cf. ἄντην); as prep., w. gen., Ἤλιδος ἄντα, *over against*, B 626; ἄντα παρειάων σχομένη λιπαρὰ κρήδεμνα, 'before' her cheeks, α 334; ἄντα σέθεν, δ 160; and freq. in hostile sense, θεοὶ ἄντα θεῶν ἴσαν, Υ 75; Διὸς ἄντα πτολεμίζειν, Θ 428, etc.

ἀντ-άξιος, ον: *equivalent in value, worth;* w. gen., ἰητρὸς γὰρ ἀνὴρ πολλῶν ἀντάξιος ἄλλων, Λ 514. (Il.)

ἀντάω (cf. ἀντί, ἄντα), ipf. ἤντεον, fut. ἀντήσω, aor. ἤντησα, subj. ἀντήσομεν: *meet, encounter;* of persons, w. dat., Z 399, H 423; of things, w. gen., μάχης, δαίτης, 'come straight to,' γ 44; ὅπως ἤντησας ὀπωπῆς, 'got sight of him face to face,' δ 327.

Ἄντεια: wife of Proetus, Stheneboea in the tragic poets, Z 160†.

ἀντ-έχω: only aor. 2 mid. imp. ἀντίσχεσθε, *hold before yourselves, interpose;* τραπέζᾱς ἰῶν, tables against the arrows, χ 74†.

ἄντην (ἄντα): *opposite, in front, in* or *to the face;* ἄντην ἵστασθε (opp. φεύγειν), Λ 590; ἄντην βαλλομένων, M 152; 'in view,' ζ 221; with ἐναλίγκιος, εἰκέλη, the effect of ἄντην is largely that of emphasis, β 5, χ 240; so with ὁμοιωθήμεναι, A 187; 'openly,' ἀγαπαζέμεν ἄντην, Ω 464.

Ἀντηνορίδης: *son of Antēnor*, Helicāon, Γ 123; pl., *sons of Antēnor*, Λ 59.

Ἀντ-ήνωρ: *Antēnor*, son of Aesyētes, husband of Theāno, Γ 262, E 69 f.

ἄντηστις (ἀντάω): *meeting;* only κατ' ἄντηστιν, *at the junction* of the men's and the women's apartments, *opposite the entrance of the house*, υ 387†. (See table III. at end of volume.)

ἀντί (cf. ἄντα), never suffers elision in Homer (ἄντ' = ἄντα, ἀντί' = ἀντία): prep. w. gen., *against* (as an equivalent, not local), *instead of, in return for;* ἀντί νυ πολλῶν | λᾱῶν ἐστὶν ἀνὴρ ὅν τε Ζεὺς κῆρι φιλήσῃ, I 116, Ψ 650, Ω 254.

ἀντί', ἀντία: see ἀντίος.

ἀντι-άνειρα (ἀνήρ): only fem., nom. pl., *matching men*, of the Amazons. (Il.)

ἀντιάω, ἀντιόω (ἀντί), fut. ἀντιάσω (as if from ἀντιάζω), ἀντιόω, aor. ἀντιάσειας, etc., part. ἀντιάσᾱς, mid. ipf. ἀντιάασθε: *meet, encounter, take part in*, usually w. gen.; of persons, Η 231, etc.; of things, μάχης, ἑκατόμβης, γάμου (mid., Ω 62), etc.; w. dat., Ζ 127, Φ 431, σ 147; w. acc. (limit of motion) only in ἐμὸν λέχος ἀντιόωσαν, 'visiting,' euphemistic of the captive who shares the couch of her lord, Α 31.

ἀντί-βιος (βίη): *hostile*, only ἀντιβίοις ἐπέεσσι, Α 304, σ 415; adv., **ἀντίβιον,** with verbs of combating, Γ 20, 435, Λ 386; also **ἀντιβίην,** Α 278, Ε 220. (Both adverbs only in Il.)

ἀντι-βολέω (βάλλω), fut. ἀντιβολήσω, aor. ἀντεβόλησε (ἀντιβ.): *come in the way of, encounter, take part in* (cf. ἀντιάω); μάχης, τάφου, etc.; subject a thing, γάμος ἀντιβολήσει ἐμέθεν, σ 272; w. dat., of persons, η 19, κ 277, Π 847; seldom of things, φόνῳ, λ 416; τάφῳ, ω 87.

ἀντί-θεος, 3: *godlike*, epith. of distinction as regards rank, might, stature, beauty; applied to kings, Ε 663; to the companions of Odysseus, δ 571; to the suitors, ξ 18, and (by Zeus) even to Polyphēmus, α 30; rarely of women, ἀντιθέην ἄλοχον (Penelope), λ 117.

ἀντί-θυρος (θύρη): *over against the door*, only κατ' ἀντίθυρον κλισίης, in a position opposite the entrance of the hut, π 159†.

Ἀντί-κλεια: *Anticlēa*, daughter of Autolycus, wife of Laertes and mother of Odysseus, λ 85, ο 358.

Ἄντι-κλος: name of a Greek warrior in the wooden horse, δ 286.

ἀντι-κρῦ, ἀντικρύς: *opposite, straightforward, straight through*; ἀντικρὺ μάχεσθαι, Ε 130, 819; w. gen., ὀιστὸν ἴαλλεν | Ἕκτορος ἀντικρῦ, Θ 301; ἀποφάναι, 'outright,' Η 362; ἀντικρῦ δ' ἀπάραξε, 'completely' off, Π 116, Ψ 866; often joined w. foll. prep., παραί, διά, κατά, ἀνά.

Ἀντί-λοχος: *Antilochus*, son of Nestor, Δ 457, Ν 554, Π 320, Ν 93, Ο 569, Ε 565, γ 452, δ 187.

Ἀντί-μαχος: a Trojan, Δ 123, 132, 138, Μ 188.

Ἀντί-νοος: *Antinous*, son of Eupeithes, α 383; prominent among the suitors of Penelope, and the most insolent of them, β 84, π 418, χ 22, ω 424.

ἀντίον: see ἀντίος.

Ἀντι-όπη: daughter of Asōpus, mother of Amphīon and Zethus, λ 260.

ἀντίος, 3 (ἀντί): *opposite*; freq. w. verbs of motion, and usually followed by gen., sometimes by dat.; in both friendly and unfriendly sense; οὐκ ἀθρῆσαι δύνατ' ἀντίη, 'over towards' him, τ 478; ἀντίος ἦλθε θέων, came running to 'meet' him, Ζ 54, Λ 535, Β 185; dat., Η 20; *against*, εἰ μή τις Δαναῶν νῦν Ἕκτορος ἀντίος εἶσιν, Η 28; so ἵστασθαι, ἀίσσειν, ἔγχε' ἀεῖραι, etc., dat., Ο 584, Υ 422.—Adv., **ἀντίον, ἀντία,** in same senses, and reg. w. gen.; ὅστις σέθεν ἀντίον εἴπῃ, *against*, Α 230; ἵν' ἀντίον αὐτὸς ἐνίσπῃ, 'in my presence,' ρ 529; δίφρον ἀντί' Ἀλεξάνδροιο θεὰ κατέθηκε, Γ 425.

ἀντιόω: see ἀντιάω.

ἀντι-πέραιος (πέρην): only neut. pl. as subst., *places opposite*, Β 635†.

ἀντίσχεσθε: see ἀντέχω.

ἀντι-τορέω, only aor.: *bore through in front*; δορὺ χροὸς ἀντετόρησεν, Ε 337; w. acc., δόμον ἀντιτορήσᾱς, 'breaking into,' Κ 267.

ἄν-τιτος (ἀνά, τίω): *in requital*, ἔργα, works 'of retribution,' 'vengeance,' ρ 51.

Ἀντι-φάτης: (1) a Trojan, Μ 191.—(2) a Greek, son of Melampus, ο 242.—(3) king of the Laestrȳgons (acc. -ῆα), κ 114.

ἀντι-φερίζω: *match oneself against, vie with*, τινί, Φ 357, 488. (Il.)

ἀντι-φέρομαι: *oppose oneself to, measure oneself with*, τινί (τὶ, acc. of specification), Φ 482. (Il.)

Ἀντί-φονος: a son of Priam, Ω 250†.

Ἄντι-φος: (1) a son of Priam, Δ 489.—(2) son of Aegyptius, β 19.—(3) a friend of Odysseus, ρ 68.—(4) son of Talaemenes, an ally of the Trojans, Β 864.—(5) a Heraclid, son of Thessalus, a leader of Greek islanders, Β 678.

ἄντλος, ου: *bilge-water, hold* of a ship. (Od.)

ἀντολή (ἀνατέλλω): *rising*, only pl., ἀντολαὶ ἠελίοιο, μ 4†.

ἄντομαι (parallel form of ἀντάω), only pres. and ipf.: *meet, encounter* · τινί, Ο 698, Χ 203; ὅθι διπλόος ἤντετο θώρηξ, 'met double,' i. e. where the cuirass formed a double layer by meeting with the ζῶμα and overlapping it, Δ 133, Υ 415.

ἄντρον: *cave, grot.* (Od.)

Ἀντρών: a town in Thessaly, B 697†.

ἄντυξ, υγος: *rim.*—(1) the metal rim of a shield, Z 118; serving to bind together the layers of leather or metal, of which the shield was composed (see the cut).—(2) the rim of a

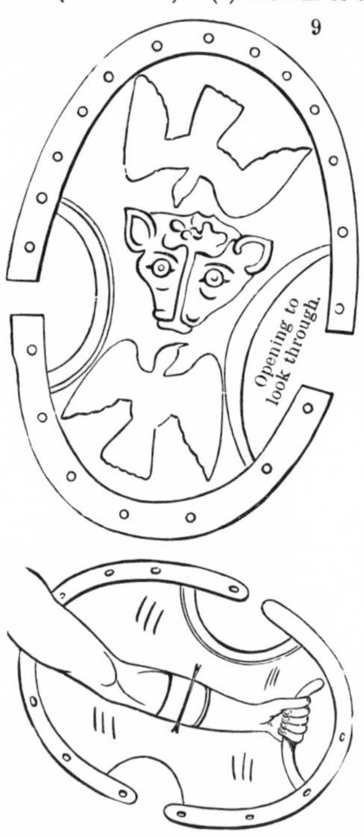

chariot, surrounding (περίδρομος) the body (δίφρος) of the car, sometimes double, E 728; it served also as a place of attachment for the reins. (See the cut.)

ἄνῡμι: see ἀνύω.

ἄνυσις (ἀνύω): *accomplishment;* ἄνυσις δ' οὐκ ἔσσεται αὐτῶν, 'success' shall not be theirs, B 347, δ 544.

ἀνύω, ἄνῡμι (ἄνω), aor. ἤνυσε, opt.

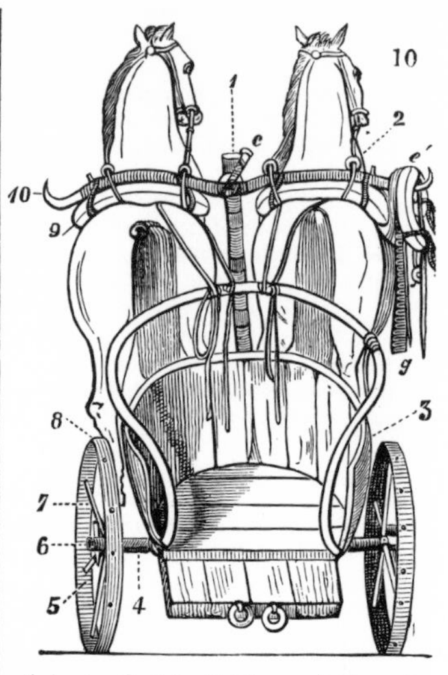

1. ῥυμός. 2. οἴηξ. 3. δίφρος. 4. ἄξων. 5. ἴτυς. 6. πλήμνη. 7. κνήμη. 8. ἐπισσωτρα. 9. ζεύγλη. 10. ζυγόν.

ἀνύσειε, pass. ipf. ἤνυτο, mid. fut. inf. ἀνύσσεσθαι: *bring to an end, accomplish;* θοῶς δέ οἱ ἤνυτο ἔργον, ε 243, abs. Δ 56, mid. π 373; ἐπεὶ δή σε φλὸξ ἤνυσεν, had 'consumed,' ω 71; of 'traversing' space (as we say, a ship 'makes' so many knots), ὅσσον τε πανημερίη γλαφυρὴ νηῦς | ἤνυσεν, δ 357, ο 294.

ἄνω, ipf. ἦνον: *complete;* ὁδόν, γ 496; pass. νὺξ ἄνεται, 'draws to a close,' K 251; ὅππως ἔργον ἄνοιτο (note the quantity), Σ 473.

ἄνω (ἀνά): *upwards,* λ 596; Λέσβος ἄνω (i. e. towards Troy, 'north'?) . . καὶ Φρυγίη καθύπερθε, Ω 544.

ἄνωγα, perf. w. pres. meaning, imp. ἄνωχθι, -ώχθω and -ωγείτω, -ωχθε and -ώχετε, inf. -ωγέμεν, plup. ἠνώγεα, ἠνώγει and -ειν, ἀνώγει (also forms that may be referred to ἀνώγω as pres. and ipf.), ἀνώγει, -ετον, subj. ἀνώγῃ, opt. ἀνώγοιμι, ipf. ἤνωγον, ἄνωγον, fut. ἀνώξω, aor. ἤνωξα: *bid, command;* foll. by acc. and inf., ἄνωχθι δέ μιν γαμέεσθαι, β 113; very seldom w. dat. of person, δέμνι' ἄνωγεν ὑποστορέσαι δμωῇσιν, υ 139; freq. joined with ἐποτρύνω, κέλομαι, and esp. w. θῡμός, (two accusatives) τά με θῡμὸς ἀνώγει, Τ 102.

ἀνῷγεν: see ἀνοίγω.

ἀνώγω: see ἄνωγα.

ἀν-ωθέω, only aor. part. ἀνώσαντες: *shove off* from land, ο 553†.

ἀν-ωιστί (ὀίω): *unexpectedly*, δ 92†.

ἀν-ώιστος (ὀίω): *unexpected*, Φ 39†.

ἀν-ώνυμος (ὄνομα): *nameless*, θ 552†.

ἄνωχθε, -θι, -θω: see ἄνωγα.

ἄξαντος, -ασθε, -εμεν, -έμεναι, -ετε: see ἄγω.

ἀξίνη: *battle-axe* of the Trojans, Ο 711. (See cut.)

11

ἄξιος, 3 (ἄγω): *of equal weight, value, worth*, with gen.; οὐδ' ἑνὸς ἄξιοί εἰμεν Ἕκτορος, Θ 234; λέβης βοὸς ἄξιος, Ψ 885; ἄξια ἄποινα, 'suitable,' i. e. precious, Ζ 46; ἄξιον, a 'good' price, υ 383.

Ἀξιός: a river in Macedonia, Φ 141, Β 849.

ἄ-ξυλος (ξύλον): *dense*, ὕλη, Λ 155†.

Ἄξυλος: son of Teuthras, from Arisbe, in Thrace, Ζ 12†.

ἄξων, ονος: *axle*, Ε 838, Π 378. (Il.)

ἀοιδή, ῆς (ἀείδω): *song, minstrelsy*; τῷ θεὸς περὶ δῶκεν ἀοιδήν, the 'gift of song', θ 44; ἀοιδῆς ὕμνον, 'strains of minstrelsy,' θ 429; concrete, 'that song,' α 351, etc. The various shades of application are not always distinct, nor is anything gained by attempting to distinguish them.

ἀοιδιάω, -άει, part. -άουσα: *sing*, κ 227 and ε 61.

ἀοίδιμος: *subject of song*, pl. (with bad sense from the context), Ζ 358†.

ἀοιδός, οῦ (ἀείδω): *singer, bard*; enumerated among the δημιοεργοί, ρ 383 ff; αὐτοδίδακτος (implying inspiration), χ 347; in Il. only Ω 720. For the high estimation in which the ἀοιδός was held, see θ 479 ff.

ἀ-ολλής, ές (εἴλω): *in throngs, (all) together;* ἀολλέες ἠγερέθοντο, Ψ 233; ἀολλέες ἦλθον ἅπᾱσαι, χ 446; πάντα φέρωμεν ἀολλέα, θ 394.

ἀολλίζω, aor. ἀόλλισαν, part. ἀολλίσσᾱσα, pass. ἀολλίσθησαν, -θήμεναι: *bring together, assemble*, Ζ 270, 287, Ο 588. (Il.)

ἄορ, ἄορος (ἀείρω), neut., but acc. pl. ἄορας, ρ 222: *sword*, 'hanger,' suspended by the ἀορτήρ, the same as ξίφος, θ 403, 406, κ 294, 321. (See cut.)

12

ἀορτήρ, ῆρος (ἀείρω): *baldric, belt*, usually for the ἄορ, and the same as τελαμών (see cut), λ 609; 'strap' for a wallet, ν 438; what the 'suspenders' were in Λ 31 is not perfectly clear.

ἀοσσητήρ, ῆρος: *defender, helper*.

ἄ-ουτος: *unwounded*, Σ 536†. See οὐτάω.

ἀπ-αγγέλλω, ipf. iter. ἀπαγγέλλεσκε, and aor.: *bring tidings, report; τινί τι*, Ι 626.

ἀπ-άγχω: *throttle*, part., τ 230†.

ἀπ-άγω, fut. ἀπάξω, aor. 2 ἀπήγαγον: *lead* or *bring away;* οἴκαδε (τινά), αὖτις πατρίδα γαῖαν, Ο 706, etc.

ἀπ-αείρομαι: only part., ἀπαειρόμενον πόλιος, *bearing away* from the city, Φ 563†.

ἀπ-αίνυμαι, ἀποαίνυμαι, only pres. and ipf.: *take away; τινός τι*, ρ 322, Ν 262.

Ἀπαισός: a town of Mysia, Β 828†. See Παισός.

ἀπ-ᾱΐσσω: only aor. part., ἀπᾱΐξᾱς, *springing from;* κρημνοῦ, Φ 234†.

ἀπ-αιτίζω: *reclaim*, β 78†.

ἀπάλαλκε, ἀπαλάλκοι: see ἀπαλέξω.

ἀ-πάλαμνος (παλάμη): *without device*, E 597†.

ἀπ-αλέξω, fut. inf. -ξήσειν, aor. 1 opt. -ξήσαιμι, aor. 2 ἀπάλαλκε, opt. ἀπαλάλκοι: *ward off, avert, keep from;* μνηστῆρας δ' ἀπάλαλκε, prayer of Penelope to Athena, δ 766; **τινά τινος**, Ω 371, X 348; with gen. of the thing, **τινὰ κακότητος**, she was not going to *keep* (save) one of them from destruction, ρ 364.

ἀπ-άλθομαι: only fut. 3 du., ἕλκε' ἀπαλθήσεσθον, shall they *be fully healed* of their wounds, Θ 405, 419.

ἀπ-αλοιάω, aor. ἀπηλοίησεν: *crush utterly;* ὀστέα, Δ 522†.

ἁπαλός, 3: *tender*, δειρή, αὐχήν, παρειαί, of women, Σ 123; χεῖρες, joined w. ἄτριπτοι, φ 151; πόδες, of Ate, T 93 (cf. 94); ἦτορ, 'life,' Λ 115; adv., ἁπαλὸν γελάσαι, the effect of wine, 'snicker,' ξ 465.

ἁπαλο-τρεφής, ές: *tender-fed*, 'fattened;' σίαλος, Φ 363†.

ἀπ-αμάω, only aor. opt. ἀπᾱμήσειε: *cut off;* λαιμόν, as children say, 'cut his neck off,' Σ 34† (v. l. ἀποτμήξειε).

ἀπαμβροτεῖν: see ἀφαμαρτάνω.

ἀπ-αμείβομαι: *answer, reply;* esp., ἀπαμειβόμενος προσέφη (προσεφώνεε), and ἀπαμείβετο φώνησέν τε. In different connection, θ 158.

ἀπ-αμύνω, aor. ἀπήμῡνα, mid. ipf. ἀπαμύνετο, aor. opt. ἀπαμῡναίμεσθα, inf. ἀπαμύνασθαι: *ward off* (τινί τι), mid., from oneself, (**τινά**) *defend oneself against;* Αἰτωλοῖσιν ἀπήμῡνεν κακὸν ἦμαρ, I 597; πόλις ᾗ (whereby) κ' ἀπαμῡναίμεσθα, O 738; χερσὶ πέποιθα | ἄνδρ' ἀπαμύνεσθαι, π 72.

ἀπ-αναίνομαι, only aor. ἀπηνήναντο, inf. ἀπανήνασθαι: *deny, disown, decline*, H 185 and κ 297.

ἀπ-άνευθε(ν): *away, apart from* (τινός); ἀπάνευθε κιών, A 35; ἕζετ' ἔπειτ' ἀπάνευθε νεῶν, A 48; βασιλῆα μάχης ἀπάνευθε φέροντες, Λ 283; 'forth from,' T 374.

ἁπάντῃ, ἀπάντη: *on every side.*

ἀπ-ανύω: only aor. ἀπήνυσαν οἴκαδ' ὀπίσσω, *accomplished* the journey home again, η 326†.

ἅπαξ: *once;* 'once for all,' μ 350. (Od.)

ἀπ-αράσσω, only aor. ἀπήραξε, ἀπάραξε: *smite off.* (Il.)

ἀπ-αρέσκομαι (ἀρέσκω), only aor. inf. ἀπαρέσσασθαι: *conciliate*, T 183†.

ἀπ-άρχομαι: *begin* a sacrifice, by cutting off hair from the forehead of the victim, γ 446, ξ 422. Cf. *κατάρχεσθαι.*

ἅ-πᾱς, -πᾱσα, -παν (stronger than πᾶς): *all*, pl. *all* (*together*), c u n c t i; ἀργύρεος ἅπᾱς, 'solid silver,' δ 616; τυχὼν φιλότητος ἁπάσης, 'nothing but kindness,' ο 158; καὶ εἰς ἐνιαυτὸν ἅπαντα, in 'a year and a day,' ξ 196.

ἄ-παστος (πατέομαι): *without* (*taste of*) *food;* ἐδητύος ἠδὲ ποτῆτος, δ 788, ζ 250.

ἀπατάω (ἀπάτη), fut. -ησω, aor. ἀπάτησα: *deceive.*

ἀπ-άτερθε(ν) (ἄτερ): *apart, away from;* ὁμίλου, E 445.

ἀπάτη, ης: *deceit;* pl., O 31.

ἀπατήλιος: *deceitful;* only neut. pl., ἀπατήλια βάζειν, εἰδέναι, ξ 127, 288.

ἀπατηλός = ἀπατήλιος, A 526†.

ἀπ-ατῑμάω, aor. ἀπητίμησε: *treat with indignity, offend deeply*, N 113†.

ἀπ-αυράω, ipf. (usually w. aor. meaning) ἀπηύρων, -ᾱς, -ᾱ, fut. ἀπουρήσουσι (v. l. ἀπουρίσσουσι), X 489, aor. part. ἀπούρᾱς: *wrest from, rob, deprive;* τινά τι, ἄμφω θῡμὸν ἀπηύρᾱ, Z 17; ἐλεύθερον ἦμαρ ἀπούρᾱς, Π 831; sometimes w. dat. of disadvantage, Ἕκτορι θῡμὸν ἀπούρᾱς, Φ 296.

ἀπαφίσκω, aor. 2 ἤπαφε, mid. opt. ἀπάφοιτο: *delude, beguile*, λ 217 and ψ 216.

ἀπέειπε: see ἀπεῖπον.

ἀπέεργε: see ἀποέργω.

ἀπειλέω, fut. -ήσω, ipf. du. ἀπειλήτην: *threaten, menace;* τινί, regularly foll. by fut. inf.; γέρας αὐτὸς ἀφαιρήσεσθαι ἀπειλεῖς, A 161; freq. w. cognate acc., ἀπειλάς, Π 201; μῦθον, A 388; less specifically, 'boast,' Θ 150 (foll. by εἶναι), θ 383; 'vow,' 'promise,' Ψ 863, 872.

ἀπειλή, ῆς, only pl.: *threats, boasting.* Cf. ἀπειλέω.

ἀπειλητήρ, ῆρος: *boaster*, pl., H 96†.

1. ἄπ-ειμι, fut. ἀπεσσεῖται, ἀπέσσεται, pres. subj. ἀπέῃσι, ipf. ἀπέην, ἄπεσαν: *be* (*distant*) *from* (τινός), *be absent, wanting;* τόσσον ἀπῆν ὅσον τε γέγωνε βοήσᾱς, ε 400; σοὶ δ' ὁδὸς οὐκέτι δηρὸν ἀπέσσεται, 'you shall not have to wait much longer for the journey,' β 285.

2. **ἄπ-ειμι,** imp. ἄπιθι, part. ἀπιών: *go away*, very often the part.; ἐγὼ μὲν ἄπειμι, 'am going,' fut., ρ 593.

ἀπ-εῖπον, ἀπέειπε (ἀπέϜ.), subj. ἀποείπω, opt. ἀποείποι, inf. ἀποειπεῖν, ἀπειπέμεν, part. ἀποειπών: (1) *speak out; μάλα γὰρ κρατερῶς ἀπέειπεν*, I 431; ἵν' ὑμῖν μῦθον ἀπηλεγέως ἀποείπω, α 373; ἀγγελίην, 'deliver,' Η 416.—(2) *say no, renounce; ὑπόσχεο καὶ κατάνευσον,* | ἢ ἀπόειπε, Α 515; μῆνιν ἀποειπών, Τ 35; πᾶσι μνηστήρεσσιν ἀπειπέμεν, 'warn them to desist,' α 91. See εἶπον.

Ἀπειραίη: *of Apeira*, γρηῦς.—**Ἀπείρηθεν**: *from Apeira.*

ἀ-πειρέσιος and **ἀπερείσιος,** 3 (πέρας, πείρατα): *unlimited, boundless, infinite*; γαῖαν ἀπειρεσίην, Υ 58; ἄνθρωποι πολλοί, ἀπειρέσιοι, τ 174; ἀπερείσι' ἄποινα, Α 13.

ἀ-πείρητος (πειράομαι): *untried, unskilful.*

ἀ-πείριτος = ἀπειρέσιος, κ 195†.

ἀ-πείρων, ονος (πέρας): *boundless, endless*; δῆμος, 'countless,' Ω 776; ὕπνος, η 286; δεσμοί, θ 340.

ἀπ-εκ-λανθάνομαι, only aor. imp. ἀπεκλελάθεσθε: *forget altogether*, ω 394†.

ἀ-πέλεθρος: *immeasurable*; ἶς, Ε 245, ι 538; neut. as adv., 'enormously far,' Λ 354.

ἀπ-εμέω: only aor. ἀπέμεσσεν, *spat out*, Ξ 437†.

ἀπεμνήσαντο: see ἀπομιμνήσκω.

ἀπένεικας: see ἀποφέρω.

ἀπέπλω: see ἀποπλώω.

ἀπερείσιος: see ἀπειρέσιος.

ἀπ-ερύκω, fut. ἀπερύξω: *hold off, keep off* or *away*, ι 119.

ἀπ-έρχομαι, aor. ἀπῆλθε, perf. ἀπελήλυθα: *come* (or *go*) *away, depart*; τινός, β 136, Ω 766.

ἀπ-ερωεύς (ἀπερωέω): *thwarter*; μενέων, Θ 361†.

ἀπ-ερωέω, aor. opt. ἀπερωήσειας: *slink away*; πολέμου, from fighting, Π 723†.

ἄπεσαν: see ἄπειμι.

ἀπέσσυτο: see ἀποσεύω.

ἀ-πευθής, έος (πεύθομαι): pass., *unascertained*; καὶ ὄλεθρον ἀπευθέα θῆκε Κρονίων, 'put even his destruction beyond ken,' γ 88 (cf. 86, 87); act., *without ascertaining*, 'uninformed,' γ 184.

ἀπ-εχθαίρω, aor. 1 subj. ἀπεχθήρω: *hate utterly*; τινά, Γ 415; causative, ὅς τέ μοι ὕπνον ἀπεχθαίρει καὶ ἐδωδὴν | μνωομένῳ, *makes hateful* to me—when I think of his loss, δ 105.

ἀπ-εχθάνομαι, aor. 2 ἀπήχθετο, inf. ἀπεχθέσθαι: *make oneself, be*, or *become hated*, β 202, Γ 454; 'mutual' enmity is implied in π 114.

ἀπ-έχω, fut. ἀφέξω, ἀποσχήσω, aor. 2 ἀπέσχον, mid. fut. ἀφέξομαι, aor. 2 ἀπεσχόμην, inf. ἀποσχέσθαι: *hold from, keep from*; act., τινός τι or τινά, ἑκὰς νήσων ἀπέχειν εὐεργέα νῆα, ο 33; ἠὼς ἥ μ' Ὀδυσῆος οἴκου ἀποσχήσει, that 'shall part' me from Odysseus' house, τ 572; also w. dat. of interest, Ω 19, υ 263; mid., τινός, 'hold aloof from,' Μ 248; 'abstain,' ι 211; 'spare,' μ 321, τ 489.

ἀπ-ηλεγέως (ἀλέγω): *without scruple*; μῦθον ἀποειπεῖν, α 373 and I 309.

ἀ-πήμαντος (πημαίνω): *unharmed*, τ 282†.

ἀπήμβροτον: see ἀφαμαρτάνω.

ἀ-πήμων, ονος (πῆμα): *without harm*; pass., ἀπήμων ἦλθε, ἀπήμονα πέμπειν τινά, 'safe and sound,' δ 487, ν 39; act., of anything that tends to safety, νόστος ἀπήμων, 'happy' return, δ 519; πομποί, 'kindly,' θ 566; οὖρος, ὕπνος, etc. The distinction of act. and pass. is rather apparent than real.

ἀπήνη, ης: *wagon*, for freight, and four-wheeled, Ω 324; with tent-like cover, ζ 70; usually drawn by mules. (See cut on following page.)

ἀπ-ηνήναντο: see ἀπαναίνομαι.

ἀπ-ηνής, ές (opp. ἐν-ηής): *unfeeling, harsh*, Α 340, τ 329; θυμός, Ο 94; νόος, Π 35; μῦθος, Ο 202.

ἀπήραξεν: see ἀπαράσσω.

ἀπηύρων: see ἀπαυράω.

ἀπ-ήωρος (ἀείρω): *hanging* (*high*) *away*; ὄζοι, μ 435†, cf. 436.

ἀ-πιθέω, only fut., and aor. ἀπίθησε: *disobey*; τινί, always with negative.

ἀπινύσσω (πινυτός): *lack understanding*, ε 342; *be unconscious*; κῆρ, acc. of specification, Ο 10.

ἄπιος (ἀπό): *distant*; **τηλόθεν ἐξ ἀπίης γαίης,** Α 270, π 18.

13

Ἀπισάων: (1) a Greek, son of Hippasus, P 348.—(2) a Trojan, son of Phausius, Λ 582.

ἀ-πιστέω (ἄπιστος): *disbelieve*, only ipf., οὔ ποτ' ἀπίστεον, 'I never despaired,' ν 339†.

ἄ-πιστος (πιστός): *faithless*, Γ 106; *unbelieving*, ξ 150.

ἀπ-ίσχω = ἀπέχω, λ 95†.

ἁπλοΐς, ίδος (ἁπλόος): *single*; χλαῖνα, to be wrapped only once about the person (opp. δίπλαξ, q. v.), Ω 230 and ω 276.

ἄ-πνευστος (πνέω): *breathless*, ε 456†.

ἀπό: *from* (a b).—I. adv. (here belong all examples of the so-called use 'in tmesi'), *off*, *away*; ἡμῖν ἀπὸ λοιγὸν ἀμῦναι, A 67; ἀπὸ δὲ χλαῖναν βάλε, B 183, etc.; a subst. in the gen. (of separation) is often added to render more specific the relation of the adv., ἀπ' ἰχῶ χειρὸς ὀμόργνῦ, E 416; πολλὸν γὰρ ἀπὸ πλυνοί εἰσι πόληος, ζ 40; thus preparing the way for the strict prepositional usage. — II. prep., w. gen., *from*, *away from*, denoting origin, starting-point, separation (distance); οὐ γὰρ ἀπὸ δρυός ἐσσι παλαιφάτου, οὐδ' ἀπὸ πέτρης, 'sprung from' tree or rock, τ 163; ἀφ' ἵππων ἆλτο χαμᾶζε, 'from his car,' Π 733; so freq. ἀφ' ἵππων, ἀπὸ νεῶν μάχεσθαι, where we say 'on'; οὐκ ἀπὸ σκοποῦ οὐδ' ἀπὸ δόξης | μῦθεῖται βασίλεια, 'wide of,' i. e. she hits the mark and meets our views, λ 344; μένων ἀπὸ ἧς ἀλόχοιο, 'away from' his wife, B 292; so ἀπ' οὔατος, ἀπ' ὀφθαλμῶν; adverbial phrase, ἀπὸ σπουδῆς, 'in earnest,' M 237. The 'temporal' meaning commonly ascribed to ἀπὸ in Θ 54 is only implied, not expressed by the preposition.

ἀποαίνυμαι: see ἀπαίνυμαι.

ἀποαιρέομαι: see ἀφαιρέομαι.

ἀπο-βαίνω, fut. ἀποβήσομαι, aor. ἀπέβην, ἀπεβήσετο: *go away*; ἐξ ἵππων (ἵππων, P 480), 'dismount'; νηός, 'disembark,' ν 281.

ἀπό-βλητος: *to be spurned, despised*, w. neg., B 361 and Γ 65.

ἀπο-βλύζω: *spirt out*; οἴνου, I 491†.

ἀπο-βρίζω, only aor. part. ἀποβρίξαντες: *sleep soundly*, ι 151 and μ 7.

ἀπο-γυιόω (γυῖον), aor. subj. ἀπογυιώσῃς: *unnerve*, Z 265†.

ἀπο-γυμνόω (γυμνός), aor. pass. part. ἀπογυμνωθέντα: *denude, strip*, κ 301†.

ἀπο-δαίομαι (δαίω), fut. inf. ἀποδάσσεσθαι, aor. ἀποδάσσασθαι: *give a share of, share with*; τινί τι, and τινί τινος, P 231, X 118, Ω 595.

ἀπο-δειροτομέω (δειρή, τέμνω), fut. -ήσω, aor. ἀπεδειροτόμησα: *cut the throat of, slaughter*; ἐς βόθρον, i. e. over the trench, so that the blood might run into it, λ 35.

ἀπο-δέχομαι, aor. ἀπεδέξατο: *accept*, A 95†.

ἀπο-διδρᾱ́σκω, aor. 2 part. ἀποδράς: *escape by stealth*; ἐκ νηός and νηός, π 65 and ρ 516.

ἀπο-δίδωμι, fut. ἀποδώσομεν, aor. ἀπέδωκε, subj. ἀποδῷσι, opt. ἀποδοῖτε, inf. ἀποδοῦναι: *give* or *deliver up, restore*; κτήματα, Γ 285; νέκυν ἐπὶ νῆας, H 84; θρέπτρα τοκεῦσιν, 'repay the debt' of nurture, Δ 478.

ἀποδίομαι: see ἐξαποδίομαι.

ἀπο-δοχμόω (δοχμός), aor. part. ἀποδοχμώσᾱς: *bend to one side*, ι 372†.

ἀποδράς: see ἀποδιδράσκω.

ἀπο-δρύφω, aor. ἀπέδρυψε, subj. ἀποδρύψωσι, aor. pass. 3 pl. ἀπέδρυφθεν: *tear off, strip off*; πρὸς πέτρῃσιν ἀπὸ χειρῶν ῥῑνοὶ ἀπέδρυφθεν, ε 435; ἵνα μή μιν ἀποδρύφοι ἑλκυστάζων, 'tear him,' i. e. abrade the skin, Ψ 187, Ω 21.

ἀπο-δύνω = ἀποδύομαι, *put off*, ipf., χ 364†.

ἀπο-δύω, fut. ἀποδύσω, aor. 1 ἀπέδυσε, aor. 2 part. ἀποδύς: act. (pres., fut., aor. 1), *strip off* (from another), τεύχεα, Δ 532, Σ 83; mid. (aor. 2), *put off* (doff), εἵματα, ε 343; ἀποδυσάμενος, ε 349; better reading ἀπολυσάμενος.

ἀποδῷσι: see ἀποδίδωμι.

ἀπο-είκω (ἀποϝ.): *yield, retire from*, Γ 406†.

ἀποεῖπον: see ἀπεῖπον.

ἀπο-εργάθω (ἀποϝ.), ipf. ἀποέργαθε (ἀπεέρ.): *keep away from, remove from*, Φ 599, φ 221.

ἀπο-έργω (ϝέργω), ipf. ἀπέεργε: *keep away from, separate*, Θ 325; 'drive away,' Ω 238.

ἀπό-ερσε (ἀπόϝ.), defective aor., subj. ἀποέρσῃ, opt. ἀποέρσειε: *sweep away, wash away*; μή μιν ἀποϝϝέρσειε μέγας ποταμός, Φ 329, 283, Ζ 348.

ἀπο-θαυμάζω, aor. ἀπεθαύμασε: *marvel at*, ζ 49†.

ἀπό-θεστος (θέσσασθαι): *scouted, despised*, ρ 296†.

ἀπο-θνήσκω, perf. part. ἀποτεθνηώς, plup. ἀποτέθνασαν: *die*; perf., *be dead*.

ἀπο-θρώσκω, only pres. part.: *leap from*, νηός, Β 702, Π 748; καπνός, 'up,' α 58.

ἀπο-θύμιος (θυμός): *displeasing*, neut. pl., Ξ 261†.

ἀπ-οικίζω, aor. ἀπῴκισε: *transfer*, from an old home to a new one, μ 135†.

ἄ-ποινα, ων (ποινή): *ransom, recompense, satisfaction*; τινός, 'for one,' Α 111, etc.

ἀποίσω: see ἀποφέρω.

ἀπ-οίχομαι: *be away, gone* (*from*), δ 109, very often the part.; 'abandon,' πολέμου, ἀνδρός, Λ 408, Τ 342.

ἀπο-καίνυμαι, only ipf.: *excel*, θ 127 and 219.

ἀπο-κείρω, only aor. 1 mid. ἀπεκείρατο: *shear away*, Ψ 141†.

ἀπο-κηδέω, only aor. part. du. ἀποκηδήσαντε: *proving remiss*, 'through your negligence,' Ψ 413†.

ἀπο-κῑνέω, aor. subj. ἀποκῑνήσωσι, iter. ἀποκῑνήσασκε: *move from*, Λ 636; τινὰ θυράων. 'dislodge,' χ 107.

ἀπο-κλῑνω, only aor. part. ἀποκλίναντα: *turn off*, 'giving a different turn' to the interpretation, τ 556†.

ἀπο-κόπτω, fut. inf. ἀποκοψέμεν, aor. ἀπέκοψα: *chop off, cut off*; παρήορον, 'cut loose' the out-running horse (cf. Θ 87), Π 474.

ἀπο-κοσμέω (κόσμος), ipf. ἀπεκόσμεον: *clear off* something that has been set on in order; ἔντεα δαιτός, η 232†.

ἀπο-κρεμάννῡμι, aor. ἀπεκρέμασε: *let droop*; αὐχένα, Ψ 879†.

ἀπο-κρῑνω, only aor. pass. ἀποκρινθέντε: *separated*, 'separating' *from* the ranks of their comrades, Ε 12†.

ἀπο-κρύπτω, aor. ἀπέκρυψα, inf. ἀποκρύψαι: *hide away, conceal*, Λ 718, Σ 465, ρ 286.

ἀποκτάμεν, ἀποκτάμεναι: see ἀποκτείνω.

ἀπο-κτείνω, aor. 1 ἀπέκτεινε, usually aor. 2 ἀπέκτανε, -έκταμεν, -έκτανον, subj. ἀποκτάνῃ, inf. ἀποκτάμεν, -τάμεναι, aor. 2 mid. (with pass. signif.) ἀπέκτατο, ἀποκτάμενος: *kill, slay*; of slaughtering animals, μ 301; ἀπέκτατο, *was slain*, Ο 437, Ρ 472; ἀποκτάμενος, *slain*, Δ 494, Ν 660, Ψ 775.

ἀπο-λάμπω, ipf. act. and mid.: *give forth a gleam, be resplendent*; τρυφάλεια, Τ 381, πέπλος, Ζ 295; impers., ὡς αἰχμῆς ἀπέλαμπε, 'such was the gleam from the spear,' Χ 319; fig., χάρις ἀπελάμπετο, σ 298.

ἀπο-λείβω· only pres. mid. ἀπολείβεται, *trickles off*, η 107†.

ἀπο-λείπω: *leave remaining*; οὐδ' ἀπέλειπεν, i. e. οὐδὲν ἀπολείπων, ι 292; *leave, quit*, δόμον· Μ 169; intrans., *be lacking, fail*, καρπός, η 117.

ἀπο-λέπω, fut. inf. ἀπολεψέμεν: *peel off*, 'lop off,' οὔατα, Φ 455† (v. l. ἀποκοψέμεν).

ἀπολέσκετο: see ἀπόλλῡμι.

ἀπο-λήγω, fut. ἀπο(λ)λήξεις, aor. subj. ἀπο(λ)λήξῃς, -ωσι, opt. ἀπο(λ)λήξειαν: *cease from, desist*, τινός, Η 263, ν 151, μ 224; with part., Ρ 565, τ 166; abs., ὡς ἀνδρῶν γενεὴ ἣ μὲν φύει ἣ δ' ἀπολήγει, 'passes away,' Ζ 146, Ν 230.

ἀπο-λιχμάω, fut. mid. ἀπολιχμήσονται: *lick off*, αἷμα, Φ 123†.

ἀπολλήξεις: see ἀπολήγω.

ἀπ-όλλῡμι, fut. ἀπολέσσω, aor. ἀπώλεσα, mid. ἀπόλλυμαι, ἀπολλύμενος, fut. inf. ἀπολεῖσθαι, aor. 2 ἀπωλόμην, ἀπόλοντο, iter. ἀπολέσκετο, opt. 3 pl. ἀπολοίατο, perf. 2 ἀπόλωλεν: I. act., lose, destroy, πατέρ' ἐσθλὸν ἀπώλεσα, β 46; οὐ γὰρ Ὀδυσσεὺς οἷος ἀπώλεσε νόστιμον ἦμαρ, α 354; κεῖνος ἀπώλεσεν Ἴλιον ἱρήν, Ε 648; ἐκπάγλως ἀπόλεσσαν (φῆρας), Α 268. — II. mid., *be lost, perish;* freq. as imprecation, ἀπόλοιτο, Σ 107, α 47.

Ἀπόλλων, Ἀπόλλωνος: *Apollo*, son of Zeus and Leto, and brother of Artemis, like her bringing sudden, painless death (see ἀγανός); god of the sun and of light, Φοῖβος, λυκηγενής, of prophecy (his oracle in Pytho, θ 79), Α 72, θ 488; but not in Homer specifically god of music and leader of the Muses, though he delights the divine assembly with the strains of his lyre, Α 603; defender of the Trojans and their capital, and of other towns in the Trojan domain, Cilla, Chryse, Α 37, Δ 507; epithets, ἀκερσεκόμης, ἀφήτωρ, διίφιλος, ἑκατηβόλος, ἕκατος, ἑκηβόλος, ἑκάεργος, ἰήιος, λᾱοσσόος, παιήων, χρῡσάορος, Σμινθεύς, Φοῖβος.

ἀπο-λούομαι (λούω), fut. ἀπολούσομαι: *wash from* (off oneself), ζ 219†.

ἀπο-λῡμαίνομαι (λῡμαίνω), *purify oneself* of pollution, by bathing as symbolical procedure, Α 313 f.

ἀπο-λῡμαντήρ, ῆρος: *defiler; δαιτῶν*, 'dinner-spoiler;' according to others, 'plate-licker,' ρ 220 and 377

ἀπο-λύω, aor. ἀπέλῡσας, subj. ἀπολύσομεν, mid. fut. ἀπολῡσόμεθα, aor. part. ἀπολῡσάμενος: I. act., *loose from, release* for ransom (Il.): ἱμάντα θοῶς ἀπέλῡσε κορώνης, φ 46; οὐδ' ἀπέλῡσε θύγατρα καὶ οὐκ ἀπεδέξατ' ἄποινα, Α 95.—II. mid., *loose from oneself, get released* for oneself, *ransom;* ἀπολῡσάμενος (κρήδεμνον), ε 349; (παῖδας) χαλκοῦ τε χρῡσοῦ τ' ἀπολῡσόμεθα, Χ 50.

ἀπο-μηνίω, fut. ἀπομηνίσει, aor. part. ἀπομηνίσᾱς: *be wrathful apart*, 'sulk in anger,' Β 772, Η 230, Τ 62, π 378.

ἀπο-μιμνήσκομαι, aor. ἀπεμνήσαντο: *remember* something in return (cf. ἀποδοῦναι), Ω 428†.

ἀπ-όμνῡμι and **ἀπομνύω,** ipf. ἀπώμνῡ and ἀπώμνυεν, aor. ἀπώμοσα: *swear not* to do; according to others, *swear* formally (solemnly), κ 345, μ 303, σ 58; ὅρκον, β 377, κ 381. (Od.)

ἀπο-μόργνῡμι, ipf. ἀπομόργνῡ, mid. aor. ἀπομόρξατο, part. ἀπομορξαμένω: *wipe off* or *away*, mid., from oneself; σπόγγῳ δ' ἀμφὶ πρόσωπα καὶ ἄμφω χεῖρ' ἀπομόργνῡ, Σ 414; ἀπομόρξατο χερσὶ παρειᾱ́ς, 'rubbed,' σ 200.

ἀπο-μῡθέομαι: only ipf., πόλλ' ἀπεμῡθεόμην, *said* much *to dissuade* thee, Ι 109†.

ἀπόναιο, ἀποναίατο: see ἀπονίνημι.

ἀπο-ναίω, only aor. subj. ἀπονάσσωσι, and aor. mid. ἀπενάσσετο: *remove*, of residence; κούρην ἄψ ἀπονάσσωσιν, 'send back,' Π 86; mid., Ὑπερησίηνδ' ἀπενάσσετο, *removed*, 'withdrew,' ο 254, Β 629.

ἀπο-νέομαι, subj. ἀπονέωνται, inf. ἀπονέεσθαι, ipf ἀπονέοντο (the ᾱ is a necessity of the rhythm, and the place of these forms is at the end of the verse): *return, go home;* in ο 308 the word applies to the real Odysseus rather than to his assumed character.

ἀπόνηθ', ἀπονήμενος: see ἀπονίνημι.

ἀπο-νίζω (**ἀπονίπτω**), aor. imp. ἀπονίψατε, part. ἀπονίψαντες, mid. pres. ἀπονίπτεσθαι, aor. ἀπονιψάμενοι: *wash off, wash clean*, mid., oneself or from oneself; ἀπονίψαντες μέλανα βροτον ἐξ ὠτειλέων, ω 189; ἀλλά μιν, ἀμφίπολοι, ἀπονίψατε, τ 317; χρῶτ' ἀπονιψαμένη, σ 172; ἱδρῶ πολλὸν ἀπενίζοντο θαλάσσῃ, Κ 572.

ἀπ-ονίνημι, mid. fut. ἀπονήσεται, aor. 2 ἀπόνητο, opt. ἀπόναιο, -αίατο, part. ἀπονήμενος: mid., *derive benefit from, get the good of* anything: (τινός), Ἀχιλλεὺς | οἷος τῆς ἀρετῆς ἀπονήσεται, Λ 763; οὐδ' ἀπόνητο, 'but had no joy' thereof, λ 324, π 120, ρ 293.

ἀπονίπτεσθαι, ἀπονίψατε: see ἀπονίζω.

ἀπο-νοστέω, only fut. inf. ἀπονοστήσειν: *return home, return*, always with ἄψ, Α 60, ω 471.

ἀπο-νόσφι(ν), also written as two words, ἀπὸ or ἄπο νόσφι: *apart, aside;* βῆναι, εἶναι, κατίσχεσθαι, Β 233; τραπέσθαι, ε 350; as prep., with gen., *apart from, far from;* usually following the governed word, ἐμεῦ ἀπονόσφιν, Α 541; φίλων ἀπονόσφιν ἑταίρων, μ 33.

ἀπ-οξύνω (ὀξύς), aor. 1 inf. ἀποξῦναι: *sharpen off, make taper;* ἐρετμά, ζ 269, ι 326 (v. l. ἀποξῦσαι).

ἀπο-ξύω (= ἀποξέω), aor. inf. ἀποξῦσαι (v. l. ἀποξῦναι), ι 326, part. ἀποξύσᾱς: *scrape off, smooth off;* fig., γῆρας, I 446†.

ἀπο-παπταίνω, fut. ἀποπαπτανέουσι: *peer away* for a chance to flee, 'look to flight,' Ξ 101.†

ἀπο-παύω, fut. ἀποπαύσει, aor. ἀπέπαυσας, mid. pres. ἀποπαύεαι, imp. ἀποπαύε(ο), fut. ἀποπαύσομαι: act., *cause to cease from, check, hinder from;* mid., *cease from, desist;* (τοὺς) ἐπεὶ πολέμου ἀπέπαυσαν, Λ 323; τοῦτον ἀλητεύειν ἀπέπαυσας, σ 114; μῆνι' Ἀχαιοῖσιν, πολέμου δ' ἀποπαύεο πάμπαν, A 422.

ἀπο-πέμπω, inf. -έμεν, fut. ἀποπέμψω, aor. ἀπέπεμψα, subj. ἀποπέμψω, imp. ἀπόπεμψον: *send away* or *off, dismiss, send away* with escort; ὥς τοι δῶρ' ἀποπέμψω, ρ 76; ἀπειλήσᾱς δ' ἀπέπεμπεν, Φ 452; ξείνους αἰδοίους ἀποπεμπέμεν ἠδὲ δέχεσθαι, τ 316.

ἀποπέσῃσι: see ἀποπίπτω.

ἀπο-πέτομαι, only aor. part. ἀποπτάμενος, -ένη: *fly away,* B 71, λ 222.

ἀπο πίπτω, only ipf. and aor. subj. ἀποπέσῃσι: *fall* (*down*) *from,* Ξ 351, ω 7.

ἀπο-πλάζω, only aor. pass. ἀπεπλάγχθην, part. ἀποπλαγχθείς: pass., *be driven from one's course, drift* (*away from*); Τροίηθεν, ι 259; κατάλεξον | ὅππῃ ἀπεπλάγχθης, θ 573; τῆλε δ' ἀπεπλάγχθη σάκεος δόρυ, 'rebounded,' X 291, N 592; cf. 578.

ἀπο-πλείω (πλέω): *sail away.*

ἀπο-πλήσσω, aor. part. ἀποπλήξᾱς: *strike off,* κ 440.

ἀπο-πλῦνω, ipf. iter. ἀποπλύνεσκε: *wash off,* 'wash up;' λάιγγας ποτὶ χέρσον, ζ 95†.

ἀπο-πλώω (πλέω), aor. 2 ἀπέπλω: *sail away from;* γαίης, ξ 339†.

ἀπο-πνείω (πνέω): *breathe forth, exhale.*

ἀπο-πρό: *away from, far from;* τινός.

ἀπο-προ-αιρέω, aor. 2 part. ἀποπροελών: *take away from;* τινός, ρ 457†.

ἀποπροέηκε: see ἀποπροΐημι.

ἀποπροελών: see ἀποπροαιρέω.

ἀπόπρο-θεν: *from afar, far away, aloof,* ρ 408.

ἀπόπρο-θι: *far away, afar.*

ἀπο-προ-ίημι, aor. ἀποπροέηκε: *let go forth from, let fly, send away;* τινὰ πόλινδε, ξ 26; ἰόν, χ 82; ξίφος χαμᾶζε, 'let fall,' χ 327.

ἀπο-προ-τέμνω, aor. 2 part. ἀποπροταμών: *cut off from;* τινός, θ 475†.

ἀποπτάμενος: see ἀποπέτομαι.

ἀπο-πτύω: *spit out,* Ψ 781; of a billow, ἀποπτύει δ' ἁλὸς ἄχνην, 'belches forth,' Δ 426.

ἀ-πόρθητος (πορθέω): *unsacked, undestroyed;* πόλις, M 11†.

ἀπ-όρνυμαι (ὄρνῡμι): *set out from;* Λυκίηθεν, E 105†.

ἀπ-ορούω, aor. ἀπόρουσε: *spring away* (*from*), 'down' from, E 20.

ἀπο-ρραίω (ῥαίω), fut. ἀπορραίσει, aor. inf. ἀπορραῖσαι: *wrest away from;* τινά τι. (Od.)

ἀπο-ρρήγνῡμι (Ϝρήγνῡμι), aor. part. ἀπορρήξᾱς: *break off, burst off.*

ἀπο-ρρῑγέω (Ϝρῑγέω), perf. with pres. signif. ἀπερρίγᾱσι: *shrink from with shuddering, be afraid,* β 52†.

ἀπο-ρρίπτω (Ϝρίπτω), aor. inf. ἀπορρῖψαι, part. ἀπορρίψαντα: *fling away;* fig., μῆνιν, I 517, Π 282.

ἀπο-ρρώξ, ῶγος (Ϝρήγνῡμι): adj., *abrupt, steep;* ἀκταί, ν 98; as subst., *fragment;* Στυγὸς ὕδατος, 'branch,' B 755, κ 514; said of wine, ἀμβροσίης καὶ νέκταρός ἐστιν ἀπορρώξ, 'morsel,' 'drop,' 'sample,' ι 359.

ἀπο-σεύομαι (σεύω), only aor. ἀπέσσυτο, -εσσύμεθα, part. ἀπεσσύμενος: *rush away, hurry away,* ι 396; δώματος, Z 390.

ἀπο-σκίδνημι (= ἀποσκεδάννῡμι), aor. ἀπεσκέδασε, mid. pres. inf. ἀποσκίδνασθαι: *scatter, disperse, dismiss,* λ 385, T 309; mid., *disperse,* Ψ 4.

ἀπο-σκυδμαίνω: *be utterly indignant at;* τινί, imp., Ω 65†.

ἀπο-σπένδω, only part.: *pour out a libation.* (Od.)

ἀπο-σταδόν and **ἀπο-σταδά** (ἵστημι): adv., *standing at a distance,* O 556 and ζ 143, 146.

ἀπο-στείχω, aor. 2 ἀπέστιχε, imp. ἀπόστιχε: *go away, depart,* A 522, λ 132, μ 143.

ἀπο-στίλβω: only part., ἀποστίλβοντες ἀλείφατος, *glistening* with oil, γ 408†.

ἀπο-στρέφω, fut. ἀποστρέψεις, part. -οντας, aor. iter. ἀποστρέψασκε, subj. ἀποστρέψῃσιν, opt. -ειεν, part. ἀπο-

στρέψᾱς: *turn* or *twist back* or *about*, reversing a former direction; (λᾶαν) ἀποστρέψασκε κραταιίς, the stone of Sisyphus, λ 597; πόδας καὶ χεῖρας, i. e. so as to tie them behind the back, χ 173; 'recall,' 'order a retreat,' K 355.

ἀπο-στυφελίζω, only aor. ἀπεστυφέλιξε, -αν: *smite back, knock back* (*from*); τινός, Σ 158. (Il.)

ἀπο-σφάλλω, only aor. subj. ἀποσφήλωσι, and opt. ἀποσφήλειε: *cause to stray* from a straight course, γ 320; met., μὴ (Μενέλᾱος) μέγα σφας ἀποσφήλειε πόνοιο, 'disappoint' them of, 'make vain' their toil, E 567.

ἀποσχέσθαι: see ἀπέχω.

ἀπο-τάμνω (=ἀποτέμνω): *cut away*, Θ 87; mid., κρέα, *cut off* for oneself (to eat), X 347.

ἀπο-τηλοῦ: *far away*, ι 117.

ἀπο-τίθημι, aor. 1 ἀπέθηκε, mid. aor. 2 ἀπεθέμην, subj. ἀποθείομαι, inf. ἀποθέσθαι: *put away*, mid., from oneself, *lay off*; δέπας ἀπέθηκ' ἐνὶ χηλῷ, Π 254; τεύχεα κάλ' ἀποθέσθαι, Γ 89, Σ 409; met., κρατερὴν ἀποθέσθαι ἐνῑπήν, E 492.

ἀπο-τίνυμαι (τίνω): *exact satisfaction from* some one for something; τινά τινος, cause one to pay you back for something, *take vengeance for*, β 73; πολέων ἀπετίνυτο ποινήν, i. e. avenged many, Π 398.

ἀπο-τίνω, fut. ἀποτίσεις, inf. -σέμεν, aor. ἀπέτῑσε, -αν, mid. fut. ἀποτίσομαι, aor. ἀπετίσατο, subj. ἀποτίσεαι: I. act., *pay back, pay for, atone for*; τῑμὴν Ἀργείοις ἀποτῑνέμεν, Γ 286; εὐεργεσίᾱς ἀποτίνειν, χ 235; τριπλῇ τετραπλῇ τ' ἀποτίσομεν, 'will make good,' A 128.—II. mid. (Od.), *exact payment* (see under ἀποτίνυμαι) or *satisfaction, avenge oneself upon, punish* (τί or τινά); κείνων γε βίᾱς ἀποτίσεαι ἐλθών, λ 118; ἀπετίσατο ποινὴν | ἰφθίμων ἑτάρων, 'for' them, ω 312.

ἀπο-τμήγω (= ἀποτέμνω), aor. opt. ἀποτμήξειε, part. ἀποτμήξᾱς: *cut off, sever*; κλῖτῡς ἀποτμήγουσι χαράδραι, 'score,' Π 390; fig., *cut off, intercept*, K 364, Λ 468.

ἄ-ποτμος (πότμος): *luckless, ill-starred*, Ω 388; sup. ἀποτμότατος, α 219.

ἀπο-τρέπω, fut. ἀποτρέψεις, -ουσι, aor. 2 ἀπέτραπε, mid. aor. 2 ἀπετράπετο: *turn away* or *back, divert from* (τινά τινος); mid., *turn away*, αὐτὸς δ' ἀπονόσφι τραπέσθαι, 'avert thy face,' ε 350; αὖτις ἀπετράπετο, 'turned back,' K 200.

ἀπο-τρῖβω: only fut., σφέλᾱ ἀποτρίψουσι πλευρά (v. l. πλευραί, the converse of the same idea), 'shall rub off,' 'polish off;' cf. 'rub down with an oaken towel,' ρ 232†.

ἀπό-τροπος (τρέπω): live *retired*, ξ 372†.

ἀπο-τρωπάω (parallel form of ἀποτρέπω), subj. -ῶμεν, -ῶσι, mid. ipf. ἀπετρωπῶντο: *turn away from* (τινός); (κύνες) δακέειν μὲν (as far as *biting* was concerned) ἀπετρωπῶντο λεόντων, Σ 585.

ἀπούρᾱς, ἀπουρήσουσι: see ἀπαυράω.

ἀπ-ουρίζω (οὖρος): only fut., ἀπουρίσσουσιν ἀρούρᾱς, *shall remove the boundary stones of* (i. e. appropriate) his fields, X 489†.

ἀπο-φέρω, fut. ἀποίσετον, inf. ἀποίσειν, aor. 1 ἀπένεικας: *bear away, bring away* or *back, carry home*; μῦθον, K 337; Κόωνδ' ἀπένεικας, by sea, Ξ 255.

ἀπό-φημι: *say out*; ἀντικρῦ, H 362; ἀγγελίην ἀπόφασθε, I 422.

ἀπέφθιθεν: see ἀποφθίνω.

ἀπο-φθινύθω: *waste away, perish*, E 643: trans., *let perish*, 'sacrifice,' θῡμόν, Π 540.

ἀπο-φθίνω, aor. mid. ἀπεφθίμην, ἀποφθίμην, ἀπέφθιτο, opt. ἀποφθίμην, imp. ἀποφθίσθω, part. ἀποφθίμενος, aor. pass. ἀπεφθίθην, 3 pl. ἀπέφθιθεν: mid. and pass., *perish, die*, Σ 499; λευγαλέῳ θανάτῳ, ο 358; λυγρὸν ὄλεθρον, ο 268.

ἀπο-φώλιος: *good-for-nothing, empty*; οὐκ ἀποφώλιος ἦα | οὐδὲ φυγοπτόλεμος, ξ 212; νόον δ' ἀποφώλιός ἐσσι, θ 177; οὐκ ἀποφώλια εἰδώς, 'no fool,' ε 182; ἀποφώλιοι εὐναί, 'unfruitful,' λ 249.

ἀπο-χάζομαι: *withdraw from*; βόθρου, λ 95†.

ἀπο-ψύχω, aor. pass. part. ἀποψῡχθείς: *leave off breathing; dry off, cool off*; εἶλεν ἀποψύχοντα, 'fainting' (opp. ἐπεὶ ἄμπνῡτο), ω 348; ἵδρῶ ἀπεψύχοντο χιτώνων, | στάντε ποτὶ **πνοιήν**, Λ 621, Χ 2; pass., ἱδρῶ ἀποψῡχθείς, Φ 561.

ἀππέμψει: see ἀποπέμπω.

ἄ-πρηκτος (πρήσσω): *without achieving*, Ξ 221; *unachieved, fruitless, endless*, Β 121, 376; and, in general, of that with which nothing can be successfully done, *hopeless, incurable* (cf. ἀμήχανος); ὀδύναι, Β 79; of Scylla, ἄπρηκτον ἀνίην, μ 223.

ἀ-πριάτην (πρίαμαι): adv., *without purchase* (ransom), Α 99; *for nothing*, ξ 317.

ἀ-προτί-μαστος (μάσσω): *untouched*, Τ 263†.

ἄ-πτερος (πτερόν): only τῇ δ' ἄπτερος ἔπλετο μῦθος, *wingless* to her was what he said, i. e. it did not escape her, she caught the idea, ρ 57, τ 29, φ 386, χ 398.

ἀ-πτήν, ῆνος (πέτομαι): *unfledged*, Ι 323†.

ἀ-πτο-επής, ές (πτοᾶ, **πτοιέω**): *fearless* (audacious) *of speech*, Θ 209†.

ἀ-πτόλεμος: *unwarlike*. (Il.)

ἅπτω, aor. part. ἅψᾱς, mid. ipf. ἥπτετο, fut. ἅψεται, aor. ἥψατο (ἅψατο), inf. ἅψασθαι, part. ἁψάμενος, aor. pass. (according to some), ἐάφθη (q. v.): I. act., *attach, fasten*, φ 408, of putting a string to a lyre.—II. mid., *fasten* for oneself, *cling to, take hold of* (τινός); ἁψαμένη βρόχον αἰπὺν ἀφ' ὑψηλοῖο μελάθρου, in order to hang herself, λ 278; ὡς δ' ὅτε τίς τε κυὼν συὸς ἀγρίου ἠὲ λέοντος | ἅψηται κατόπισθε, 'fastens on' to him from the rear, Θ 339; ἅψασθαι γούνων, κεφαλῆς, **νηῶν**, etc.; βρώμης δ' οὐχ ἅπτεαι οὐδὲ **ποτῆτος**, 'touch,' κ 379.

ἀ-πύργωτος (πύργος): *unwalled, unfortified*, λ 264†.

ἄ-πυρος (πῦρ): *untouched by fire*, kettle or tripod, Ι 122 and Ψ 267 (λευκὸν ἔτ' αὔτως, 268).

ἀ-πύρωτος = ἄπυρος (i. e. brand new), φιάλη, Ψ 270.

ἄ-πυστος (πυνθάνομαι): pass., *unheard of*; ᾤχετ' ἄιστος ἄπυστος, α 242; act., *without hearing of*; μύθων, δ 675.

ἀπ-ωθέω, fut. ἀπώσω, inf. **ἀπωσέμεν**, aor. ἀπέωσε, ἀπῶσε, subj. **ἀπώσομεν**, mid. fut. ἀπώσεται, aor. ἀπώσατο, **-ασθαι, -άμενον,** οι, ους: *push* or *thrust away* (**τινά τινος**, or **ἐκ τινός**), **mid.**, from oneself; ἀπῶσεν ὀχῆας, 'pushed back,' Ω 446; Βορέης ἀπέωσε, 'forced back,' ι 81 (cf. mid., ν 276); **θυρέων** ἀπώσασθαι λίθον, in order to get out, ι 305; μνηστῆρας ἐκ μεγάροιο, α 270.

ἄρα, ἄρ (before consonants), ῥα, ῥ' (enclitic), always post-positive: particle denoting inference or a natural sequence of ideas, *then, so then, so, naturally, as it appears*, but for the most part untranslatable by word or phrase; freq. in neg. sentences, **οὐδ'** ἄρα, **οὔτ' ἄρα**, and joined to rel. and causal words, ὅς **τ'** ἄρα, ὅς ῥά τε, **οὕνεκ'** ἄρα, ὅτι ῥα, also following **εἶτα**, γάρ, ἀλλά, **αὐτάρ**, etc.; further, in questions, and in the apodosis of sentences after **μέν** and other particles. The following examples will illustrate some of the chief usages: **οὐδ' ἄρα πως** **ἦν** | **ἐν πάντεσσ' ἔργοισι δαήμονα φῶτα** **γενέσθαι**, 'as it seems,' Ψ 670; **ἐκ δ'** **ἔθορε κλῆρος κυνέης, ὃν ἀρ' ἤθελον** **αὐτοί**, 'just the one' they wished, Η 182; **κήδετο γὰρ Δαναῶν, ὅτι ῥα θνήσκοντας** ὁρᾶτο, 'even because' she saw, Α 56; **τίς τ' ἄρ σφωε θεῶν ἔριδι** **ξυνέηκε μάχεσθαι**, 'who then'? Α 8; **αὐτὰρ ἄρα Ζεὺς δῶκε διακτόρῳ Ἀργεϊφόντῃ**, 'and then next,' Β 103; **αὐτὰρ** **ἐπεὶ πόσιος καὶ ἐδητύος ἐξ ἔρον ἕντο**, | **τοῖς ἄρα μύθων ἦρχε Γερήνιος ἱππότα** **Νέστωρ**, 'then,' not temporal, Β 433; **ὣς ἄρα φωνήσᾱς κατ' ἄρ' ἕζετο** (twice in one sentence, *ἄρα* in the phrase **κατ' ἄρ'** ἕζετο marks the sitting down as the regular sequel of making a speech), π 213.

ἀραβέω: only in the phrase ἀράβησε δὲ τεύχε' **ἐπ' αὐτῷ**, *clattered* as he fell, ω 525, and often in the Iliad.

ἄραβος: *chattering* of teeth (through fear), Κ 375†.

Ἀραιθυρέη: a town in Argolis, Β 571†.

ἀραιός: *slender, frail*, Ε 425, Σ 411; εἴσοδος, 'narrow,' κ 90.

ἀράομαι: see ἀράω.

ἀραρίσκω (root αρ), aor. ἦρσα (ἄρσα), aor. 2 ἤραρον (ἄραρον), perf. 2 ἄρηρα, part. ἀρηρώς, ἀραρυῖα, ἀρηρός, plup. ἀρήρειν, ἠρήρειν, aor. pass. 3 pl. ἄρθεν, mid. aor. 2 part. ἄρμενος: I. trans. (ipf., aor. 1 and 2 act.), *fit on* or *together, join, fit with*; rafters in building a house, Ψ 712; of constructing a wall, Π 212; joining two horns to make a bow, Δ 110; νῆ' ἄρσᾱς ἐρετῆσιν, 'fitting out' with oarsmen, α 280; pass., μᾶλλον δὲ στίχες ἄρθεν, 'closed up,' Π 211; met. (γέρας), ἄρσαντες κατὰ θῡμόν, Α 136; ἤραρε θῡμὸν ἐδωδῇ, ε 95.—II. intrans. (mid., perf. and plup.), *fit close, suit, be fitted with;* of ranks of warriors, πυργηδὸν ἀρηρότες, Ο 618; jars standing in a row against the wall, β 342; θύραι πυκινῶς ἀραρυῖαι, Ι 475; πόλις πύργοις ἀραρυῖα, 'provided with,' Ο 737; τροχὸς ἄρμενος ἐν παλάμῃσιν, potter's wheel, 'adapted' to the hands, Σ 600; met., οὐ φρεσὶν ᾗσιν ἀρηρώς, κ 553, (μῦθος) πᾶσιν ἐνὶ φρεσὶν ἤραρεν (aor. 2 here intr.), δ 777.

ἄραρον: see ἀραρίσκω.

ἀράσσω, fut. ἀράξω, aor. ἄραξα, aor. pass. ἀράχθην: *pound, batter, break;* γόμφοισιν σχεδίην, 'hammered fast'; freq. with adverbs, ἀπό, Ν 577; ἐκ, μ 422; σύν, 'smash,' Μ 384.

ἀράχνιον (ἀράχνη): *spider's web,* pl., θ 280 and π 35.

ἀράω (ἀρή), act. only pres. inf. ἀρήμεναι, χ 322; mid. fut. ἀρήσομαι, aor. ἠρησάμην: *pray* to the deity, and in the sense of *wish;* Διΐ, δαίμοσι, πάντεσσι θεοῖσι (see cut for attitude); πολλά, 'fervently'; εὐχομένη δ' ἠρᾶτο, 'lifted up her voice in prayer,' Ζ 304; with inf., χ 322, etc.; στυγερὰς ἀρήσετ' ἐρῑνῦς, 'invoke,' 'call down,' β 135; in the sense of *wish,* Ν 286, α 366, and often.

14

ἀργαλέος: *hard* to endure or deal with, *difficult;* ἕλκος, ἔργον, ἄνεμος, δεσμοί, ὁδός, etc.; ἀργαλέος γὰρ Ὀλύμπιος ἀντιφέρεσθαι, Α 589; ἀργαλέον δέ μοι ἐστὶ . . πᾶσι μάχεσθαι, Υ 356; comp., ἀργαλεώτερος, Ο 121, δ 698.

Ἀργεάδης: *son of Argeus,* Polymēlus, a Lycian, Π 417†.

Ἀργεῖος: *of Argos, Argive;* Ἥρη Ἀργείη, as tutelary deity of Argos), Δ 8, Ε 908; Ἀργείη Ἑλένη, Β 161, etc.; pl., Ἀργεῖοι, *the Argives,* freq. collective designation of the Greeks before Troy; Ἀργείων Δαναῶν, θ 578, is peculiar.

Ἀργεϊφόντης: *Argeïphontes,* freq. epith. of Hermes, of uncertain signification; the traditional interpretation, 'slayer of Argus' (root φεν) is more poetical than the modern one, 'shiner,' 'shining one' (ἀργεσ-), because it refers to a definite legend, instead of a vague mythical idea.

ἀργεννός (root ἀργ): *white* shining; ὄιες, ὀθόναι, Γ 198, 141.

ἀργεστής, ᾱο (root ἀργ): *rapid;* epith. of the south wind, Λ 306 and Χ 334.

ἀργής, ῆτος (root ἀργ), dat. ἀργῆτι and ἀργέτι, acc. ἀργῆτα and ἀργέτα: *dazzling white, glistening;* epith. of lightning, linen, fat, Θ 133, Γ 419, Λ 818.

ἀργι-κέραυνος: god *of the dazzling bolt,* epith. of Zeus. (Il.)

ἀργινόεις, acc. -εντα: *white-gleaming,* epith. of towns in Crete, because of chalk cliffs in the vicinity, Β 647, 656.

ἀργι-όδους, οντος: *white-toothed;* epith. of dogs and swine.

ἀργί-πος, ποδος: *swift-footed,* Ω 211†.

Ἄργισσα: a town in Thessaly, Β 738†.

ἄργμα (ἄρχεσθαι): only pl., ἄργματα, *consecrated pieces* of flesh, burned at the *beginning* of the sacrifice, ξ 446†.

1. Ἄργος: *Argus,* the dog of Odysseus, ρ 292†.

2. Ἄργος, εος: *Argos,* a name with some variety of application.—(1) the city of Argos in Argolis, the domain of Diomed, Β 559, Ζ 224, Ξ 119, γ 180, ο 224, φ 108; epithets, Ἀχαιικόν, ἱππόβοτον, πολύπῡρον.—(2) in wider sense, the realm of Agamemnon, who dwelt in Mycēnae, Α 30, Β 108, 115, Δ 171, Ι 22, Ν 379, Ο 30, γ 263.—(3) the entire Peloponnēsus, Ζ 152, γ 251, δ 174; and with Hellas (καθ' Ἑλλάδα καὶ μέσον Ἄργος) for the whole of Greece, α 344, δ 726, 816.—(4) Πελασγικόν, the domain of Achilles, the valley and plain of the river Penēus, Β 681, Ζ 456, Ω 437, ω 37. In some passages the name is used too vaguely to determine its exact application.

ἀργός (root ἀργ): (1) *white* shining; goose, ο 161; of oxen, 'sleek,' Ψ 30.—(2) *swift;* epith. of dogs, with and without πόδας, Α 50, β 11.

Ἄργοσδε: *to Argos.*

ἀργύρεος (ἄργυρος): (*of*) *silver, silver-mounted;* κρητήρ, Ψ 741; τελαμών, Λ 38.

ἀργυρο-δίνης (δίνη): *silver-eddying;* epith. of rivers. (Il.)

ἀργυρό-ηλος (ἧλος): ornamented *with silver nails* or *knobs, silver-studded;* ξίφος, θρόνος, φάσγανον, Β 45, η 162, Ξ 405.

ἀργυρό-πεζα: *silvery-footed;* epith. of Thetis, a Nereid fresh from the sea-waves. (Il., and ω 92.)

ἄργυρος (root ἀργ): *silver.*

ἀργυρό-τοξος (τόξον): god *of the silver bow;* epith. of Apollo; as subst., Α 37.

ἀργύφεος (root ἀργ): *white* shining, *glittering;* φᾶρος, ε 230; σπέος, of the Nereids (cf. ἀργυρόπεζα), Σ 50.

ἄργυφος = ἀργύφεος, epith. of sheep, Ω 621, κ 85.

Ἀργώ: the *Argo,* ship of the Argonauts, μ 70†.

ἀρδμός (ἄρδω): *watering, watering-place* for animals, ν 247.

Ἀρέθουσα: name of a fount in the island of Ithaca, ν 408†.

ἀρειή (ἀρή): *cursing, threatening.* (Il.)

ἄρειος: see ἀρήιος.

ἀρείων, ἄρειον (root ἀρ, cf. ἄριστος, ἀρετή): comp. (answering to ἀγαθός), *better, superior,* etc.; πλέονες καὶ ἀρείους, 'mightier,' ι 48; πρότερος καὶ ἀρείων, Ψ 588; κρεῖσσον καὶ ἄρειον, ζ 182; (παῖδες) οἱ πλέονες κακίους, παῦροι δέ τε πατρὸς ἀρείους, β 277; adv., τάχα δὲ φράσεται καὶ ἄρειον, ψ 114.

Ἀρείων: *Arīon,* name of the horse of Adrastus at the siege of Thebes, Ψ 346.

ἄ-ρεκτος (ῥέζω): *undone, unaccomplished,* Τ 150†.

ἀρέσαι, ἀρέσασθαι: see ἀρέσκω.

ἀρέσκω, act. only aor. inf. ἀρέσαι, mid. fut. ἀρέσσομαι, aor. imp. ἀρε(σ)σάσθω, part. ἀρεσσάμενος: act., *make amends,* Ι 120, Τ 138; mid, *make good* (τι) for oneself or for each other, *appease, reconcile* (τινά); ταῦτα δ' ὄπισθεν ἀρεσσόμεθ', εἴ τι κακὸν νῦν | εἴρηται, Δ 363; ἔπειτά σε δαιτὶ ἐνὶ κλισίῃς ἀρεσάσθω, with a feast of reconciliation, Τ 179.

ἀρέσθαι: see ἄρνυμαι.

ἀρετάω (ἀρετή): *come to good, thrive,* θ 329 and τ 114.

Ἀρετάων: a Trojan, slain by Teucer, Ζ 31†.

ἀρετή (root ἀρ, cf. ἀρείων, ἄριστος). subst. (answering to the adj. ἀγαθός), *excellence* (of whatever sort), *merit;* ἐκ πατρὸς πολὺ χείρονος υἱὸς ἀμείνων | παντοίᾱς ἀρετᾱ́ς, ἠμὲν πόδας ἠδὲ μάχεσθαι, all kinds of 'prowess,' Ο 642, cf. Χ 268; intellectual, ἐμῇ ἀρετῇ (βουλῇ τε νόῳ τε) | ἐκφύγομεν, μ 212; of a woman, ἐμὴν ἀρετὴν (εἶδος τε δέμας τε) | ὤλεσαν ἀθάνατοι, my 'attractions' (said by Penelope), σ 251; τῆς ἀρετῆς (β 206) includes more. The signif. *well-being, prosperity* (Υ 242, ν 45) answers to εὖ rather than to ἀγαθός.

ἀρετής, ῆτος: ἀρετῆτα, a conjectural reading, see ἀνδροτής.

ἀρή, ῆς: *prayer;* and in bad sense, *curse, imprecation,* hence *calamity, destruction;* in good sense, δ 767, Ο 378, etc.; bad, Ι 566, ρ 496; ἀρὴν καὶ λοιγὸν ἀμῦναι, Ω 489; ἀρὴν ἀπὸ οἴκου ἀμῦναι, β 59.

ἄρηαι: see ἄρνυμαι.

ἀρήγω, fut. ἀρήξω: *aid, support, succor* (τινί); (ἐμοὶ) ἔπεσιν καὶ χερσὶν ἀρήξειν, Α 77. (Il.)

ἀρηγών, όνος (ἀρήγω): *helper,* fem., Ε 511 and Δ 7.

ἀρηί-θοος (Ἄρης, θοός): *swift in battle.* (Il.)

Ἀρηί-θοος: (1) father of Menesthius, the 'club-swinger,' from Bœotia, Η 10, 137.—(2) a Thracian, charioteer of Rhigmus, Υ 487.

ἀρηι-κτάμενος (Ἄρης, κτείνω): *slain by Ares* or *in battle,* Χ 72†.

Ἀρηί-λυκος (Ares-wolf): (1) father of Prothoēnor, Ξ 451.—(2) a Trojan, slain by Patroclus, Π 308.

ἀρήιος, ἄρειος (Ἄρης): *martial, warlike;* of men, Μενέλᾱος, Αἴᾱς, υἷες Ἀχαιῶν, etc.; also of weapons and armor (τεύχεα, ἔντεα); τεῖχος ἄρειον, 'martial' wall, Δ 407, Ο 736.

ἀρηί-φατος (root φεν): *slain by Ares* or *in battle.*

ἀρηί-φιλος: *dear to Ares;* epith. of Menelāus, Achilles, the Greeks, etc. (Il.)

ἀρημέναι: see ἀράω.

ἀρημένος: *overcome, overwhelmed, burdened;* ὕπνῳ καὶ καμάτῳ, ζ 2; γήραϊ λυγρῷ, Σ 435; δύῃ ἀρημένον, σ 53.

ἀρήν: see ἀρνός.

ἀρηρομένος: see ἀρόω.

Ἀρήνη: a town subject to Nestor, B 591, Λ 723.

Ἄρης, gen. Ἄρεος and Ἄρηος, dat. Ἄρει and Ἄρηι, acc. Ἄρην and Ἄρηα, voc. Ἄρες (Ἆρες, E 31, 455): *Ares* (Mars), son of Zeus and Hera, the god of war and the tumult of battle, E 890 ff; insatiate in bloodshed, headlong and planless in warfare, thus forming a contrast to Athena, with whom he is at variance, E 853 ff., Φ 400 ff.; a brother of Ἔρις, father of Δεῖμος and Φόβος; his favorite abode is among rude, warring peoples, N 301 ff., θ 361; his mien and stature imposing and magnificent, E 860, cf. 385, θ 267 ff.; fights now for the Trojans and now for the Greeks (ἀλλοπρόσαλλος); other epithets, ἆτος πολέμοιο, βροτολοιγός, δεινός, ἀνδρειφόντης, Ἐνυάλιος, θοός, θοῦρος, μιαίφονος, ὄβριμος, ταλαυρῖνος πολεμιστής, χάλκεος, etc. The name of Ares is used by personification (though not written with a capital letter in some edd.) for his element, *battle, combat;* ξυνάγειν Ἄρηα, κρίνεσθαι Ἄρηι, ἐγείρειν ὀξὺν Ἄρηα, B 381, 385, 440.

ἄρησθε: see ἄρνυμαι.

Ἀρήτη (ἀράομαι, cf. η 54, 64 f.): *Arēte,* wife of Alcinous, king of the Phaeacians, and mother of Nausicaa.

ἀρητήρ, ῆρος (ἀράομαι): *one who prays, priest.*

Ἀρητιάδης. *son of Arētus,* Nisus, π 395.

ἄρητος: doubtful word, *wished-for* (if from ἀράομαι). ἄρητον δὲ τοκεῦσι γόον καὶ πένθος ἔθηκας, 'hast awakened the desire of lamentation' (cf. ἵμερος γόου), P 37, Ω 741; according to others, for ἄρρητος (ῥηθῆναι), 'unspeakable.'

Ἄρητος: (1) a son of Nestor, γ 414.—(2) a son of Priam, P 535.

ἄρθεν: see ἀραρίσκω.

ἀρθμέω (ἀρθμός, root ἀρ), aor. part. du. ἀρθμήσαντε: *form a bond, be bound* together in friendship, H 302†.

ἄρθμιος (ἀρθμός, root ἀρ): *bound* in friendship, *allied,* π 427†.

ἀρι- (root ἀρ): inseparable intensive prefix, *very.*

Ἀρι-άδνη: *Ariadne,* daughter of Minos, king of Crete, who gave Theseus the clue to the Labyrinth, λ 321, Σ 592.

ἀρί-γνωτος (γιγνώσκω): *recognizable;* ῥεῖα δ' ἀρίγνωτος, 'right easy to recognize,' δ 207, etc.; ὦ ἀρίγνωτε συβῶτα, thou 'unmistakable,' ρ 375.

ἀρι-δείκετος (δείκνυμι, digito monstrari): *distinguished, illustrious,* λ 540; usually w. part. gen., πάντων ἀριδείκετε λαῶν, 'among,' θ 382.

ἀρί-ζηλος (δῆλος): *conspicuous, clear,* Σ 519, 219, B 318.—Adv., **ἀριζήλως,** μ 453†.

ἀριθμέω (ἀριθμός): *count, reckon up,* B 124; δίχα πάντας ἠρίθμεον, 'counted off' in two companies, κ 304.

ἀριθμός: *number.*

Ἄριμα, pl.: name of a region in Cilicia, B 783.

ἀρι-πρεπής, ές (πρέπω): *conspicuous, distinguished;* Τρώεσσιν, 'among the Trojans,' Z 477.

Ἀρίσβᾱς: a Greek, father of Leocritus, P 345†.

Ἀρίσβη: a town in the Troad; Ἀρίσβηθεν, *from Arisbe,* B 838.

ἀριστερός: *left* (opp. δεξιός), hence *sinister, ill-boding* (ὄρνῑς, υ 242); ἐπ' ἀριστερά, 'on the left,' M 240; ἐπ' ἀριστερόφιν, N 309.

ἀριστεύς, ῆος (ἄριστος): *best man, chief,* Γ 44; ἀνδρὸς ἀριστῆος, O 489; usually pl., ἀριστῆες, B 404, etc.

ἀριστεύω (ἀριστεύς), ipf. iter. ἀριστεύεσκον: *be the best* or *bravest;* usually w. inf. (μάχεσθαι); also w. gen., Z 460.

ἄριστον: *breakfast,* in Homer taken not long after sunrise; only ἐντύνοντο ἄριστον, Ω 124, π 2.

ἄριστος (root ἀρ, cf. ἀρείων, ἀρετή), ὥριστος = ὁ ἄριστος: *best, most excellent* (see the various implied meanings under ἀγαθός); Ζεύς, θεῶν ὕπατος καὶ ἄριστος, T 258; freq. w. adv. prefixed, μέγ(α), ὄχ(α), ἔξοχ(α), A 69, M 103;

often foll. by explanatory inf., dat., or acc. (*μάχεσθαι, βουλῇ, εἶδος*); *ἦ σοὶ ἄριστα πεποίηται*, 'finely indeed hast thou been treated,' Z 56.

ἀρι-σφαλής (*σφάλλω*): *slippery; οὐδός*, ρ 196†.

ἀρι-φραδής, ές (*φράζομαι*): *very plain, easy to note* or *recognize; σῆμα, ὀστέα*, Ψ 240; adv., *ἀριφραδέως*. v. l. in ψ 225.

'Αρκαδίη: *Arcadia*, a district in the Peloponnēsus, B 603.

'Αρκάς, άδος: *Arcadian*, inhabitant of Arcadia, B 611.

'Αρκεισιάδης: *son of Arceisius*, Laertes, δ 755, ω 270, 517.

'Αρκείσιος: son of Zeus, and father of Laertes, π 118.

'Αρκεσί-λᾱος: son of Lycus, and leader of the Boeotians, B 495, ο 329.

ἀρκέω (root *ἀρκ, ἀλκ*), fut. *ἀρκέσω*, aor. *ἤρκεσα*: *keep off* (*τινί τι*), hence *protect, help* (*τινί*); *ἀλλά οἱ οὔ τις τῶν γε τότ' ἤρκεσε λυγρὸν ὄλεθρον*, Z 16; *οὐδ' ὑμῖν ποταμός περ ἀρκέσει*, Φ 131, π 261.

ἄρκιος (root *ἀρκ*), *helping, to be depended upon, certain; οὔ οἱ ἔπειτα | ἄρκιον ἐσσεῖται φυγέειν κύνας ἠδ' οἰωνούς*, 'nothing shall avail him' to escape, B 393; *νῦν ἄρκιον ἢ ἀπολέσθαι | ἠὲ σαωθῆναι*, a 'sure' thing, i. e. no other alternative presents itself, O 502; so, *μισθὸς ἄρκιος*, K 304, σ 358, unless the word has here attained to its later meaning of *sufficient*. Cf. *ἀρκέω*.

ἄρκτος: *bear*, λ 611; fem., the constellation of the *Great Bear*, Σ 487, ε 273.

ἅρμα, ατος: *chariot*, esp. the war-chariot; very often in pl., and with *ἵπποι*, E 199, 237, Δ 366; epithets, *ἀγκυλον, ἐύξοον, ἐύτροχον, θοόν, καμπύλον, δαιδάλεα, κολλητά, ποικίλα χαλκῷ*. For the separate parts of the chariot, see *ἄντυξ, ἄξων, ῥυμός, ἕστωρ, ἴτυς, ἐπίσσωτρα, πλῆμναι, κνήμη, δίφρος, ζυγόν*. (See cut No. 10, and tables I. and II.)

Ἅρμα: a town in Boeotia, B 499†.

ἁρματο-πηγός (*πήγνῡμι*): *ἀνήρ, chariot-builder*, Δ 485†.

ἁρμα-τροχιή (*τροχός*): *wheel-rut*, Ψ 505†.

ἄρμενος: see *ἀραρίσκω*.

ἁρμόζω (*ἁρμός*, root *ἀρ*), aor. *ἥρμοσα*, mid. pres. imp. *ἁρμόζεο*: *fit together, join*, mid., for oneself, ε 247, 162; intrans., *fit, ἥρμοσε δ' αὐτῷ* (sc. *θώρηξ*), Γ 333.

'Αρμονίδης: a ship-builder of Troy, E 60†.

ἁρμονίη (*ἁρμόζω*): only pl., *bands, slabs*, one side flat, the other curved, serving (ε 248, 361) to bind together the raft of Odysseus; fig., *bond, compact*, X 255.

'Αρναῖος: the original name of *Irus*, σ 5†.

ἀρνειός: *ram;* with *ὄις*, κ 527, 572.

ἀρνέομαι, aor. inf. *ἀρνήσασθαι*: *deny, refuse, say no, decline, δόμεναί τε καὶ ἀρνήσασθαι*, φ 345.

ἀρνευτήρ, ῆρος: *diver*, M 385, Π 742, μ 413.

Ἄρνη: a town in Boeotia, B 507, H 9.

ἀρνός, gen. (root *ἀρν.*), no nom. sing., acc. *ἄρνα*, dual. *ἄρνε*, pl. *ἄρνες, ἀρνῶν, ἄρνεσσι, ἄρνας*: *lamb, sheep.*

ἄρνυμαι, aor. 1 *ἠράμην*, 2 sing. *ἤραο*, aor. 2 *ἀρόμην*, subj. *ἄρωμαι*, 2 sing. *ἄρηαι*, opt. *ἀροίμην* (*ἀρέσθαι* and *ἄρασθαι* are sometimes referred to *ἀείρω, αἴρω*, q. v.): *carry off* (usually for oneself), *earn, win;* freq. the pres. and ipf. of attempted action, *οὐχ ἱερήιον οὐδὲ βοείην | ἀρνύσθην*, were not 'trying to win,' X 160; *ἀρνύμενος ἥν τε ψῡχὴν καί νόστον ἑταίρων*, 'striving to achieve,' 'save,' α 5, cf. Z 446; aor. common w. *κλέος, κῦδος, εὖχος, νίκην, ἀέθλια*, etc.; also of burdens and troubles, *ὅσσ' Ὀδυσεὺς ἐμόγησε καὶ ἤρατο*, 'took upon himself,' δ 107, Ξ 130, Υ 247.

ἀροίμην: see *ἄρνυμαι*.

ἄροσις (*ἀρόω*): *ploughing, arable land.*

ἀροτήρ, ῆρος: *ploughman.*

ἄροτος: *ploughing, cultivation*, pl., ι 122.†

ἄροτρον: *plough.*

ἄρουρα (*ἀρόω*): cultivated *land* (pl., *fields*), *ground, the earth; τέμει δέ τε τέλσον ἀρούρης* (sc. *ἄροτρον*), N 707; *ὅτε φρίσσουσιν ἄρουραι*, Ψ 599; *πλησίον ἀλλήλων, ὀλίγη δ' ἦν ἀμφὶς ἄρουρα*, Γ 115; *ζείδωρος ἄρουρα*, δ 229, τ 593 (personified, B 548).

ἀρόω, perf. pass. part. *ἀρηρομένη*: *plough*, ι 108, Σ 548.

ἁρπάζω, fut. ἁρπάξω, aor. ἥρπαξα, ἥρπασα: *seize, snatch;* esp. of robbery, abduction, and attacks of wild animals, ὅτε σε πρῶτον Λακεδαίμονος ἐξ ἐρατεινῆς | ἔπλεον ἁρπάξᾱς, the 'rape' of Helen, Γ 444; ὡς ὅδε (αἰετός) χῆν' ἥρπαξε, ο 174; κῦμα μέγ' ἁρπάξαν, ε 416.

ἁρπακτήρ, ῆρος: *robber,* Ω 262†.

ἁρπαλέος: *eagerly grasped;* κέρδεα, θ 164; adv., **ἁρπαλέως,** *greedily,* ξ 110. (Od.)

Ἁρπαλίων: son of Pylaemenes, N 644.

ἅρπη: a bird of prey, perhaps *falcon,* Τ 350†.

ἅρπυια: *harpy,* 'snatcher;' the horses of Achilles had Zephyrus as sire and the harpy Podargē as dam, Π 150; usually pl., **ἅρπυιαι**: supernatural powers, by whom those who had mysteriously disappeared were said to have been snatched away (perhaps a personification of storm-winds), α 241.

ἄ-ρρηκτος (ϝρήγνῡμι): *unbreakable, indissoluble, indestructible;* πέδαι, δεσμοί, τεῖχος, πόλις, νεφέλη, Υ 150; φωνή, 'tireless,' Β 490.

ἄ-ρρητος (root ϝερ, ῥηθῆναι): *unspoken, unspeakable.*

ἄρσην, ενος: *male.*

Ἀρσί-νοος: father of Hecamēde, of the island of Tenedos, Λ 626†.

ἀρσίπος: see ἀερσίπος.

Ἀρτακίη: name of a fountain in the country of the Laestrȳgons, κ 108†.

ἀρτεμής, ές: *safe and sound,* Ε 515, ν 43.

Ἄρτεμις: *Artemis* (Diana), daughter of Zeus and Leto, and sister of Apollo; virgin goddess of the chase, and the supposed author of sudden painless deaths of women (see ἀγανός); women of fine figure are compared to Artemis, δ 122, ρ 17, 37, τ 56, cf. ζ 151 ff.; her favorite haunts are wild mountainous regions, Erymanthus in Arcadia, Taÿgetus in Laconia, ζ 102; epithets, ἁγνή, ἰοχέαιρα, χρῡσηλάκατος, χρῡσήνιος, χρῡσόθρονος, ἀγροτέρη, κελαδεινή.

ἀρτι-επής, ές (ϝέπος): *ready of speech,* Χ 281†.

ἄρτιος (root ἀρ): *suitable;* only pl., ἄρτια βάζειν, 'sensibly,' Ξ 92, θ 240; ὅτι οἱ φρεσὶν ἄρτια ᾔδῃ, was a 'congenial spirit,' Ε 326, τ 248.

ἀρτί-πος: *sound-footed, nimble-footed,* Ι 505, θ 310.

ἀρτί-φρων (φρήν): *accommodating,* ω 261†.

ἄρτος: *bread.* (Od.)

ἀρτῡ́νω, ἀρτύω (root ἀρ), ipf. ἤρτυον, fut. ἀρτυνέω, aor. part. ἀρτῡ́νᾱς, mid. aor. ἠρτῡνάμην, pass. aor. ἀρτύνθην: *put in place, make ready, prepare;* πυργηδὸν σφέας αὐτοὺς ἀρτῡ́ναντες, ('forming close ranks,' cf. Ο 618), Μ 43; ἀρτύνθη, 'was made ready,' 'began,' Λ 216; esp. of craft, δόλον, ψεύδεα, ὄλεθρόν τινι ἀρτύειν; mid., ἠρτῡ́ναντο δ' ἐρετμὰ τροποῖς ἐν δερματίνοισιν, 'their' oars, δ 782; πυκινὴν ἠρτῡ́νετο βουλήν, 'was framing,' Β 55.

Ἀρύβᾱς: a Phoenician of Sidon, ο 426†.

ἀρχέ-κακος: *beginning mischief,* Ε 63†.

Ἀρχέ-λοχος: a Trojan, son of Antēnor, Ξ 464.

Ἀρχε-πτόλεμος: son of Iphitus, charioteer of Hector, Θ 128.

ἀρχεύω: *be commander, command,* w. dative. (Il.)

ἀρχή (ἄρχω): *beginning;* εἵνεκ' ἐμῆς ἔριδος καὶ Ἀλεξάνδρου ἕνεκ' ἀρχῆς, and 'its beginning by Alexander,' said by Menelāus, making Paris the aggressor, Γ 100; ἐξ ἀρχῆς, 'of old.'

ἀρχός: *leader, commander.*

ἄρχω, reg. in act. and mid., but without perf., and without pass.: I. act., *lead off, begin* (for others to follow), *lead, command;* τοῖς ἄρα μῡ́θων ἦρχε, 'was the first' to speak; ἦρχ' ἀγορεύειν, ἦρχε δ' ὁδοῖο, 'lead the way,' ε 237; πάντες ἅμα, Ζεὺς δ' ἦρχε, 'headed by Zeus,' Α 495; in the sense of 'commanding,' foll. by dat., ἦρχε δ' ἄρα σφιν | Ἕκτωρ, Π 552, etc.; with part., ἐγὼ δ' ἦρχον χαλεπαίνων, 'was the first to offend,' 'began the quarrel,' Β 378, Γ 447, different from the inf.—II. mid., *begin* something that one is himself to continue; ἤρχετο μῡ́θων, began 'his' or 'her' speaking; ἤρχετο μῆτιν ὑφαίνειν, etc.; ἔκ τινος ἄρχεσθαι, make a beginning 'with' something, or 'at' some point, sometimes gen. without a prep., σέο δ' ἄρξομαι, Ι 97, φ 142; of ritual observance (beginning a sacrifice), πάντων ἀρχόμενος μελέων, ξ 428 (cf. ἀπάρχομαι).

ἀρωγή (ἀρήγω): *help, aid* in battle; τί μοι ἔριδος καὶ ἀρωγῆς, 'why should I concern myself with giving succor?' Φ 360.

ἀρωγός (ἀρήγω): *helper, advocate*, σ 232, Σ 502.

ἆσαι: see (1) ἀάω, (2) ἄω.

ἆσαιμι: see ἄω.

Ἀσαῖος: a Greek, slain by Hector, Λ 301†.

ἄσαμεν: see ἄεσα.

ἀσάμινθος: *bath-tub.*

ἆσασθαι: see ἄω.

ἄσατο: see ἀάω.

ἄ-σβεστος (σβέννῡμι): *inextinguishable;* φλόξ, Π 123; mostly metaph., γέλως, μένος, βοή, κλέος.

ἄσεσθαι: see ἄω.

ἀ-σήμαντος (σημαίνω): *without a guide* (shepherd); μῆλα, Κ 485† (cf. Ο 325).

ἆσθμα, ατος: hard *breathing, panting.* (Il.)

ἀσθμαίνω: *pant, gasp.* (Il.)

Ἀσιάδης: *son of Asius.*

Ἀσίνη: a town in Argolis, Β 560†.

ἀ-σινής, ές (σίνομαι): *unmolested,* λ 110 and μ 137.

1. Ἄσιος: adj., *Asian,* λειμών, a district in Lydia, from which the name Asia was afterwards extended to the whole continent, Β 461.

2. Ἄσιος: (1) a Phrygian, son of Tymas, and brother of Hecuba, Π 717.—(2) son of Hystacus, from Arisbe, an ally of the Trojans, Μ 95.

ἄσις: *slime,* Φ 321†.

ἄ-σῖτος: *without food,* δ 788†.

Ἀσκάλαφος: a son of Ares, one of the Argonauts, Β 512.

Ἀσκανίη: (1) a district in Phrygia, Β 863.—(2) in Bithynia or Mysia, Ν 793.

Ἀσκάνιος: (1) leader of the Phrygians, Β 862.—(2) son of Hippotion, Ν 792.

ἀ-σκελής, ές (σκέλλω): *withered, wasted,* κ 463; adv., ἀσκελές, *obstinately, persistently,* α 68, δ 543; **ἀσκελέως,** *unceasingly,* with αἰεί, Τ 68.

ἀσκέω, ipf. 3 sing. ἤσκειν (for ἤσκεεν), aor. ἤσκησα, perf. pass. ἤσκημαι: *work out* with skill, aor., *wrought,* Σ 592; χιτῶνα πτύσσειν καὶ ἀσκεῖν, 'smooth out,' α 439; the part., ἀσκήσᾱς, is often used for amplification, 'elaborately,' γ 438, Ξ 240.

ἀ-σκηθής, ές: *unscathed;* ἀσκηθέες καὶ ἄνουσοι, ξ 255.

ἀσκητός (ἀσκέω): *finely* or *curiously wrought,* ψ 189; νῆμα, 'fine-spun,' δ 134.

Ἀσκληπιάδης: *son of Asclepius,* Machāon, Δ 204, Λ 614, Ξ 2.

Ἀσκληπιός: *Asclepius* (Aesculapius), a famous physician, prince of Thessalia, father of Podaleirius and Machāon, Β 731, Δ 194, Λ 518.

ἄ-σκοπος (σκοπέω): *inconsiderate,* Ω 157.

ἀσκός: *leather bottle,* usually a goat skin (see cut, after a Pompeian painting), Γ 247; βοός, a skin to confine winds, κ 19.

15

ἄσμενος (root σϝαδ, ἁνδάνω): *glad;* ἐμοὶ δέ κεν ἀσμένῳ εἴη, 'twould 'please me' well, Ξ 108.

ἀσπάζομαι, only ipf. ἠσπάζοντο: *greet warmly,* by drawing to one's embrace, *make welcome;* χερσίν, γ 35; χερσίν ἐπέεσσί τε, τ 415; δεξιῇ ἐπέεσσί τε, Κ 542.

ἀσπαίρω: *move convulsively, quiver;* mostly of dying persons and animals; πόδεσσι, χ 473, τ 231.

ἄ-σπαρτος (σπείρω): *unsown,* ι 109 and 123.

ἀσπάσιος (ἀσπάζομαι): (1) *welcome;* τῷ δ' ἀσπάσιος γένετ' ἐλθών, Κ 35, ι 466; so νύξ, γῆ, βίοτος, ε 394 (cf. 397).—(2) *glad, joyful,* Φ 607, ψ 238. —Adv., **ἀσπασίως,** ν 33, Η 118.

ἀσπαστός: *welcome;* ἀσπαστόν, 'a grateful thing,' ε 398.

ἄ-σπερμος (σπέρμα): *without offspring,* Υ 303†.

16

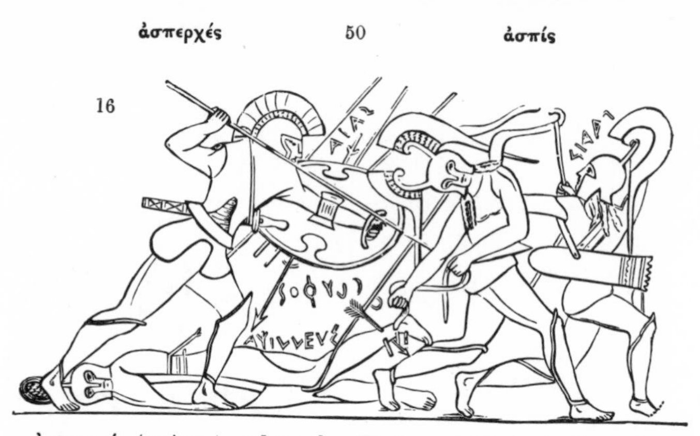

ἀ-σπερχές (σπέρχω): *vehemently; 'busily,'* Σ 556.

ἄ-σπετος (root σεπ, ἔσπετε): *unspeakable, inexpressible*, with regard to size, numbers, or quality; hence, *immense, endless;* ὕλη, αἰθήρ, δῶρα, etc.; ἁλμυρὸν ὕδωρ | ἄσπετον, 'vast as it is,' ε 101; in ἄσπετον οὖδας the epith. is regularly due to the pathos of the situation, Τ 61, ν 395, etc.; κλαγγὴ συῶν, 'prodigious squealing,' ξ 412; adv., τρεῖτ' ἄσπετον, Ρ 332.

17

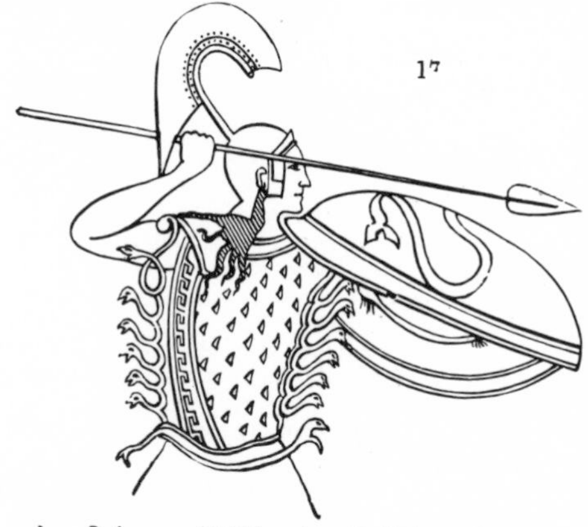

ἀσπιδιώτης: *shield-bearing*, Β 554 and Π 167.

ἀσπίς, ίδος: *shield*.—(1) the larger, oval shield, termed ἀμφιβρότη, ποδηνεκής. It is more than 2 ft. broad, 4½ ft. high, and weighed about 40 lbs. (For Agamemnon's shield, see Λ 32–40). The large shield was held over the left shoulder, sustained by the τελαμών and by the πόρπαξ, or ring on the inside.—(2) the smaller, circular shield, πάντοσ' ἐίση (see cut), with only two handles, or with one central handle for the arm and several for the hand (see cut No. 12). It was of about half the size and weight of the larger ἀσπίς, cf. the description of Sarpēdon's shield, Μ 294 ff. The shield consisted generally of from 4 to 7 layers of ox-hide (ῥῖνοί, Ν 804); these were covered by a plate of metal, and the whole was firmly united by rivets, which projected on the outer, convex side. The head of the central rivet, larger than the rest, was the ὀμφαλός or *boss*, and was usually fashioned into the form of a head. Instead of the plate above mentioned, concentric metal rings (δινωτής, εὔκυκλος) were sometimes substituted. The rim was called ἄντυξ, and the convex surface of the shield bore some device analogous to an heraldic coat of arms, Ε 182, Λ 36, cf. Ε 739. The shield of Achilles (Σ 478–608), in describing which the poet naturally did not choose to confine himself to realities, does not correspond exactly to either of the two ἀσπίδες described above.

ἀσπιστής = ἀσπιδιώτης, only pl., *warriors*. (Il.)

Ἀσπληδών: a town in Boeotia, B 511†.

ἀ-σπουδί (σπουδή): *without exertion;* always in the phrase μὴ μὰν ἀσπουδί γε, at least not 'without a struggle,' Θ 512, Ο 476, Χ 304.

ἄσσα = τινά.

ἅσσα = ἅ τινα.

Ἀσσάρακος: son of Tros, and grandfather of Anchīses, Υ 232 f.

ἆσσον (comp. of ἄγχι), double comp. **ἀσσοτέρω**: *nearer*, w. gen.; usually with ἰέναι, Α 335.

ἄσταχυς, υος: *ear of grain*, pl., B 148†.

ἀ-στεμφέως: *firmly, fast;* ἔχειν, δ 419, 459.

ἀ-στεμφής, ές: *firm, unyielding*, B 344; as adv., *still*, Γ 219.

Ἀστέριον: a town in Thessaly, B 735†.

Ἀστερίς (Star Island): a (probably fabulous) islet S. of Ithaca, δ 846†.

ἀστερόεις (ἀστήρ): *starry;* οὐρανός, Δ 44, etc.; then, 'spangled,' 'star-like,' θώρηξ, Π 134; δόμος, Σ 370.

Ἀστεροπαῖος: son of Pelagon, leader of the Paeonians, Μ 102, Φ 179.

ἀστεροπή: *lightning*. (Il.)

ἀστεροπητής: god *of the lightning*, epith. of Zeus. (Il.)

ἀστήρ, έρος, dat. pl. ἀστράσι: *star;* ἀστὴρ ὀπωρῖνός, the dog-star, Sirius, Ε 5; of a 'shooting-star,' Δ 75.

ἀστός (ἄστυ): *citizen*, pl., Λ 242 and ν 192.

ἀστράγαλος: *neck-vertebra*, κ 560; pl., *game of dice* (cf. our 'jack-stones'), Ψ 88. (See cut, after an ancient painting in Resina.)

18

ἀστράπτω, aor. part. ἀστράψᾱς: *lighten, hurl lightning*. (Il.)

ἄστρον (ἀστήρ): *constellation*, only pl., 'stars.'

ἄστυ, εος (ϝάστυ): *city* (esp. as a fortified dwelling-place); εἰς ὅ κεν ἄστυ κιχείομεν Ἰλίου ἱρῆς, Φ 128; πολλῶν δ' ἀνθρώπων ἴδεν ἄστεα, α 3; ὅππως κε πόλιν καὶ ἄστυ σαώσεις, i. e. his country and its capital, Ρ 144, cf. ζ 177 f.—ἄστυδε, *to the city*.

Ἀστύαλος: a Trojan, Ζ 29†.

Ἀστυ-άναξ (Master of the City): *Astyanax*, a name given by the Trojans to Scamandrius, the son of Hector, in honor of his father, Ζ 402 f.

ἀστυ-βοώτης (βοάω): *calling throughout the city*, Ω 701†.

Ἀστύ-νοος: (1) a Trojan leader, Ε 144†.—(2) a Trojan, son of Protiāon, Ο 455†.

Ἀστυ-όχεια: mother of Tlepolemus, B 658†.

Ἀστυ-όχη: mother of Ascalaphus and Ialmenus, B 513†.

Ἀστύ-πυλος: a Paeonian, Φ 209†.

ἀσυφηλός: doubtful word, *rude*, Ι 647 (as adv.) and Ω 767.

ἀ-σφαλέως (ἀσφαλής): *without swerving, steadily;* ἀγορεύειν, 'without faltering,' θ 171.

ἀ-σφαλής (σφάλλω): only neut. as adv. (= ἀσφαλέως), ἀσφαλὲς αἰεί, 'forever without end,' ζ 42.

Ἀσφαλίων: a servant of Menelāus, δ 216†.

ἀσφάραγος: *windpipe*, Χ 328†.

ἀσφοδελός: λειμών, the *asphodel* meadow, in the nether world, λ 539. (The asphodel is a liliaceous plant, with pale bluish flowers, it was planted about graves in Greece by the ancients as now.) (Od.)

ἀσχαλάω, ἀσχάλλω: *be impatient, vexed, fret;* with causal gen. (τ 159, 534), also with part., α 304, β 193; γέροντα μαγις ἔχον ἀσχαλόωντό, 'beside himself' with grief, Χ 412.

ἄ-σχετος (σχεῖν) and **ἀάσχετος**: *irresistible;* πένθος, 'overpowering,' Π 549, Ω 708.

Ἀσωπός: a river in Boeotia, Δ 383.

ἀ-τάλαντος (τάλαντον): *like* in weight, *equal*.

ἀταλά-φρων (ἀταλός, φρήν): *merry-hearted*, Ζ 400†.

ἀτάλλω: *skip, gambol;* κήτεα, Ν 27† (cf. Psalm 104, 26).

ἀταλός (ἀτάλλω): *frisking, merry;* ἀταλὰ φρονέοντες, 'light-hearted,' Σ 567, cf. λ 39.

ἀτάρ (ἀτᾰρ, ε 108, τ 273): *but yet, but, however;* freq. corresponding to μέν in the previous clause, Α 166, Ζ 86, 125; to ἤ μήν, Ι 58; but often without preceding particle, and sometimes with no greater adversative force than δέ, e. g. μάψ, ἀτὰρ οὐ κατὰ κόσμον, i. e. οὐδὲ κατὰ κ., Β 214, γ 138; in apod., like δέ, Μ 144. ἀτάρ is always the first word in the clause, but a voc. is not counted, Ἕκτορ, ἀτὰρ σύ μοί ἐσσι πατὴρ καὶ πότνια μήτηρ, 'but *thou*, Hector.' With this arrangement there is nothing peculiar in the force of the particle; it refers here, as always, to what precedes (expressed or implied) even when the voc. introduces the whole passage, Ἕκτορ, ἀτάρ που ἔφης, 'doubtless thou didst *think*,' etc., Χ 331, cf. δ 236. (Weakened form of αὐτάρ).

ἀ-ταρβής, ές (τάρβος): *fearless*, Ν 299†.

ἀ-τάρβητος (ταρβέω): *undaunted*, Γ 63†.

ἀταρπιτός (ἀταρπός): *path*, Σ 565 and ρ 234.

ἀταρπός: *by-path, path*, Ρ 743 and ξ 1.

ἀταρτηρός: doubtful word, *harsh, abusive, mischievous*, Α 223, β 243.

ἀτασθαλίη (ἀτάσθαλος): pl., criminal *folly, infatuation, wickedness*, α 7.

ἀτασθάλλω: *act wickedly, wantonly*, σ 57 and τ 88.

ἀτάσθαλος (cf. ἄτη): *wicked, wanton*, Χ 418, mostly of actions, χ 314; esp. in pl., ἀτάσθαλα ῥέζειν, μηχανᾶσθαι, γ 207.

ἅτε, ἅ τε: never as adv. in Homer, see ὅς τε.

ἀ-τειρής, ές (τείρω): *not to be worn out, unwearied, unyielding;* χαλκός, and of persons, μένος, κραδίη, Γ 60.

ἀ-τέλεστος (τελέω): *unended, unaccomplished, fruitless;* adv., *without end*, π 111.

ἀ-τελεύτητος (τελευτάω): *unfinished, unaccomplished, unfulfilled.*

ἀ-τελής, ές (τέλος): *unaccomplished, unconsummated*, ρ 546†.

ἀτέμβω: *stint, disappoint*, υ 294, φ 312; θῡμόν, β 90; pass., *be deprived, disappointed of, go without;* τινός, Λ 705, Ψ 445.

ἄτερ: *without, apart from*, w. gen.

ἀ-τέραμνος (τείρω): *hard, inexorable*, ψ 167†.

ἀ-τερπής, ές (τέρπω): *joyless.*

ἄ-τερπος = ἀτερπής, Ζ 285†.

ἀτέω: only part., ἀτέοντα, *foolhardy*, Υ 332†.

ἄτη (ἀάω): ruinous *mischief, ruin*, usually in consequence of blind and criminal *folly, infatuation;* ἤ με μαλ' εἰς ἄτην κοιμήσατε νηλέι ὕπνῳ (addressed to the gods by Odysseus; while he slept his comrades had laid hands on the cattle of Helius), μ 372, cf. Β 111, Θ 237; τὸν δ' ἄτη φρένας εἷλε, 'blindness' (cf. what follows, στῆ δὲ ταφών: Patroclus stands dazed by the shock received from Apollo), Π 805; εἵνεκ' ἐμεῖο κυνὸς καὶ Ἀλεξάνδρου ἕνεκ' ἄτης (said by Helen), Ζ 356; pl., ἐμὰς ἄτᾱς κατέλεξας, Ι 115, Κ 391, Τ 270. The notions of folly and the consequences of folly are naturally confused in this word, cf. Ω 480, and some of the passages cited above.—Personified, Ἄτη, *Ate*, the goddess of infatuation, πρέσβα Διὸς θυγάνηρ Ἄτη, ἣ πάντας ἀᾶται, Τ 91 (see what follows as far as v. 130, also Ι 500 ff.).

ἀ-τίζω (τίω): part., *unheeding*, Υ 166†.

ἀ-τῑμάζω (τῑμή), ipf. iter. ἀτῑμάζεσκον, aor. ἠτίμασα: *treat with disrespect, dishonor, maltreat;* Ἀτρείδης ἠτῑμασεν ἀρητῆρα (the best reading, vulg. ἠτίμησ'), Α 11.

ἀ-τῑμάω = ἀτῑμάζω.

ἀ-τίμητος: *unhonored, slighted*, Ι 648 and Π 59.

ἀ-τῑμίη: *contumely*, only pl., ἀτῑμίῃσιν (the quantity a necessity of the rhythm), ν 142†.

ἄ-τῑμος, comp. -ότερος, sup. -ότατος =ἀτίμητος, also *without compensation;* as adv., π 431, see τῑμή.

ἀτιτάλλω, aor. ἀτίτηλα: *rear, cherish;* of children, Ω 60, etc.; of animals, 'feed,' 'keep,' Ζ 271, ο 174.

ἄ-τῑτος (τίω): *unpaid, unavenged.*

Ἄ-τλᾱς (τλῆναι): *Atlas*, the father of Calypso, a god who knows the depths of the sea and holds the pillars that keep heaven and earth asunder, α 52, η 245.

ἄ-τλητος (τλῆναι): *unendurable*, I 3 and T 367.

ἄτος (for ἄ-ατος, ἄω): *insatiable.*

ἀτραπιτός = ἀταρπιτός, *path*, ν 195†.

Ἀτρείδης, ᾱο or εω: *son of Atreus*, *Atrīdes*, meaning Agamemnon when not otherwise specified; dual. Ἀτρείδᾱ, pl. Ἀτρεῖδαι, *the sons of Atreus*, *the Atrīdæ*, Agamemnon and Menelāus.

Ἀτρείων, ωνος=Ἀτρείδης.

ἀτρεκέως: *unerringly*, *truly.*

ἀτρεκής, ές: only neut., as adv., *exactly*, *true*, *real.*

ἄτρεμα(ς) (τρέμω): adv., *motionless*, *quiet*, *still.*

Ἀτρεύς, έος: *Atreus*, son of Pelops and Hippodamīa, father of Agamemnon and Menelāus; his sceptre, B 105.

ἄ-τριπτος (τρίβω): *unworn* by toil, *unhardened*, *soft*, φ 151†.

ἄ-τρομος (τρέμω): *intrepid*, *fearless.* (Il.)

ἀτρύγετος: *barren*; epith. of the sea, and once of the sky, P 425. This is the ancient and traditional interpretation of the word, but according to some moderns it means *restless.*

Ἀτρῡτώνη: *Atrytōne*, a name of Athēna, perhaps meaning the 'unwearied,' 'invincible;' always Διὸς τέκος Ἀτρυτώνη, B 157.

ἄττα: a term of endearment used in addressing elders, 'father,' 'uncle.'

ἀτύζομαι, only part. pres. and aor. ἀτυχθείς: *bewildered*, *dazed*, *distraught*, the effect of fear, grief, etc.; ἥμεθ' ἀτυζόμεναι, 'shocked,' while the suitors were being killed, ψ 42; ἀτυζομένην ἀπολέσθαι, in a 'dead fit,' Andromache, X 474; w. acc., πατρὸς ὄψιν ἀτυχθείς, 'terrified at,' Z 468; ἀτυζόμενοι φοβέοντο, Z 41; hence with motion implied in the word itself, (ἵππω) ἀτυζομένω πεδίοιο, 'scouring wildly' o'er the plain, π. gen. of place, Z 38, etc.

Ἀτυμνιάδης: *son of Atymnius*, Mydon, E 581†.

Ἀτύμνιος: (1) father of Mydon, a Paphlagonian, E 581.—(2) son of Amisodarus, of Caria, Π 317, 328.

αὖ: *again*, *on the contrary*, *on the other hand;* temporal, A 540, υ 88, etc.; oftener denoting sequence or contrast, δ' αὖ, δεύτερον αὖ, νῦν αὖ, etc.; sometimes correl. to μέν, Λ 109, δ 211, and scarcely stronger than δέ, B 493, Λ 367.

αὐαίνω (αὔω): only aor. pass. part. αὐανθέν, *when it was dry*, ι 321†.

αὐγάζομαι (αὐγή): *discern*, Ψ 458†.

Αὐγειαί: (1) a town in Laconia, B 583†.—(2) in Locris, B 532†.

Αὐγείᾱς: *Augēas*, a king in Elis, known from the cleansing of his stables by Heracles; father of Agasthenes, Phyleus, and Agamēde, Λ 701, 739.

αὐγή, ῆς: *beam*, *gleam*, *glow*; esp. of the sun, ὑπ' αὐγὰς Ἠελίοιο, β 181.

Αὐγηιάδης: *son of Augēas*, Agasthenes, B 624†.

αὐδάω, impf. αὔδᾱ, ipf. 3 sing. ηὔδᾱ, aor. iter. αὐδήσασκε, part. αὐδήσᾱς: *speak* loud and clear, cf. αὐδή, Στέντορι εἰσαμένη μεγαλήτορι, χαλκεοφώνῳ, | ὃς τόσον αὐδήσασχ' ὅσον ἄλλοι πεντήκοντα, E 786; τοῦ δὲ Ποσειδάων μεγάλ' ἔκλυεν αὐδήσαντος, 'heard his loud boastful utterance,' δ 505; ὁμοκλήσᾱς ἔπος ηὔδᾱ, Z 54; often w. acc. in the phrase ἀντίον ηὔδᾱ, 'addressed.'

αὐδή, ῆς: *voice*, properly the human voice with reference to its pleasing effects; τοῦ καὶ ἀπὸ γλώσσης μέλιτος γλυκίων ῥέεν αὐδή, of Nestor as orator, A 249; θεοῖς ἐναλίγκιος αὐδήν, Phemius, the minstrel, α 371; said of a bird, ἣ δ' (the bowstring) ὑπὸ κᾱλὸν ἄεισε, χελῑδόνι εἰκέλη αὐδήν, φ 411.

αὐδήεις, εσσα: *possessed of voice*, *voiceful*, esp. with regard to the power of song, Circe, κ 136, Calypso, μ 449, Ino, ε 334; Λευκοθέη, ἣ πρὶν μὲν ἔην βροτὸς αὐδήεσσα, i. e. a 'tuneful' mortal, not a 'mortal speaking with human voice;' of Xanthus, the horse of Achilles, αὐδήεντα δ' ἔθηκε θεά, 'endowed him with voice' (i. e. human as contrasted with equine utterance).

αὐερύω (ἀνά, Ϝερύω), aor. αὐέρυσα: *draw up* or *back;* of drawing a bow, Θ 325; loosening props, M 261; and esp. of bending back the heads of victims, for the knife, A 459.

αὖθ': (1) =αὖτε, before an aspirated vowel.—(2) =αὖθι before a vowel.

αὖθι: (*right*) *there*, (*right*) *here*, A 492, H 100; often foll. by a prep. with subst., specifying the place, αὖθι παρ' ἄμμι, I 427; αὖθι μενῶ μετὰ τοῖσι, K 62; αὖθ' ἐπὶ τάφρῳ, Λ 48; ἐν Λακεδαίμονι αὖθι, Γ 244; of time, *on the spot*, i. e. 'at once,' σ 339, E 296.

αὐιαχός (ϝιαχή): *shouting loudly together*, pl., N 41†.

αὔλειος: *belonging to the αὐλή, of the court.* (Od.)

αὐλή, ῆς: *court-enclosure, court, court-yard, farm-yard;* the αὐλή of a mansion had gate-way, portico, stables, slave-quarters, altar, and rotunda (θόλος); see table III. An αὐλή is attributed to the cabin of Eumaeus, the swine-herd, ξ 5, to the tent of Achilles, Ω 452, and even to the cave of Polyphēmus, ι 239.

αὔλη (αὐλός): *music of flutes;* αὔλῃ a conjectural reading for αὐλῇ, κ 10.

αὐλίζομαι (αὐλή): only part., αὐλιζομενάων, *being penned in*, of cattle and swine. (Od.)

αὖλις, ιδος: *place of rest;* 'encampment,' I 232; 'roosting-place,' χ 470.

Αὐλίς: *Aulis*, a town in Boeotia, on the Euripus, the rendezvous of the Greeks before sailing for Troy, B 303.

αὐλός: *flute*, a wind-instrument more like the clarinet than the modern transverse flute, Σ 495, K 13; then any *tube, channel*, as the 'socket' in which the point of a lance was fitted, P 297; 'holes' or 'eyes,' receiving the tongue of a buckle, τ 227; of a 'jet' of blood, χ 18.

αὐλῶπις, ιδος (αὐλός): *with upright tube*, to receive the plume of a helmet, E 182. (Il.) (See cuts 16, 17.)

αὖος: *dry*, neut. as adv., of sound, *hoarse, grating*, M 160, N 441.

ἄ-υπνος: *sleepless.*

αὔρη (ἄϝημι): *breeze*, ε 469†.

αὔριον: *to-morrow;* ἐς αὔριον, αὔριον ἔς, H 318.

ἀυσταλέος (αὖος): *dry, unanointed, unkempt*, squalidus, τ 327†.

αὐτ-άγρετος (αὐτός, ἀγρέω): *self-taken, attainable*, 'if men could have every wish,' π 148†.

αὖταρ (αὖτε, ἄρα): *but, however*, marking a contrast or transition like δέ, and weightier than δέ only in being disyllabic and not post-positive (cf. ἤτοι); answering to ἤτοι or μέν in a previous clause, ω 155, A 68, etc.; often at the beginning of a sentence without distinct correlation, esp. **αὖταρ** ἐπεί, Γ 1.

αὖτε (αὖ τε): *again, on the other hand, however, but;* εἴ ποτε δὴ αὖτε, A 340; ὁππότ' ἂν αὖτε, θ 444, and esp. in questions of impatient tone, τίπτ' αὖτ' εἰλήλουθας, A 202; τέων αὖτε βροτῶν ἐς γαῖαν ἱκάνω, 'whose country am I come to *now?*' ζ 119; very often denoting contrast or transition, like δέ, νῦν αὖτε, ἔνθ' αὖτε, δ' αὖτε, and correlating to μέν, Γ 241; also in apod., Δ 321.

ἀΰτέω (ἀϋτή), only ipf. ἀΰτει, ἀΰτευν: *call aloud;* with μακρόν, μέγα, Υ 50, Φ 582; with acc., Λ 258; of inanimate things, *sound, resound;* κόρυθες, M 160. Cf. αὔω 2.

ἀϋτή: loud, far-reaching *call, cry;* ὥς τε με κουράων ἀμφήλυθε θῆλυς ἀϋτή (the outcry of the maidens, when the ball with which they were playing fell into the river, had awakened Odysseus), ζ 122; esp. the *battle-cry*, and so, suggestively, for battle itself, δεινῆς ἀκόρητοι ἀϋτῆς, N 621; μεμαυῖ' ἔριδος καὶ ἀϋτῆς, E 732; ὀψείοντες ἀϋτῆς καὶ πολέμοιο, Ξ 37.

αὐτ-ῆμαρ: *on the same day.*

αὐτίκα (αὐτός): *forthwith, straightway.*

αὖτις (αὖ), Attic αὖθις: *again, back again, anew;* often πάλιν αὖτις, ἂψ αὖτις, δεύτερον αὖτις, and standing alone, αὖτις ἰών, going 'back,' Θ 271, etc.; ταῦτα μεταφρασόμεσθα καὶ αὖτις, *by and by*, A 140; also merely transitional, τοῖς δ' αὖτις μετέειπε, ο 439, σ 60.

ἀυτμή: *breath, blast, fumes;* of breathing, I 609, K 89; wind, λ 400, 407 (from the bellows, Σ 471); fire, Φ 366, ι 389 (smoky, π 290); savors, fragrances, M 369, Ξ 174, μ 369.

ἀυτμήν, ένος: *breath, blast;* of men and winds, Ψ 765, γ 289.

αὐτο-δίδακτος (διδάσκω): *self-taught*, epith. of the inspired bard, χ 347†.

αὐτό-διον (αὐτός): *on the spot, straightway*, θ 449†.

αὐτό-ετες (ϝέτος): *in the same year*, γ 322†.

αὐτόθ'=αὐτόθι.

αὐτόθεν: *from* (*right*) *there* or *here, from where he* or *she was;* (μετέειπεν) αὐτόθεν ἐξ ἕδρης, οὐδ' ἐν μέσσοισιν ἀναστάς, T 77, φ 420.

αὐτόθι: (*right*) *there*, (*right*) *here*, *on the spot;* often with more definite limitation following, *αὐτόθι μίμνει | ἀγρῷ*, λ 187, so ἐν w. dat., ι 29, I 617.

αὐτο-κασιγνήτη: *own sister*, κ 137†.

αὐτο-κασίγνητος: *own brother*. (Il.)

Αὐτό-λυκος: *Autolycus*, father of Anticlēa, and grandfather of Odysseus; he dwelt on Parnassus and was gifted with the sly arts that were inherited by his grandson, τ 394–466, K 267.

αὐτό-ματος (root *μα*, *μέμαα*): *self-moving moving of oneself*. (Il.)

Αὐτο-μέδων: son of Diōres, charioteer of Achilles, P 536, Π 145.

Αὐτο-νόη: a handmaid of Penelope, σ 182†.

Αὐτό-νοος: (1) a Greek, Λ 301†.—(2) a Trojan, Π 694†.

αὐτο-νυχί: *this very night*, Θ 197.

αὐτός, ή, ό: *same*, *self*.—(1) pronoun of identity, *ἦρχε δὲ τῷ αὐτὴν ὁδὸν ἥν περ οἱ ἄλλοι* (the *same* way, like *τὴν αὐτήν* in Attic), θ 107, M 225. (The article when joined to *αὐτός* in Homer is demonstrative, e. g. *τὼ δ' αὐτὼ μάρτυροι ἔστων*, 'these' two men themselves, not 'the same' two, A 338, π 334; once occurs crasis, *ὡὑτὸς* **ἀνήρ**, 'that' same man, E 396).—(2) pronoun of emphasis and antithesis, as one person is contrasted with another, or with some possession or part of himself, the extent to which this antithetic idea is carried forming a highly characteristic feature of the Homeric style; *πολλὰς δ' ἰφθίμους ψῡχὰς Ἄϊδι προΐαψεν | ἡρώων, α ὐ τ ο ὺ ς δὲ ἑλώρια τεῦχε κύνεσσιν*, hurled their souls to Hades, but made *them*, i. e. their bodies, a prey to dogs, A 4; *εἰσενόησα βίην Ἡρακληείην | εἴδωλον· α ὐ τ ὸ ς δὲ μετ' ἀθανάτοισι θεοῖσιν | τέρπεται, κτλ.*, Heracles himself in heaven, his ghost in hell, λ 602; *δησάντων σε ὀρθὸν ἐν ἱστοπέδῃ, ἐκ δ' α ὐ τ ο ῦ πείρατ' ἀνήφθω*, let them tie you standing up on the mast-block, with the rope ends fastened to (the mast) *itself*, μ 51; *Πριάμοιο δόμον ξεστῇς αἰθούσῃσι τετυγμένον, αὐτὰρ ἐν α ὐ τ ῷ*, i. e. in the *house itself*, as distinguished from its corridor, Z 243, and so continually. (The occurrence of *αὐτός* in the oblique cases as simple unemphatic personal pronoun is denied altogether to Homer by some scholars, and in most of the seeming instances an emphasis or contrast may be detected, as clearly e. g. Γ 365; still the approach to the later use is sometimes uncomfortably close, e. g. B 347).—Here belong such expressions as *ὑπὸ λόφον αὐτόν*, 'directly' under the plume, N 615, κ 158; *δύω ἵππους αὐτοῖσιν ὄχεσφιν*, 'chariot and all,' Θ 290; *αὐτός περ ἐών*, 'by himself,' i. e. *alone*, Θ 99, ξ 8, 450.—Here, too, belong the *reflexive* uses, δ 247, etc.; *αὐτῶν γὰρ ἀπωλόμεθ' ἀφραδίῃσιν*, by our *own* folly, κ 27; *τὴν αὐτοῦ φιλέει*, loves his *own*, I 342, β 125; similarly, *αὐτῶν γὰρ σφετέρῃσιν ἀτασθαλίῃσιν ὄλοντο*, α 7; *τὰ σ(ὰ) αὐτῆς ἔργα κόμιζε*, Z 490, 'their own,' 'thine own.'

αὐτο-σταδίη (*ἵστημι*): *hand to hand fight*, N 325†.

αὐτο-σχεδά = *αὐτοσχεδόν*.

αὐτο-σχεδίη (*σχεδόν*): *close combat;* adv., *αὐτοσχεδίην*, 'at close quarters.'

αὐτο-σχεδόν: *hand to hand*, *μάχεσθαι*, etc.

αὐτοῦ = *αὐτόθι*. Usually with following specification, *αὐτοῦ ἐνὶ Τροίῃ*, B 237; *ἀλλά που αὐτοῦ | ἀγρῶν*, somewhere *there* 'in the country,' i. e in the island of Ithaca, though not in town, δ 639; with temporal effect, O 349, Φ 425, δ 703, σ 212.

αὐτόφι(ν) = *αὐτῷ*, Γ 255; = *αὐτῶν*, Λ 44; = *αὐτοῖς*, N 42; always with a preposition.

Αὐτό-φονος: father of Polyphontes, of Thebes, Δ 395†.

αὐτο-χόωνος (*χόανος*, *melting-pit*): *just as it was cast*, of a massive quoit in its rough state, Ψ 826†.

αὔτως (*αὐτός*): *in the same way*, *just as it is*, *merely*, *in vain;* a word admitting great variety of paraphrase, but in signification always answering to some force of *αὐτός*. *γυμνὸν ἐόντα | αὔτως ὥς τε γυναῖκα*, all unarmed, 'exactly' like a woman, X 125; *ἄπυρον λέβητα, λευκὸν ἔτ' αὔτως*, still 'quite' bright, Ψ 268; *ὀκνείω δ' ἵππων ἐπιβαίνεμεν, ἀλλὰ καὶ αὔτως | ἀντίον εἶμ' αὐτῶν*, 'just as I am,' E 256; *ἡ δὲ καὶ αὔτως μ' αἰὲν νεικεῖ*, even 'as it is,' i. e. without special provocation, A 520; ἀλλ' αὔτως ἄχθος ἀρούρης, a 'mere' burden to the ground, υ 379; αὔτως γάρ ῥ' ἐπέεσσ' ἐριδαίνομεν, 'just as we do,' i. e. to no purpose, B 342.

αὐχένιος (αὐχήν): *of the neck; τένοντες*, γ 450†.

αὐχήν, ένος: *neck*, of men and animals.

αὐχμέω (αὐχμός): *be dry, unanointed, squalid*, ω 250†.

1. **αὔω, αὔω**: *kindle; ἵνα μή ποθεν ἄλλοθεν αὔοι*, that he might not have to 'get a light' elsewhere, ε 490†.

2. **αὔω**, ipf. αὖον, aor. ἤῡσα, ἄῡσα, inf. ἀῦσαι, part. ἀΰσᾱς: *call aloud*, with exertion of the voice, *halloo*; often with μακρόν, 'afar,' Γ 81, etc.; ἔνθα στᾶσ' ἤῡσε θεᾶ μέγα τε δεινόν τε | ὄρθια, Λ 10; with acc., Λ 461, N 477, ι 65; of inanimate things, *resound, ring*, N 409. Cf. ἀϋτή.

ἀφ-αιρέω, ἀπο-αιρέω, aor. ἀφεῖλον, mid. pres. imp. ἀποαίρεο, fut. inf. ἀφαιρήσεσθαι, aor., 2 sing., ἀφείλεο, pl. ἀφέλεσθε: *take away* (τινός τι), mid., for oneself, esp. forcibly or wrongfully (τινά τι or τινί τι); ὡς ἔμ' ἀφαιρεῖται Χρῡσηίδα Φοῖβος Ἀπόλλων, A 182; αὐτὰρ ὃ τοῖσιν ἀφείλετο νόστιμον ἦμαρ, α 9.

ἄ-φαλος: *without crest; κυνέη*, K 258†.

ἀφ-αμαρτάνω, only aor. 2 ἀφάμαρτε and ἀπήμβροτε: *miss* (fail to hit), *lose; καὶ βάλεν, οὐδ' ἀφάμαρτε*, Λ 350; ἐμοὶ δέ κε κέρδιον εἴη | σεῦ ἀφαμαρτούσῃ χθόνα δύμεναι, 'bereft' of thee, Z 411.

ἀφ-αμαρτο-επής: *missing* the point *in speech*, 'rambling speaker,' Γ 215†.

ἀφ-ανδάνω: *displease; μῦθος ἀφανδάνει*, π 387†.

ἄ-φαντος (φαίνω): *unseen*, 'leaving no trace,' (Il.)

ἄφαρ: *instantly, at once*, β 169, P 417; ᾦδ' ἄφαρ, K 537; ἄφαρ αὐτίκα, Ψ 593.

Ἀφαρεύς: a Greek, son of Calētor, N 541.

ἀφ-αρπάζω: *seize away from*, aor. inf., N 189†.

ἀφάρτερος (comp. of ἄφαρ): *swifter*, Ψ 311†.

ἀφαυρός, -ότερος, -ότατος: *insignificant, weakly*, H 235, υ 110.

ἀφάω (ἅπτω): only part., ἀφόωντα, *busy with handling; τόξα*, Z 322†.

Ἀφείδᾱς: an assumed, fictitious name, ω 305†.

ἀφείη: see ἀφίημι.

ἄφενος, neut.: large *possessions, riches*.

ἀφέξω, ἀφέξομαι: see ἀπέχω.

ἄφ-ημαι: only part., ἀφήμενος, *sitting apart*, O 106†.

ἀφήτωρ, ορος (ἀφίημι): the *archer*, viz. Apollo, I 404†.

ἄ-φθιτος (φθίω): *unwasting, imperishable*.

ἀφ-ίημι, imp. 2 pl. ἀφίετε, part. fem. ἀφῑεῖσαι, ipf. 3 sing. ἀφίει, fut. ἀφήσω, aor. ἀφέηκα, ἀφῆκα, 3 du. ἀφέτην, subj. ἀφέῃ, opt. ἀφείη, part. ἀφείς, mid. ipf. ἀφίετο: *let go from*.—I. act., of sending away persons, A 25, B 263; hurling missiles, lightning, Θ 133; lowering a mast, ἱστὸν προτόνοισι, A 434; grapes shedding the flower, ἄνθος ἀφῑεῖσαι, η 126; met., of 'dismissing' thirst, Λ 642; 'relaxing' force, N 444. —II. mid., δειρῆς δ' οὔ πω πάμπαν ἀφίετο πήχεε λευκώ, 'let go her' arms from his neck, ψ 240.

ἀφ-ικάνω: *be come to, arrived at* (from somewhere); δεῦρο, πρός τι, always with perf. signif., exc. ι 450, and in Od. always w. acc. of end of motion.

ἀφ-ικνέομαι, fut. ἀφίξομαι, aor. ἀφῑκόμην, perf. inf. ἀφῖχθαι: *come to, arrive at, reach* (one point from another); usually w. acc., sometimes w. prepositions; τοῦτον (δίσκον) νῦν ἀφίκεσθε, 'come up to' that now, θ 255; met., ὅτε μ' ἄλγος ἀφίκετο, Σ 395.

ἀφ-ίστημι, aor. 2 ἀπέστην, perf. ἀφέστατε, ἀφεστᾶσι, opt. ἀφεσταίη, part. ἀφεστᾱώς, plup. ἀφεστήκει, ἀφέστασαν, mid. aor. 1 subj. ἀποστήσωνται: of act. only intrans. forms occur, *stand off* or *away* (τινός); παλίνορσος, Γ 33; νόσφιν, λ 544; mid., aor. 1, causative, *get weighed out for oneself*, 'demand pay for,' χρεῖος, N 745.

ἄφλαστον: aplustre, an ornamental knob on the stern of a ship, O 717†.

ἀφλοισμός: *foam, froth*, O 607†.

ἀφνειός (ἄφενος), -ότεροι, -ότατος: *wealthy, rich in* (τινός).

ἀφ-οπλίζω: only mid. ipf. ἀφωπλίζοντο, *divested themselves of their armor;* ἔντεα. Ψ 26†.

ἀφ-ορμάομαι, only aor. pass. opt. and part. ἀφορμηθεῖεν, -θέντες: *start from, depart,* B 794, β 375.

ἀφόωντα: see ἀφάω.

ἀ-φραδέω: *be foolish.*

ἀ-φραδής, ές (φράζομαι): *inconsiderate, foolish, senseless,* β 282, λ 476.—Adv., **ἀφραδέως.**

ἀ-φραδίη (φράζομαι): *ignorance, folly;* dat. sing., B 368, elsewhere only dat. plural.

ἀ-φραίνω (φρήν): *be senseless, mad, foolish.*

ἀφρέω (ἀφρός): *foam;* only ipf. ἄφρεον δὲ στήθεα (sc. ἵπποι), 'their breasts were covered with foam,' Λ 282†.

ἀ-φρήτωρ (φρήτρη): *without clan* or *clansmen;* ἀφρήτωρ, ἀθέμιστος, ἀνέστιος, 'friendless, lawless, homeless,' I 63†.

Ἀφροδίτη: *Aphrodīte* (Venus), goddess of love, daughter of Zeus and Diōne, E 370, and in the Odyssey wife of Hephaestus, θ 267 ff.; her magic girdle described, Ξ 214 ff.; attended by the Graces, σ 192. She favors the Trojans in the war of which she was herself the cause, and in protecting her son Aenēas receives a wound from Diomed, E 331.—The name of Aphrodīte is used once by personification for her works, *love,* χ 444. Cf. Ἄρης.

ἀ-φρονέω: *be foolish,* part., O 104†.

ἀφρός: *foam.* (Il.)

ἀ-φροσύνη: *folly;* pl., *foolish behavior.*

ἄ-φρων (φρήν): *thoughtless, foolish.*

ἄ-φυλλος (φύλλον): *leafless,* B 425†.

ἀφύξειν: see ἀφύσσω.

ἀφυσγετός: *mud,* Λ 495†.

ἀφύσσω, fut. ἀφύξω, aor. ἤφυσα, part. ἀφύσσᾱς, mid. aor. ἠφυσάμην, ἀφυσσάμην, part. ἀφυσσάμενος: *draw* (water or wine), mid., for oneself, often by *dipping* from a larger receptacle into a smaller (ἀπὸ or ἔκ τινος, or τινός); οἰνοχόει γλυκὺ νέκταρ, ἀπὸ κρητῆρος ἀφύσσων, for the other gods, A 598; ἀφυσσάμενοι μέλαν ὕδωρ, for their own use, on ship-board, δ 359; διὰ (adv.) δ' ἔντερα χαλκὸς | ἤφυσε, pierced and 'opened,' (cf. 'dip into' him), N 508, P 315, Ξ 517; met., ἄφενος καὶ πλοῦτον ἀφύξειν, 'draw off,' i. e. accumulate riches for another man, A 171.

Ἀχαιαί: *Achaean women.* (Od.)

Ἀχαιάς, άδος: *Achaean woman.*

Ἀχαιικός: *Achaean.*

Ἀχαιίς, ίδος: *Achaean* (γαῖα), and without γαῖα, *Achaea,* i. e. Northern Greece; pl., as subst., *Achaean women;* contemptuously, Ἀχαιΐδες, οὐκέτ' Ἀχαιοί, B 235, H 96.

Ἀχαιοί: the *Achaeans,* the chief tribe of Greeks in Thessaly, Messēne, Argos, and Ithaca; mostly as a collective appellation of the Greeks before Troy, A 2, etc.; epithets, ἀρηίφιλοι, δῖοι, ἑλίκωπες, ἐυκνήμῖδες, κάρη κομόωντες, μεγάθῡμοι, μένεα πνείοντες, χαλκοχίτωνες.

ἄ-χαρις, comp. ἀχαρίστερος: *unpleasant, unwelcome,* υ 392†.

ἀ-χάριστος = ἄχαρις, neut. pl., θ 236†.

Ἀχελώιος = Ἀχελῷος: *Achelōus,* river-god; (1) in Greece, Φ 194.—(2) in Phrygia, Ω 616†.

ἄχερδος: *wild pear-tree, prickly pear,* ξ 10†.

ἀχερωίς: *white poplar,* N 389. (Il.)

Ἀχέρων, οντος: *Acheron,* river of the nether world, into which flow Pyriphlegethon and Cocȳtus, κ 513†.

ἀχεύω (ἄχος): only part., *grieving,* usually w. causal gen., ξ 40; τοῦγ' εἵνεκα θῡμὸν ἀχεύων, 'troubling his soul,' acc. of specification, φ 318.

ἀχέω = ἀχεύω, only part., ἀχέων, ἀχέουσα.

ἄχθομαι (ἄχθος), ipf. ἤχθετο (see also ἔχθομαι): (1) *be laden;* νηῦς ἤχθετο τοῖσι νέεσθαι, ο 457†.—(2) *be distressed, afflicted;* ὀδύνῃσι, E 354; κῆρ, 'at heart,' and w. obj. (cognate) acc., ἄχθομαι ἕλκος, distressed 'by,' E 361, cf. N 352.

ἄχθος, εος (root ἀχ): *burthen, weight,* Υ 247, γ 312; prov., ἄχθος ἀρούρης, a useless 'burden to the ground,' Σ 104, υ 379.

Ἀχιλεύς, Ἀχιλλεύς, ῆος, dat. -ῆι and -εῖ: *Achilles,* son of Peleus and Thetis, king of the Myrmidons, and the hero of the Iliad, as announced in A 1. For his relations to Phoenix and Cheiron the centaur, see I; his destiny, I 410 ff.; expedition against Troy, B 681; forays, I 328, A 392, B 690; death of Patroclus, Π 827; μηνίδος ἀπόρρησις, Τ 56; Ἕκτορος ἀναίρεσις, Χ; Ἕκτορος λύτρα, Ω. The death of Achilles is mentioned in the Odyssey, ε 310, ω 37 ff. Epithets, δαΐφρων, διίφιλος, θεοείκελος, θεοῖς ἐπιείκελος, πελώριος, ποδάρκης, ποδώκης, πτολίπορθος, ῥηξήνωρ, πόδας ταχύς, and ὠκύς. (See cut from Panathenaic Amphora.)

19

ἀχλύς, ύος: *mist, darkness*, η 41, Ε 127, υ 357; often met., of death, swooning, Ε 696, Π 344.

ἀχλύω: only aor., ἤχλῦσε, *grew dark*, μ 406. (Od.)

ἄχνη: *foam* of the sea, Λ 307; *chaff*, pl., Ε 499.

ἄχνυμαι (root ἀχ), ipf. ἄχνυτο: *be distressed, grieve;* τινός, 'for' some one; often w. acc. of specification (κῆρ); also κῆρ ἄχνυται, ἄχνυται θῡμὸς ἐνὶ στήθεσσιν ἐμοῖσιν, Ξ 38, ξ 170. Cf. ἀκαχίζω.

ἄ-χολος: *without wrath;* νηπενθές τ' ἄχολόν τε, 'cure for grief and gall,' δ 221†.

ἄχομαι = ἄχνυμαι, σ 256 and τ 129.

ἄχος, εος (root ἀχ): *anguish, distress*, for oneself or for another (τινός), pl. ἄχεα, *woes;* ἀλλά μοι αἰνὸν ἄχος σέθεν ἔσσεται, ὦ Μενέλᾱε, | αἴ κε θάνῃς, Δ 169; so ἄχος γένετό τινι, ἀμφεχύθη, εἷλεν, ἔλαβέ τινα, θῡμὸν ἵκᾱνεν, etc.; ἔχω ἄχε' ἄκριτα θῡμῷ, Γ 412, Ζ 413, τ 167.

ἀ-χρεῖος: *useless, aimless;* only neut. as adv., of the *foolish* look of the punished Thersites, Β 269, the *forced* laugh of Penelope, σ 163.

ἀ-χρημοσύνη: *indigence, want*, ρ 502†.

ἄχρι(ς): *quite, quite close*, Δ 522, Π 324, Ρ 599; *until*, σ 370.

ἀχυρμιή (ἄχυρον): *place where chaff falls, chaff-heap*, pl., Ε 502†.

ἄψ: *back, backward, back again, again;* freq. with verbs of motion, ἂψ ἰέναι, ἀπιέναι, ἀπονοστεῖν, στρέφειν, etc.; so ἂψ διδόναι, ἀφελέσθαι, ἂψ ἀρέσαι, Ι 120; ἂψ πάλιν, ἂψ αὖθις, Σ 280, Θ 335.

Ἀψευδής: a Nereid, Σ 46†.

ἀψίς, ῖδος: *mesh*, pl., Ε 487†.

ἀψό-ρροος (ῥέω): *back-flowing;* of the stream of Oceanus that returns into itself, Σ 399†.

ἄψ-ορρος (ὄρνῡμι): *returning, back again, back;* with verbs of motion, ἄψορροι ἑκίομεν, Φ 456; mostly neut. sing. as adv., ἄψορρον βῆναι, καταβῆναι, προσέφην, ι 501.

ἅψος, εος (ἅπτω): *joint, limb;* λύθεν δέ οἱ ἅψεα πάντα, her 'members' were relaxed in sleep, δ 794 and σ 189.

ἄω, inf. ᾄμεναι, fut. inf. ᾄσειν, aor. opt. ᾄσαιμι, subj. ᾄσῃ, inf. ᾄσαι, mid. fut. ᾄσεσθε, aor. inf. ᾄσασθαι: trans., *satiate;* τινά τινος, Ε 289; τινί, Λ 817; intrans., and mid., *sate oneself*, Ψ 157, Ω 717; met., (δοῦρα) λιλαιόμενα χροὸς ᾄσαι, eager to 'glut' themselves with flesh, Λ 574, Φ 70.

ἄωρος (ἀείρω), cf. μετέωρος: *dangling;* of the feet of Scylla, μ 89†.

ἄωρτο: see ἀείρω.

ἀωτέω: *sleep soundly*, w. ὕπνον, 'sunk in slumber,' Κ 159 and κ 548.

ἄωτος or **ἄωτον** (ἄϝημι): *floss, fleece;* of wool, α 443, ι 434; and of the 'nap' of linen, Ι 661.

B.

βάδην (*βαίνω*): *step by step*, N 516†.

βάζω, perf. pass. *βέβακται*: *talk*, *speak*, mostly with reference to one's way of thinking, and consequently of expressing himself; *ἄρτια, πεπνῡμένα, εὖ βάζειν*, and often in bad sense, *ἀνεμώλια, μεταμώνια, ἀπατήλια βάζειν, πάϊς ὣς νήπια βάζεις*, *pratest*, δ 32; *οὔτε ποτ' εἰν ἀγορῇ διχ' ἐβάζομεν οὔτ' ἐνὶ βουλῇ*, 'expressed divided sentiments,' γ 127; *ἔπος δ' εἴπερ τι βέβακται | δεινόν*, 'if a harsh word has been spoken,' θ 408.

βαθυ-δῑνήεις, *εντος* (*δίνη*): *deep-eddying*.

βαθυ-δίνης = *βαθυδῑνήεις*, epith. of rivers; *Ὠκεανός*, κ 511.

βαθύ-ζωνος (*ζώνη*): *deep-girdled*, i. e. with girdle low down over the hips, epith. of women. (See cut.)

20

Βαθυ-κλῆς: a Myrmidon, son of Chalcon, Π 594†.

βαθύ-κολπος: *deep-bosomed*, i. e. with deep folds in the garment, above the girdle over which the folds fell; epith. of Trojan women. (Il.) (See cut.)

βαθύ-λειμος (*λειμών*): *with deep* (grassy) *meadows*, epith of towns. (Il.)

βαθυ-λήιος (*λήιον*): *with deep* (high-waving) *grain*, Σ 550†.

βαθύνω: *deepen, hollow out*, Ψ 421†.

βαθυ-ρρείτης, ᾱο (*ῥέω*): *deep-flowing, deep-streaming; Ὠκεανός*, Φ 195†.

βαθύ-ρροος = *βαθυρρείτης*.

βαθύς, *εῖα, ύ*, gen. *βαθείης* and *βαθέης*, acc. *βαθεῖαν* and *βαθέην*, sup. *βάθιστος*: *deep; αὐλή*, deep as regards its high environments, E 142, ι 239; similarly *ἠιών*, or, as others interpret, 'deep-bayed,' B 92; naturally w. *Τάρταρος, λήιον, ὕλη, ἀήρ, λαῖλαψ*, etc.; met., *τὸν δ' ἄχος ὀξὺ κατὰ φρένα τύψε βαθεῖαν*, 'in the depths' of his heart, alta mente, T 125.

βαθύ-σχοινος: *deep* (grown) *with reeds*, Δ 383†.

βαίνω, fut. *βήσομαι*, aor. 1 *ἔβησα*, aor. 2 *ἔβην* or *βῆν, βῆ*, du. *ἐβήτην, βήτην, βάτην*, pl. *ἔβησαν, βῆσαν, ἔβαν, βάν*, subj. *βῶ, βείω, βήῃς, βήῃ*, inf. *βήμεναι*, perf. *βέβηκα*, 3 pl. *βεβάᾱσι*, inf. *βεβάμεν*, part. *βεβαώς, -ῶτα*, fem. *βεβῶσα*, plup. 3 sing. *βεβήκειν*, 3 pl. *βέβασαν*, mid. aor. (*ἐ*)*βήσετο*: *walk, step, go*, perf., *tread, stand* (have a footing), strictly of moving the legs apart, hence to denote the attitude of standing over to protect one, *ἀμφὶ δ' ἄρ' αὐτῷ βαῖνε λέων ὥς*, E 299; hence, too, the phrase *βῆ δ' ἰέναι, βῆ δὲ θέειν*, 'started for to go,' a graphic periphrasis for *ᾔει*, etc.; often in the sense of departing, *ἣ δ' Οὔλυμπόνδε βηβήκει*, 'was gone,' A 221; *ἐννέα βεβάᾱσιν ἐνιαυτοί*, 'have passed,' B 134; *πῇ δὴ συνθεσίαι τε καὶ ὅρκια βήσεται ἥμιν*, 'what is to become of?' B 339; so, *ἔβαν φέρουσαι, βῆ φεύγων*, etc.; *βήσετο δίφρον*, 'mounted,' apparently trans., really w. acc. of limit of motion, Γ 262; causative, aor. 1 act., *φῶτας ἐείκοσι βῆσεν ἀφ' ἵππων*, *made to go*, 'brought' down from their cars, Π 180; *βῆσαι ἵππους ἐπὶ Βουπρασίου*, 'bring' horses to B., Λ 756.

βάλανος, *ἡ*: *acorn*.

Βαλίος: name of one of the horses of Achilles, T 400.

βάλλω, fut. *βαλῶ*. *βαλέω*, aor. *ἔβαλον, βάλον*, subj. *βάλησθα*, opt. *βάλοι-*

σθα, plup. 3 sing. βεβλήκειν, pass. perf. 3 pl. βεβλήαται, plup. βεβλήατο (also, but only w. metaph. signif., βεβόλητο, βεβολήατο, βεβολημένος), mid. aor. with pass. signif., βλῆτο, subj. βλήεται, opt. 2 sing. βλεῖο, part. βλήμενος: *throw, cast*, mid., something pertaining to oneself; hence often in the sense of *shoot, hit; καὶ βάλεν οὐδ' ἀφάμαρτε*, N 160; ἕλκος, τό μιν βάλε Πάνδαρος ἰῷ (μίν is the primary obj.), E 795; metaph., φιλότητα μετ' ἀμφοτέροισι βάλωμεν, 'strike,' 'conclude,' Δ 16; σὺ δ' ἐνὶ φρεσὶ βάλλεο σῇσιν, 'bear in mind' (note the mid.), A 297, etc. The various applications, literal and metaphorical, are numerous but perfectly intelligible.—Intrans., ποταμὸς εἰς ἅλα βάλλων, Λ 722; ἵπποι περὶ τέρμα βαλοῦσαι, Ψ 462; mid. aor., with pass. signif., βλήμενος ἢ ἰῷ ἢ ἔγχεϊ, Θ 514; pass., of the mind only, ἄχεϊ μεγάλῳ βεβολημένος ἦτορ, 'stricken,' I 9, 3, κ 347.

βαμβαίνω: *totter* with fear, or, as others interpret, *stammer*, part., K 375†.

βάν: see βαίνω.

βάπτω: *dip*, ι 392†.

βαρβαρό-φωνος: *rude* (*outlandish*) *of speech*, B 867.

βάρδιστος: see βραδύς.

βαρέω: see βαρύνω.

βαρύθω: *be heavy*, by reason of a wound; ὦμος, Π 519†.

βαρύνω, ipf. or aor. 1 (ἐ)βάρῦνε, pass aor part. βαρυνθείς, perf. 2 βεβαρηώς: *weigh down, oppress by weight*; εἵματα γάρ ῥ' ἐβάρῦνε, while swimming, ε 321; κάρη πήληκι βαρυνθέν, Θ 388; mid., οἴνῳ βεβαρηότες, 'drunken,' γ 139, τ 122.

βαρύς, εῖα, ύ: *heavy*, oftener figurative than literal; σχέθε χεῖρα βαρεῖαν, stayed his 'heavy hand,' suggesting power, A 219; βαρείᾱς χεῖρας ἐποίσει, 'violent' hands, A 89; of 'grievous' pains, E 417; 'dread' fates, Φ 548; 'low,' 'gruff' voice, ι 257, etc.; adv., βαρύ and βαρέα στενάχειν, sigh 'deeply.'

βαρυστενάχων: see βαρύς, fin.

βασίλεια: *queen*; the queen's daughter, the *princess*, is termed βασίλεια in ζ 115; βασίλεια γυναικῶν, 'queen among women' (cf. δῖα γυναικῶν), λ 258.

βασιλεύς, ῆος: *king*, exercising the functions of commander-in-chief, priest, and judge; pl., βασιλῆες, *kings, nobles, chiefs*, termed σκηπτοῦχοι, διογενεῖς, διοτρεφεῖς.—Used adjectively w. ἀνήρ, Γ 170; ἄναξ, υ 194; hence comp. βασιλεύτερος, sup. βασιλεύτατος, *more, most kingly, princely*.

βασιλεύω: *be king* or *queen*, Z 425.

βασιλήιος: *royal*; γένος, Π 401†.

βασιληίς, ίδος: *royal*; τῑμή, Z 193†.

βάσκω (βαίνω): only imp., in the phrase βάσκ' ἴθι, *haste and fly!* addressed to the Dream-god, to Iris, and to Hermes, B 8, Ω 144, 336.

βαστάζω: *raise* (move by lifting), λ 594, (weigh in the hands), φ 405.

βάτην: see βαίνω.

Βατίεια (βάτος, 'Thorn-hill'): name of a height on the plain of Troy, before the city, B 813†.

βάτος, ἡ: pl., *thorn-bushes, thorns*, ω 230†.

βεβάᾱσι, βέβαμεν, βεβαώς: see βαίνω.

βεβαρηότα: see βαρύνω.

βεβίηκε: see βιάζω.

βεβλήαται, βεβολήατο, βεβολημένος: see βάλλω.

βεβρώθω (parallel form of βιβρώσκω): *eat, devour*, only opt., Δ 35†.

βεβρωκώς, βεβρώσεται: see βιβρώσκω.

βέῃ, βείομαι: see βέομαι.

βείω: see βαινω.

βέλεμνον = βέλος, only plural.

Βελλεροφόντης: *Bellerophon*, a Corinthian and Lycian hero, son of Glaucus and grandson of Sisyphus; his story, Z 153-197.

βέλος, εος (βάλλω): *missile, shot*; anything thrown, whether a *shaft* (arrow or dart), a stone, or the footstool hurled at Odysseus in ρ 464; of the effects of a shot, Θ 513; βέλος ὀξύ, sharp 'pang,' Λ 269; ἐκ βελέων, out of 'range.'

βέλτερος: *better*, only neut. sing., βέλτερον (ἐστί), foll. by inf., βέλτερον εἰ, ζ 282.

βένθος, εος (βαθύς): *depth*, also pl., *depths*; θαλάσσης πάσης βένθεα οἶδεν, α 53; βένθεα ὕλης, ρ 316; ἁλὸς βένθοσδε, 'into deep water,' δ 780.

βέομαι, βείομαι, 2 sing. βέῃ, pres. w.

fut. signif.: *shall* (*will*) *live*, Ο 194, Π 852, Χ 22, 431, Ω 131.

βέρεθρον: *abyss*, *chasm*, Θ 14, μ 94.

βῆ: see βαίνω.

βηλός (βαίνω): *threshold*. (Il.)

βῆμεν, βήμεναι: see βαίνω.

βήσαμεν, βῆσε, βήσετο: see βαίνω.

Βῆσσα: a town in Locris, Β 532†.

βῆσσα (βαθύς): *glen*, *ravine*; οὔρεος ἐν βήσσῃς, Γ 34, etc.

βητ-άρμων, ονος (βαίνω, root ἀρ): *dancer*, pl., θ 250 and 383.

βιάζω and **βιάω** (βίη), pres. 2 pl. βιάζετε, perf. βεβίηκα, mid. and pass. pres. βιάζεται, βιόωνται, opt. βιῴατο, ipf. βιάζετο, βιόωντο, mid. fut. βιήσομαι, aor. (ἐ)βιήσατο, part. βιησάμενος: *force*, *constrain*, mid., *overpower*, *treat with violence*; met., ἄχος βεβίηκεν Ἀχαιούς, 'overwhelmed,' Κ 145; pass. βιάζεσθαι βελέεσσιν, Λ 576; ὄνος παρ' ἄρουραν ἰὼν ἐβιήσατο παῖδας, 'forces his way in spite of the boys,' Λ 558; νῶι ἐβιήσατο μισθόν, 'forcibly withheld from us' (two accusatives as w. a verb of depriving), Φ 451; ψεύδεσσι βιησάμενος, 'overreaching,' Ψ 576.

βίαιος: *violent*; ἔργα, 'deeds of violence,' β 236.—Adv., **βιαίως**. (Od.)

Βίᾱς: (1) father of Laogonus and Dardanus, Υ 460.—(2) a leader of the Athenians, Ν 691.—(3) a Pylian, Δ 296.

βιάω: see βιάζω.

βιβάω, βιβάσθω, βίβημι (parallel forms of βαίνω), pres. part. βιβάσθων and βιβάς, acc. βιβάντα and βιβῶντα, fem. βιβῶσα: *stride* along, *stalk*; usually μακρὰ βιβάς, 'with long strides,' ὕψι βιβάντα, Ν 371.

βιβρώσκω, perf. part. βεβρωκώς, pass. fut. βεβρώσεται: *eat*, *devour*; χρήματα βεβρώσεται, β 203.

βίη, ης, dat. βίηφι: *force*, *violence*, in the latter sense usually pl., sing. ψ 31; βίη καὶ κάρτος, δ 415; οὐκ ἴς οὐδὲ βίη, σ 4; ἀρετῇ τε βίῃ τε, Ψ 578; rarely of the mind, οὐκ ἔστι βίη φρεσί, Γ 45; often in periphrases w. gen. of proper name, or w. adj., βίη Ἡρᾱκληείη, Αἰνείᾱο βίη, the might of Heracles, i. e. the mighty Heracles, etc.; βίῃ, *by force*, *in spite of*, βίῃ ἀέκοντος, δ 646, Α 430.

Βι-ήνωρ: a Trojan, Λ 92†.

βίος: *life*. (Od.)

βιός, οῖο: *bow*.

βίοτος (βίος): *life*, *livelihood*, *substance*, *goods*; πότμος βιότοιο, Δ 170; βίοτον καὶ νόστον, α 287; ἀλλότριον βίοτον νήποινον ἔδουσιν, α 160; βίοτος καὶ κτήματα, β 123.

βιόω, aor. 2 inf. βιῶναι, imp. 3 sing. βιώτω, mid. aor. ἐβιωσάμην: *live*; mid., causative, σὺ γάρ μ' ἐβιώσαο, 'didst save my life,' θ 468.

βιῴατο, βιόωνται, βιόωντο: see βιάζω.

βλάβομαι: see βλάπτω.

βλάπτω, βλάβω, aor. ἔβλαψα, βλάψα, pass. pres. βλάβεται, perf. part. βεβλαμμένος, aor. 1, 3 pl., ἐβλάφθησαν, part. βλαφθείς, aor. 2 ἐβλάβην, 3 pl. ἔβλαβεν, βλάβεν: *impede*, *arrest*; τόν γε θεοὶ βλάπτουσι κελεύθου, α 195; (ἵππω) ὄζῳ ἐνὶ βλαφθέντε, 'caught' in, Ζ 39, Ο 647; βλάψε δέ οἱ φίλα γούνατα, Η 271; so pass., βλάβεται γούνατα, 'totter,' ν 34; βεβλαμμένον ἦτορ, 'arrested in life's flow,' i. e. 'wounded in the heart,' Π 660; metaph., *harm* the mind, *infatuate*; τὸν δέ τις ἀθανάτων βλάψε φρένας, ξ 178; and without φρένας, (Ἄτη) βλάπτουσ' ἀνθρώπους, Ι 507; pass., βλαφθείς, Ι 512.

βλεῖο: see βάλλω.

βλεμεαίνω: *exult haughtily in*, *rave with*; regularly with σθένεϊ, also (θῡμός) περὶ σθένει βλεμεαίνει, the heart 'beats high' in its strength, Ρ 22.

βλέφαρον: *eyelid*, only dual and pl.

βλήεται, βλήμενος: see βάλλω.

βλῆτρον: *rivet* (or *ring*, *band*), Ο 678†.

βληχή: *bleating*, μ 266†.

βλοσυρός: doubtful word, *ferocious*, Η 212; perh. 'bushy,' Ο 608.

βλοσυρ-ῶπις (ὤψ): *with ferocious looks*, epith. of the Gorgon, Λ 36†.

βλωθρός: *tall*, of trees.

βλώσκω (for μλώσκω, root μολ), aor. 2 ἔμολον, subj. μόλῃ, part. μολών, -οῦσα; perf. μέμβλωκα: *go*, *come*.

βο-άγριον: *shield of ox-hide*, pl., Μ 22 and π 296.

Βοάγριος: a river in Locris, Β 533.

βοάω (βοή), βοάᾳ, βοόωσιν, inf. βοᾶν, part. βοόων, aor. (ἐ)βόησα, part. βοήσᾱς, βώσαντι: *shout*; μέγα, μακρά ('afar'), σμερδνόν, σμερδαλέον, ὀξύ, etc.; of things, **κῦμα, ἠιόνες**, 'resound,' 'roar,' Ξ 394, Ρ 265.

βόειος, βόεος (βοῦς): *of an ox* or *of oxen;* δέρμα, νεῦρα, and ('of ox-hide,' 'leather') ἱμάντες, κνημῖδες, ω 228.—As subst., **βοείη, βοέη,** *ox-hide, hide.*

βοεύς, ῆος (βοῦς): *thong of ox-hide,* on sails, β 426, ο 291.

βοή, ῆς: *shout, shouting, outcry;* freq. of the battle-cry, βοὴν ἀγαθός, i. e. good at fighting; also of a call to the rescue, alarm, κ 118, ξ 226, χ 77; and of a cry of pain, Z 465, ω 48, ι 401; βοὴν ἔχον (φόρμιγγες), 'kept sounding.' Σ 495.

Βοηθοΐδης: *son of Boethoüs,* Eteōneus. (Od.)

βοη-θόος (βοή, θέω): *running to the shout, battle-swift;* ἅρμα, P 481, and of men. (Il.)

βο-ηλασίη (βοῦς, ἐλαύνω): *cattle-lifting,* Λ 672†.

βοητύς, ύος (βοάω): *clamor,* α 369†.

βόθρος: *hole* in the ground; for planting trees, for sacrificial blood, λ 25; of a natural trough for washing clothes, ζ 92.

Βοίβη: a town in Thessaly, B 712†. —Hence **Βοιβηῒς** λίμνη, B 711†.

Βοιώτιος: *Boeotian;* subst. **Βοιωτοί,** *Boeotians.*

βολή (βάλλω): *throw, throwing, pelting,* only pl.; ὀφθαλμῶν βολαί, 'glances,' δ 150. (Od.)

βόλομαι: see βούλομαι.

βομβέω: of sounds that ring in the ears, *hum;* of a quoit whizzing through the air, θ 190; of oars dragging and 'rustling' in the water, μ 204.

βοόων: see βοάω.

βορέης, ᾱο, βορέω: *north wind;* epithets, αἰθρηγενέτης, αἰθρηγενής, ἀκρᾱής, κραιπνός.—Personified, *Boreas;* Βορέῃς (– –) καὶ Ζέφυρος, I 5, Ψ 195.

βόσις (βόσκω): *food;* ἰχθύσιν, T 268†.

βόσκω, fut. βοσκήσω, mid. ipf. (ἐ)βόσκετο, iter. βοσκέσκοντο: I. act., *feed, pasture;* of the herdsman, βοῦς βόσκ' ἐν Περκώτῃ, O 548, and of the element that nourishes, (νῆσος) βόσκει αἶγας, ι 124; Ἀμφιτρίτη κήτεα, μ 97; γαῖα ἀνθρώπους, λ 365, etc.—II. mid., *feed, graze,* δ 338, φ 49.

βοτάνη (βόσκω): *fodder, grass,* N 493 and κ 411.

βοτήρ, ῆρος: *shepherd,* pl., ο 504†.

βοτόν: only pl., βοτά, *flocks,* Σ 521†.

βοτρῡδόν (βότρυς): *in clusters;* of swarming bees, B 89†.

βότρυς, υος: *cluster of grapes,* pl., Σ 562†.

βού-βοτος: *kine-pasture,* ν 246†.

βού-βρωστις (βοῦς, βιβρώσκω): *ravenous hunger,* Ω 532†.

βουβών, ῶνος: *groin,* Δ 492†.

βου-γάϊος: *braggart, bully;* a term of reproach, N 824, σ 79.

Βούδειον: a town in Phthia, Π 572†.

βουκολέω (βουκόλος), ipf. iter. βουκολέεσκες: act., *pasture, tend cattle;* mid., *graze,* ἵπποι ἕλος κάτα βουκολέοντο, Y 221.

Βουκολίδης: *son of Bucolus,* Sphelus, O 338†.

Βουκολίων: a son of Laomedon, Z 22†.

βου-κόλος (βοῦς, root κελ): *cattle-driver, herdsman;* with ἄνδρες, N 571; ἀγροιῶται, λ 293.

βουλευτής: *counsellor;* γέροντες, elders *of the council* (βουλή), Z 114†.

βουλεύω (βουλή), fut. inf. βουλευσέμεν, aor. (ἐ)βούλευσα: *hold counsel, deliberate, advise, devise;* abs., B 347; βουλήν, βουλᾶς βουλεύειν, I 75, K 147; βουλεύειν τινι, I 99; ὁδὸν φρεσὶ βουλεύειν, α 444; κακόν τινι, ε 179; foll. by inf., I *thought* to, ι 299; by ὅπως, ι 420; mid., *devise, determine upon,* ἀπάτην, B 114, I 21.

βουλή: (1) *counsel, plan, decree;* βουλὴ δὲ κακὴ νίκησεν ἑταίρων, κ 46; Διὸς δ' ἐτελείετο βουλή, the 'will' of Zeus, A 5; οὔ τοι ἄνευ θεοῦ ἥδε γε βουλή, β 372, also in plural.—(2) the *council* of nobles or elders, γερόντων, B 53, 194, 202, γ 127, distinguished from the ἀγορά, or assembly.

βουλη-φόρος: *counsel-bearing, counselling;* ἀγοραί, ι 112; ἀνήρ, A 144; ἄναξ, M 414; also subst., *counsellor,* E 180, H 126.

βούλομαι, βόλομαι (βόλεται, βόλεσθε, ἐβόλοντο): *will, wish, prefer;* Τρώεσσι δὲ βούλετο νίκην, H 21, etc.; often with foll. ἤ, βούλομ' ἐγὼ λαὸν σῶν ἔμμεναι ἢ ἀπολέσθαι, A 117.

βου-λῡτός (βοῦς, λύω): time of *unyoking oxen* from the plough; ἠέλιος μετενίσσετο βουλῡτόνδε, began to verge towards *eventide,* Π 779, ι 58.

βου-πλήξ, ῆγος (πλήσσω): *ox-goad,* Z 135†.

Βουπράσιον: an ancient town of Elis, B 615.

βοῦς, βοός; acc. βοῦν (βῶν), pl. dat. βουσί and βόεσσι, acc. βόας and βοῦς: *cow* or *ox,* pl., *kine, cattle;* βοῦς ἄρσην, H 713, τ 420; ταῦρος βοῦς, P 389; usual epithets, ἀγελαίη, ἄγραυλος, εἰλίποδες, ἕλικες, ἐρίμῡκοι, ὀρθόκραιραι.—Also, as fem. subst., *ox-hide, shield of ox-hide,* acc. βῶν, H 238, 474, M 137.

βου-φονέω: *slaughter cattle,* H 466†.

βο-ῶπις, ιδος (βοῦς, ὤψ): *ox-eyed;* epith. of women (cf. 'eyes of a gazelle,' 'ox-eyed daisy'), H 10, Σ 40; often βοῶπις πότνια Ἥρη.

Βοώτης (= βούτης, Herdsman): *Boötes,* the constellation Arctūrus, ε 272†.

βραδύς, εῖα, ύ, sup. βάρδιστος: *slow.*

βραδυτής, ῆτος: *slowness,* T 411†.

βραχίων, ονος: *arm;* πρυμνός, *upper arm, shoulder.*

(βράχω), aor. ἔβραχε, βράχε: *clash, crack, bray,* (a word whose applications are difficult to reconcile); of armor, an axle, E 838; the earth (cf. 'crack of doom'), Φ 387; a river, Φ 9; a door, Φ 49; the wounded Ares, E 859, 863 a horse, Π 468.

βρέμω, mid. βρέμεται: *roar.*

βρέφος: *unborn young* (of a mule foal), Ψ 266†.

βρεχμός: *forehead,* E 586†.

Βριάρεως: *Briareus,* a hundred-armed water-giant, A 403.†

βριαρός (root βρι): *heavy.* (Il.)

βρίζω: *be drowsy, nod;* part. fig., 'napping,' Δ 223†.

βρι-ήπυος (ἠπύω): *loud-shouting,* N 521†.

βρῑθοσύνη (βρίθω): *weight,* E 839 and M 460.

βρῑθύς, εῖα, ύ: *heavy, ponderous.*

βρίθω (root βρι), ipf. βρῖθον, aor. ἔβρῑσα, perf. βέβρῑθα: *be heavy, weighed down;* σταφυλῇσι μέγα βρίθουσα ἀλωή, Σ 561, and once mid., μήκων καρπῷ βρῑθομένη, Θ 307; with gen., ταρσοὶ τῡρῶν βρῖθον, ι 219; τράπεζαι σίτου βεβρίθᾱσι, etc.; met., ἔρις βεβρῑθυῖα (= βρῑθεῖα), Φ 385.—Also *fall heavily upon, charge,* M 346, etc.; *preponderate, be superior* (by giving the most presents), ζ 159.

Βρῑσεύς: *Briseus,* king and priest in Lyrnessus, the father of Brisēis, A 392, I 132, 274.

Βρῑσηίς, ίδος: *Brisēis, daughter of Briseus,* a captive beloved by Achilles, A 184, T 282. (See cut, after a Panathenaic Amphora.)

βρομέω: *buzz,* Π 642†.

βρόμος (βρέμω): *roar, crackling,* Ξ 396†.

βροντάω, aor. (ἐ)βρόντησε: *thunder,* only with Ζεύς as subject.

βροντή, ῆς: *thunder.*

βρότεος (βροτός): *human;* φωνή, τ 545†.

βροτόεις (βρότος): *bloody, gory.* (Il.)

βροτο-λοιγός: *man-destroying;* epith. of warriors and of Ares.

βροτός (for μροτός, root μερ, μορ): *mortal;* βροτὸς ἀνήρ, βροτοὶ ἄνδρες, and as subst., *mortal man;* epithets, θνητοί, γ 3; δειλοί, ὀιζῡροί, μέροπες, ἐπιχθόνιος.

βρότος: *blood* (from a wound), *gore.*

βροτόω: only perf. pass. part. βεβροτωμένα, *made gory,* λ 41†.

βρόχος: *noose,* λ 278 and χ 472.

Βρῡσειαί: a town in Laconia, B 583†.

βρῡχάομαι, perf. w. pass. signif., *βέβρῡχα*, part. *βεβρῡχώς*, plup. 3 sing. *ἐβεβρύχειν*: *bellow, moan* · of waves, and of mortally wounded men, Π 486, ε 412.

βρύω: *teem, swell*, P 56†.

βρώμη, ης (*βιβρώσκω*): *food.* (Od.)

22

βρῶσις, ιος: *eating, food.*

βρωτύς, ύος: *food.*

βύβλινος (*βύβλος*): *made of papyrus*; ὅπλον νεός, φ 391†.

βύκτης (*βύζω*): *whistling, howling*, of winds, κ 20†.

βυσσο-δομεύω (*βυσσός, δέμω*): *build in the depths, brood*, always in bad sense; *κακὰ φρεσί*, ρ 66. (Od.)

βυσσός (= *βύθος*): the *deep, depths*, Ω 80†.

βύω: only perf. pass. part. *βεβυσμένον*, *stuffed full*, δ 134†.

βῶλος. *clod*, σ 374†.

βωμός (*βαίνω*): *step, pedestal*, η 100, *stand, platform, rack*, Θ 441, and esp. *altar*. (See cut.)

Βῶρος: (1) a Maeonian, father of Phaestus, E 44†.—(2) son of Periēres, husband of Polydōra, the daughter of Peleus, Π 177.

βῶν: see *βοῦς*.

βώσαντι: see *βοάω*.

βωστρέω: *call loudly upon*, μ 124†.

βωτι-άνειρα: *nourishing heroes*, A 155†.

βώτωρ, ορος (*βόσκω*): *shepherd*; pl., and w. *ἄνδρες*, M 302, ρ 200.

Γ.

γαῖα, γῆ: *earth, land;* distinguished from the heavens, (*κίονες*) *αἳ γαῖάν τε καὶ οὐρανὸν ἀμφὶς ἔχουσιν*, α 54; geographically, *Ἀχαιΐδα γαῖαν*, esp. native land, *πατρίδα γαῖαν*, pl., *οὐδέ τις ἄλλη* | *φαίνετο γαιάων ἀλλ' οὐρανὸς ἠδὲ θάλασσα*, ξ 302; as substance, *χυτὴ γαῖα*, for a grave, Z 464; *κωφὴ γαῖα*, 'silent dust,' Ω 54; prov., *ὑμεῖς πάντες ὕδωρ καὶ γαῖα γένοισθε*, H 99. The form *γῆ* is of less common occurrence, ν 233, ψ 233, Φ 63.—Personified, **Γαῖα,** O 36; *Γῆ*, Γ 104, T 259.

Γαιήιος, *υἱός*: son *of Earth*, η 324† (cf. λ 576).

γαιή-οχος (*ἔχω*): *earth-holding;* epith. of Poseidon.

γαίω: only part., *κύδεϊ γαίων*, *exulting in* his glory. (Il.)

γάλα, *γάλακτος*: *milk.*

γαλα-θηνός (*θῆσθαι*): *milk-sucking, sucking; νεβροί*, δ 336 and ρ 127.

Γαλάτεια (cf. *γαλήνη*): *Galatēa*, a Nereid, Σ 45†.

γαλήνη, ης: *calm* surface of the sea; *ἄνεμος μὲν ἐπαύσατο, ἡ δὲ γαλήνη* | *ἔπλετο νηνεμίη, κοίμησε δὲ κύματα δαίμων*, μ 168.

γαλόως, dat. sing. and nom. pl. *γαλόῳ*: *husband's sister*. Il.

γαμβρός (*γαμέω*, 'relative by marriage): *son-in-law*, Z 249; *brother-in-law*, N 464 and E 474.

γαμέω, fut. *γαμέω*, aor. *ἔγημε, γῆμε*, mid. *γαμέεσθαι*, fut. *γαμέσσεται*, aor. opt. *γήμαιτο*, inf. *γήμασθ(αι)*: *marry;* act. of the man, mid. of the woman (n u b e r e); once mid. of the parents, 'get a wife for their son,' I 394.

γάμος: *marriage, wedding, marriage-feast.*

γαμφηλή, ῆς: only pl. and of animals, *jaws.* (Il.)

γαμψ-ῶνυξ, υχος (ὄνυξ): *with crooked claws, talons,* αἰγυπιοί.

γανάω: *shine, be bright.*

γάνυμαι (γάνος), fut. γανύσσομαι: *be glad.*

Γανυμήδης: *Ganymede*, son of Tros, and cup-bearer of Zeus, E 266, Υ 232.

γάρ (γέ, ἄρα): *for, namely;* but often not to be translated, as in strong asseverations (esp. ἦ γάρ), A 293, 342, 355, and in questions, ὦ Κίρκη, πῶς γάρ με κέλεαι σοὶ ἤπιον εἶναι, 'how *canst* thou bid me?' κ 337; similarly after interjections, and in wishes, αἲ γάρ, εἰ or εἴθε γάρ. The causal (*for*) and explanatory (*namely*) uses need no illustration. ἀλλὰ . . . γάρ, *but yet, but really,* H 242, κ 202; freq. in combination (γάρ) δή, οὖν, ῥά, τέ, τοί.

Γάργαρον: name of the south peak of mount Ida in the Troad. (Il.)

γαστήρ, έρος (also gen. γαστρός, dat. -τρί): *belly; the womb,* Z 58; met. for hunger, ζ 133, etc.; *paunch, haggis,* σ 44.

γάστρη: *belly* of a caldron.

γαυλός: *milk-pail,* ι 223†.

γέ: enclitic particle, used to give prominence to a word or a statement; sometimes to be translated, *at least, at any rate,* but for the most part untranslatable, and only to be represented in English orally by the tone, in writing by italics; εἰ ζ ω ό ν γ' Αἴγισθον ἐνὶ μεγάροισιν ἔτετμεν | Ἀτρείδης, 'had Menelāus found Aegisthus at home *alive!*' γ 256; εἴπερ γάρ τε χ ό λ ο ν γε καὶ αὐτῆμαρ καταπέψῃ | ἀλλά τε καὶ μετόπισθεν ἔχει κότον, 'though he swallow his *wrath* . . . yet he retains a grudge, etc.,' A 81; hence γε may convert a slight word into a strong one, lending, as it does, another syllable, and preserving the acute tone, ὃ becomes ὅ γε, σὲ becomes σέ γε, etc.; even by preventing elision it is a means of force, you may call it a 'stop-gap,' yet it is not otiose. With other particles, ἄρα γε, εἴ γε, πρίν γε, πάρος γε, ἐπεί γε, etc.; freq. in neg. sentences, where it may sometimes be translated by an interjected *no*, as in affirmative sentences occasionally by *yes.* For repetition of γέ, cf. E 287 f.

γέγαα, γεγάᾱσι, γεγαώς: see γίγνομαι.

γέγηθα: see γηθέω.

γέγωνα, γεγωνέω, γεγώνω: the perf. w. pres. signif., inf. γεγωνέμεν, part. γεγωνώς, plup. (or ipf.) ἐγεγώνει, pres. inf. γεγωνεῖν, ipf. ἐγέγωνε, (ἐ)γεγώνευν: *make oneself heard* by a call; οὔ πώς οἱ ἔην βώσαντι γεγωνεῖν, M 337; ὅσσον τε γέγωνε βοήσᾱς (sc. τὶς), ε 400; *call, cry out to,* γέγωνέ τε πᾶν κατὰ ἄστυ, Ω 703; Κίκονες Κικόνεσσι γεγώνευν, ι 47.

γείνομαι (root γα), aor. ἐγεινάμην: pres. and ipf., *be born;* aor. causative, *bear, beget,* of both father and mother; ἐπὴν δὴ γείνεαι αὐτός, after thou hast thyself *created* them, υ 202.

γείτων, ονος: *neighbor.* (Od.)

γελαστός (γελάω): *ridiculous;* ἔργα, doings that bring ridicule upon the speaker, θ 307†.

γελάω, γελόω, part. γελόωντες, γελώοντες, ipf. 3 pl. γελώων, aor. (ἐ)γέλα(σ)σεν, 3 pl. γέλα(σ)σαν, part. γελά(σ)σᾱς: *laugh,* ἡδύ, 'heartily;' ἁπαλόν, ἀχρεῖον, δακρυόεν, χείλεσιν, only 'with the lips,' i. e. not from the heart, O 101; fig., γέλασσε δὲ πᾶσα περὶ χθὼν | χαλκοῦ ὑπὸ στεροπῆς, T 362; ἐμὸν δ' ἐγέλασσε φίλον κῆρ, 'laughed within me,' ι 413.

γελοιάω: γελοίων, γελοίωντες, restored readings γελώων, γελώοντες, see γελάω.

γελοίιος (γέλως): *laughable,* B 215†.

γέλος: see γέλως.

γελόω, γελόωντες, γελώοντες: see γελάω.

γέλως, γέλος, dat. γέλῳ, acc. γέλω and γέλον: *laughter;* γέλῳ ἔκθανον, 'laughed themselves to death,' σ 100.

γενεή, ῆς: *birth, lineage, race;* γενεῇ ὑπέρτερος, 'rank,' Λ 786; ὁπλότερος, 'age,' B 707; 'breed' of horses, E 265; 'generation,' Z 149, pl. A 250.

γενέθλη, ης (parallel form of γενεή): *race, stock;* ἀργύρου, 'home,' B 857.

γενειάς, άδος (γένειον): pl., *beard,* π 176†.

γενειάω: only aor. part. γενειήσαντα, just *getting a beard,* σ 176 and 269.

γένειον: *chin; γένειον λαβεῖν, ἅψασθαι*, done in supplicating a person, Α 501. (See cut under γουνόομαι.)

γένεσις: *generation, origin; Ὠκεανόν, θεῶν γένεσιν*, Ξ 201, 246, 302.

γενετή, ῆς: *birth; ἐκ γενετῆς*, 'from the hour of birth,' σ 6.

γενναῖος (γέννα): *according to* one's *birth, native* to one; *οὐ γάρ μοι γενναῖον*, 'not my way,' Ε 253†.

γένος, εος (root γα): *family, race, extraction; ἡμιθέων, ἀνδρῶν, βοῶν γένος*, and of the individual, 'scion,' *ἀνὴρ . . . σὸν γένος*, Τ 124, etc.; *γένει ὕστερος*, 'birth,' 'age,' Γ 215; *γένεα*, 'generations,' γ 245.

γέντο, defective aor. 3 sing: *grasped*. (Il.)

γένυς, υος, acc. pl. *γένῡς*: *under jaw, jaw*, of men and animals.

γεραιός: *old, aged, venerable;* only subst. in Homer, *δῖε γεραιέ*, Ω 618; *Φοῖνιξ ἄττα, γεραιὲ διοτρεφές*, Ι 607; *παλαιγενές*, Ρ 561; *γεραιαί*, Ζ 87.—Comp., **γεραίτερος.**

γεραίρω: *honor* (with a γέρας), *show honor to*, Η 321, ξ 437.

Γεραιστός: name of the promontory at the S. extremity of Euboea, now Geresto, γ 177†.

γέρανος, ἡ: *crane*. (Il.)

γέραρος, comp. *γεραρώτερος*: *stately*, Γ 170 and 211.

γέρας, αος, pl. *γέρα*: *gift of honor, honor, prerogative;* nobles and esp. the king received *γέρα* from the commonalty, *γέρας θ' ὅ τι δῆμος ἔδωκεν*, η 150; of the kingly office itself, Υ 182, λ 175; of offerings to the gods, and burial honors of the dead, *τὸ γὰρ γέρας ἐστὶ θανόντων*.

Γερήνιος: *Gerenian*, epith. of Nestor, from Gerenia in Laconia or Messenia; *Γερήνιος ἱππότα Νέστωρ*, also *Νέστωρ . . . Γερήνιος, οὖρος Ἀχαιῶν*, γ 411, etc.

γερούσιος: *pertaining to* the council of *the elders, senatorial; οἶνος*, ν 8; *ὅρκος*, Χ 119.

γέρων, οντος, voc. *γέρον*: *old man* (s e n e x), and specially, mostly in pl., *elders*, members of the council (*βουλὴ γερόντων*), cf. Lat. s e n a t o r.—As adj., *πατὴρ γέρων*, Α 358, neut. *γέρον σάκος*, χ 184.

γεύομαι (γεύω), fut. *γεύσομαι*, aor. inf. *γεύσασθαι*: *taste*, with gen., met., *γευσόμεθ' ἀλλήλων ἐγχείῃσιν*, Υ 258; *χειρῶν*, 'fists,' υ 181.

γέφῡρα, only pl.: *dams, dikes; τὸν δ' οὔτ' ἄρ τε γέφῡραι ἐεργμέναι ἰσχανόωσι*, Ε 88; met., *πτολέμοιο γεφῦραι*, 'bridges of war,' the lanes between files and columns on the battle-field.

γεφῡρόω, aor. *γεφύρωσε*: *dam up* a river, Φ 245; *κέλευθον*, 'make a causeway,' Ο 357.

γῆ, Γῆ: see *γαῖα*.

γηθέω, aor. *γήθησα*, perf. *γέγηθα*: *rejoice, be glad;* freq. w. part., *γήθησεν ἰδών*, etc.; sometimes w. acc., *τάδε*, ι 77; acc. of part., *εἰ νῶι . . . Ἕκτωρ γηθήσει προφανέντε*, Θ 378.

γηθοσύνη (γηθέω): *joy, gladness*, dat., Ν 29 and Φ 390.

γηθόσυνος: *glad*.

γηράς: see *γηράσκω*.

γῆρας, αος, dat. *γήραϊ* and *γήραι*: *old age*.

γηράσκω, aor. 2 *ἐγήρᾱ*, part. *γηράς*: *grow old;* of fruit, 'ripen,' η 120.

γῆρυς: *speech*, Δ 437†.

Γίγαντες: the *Giants*, a wild race related to the gods, η 59, 206, and κ 120.

γίγνομαι (root γα), aor. iter. *γενέσκετο*, perf. *γέγονε*, 3 pl. *γεγάᾱσι*, inf. *γεγάμεν*, part. acc. sing. *γεγαῶτα*, pl. *-ῶτας*, plup. *γεγόνει*: *become*, (of men) *be born;* the word admits of great variety in paraphrase, but never departs from its meaning of *come into being; ἄνθεα γίγνεται*, 'grow'; *κλαγγὴ γένετο*, 'arose,' 'was heard'; *ποθὴ Δαναοῖσι γένετο*, 'filled,' 'they felt'; *νῶι νόστον ἔδωκε νηυσὶ γενέσθαι*, i. e. the accomplishment of it, δ 173; *οὐκ ἂν ἔμοιγε | ἐλπομένῳ τὰ γένοιτο*, I may hope, but this will not 'happen,' γ 228; *πάντα γιγνόμενος*, Proteus, 'turning into' every shape, δ 417; *ἐπὶ νηυσὶ γενέσθαι*, 'get' upon the ships, and thus often implying motion, e. g. *πρὸ ὁδοῦ γένοντο*, 'progressed,' Δ 382; never of course the same as *εἶναι*, but the perf. is sometimes a strong equivalent of the verb of existence, *τοῖς οἳ νῦν γεγάᾱσι*, who 'live' now, ω 84, ν 160, etc.

γιγνώσκω, fut. *γνώσομαι, γνώσεαι*, aor. *ἔγνων*, subj. *γνώω, -ομεν, -ωσι*, inf. *γνώμεναι*: *come to know*, (*learn to*) *know*, the verb of *insight; γιγνώσκων ὅ τ' ἄναλκις ἔην θεός*, 'perceiving,' E 331; *ἀμφὶ ἓ γιγνώσκων ἑτάρους*, 'recognizing,' O 241; *ὁμηλικίην ἐκέκαστο | ὄρνῑθας γνῶναι*, in 'understanding' birds, β 159.

γλάγος, *τό* (*γάλα*): *milk*, B 471 and Π 643.

γλακτο-φάγος (*φαγεῖν*): *living on milk*, N 6†.

Γλαύκη: a Nereid, Σ 39†.

γλαυκιάω: only part., *with gleaming* or *glaring eyes*, of a lion, Υ 172†.

γλαυκός: *gleaming* (but with reference to the effect of color, grayish-blue); *θάλασσα* (cf. 'old ocean's gray and melancholy waste'), Π 34†.

Γλαῦκος: *Glaucus*.—(1) the son of Sisyphus, and father of Bellerophon, Z 154 ff.—(2) grandson of Bellerophon, and a leader of the Lycians, H 13, Z 119.

γλαυκ-ῶπις, *ιδος*: *gleaming-eyed* (and with reference to the color, grayish-blue); epith. of the warlike goddess Athēna.

Γλαφύραι: a town in Thessaly, B 712†.

γλαφυρός: *hollow;* often of ships; of the *φόρμιγξ*, θ 257; a grotto, Σ 402, β 20; a harbor, μ 305.

γλήνη: *pupil* of the eye, ι 390; as term of reproach, *κακὴ γλήνη*, 'doll,' 'girl,' *coward*, Θ 164.

γλῆνος, *εος*: pl., *jewelry*, Ω 192†.

Γλίσᾱς, *αντος*: a town in Boeotia, B 504†.

γλουτός: *rump, buttock*, E 66, Θ 340. (Il.)

γλυκερός (comp. *γλυκερώτερος*) = *γλυκύς*.

γλυκύθῡμος: *sweet-tempered*, Υ 467†.

γλυκύς, *εῖα, ύ*, comp. *γλυκίων*: *sweet; νέκταρ*, A 598; metaph., *ὕπνος, ἵμερος, αἰών*.

γλυφίς, *ίδος* (*γλύφω*): *notch* of an arrow; besides the notch for the string there were others to secure a firm hold with the fingers in drawing the bow, Δ 122, φ 419.

γλῶσσα, *ης*: *tongue, language*, B 804, Δ 438.

γλωχίς, *ῖνος* (*γλῶσσα*): any *tongue-like point;* of the end of a yoke-strap, Ω 274†. (See cut under *ζυγόν*, letter *b*, No. 45.)

γναθμός: *jaw, cheek;* for υ 347, see *ἀλλότριος*.

γναμπτός (*γνάμπτω*): *bent, bending;* of the limbs of living beings, *supple*, ν 398; met., *νόημα*, 'placable,' Ω 41.

γνάμπτω, aor. *γνάμψα*: *bend.*

γνήσιος (*γίγνομαι*): *genuine, legitimate.*

γνύξ (*γόνυ*): adv., *with bent knee, upon the knee.*

γνῷ, γνώμεναι, γνῶομεν: see *γιγνώσκω*.

γνώριμος: *known* to one, an 'acquaintance,' π 9†.

γνωτός: *known;* also, *related* by blood, Γ 174; *brother*, P 35, etc.

γοάω (*γόος*), inf. *γοήμεναι*, part. *γοόων, γοόωντες* (*γοῶντες*), ipf. *γόον, γόων*, iter. *γοάασκεν*, fut. *γοήσεται*: *wail*, esp. in lamentation for the dead; w. acc., *bewail*, *τινά*, Z 500, etc.; *πότμον*, Π 857.

γόμφος: wooden *nail, peg*, pl., ε 248†.

γονή: *offspring*, Ω 539 and δ 755.

Γονόεσσα: a town in Achaea, near Pellēne, B 573†.

γόνος, *ὁ*: *birth, origin;* then *offspring* (son), *young*, δ 12, Z 191, μ 130.

γόνυ, gen. *γούνατος* and *γουνός*, pl. *γούνατα* and *γοῦνα*, gen. *γούνων*, dat. *γούνασι* and *γούνεσσι*: *knee; γόνυ κάμπτειν*, phrase for sitting down to rest, *ἐπὶ γούνεσσι καθίσσᾱς*, taking upon the 'lap,' I 488, E 370; freq. as typical of physical strength, *εἰσόκε μοι φίλα γούνατ' ὀρώρῃ*, so long as my 'knees can spring,' so long as my strength shall last; but oftenest of suddenly failing strength, swooning, death, *πολλῶν ἀνδρῶν ὑπὸ γούνατ' ἔλῡσεν* (Helen caused the death of many men); *λύτο γούνατα*, δ 703, 'knees were relaxed,' of Penelope. From the custom of embracing the knees in supplication come the phrases *γοῦνα* or *γούνων λαβεῖν, ἅψασθαι, ὑπὲρ γούνων* or *γούνων λίσσεσθαι*, 'by' the knees, 'by your life'; hence *θεῶν ἐν γούνασι κεῖται*, 'rests with' the gods, 'in the gift' of the gods, α 267.

γόον: see *γοάω*.

γόος: *wailing, lamentation; γόον δ' ὠίετο θῡμός*, 'his soul was engrossed with woe,' he was ready to burst into wailing, *κ* 248.

γοόω: see *γοάω*.

Γόργειος: *of the Gorgon; κεφαλή*, 'the Gorgon's head,' E 741, λ 634.

Γοργυθίων: son of Priam and Castianeira, Θ 302†.

Γοργώ, οῦς: the *Gorgon*, a monster that inspired terror by her looks, *βλοσυρῶπις, δεινὸν δερκομένη*, Λ 36.

Γόρτυς or **Γόρτῡν, ῡνος**: *Gortȳna*, a city in Crete, *γ* 294 and B 646.

γοῦν: sometimes written for *γ' οὖν*.

γουνάζομαι (*γόνυ*), fut. *γουνάσομαι*: *supplicate, beseech, implore*, strictly to kneel (clasping the knees of the person addressed, see under *γόνυ*), *γούνων γουνάζεσθαι*, X 345, cf. 338 (*ὑπὲρ γούνων*).

γούνατα, γούνασι, γούνεσσι: see *γόνυ*.

Γουνεύς: leader of two tribes of Pelasgians, B 748†.

γουνόομαι (*γόνυ*)=*γουνάζομαι*, q. v.; foll. by fut. inf. from the sense of 'vowing' implied, *κ* 521. (See cut, from ancient gem, representing Dolon and Ulysses.)

23

γουνός: probably (if from *γόνυ*) *curve, slope;* of hilly places, *γουνὸν Ἀθηναίων*, λ 323 (cf. Hdt. iv. 99); *ἀλωῆς*, *α* 193, Σ 57.

γραῖα: *old woman*, *α* 438†.

Γραῖα: a town in Boeotia, B 498†.

γραπτύς, ύος, acc. pl. *γραπτῦς*: *scratch*, *ω* 229†.

γράφω, aor. *γράψε*: *scratch, graze; ὀστέον*, reached by the point of the lance, P 599; *σήματα ἐν πίνακι*, symbols graven on a tablet, Z 169.

Γρήνῑκος· the river *Granīcus*, which rises in Mount Ida, M 21†.

γρηῦς, γρῆυς, dat. *γρηΐ*, voc. *γρηῦ* and *γρῆυ*: *old woman*.

γύαλον: *convexity*, of cuirass; *γυάλοισιν ἀρηρότα*, fitted together of *convex plates*, O 530. See *θώρηξ*. (Il.)

Γυγαίη: *λίμνη*, the *Gygaean* lake, in Lydia, near Sardis, Υ 391. Also the nymph of this lake, B 865.

γυῖον: only pl., *joints, ποδῶν γυῖα*, N 512; then, *limbs, members, γυῖα λέλυνται* (see *γόνυ*), *κάματος ὑπήλυθε γυῖα, γυῖα ἐλαφρὰ θεῖναι*, E 122; *ἐκ δέος εἵλετο γυίων*, ζ 140.

γυιόω, fut. *γυιώσω*: *lame*, Θ 402 and 416.

γυμνός: *naked; τόξον*, taken from its case, λ 607; *ὀιστός*, from the quiver, as we say 'naked sword,' φ 417; then, usually, *unarmed*, Φ 50, X 124.

γυμνόω, mid. pres. *γυμνοῦσθαι*, pass. aor. (*ἐ*)*γυμνώθην*: *strip, denude;* in Hom. only mid. and pass., ζ 222; *ῥακέων ἐγυμνώθη*, 'threw off,' we should say, *χ* 1. Usually of being 'disarmed,' *γυμνωθέντα βραχίονα*, i. e. unprotected by the shield, M 389; *τεῖχος ἐγυμνώθη*, M 399.

γυναικεῖος (*γυνή*); *of women; βουλαί*, λ 437†.

γυναι-μανής (*μαίνομαι*): *woman-mad;* Paris, Γ 39. (Il.)

γύναιος = *γυναικεῖος, δῶρα*, λ 521 and *ο* 247.

γυνή, *γυναικός*: *woman; γυνὴ ταμίη, δέσποινα, γρηῦς, ἀλετρίς, δμωαὶ γυναῖκες*, etc.; *wife*, Z 160, etc.

Γῦραί: *πέτραι*, the *Gyraean* rocks,

24

near Naxos, where the lesser Ajax was shipwrecked, δ 500.—Hence, adj., **Γῡραῖος,** Γῡραίη πέτρῃ, δ 507.

γῡρός: ἐν **ὤμοισιν,** *round*-shouldered, τ 246†.

Γυρτιάδης: *son of Gyrtius*, Hyrtius, Ξ 512†.

Γυρτώνη: a town in Pelasgiōtis, on the river Penēus, B 738†.

γύψ, du. γῦπε, pl. nom. γῦπες, dat. γύπεσσι: *vulture.*

γωρῡτός: *bow-case*, φ 54†. (See cuts, No. 24, from Greek and Assyrian representations.)

Δ.

δα-: an inseparable prefix, with intensive meaning, cf. δά-σκιος.

ΔΑ (the root of διδάσκω), aor. 2 act. δέδαε, aor. 2 pass. ἐδάην, subj. δαείω, δαῶμεν, inf. δαῆναι, δαήμεναι, fut. δαήσομαι, perf. δεδάηκα, part. δεδαώς, δεδαηκότες, mid. aor. inf. δεδάασθαι: (1) *teach*, only aor. 2 act. δέδαε (τινά τι), ζ 233, θ 448, χ 160, w. inf., υ 72.—(2) *learn, be instructed*, the other forms; w. gen., πολέμοιο δαήμεναι, 'become skilled in,' Φ 487; ἐμεῦ δαήσεαι, 'from me,' τ 325; w. acc. οὐ δεδαηκότες ἀλκήν, β 61; δεδάασθαι γυναῖκας, 'find out,' π 316.

δαήμων, ονος (root δα): *skilled in;* w. gen., also ἔν τινι.

δαῆναι, δαήσεαι, δαῶμεν: see ΔΑ.

δᾱήρ, έρος, voc. δᾶερ: *husband's brother;* δᾱέρων πολὺ φίλτατε πάντων, Ω 762; the same scansion also v. 769. (Il.)

δάηται: see δαίω 1.

δαί: used colloquially in questions; τίς δαὶ ὅμῑλος ὅδ' ἔπλετο, '*pray*, what throng is this?' α 225 (vulg. δέ), ω 299, K 408 (vulg. δ' αἰ).

δαΐ: see δαΐς.

δαιδάλεος (root δαλ): *cunningly* or *skilfully wrought* or *decorated.*

δαιδάλλω (root δαλ): *elaborate skilfully, decorate.*

δαίδαλον (root δαλ): *cunning work, piece of artistic workmanship;* usually pl.

Δαίδαλος (root δαλ): a typical name, *Daedalus*, a famous artist of Crete, Σ 592†.

δαΐζω (δαίω 2), fut. δαΐξω, pass. perf. part. δεδαϊγμένος: *cleave, cut asunder;* of carving, ξ 434, but usually of wounding, hence *cut down, slay*, Φ 147; pass. δεδαϊγμένον ὀξέι χαλκῷ, Σ 236, etc.; metaph., two expressions are to be distinguished, ἐδαΐζετο θῡμός, 'rent' with cares, sorrows, I 9, ν 320, and ὥρμαινε δαϊζόμενος κατὰ θῡμὸν | διχθάδια, a 'divided' mind, Ξ 20.

δαϊ-κτάμενος: *killed in battle*, Φ 146 and 301.

δαιμόνιος, in Hom. only voc., δαιμόνιε, δαιμονίη, δαιμόνιοι: *under the influence of a δαίμων, possessed;* used in both good and bad sense, and to be translated according to the situation described in the several passages where it occurs, A 561, B 190, 200, Γ 399, Δ 31, Z 407, Ω 194, δ 774, κ 472, σ 15, ψ 174.

δαίμων, ονος: *divinity, divine power;* sometimes equivalent to θεός, but esp. of the gods in their dealings with men, Γ 420; σὺν δαίμονι, 'with the help of God,' κακὸς δαίμων, δαίμονος αἶσα κακή, etc.; hence freq. 'fate,' 'destiny,' πάρος τοι δαίμονα δώσω, thy 'death,' Θ 166.

δαίνυ(ο): see δαίνῡμι.

δαίνῡμι (δαίω 2), imp. 2 sing. **δαίνῡ,** part. δαινύντα, ipf. δαίνῡ, fut. inf. δαίσειν, mid. pres. opt. δαινῦτο, -ύατο, aor. part. δαισάμενος: I. act., *divide, distribute* food, to each his portion, said of the host; δαίνῡ δαῖτα γέρουσιν, I 70; hence, 'give a feast, τάφον, γάμον, funeral, marriage-feast, γ 309, T 299.—II. mid., *partake of* or *celebrate* a feast, *feast* (*upon*); abs., O 99, Ω 63; w. acc., δαῖτα, εἰλαπίνην, **κρέα καὶ μέθυ,** ι 162.

1. δαΐς, *ίδος* (*δαίω* 1): *torch,* only pl. (The torch consisted of a number of pine splinters bound together. See cut.)

25

2. δαΐς: *combat,* only dat., *ἐν δαῒ λυγρῇ, λευγαλέῃ,* N 286, Ξ 387.

δαίς, *δαιτός* (*δαίνῡμι*): *feast, banquet, meal;* once (in a simile) of a wild animal, Ω 43.

δαίτη = *δαίς*: *δαίτηθεν, from the feast,* κ 216.

δαιτρεύω (*δαιτρός*): *distribute;* esp. of carving meat; of booty, Λ 688.

δαιτρόν: *portion,* Δ 262†.

δαιτρός: *carver.* (See cut.)

26

δαιτροσύνη: *art of carving and distributing,* π 253†.

δαιτύμων, *ονος* (*δαιτύς*): *banqueter,* pl. (Od.)

δαιτύς, *ύος* = *δαίς,* Χ 496.†

Δαίτωρ: a Trojan, Θ 275†.

δαΐ-φρων, *ονος*: (if from *δαίω* 1) *fiery-hearted;* in Il., of warriors; in Od., in other relations, θ 373, ο 356.

1. δαίω, perf. *δέδηα,* plup. *δεδήειν,* mid. aor. subj. *δάηται*: I. trans. (act. exc. perf.), *kindle, set in a blaze; δαῖέ οἱ ἐκ κορυθός τε καὶ ἀσπίδος ἀκάματον πῦρ,* the goddess 'made fire blaze' from his helmet, etc., Ε 5, 7, so pass., Φ 376. — II. intrans. (mid. and perf.), *blaze,* Φ 375, Σ 227, etc.; met. *ὄσσε, πόλεμος, ἔρις, μάχη ἐνοπή τε,* Μ 35; *Ὄσσα,* Β 93; *οἰμωγή,* υ 353.

2. δαίω, only pres. and ipf. mid. and pass., and perf. *δεδαίαται*: *divide,* mid. *distribute,* ο 140 and ρ 332; *ἀλλά μοι ἀμφ' Ὀδυσῆι δαΐφρονι δαίεται ἦτορ,* my heart is 'rent' (cf. *δαΐζω*), α 48.

δάκνω, only aor. 2 *δάκε,* inf. *δακέειν*: *bite,* Σ 585; met., *φρένας,* 'stung,' Ε 493. (Il.)

δάκρυ, pl. *δάκρυα,* dat. *δάκρυσι*: *tear.*

δακρυόεις, *εσσα, εν*: *weeping, tearful; δακρυόεν γελάσᾱσα,* 'through her tears,' Ζ 484; applied to *πόλεμος, μάχη,* Ε 737.

δάκρυον=*δάκρυ.* **δακρυόφιν,** seven times.

δακρυ-πλώω: *swim* with tears; of effect of intoxication on the eyes, τ 122†. (Also written as two words.)

δακρυχέων, *ουσα*: now written as two words, see *χέω.*

δακρύω, aor. *ἐδάκρῡσα,* pass. perf. *δεδάκρῡμαι*: *weep,* aor. *burst into tears;* perf. pass., *be in tears,* Π 7.

δᾱλός (*δαίω* 1): *fire-brand.*

δαμάζω: see *δάμνημι.*

δάμαρ, *δάμαρτος* (*δάμνημι*): *wife,* always w. gen. of the husband. Cf. opp. *παρθένος ἄδμης.*

δάμνημι, δαμνάω, ipf. (*ἐ*)*δάμνᾱ,* fut. *δαμᾷ, δαμάᾳ, δαμόωσι,* aor. *ἐδάμα(σ)σα,* pass. *δάμναμαι,* 2 sing. *δαμνᾷ,* pass. aor. 1 *ἐδμήθην,* imp. *δμηθήτω,* part. *δμηθείς,* also *ἐδαμάσθην, δαμνάσθη,* aor. 2 *ἐδάμην, δάμη,* 3 pl. *δάμεν,* subj. *δαμείω, δαμήῃς, -ήῃ, -ήετε,* opt. *δαμείη,* 3 pl. *-εῖεν,* inf. *-ῆναι, -ήμεναι,* part. *-είς,* perf. *δεδμήμεσθα,* part. *δεδμημένος,* plup. *δεδμήμην, δέδμητο, δέδμηντο, δεδμήατο,* mid. aor. (*ἐ*)*δαμασσάμην,* subj. *δαμάσσεται,* etc.: *tame, subdue,* mid., for oneself; of taming, 'breaking' animals, Ρ 77, δ 637 (cf. *ἱπποδάμος*); subjecting as a wife, Σ 432, Γ 301 (cf. *δάμαρ*); and, generally, of 'reducing to subjection,' 'overcoming,' in war or otherwise, 'laying low' in battle; of things as well as of persons, **τὸν** *δ' οὐ βέλος ὠκὺ δάμασσεν,* Ε 106, 391; met., *ἔρος θῡμόν,* Ξ 316, etc.; pass. freq. in all the above relations.

Δάμασος: a Trojan, Μ 183.

Δαμαστορίδης: *son of Damastor.* —(1) Tlepolemus, Π 416. —(2) Agelāus, a suitor of Penelope, υ 321.

δαμείω, δάμεν, δαμήῃ, δαμήμεναι, δαμόωσι: see *δάμνημι.*

Δανάη: *Danaë,* daughter of Acrisius, and mother of Perseus, Ξ 319.

Δαναοί: the *Danaäns,* freq. collective designation of the Greeks before Troy.

δᾱνός (*δαίω* 1): *dry,* ο 322†.

δάος, τό (δαίω 1): *fire-brand, torch.* (See cut.)

27

δά-πεδον (πέδον): *ground, pavement,* floor beaten down hard, esp. in houses, δ 627, *floor.*

δάπτω, fut. δάψω, aor. ἔδαψα: *tear, rend, devour;* strictly of wild animals; fig. of the spear, and of fire, Ψ 183. (Il.)

Δαρδανίδης: *son* or descendant *of Dardanus;* Priam, Ilus.

Δαρδανίη: *Dardania,* the city founded by Dardanus, Υ 216†.

Δαρδάνιαι, πύλαι, the *Dardanian* gate of Troy, Ε 789, Χ 194, 413.

Δαρδάνιοι, Δάρδανοι, Δαρδανίωνες, fem. **Δαρδανίδες**: *Dardanians.* inhabitants of Dardania; often named in connection with the Trojans, as representatives of the allies, Β 819, 839, Γ 456.

Δάρδανος: (1) son of Zeus, the founder of Dardania, and progenitor of the Trojans, Υ 215, 219, 304.—(2) son of Bias, Υ 460†.

δαρδάπτω (= δάπτω): *devour,* Λ 479; fig., ξ 92, π 315.

Δάρης: a priest of Hephaestus, Ε 9 and 27.

δαρθάνω, aor. ἔδραθε: *sleep,* υ 143†.

δασάσκετο, δάσασθαι: see δατέομαι.

δά-σκιος (σκιά): *thick-shaded,* Ο 273 and ε 470.

δασμός (δατέομαι): *division,* of booty, Α 166†.

δάσονται, δάσσατο: see δατέομαι.

δασπλῆτις: doubtful word, *hard-smiting;* epith. of the Erinnys, ο 234†.

δασύ-μαλλος: *thick-fleeced,* ι 425†.

δασύς, εῖα, ύ: *thick, shaggy,* ξ 49 and 51.

δατέομαι (δαίω 2), ipf. 3 pl. δατεῦντο, fut. δάσονται, aor. δασσάμεθα, ἐδάσαντο, iter. δασάσκετο, perf. pass. 3 sing. δέδασται: *divide with each other, divide (up);* πατρώια, μοίρᾱς, ληίδα, κρέα, etc.; of simply 'cutting asunder,' α 112, τὸν μὲν Ἀχαιῶν ἵπποι ἐπισσώτροις δατέοντο, Υ 394; χθόνα ποσσὶ δατεῦντο (ἡμίονοι), Ψ 121; met., Τρῶες καὶ Ἀχαιοὶ | ἐν μέσῳ ἀμφότεροι μένος Ἄρηος δατέονται, Σ 264.

Δαυλίς: a town in Phocis, Β 520†.

δάφνη: *laurel, bay,* ι 183†.

δα-φοινός and **δα-φοινεός**: *(blood) red,* Σ 538; of serpent, jackal, lion, Β 308, Κ 23, Λ 474.

δέ: *but, and;* strictly neither adversative nor copulative, but used to *offset* statements or parts of statements; such offsetting or coördination ('parataxis') by means of δέ, when it appears in place of the to us more familiar subordination of ideas ('hypotaxis'), gives rise to the translation 'while,' 'though,' 'for,' etc. Hence δέ appears even in the apodosis of conditional or temporal sentences, οἳ δ' ἐπεὶ οὖν ἤγερθεν . . τοῖσι δ' ἀνιστάμενος μετέφη, when they were all assembled, 'then' arose Achilles, Α 57, 137. The other extreme, of an apparently adversative force, is best seen in negative sentences where δέ is (rarely) used for ἀλλά, ι 145. With other particles, καί ('also') δέ, (δέ) τε, ἄρα, αὖ, δή. δέ is placed as second (or third) word in its clause, but a vocative is not counted, γ 247.

-δε: inseparable enclitic suffix, appended to accusatives, denoting direction *towards;* e. g. οἰκόνδε, doubled in ὅνδε δόμονδε, with ellipsis of δόμον in Ἄιδόσδε.

δέατ(ο): defective ipf., *appeared, seemed,* ζ 242†. Cf. δοάσσατο.

δέγμενος: see δέχομαι.

δέδαα, δεδάηκα: see ΔΑ.

δεδαίαται, δέδασται: see δατέομαι.

δεδαϊγμένος: see δαΐζω.

δέδηε, δεδήει: see δαίω 1.

δεδίᾱσι: see δείδω.

δεδίσκομαι and **δειδίσκομαι** (δείκνῡμι): *bid welcome* or *farewell* (by gesture), *pledge;* δέπαϊ, δεξιτερῇ χειρί. (Od.)

δεδμήατο, δεδμημένος: see δάμνημι.

δεδοκημένος: see δοκάω.

δέδορκε: see δέρκομαι.

δεδραγμένος: see δράσσομαι.

δέελος = δῆλος, Κ 466†.

δεῖ (δέω): τί δὲ δεῖ πολεμιζέμεναι Τρώεσσιν | Ἀργείους; 'Why should the Greeks be warring with the Trojans?' Ι 337. Elsewhere χρή in Homer.

δείδεκτο, δειδέχαται: see δείκνῡμι.

δειδήμων, ονος (δείδω): *timid, pusillanimous,* Γ 56†.

δείδια, δείδιθι: see δείδω.

δειδισκόμενος: see δεδίσκομαι.

δειδίσσομαι (δείδω), fut. inf. δειδίξεσθαι, aor. inf. δειδίξασθαι: trans., *terrify, scare;* intrans., *be terrified* (in a panic), only B 190. (Il.)

δείδοικα: see δείδω.

δείδω (root δϝι), fut. δείσομαι, aor. ἔδεισα (ἔδϝεισα, hence often — — ⏑), perf. δείδοικα and δείδια, δείδιμεν, imp. δείδιθι, plup. ἐδείδιμεν, and (as if ipf.) δείδιε: *stand in awe of, dread, fear*, trans. or intrans.; Δία ξένιον δείσᾱς, ξ 389; ὅ πού τις νῶι τίει καὶ δείδεε θῡμῷ, π 306; often in the ordinary sense of fearing, ὣς ἔφατ', ἔδϝεισεν δ' ὁ γέρων, A 33.

δειελιάω (δείελος): only aor. part., δειελιήσᾱς, *having made an evening meal*, ρ 599†.

δείελος (δείλη): *pertaining to the late afternoon;* δείελον ἦμαρ (=δείλη), ρ 606; subst., δείελος ὀψὲ δύων, Φ 232 (=δείελον ἦμαρ).

δεικανάομαι (δείκνῡμι)=δειδίσκομαι. δεπάεσσιν, ἔπεσσι, O 86, ω 410.

δείκνῡμι, fut. δείξω, aor. ἔδειξα, δεῖξα, mid. perf. δείδεγμαι, plup. δείδεκτο, 3 pl. δειδέχατο: *show, point out*, act. and mid.; σῆμα, τέρας, 'give' a sign, γ 174; mid. also=δειδίσκομαι, q. v.; κυπέλλοις, δεπάεσσι, μῡθοις, I 671, η 72.

δείλη: *late afternoon* or *early evening;* ἔσσεται ἢ ἠὼς ἢ δείλη ἢ μέσον ἦμαρ, Φ 111†.

δείλομαι: *verge towards setting;* only ipf., δείλετο τ' ἠέλιος, 'was westering,' H 289†.

δειλός (root δϝι): (1) *cowardly*, A 293, N 278.—(2) *wretched* (*wretch*), *miserable;* esp. in phrase δειλοῖσι βροτοῖσιν, and ἆ δειλέ, δειλώ, δειλοί.

δεῖμα (δείδω): *fear*, E 682†.

δείματο, δείμομεν: see δέμω.

Δεῖμος (δείδω): *Terror*, a personification, Δ 440. (Il.)

δεινός (root δϝι): *dreadful, terrible;* often adv., δεινὸν ἄῡσαι, δεινὰ ἰδών, etc.; in good sense, δεινός τ' αἰδοῖός τε, i. e. commanding reverence, θ 22; cf. Γ 172, where the scansion is to be noted, ἑκυρὲ δϝεινός τε.

δείους, gen.: see δέος.

δειπνέω (δεῖπνον), plup. δεδειπνήκει(ν): *take a meal.*

δείπν-ηστος (δειπνέω): *meal-time* (afternoon), ρ 170†.

δειπνίζω, aor. part. δειπνίσσᾱς: *entertain at table*, δ 435 and λ 411.

δεῖπνον (cf. δάπτω): the principal *meal* of the day (usually early in the afternoon, cf. ἄριστον, δόρπον), *mealtime, repast;* of food for horses, B 383.

δείρᾱς: see δέρω.

δειρή, ῆς: *neck, throat.*

δειρο-τομέω (τέμνω): *cut the throat, behead.*

Δεισ-ήνωρ: a Lycian, P 217†.

δέκα: *ten.*

δεκάκις: *ten times.*

δέκας, αδος: *a company of ten, decade.*

δέκατος: *tenth;* ἐς δεκάτους ἐνιαυτούς, for ἐς δέκα ἐνιαυτούς or δέκατον ἐνιαυτόν, Θ 404.

δεκά-χῑλοι: *ten thousand.*

δέκτης (δέχομαι): *beggar, mendicant*, δ 248†.

δέκτο: see δέχομαι.

δελφίς, ῖνος: *dolphin*, Φ 22 and μ 96.

δέμας (δέμω): *frame, build* of body; joined with εἶδος, φυή, and freq. with adjectives as acc. of specification, μῑκρός, ἄριστος, etc.—As adv., *like* (i n s t a r), μάρναντο δέμας πυρὸς αἰθομένοιο, Λ 596.

δέμνιον: pl., *bedstead, bed.*

δέμω, aor. ἔδειμα, subj. δείμομεν, pass. perf. part. δεδμημένος, plup. (ἐ)δέδμητο, mid. aor. (ἐ)δείματο: *build, construct*, mid. for oneself.

δενδίλλω: only part., *directing sidelooks*, 'with significant looks,' 'winks,' I 180†.

δένδρεον: *tree;* δενδρέῳ, δενδρέων, Γ 152, τ 520.

δενδρήεις, εσσα, εν: *full of trees, woody.*

Δεξαμένη ('Cistern'): a Nereid, Σ 44†.

Δεξιάδης: *son of Dexius*, Iphinous, H 15.

δεξιή (fem. of δεξιός): *right hand*, then *pledge* of faith.

δεξιός: *right*-hand side, hence *propitious* (cf. ἀριστερός), ὄρνῑς, ο 160; ἐπὶ δεξιά, δεξιόφιν, 'on the right,' N 308.

δεξιτερός = δεξιός. δεξιτερῆφι, Ω 284, ο 148. Subst., δεξιτερή = δεξιή.

δέξο: see δέχομαι.

δεόντων: see δέω 2; better reading διδέντων, see δίδημι.

δέος, gen. δειους (root δϜι): *fear, dread.*

δέπας (cf. δάπτω), dat. δέπαϊ and δέπαι, pl. δέπᾱ, gen. δεπάων, dat. δεπάεσσι and δέπασσι: drinking *cup, beaker;* a remarkable one described, Λ 632 ff. (See cut.)

28

δέρκομαι, ipf. iter. δερκέσκετο, aor. 2 ἔδρακον, perf. w. pres. signif. δέδορκα: *look, see,* strictly of the darting glance of the eye; πῦρ ὀφθαλμοῖσι δεδορκώς, τ 446; δεινὸν δερκομένη, 'with dreadful glance,' of the Gorgon, Λ 37; typically of life, ἐμεῦ ζῶντος καὶ ἐπὶ χθονὶ δερκομένοιο, while I live and 'see the light of day,' Α 88, π 439; with obj. accusative, Ν 86, Ξ 141.

δέρμα, ατος (δέρω): *skin, hide, leather;* seldom of the living man, Π 341, ν 431.

δερμάτινος: *leathern.*

δέρον: see δέρω.

δέρτρον: *membrane* enclosing the bowels; δέρτρον ἔσω δύνοντες, 'penetrating the vitals,' λ 579†.

δέρω, ipf. ἔδερον, δέρον, aor. ἔδειρα: *flay.*

δέσμα, ατος (δέω 2): only pl., *bonds;* of a woman's *head-band,* Χ 468. (See cut No. 8).

δεσμός (δέω 2): any (*means of*) *binding, fastening, fetter, imprisonment,* pl., *bonds; ἄνευ δεσμοῖο μένουσιν | νῆες,* i. e. without mooring, ν 100; of a latch-string, φ 241, etc.

δέσποινα (fem. of δεσπότης): *mistress;* with γυνή and ἄλοχος, 'lady,' γ 403, η 347.

δετή (δέω 2): pl., *faggots; καιόμεναι,* Λ 554 and Ρ 663.

δευήσεσθαι: see δεύω.

Δευκαλίδης: *son of Deucalus* (*Deucalion*), Idomeneus, Μ 117.

Δευκαλίων: *Deucalion.*—(1) son of Minos, king of Crete, Ν 451 ff., τ 180 ff.—(2) a Trojan, Υ 478.

δεῦρο, δεύρω: *hither;* often w. imp., or subj. of exhortation, and sometimes in hortatory sense without a verb, ἀλλ' ἄγε δεῦρο, εἰ δ' ἄγε δεῦρο, etc.; also without definite reference to motion, δεῦρ' ἄγε πειρηθήτω, 'come on,' let him try, θ 205, 145.

δεύτατος (sup. of δεύτερος): *last.*

δεῦτε: adv. of exhortation, *come on;* δεῦτε, φίλοι, Ν 481; δεῦτ' ἴομεν πόλεμόνδε, Ξ 128. Cf. δεῦρο, fin.

δεύτερος: *second, next; τὰ δεύτερα,* 'the second prize,' Ψ 538.—Adv., **δεύτερον,** *secondly, again.*

1. **δεύω,** ipf. ἔδευε, δεῦε, iter. δεύεσκον, pass. pr. δεύεται, ipf. δεύετο, -οντο: *wet, moisten;* as mid., (λάρος) πτερὰ δεύεται ἅλμῃ, ε 53.

2. **δεύω** (δέϜω), of act. only aor. 1 ἐδεύησε, mid. δεύομαι, opt. 3 pl. δευοίατο, ipf. ἐδευόμην, fut. δευήσομαι: act. (aor. 1), *lack;* ἐδεύησεν δ' οἰήιον ἄκρον ἱκέσθαι, 'came short' of reaching the end of the rudder, ι 540; mid., *be lacking* or *wanting in, be without* or *away from, inferior to* (τινός); οὐδέ τι θῦμὸς ἐδεύετο δαιτὸς ἐίσης, Α 468, etc.; also abs., δευόμενος, Α 134; μάχης ἄρα πολλὸν ἐδεύεο, Ρ 142, Ν 310; πάντα δεύεαι Ἀργείων, Ψ 484.

δέχαται, δέχθαι: see δέχομαι.

δέχομαι, 3 pl. δέχαται, fut. δέξομαι, aor. (ἐ)δεξάμην, perf. δέδεγμαι, imp. δέδεξο, fut. perf. δεδέξομαι, aor. 2 ἐδέγμην, ἔδεκτο, δέκτο, imp. δέξο, inf. δέχθαι, part. δέγμενος: *receive, accept, await;* of taking anything from a person's hands (τινός τι or τινί τι), δέξατό οἱ σκῆπτρον, Β 186; so of accepting sacrifices, receiving guests hospitably, 'entertain,' ξείνους αἰδοίους ἀποπεμπέμεν ἠδὲ δέχεσθαι, ν 316; in hostile sense, of receiving a charge of the enemy (here esp. δέχαται, δέδεγμαι, ἐδέγμην, δέγμενος, δεδέξομαι), τόνδε δεδέξομαι δουρί, Ε 238; in the sense of 'awaiting' (here esp. aor. 2) freq. foll. by εἰσόκε, ὁπότε, etc.; δέγμενος Αἰακίδην, ὁπότε λήξειεν ἀείδων, 'waiting till Achilles should leave off singing,' Ι 191.—Intrans., ὥς μοι δέχεται κακὸν ἐκ κακοῦ αἰεί, 'succeeds,' Τ 290.

δέψω, aor. part. δεψήσᾱς: *knead* (to soften), μ 48†.

1. **δέω** (δέϜω): only aor., δῆσεν, *stood in need of,* Σ 100†. (δεῖ, see separately.)

2. **δέω,** imp. 3 pl. δεόντων (better reading διδέντων), ipf. δέον, fut. inf. δήσειν, aor. ἔδησα, δῆσα, mid. ipf. δέοντο, aor. ἐδήσατο, iter. δησάσκετο, plup. δέδετο, δέδεντο: *bind, fasten;* mid., for oneself, ὅπλα ἀνὰ νῆα, 'making fast their' tackle, β 430; metaph., ἡμέτε-

ρον δὲ μένος καὶ χεῖρας ἔδησεν, Ξ 73; ὅς τίς μ' ἀθανάτων πεδάᾳ καὶ ἔδησε κελεύθου (gen. of separation), δ 380, θ 352.

δή: *now, just, indeed, really*, etc.; a particle marking degree of time, quality, or emphasis, mostly untranslatable by a single word; postpositive except in the initial phrases δὴ τότε, δὴ γάρ, δὴ πάμπαν, Τ 342; καὶ δή μοι γέρας αὐτὸς ἀφαιρήσεσθαι ἀπειλεῖς, and 'here now,' Α 161; ὀκτὼ δὴ προέηκα ὀιστούς, 'full eight already,' Θ 297 (so often w. numerals); appended to adverbs of time, ὅτε δή, ὀψὲ δή, to adjectives (esp. superlatives, κάρτιστοι δή, 'the very mightiest'), to relative and interrogative pronouns, and to other particles, ὡς δή, ironical; εἰ δή, if 'really'; ἀλλὰ δή, (γὰρ) δή (scilicet enim); esp. in wishes or commands, μὴ δή, 'only'; ἴθι δή, ἄγε δή, etc. δή often coalesces with a following long vowel or diphthong ('synizesis'), δὴ αὖτε, δὴ οὕτως (not to be written δ').

δηθά, δήθ': *long, a long time.*

δηθύνω (δηθά): *linger, tarry.*

Δηι-κόων: a Trojan, Ε 533 ff.

δήιος (δαίω 1): *burning, blazing*; πῦρ, Β 415; met., *destroying, hostile*, pl., *enemies*, Β 544; δήιον ἄνδρα, Ζ 481. To be read with synizesis in several forms, δηίοιο, δηίῳ, etc.

Δηιοπίτης: a son of Priam, Λ 420†.

δηιοτής, ῆτος (δήιος): *conflict, combat.*

Δηί-οχος: a Greek, Ο 341†.

δηιόω, δηόω (δήιος), opt. 3 pl. δηιόῳεν, pass. ipf. 3 pl. δηιόωντο: *slay, cut down, destroy*; with acc., and often also dat. instr., ἔγχεϊ, χαλκῷ, etc.; ἔγχεϊ δηιόων περὶ Πατρόκλοιο θανόντος, 'battling,' Σ 195.

Δηί-πυλος: companion at arms of Sthenelus, Ε 325†.

Δηί-πυρος: a Greek, Ν 576.

Δηί-φοβος: *Deïphobus*, son of Priam and Hecuba, a prominent warrior of the Trojans, Μ 94, δ 276.

δηλέομαι, fut. δηλήσομαι, aor. (ἐ)δηλήσαντο: *harm, slay, lay waste*; τινὰ χαλκῷ, χ 368; καρπόν, Α 156; abs., Ξ 102; met., μή τις ὑπερβασίῃ Διὸς ὅρκια δηλήσηται, Γ 107.

δήλημα: *destruction*; of winds, δηλήματα νηῶν, 'destroyers,' μ 286.

δηλήμων, ονος: *harming, destructive;* subst., *destroyer*, σ 85.

Δῆλος: *Delos*, the island sacred as the birthplace of Apollo and Artemis, ζ 162†.

δῆλος: *clear, evident;* δῆλον, υ 333†.

Δημήτηρ, Δημήτερος and Δήμητρος: *Demēter* (Ceres), Ξ 326, ε 125, Β 696.

δημιο-εργός (Ϝέργον): *worker for the community, craftsman;* of the seer, physician, joiner, bard, ρ 383 ff.

δήμιος, 2 (δῆμος): *pertaining to the community, of the people, public;* πρῆξις δ' ἥδ' ἰδίη, οὐ δήμιος, γ 82; δήμια πίνουσιν, 'the public wine' (cf. γερούσιος οἶνος, Δ 259), Ρ 250.

δημο-βόρος (βιβρώσκω): *people-devouring*, epithet of reproach, Α 231†.

δημο-γέρων: *elder of the people;* of Trojan worthies, Γ 149 and Λ 372.

Δημό-δοκος: *Demodocus*, the blind bard of the Phaeacians, θ 44. (Od.)

δημόθεν: *from among the people*, τ 197†.

Δημο-κόων: a son of Priam, Δ 499†.

Δημο-λέων: a son of Antēnor, Υ 395†.

Δημο-πτόλεμος: a suitor of Penelope, χ 266.

δῆμος: *land*, then *community, people;* Λυκίης ἐν πίονι δήμῳ, Π 437; Φαιήκων ἀνδρῶν δῆμόν τε πόλιν τε, ζ 3; fig. δῆμον ὀνείρων, ω 12; βασιλῆά τε πάντα τε δῆμον, θ 157; δήμου ἄνδρα, Β 198 (opp. βασιλῆα καὶ ἔξοχον ἄνδρα, v. 188); δῆμον ἐόντα (= δήμου ἄνδρα), Μ 213.

δημός: *fat;* of men, Θ 380, Λ 818.

Δημ-οῦχος: a Trojan, son of Philētor, Υ 457.

δήν (δϜήν, cf. diu): *long, a long time;* οὔτι μάλα δϜήν, | Ν 573; οὐδ' ἄρ' ἔτι δϜήν, | β 36. Note the scansion.

δηναιός (δϜήν): *long-lived*, Ε 407†.

δῆνος: only pl., δήνεα, *counsels, arts.*

δηόω: see δηιόω.

δηριάομαι, δηρίομαι (δῆρις), inf. δηριάασθαι, imp. δηριαάσθων, ipf. δηριόωντο, aor. δηρίσαντο, aor. pass. dep. δηρινθήτην: *contend;* mostly with arms, τὼ περὶ Κεβριόναο λέονθ' ὣς δηρινθήτην, Π 756; less often with words, ἐκπάγλοις ἐπέεσσιν, θ 76, 78, Μ 421.

δῆρις: *contention, strife.*

δηρός (δϝήν): *long;* χρόνον, Ξ 206, 305; usually adv., **δηρόν**, ἐπὶ δϝηρόν, Ι 415.

δησάσκετο: see δέω 2.

δῆσε: see δέω 1 and δέω 2.

δήω, pres. w. fut. signif., only δήεις, δήομεν, δήετε: *shall* or *will find, reach.*

Δία: see Ζεύς.

διά (cf. δύο): *between, through,* originally denoting severance. — I. adv. (here belong the examples of 'tmesis' so-called), διὰ δ' ἔπτατο πικρὸς ὀιστός, Ε 99; διά τ' ἔτρεσαν ἄλλυδις ἄλλος (defined by ἄλλυδις ἄλλος), Ρ 729; διὰ κτῆσιν δατέοντο, 'between' themselves, Ε 158; κλέος διὰ ξεῖνοι φορέουσιν, 'abroad,' τ 333; freq. with an explanatory gen. in the same clause, thus preparing the way for the strict prepositional use, διὰ δ' ἧκε σιδήρου, φ 328; διὰ δ' αὐτοῦ πεῖρεν ὀδόντων, Π 405; with another adv., διὰ δ' ἀμπερές, 'through and through,' Λ 377, etc.—II. prep., (1) w. gen., (αἴγλη) δι' αἰθέρος οὐρανὸν ἷκεν, Β 458; διὰ νήσου ἰών, 'along through,' μ 335; ὃ δ' ἔπρεπε καὶ διὰ πάντων, 'among,' 'amid,' Μ 104.—(2) w. acc., local (temporal) and causal; διὰ δώματα ποιπνύοντα, Α 600; fig., μῦθον, ὃν οὔ κεν ἀνήρ γε διὰ στόμα πάμπαν ἄγοιτο, Ξ 91; μή πως καὶ διὰ νύκτα καρηκομόωντες Ἀχαιοὶ | φεύγειν ὁρμήσωνται, 'during' the night, Θ 511; δι' ἀτασθαλίᾱς ἔπαθον κακόν, 'by reason of,' ψ 67; καὶ νήεσσ' ἡγήσατ' Ἀχαιῶν Ἴλιον εἴσω | ἣν διὰ μαντοσύνην, 'through,' 'by means of,' Α 72.—The first syllable of διά is lengthened at the beginning of some verses, Γ 357, Δ 135, Η 251, Λ 435.

δια-βαίνω, inf. διαβαινέμεν, aor. 2 διέβην, inf. διαβήμεναι, part. διαβάς: *step apart* (of the position of the legs, see βαίνω); εὖ διαβάς, 'planting himself firmly,' Μ 458; *go through, cross,* τάφρον, Μ 50; εἰς Ἦλιδα, δ 635.

δια-γιγνώσκω, aor. 2 inf. διαγνῶναι: *recognize distinctly, distinguish.* (Il.)

δια-γλάφω, aor. part. διαγλάψᾱσα: *scoop out,* δ 438†.

δι-άγω, aor. 2 διήγαγον: *carry across* or *over,* υ 187†.

δια-δέρκομαι, aor. opt. διαδράκοι: *look through at,* Ξ 344†.

δια-δηλέομαι, aor. διεδηλήσαντο: *tear in pieces,* ξ 37†.

δι-άει: see διάημι.

δια-είδομαι (διαϝ.), fut. διαείσεται: *appear through, be discernable,* Ν 277; causative, ἣν ἀρετὴν διαείσεται, 'will give his prowess to be seen,' Θ 535.

διαειπέμεν: see διεῖπον.

δι-άημι, ipf. διάει (διάη): *blow through,* ε 478 and τ 440.

δια-θειόω (θέειον): *fumigate* with sulphur, χ 494†.

δια-θρύπτω, aor. pass. part. διατρυφέν: *break in pieces, shiver,* Γ 363†.

διαίνω, aor. ἐδίηνε: *wet, moisten.* (Il.)

δια-κείρω, aor. inf. διακέρσαι: *cut short, frustrate,* Θ 8†.

δια-κλάω, aor. part. διακλάσσᾱς: *break in twain,* Ε 216†.

δια-κοσμέω, aor. mid. διεκοσμήσαντο, aor. pass. opt. διακοσμηθεῖεν: *dispose, marshal, put in order,* mid., μέγαρον, χ 457.

δια-κριδόν (κρίνω): *decidedly;* ἄριστος, Μ 103 and Ο 108.

δια-κρίνω, fut. διακρινέει, aor. διέκρῑνε, opt. διακρίνειε, pass. aor. διεκρίθην, 3 pl. διέκριθεν, opt. διακρινθεῖτε, inf. διακρινθήμεναι, part. -θέντε, -θέντας, perf. part. διακεκριμένος, mid. fut. inf. διακρινέεσθαι: *part, separate, distinguish;* (αἰπόλια) ἐπεί κε νομῷ μιγέωσιν, Β 475; of parting combatants, μαχησόμεθ' εἰσόκε δαίμων | ἄμμε διακρίνῃ, Η 292; 'distinguish,' θ 195; freq. in passive.

διάκτορος: *runner, guide;* epith. of Hermes as messenger of the gods and conductor of men and of the shades of the dead, Ω 339, ω 1. (Formerly connected with διάγω, now generally with διώκω. The traditional derivation is not less probable because more obvious.)

δια-λέγομαι: only aor. mid., τίη μοι ταῦτα φίλος διελέξατο θῡμός, thus 'hold converse' with me, Λ 407, Ρ 97, Χ 122.

δι-αμάω, aor. διάμησε: *cut through,* Γ 359 and Η 253.

διαμελεϊστί: see μελεϊστί.

δια-μετρέω: *measure off,* Γ 315†.

δια-μετρητός: *measured off, laid off,* Γ 344†.

δια-μοιράομαι (μοῖρα): *portion out,* ξ 434†.

δι-αμ-περές (πείρω): *piercing through, through and through;* 'in unbroken succession,' Η 171, χ 190, ξ 11; of time, *forever, constantly,* with αἰεί, ἤματα πάντα, Ο 70, δ 209. (Sometimes διὰ δ' ἀμπερές, Λ 377, Ρ 309, φ 422.)

δι-άν-διχα (δίχα): *between two ways, in two ways;* μερμηρίζειν, 'between two resolves,' foll. by ἤ, ἤ, Ν 455; σοὶ δὲ διάνδιχα δῶκε, 'a divided gift' (i. e. only one of two gifts), Ι 37.

δι-ανύω, aor. διήνυσεν: *finish,* ρ 517.

δια-πέρθω, aor. 1 διέπερσα, aor. 2 διέπραθον: *utterly sack* or *destroy;* aor. mid. διεπράθετο, w. pass. signif., Ο 384.

δια-πέτομαι, aor. διέπτατο: *fly through, fly away out,* α 320.

δια-πλήσσω, aor. inf. διαπλῆξαι: *strike asunder, cleave, split.*

δια-πορθέω = διαπέρθω, Β 691†.

διαπραθέειν: see διαπέρθω.

δια-πρήσσω: *pass through* or *over, accomplish, finish;* with part., Ι 326, ξ 197.

δια-πρό: *right through, through and through,* with and without gen.

δια-πρύσιον: adv., reaching *far and wide,* Ρ 748; *piercingly,* ἤϋσεν, Θ 227.

δια-πτοιέω: *startle and scatter,* σ 340†.

δι-αρπάζω: *seize and tear to pieces,* Π 355†.

δια-ρραίω, fut. διαρραίσω, aor. inf. διαρραῖσαι: *utterly shatter, overthrow, destroy;* fut. mid. w. pass. signif., Ω 355.

δια-ρρίπτω (ϝρίπτω): *shoot through,* τ 575†.

δια-σεύομαι: only aor. 3 sing. διέσσυτο, *rushed through, hastened through;* with acc. and w. gen.

δια-σκίδνημι, 3 pl. διασκίδνᾶσι, aor. διεσκέδασε, opt. διασκεδάσειε: *scatter, disperse;* νῆα, 'scatter in fragments,' 'shatter,' η 275; fig., ἀγλαΐᾱς, 'scatter to the winds,' put an end to, ρ 244.

δια-σκοπιάομαι: *spy out,* Κ 388 and Ρ 252.

δια-σχίζω, aor. act. διέσχισε, aor. pass. διεσχίσθη: *cleave asunder, sever,* ι 71 and Π 316.

δια-τμήγω, aor. inf. διατμῆξαι, aor. 2 διέτμαγον, aor. 2 pass. διετμάγην, 3 pl. διέτμαγεν: *cut apart, cleave, separate;* διατμήξᾱς, sc. Τρῶας, Φ 3; fig., νηχόμενος μέγα λαῖτμα διέτμαγον, η 276, ε 409; freq. pass. as dep., τώ γ' ὡς βουλεύσαντε διέτμαγεν, 'parted,' Α 531.

δια-τρέχω, aor. 2 διέδραμον: *run through* or *over,* γ 177 and ε 100.

δια-τρέω, aor. διέτρεσαν: *flee in different directions, scatter in flight.* (Il.)

δια-τρίβω, aor. part. διατρίψᾱς: *rub apart,* ῥίζαν χερσί, Λ 846; met., *waste time, delay, put off;* διατρίβειν Ἀχαιοὺς γάμον (acc. of specification), β 204; ὁδοῖο (gen. of separation, sc. ἑταίρους), β 404.

δια-τρύγιος (τρύγη): *bearing* (strictly, 'to be gathered') *in succession,* ω 342†.

διατρυφέν: see διαθρύπτω.

δια-φαίνομαι: *be visible through,* τινός, Θ 491, Κ 199; *glow throughout,* ι 379.

δια-φθείρω, fut. διαφθέρσει, perf. διέφθορας: *utterly destroy;* perf., intrans., 'thou art doomed,' Ο 128.

δια-φράζω, only aor. 2 διεπέφραδε: *indicate distinctly, tell fully, give directions,* ζ 47.

δι-αφύσσω, aor. διήφυσε: *draw off entirely, consume; tear away* (by ripping), πολλὸν δὲ διήφυσε σαρκὸς ὀδόντι (σῦς), τ 450. Cf. ἀφύσσω.

δια-χέω: only aor. 3 pl. διέχευαν, *quartered* (cut in large pieces, opp. μίστυλλον).

διδάσκω (root δα), aor. (ἐ)δίδαξα, pass. perf. inf. δεδιδάχθαι: *teach,* pass., *learn;* διδασκόμενος πολέμοιο, 'a beginner, tiro in fighting,' Π 811.

δίδημι (parallel form of δέω 2), ipf. 3 sing. δίδη, imp. διδέντων (v. l. δεόντων): *bind,* Α 105 and μ 54.

διδυμάων, ονος: only dual and pl., *twin-brothers, twins;* with παῖδε, Π 672.

δίδυμος (δύο): *twofold;* pl. subst., *twins,* Ψ 641.

δίδωμι, διδόω, besides reg. forms also διδοῖς, διδοῖσθα, inf. διδόμεν, διδοῦναι, imp. δίδωθι, δίδου, ipf. (ἐ)δίδου, 3 pl. δίδοσαν, δίδον, fut. διδώσομεν, inf. διδώσειν, δωσέμεναι. aor. 3 pl. δόσαν, subj. δώῃ, δώομεν, δώωσιν, inf. δόμεν(αι), aor. iter. δόσκον: *give, grant,* pres. and ipf. *offer,* ἕδνα διδόντες, υ

378; freq. w. epexegetical inf., (**κυνέην**) δῶκε ξεινήιον εἶναι, K 269; of 'giving over' in bad sense, κυσίν, ἀχέεσσι, etc.; giving in marriage, δ 7.

δίε: see δίω.

διέδραμον: see διατρέχω.

δι-εῖπον, διαεῖπον (ϝεῖπον), inf. διαειπέμεν, imp. δίειπε: *tell* or *talk over fully*, K 425 and δ 215.

δι-είρομαι: *inquire of* or *question fully*, τὶ, and τινά τι.

δι-έκ: *out through*, τινός.

δι-ελαύνω, only aor. διήλασε: *drive through, thrust through*, τινός τι.

διελθέμεν: see διέρχομαι.

δίεμαι (cf. δίω), 3 pl. δίενται, inf. δίεσθαι: *be scared away, flee*; σταθμοῖο δίεσθαι, 'from the fold,' M 304; πεδίοιο δίενται, 'speed over the plain,' Ψ 475.

δι-έξ-ειμι (εἶμι): *go out through*, Z 393†.

δι-εξ-ερέομαι: *inquire thoroughly about*, K 432†.

διεπέφραδε: see διαφράζω.

διέπραθον: see διαπέρθω.

διέπτατο: see διαπέτομαι.

δι-έπω, ipf. δίεπε, διείπομεν: *follow up, move through, attend to*; κοιρανέων δίεπε στρατόν, B 207; σκηπανίῳ δίεπ' ἀνέρας, i. e. in order to disperse them, Ω 247.

δι-έργω, only ipf. διέϝεργον: *hold apart*, M 424†.

δι-ερέσσω: only aor. διήρεσα, *paddled hard*, χερσί, μ 444 and ξ 351.

διερός: doubtful word, *living*, ζ 201, *quick*, ι 43.

δι-έρχομαι, fut. inf. διελεύσεσθαι, aor. διῆλθον: *pass through*, with acc. and with gen.

δι-έσσυτο: see διασεύομαι.

διέτμαγεν: see διατμήγω.

δι-έχω, only aor. 2 διέσχε, intrans.: *reach through, penetrate through.*

δίζημαι, fut. διζησόμεθα: *go to seek, seek, seek to win*, w. acc.; abs., ἕκαστος μνάσθω ἐέδνοισιν διζήμενος, π 391.

δί-ζυξ, υγος (ζεύγνῡμι): pl., *yoked two abreast*, E 195 and K 473.

δίζω (δίς): only ipf. δίζε, *was in doubt, debated*, Π 713†.

Δίη: a small island near Cnossus in Crete, λ 325.

διηκόσιοι: *two hundred.*

δι-ηνεκής, ές (ἤνεγκα): *continuous, unbroken, long.*—Adv., **διηνεκέως,** *from beginning to end, at length, minutely.*

διήρεσα: see διερέσσω.

δίηται: see δίω.

δι-ικνέομαι, fut. διίξομαι, aor. 2 sing. διίκεο: *go through*, in narration, I 61 and T 186.

διῑ-πετής, έος (Διός, πίπτω): *fallen from Zeus*, i. e. *from heaven*, epith. of rivers.

δι-ίστημι, only intr., aor. 2 διαστήτην, διέστησαν, part. διαστάντες, perf. διέσταμεν, mid. ipf. διίστατο: *stand apart, separate*; met., διαστήτην ἐρίσαντε, A 6.

διΐ-φιλος: *dear to Zeus*; epith. of heroes, once of heralds, Θ 517, and once of Apollo, A 86.

δικάζω (δίκη), aor. δίκασαν, imp. δικάσσατε: act., of the judge, *pronounce judgment, decide;* mid., of the parties, *seek justice, contend*, λ 545, μ 440.

δίκαιος (δίκη), -ότερος, -ότατος: *right, righteous, just.*—Adv., **δικαίως.**

δικασ-πόλος (πέλω): *dispenser of justice, judge;* with ἀνήρ, λ 186.

δίκη: *usage, custom*, hence *right, justice;* αὕτη δίκη ἐστὶ βροτῶν, the 'inevitable way,' λ 218; μνηστήρων οὐχ ἥδε δίκη τὸ πάροιθε τέτυκτο, σ 275; ἣ γὰρ δίκη, ὁππότε πάτρης | ἧς ἀπέῃσιν ἀνήρ, τ 168; δίκῃ ἠμείψατο, 'in the way of justice,' 'with an appeal to justice,' Ψ 542; pl., *judgments, decisions*, λ 570.

δι-κλίς, ίδος (κλίνω): *double-folding*, of doors and gates, M 455. (See cut, representing ancient Egyptian doors.)

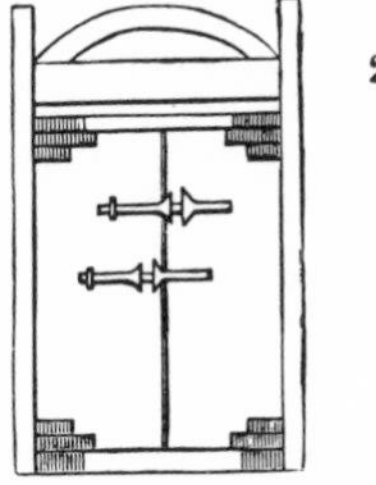
29

δίκτυον: *net*, for fishing, χ 386†.

δῑνεύω and **δῑνέω** (δίνη), ipf. ἐδίνευον, (ἐ)δίνεον, iter. δῑνεύεσκε, aor. part. δῑνήσᾱς, pass. ipf. ἐδῑνεόμεσθα, aor. δῑνηθήτην, -θῆναι, -θείς: *turn* *round and round, whirl;* of a quoit, ἧκε δὲ δῑνήσᾱς, sent it 'whirling,' i. e. making it whirl, Ψ 840; of 'twirling' the heated stake thrust into the eye of the Cyclops, ἐν ὀφθαλμῷ δῑνέομεν, ι 388; intrans. and pass., of dancers and tumblers, Σ 494, δ 19; birds circling in the air, Ψ 875; eyes rolling, T 680; and persons roaming about, ι 153.

δίνη: *eddy*, of a river, Φ.

δῑνήεις, εντος: *eddying.*

δῑνωτός (δῑνόω): *turned, rounded;* freely applied to ornamental work, N 407, τ 56.

διο-γενής, έος: *descended from Zeus, Zeus-born*, epith. of kings.

Διόθεν: *from Zeus, by command of Zeus.*

δι-οϊστεύω, fut. inf. διοϊστεύσειν, aor. διοΐστευσα: *shoot an arrow through*, τινός, τ 578, etc.; of shooting across an interval, i. e. from one cliff to another, μ 102.

Διο-κλῆς: son of Orsilochus of Pherae, γ 488.

δι-όλλῡμι: only perf. 2, οὐδ' ἔτι κᾱλῶς | οἶκος ἐμὸς διόλωλε, 'it is no longer fair the way my house *has gone to ruin*, β 64.

Διο-μήδη: a slave of Achilles, daughter of Phorbas of Lesbos, I 665†.

Διο-μήδης: *Diomed*, the son of Tydeus, and one of the most brilliant of the Homeric heroes. Book E receives its title from his exploits (Διομήδους ἀριστεῖᾱ), but they are prominent elsewhere also. Diomed and Glaucus, Z 119–236. He returned in safety to Argos, γ 180 ff.

Δίον: a town in Euboea, B 538†.

Διόνῡσος: see Διώνῡσος.

δι-οπτεύω: only fut. part., διοπτεύσων, *to spy about*, K 451†.

δι-οπτήρ, ῆρος: *scout*, K 562†.

δῖος, δῖα, δῖον (δῖϝος, Διός): *divine*, an epithet applied with great freedom and with consequent weakening of force; only fem. as applied to gods, δῖα θεά, K 290; δῖ' Ἀφροδίτη, so δῖα θεάων, also δῖα γυναικῶν, 'divine of women'; applied to Charybdis, μ 104; to the swineherd Eumaeus ('noble'), π 56; to one of Hector's horses, Θ 185; also to inanimate things, the sea, earth, lands, rivers.

Δῖος: a son of Priam, Ω 251.

διο-τρεφής, έος (τρέφω): *nourished by Zeus, Zeus-nurtured;* epith. of kings (cf. διογενής), and of other illustrious persons; αἰζηοί, B 660; of the river Scamander, Φ 223; and of the Phaeacians as related to the gods, ε 378.

δί-πλαξ, ακος (πλέκω): *doubled, laid double*, δημός, Ψ 243; as subst., sc. χλαῖνα, *double mantle*, Γ 126.

δι-πλόος: *double.*

δί-πτυξ, υχος (πτύσσω): *folded double* (in two layers), κνίση, A 461, etc.

δί-πτυχος = δίπτυξ, λώπη, see δίπλαξ.

δίς (δϝίς, δύο): *twice*, ι 491†.

δισ-θανής, έος: *twice-dying*, μ 22†.

δισκέω: *hurl the discus*, θ 188†.

δίσκος (δικεῖν): *discus, quoit*, of metal or stone.—Hence **δίσκουρα** (οῦρον), n. pl., *a quoit's cast*, Ψ 431, 523. —(For the attitude in throwing the quoit, see cut, after Myron's famous statue of the Discobolus.)

δῑφάω: *dive after;* τήθεα, Π 747†.

δίφρος: (1) *chariot-box, chariot;* usually war-chariot, but for travelling, γ 324. (See cut No. 10).—(2) *stool*, low *seat* without back or arms.

δίχα: *in two (parts), twofold;* met., 'in doubt,' 'at variance,' δίχα μερμηρίζειν, θῡμὸν ἔχειν, βάζειν, etc.

διχθά = δίχα.

διχθάδιος: *twofold, double.*

δίψα: *thirst.* (Il.)

διψάω: only part., διψάων, *thirsting*, λ 584†.

δίω, ipf. δίε, δίον, mid. subj. δίηται, δίωνται, opt. δίοιτο: act., intrans., *flee*,

Χ 251; *fear, be afraid;* mid., causative, *scare* or *drive away;* of the hound, οὔ τι φύγεσκε κνώδαλον ὅττι δίοιτο, that he 'started,' 'chased,' ρ 317; ἐπεί κ' ἀπὸ ναῦφι μάχην ἐνοπήν τε δίηται, 'repel,' Π 246.

δι-ωθέω: only aor. διῶσε, *forced away, tore away,* Φ 244†.

διώκω: trans., *pursue, chase, drive,* intr., *speed, gallop;* ἅρμα καὶ ἵππους | Οὔλυμπόνδε δίωκε, Θ 439; pass., νηῦς ῥίμφα διωκομένη, 'sped,' ν 162; mid. trans., Φ 602, σ 8; act. intr. often.

Διώνη: the mother of Aphrodīte, Ε 370.

Διώνῡσος: *Dionȳsus* (*Bacchus*), the god of wine, Ζ 132 ff., Ξ 325, λ 325, ω 74.

Διώρης: (1) son of Amaryncеus, a leader of the Epeians, Β 622.—(2) father of Automedon, Ρ 429.

δμηθείς, δμηθήτω: see δάμνημι.

δμῆσις (δάμνημι): *taming,* Ρ 476†.

δμήτειρα (δάμνημι): *subduer;* νύξ, Ξ 259†.

Δμήτωρ ('Tamer'): a name feigned by Odysseus, Ρ 443.

δμωή (δάμνημι): *female slave;* often by capture in war, ζ 307; freq. δμωαὶ γυναῖκες.

δμώς, ωός (δάμνημι): *slave;* often by capture in war, δ 644, π 140; δμῶες ἄνδρες, μ 230.

δνοπαλίζω: doubtful word, ἀνὴρ δ' ἄνδρ' ἐδνοπάλιζεν, *hustled,* Δ 472; ἠῶθέν γε τὰ σὰ ῥάκεα δνοπαλίζεις, you *will bundle on* your rags, ξ 512.

δνοφερός (δνόφος): *dark, dusky.*

δοάσσατο, defective aor., subj. δοάσσεται: *seem, appear.* Cf. δέατο.

δοιή: only ἐν δοιῇ, *in perplexity,* Ι 230.

δοιοί, δοιαί, δοιά: *twofold, two.*

δοιώ: *a pair, two.*

δοκάω, δοκεύω, aor. part. δοκεύσᾱς, mid. perf. δεδοκημένος: *observe sharply, watch;* τινά, Ψ 325, ε 274; abs., ἑστήκει δεδοκημένος, 'on the watch,' Ο 730.

δοκέω, aor. δόκησε: *think, fancy,* usually *seem;* δοκέω νῑκησέμεν Ἕκτορα δῖον, Η 192; δοκέει δέ μοι ὧδε καὶ αὐτῷ | λώϊον ἔσσεσθαι, Ζ 338.

δοκός, ἡ (δέχομαι): *beam,* esp. of a roof, χ 176.

δόλιος (δόλος): *deceitful, deceiving.* (Od.)

Δόλιος: a slave of Penelope.

δολίχ-αυλος (αὐλός): *with long socket;* αἰγανέη, ι 156†.

δολιχ-εγχής, έος (ἔγχος): armed *with long spears,* Φ 155†.

δολιχ-ήρετμος (ἐρετμός): *long-oared,* making use *of long oars;* epith. of ships, and of the Phaeacian men. (Od.)

δολιχός: *long,* both of space and time, δόρυ, ὁδός, νοῦσος, νύξ, ψ 243; adv., δολιχόν, Κ 52.

δολιχό-σκιος (σκιή): *long-shadowy,* casting a long shadow, epith. of the lance.

δολόεις, εσσα, εν (δόλος): *artful;* fig., δέσματα, θ 281.

δολο-μήτης and **δολόμητις,** voc. δολομῆτα: *crafty, wily.*

Δόλοπες: see Δόλοψ.

Δολοπίων: a Trojan, priest of Scamander, father of Hypsēnor, Ε 77†.

δόλος: *bait, trick, deceit;* ἰχθῦσι, μ 252; of the wooden horse, θ 276; δόλῳ, 'by craft,' 'stratagem,' opp. ἀμφαδόν, α 296; βίηφι, ι 406; pl., *wiles,* ι 19, 422, Γ 202; δόλον (δόλους) ὑφαίνειν, τεύχειν, ἀρτύειν, τολοπεύειν.

δολο-φρονέων, -έουσα: *devising a trick, artful-minded.*

δολο-φροσύνη: *wile,* Τ 97 (pl.) and 112.

Δόλοψ, οπος: (1) pl., the *Dolopians,* Ι 484.—(2) *a.* A Trojan, the son of Lampus, Ο 525. *b.* A Greek, the son of Clytius, Λ 302.

Δόλων (δόλος): *Dolon,* the spy, son of Eumēdes, Κ 314 ff., hence the name of the book, Δολώνεια. (See cut, No. 23).

δόμονδε: adv., *into the house,* χ 479; *homeward, home,* Ω 717; ὅνδε δόμονδε, *to his house, to his home.*

δόμος (δέμω): *house, home,* denoting a dwelling as a whole; usually sing. of temples, and when applied to the abodes of animals, but often pl. of dwellings of men; (Ἀθηναίης) ἱεροῖο δόμοιο, Ζ 89, Η 81; Ἄιδος δόμος, also Ἀίδᾱο δόμοι, (μήλων) πυκινὸν δόμον, Μ 301; οὐδ' ἀπολείπουσιν κοῖλον δόμον (σφῆκες), Μ 169.

δονακεύς (δόναξ): *thicket of reeds,* Σ 576†.

δόναξ, ακος: *reed; shaft* of an arrow, Λ 584.

δονέω, aor. ἐδόνησα: *move to and fro, agitate, shake;* of the wind driving the clouds before it, **νέφεα σκιόεντα** δονήσᾱς, M 157.

δόξα (δοκέω): *expectation, view;* οὐδ' ἀπὸ δόξης, K 324 and λ 344. See ἀπό, ad fin.

δορός (δέρω): *leather bag,* β 354 and 380.

δορπέω, fut. -ήσομεν, ipf. 3 du. δορπείτην: *sup.*

δόρπον: *evening meal* or *meal-time, supper;* pl., δόρπα, Θ 503.

δόρυ, gen. δούρατος and δουρός, dat. δούρατι and δουρί, du. δοῦρε, pl. δούρατα and δοῦρα, dat. δούρασι and δούρεσσι: (1) *wood, beam,* and of a living *tree,* ζ 167; of timber, esp. for ships, δοῦρα **τέμνειν, τάμνεσθαι,** ε 162, 243, Γ 61; ἐλάτης, Ω 450; δόρυ **νήιον, νήια** δοῦρα, δοῦρα **νηῶν,** P 744, ι 498, B 135, ε 370.—(2) *shaft* of a spear, *spear;* of ash, **μείλινον,** E 666.

Δόρυ-κλος: a natural son of Priam, Λ 489†.

δόσις (δίδωμι): *gift, boon.*

δόσκον: see δίδωμι.

δοτήρ, ῆρος: *giver,* pl., T 44 and θ 325.

δούλειος (δοῦλος): *slave like, servile,* ω 252†.

δούλη: *female slave.*

δούλιος: only δούλιον **ἦμαρ,** the day *of servitude.*

Δουλίχιον (δολιχός, 'Long-land'): *Dulichium,* an island in the Ionian Sea, S. E. of Ithaca, B 625, α 246.—**Δουλίχιόνδε,** *to Dulichium,* B 629.—**Δουλιχιεύς,** *an inhabitant of Dulichium,* σ 424.

δουλιχό-δειρος (δολιχός, δειρή): *long-necked,* B 460 and O 692.

δουλοσύνη (δοῦλος): *slavery,* χ 423†.

δουπέω (δοῦπος), old form γδουπέω: **ἐπὶ** (adv.) δ' ἐγδούπησαν 'Αθηναίη τε **καὶ** Ἥρη, *thundered,* Λ 45 (cf. ἐρίγδουπος); often δούπησεν δὲ **πεσών,** fell with a *thud,* and without **πεσών,** δουπῆσαι, N 426; δεδουπότος Οἰδιπόδᾱο | ἐς τάφον, Ψ 679. See δοῦπος.

δοῦπος (cf. **κτύπος**): any dull, heavy sound, as the *thunder* at the gates of a besieged town, ἀμφὶ **πύλᾱς** ὅμαδος **καὶ** δοῦπος ὀρώρει | πύργων **βαλλομένων,** I 573; of the *din* of battle, compared to the echo of woodmen's axes, Π 635; the *roar* of the sea, ε 401; or of a mountain torrent, Δ 455. Cf. δουπέω.

δουράτεος (δόρυ): *wooden;* ἵππος, θ 493, 512.

δουρ-ηνεκής (δόρυ, ἤνεγκον): *a spear's throw,* neut. as adv., K 357†.

δουρι-κλειτός and **δουρι-κλυτός**: *renowned in the use of the spear.*

δουρι-κτητός (κτάομαι): *acquired by the spear, captured in battle,* I 343†.

δοῦρα, δούρατος: see δόρυ.

δουρο-δόκη (δέχομαι): *spear-receiver, case* or *stand for spears,* perhaps a ring on a column in the vestibule, α 128†.

δόχμιος and **δοχμός**: *oblique, sideways;* δόχμια as adv., Ψ 116; δοχμὼ ἀίσσοντε, M 148.

δράγμα (δράσσομαι): *handful* of grain cut by the sickle, Λ 69 and Σ 552.

δραγμεύω (δράγμα): *gather handfuls* of grain, as they fall from the sickle, Σ 555†.

δραίνω (δράω): *wish to act* or *do* anything, K 96†.

Δρακίος: a leader of the Epeians, N 692.

δράκων, οντος (δέρκομαι): *snake, serpent.*

δράσσομαι, perf. part. **δεδραγμένος**: *grasp* with the hand, N 393 and Π 486.

δρατός (δέρω): *flayed,* Ψ 169.

δρᾶω, opt. **δρώοιμι**: *work, do work* as servant (δρηστήρ), ο 317†.

δρεπάνη and **δρέπανον**: *sickle,* Σ 551 and σ 368.

δρέπω, aor. mid. part. δρεψάμενοι: *pluck, cull,* μ 357†.

Δρῆσος: a Trojan, Z 20†.

δρηστήρ, ῆρος (δράω): *workman, servant.*—Fem., **δρήστειρα,** *workwoman, female servant.* (Od.)

δρηστοσύνη (δρηστήρ): *work, service,* ο 321†.

δρῑμύς, εῖα, ύ: *pungent, stinging, sharp;* ἀνὰ ῥῖνας δέ οἱ ἤδη | δρῑμὺ **μένος προύτυψε,** of the 'peppery' sensation in the nose caused by emotion, ω 319; **χόλος,** Σ 322; **μάχη,** O 696.

δρίος (cf. δρῦς) = δρῡμός, ξ 353†.

δρόμος (δραμεῖν): *running, race, race-course.*

Δρύᾱς: (1) king of the Lapithae, Α 263†.—(2) father of Lycurgus, Ζ 130†.

δρύινος (δρῦς): *oaken*, φ 43†.

δρῡμός, pl. δρυμά (δρῦς): *oak-thicket, coppice.*

δρύ-οχος (δρῦς, ἔχω): pl., *ribs* of a ship or boat, τ 574†. (See cut.) Later the same word designates the keelson, as holding fast the ribs, the lower ends of which are inserted into it. (See cut, where *f e* designates the *stem; b g, keelson; i h, mast; o, o, o, ribs.*)

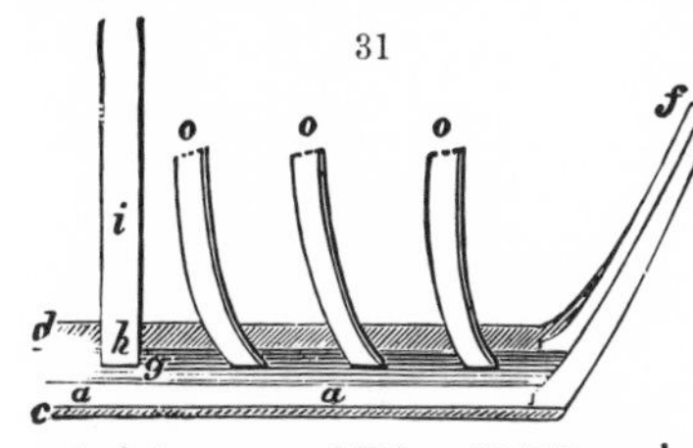

Δρύοψ: a son of Priam, Υ 455.

δρύπτω, aor. δρύψε, aor. mid. part. δρυψαμένω, aor. pass. δρύφθη: *lacerate, tear;* mid., reciprocal, παρειάς, 'each other's cheeks,' β 153.

δρῦς, υός (δόρυ): *tree, oak;* prov., οὔ πως νῦν ἔστιν ἀπὸ δρυὸς οὐδ' ἀπὸ πέτρης ὀαρίζειν, Χ 126; οὐκ ἀπὸ δρυὸς οὐδ' ἀπὸ πέτρης ἐσσί, τ 163. From *tree* or rock, in both proverbs.

δρυ-τόμος (τέμνω): *woodcutter, woodman;* with ἀνήρ, Λ 86.

δρώοιμι, δρώωσι: see δράω.

δῦ: see δύω.

δυάω (δύη): *plunge in misery*, υ 195†.

δύη: *misery, misfortune.* (Od.)

Δύμᾱς: (1) a Phrygian, the father of Hecuba, Π 718.—(2) a Phaeacian, ζ 22†.

δῦμεναι: see δύω.

δύναμαι, δυνάμεσθα, fut. δυνήσομαι, aor. (ἐ)δυνήσατο, pass. δυνάσθη: *be able, have power, avail;* θεοὶ δέ τε πάντα δύνανται, κ 306; ἀνδρὸς μέγα δῡναμένοιο, 'very powerful,' λ 414, α 276.

Δῡναμένη: a Nereid, Σ 43†.

δύναμις: *power, strength.*

δύνω and **δύω**, fut. δύσω, ipf. δῦνε, iter. δύσκε, aor. 1 ἔδῡσα, aor. 2 ἔδῡν, δῦ, subj. δύω, opt. δύη, inf. δῦναι, δῦμεναι, part. δύντα, perf. δέδῡκε, mid. δύομαι, fut. δύσομαι, aor. ἐδύσατο, δύσετο, opt. δῡσαίατο: *go into* or *among, enter*, and (apparently trans.) *put on, don*, χιτῶνα, τεῦχεα, θώρηκα, and with prepositions; with reference to place the verb is either abs. (ἠέλιος δ' ἄρ' ἐδῡ, δύσετο δ' ἠέλιος, *set*), or foll. by acc. of limit of motion, or by prepositions (εἰς, εἴσω, ἐν); freq. πόλεμον, μάχην, ὅμῑλον, so χθόνα δῦμεναι, δῦτε θαλάσσης εὐρέα κόλπον, Σ 140; δόμον Ἄιδος εἴσω, Γ 322; and of persons, δύσεο δὲ μνηστῆρας, ρ 276, etc.; met., of feelings, κάματος γυῖα δέδῡκεν, Ε 811; Μελέαγρον ἔδῡ χόλος, Ι 553; ἐν (adv.) δέ οἱ ἦτορ δῦν' ἄχος, Τ 367; fut. act. and aor. 1 act. are trans., ἀπὸ (adv.) μὲν φίλα εἵματα δύσω (σέ), Β 261; ἐκ μέν με εἵματ' ἔδῡσαν, 'stripped' me of, ξ 341.

δύο, δύω, indeclinable in Homer: *two;* proverb, σύν τε δύ' ἐρχομένω καί τε πρὸ ὃ τοῦ ἐνόησεν, 'two together going, hasteneth the knowing' (lit. one notes before the other), Κ 224.

δυοκαίδεκα: *twelve.*

δυόωσι: see δυάω.

δυσ-: inseparable prefix, opp. εὖ, cf. *un*-rest, *mis*-chance.

δυσ-αής, έος (ἄημι): *ill-blowing;* of contrary or tempestuous winds.

δυσ-άμ-μορος: *most miserable.* (Il.)

δυσ-αριστο-τόκεια (τίκτω): *unhappy mother of an heroic son*, Σ 54†.

δύσεο, δύσετο: see δύνω.

δύσ-ζηλος: *very jealous* or *suspicious*, η 307†.

δυσ-ηλεγής, έος: (if from ἄλγος), *painful, grievous*, epith. of war and of death, Υ 154 and χ 325.

δυσ-ηχής, έος (ἠχέω): *ill-sounding* (h o r r i s o n u s), epith. of war and of death in war. (Il.)

δυσ-θαλπής, έος (θάλπος): *ill-warming, chilly*, Ρ 549.

δυσ-κέλαδος: *ill-sounding;* φόβος, attended by the cries of pursuers and pursued, Π 357†.

δυσ-κηδής, έος (κῆδος): *troublous;* νύξ, ε 466†.

δυσ-κλέης (κλέος), acc. δυσκλέα: *inglorious*, Β 115 and Ι 22.

δύσκον: see δύνω.

δυσ-μενέων (*μένος*): *bearing ill-will.* (Od.)

δυσ-μενής, έος: *hostile*, subst., *enemy.*

δυσ-μήτηρ: only voc., my mother, yet *no mother*, ψ 97†.

δύσ-μορος: *ill-fated.*

Δύσ-παρις: *hateful Paris*, voc., Γ 39 and Ν 769.

δυσ-πέμφελος: word of doubtful meaning, *boisterous*, *angry* sea, Π 748†.

δυσ-πονής, έος (*πόνος*): *toilsome*, ε 493†.

δύστηνος: *unhappy*, *miserable.*

δυσ-χείμερος (*χεῖμα*): *wintry;* of Dodōna, Β 750 and Π 234.

δυσ-ώνυμος (*ὄνομα*): *of evil name* or *omen*, *ill-named.*

δυσ-ωρέω (*ὥρᾱ*): *keep wearisome watch*, Κ 183†.

δύω, δύων: see *δύνω.*

δύω: *two*, see *δύο.*

δυώδεκ(α) = *δυοκαίδεκα*, Κ 488, Β 637; **δυωδέκατος** = *δωδέκατος*, Α 493.

δυωδεκά-βοιος: *worth twelve oxen*, Ψ 703†.

δυω-και-εικοσί-μετρος: *holding twenty-two measures*, Ψ 264†.

δυω-και-εικοσί-πηχυς, υ: *twenty-two cubits long*, Ο 678†.

δῶ = *δῶμα.*

δώδεκα: *twelve;* with *πάντες, πᾶσαι*, 'twelve in all'; **δωδέκατος**, *twelfth.*

Δωδωναῖος: *of Dodōna*, epith. of Zeus, Π 233.

Δωδώνη: *Dodōna*, in Epīrus, site of an ancient oracle of Zeus, ξ 327, Β 750.

δώῃ(σι): see *δίδωμι.*

δῶμα, ατος (*δέμω*, 'building'): (1) *house*, *palace*, *mansion*, often pl., *δώματα*, *house* as consisting of rooms.—(2) *room*, esp. the largest apartment or men's dining-hall (*μέγαρον*), χ 494; so perhaps in pl., Α 600.

δωρέομαι: *give*, *bestow*, Κ 557†.

δωρητός: *open to gifts*, *reconcilable*, Ι 526†.

Δωριεύς, pl. **Δωριέες**: *Dorians*, τ 177†.

Δώριον: a town subject to Nestor, Β 594†.

Δωρίς: a Nereid, Σ 45†.

δῶρον (*δίδωμι*): *gift*, *present.*

δωτήρ, ῆρος: pl., *givers*, θ 325†

δωτίνη = *δῶρον.*

Δωτώ: a Nereid, Σ 43†.

δώτωρ, ορος = *δωτήρ*, θ 335†.

δώωσι: see *δίδωμι.*

E.

ἔ': a false reading for *ἔα* = *ἦν*, ξ 222.

ἕ, enclitic, **ἑέ**: see *οὗ.*

ἔα: see *εἰμί.*

ἔᾱ: see *ἐάω.*

ἐάγην: see *ἄγνῡμι.*

ἑᾱδότα: see *ἁνδάνω.*

ἐάλην: see *εἴλω.*

ἑᾱνός (*Fέννῡμι*): *enveloping*, *clinging*, hence *soft* or *fine;* epith. of clothing and woven fabrics; also of tin, 'pliant,' Σ 613.

ἑανός, εἱανός (*Fέννῡμι*): *robe*, garment of goddesses and women of distinction.

ἔαξε: see *ἄγνῡμι.*

ἔαρ (*Fέαρ*, ver): *Spring; ἔαρος νέον ἱσταμένοιο*, τ 519.

ἔᾱσιν: see *εἰμί.*

ἕαται, ἕατο: see *ἧμαι.*

ἐάφθη: defective aor. pass., a doubtful word, used twice, *ἐπὶ δ' ἄσπις ἐάφθη καὶ κορύς*, Ν 543 (similarly Ξ 419), *followed.*

ἐάω, εἰάω, ἐῶ, εἰῶ, ἐάᾳς, etc., ipf. *εἴων, εἴᾱς, εἴᾱ, ἔᾱ*, iter. *εἴασκον, ἔασκες*, fut. *ἐάσω*, aor. *εἴᾱσα, ἔᾱσας*, etc.: *let*, *permit*, *let alone*, *let be*, *οὐκ ἐᾶν*, *prevent*, *forbid; εἴπερ γὰρ φθονέω τε καὶ οὐκ εἰῶ διαπέρσαι* (note *οὐκ εἰῶ* in the condition), Δ 55, Β 132, 832; *παύε', ἔᾱ δὲ χόλον*, 'give up' thy wrath, Ι 260; *ἵππους ἔᾱσε*, 'left standing,' Δ 226; *τὸν μὲν ἔπειτ' εἴᾱσε*, him he 'let lie,' Θ 317: with inf. of the omitted act., *κλέψαι μὲν ἐάσομεν*, 'we will dismiss' the plan of stealth, Ω 71.—Some forms are often to be read with synizesis, ἐᾷ, ἔᾱ, ἐῶμεν, ἐάσουσιν.

ἐάων: see ἐύς.

ἑβδόματος and **ἕβδομος**: *seventh; ἑβδομάτῃ, on the seventh day*, κ 81, ξ 252.

ἔβλητο: see βάλλω.

ἐγγεγάᾱσι: see ἐγγίγνομαι.

ἐγ-γείνομαι: *engender*, T 26†.

ἐγ-γίγνομαι: only perf. ἐγγεγάᾱσιν, *are in, live in* or *there*.

ἐγ-γυαλίζω (γύαλον), fut. -ξω, aor. ἐγγυάλιξε: *put into the hand, hand over, confer*, τῑμήν, κῦδος, etc.; κέρδος, 'suggest,' 'help us to,' ψ 140.

ἐγγυάομαι: δειλαί δειλῶν ἐγγύαι ἐγγυάασθαι, 'worthless *to receive* are the pledges of the worthless,' θ 351†; ἐγγυάω, 'give pledge.'

ἐγγύη: *surety, pledge*, see ἐγγυάομαι.

ἐγγύθεν (ἐγγύς): *from near, near;* of time, T 409; of relationship, η 205.

ἔγγυθι = ἐγγύς.

ἐγγύς: *near*, of time or space, with gen. or without.

ἐγδούπησαν: see δουπέω.

ἐγείρω, aor. ἤγειρα, ἔγειρε, mid. part. ἐγειρόμενος, aor. ἔγρετο, imp. ἔγρεο, inf. (w. accent of pres.) ἔγρεσθαι, part. ἐγρόμενος, perf. 3 pl. ἐγρηγόρθᾱσι, inf. (w. irreg. accent) ἐγρήγορθαι, pass. aor. 3 pl. ἔγερθεν: I. act., *awaken, wake, arouse;* τινὰ ἐξ ὕπνου, ὑπνώοντας, E 413, ε 48; Ἄρηα, πόλεμον, πόνον, μένος, νεῖκος, O 232, 594, P 554.—II. mid., *awake*, perf. *be awake;* ἔγρετο εὕδων, ν 187; ἔγρεο, 'wake up!'; ἐγρήγορθε ἕκαστος, 'keep awake,' every man! H 371.

ἔγκατα, dat. ἔγκασι: *entrails*.

ἐγ-κατα-πήγνῡμι, aor. ἐγκατέπηξα: *thrust firmly in*, ξίφος κουλεῷ, λ 98†.

ἐγ-κατα-τίθημι, aor. ἐγκάτθετο, imp. ἐγκάτθεο: *deposit in, place in*, ἱμάντα κόλπῳ, Ξ 219; met., ἄτην θῡμῷ, 'conceive' infatuation, ψ 223; τελαμῶνα ἐῇ ἐγκάτθετο τέχνῃ, 'conceived in (by) his art,' or perhaps better 'included in (among the specimens of) his art,' λ 614.

ἔγ-κειμαι, fut. ἐγκείσεαι: *lie in*, εἵμασι, X 513†.

ἐγκεράσᾱσα: see ἐγκίρνημι.

ἐγ-κέφαλος (κεφαλή): *brain*.

ἐγ-κίρνημι, aor. part. ἐγκεράσᾱσα: *mix in*, οἶνον, Θ 189†.

ἐγκλάω: see ἐνικλάω.

ἐγ-κλῑνω: only perf. pass. (met.), πόνος ὔμμι ἐγκέκλιται, *rests upon* you, Z 78†.

ἐγ-κονέω: *be busy*, only pres. part., στόρεσαν λέχος ἐγκονέουσαι, 'in haste,' Ω 648, η 340, ψ 291.

ἐγ-κοσμέω: *put in order within*, νηὶ τεύχεα, ο 218†.

ἐγ-κρύπτω, aor. ἐνέκρυψε: *hide in, bury in*, δᾱλὸν σποδιῇ, ε 488†.

ἐγ-κύρω, aor. ἐνέκυρσε: *meet, fall in with*, N 145†.

ἔγρεο, -ετο, -εσθαι, ἐγρήγορθαι: see ἐγείρω.

ἐγρηγορόων, as if from ἐγρηγοράω: remaining *awake*, K 182.

ἐγρήσσω (ἐγείρω): *watch, keep watch.*

ἐγχείη (ἔγχος): *lance.*

ἐγχείῃ: see ἐγχέω.

ἔγχελυς, υος: *eel.*

ἐγχεσί-μωρος: word of doubtful meaning, *mighty with the spear.*

ἐγχέσ-παλος (πάλλω): *spear-brandishing.*

ἐγ-χέω, aor. subj. ἐγχείῃ, aor. mid. ἐνεχεύατο: *pour in*, mid. for oneself, ι 10, τ 387.

ἔγχος, εος: *spear, lance;* used for both hurling and thrusting, and regarded as the most honorable weapon; the shaft, δόρυ, was of ash, about 7 ft. long; the upper end, καυλός, was fitted with a bronze socket, αὐλός, into which the point, ἀκωκή, αἰχμή, was inserted, Π 802, being held fast by the πόρκης; the lower end, οὐρίαχος, was furnished with a ferule or spike, σαυρωτήρ, for sticking into the earth. The warrior usually carried two spears—for hurling, at a distance of about 12 paces, and for thrusting from above. Hector's spear was 16 ft. long, Z 319. (See also σῦριγξ, and cut 19.)

ἐγχρίμπτω, ἐνιχρίμπτω, aor. part. ἐγχρίμψᾱς, mid. ipf. ἐγχρίμπτοντο, pass. aor. imp. ἐγχριμφθήτω, part. ἐγχριμφθείς, ἐνιχριμφθέντα: *press close to, draw near;* of running close to the turning-post in a race, Ψ 334, 338; grazing the bone by a lance-point, E 662; crowding close in combat, P 413; approaching very near, N 146.

ἐγώ, ἐγών, besides the usual forms,

also gen. ἐμεῖο, ἐμεῦ, ἐμέο, μευ, ἐμέθεν: *I, me.*

ἐδάην: see ΔΑ.

ἐδανός (Ϝεδανός, ἡδύς): *sweet*, Ξ 172†.

ἐδάσατο, -σσατο: see δατέομαι.

ἔδαφος: *floor*, of a ship, ε 249†.

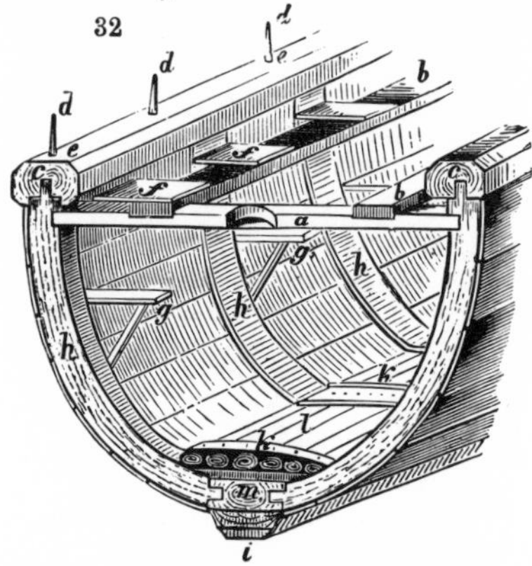

(See cut 32.) *a*, μεσόδμη, *mast-box; b, beams running parallel to c*, ἐπηγκενίδες, *gunwale; d*, κληῖδες, *row-lock, thole-pin; e*, σκαλμοί, part of the gunwale on which the oar rests, *bed of the oar; f*, ζυγά, *thwarts* (should cross the vessel); *g*, θρῆνυς, *braces* for the feet; *h*, ἴκρια, *ribs; i*, τρόπις, *keel; k*, ἁρμονιαί, *slabs*, sustaining the floor; *l*, ἔδαφος, *floor; m, keelson*, was probably not distinguished from *i, keel.* (See also plate No. IV., at end of vol.)

ἔδδεισε, ἐδείδιμεν: see δείδω.

ἐδέδμητο: see δέμω.

ἔδεκτο: see δέχομαι.

ἐδητύς, ύος (ἔδω): *food.*

ἔδμεναι: see ἔδω.

ἔδνον (Ϝέδνον), only pl. ἔδνα, **ἔεδνα**: (1) *bridal gifts*, presented by the suitor to the father of the bride, as if to purchase her. —(2) *dowry* of the bride, given to her by her father, α 277.

ἐδνοπάλιζεν: see δνοπαλίζω.

ἐδνόω, ἐεδνόω (ἔδνον): aor. mid. opt. ἐεδνώσαιτο: *portion off*, θύγατρα, said of the father, β 53.

ἐδνωτής, ἐεδνωτής: *giver of dowry*, the father of the bride.

ἔδομαι: see ἔδω, ἐσθίω.

ἕδος, εος (root ἑδ): (1) *sitting; οὐχ* ἕδος ἐστί, 'it's no time for sitting,' Λ 648. —(2) *sitting-place, seat, abode;* ἀθανάτων ἕδος, of Olympus, Ε 360; so 'site,' 'situation,' Ἰθάκης ἕδος (a periphrasis for the name of the place merely), ν 344.

ἔδραθον: see δαρθάνω.

ἔδραμον: see τρέχω.

ἕδρη (root ἑδ): *seat, stool* (see cut 33; also 75), Τ 77; pl. ἕδραι, rows of *seats*, e. g. stone benches in the ἀγορά, θ 16; and elsewhere, e. g. γ 7; τίειν ἕδρῃ, honor 'with a seat,' i. e. show to a place of honor.

ἑδριάομαι (ἕδρη), ipf. ἑδριόωντο: *sit down, take seats* in council, Κ 198, η 98.

ἔδυν: see δύνω.

ἔδω, inf. ἔδμεναι, ipf. ἔδον, iter. ἔδεσκε, fut. ἔδομαι, perf. part. ἐδηδώς, pass. perf. ἐδήδοται: *eat;* of both men and animals; metaph., 'consume,' 'devour,' 'gnaw;' οἶκον, κτήματα, α 375; ἄλλοι δ' ἡμέτερον κάματον νήποινον ἔδουσιν, 'the fruits of our toil,' ξ 417; θυμὸν ἔδων, βρώμης δ' οὐχ ἅπτεαι, κ 379, ι 75.

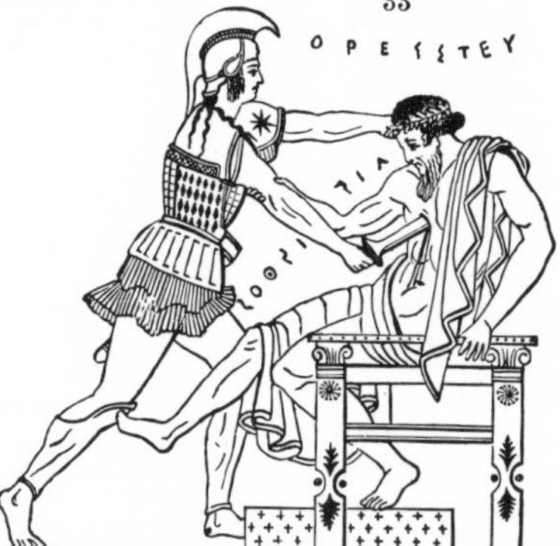

ἐδωδή (ἔδω): *food, meat, fodder.*

ἐέ: see οὗ.

ἔεδνα, ἐεδνόω, ἐεδνωτής: see ἔδνον, ἐδνόω, ἐδνωτής.

ἐεικοσά-βοιος (ἐϝεικ.): *worth twenty cattle*, α 431 and χ 57.

ἐείκοσι(ν): see εἴκοσιν.

ἐεικόσ-ορος (ἐϝεικ.): *twenty-oared*, ι 322†.

ἐεικοστός = εἰκοστός.

ἐείλεον: see εἴλω.

ἐεισάμενος, ἐείσαο, -ατο: see (1) εἴδω. (2) εἶμι.

ἐεισάσθην: see εἶμι.

ἐέλδομαι, ἐέλδωρ: see ἔλδομαι, ἔλδωρ.

ἐέλμεθα, ἐελμένος, ἐέλσαι: see εἴλω.

ἐέλπομαι: see ἔλπομαι.

ἐεργάθω· see ἐργάθω.

ἔεργε, ἐεργμένος: see ἔργω.

ἐέργνῡμι · see κατέργνῡμι.

ἐερμένος: see εἴρω.

ἐέρση, ἐερσήεις: see ἔρση, ἐρσήεις.

ἔερτο: see εἴρω.

ἐέρχατο: see ἔργω.

ἐέσσατο, ἔεστο: see ἕννῡμι.

ἐέσσατο: see εἷσα.

ἕζομαι (root ʽεδ), 2 sing. ἕζεαι, imp. ἕζεο, ἕζευ, ipf. ἑζόμην: *sit down, take a seat;* in dodging a spear, Χ 275; fig., of the sinking of the scale, κῆρες ἐπὶ χθονὶ ἑζέσθην, Θ 74.

ἔῃ: see εἰμί.

ἕηκε: see ἵημι.

ἔην: see εἰμί.

ἑήνδανε: see ἁνδάνω.

ἐῆος: see ἐύς.

ἕης: see ὅς.

ἑῆς: see ἑός.

ἔησθε, ἔῃσι: see εἰμί.

ἔθ' = ἔτι.

ἔθειρα, only pl. ἔθειραι: *horse-hair*, of the mane and tail of horses, and of the plume of a helmet.

ἐθείρω: *till*, ἀλωήν, Φ 347†.

ἐθελοντήρ, ῆρος: *volunteer*, β 292†.

ἐθέλω, subj. ἐθέλωμι, ipf. ἔθελον, ἤθελετον, iter. ἐθέλεσκες, fut. ἐθελήσω, aor. ἐθέλησα: *will, wish, choose*, with neg., *be unwilling, refuse;* οὐδ' ἔθελε προρέειν (ὕδωρ), Φ 366, Α 112; so οὐκ ἐθέλων, πολλὰ μάλ' οὐκ ἐθέλοντος, 'sorely against his will;' in prohibitions w. μή (n o l i), μήτε σύ, Πηλείδη ἔθελ' ἐριζέμεναι βασιλῆι, Α 277; foll. by ὄφρα, Α 133.

ἔθεν = οὗ.

ἐθηεύμεθα: see θηέομαι.

ἔθνος (ϝέθνος): *company, band, host;* of men, ἑτάρων, λᾱῶν, νεκρῶν, also of 'swarms,' 'flocks,' of bees, flies, birds, etc.

ἔθορον: see θρώσκω.

ἔθρεψα: see τρέφω.

ἔθω (σϝέθω), part. ἔθων, perf. 2 εἴωθα, ἔωθε: *be accustomed, wont ;* κακὰ πόλλ' ἔρδεσκεν ἔθων, 'was in the habit of continually working mischief,' Ι 540; οὓς παῖδες ἐριδμαίνωσιν ἔθοντες, 'as is their wont,' Π 260; ὑφ' ἡνιόχῳ εἰωθότι, 'their accustomed driver, Ε 231.

εἰ: *if, if only, whether;* conjunction used in the expression of a wish or a condition, and in indirect questions.—I. As particle of wishing, εἰ or εἰ γάρ, *would that, O that*, is foll. by the optative.—II. Interrogatively, *whether*, foll. by such construction as the meaning requires, e. g., κατάλεξον | εἰ καὶ Λᾱέρτῃ αὐτὴν ὁδὸν ἄγγελος ἔλθω, 'am to go,' π 138.—III. In conditional clauses εἰ (εἰ μή), and with the subj. often (sometimes w. the opt.) εἴ κεν, rarely w. ἄν, εἰ δ' ἂν ἐμοὶ τῑμὴν Πρίαμος Πριάμοιό τε παῖδες | τίνειν οὐκ ἐθέλωσιν, Γ 288. Conditions of which the conclusion is vague are sometimes regarded as interrogative, e. g. ἀναπεπταμένᾱς ἔχον ἀνέρες, εἴ τιν' ἑταίρων | ἐκ πολέμου φεύγοντα σαώσειαν, they held the gates open, *in case* they might be able to save some fugitive, Μ 122; thus often εἴ που or εἴ πως, 'in the hope that,' 'on the chance that,' etc. —With other particles, εἰ καί, *if also* (or denoting concession, *though*), καὶ εἰ (οὐδ' εἰ, μηδ' εἰ), *even if*, denoting opposition; εἴ τε . . εἴ τε (sive . . sive), ὡς εἰ, ὡς εἴ τε, εἰ δή, εἴ περ, εἴ γε (q. v.); in εἰ δ' ἄγε (q. v.), εἰ is probably an interjection.

εἰαμένη (cf. ἧμαι): *low-lying pasture* or *water-meadow;* ἐν εἰαμένῃ ἕλεος μεγάλοιο, Δ 483 and Ο 631, once mentioned as the home of a poplar-tree, and once as a pasture for kine.

εἰανός: see ἑανός.

εἰαρινός (ϝέαρ): *of Spring, vernal*, ὥρη, ἄνθεα, νοτίαι.

εἴᾱσα, εἴασκον: see ἐάω.

εἴαται, εἵατο: see ἧμαι.

εἴατο: see εἰμί.

εἴβω (cf. λείβω), ipf. εἶβον: *shed, let fall*, always with δάκρυον.

εἰ γάρ: see εἰ, I.

εἴ γε: *if, since* (siquidem); usually separated as εἰ ἐτεόν γε, but εἴ γε μέν, ε 206; cf. E 258.

εἰ δ' ἄγε (ἄγετε): *come! come on!* εἰ is probably an interjection, cf. εἶα.

εἰδάλιμος (εἶδος): *beautiful in form*, ω 279†.

εἶδαρ, ατος (ἔδω): *food, fodder, viands*, E 369, α 140.

Εἰδοθέη: *Eidothea*, a sea-goddess, the daughter of Proteus, δ 366.

εἴδομαι, εἶδον: see εἴδω, I.

εἶδος, εος (ϝιδ), dat. εἴδεϊ: *appearance, looks*, esp. of the human countenance, and mostly with a suggestion of beauty; freq. as acc. of specification with adjectives, and often coupled w. μέγεθος, φυή, δέμας. Of a dog, ταχὺς θέειν ἐπὶ εἴδεϊ τῷδε, a fast runner 'with all that good looks,' ρ 308.

εἴδω (root ϝιδ): an assumed pres., answering to the tenses enumerated below, meaning (I) *see, seem*, and (II) *know*.—I. (1) *see, look*, aor. 2 **εἶδον, ἴδον**, subj. ἴδω, **ἴδωμι**, opt. ἴδοιμι, imp. ἴδε, inf. ἰδεῖν, **ἰδέειν**, part. ἰδών, mid. aor. 2 **ἰδόμην, ἴδοντο**, εἴδοντο, subj. **ἴδωμαι**, opt. ἴδοιτο, imp. ἴδεσθε, inf. ἰδέσθαι.—(2) *seem, appear, be like*, pres. εἴδεται, part. εἰδόμενος, aor. 1 2 sing. ἐείσαο, 3 sing. **ἐείσατο**, εἴσατο, opt. εἴσαιτο, part. εἰσάμενος, ἐεισάμενος. The meanings need no special illustration; a difference between act. and mid. of signif. *see* is not to be sought. Metaph., ὄφρα ϝίδωμαι ἐνὶ φρεσὶν ἠδὲ δαείω, Φ 71. Denoting resemblance, εἴσατο δὲ φθογγὴν υἷι Πριάμοιο Πολίτῃ, B 791, etc.—II. *know*, perf. **οἶδα**, οἶσθα (οἶδας), ἴδμεν, ἴστε, ἴσᾱσ(ι), subj. εἰδῶ, εἰδέω, εἴδομεν, εἴδετε, εἰδῶσι, opt. εἰδείην, imp. ἴσθ(ι), **ἴστω**, inf. **ἴδμεναι**, ἴδμεν, part. εἰδώς, εἰδυῖα, ἰδυῖα, plup. ᾔδε(α), ἠείδης and ᾔδησθα, ᾔδη and ᾔδεε(ν) and ἠείδη, 3 pl. ἴσαν, fut. εἴσομαι, εἰδήσω, inf. εἰδήσειν, εἰδησέμεν: The meaning *know* comes as the result of *have seen* (cf. nosco, novi); with acc. οἶδα may mean 'be skilled in,' and w. inf. 'know how,' see esp. H 237–241; special phrase, χάριν εἰδέναι, 'be grateful,' 'thankful'; another special signif., peculiar to Homer, is when the word denotes *disposition* or *character, turn of mind;* φίλα εἰδότες ἀλλήλοισι, γ 277; ἤπια εἰδέναι, so αἴσιμα, ἄρτια, ἀθεμίστια ϝειδώς, 'a lawless spirit,' ι 189.

εἴδωλον (εἶδος): *shape, phantom*, E 449, δ 796; esp. pl., of the *shades* in the nether world, βροτῶν εἴδωλα καμόντων, λ 476.

εἶθαρ: *immediately*.

εἴθε: *would that! Oh, that!* See αἴθε.

εἰ καί: see εἰ, ad fin.

εἴ κεν: see εἰ, also ἄν and κέν.

εἶκε: see (1) εἴκω, (2) ἔοικα.

εἴκελος (ϝεικ., ἔοικα): *like*, τινί. Cf. ἴκελος.

εἰκοσάκις: *twenty times.*

εἴκοσι(ν), ἐείκοσι (ϝεικ., viginti): *twenty.*

εἰκοσιν-ήριτος: *twenty-fold*, X 349†.

εἰκοστός, ἐεικοστός: *twentieth.*

ἔικτο, ἔικτον, ἐίκτην, εἰκυῖα: see ἔοικα.

εἴκω (ϝείκω), imp. εἶκε, part. εἴκων, aor. εἶξα, iter. εἴξασκε: *yield, give way, withdraw* (from anything, τινός, before one, τινί), *be inferior* (to one, τινί, in some respect, τὶ, sometimes τινί); εἰσορόων χρόα κᾱλόν, ὅπῃ ϝείξειε μάλιστα, where it, i. e. the body of Hector, would best 'yield' to a blow, X 321; εἴ πέρ τίς σε βίῃ καὶ κάρτεϊ ϝείκων | οὔ σε τίει, 'yielding' to violent impulses, ν 143; μηδ' εἴκετε χάρμης | Ἀργείοις, 'fall not back from battle before the Greeks,' Δ 509; ἀνδρῶν δυσμενέων ὅ τέ μοι ϝείξειε πόδεσσιν, whoever 'was inferior' to me in running, ξ 221; aor. 1 trans., εἶξαι ἡνία ἵππῳ, 'give him free rein,' Ψ 337.

εἰλαπινάζω (εἰλαπίνη): *feast, be at the banquet.*

εἰλαπιναστής: *banqueter, guest*, P 577†.

εἰλαπίνη: *festal banquet.*

εἶλαρ (ϝειλ., εἴλω): means of *defence, protection;* κύματος, 'against the wave,' ε 257.

εἰλάτινος: *of pine* or *fir* wood.

Εἰλείθυια: *Eilithyia*, daughter of Hera, τ 188; usually pl., **Εἰλείθυιαι**, the *goddesses of child-birth.*

Εἰλέσιον: a town in Boeotia, B 499†.

εἰλέω: see εἴλω.

εἰλήλουθα, εἰλήλουθμεν: see ἔρχομαι.

εἰλί-πος (εἴλω, πούς), only pl. acc

εἰλίποδας, dat. εἰλιπόδεσσι: *close-footed* or *trailing-footed;* epith. of kine, with reference to their peculiar rolling gait.

εἰλίσσω: see ἑλίσσω.

εἶλον, εἱλόμην: see αἱρέω.

εἰλύαται: see εἰλύω.

εἴλῡμα (Ϝειλύω): *wrapper*, ζ 179†.

εἰλῡφάζω (Ϝειλ.): *whirl about; φλόγα*, Υ 492†.

εἰλυφάω = εἰλῡφάζω, Λ 156†.

εἰλύω (Ϝειλύω), fut. εἰλύσω, pass. perf. εἴλῡμαι, 3 pl. εἰλύαται, part. εἰλῡμένος, plup. εἴλῡτο: *wrap, envelop, cover.*

εἴλω, εἰλέω (Ϝειλέω), subj. εἰλέωσι, part. εἰλεῦντα, ipf. εἴλει, εἴλεον, ἐείλεον, aor. 3 pl. ἔλσαν, inf. ἔλσαι, ἐέλσαι, part. ἔλσᾱς, pass. pres. part. εἰλόμενοι, ipf. εἰλεῦντο, aor. ἐάλη, 3 pl. ἄλεν, inf. ἀλήναι, ἀλήμεναι, part. ἀλείς, perf. ἐέλμεθα, part. ἐελμένος: I. act. and pass., *crowd together, hem in, shut up* or *off;* (Orīon the hunter) θῆρας ὁμοῦ εἰλεῦντα, λ 573; (δμωᾱς) εἴλεον ἐν στείνει, ὅθεν οὔ πως ἦεν ἀλύξαι, χ 460; κατὰ πρύμνᾱς τε καὶ ἀμφ' ἅλα ἔλσαι Ἀχαιούς, Α 409; ὅν περ ἄελλαι | χειμέριαι εἰλέωσιν, 'hold storm-bound,' Β 294; (νῆα) κεραυνῷ | Ζεὺς ἔλσᾱς ἐκέασσε, 'with a crushing blow,' ε 132; (Ἄρης) Διὸς βουλῇσιν ἐελμένος, 'held close,' Ν 523.—II. mid., *crowd* or *collect together, crouch, gather oneself* for a spring; ἔστασαν ἀμφὶ βίην Διομήδεος εἰλόμενοι, Ε 782; οἳ δή τοι εἰς ἄστυ ἄλεν, Χ 12; χειμέριον ἀλὲν ὕδωρ, 'accumulated,' Ψ 420; τῇ (ἀσπίδι) ὕπο πᾶς ἐάλη, 'crouched,' Ν 408; ἐνὶ δίφρῳ ἧστο ἀλείς, 'cowering close,' Π 403; Ἀχιλῆα ἀλεὶς μένεν, i. e. all ready to charge upon him, Φ 571, ω 538.

εἷμα (Ϝέννῡμι): *garment*, of any sort; pl., εἵματα, *clothing;* freq as pred. noun, παρ' δ' ἄρα οἱ φᾶρός τε χιτῶνά τε Ϝείματ' ἔθηκαν, 'as clothing,' i. e. 'to wear,' ζ 214.

εἶμαι: see ἕννῡμι.

εἵμαρται, εἵμαρτο: see μείρομαι.

εἰμέν: see εἰμί.

εἱμένος: see ἕννῡμι.

εἰ μή: *if not, unless, except*, μ 326.

εἰμί, 2 sing. ἐσσί, εἰς (never εἶ), 1 pl. εἰμέν, 3 pl. ἔᾱσι, subj. ἔω, εἴω, 3 ἔῃσι, ᾖσι, 3 pl. ἔωσι, ὦσι, opt. 2 ἔοις, 3 ἔοι, inf. ἔ(μ)μεν(αι), part. ἐών, ἐοῦσα, ἐόν, ipf. ἔα, ἦα, ἔον (ἔην), 2 ἔησθα, ἦσθα, 3 ἔην, ἤην, ἦεν, du. ἤστην, pl. ἔσαν, iter. ἔσκον, fut. ἔ(σ)σομαι, ἔ(σ)σεαι, ἔ(σ)σεται, ἐ(σ)σόμεθα: as copula, meaning *to be*, forms of the pres. ind. are enclitic, with the exception of ἔᾱσι. But they are not enclitic in the meaning *exist, be possible;* so at the beginning of a sentence, and ἔστι after οὐκ, καί, εἰ, and ὡς. Ζεῦ πάτερ, ἦ ῥα ἔτ' ἔστε θεοί, 'ye do then still *exist*,' ω 352; εἴ τί που ἔστι, πίθοιό μοι, 'if it be anywise *possible*,' δ 193. εἶναι is used in Hom. as elsewhere to form periphrastic tenses, τετληότες εἰμέν (=τετλήκαμεν), Ε 873; βλήμενος ἦν, Δ 211; and it is the usual verb to denote *possession*, εἰσίν μοι παῖδες, Κ 170; ὄφρα οἱ εἴη πίνειν, 'have (a chance) to drink,' ι 248; phrases, ἔνδον ἐόντων, 'of her store'; ὅπως ἔσται τάδε ἔργα, 'what turn affairs will take'; εἴη κεν καὶ τοῦτο, 'this might well come to pass'; ἐμοὶ δέ κεν ἀσμένῳ εἴη, 'it would please me well'; καὶ ἐσσομένοισι πυθέσθαι, 'for future generations,' 'for posterity to hear'; εἴ ποτ' ἔην γε, 'if indeed he ever *was*'—as if his existence had been but a dream after all.—Ellipsis of ἐστί is freq., of other forms rare, sc. ἔῃ, Ξ 376.

εἶμι, 2 sing. εἶσθα, subj. ἴησθα, ἴῃς, ἴῃσι, ἴομεν, ἴωσι, opt. ἴοι, ἰείη, inf. ἴ(μ)μεν(αι), ipf. ᾔιον, ᾔια, ᾔιες, ἴες, ᾔιεν, ᾖε, ἴε, ᾔομεν, ᾔισαν, ἴσαν, ᾔιον, fut. εἴσομαι, aor. mid (ἐ)είσατο: *go*, the pres. w. fut. signif., but sometimes w. pres. signif., esp. in comparisons, e. g. Β 87. The mid. form peculiar to Homer has no peculiar meaning, Ἕκτωρ ἄντ' Αἴαντος ἐείσατο, *went* to meet Ajax, Ο 415.

εἰν = ἐν.

εἰνα-ετες (ἐννέα, Ϝέτος): adv., *nine years.*

εἰνάκις: *nine times*, ξ 230†.

εἰν-άλιος (ἅλς): *in* or *of the sea, sea-.* (Od.)

εἰνά-νυχες (ἐννέα, νύξ): adv., *nine nights long*, Ι 470†.

εἰνάτερες (Ϝειν.): *brothers' wives* (Il.)

εἴνατος (ἐννέα): *ninth.*

εἵνεκα = ἕνεκα.

εἰνί = ἐν.

εἰν-όδιος (ὁδός): *in the way* Π 260†.

εἰνοσίγαιος = ἐννοσίγαιος.

εἰνοσί-φυλλος (ἔνοσις, φύλλον): *leaf-shaking, with quivering foliage,* epith. of wooded mountains.

εἴξασκε: see εἴκω.

εἶο: see οὗ.

εἰοικυῖαι: see ἔοικα.

εἷος = ἕως.

εἶπα, εἰπέμεν(αι): see εἶπον.

εἴπερ, εἴ περ: *if really, if;* mostly in a concessive sense.

εἶπον (root Ϝεπ, cf. v o c o), ἔειπον, iter. εἴπεσκεν, subj. εἴπωμι, εἴπῃσθα, aor. 1 εἶπα, 2 pl. εἴπατε: *speak, say;* strictly of an utterance with regard to its tenor and ethical expression rather than to the subject-matter (cf. ἔπος); hence the word may signify 'command' with foll. inf., εἰπεῖν τε γυναιξὶν | κληῖσαι μεγάροιο θύρᾱς, φ 235; with nearer indication of the feeling, εὐχόμενος δ' ἄρα εἶπεν, η 330; ὀχθήσᾱς δ' ἄρα εἶπε, Σ 5; εἶπε δ' ἄρα κλαίουσα, Τ 286; freq. w. obj., ἔπος, μῦθον, ἀγγελίην, etc.; so w. acc. of person named, οὐδ' ἢν 'Αγαμέμνονα εἴπῃς, 'pronounce the name of,' 'name,' Α 90; ἔσται μὰν ὅτ' ἂν αὖτε φίλην γλαυκῶπιδα εἴπῃ, i. e. when I shall hear him call me by this name, Θ 373, τ 334.

εἴ που, εἴ πως see εἰ.

εἰράων: see εἴρη.

εἴργω: see ἔργω.

εἴρερος (root σερ, cf. s e r v u s): *bondage,* θ 529.

εἰρεσίη (ἐρέσσω): *rowing.* (Od.)

Εἰρέτρια. *Eretria,* in Euboea, Β 537†

εἴρη · *meeting-place* (equiv. to ἀγορά), pl., Σ 531†.

εἴρηαι: see εἴρομαι.

εἰρήνη (εἴρηται): *peace;* ἐπ' εἰρήνης, 'in time of peace.'

εἴρηται: see (1) εἴρω 1.—(2) εἴρομαι.

εἴριον: see ἔριον.

εἰρο-κόμος (κομέω): *wool-carder,* Γ 387†.

εἴρομαι, εἴρεαι, subj. εἴρωμαι, -ηαι, -ηται, -ώμεθα, imp. εἴρεο, εἰρέσθω, inf. εἴρεσθαι, part. εἰρόμενος, ipf. εἴρετο, -οντο, fut. εἰρήσομαι: *ask, inquire,* often τινά τι, also ἀμφί τινι, περί τινος, etc.; and w. acc. of thing inquired about or for, φυλακᾱς δ' ἃς εἴρεαι, Κ 416, Ζ 239, λ 542.

εἰρο-πόκος (πέκω): *woolly-fleeced, woolly,* ι 443 and Ε 137.

εἶρος: *wool, fleece,* δ 135 and ι 426.

εἰρύαται: see ἐρύομαι.

1. εἴρω (root Ϝερ, cf. verbum), pres. rare (ν 7), fut. ἐρέω, -έει, -έουσι, part. ἐρέων, ἐρέουσα, pass. perf. εἴρηται, part. εἰρημένος, plup. εἴρητο, fut. εἰρήσεται, aor. part. dat. sing. ῥηθέντι: *say, speak, declare;* strictly with regard merely to the words said; *announce, herald,* ('Ηώς) Ζηνὶ φόως ἐρέουσα, Β 49; ('Εωσφόρος) φόως ἐρέων ἐπὶ γαῖαν, Ψ 226.

2. εἴρω (root σερ, cf. s e r o), only pass. perf. part. ἐερμένος, plup. ἔερτο: *string,* as beads; μετὰ (adv.) δ' ἠλέκτροισιν ἔερτο, at intervals 'was strung' with beads of amber, ο 460; ὅρμος ἠλέκτροισιν ἐερμένος, σ 296; γέφῡραι ἐερμέναι, 'joined' in succession, Ε 89.

εἰρωτάω (εἴρομαι), ipf. εἰρώτᾱ: *ask,* τινά τι. (Od.)

εἰς, ἐς (εἰς before a consonant only in εἰσβαινω): *into.*—I. adv. (the so-called 'tmesis'), ἐς δ' ἤλθον, ἐς δ' ἐρέτᾱς ἀγείρομεν, Α 142; an acc. in the same clause may specify the relation of the adv., thus preparing the way for a true prepositional use, τὼ δ' εἰς ἀμφοτέρω Διομήδεος ἅρματα (acc. of end of motion) βήτην, Θ 115, β 152.—II. prep. w. acc., *into, to, for,* ἐς ἀλλήλους δὲ ἴδοντο, 'towards' each other, into each other's faces, Ω 484; of purpose, εἰπεῖν εἰς ἀγαθόν, 'for' a good end, Ι 102; εἰς ἄτην, 'to' my ruin, μ 372; of time, εἰς ἐνιαυτόν, i. e. up to the end of a year, δ 595; so εἰς ὅ κε, *until;* distributively, αἰει εἰς ὥρᾱς, 'season after season' (cf. i n d i e s), ι 135. Apparently w. gen., by an ellipsis, εἰς 'Αιδāο (sc. δόμον), ἐς Πριάμοιο, and by analogy, εἰς Αἰγύπτοιο (sc. ὕδωρ), εἰς ἡμετέρου, β 55, etc.

εἶς: see εἰμί.

εἷς, μία, ἕν: *one;* τούς μοι μία γείνατο μήτηρ, 'one and the same' mother as my own, Τ 293; adv. phrase, ἐς μίαν βουλεύειν, be 'at one' again in counsel, Β 379.

εἶσα (root 'εδ-), defective aor., imp. εἶσον, inf. ἕσσαι, part. ἕσᾱς, ἕσᾱσα, mid. ἐέσσατο: *cause to sit, sit down, settle;* ἐς θρόνον εἶσεν ἄγων, i. e. gave her a seat, α 130; λόχον, 'lay' an ambuscade, δ 531; δῆμον Σχερίῃ, 'settled' them in Scheria, ζ 8; ἐπὶ βουσὶν εἷσέ με, 'established' me in charge of), υ 210; mid., ἐπὶ νηὸς ἐέσσατό με, 'took me on board' of his ship, ξ 295.

εἰσ-αγείρομαι, ipf. ἐσαγείρετο, aor. -ατο: *gather together in* or *for;* of a crew, ξ 248; met., νέον δ' ἐσαγείρετο θῡμόν, 'was collecting' his powers, coming to life, O 240.

εἰσ-άγω, ἐσάγω, ipf. -ῆγον, aor. 2 -άγαγον (-ήγαγε): *lead or bring in;* w. acc. of the place whither, δώματα, δόμον, Κρήτην, εἰσήγαγ' ἑταίρους, γ 191.

εἰσ-αθρέω, aor. opt. ἐσαθρήσειεν: *descry*, Γ 450†.

εἰσ-ακούω, aor. ἐσάκουσε: *give ear*, Θ 97.

εἰσ-άλλομαι, aor. 1 ἐσήλατο, aor. 2 ἐσᾶλτο: *leap into* or *at*. (Il.)

εἰσάμενος: see εἴδω, I.

εἰσ-ανα-βαίνω, opt. -νοι, ipf. -ανέβαινον, aor. 2 -ανέβησαν, inf. -βῆναι, part. -βᾶσα: *go up* or *back to, ascend to, mount.*

εἰσ-αν-άγω: *lead away into* bondage, τινὰ εἴρερον, θ 529†.

εἰσ-αν-εῖδον: *look up into*, Π 232 and Ω 307.

εἰσ-άν-ειμι (εἶμι): only part., *climbing* the sky, ἠέλιος οὐρανόν, Η 423†.

εἰσ-άντα, ἐσάντα: *in the face, straight at, straight forward.*

εἴσατο: see (1) εἴδω, I.—(2) εἶμι.

εἰσ-αφ-ικᾱ́νω = εἰσαφικνέομαι.

εἰσ-αφ-ικνέομαι, aor. opt. -ίκοιτο, subj. -ίκηαι, -ίκηται, inf. -κέσθαι: *arrive at, reach.*

εἰσ-βαίνω, ἐσβαίνω, aor. 2 opt. ἐσβαίη, part. ἐσβάντες: *enter*, esp. *go on board* ship, *embark.*

εἰσ-δέρκομαι, aor. ἐσέδρακον: *look at, discern.*

εἰσ-δύομαι, fut. ἐσδύσεαι: *enter into*, to take part in, ἀκοντιστύν, Ψ 622†.

εἰσεῖδον: see εἰσοράω.

εἴσ-ειμι (εἶμι): *go into, enter;* μετ' ἀνέρας, 'among the men,' Σ 184; w. acc., οὐδ' Ἀχιλῆος | ὀφθαλμοὺς εἴσειμι, 'into his sight,' Ω 463.

εἰσ-ελαύνω, εἰσελάω, part. -άων, aor. 3 pl. εἰσέλασαν, part. εἰσελάσαντες: *drive in;* of a ship, *run* or *row in.*

εἰσ-ερύω, aor. part. εἰσερύσαντες: *drag into*, νῆα σπέος, μ 317†.

εἰσ-έρχομαι, fut. ἐσελεύσομαι, aor. 2 εἰσῆλθον, ἐσήλυθον: *come* or *go into, enter;* metaph., μένος ἄνδρας εἰσέρχεται, πείνη δῆμον, ο 407.

ἐΐση (Ϝῖσος), only fem. forms: *equal;* epith. of δαίς, 'equally divided' feast, A 468; νῆες ἐΐσαι, 'balanced,' 'symmetrical,' A 306; ἀσπὶς πάντοσ' ἐΐση, i. e. circular, Γ 347; ἵπποι, exactly matched in size, B 765; φρένες ἔνδον ἐΐσαι, a 'well-balanced' mind, λ 337.

εἶσθα: see εἶμι.

εἰσ-θρώσκω, aor. 2 ἔσθορε: *spring in.* (Il.)

εἰσῑέμεναι: see εἰσίημι.

εἰσ-ίζομαι, subj. ἐσίζηται: *place oneself in* an ambuscade, N 285†.

εἰσ-ίημι: only mid. pres. part. εἰσῑέμεναι, *seeking to enter*, χ 470†.

εἴσ-ιθμη (εἶμι): *way in, entrance*, ζ 264†.

εἰσ-κατα-βαίνω, part. ἐσκαταβαίνων: *go down into*, ὄρχατον, ω 222†.

ἐΐσκω, ἴσκω (ϜεϜ., cf. Ϝίκελος), ἴσκουσι, part. ἴσκοντες, ipf. ἤισκον, ἔισκον, ἴσκον: *make like, deem* or *find like, compare to, judge* as to likeness or similarity; ἄλλῳ δ' αὐτὸν φωτὶ κατακρύπτων ἤισκεν, 'made himself look like' another man, δ 247; ἐμὲ σοὶ Ϝίσκοντες, i. e. taking me for thee, Π 41; τὸ μὲν ἄμμες ἐΐσκομεν ὅσσον θ' ἱστὸν νηός, 'we judged it to be as large,' ι 321; ἐΐσκομεν ἄξιον εἶναι | τρεῖς ἑνὸς ἀντὶ πεφάσθαι, 'deem it a fair equivalent,' N 446, Φ 332.

εἰσ-μαίομαι: only aor. (metaph.), θανὼν μάλα με ἐσμάσσατο θῡμόν, 'searched into,' i. e. carried grief to my heart, P 564 and Υ 425.

εἰσ-νοέω, aor. εἰσενόησα: *perceive.*

εἴσ-οδος: *entrance*, κ 90†.

εἰσ-οιχνέω (οἴχομαι), 3 pl. -εῦσι, part. -εῦσαν: *enter.* (Od.)

εἰσόκε(ν), εἰς ὅ κεν: *until, as long as.*

εἴσομαι: see (1) εἶμι.—(2) εἴδω, II.

εἰσ-οράω, εἰσορόωσι, opt. -ορόῳτε, part. -ορόων and -ῶν, aor. εἰσεῖδον, ἔσιδον, iter. ἐσίδεσκεν, fut. ἐσόψομαι: *look upon, behold*, act. and mid.; the part. is often added to verbs by way of amplification, σέβας μ' ἔχει εἰσορόωντα, ζ 161; so the inf. epexegetically, ὀξύτατον πέλεται φάος εἰσοράασθαι, Ξ 345.

ἐΐσος: see ἐΐση.

εἰσόψομαι: see εἰσοράω.

εἰσ-πέτομαι, aor. εἰσέπτατο: *fly into*, Φ 494†.

εἰσ-φέρω, ipf. ἔσφερον; *carry in*, mid., (ποταμὸς) πεύκᾱς ἐσφέρεται, 'sweeps into its current,' Λ 495.

εἰσ-φορέω, ipf. ἐσφόρεον: parallel form of εἰσφέρω.

εἰσ-χέω: only aor. mid. (metaph.), ἐσέχυντο κατὰ πύλᾱς, they *poured in* at the gates, Μ 470 and Φ 610.

εἴσω and **ἔσω** (εἰς): *towards within, into;* often following an acc. of end of motion, Ἴλιον εἴσω, οὐρανὸν εἴσω, etc.; w. gen., η 135, θ 290.

εἰσ-ωπός (ὤψ): *face to face with, directly in front of,* νεῶν, Ο 653†.

εἶται: see ἕννῡμι.

εἴ τε: see εἰ.

εἶτε = εἴητε, see εἰμί.

εἰῶ = ἐάω.

εἴωθα: see ἔθω.

εἴων: see ἐάω.

εἵως = ἕως.

ἐκ, before vowels **ἐξ:** *out.*—I. adv. (here belong the examples of 'tmesis' so-called), ἐκ δ' εὐνᾱς ἔβαλον, Α 436; ἐκ δ' ἔσσυτο λᾱός, Θ 58; a gen. in the same clause may specify the relation of the adverb, thus forming a transition to the true prepositional use, ἐκ δ' ἄγαγε κλισίης (gen. of place whence) Βρῑσηίδα, Α 346.—II. prep. w. gen., *out of, (forth) from;* of distance or separation, ἐκ βελέων, 'out of range,' Λ 163; ἐκ καπνοῦ, 'out of,' 'away from' the smoke, π 288; often where motion is rather implied than expressed, as with verbs of beginning, attaching or hanging, ἐκ δὲ τοῦ ἀρχόμενος, 'beginning with that,' ψ 199; ἐκ πασσαλόφι κρέμασεν φόρμιγγα, θ 67; τῆς δ' ἐξ ἀργύρεος τελαμὼν ἦν, 'attached to it,' Λ 38; ἐξ ἑτέρων ἕτερ' ἐστίν, 'one set of buildings adjoining another,' ρ 266; hence temporal, ἐκ τοῦδε, ἐξ οὗ, *since;* often causal, ἐξ ἀρέων μητρὸς κεχολωμένος, 'in consequence of,' Ι 566; sometimes nearly equiv. to ὑπό, i. e. source for agency, πάσχειν τι ἔκ τινος, ἐφίληθεν ἐκ Διός, Β 669; phrases, ἐκ θῡμοῦ φιλεῖν, ἐξ ἔριδος μάχεσθαι, etc.—ἐκ is accented ('anastrophe') when it follows its case, καύματος ἔξ, Ε 865, Ξ 472, ρ 518.

Ἑκάβη: *Hecuba*, the wife of Priam, daughter of Dymas, a Phrygian king, Ζ 293, Π 718. (Il.)

ἑκά-εργος (ϝεκάς, ϝέργον): *far-working, far-worker,* epith. of Apollo, the 'far-darter.' Some moderns are disposed to set aside the traditional interpretation in favor of new ones, in regard to which, however, they do not agree among themselves.

ἐκάην: see καίω.

ἕκαθεν (ϝεκάς): *from far away, afar, far.*

Ἑκαμήδη: daughter of Arsinous, and slave of Nestor, Λ 624.

ἑκάς (ϝεκάς): adv., *far, remote;* freq. w. gen., *far from.*—Comp., **ἑκαστέρω,** sup. **ἑκαστάτω.**

ἑκάστοθι: *in each place,* 'in each division,' γ 8†.

ἕκαστος (ϝεκ.): *each, each one;* in sing. regularly w. pl. vb., and in app. to pl. subjects, οἳ μὲν κακκείοντες ἔβαν οἶκόνδε ϝέκαστος, 'each to his home,' Α 606; pl., less common and strictly referring to each of several parties or sets of persons, Γ 1; sometimes, however, equiv. to the sing., ξ 436.

ἑκάτερθε(ν) (ϝεκ.): *from* or *on both sides.*

ἑκατη-βελέτης, ᾱο = ἑκατηβόλος, Α 75†.

ἑκατη-βόλος (ϝέκατος, βάλλω): *far-darting,* epithet of Apollo; subst., the 'far-darter,' Ο 231.

ἑκατόγ-χειρος: *hundred-handed,* Α 402†.

ἑκατό-ζυγος: *with a hundred benches,* νηῦς, an hyperbole, Υ 247†.

ἑκατόμ-βη (βοῦς): *hecatomb;* properly, 'sacrifice of a hundred oxen,' but the number is a round one, as the hecatombs mentioned always contain less than 100 head; hence for 'sacrifice' generally, Β 321, etc.

ἑκατόμ-βοιος: *worth a hundred oxen;* 'the value of a hundred oxen,' ἑκατόμβοιον, Φ 79. (Il.)

ἑκατόμ-πεδος, ἑκατόμποδος (πούς): *a hundred feet each way,* Ψ 164†.

ἑκατόμ-πολις: *hundred-citied,* in round numbers (cf. τ 174), epith. of Crete, Β 649†.

ἑκατόμ-πυλος: *hundred-gated,* epith. of Egyptian Thebes, Ι 383†.

ἑκατόν: *hundred;* freq. as a round number, alone and in compounds.

ἕκατος (ϝεκάς): *far*-working, subst., the *far*-worker; epith. of Apollo; cf ἑκάεργος, ἑκατηβόλος. (Il.)

ἐκ-βαίνω, aor. 1 part. ἐκβήσαντες, aor. 2 imp. ἔκβητε: *go out*, esp. *go ashore, disembark;* aor. 1 trans., 'putting you ashore,' ω 301.

ἐκ-βάλλω, ipf. ἔκβαλλε, aor. 2 ἔκβαλον: *throw* or *cast out* or *forth, let fall;* χειρὸς ἔγχος, the spear from the hand, Ξ 419; so of striking something from the hand of another, etc.; of felling trees, ε 244; metaph., ἔπος, Σ 324, δ 503.

ἔκ-βασις: *landing-place*, ε 410†.

ἐκ-βλώσκω, aor. 2 ἔκμολεν: *go forth*, Λ 604†.

ἐκγεγάμεν, ἐκγεγάτην, ἐκγεγαώς: see ἐκγίγνομαι.

ἐκ-γελάω, aor. part. ἐκγελάσᾱς: *laugh out;* ἡδύ, 'heartily,' π 345.

ἐκ-γίγνομαι, aor. ἐξεγένοντο, perf. du. ἐκγεγάτην, inf. ἐκγεγάμεν, part. ἐκγεγαῶτι: *spring from*, perf. *be descended from*, τινός.

ἔκ-γονος: *offspring, child.*

ἐκ-δέρκομαι: *look forth from*, Ψ 477†.

ἐκ-δέρω, aor. part. ἐκδείρᾱς: *flay*, κ 19†.

ἐκ-δέχομαι: *receive from*, τινί τι, Ν 710†.

ἐκ-δέω, ipf. ἔκδεον, aor. inf. ἐκδῆσαι, part. ἐκδήσᾱς: *bind* or *tie to;* w. gen., Ψ 121.

ἔκ-δηλος: *conspicuous*, Ε 2†.

ἐκ-δια-βαίνω, aor. 2 part. ἐκδιαβάντες: *pass quite over*, Κ 198†.

ἐκ-δίδωμι, aor. 2 imp. ἔκδοτε: *deliver over*, Γ 459†.

ἐκ-δύνω, ἐκδύω, ipf. ἐκδῡνε, aor. opt. ἐκδῦμεν, part. ἐκδύς, mid. ipf. ἐξεδύοντο: *get out from, put off, doff;* ἐκδὺς μεγάροιο, χ 334; ἔκδῡνε χιτῶνα, α 437; τεύχεα τ' ἐξεδύοντο, Γ 114; metaph., ὄλεθρον, 'escape,' Π 99.

ἐκεῖθι: *there*, ρ 10†.

ἐκεῖνος, η, ο, and **κεῖνος**: *that one* (ille), *he, she;* κεῖνος μέν τοι ὅδ' αὐτὸς ἐγώ, πάτερ, ὃν σὺ μεταλλᾷς, 'I myself here am *he*,' ω 321; freq. deictic, κεῖνος ὅ γε, *yonder* he is, Γ 391, Ε 604.—Adv., **κείνῃ,** *there*, ν 111.

ἐκέκαστο: see καίνυμαι.

ἐκέκλετο: see κέλομαι.

ἐκέκλιτο: see κλίνω.

ἔκηα: see καίω.

ἐκη-βολίη (ϝεκάς, βάλλω): *shooting far*, pl., attribute of a hunter, Ε 54†.

ἐκη-βόλος = ἑκατηβόλος, epithet of Apollo.

ἕκηλος (ϝεκ.) and **εὔκηλος**: *of good cheer, free from care, at ease;* often negatively, 'undisturbed,' 'unmolested,' Ζ 70, Ρ 340; iron., ἕκηλος ἐρρέτω, 'let him go to perdition at his leisure,' Ι 376.

ἕκητι (ϝέκητι): *by the will* or *grace* (of a god). (Od.)

ἐκ-θνήσκω: only aor. ἔκθανον γέλῳ, *died* a-laughing, σ 100†.

ἐκ-θρώσκω, aor. ἐξέθορε, ἔκθορε: *spring* or *leap forth.*

ἐκ-καθαίρω: *clean out*, Β 153†.

ἑκ-καιδεκά-δωρος: *sixteen palms* (δῶρα) *long*, of the horns of a wild goat, Δ 109†.

ἐκ-καλέω, aor. part. -έσᾱς, -αντες: *call out* or *forth*, mid., to oneself.

ἐκ-κατα-πάλλω: only aor. mid. ἐκκατέπαλτο, *darted down from;* οὐρανοῦ, Τ 351†.

ἐκ-κατ-εῖδον, part. ἐκκατιδών: *look down from*, Περγάμου, Δ 508 and Η 21.

ἐκ-κλέπτω, aor. ἐξέκλεψεν: *steal away*, Ε 390†.

ἐκ-κυλίω: only aor. pass. ἐξεκυλίσθη, *rolled* (*headlong*) *down from*, ἐκ δίφρου, Ζ 42 and Ψ 394.

ἐκ-λανθάνω, aor. 2 ἐκλέλαθον, mid. aor. ἐκλάθετο, ἐξελάθοντο, subj. ἐκλελάθωνται, opt. -οιτο, inf. -έσθαι: act., causative, *make to forget utterly;* τινά τι, Β 600; mid., *forget utterly;* τινός, also w. inf., κ 557.

ἐκλέεο: see κλείω 1.

ἔκ-λησις (λήθω): *forgetting* and forgiving, ω 485†.

ἐκ-λύω, mid. fut. ἐκλῡσομαι, pass. aor. ἐξελύθη, Ε 293 (v. l. ἐξεσύθη): *loose from*, mid., *set free from*, w. gen., κ 286.

ἐκ-μείρομαι: only perf., θεῶν ἐξέμμορε τῑμῆς, *has won a high share* in the honor of the gods, ε 335† (v. l. θεῶν ἔξ).

ἔκμολεν: see ἐκβλώσκω.

ἐκ-μυζάω, aor. part. ἐκμυζήσᾱς: *suck out*, Δ 218†.

ἐκ-νοστέω, aor. part. ἐκνοστήσᾱς: *return from*, μάχης (v. l. μάχης ἔκ).

ἔκ-παγλος, sup. ἐκπαγλότατος: *terrible*, both of persons and of things; adv., **ἔκπαγλον, ἔκπαγλα, ἐκπάγλως,**

terribly, but often colloquially weakened, 'exceedingly,' ἔκπαγλα φιλεῖν, Γ 415 (cf. *αἰνά*, *αἰνῶς*).

ἐκ-παιφάσσω (φάος): only inf. (metaph.), *shine forth*, of brilliant performance, or perhaps of lightning swiftness, Ε 803†.

ἐκ-πάλλω: only aor. mid., ἔκπαλτο, *spirted out*, Υ 483†.

ἐκ-πατάσσω: *strike out*; only pass. perf. part. (metaph.), φρένας ἐκπεπαταγμένος, 'bereft of sense,' σ 327† (cf. ἐκπλήσσω).

ἐκ-πέμπω, aor. ἔκπεμψα: *send out* or *away*, mid., from oneself; *conduct forth*, Ω 681.

ἐκπέποται: see ἐκπίνω.

ἐκ-περάω, ἐκπεράᾳ, -όωσι, aor. ἐξεπέρησε: *pass through*, of arrow or spear; *traverse*, of the sea.

ἐκ-πέρθω, fut. ἐκπέρσω, aor. 1 subj. ἐκπέρσωσι, aor. 2 ἐξεπράθομεν: *utterly destroy*, *pillage from*; πολίων, Α 125.

ἐκπεσέειν: see ἐκπίπτω.

ἐκπεφυυῖαι: see ἐκφύω.

ἐκ-πίνω, aor. 2 ἔκπιον, perf. pass. ἐκπέποται: *drink up*, *drink dry*. (Od.)

ἐκ-πίπτω, aor. 2 ἔκπεσον, inf. -σέειν: *fall out*, *fall down* (*from*).

ἐκ-πλήσσω, pass. aor. 2 3 pl. ἔκπληγεν: *strike out*, regularly metaph., *dismay*, *terrify*, with and without φρένας, Σ 225.

ἐκ-ποτέομαι (πέτομαι): *flutter down from* the sky (Διός), of snow-flakes, Τ 357†.

ἐκ-πρεπής, έος (πρέπω): *conspicuous*, *distinguished*, Β 483†.

ἐκ-προ-καλέω: only aor. mid. part., ἐκπροκαλεσσαμένη, *having called him forth to herself*, β 400†.

ἐκ-προ-λείπω: only aor. 2 part. ἐκπρολιπόντες, *going forth and leaving*, the wooden horse, θ 515†.

ἐκ-πτύω: only aor. ἐξέπτυσε, *spat forth*, salt water, ε 322†.

ἐκ-πυνθάνομαι: only aor. 2 inf., *search out*, Κ 308 and 320.

ἐκρέμω: see κρέμαμαι.

ἐκ-ρήγνῡμι, aor. ἐξέρρηξα: *break* or *burst away*, foll. by part. gen., Ψ 421; of 'snapping' a bowstring, Ο 469.

ἐκ-σαόω, aor. ἐξεσάωσεν: *save* (*from*), τινά (τινος).

ἐκ-σεύω, aor. mid. ἐξέσσυτο, pass. ἐξεσύθη: mid., *rush* or *hasten forth*; w. gen., Η 1, ι 373; fig., βλεφάρων ἐξέσσυτο ὕπνος, μ 366.

ἐκ-σπάω, aor. ἐξέσπασε, mid. part. ἐκσπασσαμένω: *pull out*, mid., something that is one's own, Η 255.

ἐκ-στρέφω, aor. ἐξέστρεψε: *twist* or *wrench out of*; ἔρνος βόθρου, Ρ 58†.

ἔκτα, ἔκταθεν: see κτείνω.

ἐκτάδιος, 3 (τείνω): *broad*; 'with ample folds,' χλαῖνα, Κ 134†.

ἐκ-τάμνω, subj. ἐκτάμνῃσι, aor. ἐξέταμον, ἔκταμε: *cut out*, *hew out*, *fell* trees, ι 320; of the havoc wrought by wild boars, Μ 149.

ἔκταν: see κτείνω.

ἐκ-τανύω, aor. ἐξετάνυσσα, pass. ἐξετανύσθην: *stretch out*, 'lay low,' Ρ 58; mid., *fall prone*, Η 271.

ἐκ-τελέω, ἐκτελείω, aor. ἐξετέλεσσα, pass. ipf. ἐξετελεῦντο, perf. ἐκτετέλεσται: *bring to an end*, *finish*, *fulfil*, *consummate*, *achieve*; ὅ μοι οὔ τι θεοὶ γόνον ἐξετέλειον | ἐξ ἐμοῦ, 'granted me no offspring of my own,' Ι 493.

ἐκ-τίθημι, aor. 2 part. ἐκθείς: *put* or *set out*, ψ 179†.

ἔκτοθεν: *outside*, w. gen., 'separate from,' α 133; in ι 239 the MSS. have ἔντοθεν. (Od.)

ἔκτοθι: *outside*, 'far from,' νηῶν, Ο 391, Χ 439.

Ἑκτόρεος: *of Hector*, Β 416.

Ἑκτορίδης: *son of Hector*, Astyanax, Ζ 401.

ἐκτός (ἐκ): *outside*, Δ 151; w. gen., *outside of*, Ψ 424, and w. ἀπό, 'apart from,' Κ 151.

ἕκτος: *sixth*.

ἔκτοσε: *out of*, w. gen., ξ 277†.

ἔκτοσθε(ν): *outside*, Η 341; w. gen., *outside of*.

ἔκτυπε: see κτυπέω.

Ἕκτωρ, ορος: *Hector*, son of Priam and Hecuba, Χ 80, 405, 430, Ω 747; husband of Andromache, Ζ 390, Ω 723; and father of Astyanax. Hector was the mainstay of Troy in the war, οἶος γὰρ ἐρύετο Ἴλιον Ἕκτωρ, Ζ 403. He was slain by Achilles in revenge for the killing of Patroclus, Σ 115, Χ 326, 331, 361.

ἑκυρή (Ϝεκ.): *mother-in-law*.

ἑκυρός (Ϝεκ.): *father-in-law*.

ἐκ-φαίνω, fut. ἐκφανεῖ, pass. aor. ἐξεφαάνθη, 3 pl. -φάανθεν, aor. 2 ἐξεφάνη:

act., *bring to light*, Τ 104; mid. and pass., *shine out*, *sparkle*, Τ 17; *appear*, *come to light*, μ 441.

ἐκ-φέρω, ipf. ἐξέφερον, ἔκφερε, fut. 3 pl. ἐξοίσουσι: *bear* or *carry out* or *off*; of bearing away a prize, Ψ 785; stolen property, ο 470; bringing payment to maturity, Φ 450; and esp. of carrying forth the dead for burial, Ω 786; intrans., *take the lead*, in racing, Ψ 376, 759.

ἐκ-φεύγω, aor. 2 ἐξέφυγον, ἔκφυγε: *flee* or *fly from*, *escape from*, *escape*; w. gen., ἁλός, ἔνθεν, ψ 236, μ 212, or transitively w. acc., ὁρμήν, κῆρας, γάμον, Ι 355, δ 512, τ 157; freq. of the weapon flying from the hand of him who hurls it, Ε 18, etc.

ἔκ-φημι, only pres. inf. mid. ἔκφασθαι: *speak out*, *utter* (ἔπος), ν 308 and κ 246.

ἐκ-φθέγγομαι: only aor. ἐκφθέγξατο, *called out from*, Φ 213.

ἐκ-φθίνω: only pass. plup. ἐξέφθιτο, *had been consumed out of* the ships, ι 163 and μ 329.

ἐκ-φορέω (φέρω): *carry forth from*; νέκυας οἴκων, χ 451; mid., *move forth from*, νηῶν, Τ 360.

ἔκφυγε: see ἐκφεύγω.

ἐκ-φύω: only perf. part. (intrans.) ἐκπεφυυῖαι, *growing out of*, κεφαλαὶ αὐχένος, Λ 40†.

ἐκ-χέω, mid. aor. 1 ἐκχεύατο, aor. 2 ἐξέχυτο and ἔκχυτο, part. ἐκχύμενος, pass. plup. ἐξεκέχυντο: *pour out*; mid., something that is one's own, ὀιστούς, χ 3; or intrans., *stream* or *pour forth*, ὕδατος ἐκχυμένοιο, Φ 300; met., of meshes 'hanging down,' θ 279; men or animals 'pouring forth' in numbers, θ 515.

ἑκών, ἑκοῦσα (Ϝεκ.): *willingly*, *intentionally*, *of one's own will*; ἑκὼν ἀέκοντί γε θῡμῷ, i. e. not by compulsion, and yet reluctantly, Δ 43; ἑκὼν δ' οὐκ ἄν τις ἕλοιτο (δῶρα θεῶν), i. e. they cannot be got otherwise than from the gift of the gods, Γ 66.

ἐλάᾱν: see ἐλαύνω.

ἐλαίη: *olive-tree*; ἱερή, sacred to Athēna, ν 372.

ἐλαΐνεος, ἐλάϊνος: *of olive-wood*.

ἔλαιον: *olive-oil*; εὐῶδες, β 339; ῥοδόεν, Ψ 186. See λίπα.

ἔλα(σ)σα, ἐλάσασκε: see ἐλαύνω.

Ἔλασος: a Trojan, Π 696.

ἐλάσσων (ἐλαχύς), irreg. comp of μῑκρός: only neut. ἔλασσον, *less*, Κ 357†.

ἐλαστρέω (parallel form of ἐλαύνω): *drive*; ζεύγεα, Σ 543†.

ἐλάτη: *pine* or *fir*; pl., 'oars of pine,' Η 5, μ 172.

ἐλατήρ, ῆρος (ἐλάω): *driver*, *charioteer*. (Il.)

Ἔλατος: (1) an ally of the Trojans, Ζ 33.—(2) a suitor of Penelope, χ 267.

Ἐλατρεύς ('Rower'): a Phaeacian, θ 111, 129.

ἐλαύνω, ἐλάω, inf. ἐλάᾱν, ipf. ἔλων, fut. ἐλόωσι, aor. ἤλασσε, ἔλασσε, iter. ἐλάσασκε, pass. plup. ἠλήλατο, ἐλήλατο, 3 pl. ἐληλάδατο or ἐληλέ(δ)ατο: *drive*, *impel*, *strike*, mid., for oneself, δ 637, Κ 537, etc.; freq. of 'rowing' a vessel, with and without νῆα, ν 22, pass. ν 155; so of driving horses, without obj. expressed, Ε 264; μάστῑξεν δ' ἐλάᾱν, γ 484; hence apparently often intrans., πόντον ἐλαύνοντες, Η 6, Ν 27, η 319; of 'driving away' cattle, horses, etc., Α 154; in the sense *strike* the verb occurs often, esp. of 'forging,' Μ 296; of 'drawing,' or 'laying out' a fence or wall, or a swath in reaping, ἕρκος, τεῖχος, τάφρον, Η 450, Ι 349, Σ 564; σταυρούς, ξ 11; χάλκεοι τοῖχοι ἐληλέδατο, 'were extended,' η 86; ὄγμον, Λ 68; metaph., of 'persecuting,' ε 290; being 'racked' with pain, Π 518; 'raising' a din, Α 575.

ἐλαφη-βόλος: (ἀνήρ) *deer-hunter*, Σ 319†.

ἔλαφος, ὁ and ἡ: *stag* or *hind*, Γ 24; a symbol of cowardice, Α 225.

ἐλαφρός, -ότερος, -ότατος: *light* (moving), *nimble*; of the swift wind, Τ 416; *light* (of weight), Μ 450; met., πόλεμος, Χ 287. — Adv., **ἐλαφρῶς,** *lightly*, *easily*, ε 240.

ἔλαχε: see λαγχάνω.

ἐλαχύς, ἐλάχεια (cf. ἐλάσσων): *small*, ι 116, κ 509, v. l. λάχεια.

ἐλάω: see ἐλαύνω.

ἔλδομαι (Ϝελδ.), **ἐέλδομαι**: *desire*, *long for*; τινός, Ξ 276, ε 210, etc.; also τὶ, α 409, and w. inf., Ν 638, υ 35; in pass. signif., Π 494.

ἔλδωρ, ἐέλδωρ (ἐϜελδ.): *desire*, *wish*.

ἕλε: see αἱρέω.

ἐλεαίρω (ἔλεος), ipf. ἐλέαιρεν, iter. ἐλεαίρεσκον: *pity, feel compassion; οὐκ ἐλεαίρεις ἄνδρας . . μισγέμεναι κακότητι*, 'thou dost unpityingly involve men in trouble,' υ 202.

ἐλεγχείη = ἔλεγχος. 'Devote to *shame*,' 'cover with *shame*,' X 100, ξ 38.

ἐλεγχής, έος: *despicable; ἐλέγχιστος, most infamous*, B 285.

ἔλεγχος: *shame, reproach, disgrace;* pl., φ 333; pl. as term of reproach (abstr. for concrete), κάκ' ἐλέγχεα, *miscreants, cowards*, B 235, Ω 260.

ἐλέγχω: *dishonor, bring disgrace upon*, φ 424; τῶν μὴ σύ γε μῦθον ἐλέγξῃς | μηδὲ πόδας, 'put not to shame their words and mission,' i. e. by making them vain, I 522.

ἑλέειν: see αἱρέω.

ἐλεεινός, -ότερος, -ότατος: *pitiable, piteous;* neut., and esp. pl., as adv., *pitifully*, θ 531, X 37, B 314.

ἐλεέω, fut. ἐλεήσει, aor. ἐλέησε: *pity, have compassion* or *pity upon;* τινά, also τί, Z 94; w. part., O 44, P 346, ε 336.

ἐλεήμων: *compassionate*, ε 191†.

ἐλεητύς, ύος = ἔλεος, ξ 82 and ρ 451.

ἔλεκτο: see λέγω.

ἐλελίζω, aor. ἐλέλιξε, mid. aor. part. ἐλελιξάμενος, pass. plup. ἐλέλικτο, aor. ἐλελίχθη, 3 pl. ἐλέλιχθεν: *set quivering* or *quaking, whirl round and round*, mid. intrans.; μέγαν δ' ἐλέλιξεν Ὄλυμπον, 'made Olympus tremble,' A 530, Θ 199; ἐλελίχθη γυῖα, 'quaked,' X 448; of a spear brandished in the hand, σειόμενον ἐλέλικτο, N 558; of a serpent 'coiled,' Λ 39; Odysseus' ship is made to 'spin' by the lightning, his raft by a great wave, μ 416, ε 314; esp. of facing about and 'rallying' in the fray, οἱ δ' ἐλελίχθησαν καὶ ἐναντίοι ἔσταν Ἀχαιῶν, Z 106, P 278.

Ἑλένη: *Helen*, the wife of Menelāus, daughter of Zeus and Leda, Γ 199, 426, and sister of Castor and Pollux, Γ 238. Often w. the epithet Ἀργείη, B 161, δ 184; Γ 91, 121, Ω 761, δ 12, 219, 279. Helen returned to her home in Sparta after the war, and in the Odyssey is seen living happily with Menelāus, δ, ο.

Ἕλενος: *Helenus.*—(1) a son of Priam, the best seer of the Trojans, Z 76, N 576, Ω 249.—(2) a Greek, son of Oenopion, E 707.

ἑλεό-θρεπτος: *growing in marshes*, B 776†.

ἔλεος: *pity, compassion*, Ω 44†.

ἐλεός: *meat-board, dresser*, I 215 and ξ 432.

ἕλεσκον: see αἱρέω.

ἑλετός (ἑλεῖν): *to be caught;* ἀνδρὸς ψῡχὴ πάλιν ἐλθεῖν οὔτε λεϊστὴ οὔθ' ἑλετή, 'the breath of life comes not back by plundering or capture,' I 409†.

ἑλεῦ = ἑλοῦ, see αἱρέω.

ἐλεύθερος: *free;* ἐλεύθερον ἦμαρ, 'the day of freedom' (= ἐλευθερία), Z 455, cf. δούλιον ἦμαρ; κρητήρ, 'bowl of freedom,' celebrating its recovery, Z 528.

ἐλεφαίρομαι: *delude, deceive*, Ψ 388; with a play upon ἐλέφᾱς, τ 565.

ἐλέφᾱς, αντος: *ivory*, Δ 141, E 583, δ 73, θ 404; a symbol of whiteness, σ 196, ψ 200.

Ἐλεφήνωρ: son of Chalcōdon, leader of the Abantes, B 540, Δ 467.

Ἐλεών: a town in Boeotia, B 500.

ἐληλάδατο, ἐλήλαται, ἐλήλατο, ἐληλέατο, ἐληλέδατο: see ἐλαύνω.

ἐληλουθώς, ἐλθέμεν(αι): see ἔρχομαι.

Ἑλικάων: a son of Antēnor, husband of Laodice, Γ 123.

Ἑλίκη: a town in Achaea, containing a shrine of Poseidon, B 575, Θ 203.

Ἑλικώνιος: *Heliconian;* ἄναξ, i. e. Poseidon, Υ 404.

ἑλικ-ῶπις, ιδος, and **ἑλίκ-ωψ**, ωπος (Ϝέλιξ, ὤψ): *quick-eyed*, or, according to others, *with arched eye-brows*, A 98, 389.

ἕλιξ (Ϝελίσσω): *bent around*, as epith. of kine, *crumple-horned;* joined with εἰλίποδας, I 466, α 92, and with εὐρυμέτωποι, λ 289, μ 355.—Subst., **ἕλικες** γναμπταί, *armlets* bent into a spiral. (See cut No. 2.)

ἑλίσσω (Ϝελ.), inf. ἑλισσέμεν, aor. part. ἑλίξᾱς, mid. ipf. εἱλίσσετο, ἑλίσσετο, aor. part. ἑλιξάμενος, pass. ἑλιχθέντων: *curl, wind, turn*, mid. intrans., causative, 'making it roll,' N 204; of a serpent 'coiling' himself, ἑλισσόμενος περὶ χειῇ, X 95; savor of a sacrifice curling upwards, ἑλισσομένη περὶ καπνῷ, Α 317; of turning the goal in a race, Ψ 309; then of persons going around, turning to and fro, facing about and 'rallying,' Φ 11, Ψ 320, Μ 74.

ἑλκεσί-πεπλος: *with trailing robe*, epith. of Trojan women. (Il.)

ἑλκε-χίτων, ωνος: *with trailing tunic*, Ν 685†.

ἑλκέω (ἕλκω), ipf. ἕλκεον, fut. ἑλκήσουσι, aor. ἥλκησε, aor. pass. part. ἑλκηθείσᾱς: *drag, drag away* (as captive), Χ 62; of dogs pulling and tearing, Ρ 558, Χ 336; of maltreating or outraging, λ 580.

ἑλκηθμός (ἑλκέω): *dragging away* into captivity, Ζ 465†.

ἕλκος, εος: *wound, sore*, Τ 49; ὕδρου, 'from the serpent,' Β 723.

ἑλκυστάζω: parallel form of ἑλκέω, Ψ 187 and Ω 21.

ἕλκω, inf. ἑλκέμεν(αι): *draw, drag*, mid., something of one's own; of drawing a bow, Δ 122, φ 419; 'raising' the balance, and 'hoisting' sails, Χ 212, ο 291; 'tugged at it,' Μ 398; pass., 'trailing,' Ε 665; 'wrenched,' Ψ 715; mid., of drawing one's sword, tearing one's hair, etc., Κ 15, Ρ 136, τ 506.

ἔλλαβε: see λαμβάνω.

Ἑλλάς, άδος: *Hellas*, understood by the ancients to be a Thessalian city and district in Phthiōtis, under the sway of Achilles, Β 684; now more correctly described as the tract between the Asōpus and the Enīpeus; coupled with Phthia, Ι 395; the realm of Peleus, λ 496; καθ' Ἑλλάδα καὶ μέσον Ἄργος (all Greece), see Ἄργος, epithets, καλλιγύναικα, εὐρυχόροιο, Β 683, Ι 447, 478.

ἐλλεδανός (εἴλω): *straw band* for bundles of grain, Σ 553†.

Ἕλληνες: the *inhabitants of Hellas*, Β 684; see Μυρμιδόνες and Πανέλληνες.

Ἑλλήσ-ποντος ('Sea of Helle'): the *Hellespont*, with adjacent bodies of water, ω 82.

ἐλλισάμην, ἐλίσσετο: see λίσσομαι.

ἐλλιτάνευε: see λιτανεύω.

ἐλλός, ἐλλός: *young deer*, τ 228†.

ἕλοιμι, ἕλον, ἑλόμην: see αἱρέω.

ἕλος, εος (Ϝέλος): *meadow-land, marsh*, Δ 483, ξ 474.

Ἕλος (Ϝέλος, cf. Veliae): (1) in Laconia, a maritime city, named from its marshes, Β 584.—(2) a town of the Pylians, Β 594.

ἐλόωσι: see ἐλαύνω.

Ἐλπήνωρ ('Hopeful'): *Elpēnor*, a companion of Odysseus, κ 552, λ 51, 57.

ἐλπίς, ίδος (Ϝελπίς): *hope; ἔτι γὰρ καὶ ἐλπίδος αἶσα*, 'share' of hope, the 'boon' of hope, 'room' for hope, τ 84.

ἔλπω (Ϝέλπω), usually mid. ἔλπομαι, ἐέλπεται, ipf. ἔλπετο, perf. ἔολπα (ϜέϜολπα), plup. ἐώλπει: act., *make to hope, give hopes*, β 91, ν 380; mid., *hope, expect*, also 'think,' Ι 40, Ν 309, Τ 328, ι 419, φ 314; even in bad sense, implying *fear* or apprehension, Ο 110; w. acc. νίκην, Ν 609, Ο 539; τοῦτο, φ 317; foll. by inf., fut. in the meaning *hope*, in other meanings by tenses referring to the past, Η 199, etc., freq. θῡμῷ, κατὰ θῡμόν, ἐνὶ φρεσί, also θῡμὸς ἔλπεται, Ο 701.

ἐλπωρή = ἐλπίς. (Od.)

ἔλσαι, ἔλσᾱς: see εἴλω.

ἐλύω (Ϝελύω), aor. pass. ἐλύσθη, part. ἐλυσθείς: *wind, roll up;* pass., of a chariot-pole dragging in curves, 'wiggling,' along the ground, Ψ 393; of Priam bent prostrate at the feet of Achilles, Ω 510; Odysseus curled up under the belly of the ram, ι 433.

ἕλχ' = ἕλκε, see ἕλκω.

ἔλων: see ἐλαύνω.

ἕλωρ (Ϝελεῖν): *prey, spoil*, of wild beasts, birds, enemies; pl., Πατρόκλοιο ἕλωρα ἀποτίνειν, pay the penalty 'for taking and slaying' (ἑλεῖν) Patroclus, Σ 93.

ἑλώριον = ἕλωρ, pl., Α 4†.

ἐμβαδόν: *on foot* (over the sea), Ο 505†.

ἐμ-βαίνω, ipf. ἔμβαινον, aor. 2 ἔμβη, -ητον, subj. ἐμβήῃ, perf. part. ἐμβεβαῶτα, -υῖα, plup. ἐμβέβασαν: *set foot in, step into* or *upon, mount, go on board; ἔμβη νηὶ* Πύλονδε, 'embarked for Pylos,' δ 656; μή τις θεῶν ἐμβήῃ, 'come in thy way,' Π 94; Antilochus to his horses, ἔμβητον καὶ σφῶι, 'go in!' Ψ 403; perf., *stand upon* (see βαίνω), ἵπποισιν καὶ ἅρμασιν ἐμβεβαῶτα, Ε 199; of the leaden sinker 'mounted' upon the horn guard of a fish-hook, Ω 81.

ἐμ-βάλλω, ipf. ἐνέβαλλε, aor. 2 ἔμβαλον, inf. ἐμβαλέειν: *throw* or *cast in; πῦρ νηί*, O 598; *τινὰ πόντῳ*, Ξ 258; *τὶ χερσίν*, 'put' or 'give into' the hands, Ξ 218, β 37, etc.; *βροτοῦ ἀνέρος ἔμβαλον εὐνῇ*, 'brought thee to the couch of a mortal,' Σ 85; metaph., *νεῖκός τισι*, Δ 444; *ἵμερον θυμῷ*, 'infuse,' 'inspire with,' Γ 139; intrans., *κώπῃς*, 'lay to' the oars, ι 489; mid., *μῆτιν ἐμβάλλεο θυμῷ*, 'lay to heart,' Ψ 313; *φύξιν*, 'take thought of,' K 447.

ἐμ-βασιλεύω: *be king in, rule therein*, B 572 and ο 413.

ἐμβέβασαν, ἐμβεβαώς, ἐμβήῃ, ἔμβη: see ἐμβαίνω.

ἐμ-βρέμομαι: only pres. 3 sing., the wind *roars in* the sail, O 627†.

ἔμβρυον: *new-born lamb*. (ι).

ἐμέθεν, ἐμεῖο, ἐμέο, ἐμεῦ: see ἐγώ.

ἐμέμηκον: see μηκάομαι.

ἔμεν(αι): see εἰμί.

ἔμεν(αι): see ἵημι.

ἐμέω: *spew* or *spit out*, O 11†.

ἔμικτο: see μίγνυμι.

ἔμμαθε: see μανθάνω.

ἐμ-μαπέως: *instantly*, E 836 and ξ 485.

ἐμ-μεμαώς, υῖα, du. -ῶτε, pl. -ῶτες (μέμαα): *eager, vehement*.

ἔμμεν(αι): see εἰμί.

ἐμ-μενές (μένω): always ἐμμενὲς αἰεί, *continually* ever.

ἔμμορε: see μείρομαι.

ἔμ-μορος (μείρομαι): *sharing in*, τιμῆς, pl., θ 480†.

ἐμός, ή, όν, no voc.: *my, mine;* rarely with art., Λ 608, δ 71; οὑμός (= ὁ ἐμός), Θ 360; strengthened by gen. of αὐτός, ἐμὸν αὐτοῦ χρεῖος, 'my *own*,' β 45; equiv. to obj. gen., ἐμὴ ἀγγελίη, 'about me,' T 336.

ἐμ-πάζομαι, ipf. ἐμπάζετο: *care for*, w. gen. (acc., π 422); usually with negative.

ἔμ-παιος: *conversant with*, τινός, υ 379 (ἔμπᾰιον) and φ 400.

ἐμ-πάσσω: *sprinkle in;* only ipf. (fig.) ἐνέπασσε, 'was weaving in,' Γ 126 and X 441.

ἔμ-πεδος (πέδον): *firmly standing* or *footed*, ψ 203, N 512; *firm, immovable, unshaken*, M 9, 12; so of the mind, βίη, μένος, φρένες, 'unimpaired,' κ 493; ἔμπεδος οὐδ' ἀεσίφρων (Πρίαμος), Υ 183; 'sure,' 'certain,' τ 250, θ 30; of time, 'lasting,' 'constant,' Θ 521, θ 453; and metaph., ἦτορ, φρένες, Z 352, σ 215.—Neut. **ἔμπεδον** as adv., with the same meanings, στηρίξαι *firmly*, μ 434; μένειν, without leaving the spot, E 527; θέειν, 'constantly,' N 141, ν 86.

ἐμπεσεῖν: see ἐμπίπτω.

ἔμπης: *wholly, nevertheless;* the former meaning is denied by some scholars, and there are but very few passages to which the latter meaning is not applicable, e. g. σ 354, τ 37; in its common signif. of *still, yet, nevertheless*, ἔμπης may be placed after the concessive part. (precisely like ὅμως in Att.), and freq. at the end of the verse, though grammatically and in sense belonging to the leading verb; Τρωσὶ μὲν εὐκτὰ γένηται (ἐπικρατέουσι περ) ἔμπης, Ξ 98, I 518, etc. καὶ ἔμπης, ε 205; ἀλλ' ἔμπης, Θ 33; δ' ἔμπης correl. to μέν, A 562.

ἐμ-πίπλημι, imp. ἐμπίπληθι, fut. inf. ἐμπλησέμεν, aor. ἐνέπλησε, imp. ἔμπλησον, subj. ἐνιπλήσῃς, part. ἐμπλήσᾶς, mid. aor. ἐμπλήσατο, inf. ἐνιπλήσασθαι, part. ἐμπλησάμενος, aor. 2 (w. pass. signif.), ἔμπλητο, -ντο: *fill full* (τί τινος), mid., *fill* or *sate oneself;* fig., θυμὸν ὀδυνάων, τ 117; υἷος ἐνιπλησθῆναι ὀφθαλμοῖσιν, 'have the satisfaction of looking on my son,' λ 452; aor. 2 mid. as pass., ἔμπληντο βροτῶν ἀγοραί, θ 16.

ἐμ-πίπτω, aor. ἔμπεσε: *fall into* or *upon; πῦρ ἔμπεσε νηυσίν*, Π 113; ἐν ὕλῃ, Λ 155; freq. in hostile sense, ἔμπεσ' ἐπικρατέως, 'charge,' Π 81; metaph., χόλος, δέος ἔμπεσε θυμῷ, I 436, Ξ 207; ἔπος μοι ἔμπεσε θυμῷ, 'came to my mind,' μ 266.

ἔμ-πλειος and **ἐνί-πλειος**: *filled with, full*. (Od.)

ἐμ-πλήγδην (ἐμπλήσσω): *at random*, υ 132†.

ἔμ-πλην (πέλας): *hard by*, w. gen., B 526†.

ἐμπλήσατο, ἔμπλητο, -ντο: see ἐμπίπλημι.

ἐμπλήσσω: see ἐνιπλήσσω.

ἐμ-πνέω, ἐμπνείω, aor. ἐνέπνευσε, ἔμπνευσε: *breathe upon*, P 502; met., *inspire*, μένος, θάρσος, etc.; of an inspiring 'suggestion,' τ 138 (ἔμπνυτο, ἐμπνύνθη, v. l. ἀμπ., see ἀναπνέω.)

ἐμ-ποιέω: only ipf. ἐνεποίεον, *fitted into*, Η 438.

ἐμ-πολάω: only mid. ipf., ἐμπολόωντο, *gained for themselves by trading*, ο 456†.

ἔμ-πορος: *passenger*, on board another's ship, β 319 and ω 300.

ἐμ-πρήθω, ἐνιπρήθω, ipf. ἐνέπρηθον, ἐνιπρήσω, fut. inf. ἐμπρήσειν, aor. ἐνέπρησε, ἔμπρησε, subj. ἐνιπρήσωσι: (1) of wind, *blow into, fill* the sail, β 427. —(2) of fire, *kindle; νῆας, ἄστυ, νεκρούς*, Θ 182; usually with πυρί, also πυρός (part. gen.), Ι 242, Π 82.

ἐμ-πυρι-βήτης (πῦρ, βαίνω): *standing over the fire; τρίπος*, Ψ 702†.

ἐμ-φορέω: only mid. ipf., ἐμφορέοντο, *were borne about* in the waves, μ 419 and ξ 309.

ἔμ-φῦλος: *of the same tribe*, ο 273†.

ἐμ-φύω, aor. ἐνέφῦσε, perf. 3 pl. ἐμπεφύᾱσι, part. fem. ἐμπεφυυῖα: trans. (aor. 1 act.), *implant*, metaph., θεός μοι ἐν φρεσὶν οἴμᾱς, χ 348; intrans., *grow in* or *upon*, τρίχες κρᾱνίῳ, Θ 84; fig., ἐμπεφυυῖα, 'clinging closely,' Α 513.

ἐν, ἐνί, εἰν, εἰνί: *in*.—I. adv., *in, therein, among* them, Ε 740, etc.; esp. the form ἔνι, for ἔνεστι, ἔνεισι, πολέες δ' ἔνι μῦθοι, Υ 248. Here belong all examples of 'tmesis' so-called, ἐν δ' ἔπεσε, 'fell on' the throng, Ο 624. The adv. may be defined in its relation by a dative in the same clause, thus showing an approach to the true prepositional use, ἐν δέ τε θῡμὸς στήθεσιν ἄτρομός ἐστιν, *in* them, viz., in their breasts, Π 162.—II. prep. w. dat., *in, on, among;* not only of place and persons, ἐν Δαναοῖσι, ἐν ἀθανάτοισι, ἐνὶ στρατῷ, ἐν πᾶσιν, β 194; but also of conditions, physical and mental, ἐν φιλότητι, ἐν πένθεϊ, ἐν δοιῇ, Ι 230. Of time, ὥρῃ ἐν εἰαρινῇ, Π 643, σ 367; instead of a causal or an instrumental expression, ἐν ὀφθαλμοῖς ὁρᾶν, Α 587, Γ 306, κ 385; κατακτείνεσθαι ἀνδρῶν ἐν παλάμῃσιν, Ε 558, Ω 738, etc.; often with verbs of motion, the state of rest after motion taking the place of movement into, ἐν γούνασι πίπτειν, Ε 370; ἐν χερσὶ τιθέναι, etc.; elliptical, ἐνὶ Κίρκης, sc. οἴκῳ, κ 282, esp. εἰν 'Αΐδᾱο. When ἐνί follows its case, it is written ἔνι ('anastrophe'), Ι 53.

ἐναίρω (ἔναρα), inf. ἐναιρέμεν, mid. aor. ἐνήρατο: act. and mid., *slay* in battle; once of killing game, κατ' οὔρεα θῆρας ἐναίρειν, Φ 485; fig., μηκέτι χρόα κᾶλὸν ἐναίρεο, 'disfigure,' τ 263.

ἐν-αίσιμος: *fateful, favorable* (opp. παραίσιος), Β 353, β 182, 159; then *proper, seemly, just* (ἐν αἴσῃ, κατ' αἶσαν, κατὰ μοῖραν), ἀνήρ, Ζ 521; φρένες, σ 220; δῶμα, Ω 425; neut. sing. as adv., ἐναίσιμον ἐλθεῖν, 'opportunely,' Ζ 519; predicative, β 122, η 299.

ἐν-αλίγκιος: *like*, τινί τι, to some one in some respect, α 371; ἄντην, in countenance.

ἐνάλιος: see εἰνάλιος.

ἐν-αμέλγω: only ipf., ἐνάμελγεν, *milked therein*, ι 223†.

ἔν-αντα: *over against; τινός*, Υ 67†.

ἐν-αντί-βιον: *with hostile front against*, ξ 270, ρ 439, Υ 130.

ἐν-αντίος, 3: *opposite*, of motion and position, in friendly sense or hostile, *against*, Ζ 247, ψ 89, κ 89, Ε 497; of the 'manifest' appearance of a deity, ζ 329; adv., **ἐναντίον**, ἐναντίον ὧδε κάλεσσον, summon him hither 'into my presence,' τ 544; freq. ἐναντίον ἐλθεῖν τινός, go 'to meet,' or 'against.'

ἔναξε: see νάσσω.

ἔναρα, τα: *spoils* (armor taken from the slain foe), *booty*, Ο 347, Ι 188.

ἐν-αργής, ές: *visible, manifest*, δ 841, η 201; χαλεποὶ δὲ θεοὶ φαίνεσθαι ἐναργεῖς, it is hazardous when the gods appear 'in their true forms,' Υ 131.

ἐν-αρηρώς (root ἀρ), ός: *well fitted in*, ε 236†.

ἐναρίζω (ἔναρα), ipf. ἐνάριζε, aor. ἐνάριξα: *strip of armor, despoil; τινά τι*, Ρ 187, Χ 323, Μ 195, Ο 343; then, usually, *slay* in battle, *kill*, Ε 155, Π 731, Α 191. (Il.)

ἐν-αρίθμιος: *filling up the number*, μ 65; *of account* (ἐν ἀριθμῷ), Β 202.

ἔνατος, εἴνατος: *ninth*.

ἔν-αυλος (αὐλός): *channel, river-bed* (of the streams in the Trojan plain, dry in summer), *water-course*, Π 71, Φ 283, 312.

ἐν-δείκνῡμι: only fut. mid., ἐνδείξομαι, *I will declare it*, Τ 83.

ἕν-δεκα: *eleven*, round number in Φ 45.

ἐνδεκά-πηχυς, υ: *eleven cubits long*, Ζ 319 and Θ 494.

ἐνδέκατος: *eleventh; ἐνδεκάτῃ, on the eleventh day*, often as round number after mentioning ten days, Ω 666, β 374, δ 588.

ἐν-δέξιος: *on the right, favorable*, I 236; adv. **ἐνδέξια,** *from left to right*, regarded as the lucky direction in pouring wine, drawing lots, etc., Α 597, Η 184, ρ 365; cf. ἐπιδέξια.

ἐν-δέω, aor. ἐνέδησε: *bind* or *tie in* or *on*, Ο 469, ε 260; fig., 'involve,' 'entangle,' Β 111, Ι 18.

ἐν-δίημι: only ipf., αὔτως ἐνδίεσαν κύνας, merely *tried to set on* the dogs, Σ 584†.

ἔνδῖνα, pl.: *entrails*, Ψ 806†.

ἔν-δῖος (cf. Διός): *at midday*, δ 450 and Λ 726.

ἔνδοθεν: *from within, within*; w. gen., Ζ 247.

ἔνδοθι: *within*, Ζ 498; w. gen., Σ 287; opp. θύρηφιν, χ 220; often = ἐν φρεσί, with θῦμός, μῆτις, νόος.

ἔνδον: *within*, esp. *in the house, tent*, etc., Σ 394; *at home*, π 355, 462, φ 207, ψ 2; Διὸς ἔνδον, *in the house* of Zeus, Υ 13, Ψ 200.

ἐν-δουπέω, aor. ἐνδούπησα: *fall with a heavy sound*, 'plump down,' μ 443 and ο 479.

ἐνδυκέως: *duly, attentively, kindly*; τρέφειν, Ψ 90; φείδεσθαι, Ω 158; ὁμαρτεῖν, Ω 438; oftener in Od., with φιλεῖν, πέμπειν, λούειν, κομεῖν, etc.; ἐνδυκέως κρέα τ' ἤσθιε πῖνέ τε οἶνον, 'with a relish,' ξ 109.

ἐν-δύνω and **ἐνδύω,** ipf. ἐνέδῦνε, aor. 2 part. ἐνδῦσα: *put on, don*, Β 42, Ε 736, Θ 387.

ἐνέηκα: see ἐνίημι.

ἐνεῖκαι: see φέρω.

ἔν-ειμι (εἰμί), ἔνεστι, ἔνειμεν, ἔνεισι, opt. ἐνείη, ipf. ἐνῆεν, ἐνέην, ἔνεσαν: *be in* or *on*; w. dat., κ 45, or adv., Ω 240; ἔν τινι, Ζ 244; ὀλίγος δ' ἔτι θῦμὸς ἐνῆεν, 'there was little life remaining in me,' Α 593; εἰ χάλκεόν μοι ἦτορ ἐνείη, 'had I a heart of bronze within me,' Β 490.

ἕνεκα, ἕνεκεν, εἵνεκα: *on account of, for the sake of, because of*, w. gen.; placed before or after its case.

ἐνέκυρσε: see ἐγκυρέω.

ἐνενήκοντα: *ninety*.

ἐνένῖπον, ἐνένιπτε: see ἐνίπτω.

ἐνέπω and **ἐννέπω** (root σεπ), imp. ἔννεπε, opt. ἐνέποιμι, part. ἐνέπων, -οντα, -οντε, -τες, fem. -ουσα, ipf. ἔννεπε, aor. ἔνισπον, ἔνισπες, ἔνισπε, opt. -οις, -οι, subj. -ω, -ῃ, imp. ἔνισπε and ἐνίσπες, inf. -εῖν, fut. ἐνίψω and ἐνισπήσω: *relate*, reg. w. acc. of the thing which forms the theme of the narration, μῦθον, ὄνειρον, ἄνδρα, α 1; μύθοισιν τέρποντο πρὸς ἀλλήλους ἐνέποντες (sc. μύθους), Λ 643, ψ 301.

ἐν-ερείδω, aor. ἐνέρεισαν: *thrust into*; τινί τι, ι 383†.

ἔνερθε(ν), νέρθε(ν): *from below*, Υ 57 (opp. ὑψόθεν); *below*, Ξ 274; w. gen., Θ 16; after its case, Λ 234, 252.

ἔνεροι: *those below* the earth (i n f e r i), both gods and the shades of the dead, Ο 188, Υ 61.

ἐνέρτερος, comp. of ἔνεροι: *deeper down, lower*, Ε 898; ἐνέρτεροι θεοί (= οἱ ἔνερθε θεοί), the *nether* gods, Ο 225.

ἔνεσαν: see ἔνειμι.

ἐνεστήρικτο: see ἐνστηρίζω.

ἐν-ετή (ἐνίημι): *clasp*, a species of περόνη, Ξ 180†.

Ἐνετοί: a tribe of the Paphlagonians, Β 852†.

ἐν-εύδω: *sleep in* or *on*. (Od.)

ἐν-εύναιον: *sleeping-place, bed*, ξ 51; pl., *bedclothes*, π 35.

ἐν-ηείη (ἐνηής): *gentleness, amiability*, Ρ 670†.

ἐν-ηής, έος: *gentle, amiable*, Ψ 252, θ 200.

ἔν-ημαι, ipf. ἐνήμεθα: *sit within*, δ 272†.

ἐνήρατο: see ἐναίρω.

ἐν-ήνοθε (cf. ἄνθος), defective perf. w. pres. signif.: *swells there, steams there, rises there*, ρ 270†.

ἔνθα: I. demonstr., *there, thither, then*; of place, usually denoting rest, Α 536, γ 365; less often direction, ἔνθ' ἐλθών, Ν 23; ἔνθα καὶ ἔνθα, 'here and there,' 'to and fro,' 'in length and breadth,' Β 476, 462, β 213, Η 156, κ 517; ἢ ἔνθ' ἢ ἔνθα κίοντα, 'going or coming,' κ 574; often temporal, *thereupon*, ἔνθα ἔπειτα, κ 297; ἔνθ' αὖ, Ε 1; introducing apodosis, Β 308.—II. relative, *where*, Α 610; ἔνθ' ἄρα, χ 335; ἔνθα περ, ν 284; ἔνθα τε, ν 107, Β 594.

ἐνθάδε: *hither, thither*, Δ 179, π 8; *here, there*, Β 296, β 51; ἐνθάδ' αὖθι, *here* on the spot, Ψ 674, ε 208.

ἔνθεν: I. demonstr., *thence, then, thereupon*, both local and temporal, K 179, N 741; ἔνθεν . . ἑτέρωθι δέ, 'on this side . . on the other,' μ 235, 59, 211; ἔνθεν ἐμοὶ γένος, ὅθεν σοί, Δ 58. —II. relative, *whence*. Ω 597; (οἶνον) ἔνθεν ἔπῑνον, 'whereof,' δ 220, τ 62; correl. to ἔνθα, ε 195.

ἔνθενδε: *from here, from there, thence*.

ἐν-θρώσκω, aor. ἔνθορε: *spring in* or *upon*, w. dat., O 623, Ω 79; λὰξ ἔνθορεν ἰσχίῳ, 'with a kick at his hip,' ρ 233.

ἐν-θῡ́μιος: *taken to heart*, 'subject of anxiety,' ν 421†.

ἐνί, ἔνι: see ἐν.

ἐνιαύσιος: *yearling*, π 454†.

ἐνιαυτός: *year*. Perhaps originally a less specific term than ἔτος, ἔτος ἦλθε περιπλομένων ἐνιαυτῶν, 'as time and seasons rolled round,' α 16; Διὸς ἐνιαυτοί, B 134 (cf. ξ 93).

ἐν-ιαύω: only ipf., ἐνίαυε, *used to sleep there* or *among*, ι 187 and ο 557.

ἐν-ίημι, ἐνίησι, imp. ἐνίετε, fut. ἐνήσω, aor. ἐνῆκα, ἐνέηκε, part. fem. ἐνεῖσα: *let go in* or *into, let in;* of sending men into battle to fight, Ξ 131; throwing fire upon, setting fire to, ships, M 441; launching a ship in the sea, β 295; often w. dat., νηυσίν, πόντῳ, rarely ἔν τινι; metaph., of inspiring feelings, θάρσος τινὶ ἐν στήθεσσιν, P 570; filling one with any sentiment, τινὶ ἀναλκίδα θῡμόν, Π 656; κότον, Π 449; μένος, ν 387; plunging in troubles, πόνοισι, K 89; leading to concord, ὁμοφροσύνῃσιν, O 198.

Ἐνιῆνες: a tribe dwelling about Dodōna, B 749†.

ἐνι-κλάω, inf. ἐνικλᾶν: *break within, frustrate*, Θ 408 and 422.

Ἐνῑπεύς: river-god, river in Phthiōtis, λ 238†.

ἐνῑπή (ἐνίπτω): *rebuke, reprimand*.

ἐνίπλειος: see ἔμπλειος.

ἐνιπλησθῆναι, -πλήσωσι: see ἐμπίπλημι.

ἐνι-πλήσσω, aor. subj. ἐνιπλήξω: intrans., *dash into, rush into;* τάφρῳ, ἕρκει, M 72, χ 469.

ἐνιπρήθω: see ἐμπρήθω.

ἐνίπτω, opt. ἐνίπτοι, imp. ἔνιπτε, aor. 2 ἐνένῑπε and ἠνίπαπε: *chide, rebuke, upbraid;* Odysseus chides himself, to repress his wrath, κραδίην ἠνίπαπε μύθῳ· | 'τέτλαθι δή, κραδίη,' υ 17; usually w. specifying terms in dat., χαλεποῖσιν ὀνείδεσιν, ὀνειδείοις ἐπέεσσιν, χαλεπῷ or κακῷ μύθῳ, B 245, Γ 438, P 141, σ 326.

ἐνι-σκίμπτω, aor. part. ἐνισκίμψαντε, aor. pass. ἐνισκίμφθη: *lean on, hold close to*, P 437; pass., *stick in*, P 528, Π 612.

Ἐνίσπη: a town in Arcadia, B 606.

ἐνισπήσω, ἔνισπον, ἐνίσπες: see ἐνέπω.

ἐνίσσω, inf. ἐνισσέμεν, ipf. ἐνίσσομεν, pass. part. ἐνισσόμενος: parallel form of ἐνίπτω.

ἐνιχριμφθέντα: see ἐγχρίμπτω.

ἐνίψω: see ἐνέπω.

ἐννέα: *nine*.

ἐννεά-βοιος: *worth nine cattle*, Z 236†.

ἐννεα-καί-δεκα: *nineteen*, Ω 496†.

ἐννεά-πηχυς, υ: *nine cubits long*.

ἐννεά-χῑλοι: *nine thousand*.

ἔννεον: see νέω.

ἐννε‿όργυιος: *nine fathoms long*, λ 312†.

ἐνν-εσίη: dat. pl., *at the command;* τινός, E 894.

ἐννέ‿ωρος: *nine years old*, the number being a round one, Σ 351, κ 19; in τ 179 perhaps meaning 'in periods of nine years.'

ἐννήκοντα: *ninety*, τ 174†.

ἐνν-ῆμαρ: *nine days long*.

Ἔννομος: (1) a soothsayer, chief of the Mysians, slain by Achilles, B 858, P 218.—(2) a Trojan, slain by Odysseus, Λ 422.

ἐννοσί-γαιος (ἔνοσις, γαῖα): *earth-shaker*, epithet of Poseidon, god of the sea, as causer of earthquakes; joined with γαιήοχος, I 183.

ἔννῡμι (Ϝέννυμι), fut. ἕσσω, aor. ἕσσα, imp. ἕσσον, inf. ἕσσαι, part. ἕσσᾱς, mid. and pass., pres. inf. ἕννυσθαι, ipf. ἕννυτο, aor. ἕ(σ)σατο, ἐέσσατο, inf. ἕσασθαι, part. ἑσσάμενος, perf. εἷμαι, ἕσσαι, εἷται, part. εἱμένος, plup. 2 sing. ἕσσο, 3 ἕστο, ἕεστο, du. ἕσθην, 3 pl. εἵατο: *clothe, put on clothing*, mid., on oneself, pass. (esp. perf. and plup.), *be clothed in, wear;* act., of clothing another, ἕσσᾱς με χλαῖναν τε χιτῶνά τε, ξ 396; thus regularly w. two accusatives, E 905, ο 338, π 79; mid. w. acc., or acc.

and dat., χροῒ χαλκόν, Τ 233; also περὶ χροΐ, Η 207; ἀμφ' ὤμοισιν, Κ 177; pass. w. acc. of thing retained, τεύχεα εἱμένος, κακὰ εἱμένος, ἀείκεα ἕσσο, 'shockingly clothed,' Δ 432, τ 327, π 199; fig., ἦ τέ κε λάϊνον ἕσσο χιτῶνα, 'hadst been clad in a coat of stone' (stoned to death), Γ 57; φρεσὶν εἱμένος ἀλκήν, Υ 381.

ἐν-νύχιος, ἔννυχος (Λ 716†): *in the night time.*

ἐν-οινο-χοέω: *pour* (*wine*) *in*, part., γ 472†.

ἐν-οπή (ὄψ): *voice*, κ 147, *outcry;* attributed to musical instruments, αὐλῶν συρίγγων τ' ἐνοπήν, Κ 13; esp. of the cry of battle, Γ 2, and figuratively for battle itself, Μ 35; of grief, ἐνοπήν τε γόον τε, Ω 160.

Ἐνόπη: a town in Messenia, subject to Agamemnon, Ι 150, 292.

ἐν-όρνῡμι, aor. ἐνῶρσα, part. ἐνόρσᾱς, mid. aor. 2 ἐνῶρτο: *rouse* or *excite in;* τινὶ γόον, φύζαν, Ζ 499, Ο 62; mid., *arise in* or *among;* ἐνῶρτο γέλως μακάρεσσι θεοῖσιν, Α 599, θ 326.

ἐν-ορούω, aor. ἐνόρουσα: *spring upon, rush* or *charge upon*, w. dat.; of warriors, of a lion, Π 783, Κ 486.

ἔν-ορχος: *uncastrated*, Ψ 147†.

ἐνοσί-χθων = ἐννοσίγαιος.

ἐνσκίμπτω: see ἐνισκίμπτω.

ἐν-στάζω: *drop in*, only perf. pass., ἐνέστακται, *has been infused* in thy veins, β 271†.

ἐν-στηρίζω: only plup. pass., ἐνεστήρικτο, *remained sticking fast*, Φ 168.

ἐν-στρέφω: only mid., ἐνστρέφεται ἰσχίῳ, *turns* (*plays*) *in the* hip-joint, Ε 306†.

ἐν-τανύω (= ἐντείνω), aor. ἐντάνυσε, mid. aor. inf. ἐντανύσασθαι: *stretch tight in*, regularly (act. and mid.) *string* a bow; νευρὴν ἐντανύσαι, of *stretching* the string *in* the bow to string it, not pulling it to shoot, τ 587, φ 97, ω 171; then βιόν, τόξον, τ 577, φ 75, 114, 150, 403; pass., φ 2. (See cut No. 34, from an antique gem.)

ἐν-ταῦθα: *hither*, Ι 601†.

ἐν-ταυθοῖ: *here.*

ἔντεα, pl.: *harness, armor, weapons;* esp. the breast-plate, Γ 339, Κ 34, 75; ἔντεα ἀρήια, 'fighting gear,' Κ 407, ψ 368; of table-furniture, ἔντεα δαιτός, η 232.

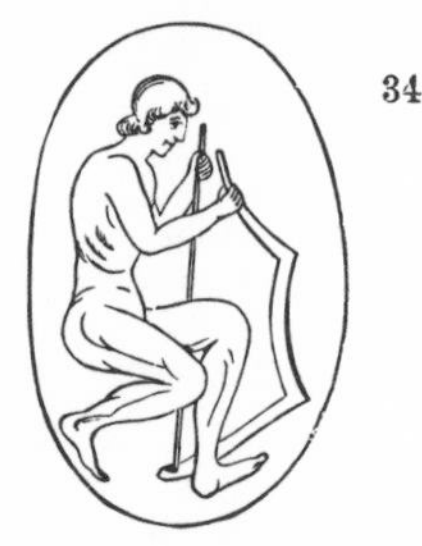

34

ἐν-τείνω, only pass. perf. and plup.: *stretch within;* δίφρος ἱμᾶσιν ἐντέταται, 'is plaited' with gold and silver straps, Ε 728; κυνέη ἱμᾶσιν ἐντέτατο, 'was lined with tightly-stretched straps,' Κ 263, cf. Ψ 335, 436.

ἔντερον: *gut*, οἰός, used for harp-string, φ 408; pl., *bowels.*

ἐντεσί-εργος (ἔντεα, ϝέργον): *working in harness*, Ω 277†.

ἐντεῦθεν: *thence*, τ 568†.

ἐν-τίθημι, fut. ἐνθήσω, aor. inf. ἐνθέμεναι, mid. ipf. ἐντιθέμεσθα, aor. 2 ἔνθετο, imp. ἔνθεο, part. ἐνθεμένη: *put* or *place in* or *on*, mid., for oneself, or something of one's own; of putting provisions on board a ship, ε 166; clothing on a bed, Ω 646, etc.; mid., of a mother laying her son upon the bier, Φ 124; metaph., μή μοι πατέρας ποθ' ὁμοίῃ ἔνθεο τῑμῇ, 'hold in esteem,' Δ 410; ἵλαον ἔνθεο θῡμόν, 'take on,' Ι 639; χόλον θῡμῷ, 'conceive,' Ι 326, ω 248; μῦθον θῡμῷ, 'take to heart,' α 361.

ἔντο: see ἵημι.

ἐντός: *within;* w. gen., λιμένος ἐντός, Α 432, etc.

ἔντοσθε(ν) and **ἔντοθεν** = ἐντός.

ἐν-τρέπω: only pass. (met.), ἐντρέπεται ἦτορ, *is moved*, Ο 554 and α 60.

ἐν-τρέχω: *run in*, 'play freely in' the armor, Τ 385†.

ἐν-τροπαλίζομαι (frequentative of ἐντρέπομαι): only part., *turning frequently about.* (Il.)

ἐντῦνω, ἐντύω (ἔντεα), ipf. ἔντῡνον, ἔντυον, aor. 1 imp. ἔντῡνον, part. ἐντύνᾱσα, mid. subj. 2 sing. ἐντύνεαι, aor. part. ἐντῡνάμενος: *harness*, Ε 720; *make ready*, mid., for oneself, *adorn oneself;* of preparing a bed, ψ 289; a drink, Ι 203; striking up a song, μ

183; mid., δαῖτα, γ 33; ἦλθ' ἐντῡναμένη (Κίρκη), μ 18, cf. Ξ 162.

ἐν-τυπάς (τύπτω): adv., *closely wrapped in* his mantle, Ω 163†.

Ἐνῡάλιος (Ἐνῡώ): *Enyalius*, epith. of Ares as god of battle, usually subst.; adj., P 211; Ἐνῡαλίῳ ἀνδρεϊφόντῃ, 'synizesis,' B 651, etc.

Ἐνῡεύς: king of Scyros, slain by Achilles, I 668†.

ἐν-ύπνιος: *in sleep*, only neut. as adv., B 56.

Ἐνῡώ: *Enyo* (Bellōna), battle personified, a companion of Ares, E 333, 592.

ἐν-ωπαδίως: *face to face, clearly*, ψ 94†.

ἐν-ωπῇ (ὤψ): *in view, openly*, E 374 and Φ 510.

ἐν-ώπια (ὤψ, cf. 'façade'): the *side-walls* of the vestibule, epith. παμφανόωντα, perhaps because painted white. See plate III. A and B.

ἕξ: *six*.

ἐξ-αγγέλλω, aor. 1 ἐξήγγειλεν: *bring news out, report* a fact, E 390†.

ἐξ-αγορεύω: *relate*, λ 234†.

ἐξ-άγω, ipf. ἔξαγε, imp. ἔξαγε, aor. 2 ἐξήγαγε, -άγαγε: *lead* or *bring out*, τινά (τινος), also ἔκ τινος; of 'extending' a mound (cf. ἐλαύνω), H 336; of birth (bringing to light, into the world), Π 188.

Ἐξάδιος: one of the Lapithae, A 264†.

ἑξά-ετες (Ϝέτος): adv., *six years*, γ 115†.

ἐξ-αίνυμαι: *take out* or *away*, w. two accusatives, E 155; 'took out (of the chariot and placed) in the vessel,' ο 206.

ἐξ-αίρετος: *chosen, choice*, δ 643, B 227.

ἐξ-αιρέω, aor. 2 ἐξεῖλον and ἔξελον, mid. ipf. ἐξαιρεύμην, aor. ἐξειλόμην, -ελόμην: *take out* or *away, select, choose from*, mid., for oneself; ἔνθεν ἔξελε πέπλους, Ω 229; ἣν ἄρα μοι γέρας ἔξελον υἷες Ἀχαιῶν, Π 56; mid., φαρέτρης ἐξείλετο πικρὸν ὀιστόν, Θ 323; (Βρισηΐδα) ἐκ Λυρνησσοῦ ἐξείλετο, here not of choosing but of taking away, B 690; cf. Λ 704; so of taking away one's life, θῡμόν, O 460, T 137, λ 201; φρένας, 'wits,' Z 234; of 'choosing,' I 130, 272, ξ 232.

ἐξαίρω: see ἐξάρνυμαι.

ἐξ-αίσιος (opp. ἐναίσιος): *undue, unjust, unrighteous*, δ 670, O 577; in ρ 577 ἐξαίσιον is sometimes interpreted as an adv., 'unduly,' 'excessively.'

ἔξ-αιτος = ἐξαίρετος.

ἐξ-αίφνης = ἐξαπίνης, P 738 and Φ 14.

ἐξ-ακέομαι, aor. opt. ἐξακέσαιο: *heal completely*; 'seek to remedy,' I 507; χόλον, 'appease,' Δ 36, γ 145.

ἐξ-αλαόω (ἀλαός), aor. ἐξαλάωσα: *blind completely*. (Od.)

ἐξ-αλαπάζω, fut. -ξω, aor. ἐξαλάπαξα: *empty entirely, sack, utterly destroy*; usually of cities, once of ships, N 813.

ἐξ-άλλομαι, aor. part. ἐξάλμενος: *leap out from*, w. gen.; of taking the lead with a spring in racing, Ψ 399.

ἐξ-ανα-βαίνω: only aor. 2 part., ἐξαναβᾶσαι, *climbing up* upon (*out* of the sea), Ω 97†.

ἐξ-ανα-δύνω, aor. 2 part. -δύς, fem. pl. -δῦσαι: *emerge from*; ἁλός, δ 405, ε 438.

ἐξ-ανα-λυω, aor. inf. -λῦσαι: *release from*; θανάτοιο, Π 442 and X 180.

ἐξ-ανα-φανδόν: *quite openly*, υ 48†.

ἐξ-αν-ίημι, part. ἐξανιεῖσαι: *let go forth, send forth*, Σ 471†.

ἐξ-ανύω, aor. ἐξήνυσα: *accomplish*, Θ 370; euphem., *finish, despatch, kill*, Λ 365, Y 452.

ἐξ-απατάω, fut. inf. -ήσειν, aor. ἐξαπάτησα: *deceive utterly*.

ἐξ-απαφίσκω, aor. 2 ἐξήπαφε, subj. ἐξαπάφω, mid. aor. 2 opt. ἐξαπάφοιτο: *deceive utterly, cheat*, act. and mid., Ξ 160, I 376.

ἐξ-απίνης: *suddenly, on a sudden*.

ἐξ-απο-βαίνω: only aor. 2, *disembarked from*; νηός, μ 306†.

ἐξ-απο-δίομαι: μάχης ἐξᾱποδίωμαι, *chase out* of the battle, E 763. (The ᾱ a necessity of the rhythm.)

ἐξ-απο-δύνω: *put off*; εἵματα, ε 372†.

ἐξ-απ-όλλῡμι, aor. mid. opt. 3 pl. -λοίατο, perf. -όλωλε: *perish utterly from*, w. gen., Ἰλίου, δόμων, οὐρανοῦ, Z 60, Σ 290, υ 357.

ἐξ-απο-νέομαι: μάχης ἐξᾱπονέεσθαι, *return out* of the battle. (Il.) (ᾱ a necessity of the rhythm.)

ἐξ-απο-νίζω: only ipf., τοῦ (more

natural than τῷ) πόδας ἐξαπόνιζε, *out of which she used to wash* feet, τ 387†.

ἐξ-απο-τίνω: *pay off, satisfy in full*, Φ 412†.

ἐξ-άπτω, ipf. ἐξῆπτον, aor. part. ἐξάψᾱς: *attach to*, τινός τί, mid., *hang hold of, swing from*, Θ 20.

ἐξ-άρνυμαι, aor. ἐξήρατο: *earn, carry off* as booty *from*, κ 84, ε 39, ν 137.

ἐξ-αρπάζω, aor. ἐξάρπαξα: *snatch away* (*from*), μ 100; in Il. of rescuing men from danger, Γ 380, Υ 443, Φ 597.

ἔξ-αρχος: pl., *leaders* of the dirge, Ω 721.

ἐξ-άρχω, ipf. ἐξῆρχε, mid. -ήρχετο: *begin, lead off;* μολπῆς, γόοιο, Σ 606, 316; w. acc., βουλάς, 'be the first to propose,' 'author of,' Β 273; mid., μ 339 (see ἄρχω).

ἐξ-αυδάω: *speak out*. (Il.)

ἔξ-αυτις: *again, anew.*

ἐξ-αφ-αιρέω, mid. aor. 2 subj. ἐξαφέλησθε: *take* the life *from;* ψῡχάς, χ 444†.

ἐξ-αφύω (ἀφύω=ἀφύσσω): *draw entirely out;* οἶνον, ξ 95†.

ἐξ-εῖδον: μέγ' ἔξιδεν ὀφθαλμοῖσιν, *looked forth* with wondering eyes, Υ 342†.

ἑξείης (ἔχεσθαι): *in order, one after another*, Ο 137, Χ 240.

1. **ἔξ-ειμι** (εἰμί): *be from* or *of* (son or descendant of), ν 130.

2. **ἔξ-ειμι** (εἶμι), 2 sing. ἔξεισθα, inf. ἐξιέναι, ἐξίμεναι, ipf. ἐξῄει: *go out.*

ἐξ-εῖπον, subj. ἐξείπω, opt. -ποι, fut. ἐξερέω: *speak out.*

ἐξ-είρομαι, ipf. ἐξείρετο: *inquire of, ask for.*

ἐξεκυλίσθη: see ἐκκυλίω.

ἐξ-ελαύνω, ἐξελάω, ipf. ἐξήλαυνε, fut. inf. ἐξελάᾱν, aor. ἐξήλασε, -έλασε, 3 pl. -ήλασσαν: *drive out* or *away from*, usually w. gen.; *knock out*, ὀδόντας γναθμῶν, σ 29; seemingly intrans., 'drive,' sc. ἵππους, Ω 323 (see ἐλαύνω).

ἐξελεῖν: see ἐξαιρέω.

ἐξ-έλκω: *draw out*, w. gen., ε 432; the thread of the woof through the warp, Ψ 762.

ἐξέμεν(αι): see ἐξίημι.

ἐξ-εμέω, aor. opt. -έσειε: *belch out, disgorge*, μ 237 and 437.

ἐξ-εναρίζω, fut. -ίξει, aor. ἐξενάριξα: *strip of armor, despoil;* τινά and τεύχεα, Ε 151, 155, Η 146; then *kill, slay*, Δ 488, λ 273, χ 264.

ἐξ-ερεείνω: *make inquiry*, abs., and w. acc. of pers., or of thing, ἕκαστα, 'ask all about it,' κ 14; mid., Κ 81; fig., πόρους ἁλὸς ἐξερεείνων, 'questing,' 'exploring,' μ 259.

ἐξ-ερείπω, aor. 2 subj. ἐξερίπῃ, part. -εριποῦσα: aor. 2 intrans., *fall down* or *over*. (Il.)

1. **ἐξερέω**: see ἐξεῖπον.

2. **ἐξ-ερέω, ἐξερέομαι,** inf. ἐξερέεσθαι, only pres. forms of both act. and dep. (act. only in Od.): *inquire of, question, ask*, w. acc. of person, or of thing; 'explore,' δ 337, ρ 128, cf. μ 259; 'investigate,' α 416.

ἐξ-ερύω, aor. ἐξείρυσε, ἐξέρυσε, 3 pl. ἐξείρυσσαν: *draw out* or *away*, σ 86, χ 476; βέλος ὤμου, δόρυ μηροῦ, Ε 112, 666; but δίφρον ῥῡμοῦ, 'by the pole,' Κ 505.

ἐξ-έρχομαι, aor. ἐξῆλθον: *come* or *go out, march forth*, Ι 476, 576; πόληος, 'out of the city,' τείχεος, θύραζε, τ 68.

ἐξ-ερωέω: only aor. ἐξερώησαν (ἵπποι), have *run away*, 'bolted,' Ψ 468†.

ἐξ-εσίη (ἐξίημι): *errand, embassy*, Ω 235 and φ 20.

ἑξ-ετής, ἑος: *six years old*, Ψ 266 and 655.

ἐξ-έτι: *ever since*, w. gen.; ἐξέτι πατρῶν, 'since the times of our fathers,' θ 245.

ἐξ-ευρίσκω, aor. opt. ἐξεύροι: *find out, discover*, Σ 322†.

ἐξ-ηγέομαι, imp. -γείσθω: *lead out*, w. gen., Β 806†.

ἑξήκοντα: *sixty.*

ἐξήλασα: see ἐξελαύνω.

ἐξ-ήλατος (ἐλαύνω): *beaten out, hammered*, Μ 295†.

ἐξ-ῆμαρ: *for six days.* (Od.)

ἐξ-ημοιβός (ἀμείβω): neut. pl., *for change, changes of raiment*, θ 249†.

ἐξήπαφε: see ἐξαπαφίσκω.

ἐξηράνθη: see ξηραίνω.

ἐξήρατο: see ἐξάρνυμαι.

ἐξηρώησα: see ἐξερωέω.

ἑξῆς = ἑξείης. (Od.)

ἐξ-ίημι, aor. 2 inf. ἐξέμεν(αι): *let go out, send out*, Λ 141, λ 531.

ἐξ-ῑθύνω: *straighten*, Ο 410†.

ἐξ-ικνέομαι, aor. 2 ἐξικόμην, ἐξίκετο (ῑ, augment): *reach, arrive at, gain* (from somewhere), w. acc. of place or person, I 479, μ 166, ν 206.

ἐξίμεναι: see ἔξειμι 2.

ἐξ-ίσχω: *hold out, protrude*, μ 94†.

ἐξοίσω: see ἐκφέρω.

ἐξ-οιχνέω, 3 pl. -νεῦσι: *go forth*, I 384†.

ἐξ-οίχομαι: only 3 sing. ἐξοίχεται, *is gone away*, Z 379, 384.

ἐξ-όλλῡμι, aor 1 opt. -ολέσειε: *utterly destroy*, τ 597.

ἐξ-ονομαίνω, aor. subj. -μήνῃς, inf. -μῆναι: *call by name, name, mention*, ζ 66.

ἐξ-ονομα-κλήδην: *calling out the name, by name*, X 415.

ἐξ-όπιθε(ν): *in the rear, behind*; w. gen., P 521. (Il.)

ἐξ-οπίσω: *backwards, back* (*from*), w. gen., P 357. (Il.)—Of time, *hereafter, in future.* (The Greeks stood with their backs to the future.)

ἐξ-ορμάω: only aor. part. intrans., ἐξορμήσᾱσα, *starting away* (from the direction intended), μ 221†.

ἐξ-οφέλλω: *greatly augment*, ο 18†.

ἔξ-οχος (ἔχω): *prominent, preëminent* above or among, w. gen., Ξ 118, or w. dat. (in local sense), B 483, φ 266.—Adv., **ἔξοχον** and **ἔξοχα,** *preëminently, chiefly, most*; 'by preference,' ι 551; ἔξοχ' ἄριστοι, 'far' the best, I 638, δ 629.

ἐξ-υπ-αν-ίστημι: only aor. 2 intrans., σμῶδιξ μεταφρένου, *started up from* (*on*) his back *under* the blows of the staff, B 267†.

ἔξω: *outside, without*, P 205, κ 95; often of motion, *forth*, οἱ δ' ἴσαν ἔξω, Ω 247; freq. w. gen.

ἕξω: see ἔχω.

ἕο, ἑοῖ: see οὗ.

ἔοι: see εἰμί.

ἔοικα (ϝέϝοικα), 3 du. ἔικτον, part. ἐοικώς, εἰκώς, fem. εἰκυῖα, ἐικυῖα, ἰκυῖα, pl. εἰοικυῖαι, plup. ἐῴκειν, du. ἐίκτην, 3 pl. ἐοίκεσαν, also ἔικτο, ἤικτο (an ipf. εἶκε, Σ 520, is by some referred here, by others to εἴκω): (1) *be like, resemble*, τινί (τι), ἄντα, εἰς ὦπα, α 208, Ω 630, Γ 158; 'I seem to be singing in the presence of a god when I sing by thee' (ἔοικα = v i d e o r m i h i), χ 348.—(2) impers., *be fitting, suitable, beseem*; abs., οὐδὲ ϝέϝοικεν, A 119, and w. dat. of person, I 70, also w. acc. and inf., B 190; freq. the part. as adj., μῦθοι ἐοικότες, γ 124; ἐοικότα μῡθήσασθαι, καταλέξαι, γ 125, δ 239.

ἑοῖο: see ἑός.

ἔοις: see εἰμί.

ἔολπα: see ἔλπω.

ἔον: see εἰμί.

ἔοργας: see ἔρδω.

ἑορτή: *festival*, υ 156 and φ 258.

ἑός, ἑή, ἑόν (σϝός, cf. s u u s), gen. ἑοῦ, ἑοιο, ἑῆς: *his, her, own*; seldom w. art., Ψ 295, K 256; strengthened by gen. of αὐτός, ἑοὶ αὐτοῦ θῆτες, *his own*, δ 643.

ἐπ-αγάλλομαι: *exult in*, Π 91†.

ἐπ-αγγέλλω: *bring news to, announce*, δ 775.

ἐπ-αγείρω: *bring together*, A 126†.

ἐπάγην: see πήγνῡμι.

ἐπ-αγλαΐζομαι, fut. inf. ἐπαγλαιεῖσθαι: *glory in*, Σ 133†.

ἐπ-άγω, aor. 2 ἐπήγαγον: *lead* or *bring on*, met., *induce*, of 'setting on' dogs, τ 445; joined w. πείθειν, ξ 392.

ἐπ-αείρω, aor. 1 3 pl. ἐπάειραν, part. -αείρᾱς: *lift up* (*on*), K 80; w. gen., ἁμαξάων, 'and placed upon,' H 426, I 214.

ἔπαθον: see πάσχω.

ἐπ-αιγίζω (αἰγίς): *rush on*, of winds, B 148, ο 293.

ἐπ-αινέω, ipf. ἐπῄνεον, aor. ἐπῄνησα *give approval* or *assent, approve, commend*; abs., also w. dat. of person, Σ 312; acc. of thing, μῦθον, B 335.

ἐπ-αινός (αἰνός): only fem.; the *dread* Persephone, consort of Hades.

ἐπ-ᾱΐσσω, ipf. ἐπήΐσσον, aor. ἐπήῑξα, iter. -ᾱΐξασκε, inf. -ᾱῖξαι, mid. ἐπᾱΐσσονται, fut. inf. -ᾱΐξεσθαι: *dart* or *spring at* or *upon*; usually in hostile sense, abs., and w. gen. or dat. of the person or thing attacked; of the wind, ἐπᾱΐξᾱς, 'darting down upon' the sea, B 146; ἐπᾱΐσσοντα νεῶν, N 687, E 263; Κίρκῃ ἐπᾱῖξαι, κ 295, 322; w. acc. of end of motion, ἐπᾱῖξαι μόθον ἵππων, H 240; mid., subjective, χεῖρες, 'play' lightly, Ψ 628; 'dart in' for the prize, Ψ 773.

ἐπ-αιτέω, aor. opt. -τήσειας: *ask besides*, Ψ 593†.

ἐπ-αίτιος: *to blame*; οὔ τι μοι ὔμμες

ἐπαίτιοι, 'I have no fault to find with *you*,' A 335†.

ἐπ-ακούω, aor. ἐπάκουσα: *hearken to, hear*, with the same constructions as ἀκούω, τ 98, B 143.

ἐπ-ακτήρ, ῆρος: *hunter*, i. e. ὁ κύνας ἐπάγων, τ 435; ἄνδρες ἐπακτῆρες, P 135.

ἐπ-αλάομαι, aor. pass. subj. ἐπαληθῇ: *wander to*, w. acc. of end of motion, Κύπρον, δ 83; πόλλ' ἐπαληθείς, 'after long wanderings,' δ 81.

ἐπ-αλαστέω, part. -ήσᾶσα: *be indignant (at)*, α 252†.

ἐπ-αλέξω, fut. -ήσω: *give aid to, defend, help*, τινί, Θ 365 and Λ 428.

ἐπαληθείς: see ἐπαλάομαι.

ἐπ-αλλάσσω: only aor. part., ἐπαλλάξαντες, *entwining in each other, connecting* (the ends of the cord of war), i. e. prolonging the contest; others interpret, 'drawing the cord of war now this way, now that,' N 359†.

ἐπάλμενος: see ἐφάλλομαι.

ἔπ-αλξις, ιος (ἀλέξω): *breastwork, battlement*. (Il.)

Ἐπάλτης, a Lycian, slain by Patroclus, Π 415†.

ἐπᾶλτο: see ἐφάλλομαι.

ἐπ-αμάομαι: only aor. ἐπαμήσατο, *heaped up for himself* a bed of leaves, ε 482†. See ἀμάω.

ἐπ-αμείβω, aor. subj. ἐπαμείψομεν: *give in exchange to, exchange with*; ἀλλήλοις, Z 230; mid., νίκη δ' ἐπαμείβεται ἄνδρας, 'passes from one man to another,' Z 339. (Il.)

ἐπ-αμοιβαδίς (ἐπαμείβω): *interchangingly*, 'intertwined with each other,' ε 481†.

ἐπ-αμύντωρ, ορος: *defender*, π 263†.

ἐπ-αμῦνω, aor imp. ἐπάμῦνον: *bring aid to, come to the defence*, abs., and w. dat., E 685, Θ 414. (Il.)

ἐπ-ανα-τίθημι, aor. 2 inf. ἐπανθέμεναι: *shut again*: σανίδας, Φ 535†.

ἐπ-αν-ίστημι: only aor. 2 intrans., ἐπανέστησαν, *thereupon arose*, i. e. after him, B 85†.

ἐπ-αοιδή (ἐπαείδω): *incantation, spell*, τ 457†.

ἐπ-απειλέω, aor. ἐπηπείλησα: *direct threats against, threaten*, τινί (τι).

ἐπ-αραρίσκω, aor. 1 ἐπῆρσε, plup. ἐπαρήρει: trans. (aor. 1), *fit to* (τινί τι), Ξ 167, 339; intr. (plup.), *fit in*, M 456.

ἐπ-ᾱρή: *imprecation, curse*, pl., I 456†.

ἐπ-αρήγω: *bring help to, succor*.

ἐπαρήρει: see ἐπαραρίσκω.

ἐπ-αρκέω: *bring defence to, ward off*; τινί τι, ρ 568.

ἐπ-άρουρος (ἄρουρα): *bound to the soil* (as a serf), λ 489†.

ἐπ-αρτής, ές (root ἀρ): *equipped, ready*. (Od.)

ἐπ-αρτύω: *fit on*, θ 447.

ἐπ-άρχομαι, aor. imp. ἐπαρξάσθω, part. -ξάμενος: ritualistic word, always w. δεπάεσσιν, *make a beginning (thereto)*, 'perform the dedicatory rites' with the cups, by filling them to pour the libation, A 471, γ 340.

ἐπ-αρωγός (ἀρήγω): *helper*, λ 498†.

ἐπ-ασκέω: only perf. pass., ἐπήσκηται δέ οἱ αὐλὴ | τοίχῳ καὶ θριγκοῖσι, 'it (the house, οἱ) has a court *skilfully adjoined* with wall and coping,' ρ 266†.

ἐπ-ασσύτερος (ἆσσον): *closer and closer, close together*, Δ 423; *in quick succession*, A 383, π 366.

ἔπ-αυλος (αὐλή, 'adjoining the court'): pl., *cattle stalls, stables*, ψ 358†.

ἐπ-αυρίσκω, aor. 2 subj. ἐπαύρῃ, inf. ἐπαυρεῖν, ἐπαυρέμεν, mid. pres. ἐπαυρίσκονται, fut. inf. -ρήσεσθαι, subj. aor. 2 ἐπαύρηαι and ἐπαύρῃ, 3 pl. ἐπαύρωνται: I. act., *acquire, obtain*, Σ 302, ρ 81; fig., often of missiles, 'reach,' 'touch,' χρόα, Λ 573; w. gen., λίθου, 'graze' the stone, Ψ 340.—II. mid., *partake of, enjoy*, 'reap the fruit of,' w. gen., N 733; freq. ironical, A 410, Z 353; w. acc., *bring on oneself*, ρ 81.

ἐπ-αφύσσω, aor. ἐπήφυσε: *draw* or *dip* (water) *upon*, τ 388†.

ἐπ-εγείρω, aor. mid. ἐπέγρετο, part. ἐπεγρόμενος: *awaken* (*at* some juncture), χ 431; mid., *wake up* (*at*), K 124, υ 57.

ἐπέδραμον: see ἐπιτρέχω.

ἐπέην: see ἔπειμι 1.

ἐπεί: temporal and causal conjunction.—I. temporal, *when, after*; of definite time, foll. by ind., freq. aor. (where we use plup.), A 57; but also by other tenses, A 235; of indefinite time (conditional), with the usual constructions that belong to relative words (see ἄν, κέν).—II. causal, *since*, *for*, foll. by ind.—With other words, ἐπεὶ πρῶτον, πρῶτα, 'after once,' 'as soon as,' ἐπεὶ ἄρ, ἐπεὶ δή (ἐπειδή), ἐπεὶ ἤ (ἐπειή), ἐπεὶ οὖν, ἐπεί περ, ἐπεί τοι, see the several words. ἐπεὶ οὐ is to be read with 'synizesis,' except in ε 364, θ 585. ἐπεί stands at the beginning of some verses, as if ἐππεί.

Ἐπειγεύς: a Myrmidon, the son of Agacles, slain by Hector, Π 571.

ἐπείγω, ipf. ἔπειγον, pass. ἐπείγετο: I. act. and pass., *press hard, oppress, impel, urge on;* of weight, ὀλίγον δέ μιν ἄχθος ἐπείγει, Μ 452; old age, χαλεπὸν κατὰ γῆρας ἐπείγει, Ψ 623; wind driving a ship before it, ἔπειγε γὰρ οὖρος ἀπήμων, μ 167; hurrying on a trade, ο 445; pass. ἐπείγετο γὰρ βελέεσσιν, 'hard pressed,' Ε 622; λέβης ἐπειγόμενος πυρὶ πολλῷ, i. e. made to boil in a hurry, Φ 362.—II. mid., *press on, hasten;* of winds driving fast, ἐπειγομένων ἀνέμων, Ε 501; μή τις ἐπειγέσθω οἰκόνδε νέεσθαι, Β 354; esp. freq. the part., 'hastily,' Ε 902, λ 339; and w. gen., 'eager for,' 'desirous of,' ὁδοῖο, α 309, etc.; with acc. and inf., ν 30. The mid. is also sometimes trans. (subjectively), 'hasten on for oneself,' γάμον, β 97, τ 142, ω 132.

ἐπειδάν: *when*, Ν 285†.

ἐπειδή: *when, after, since*, the δή being hardly translatable, see ἐπεί. Less often causal than temporal, η 152.

ἐπειή: see ἐπεί and ἤ. Always causal.

1. ἔπ-ειμι (εἰμί), opt. ἐπείη, ipf. 3 sing. ἐπέην and ἐπῆεν, 3 pl. ἔπεσαν, fut. ἐπέσσεται: *be upon, be remaining*, Β 259, β 344, δ 756. See ἔπι, under ἐπί.

2. ἔπ-ειμι (εἶμι), ἔπεισι, part. ἐπιών, ipf. ἐπήιε, ἐπήισαν, ἐπῇσαν, mid. fut. ἐπιείσομαι, aor. part. ἐπιεισαμένη: *go* or *come upon* or *at;* abs., or w. acc. of place or person, ἀγρόν, ψ 359; met., πρίν μιν καὶ γῆρας ἔπεισιν, 'shall come upon' her, Α 29; also w. dat., τοῖς ὀρυμαγδὸς ἐπήιεν, 'came to their ears,' Ρ 741; esp. in hostile sense, *attack*, w. acc. or dat., Λ 367, Ν 482.

Ἐπειοί: the *Epeians*, a tribe in North Elis, Λ 732, Ν 686, Δ 537.

Ἐπειός: *Epeius*, son of Panopeus, the builder of the wooden horse, Ψ 665, 838, λ 523.

ἐπείπερ: see ἐπεί and πέρ.

ἔπειτα (ἐπί, εἶτα): *thereupon, then, in that case;* of time or of sequence, often correl. to πρῶτον, Ζ 260; and joined with *αὐτίκα, αἶψα, ὦκα*, also ἔνθα δ' ἔπειτα, Σ 450; referring back to what has been stated (or implied), 'so then,' 'accordingly,' 'after all,' α 65, 106, γ 62; after a part., Ξ 223, Λ 730; freq. introducing an apodosis emphatically, 'in that case,' α 84, and after temporal clauses, esp. δὴ ἔπειτα, θ 378; τότ' ἔπειτα.

ἐπεκέκλετο: see ἐπικέλομαι.

ἐπέκερσε: see ἐπικείρω.

ἐπ-ελαύνω, pass. plup. ἐπελήλατο: *forge* or *weld on*, Ν 804, Ρ 493. See ἐλαύνω.

ἐπέλησε: see ἐπιλανθάνω.

ἐπ-εμ-βαίνω: only perf. part. ἐπεμβαώς, *standing upon;* οὐδοῦ, Ι 582†. See βαίνω.

ἐπενεῖκαι: see ἐπιφέρω.

ἐπένειμε: see ἐπινέμω.

ἐπενήνεον: see ἐπινηνέω.

ἐπ-εν-ήνοθε (cf. ἄνθος): defective perf. w. signif. of ipf. or pres., *grew upon*, Β 219, Κ 134; of a perfume, *rises upon*, 'floats around,' θεούς, θ 365 (cf. ἐνήνοθε).

ἐπ-εν-τανύω: only aor. part., ἐπεντανύσᾱς, *stretching high over* (a rope over the rotunda), χ 467†.

ἐπ-εντῡνω, ἐπεντύω: *harness (to)*, Θ 374; mid., *equip oneself* to win, ἄεθλα, ω 89.

ἐπ-έοικα, plup., ἐπεῴκει: *be seemly, becoming;* τινί, Δ 341; also w. acc. and inf., Α 126; regularly impers., but once w. pers. subject, 'befits,' Ι 392.

ἐπέπιθμεν: see πείθω.

ἐπέπληγον: see πλήσσω.

ἐπέπλως: see ἐπιπλώω.

ἐπεποίθει: see πείθω.

ἐπεπόνθει: see πάσχω.

ἐπέπταρε: see ἐπιπταίρω.

ἐπέπτατο: see ἐπιπέτομαι.

ἐπέπυστο: see πυνθάνομαι.

ἐπ-ερείδω, aor. ἐπέρεισε: *lean* or *bear on* hard; Athēna lends force in driving the spear of Diomed, Ε 856; Polyphēmus throws enormous strength into his effort as he hurls the stone, ι 538.

ἐπερρώσαντο: see ἐπιρρώομαι.

ἐπ-ερύω, aor. ἐπέρυσσε: *draw to*, α 441†.

ἐπ-έρχομαι, fut. inf. ἐπελεύσεσθαι, aor. ἐπῆλθον, ἐπήλυθον, perf. ἐπελήλυθα: *come* or *go to* or *upon*, *come on;* of the 'arrival' of times and seasons, κ 175, Θ 488; the 'approach' of sleep or sickness, δ 793, λ 200; and often in hostile sense, 'attack,' esp. the part., Ο 406, Δ 334; mostly w. dat., but w. acc. in the sense 'visit,' 'haunt,' 'traverse,' ἄγκεα, Σ 321; γαῖαν, δ 268; ἀγρούς, π 27; τμήδην, 'struck and grazed,' Η 262.

ἐπεσ-βολίη (ἐπεσβόλος): *forward talk*, pl., δ 159†.

ἐπεσ-βόλος (ἔπος, βάλλω, 'word-slinging'): *wordy*, *scurrilous*, Β 275†.

ἔπεσον: see πίπτω.

ἐπέσπον: see ἐφέπω.

ἐπέσσεται: see ἔπειμι 1.

ἐπέσσυται: see ἐπισεύω.

ἐπέστη: see ἐφίστημι.

ἐπέσχον: see ἐπέχω.

ἐπ-ετήσιος (Ϝέτος): *throughout all the year*, η 118†.

ἔπευ: see ἕπω.

ἐπ-ευφημέω: only aor. ἐπευφήμησαν, *added their favoring voices*, to what the priest himself had said, in favor of granting his petition, Α 22, 376.

ἐπ-εύχομαι, fut. 2 sing. ἐπεύξεαι, aor. ἐπεύξατο: (1) *pray* (*at* some juncture), *add a prayer*, κ 533, ξ 436.—(2) *boast over*, *exult* (*at*), Λ 431, Ε 119.—In both senses abs., or w. dat., and w. foll. inf.

ἔπεφνον: see φεν-.

ἐπέφραδον: see φράζω.

ἐπ-έχω, ipf. ἐπεῖχον, ἔπεχεν, aor. 2 ἐπέσχον, opt. ἐπισχοίης, imp. ἐπίσχετε, mid. aor. part. ἐπισχόμενος: *hold to*, *hold on*, *direct to* or *at*, *extend over;* of putting the feet on a foot-stool, Ξ 241, ρ 410; holding a cup to the lips, Ι 489, Χ 494, similarly 83; guiding a chariot against the enemy, Ρ 464; and, intransitively, of assailing (cf. 'have at him'), τί μοι ὧδ' ἐπέχεις, 'why so hard on me?' τ 71; then of occupying, reaching in space, Φ 407, Ψ 190, 238; *hold* in the sense of 'check,' intr. 'refrain,' Φ 244, φ 186; met., θυμόν, υ 266.—Mid., aor., *take aim*, χ 15.

ἐπ-ήβολος: *possessed of*, β 319†.

ἐπ-ηγκενίδες: *uppermost streaks* or *planks* of a ship, forming the *gunwale*, ε 253†. (See cut No. 32, letter *c*).

ἐπῆεν: see ἔπειμι 1.

ἐπ-ηετανός (αἰεί): *lasting forever*, *perennial;* ἀρδμοί, πλυνοί, ν 247, ζ 86; hence 'plentiful,' 'abundant,' σῖτος, γάλα, κομιδή, σ 360, δ 89, θ 233.—Neut. as adv., **ἐπηετανόν,** *always*, 'abundantly,' η 128, 99, κ 427.

ἐπῄιεν: see ἔπειμι 2.

ἐπήλυθον: see ἐπέρχομαι.

ἐπ-ημοιβός (ἀμείβω): *serving for a change;* χιτῶνες, ξ 513; ὀχῆες, *cross-bars*, shutting over one another in opposite directions. (See cut No. 29).

ἐπήν: *when*, *after*. See **ἐπεί,** also ἄν, κέν.

ἐπῄνεον: see ἐπαινέω.

ἔπηξα: see πήγνυμι.

ἐπ-ηπύω: *applaud*, Σ 502†.

ἐπ-ήρατος (ἐράω): *lovely*, *charming*, only of things and places, θ 366, δ 606, Σ 512.

ἐπ-ήρετμος (ἐρετμός): *at the oar*, β 403; *furnished with oars;* νῆες, δ 589, ε 16.

ἐπ-ηρεφής, έος (ἐρέφω): *overhanging*, *beetling;* πέτραι, κρημνοί, κ 131, μ 59, Μ 54.

Ἐπήριτος: a name feigned by Odysseus, ω 306†.

ἐπῆρσα: see ἐπαραρίσκω.

ἐπῇσαν: see ἔπειμι 2.

ἐπ-ητής, έος: *discreet*, *humane*, ν 332 and σ 128.

ἐπ-ήτριμος: *thick* together, *numerous;* πίπτειν, 'thick and fast,' Τ 226, Σ 211, 552.

ἐπ-ητύς, ύος (ἐπητής): *humanity*, *kindliness*, φ 306† (v. l. ἐπητέος).

ἐπί: *upon*, *on*.—I. adv., *thereon*, *on top*, *thereby*, *besides;* esp. ἔπι = ἔπεστι or ἔπεισι, οὔ τοι ἔπι δϜέος, 'thou hast nought to fear,' Α 515, θ 563. Here belong all examples of 'tmesis,' ἐπὶ δ' αἴγειον κνῆ τυρόν, grated 'on,' Λ 639, 640; the appropriate case of a subst. may specify the relation of the adv., ἐπὶ κνέφας ἤλυθε γαῖαν, darkness came 'on'—over the earth, Ω 351.—κρέ' ἔδων καὶ ἐπ' ἄκρητον γάλα πίνων, 'on top' of the meat, 'besides,' ι 297; πρὸ μέν τ' ἄλλ', αὐτὰρ ἐπ' ἄλλα, some before, some 'after,' Ν 799; ἐπὶ σκέπας ἦν ἀνέμοιο, 'withal,' ε 443.—II. prep., (1) w. gen., local, of position, *on*, *at*, or direction, *towards*, *for;* and sometimes temporal; freq. ἐφ' ἵππων, ἐπὶ νηῶν; ἐπ' ἀγροῦ, 'in the country,' 'at the farm,' α 190; ἐπ' ὄγμου, 'at the swath,' Σ 557; σιγῇ ἐφ' ὑμείων, 'by yourselves,' Η 195; ἐπὶ παιδὸς ἕπεσθαι, 'along with,' α 278; direction, νήσου ἔπι Ψυρίης, make 'for' the island, γ 171, Ε 700; time, ἐπ' εἰρήνης, ἐπὶ προτέρων ἀνθρώπων, 'in the time of,' Β 797, Ε 637.—(2) w. dat., of place, time, purpose, condition; νέμεσθαι ἐπὶ κρήνῃ, 'at' the spring, ν 408; νῆα ἐπ' ἠπείροιο ἔρυσσαν | ὑψοῦ ἐπὶ ψαμαθοῖς, high 'upon the sand,' Α 486; ἐπὶ Πατρόκλῳ τέτατο ὑσμίνη, 'over Patroclus,' Ρ 543; so of charge or mastery, ποιμαίνειν ἐπ' ὄεσσι, Ζ 25; υἱὸν ἐπὶ κτεάτεσσι λιπέσθαι, 'in charge of,' 'as master of,' Ε 154; ἐπὶ ἴστορι πεῖραρ ἑλέσθαι, 'by,' i. e. before a judge, Σ 501; freq. of hostile direction, ἧκε δ' ἐπ' Ἀργείοισι βέλος, 'at the Greeks,' Α 382; addition, ὄγχνη ἐπ' ὄγχνῃ, 'pear upon pear,' η 120, 216; of time, ἐπὶ νυκτί, 'in the night,' Θ 529; ἐπ' ἤματι, 'a day long,' Τ 229; 'day by day,' μ 105; ἐπ' ἤματι τῷδε, 'on this day,' Ν 234; cause or purpose, γαστέρας ἐπὶ δόρπῳ κατθέμεθα, 'for supper,' σ 44; ἐπ' ἀρωγῇ, Ψ 574; ἐπὶ ῥηθέντι δικαίῳ, 'at a just remark,' σ 414; condition or price, μισθῷ ἔπι ῥητῷ, Φ 445, Κ 304, Ι 602.—(3) w. acc., local, direction *to* or *at* (hostile), or extension, *over;* of purpose, *for;* and of time in extension, *for*, *up to;* ἕζεσθαι ἐπ' ἐρετμά, 'take seats at the oars,' μ 171; ἐπὶ ἔργα τρέπεσθαι, 'to work,' Γ 422; ὄρνυσθαι ἐπί τινα, 'against,' Ε 590; ἐπ' ἐννέα κεῖτο πέλεθρα, 'extending over,' λ 577; πάντας ἐπ' ἀνθρώπους ἐκέκαστο, 'the world over,' Ω 535; so ἐπὶ γαῖαν, ἐπὶ πόντον; purpose, ἀναστῆναι ἐπὶ δόρπον, Μ 439; time, παννύχιον εὕδειν καὶ ἐπ' ἠῶ καὶ μέσον ἦμαρ, η 288; so ἐπὶ χρόνον, 'for a time;' ἐπὶ δϝηρόν, 'for long.'

ἐπ-ιάλλω: *send upon;* only aor. 1, ἐπίηλεν τάδε ἔργα, 'brought to pass,' χ 49†.

ἐπιάλμενος: see ἐφάλλομαι.

ἐπιανδάνω: see ἐφανδάνω.

ἐπ-ιάχω, aor. 2 ἐπίαχον: *shout (at)*, *shout (in battle)*, Η 403, Ε 860. (Il.)

ἐπί-βαθρον (paid by an ἐπιβάτης): *fare*, *passage-money*, ο 449†.

ἐπι-βαίνω, fut. inf. ἐπιβησέμεν, aor. 1 ἐπέβησα, subj. ἐπιβήσετε, imp. ἐπίβησον, aor. 2 ἐπέβην, subj. du. ἐπιβῆτον, 1 pl. ἐπιβείομεν, mid. fut. ἐπιβήσομαι, aor. ἐπεβήσετο: *set foot on*, *mount*, *go on board;* w. gen. γαίης, ἵππων, νηῶν, εὐνῆς, κ 334; πυρῆς, Δ 99; fig., ἀναιδείης ἐπιβῆναι, 'tread the path of insolence,' χ 424, ψ 52; w. acc. Πιερίην, Ξ 226, ε 50.—Aor. 1 and fut. act., causative, τινὰ ἵππων, *make* one *mount* the car, Θ 129; πυρῆς, of bringing men to their death, Ι 546; πάτρης, bringing one home, η 223; and fig., ἐυκλείης, σαοφροσύνης, Θ 285, ψ 13.

ἐπι-βάλλω, ipf. ἐπέβαλλε, mid. pres. part. ἐπιβαλλόμενος: *throw* or *cast on;* of plying the whip, 'laying it on' the horses, ζ 320; intrans., (νηῦς) Φεὰς ἐπέβαλλε, 'touched at,' ο 297; mid., 'lay hand on,' 'aim for,' ἐνάρων, Ζ 68.

ἐπι-βάσκω: equivalent to the causative tenses of ἐπιβαίνω, *bring into;* κακῶν, Β 234†.

ἐπιβήμεναι: see ἐπιβαίνω.

ἐπι-βήτωρ, ορος: *mounter*, 'mounted warrior,' ἵππων, σ 263; designating a boar, συῶν ἐπιβήτωρ, λ 131, ψ 278.

ἐπι-βλής, ῆτος (ἐπιβάλλω): *bar*, of gate or door, Ω 453†. (See cut No. 56, and the adjacent representation of Egyptian doors; see also No. 29.)

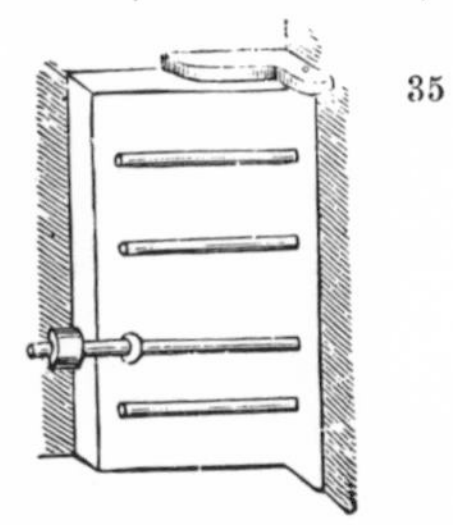
35

ἐπι-βοάω, mid. fut. ἐπιβώσομαι: *call upon*, for help, as witnesses, θεούς, α 378, Κ 463 (v. l. ἐπιδωσόμεθα).

ἐπι-βουκόλος: *herdsman (over cattle)*, *cattle-herd*. (Od.)

ἐπι-βρέμω: *set roaring*, Ρ 739†.

ἐπι-βρίθω, aor. ἐπέβρῖσα: *weigh down upon, make heavy* (with fruit), ω 344; *fall heavily* (*upon*), Η 91, Μ 286, fig., πόλεμος, Η 343.

ἐπιβωσόμεθα: see ἐπιβοάω.

ἐπι-βώτωρ, ορος: μήλων, *shepherd,* ν 222. Cf. ἐπιβουκόλος.

ἐπι-γίγνομαι: *draw on, approach,* Ζ 148†.

ἐπι-γιγνώσκω, aor. subj. ἐπιγνώῃ, -γνώωσι: *mark, recognize,* σ 30, ω 217.

ἐπι-γνάμπτω, aor. ἐπέγναμψα: *bend over;* δόρυ, Φ 178; met., *bend,* 'change,' 'bow' the will, Β 14, Ι 514, Α 569.

ἐπιγνώῃ: see ἐπιγιγνώσκω.

ἐπι-γουνίς, ίδος (γόνυ, 'above the knee'): *thigh;* μεγάλην ἐπιγουνίδα θεῖτο, 'grow a stout thigh,' ρ 225. (Od.)

ἐπι-γράβδην (ἐπιγράφω): adv., βάλε, struck *scratching,* i. e. 'grazed,' Φ 166†.

ἐπι-γράφω, aor. ἐπέγραψα: *scratch on;* 'graze,' χρόα, Ν 533; 'mark,' κλῆρον, Η 187.

Ἐπίδαυρος: *Epidaurus,* in Argolis, Β 561†.

ἐπιδέδρομε: see ἐπιτρέχω.

ἐπι-δέξιος: only neut. pl. as adv., **ἐπιδέξια,** *toward the right* (the lucky direction), φ 141; *on the right* (auspiciously), Β 353.

ἐπι-δευής, ές (ἐπιδεύομαι): *in need of, lacking, inferior to;* δαιτός, Ι 225; w. two genitives (and illustrating both meanings at once), βίης ἐπιδευέες εἰμὲν Ὀδυσῆος, φ 253.—Adv., ἐπιδευὲς ἔχειν δίκης, 'fail of,' Τ 180.

ἐπι-δεύομαι (δέομαι), ipf. ἐπεδεύετο: *lack, need, be inferior to,* w. gen. of thing or of person, Β 229, Σ 77; both together, οὐ μὲν γάρ τι μάχης ἐπεδεύετ' Ἀχαιῶν (cf. φ 253, under ἐπιδευής), Ω 385.

ἐπι-δημεύω (δῆμος): *stay at home* (in town, and not in the country), π 28†.

ἐπι-δήμιος: *at home,* α 194, Ω 262; πόλεμος, 'civil strife,' Ι 64.

ἐπι-δίδωμι, aor. ἐπέδωκε, inf. ἐπιδοῦναι, mid. fut. ἐπιδωσόμεθα, aor. 2 subj. ἐπιδώμεθα: *give besides* or *with,* Ψ 559; as dowry, Ι 147; mid., *take* (*to oneself*) *as witness,* Χ 254; 'honor with gifts'(?), Κ 463 (v. l. ἐπιβωσόμεθα).

ἐπι-δῑνέω (δίνη), aor. part. ἐπιδῑνήσᾱς, pass. -ηθέντε: *set whirling, whirl,* Γ 378, ι 538; pass., *wheel, circle* (of birds), β 151; mid., metaph., *revolve in mind, ponder,* υ 218.

ἐπι-διφριάς, άδος (δίφρος): *rim* of a chariot-box, Κ 475†. (See cut No. 10, under ἄντυξ.)

ἐπι-δίφριος (δίφρος): *in the chariot,* neut. pl., predicatively, ο 51 and 75.

ἐπιδραμεῖν, ἐπιδραμέτην: see ἐπιτρέχω.

ἐπί-δρομος (ἐπιδραμεῖν): *to be scaled;* τεῖχος, Ζ 434†.

ἐπιδώμεθα: see ἐπιδίδωμι.

ἐπι-είκελος (ϝείκελος): *like to;* θεοῖς, ἀθανάτοισιν, Α 265, Ι 485.

ἐπι-εικής, ές (ϝέϝοικα): *suitable, becoming,* ι 382; (τύμβον) ἐπιεικέα τοῖον, 'only just of suitable size,' Ψ 246; often ὡς ἐπιεικές (sc. ἐστιν).

ἐπι-εικτός, 3 (ϝείκω): *yielding,* always w. neg., μένος οὐκ ἐπιεικτόν, 'unyielding,' 'steadfast,' τ 493, Ε 892; σθένος, 'invincible,' Π 549; ἔργα, 'unendurable,' i. e. to which one must not yield, θ 307.

ἐπιειμένος: see ἐπιέννῡμι.

ἐπιείσομαι: see ἔπειμι 2.

ἐπι-έλπομαι (ϝέλπω): *have hope of,* Α 545, φ 126.

ἐπι-έννῡμι (ϝέννῡμι), aor. 1 pl. ἐπιέσσαμεν, pass. perf. part. ἐπιειμένος: *put on over;* χλαῖναν, υ 143; pass., metaph., ἐπιειμένος ἀλκήν, ἀναιδείην, *clothed in* might, etc., Η 164, Α 149.

ἐπι-ζάφελος: *raging, furious;* χόλος, Ι 525.—Adv., **ἐπιζαφέλως,** *vehemently.*

ἐπίηλε: see ἐπιάλλω.

ἐπιήνδανε: see ἐφανδάνω.

ἐπίηρα: see ἦρα.

ἐπι-ήρανος (ἦρα): *agreeable;* θυμῷ, τ 343†.

ἐπι-θαρσῡ́νω: *encourage,* Δ 183†.

ἐπιθεῖτε: see ἐπιτίθημι.

ἐπί-θημα (τίθημι): *lid* of a chest, pl., Ω 228†.

ἐπιθρέξᾱς: see ἐπιτρέχω.

ἐπι-θρώσκω: *spring upon;* νηός, Θ 515; 'jump upon' (in contempt), Δ 177; τόσσον ἐπιθρώσκουσι, *spring* so far, Ε 772.

ἐπ-ῑθύω (ἰθύς), aor. part. ἐπῑθύσαντες: *charge straight at* or *on,* Σ 175, π 297.

ἐπι-ίστωρ, ορος (root ϝιδ): *conscious of, accomplice in,* φ 26†.

ἐπίκαρ: see κάρ.

ἐπι-κάρσιος, 3 (κάρ, κάρα): *headforemost, headlong*, ι 70†.

Ἐπικάστη (καίνυμαι, the 'Notorious'): the mother of Oedipus, in the tragic poets *Jocasta*, λ 271†.

ἐπί-κειμαι, fut. ἐπικείσεται: *lie on* or *to*, i. e. 'be closed' (of doors), ζ 19; met., ἀνάγκη, 'press upon' (as we say 'be under' the necessity), Z 458.

ἐπι-κείρω, aor. ἐπέκερσε: *mow down*; φάλαγγας, Π 394†.

ἐπι-κέλλω, aor. ἐπέκελσα: *beach* a ship, νῆα, ι 138; intr., νηῦς, *run in* on the beach, ν 114, ι 148 (cf. 149).

ἐπι-κέλομαι, aor. ἐπεκέκλετο: *invoke*; Ἐρῑνῦς, I 454†.

ἐπι-κερτομέω: *mock at, deride*; part., 'jestingly,' Ω 649.

ἐπι-κεύθω, fut. -σω, aor. subj. ἐπικεύσῃς: *conceal*, always w. neg., ξ 467, δ 744, E 816.

ἐπι-κίδναμαι: only pres. 3 sing., *diffuses itself over*, B 850, H 451, 458.

ἐπι-κίρνημι, aor. inf. ἐπικρῆσαι: *mix in*, add wine to water, η 164†.

ἐπι-κλείω (κλέος): *bestow praise upon, applaud*, α 351†.

Ἐπικλῆς: a Lycian, slain by Ajax, M 379†.

ἐπί-κλησις (καλέω): *given name* ('surname'); only acc., adverbially or predicatively, mostly with καλεῖν, Ἄρκτον θ', ἣν καὶ ἄμαξαν ἐπίκλησιν καλέουσιν, 'which they call also *by the name* of the wain,' ε 273, H 138, X 506; Σπερχειῷ, αὐτὰρ ἐπίκλησιν Βώρῳ, 'but *by repute* to B.,' Π 177.

ἐπι-κλίνω: only pass. perf. part., ἐπικεκλιμέναι σανίδες, *closed* doors, M 121†.

ἐπί-κλοπος (κλέπτω): *thievish, cunning, sly rogue*; μύθων, τόξων, 'filcher' (combined skill and rascality), X 281, φ 397.

ἐπι-κλύω: *hear*, Ψ 652, ε 150.

ἐπι-κλώθω, aor. ἐπέκλωσα, mid. ἐπεκλωσάμην: *spin to*, of the Fates spinning the threads of destiny; hence *allot to, grant*, w. acc., or foll. by inf. (Od. and Ω 525.)

ἐπι-κόπτω: only fut. part., ἐπικόψων, *to fell* by a blow, γ 443†.

ἐπι-κουρέω: only fut. part., ἐπικουρήσοντα, *to give aid*, E 614†.

ἐπί-κουρος: *helper* in battle, E 478, fem., Φ 431; pl., *allies* of the Trojans.

ἐπι-κραίνω, ἐπικραιαίνω, aor. opt. ἐπικρήνειε, imp. ἐπικρήηνον: *bring to fulfilment, fulfil, accomplish*. (Il.)

ἐπι-κρατέω: *have power over, rule over*; 'have the upper hand,' Ξ 98.

ἐπι-κρατέως (κράτος): *mightily, victoriously*. (Il.)

ἐπικρήηνον, ἐπικρήνειε: see ἐπικραίνω.

ἐπικρῆσαι: see ἐπικίρνημι.

ἐπ-ίκριον: *yard* of a ship, ε 254 and 318.

ἐπι-λάμπω, aor. ἐπέλαμψε: *shine in*, P 650†.

ἐπι-λανθάνω, ἐπιλήθω, aor. ἐπέλησε, mid. ipf. ἐπελήθετο, fut. ἐπιλήσομαι: act., *make to forget*, w. gen., υ 85; mid., *forget*.

ἐπι-λείβω: *pour* wine *over*, as a libation, γ 341.

ἐπι-λεύσσω: *see ahead*, Γ 12†.

ἐπί-ληθος: *causing oblivion*; κακῶν, δ 221†.

ἐπιλήθω: see ἐπιλανθάνω.

ἐπι-ληκέω: *beat time to* a dance, θ 379†.

ἐπι-λίγδην: βλῆτο ὦμον, received a stroke *grazing* the shoulder, P 599†.

ἐπ-ιλλίζω: *wink to*, σ 11†.

ἐπι-λωβεύω (λώβη): *mock at*, β 323†.

ἐπι-μαίνομαι, aor. ἐπεμήνατο: *be mad for, madly desirous*, w. inf., Z 160†.

ἐπι-μαίομαι, imp. ἐπιμαίεο, ipf. ἐπεμαίετο, fut. ἐπιμάσσεται, aor. ἐπεμάσσατο, part. ἐπιμασσάμενος: (1) *feel over, feel for, touch up*; of the blind Polyphēmus feeling over the backs of his sheep, hoping to catch Odysseus, οἰων ἐπεμαίετο νῶτα, ι 441; Odysseus feeling for the right place to stab the sleeping Polyphēmus, χείρ' (dat.) ἐπιμασσάμενος, ι 302; the surgeon probing a wound, ἕλκος δ' ἰητὴρ ἐπιμάσσεται, Δ 190; of touching one with the magic wand, ῥάβδῳ, N 429; horses with the whip, E 748.—(2) *make for, strive for*; τινός, μ 220, ε 344, K 401.

ἐπι-μάρτυρος: *witness to* a matter, only of gods, H 76, α 273.

ἐπιμασσάμενος: see ἐπιμαίομαι.

ἐπί-μαστος (ἐπιμαίομαι): of one

who has been *handled*, hence 'filthy,' ἀλήτης, υ 377†.

ἐπι-μειδάω: only aor. part., ἐπιμειδήσᾱς, *smiling at* or *upon*, Δ 356; in bad sense, Κ 400.

ἐπι-μέμφομαι: *find fault with, blame for*, w. dat. of person, π 97; gen. (causal) of the thing, Α 65, 93, Β 225.

ἐπι-μένω, aor. imp. ἐπίμεινον, inf. ἐπιμεῖναι: *stay, wait, tarry*.

ἐπι-μήδομαι: *devise against; τινί τι*, δ 437†.

ἐπι-μῆνις: *wrath thereat*, Ε 178†. The reading of Aristarchus.

ἐπι-μηνίω: only ipf., *was at feud with*, Ν 460†.

ἐπι-μιμνήσκομαι, aor. mid. opt., ἐπιμνησαίμεθα, pass. part. ἐπιμνησθείς: *call to mind, remember*.

ἐπι-μίμνω: *wait upon, superintend; ἔργῳ*, ξ 66 and ο 372.

ἐπι-μίξ: *indiscriminately*.

ἐπι-μίσγομαι: *mingle with*, hence *come in contact with, have to do with, engage* in battle (*with* the enemy), Ε 505.

ἐπιμνησαίμεθα: see ἐπιμιμνήσκομαι.

ἐπι-μύζω (μύζω, 'say μῦ'), aor. ἐπέμυξαν: *mutter, murmur at*. (Il.)

ἐπι-νέμω, aor. ἐπένειμε: *distribute (to)*.

ἐπι-νεύω, aor. ἐπένευσα: *nod* with the helmet (of the plume), Χ 314; *nod assent* (opp. ἀνανεύω), κάρητι, Ο 75.

ἐπι-νεφρίδιος (νεφρός): *over the kidneys*, Φ 204†.

ἐπι-νέω, aor. ἐπένησε: *spin to*, i. e. allot as destiny (cf. ἐπικλώθω), Υ 128 and Ω 210.

ἐπι-νηνέω (νέω, νηέω): *heap up upon; νεκροὺς πυρκαϊῆς*, Η 428 and 431.

ἐπί-ξυνος (ξῡνός = κοινός): *common*, i. e. where several persons have rights, Μ 422†.

ἐπι-ορκέω, fut. -ήσω: *swear falsely; πρὸς δαίμονος*, in the name of a divinity, Τ 188†.

ἐπί-ορκος: *falsely sworn, false*, Τ 264; as subst., ἐπίορκον, *false oath*, Γ 279; *vain oath*, Κ 332.

ἐπι-όσσομαι: *look after, look out for* (to hinder, if possible), w. acc., Ρ 381†.

ἐπίουρα: see οὖρον.

ἐπί-ουρος (οὖρος): *guardian* or *watch over*; Κρήτῃ, 'ruler over' Crete, Ν 450; ὑῶν, 'chief swine-herd,' ν 405, ο 39.

ἐπιόψομαι: see ἐφοράω.

ἐπι-πείθομαι, ipf. ἐπεπείθετο, fut. ἐπιπείσομαι: *allow oneself to be prevailed upon*, β 103, κ 406; hence, *obey, τινί*.

ἐπι-πέλομαι: only syncopated part., ἐπιπλόμενον ϝέτος, *on-coming, on-rolling* year, η 261 and ξ 287.

ἐπι-πέτομαι, aor. ἐπέπτατο, inf. ἐπιπτέσθαι: *fly toward* or *in*, Ν 821; of an arrow, Δ 126.

ἐπι-πίλναμαι: *come nigh*, ζ 44†.

ἐπι-πλάζομαι, aor. pass. part. -πλαγχθείς: *drift over; πόντον*, θ 14†.

ἐπι-πλέω, ἐπιπλείω: *sail over*, w. acc.

ἐπι-πλήσσω, fut. inf. -ήξειν: *lay on blows*, Κ 500; metaph., *take to task, rebuke*, Μ 211, Ψ 580.

ἐπιπλόμενον: see ἐπιπέλομαι.

ἐπιπλώω, aor. 2 2 sing. ἐπέπλως, aor. 1 part. ἐπιπλώσᾱς: = ἐπιπλέω, γ 15, Ζ 291, Γ 47.

ἐπι-πνέω, ἐπιπνείω, aor. subj. ἐπιπνεύσωσι: *breathe* or *blow upon*, Ε 698; νηί, δ 357.

ἐπι-ποιμήν, ένος: pl., fem., *shepherdesses over*, μ 131†. Cf. ἐπιβουκόλος, ἐπιβώτωρ.

ἐπι-πρέπω: only 3 sing., *is to be seen, manifest in*, ω 252†.

ἐπιπροέμεν: see ἐπιπροΐημι.

ἐπι-προ-ιάλλω: only aor. ἐπιπροΐηλε, *set before* them (σφωίν), Λ 628†.

ἐπι-προ-ίημι, aor. ἐπιπροέηκα, inf. ἐπιπροέμεν: *let go forth to* or *at*; of sending a man to the war, Σ 58, 439; discharging an arrow at one, Δ 94; intrans. (sc. νῆα), *make for; νήσοισιν*, ο 299.

ἐπι-πταίρω, aor. ἐπέπταρε: *sneeze at; τινὶ ἐπέεσσιν* (at one's words, a lucky omen; πᾶσι, means that the omen applied to *all* she had said), ρ 545†.

ἐπιπτέσθαι: see ἐπιπέτομαι.

ἐπι-πωλέομαι: *go round to; στίχας*, of 'inspecting' the ranks, Δ 231; trying them, to find a chance to fight, Λ 264. (Il.)

ἐπι-ρρέζω (ϝρέζω): only ipf. iter.,

ἐπιρρέζεσκον, *were wont to do* sacrifice, ρ 211†.

ἐπι-ρρέπω (ϝρέπω): *sink toward*, of the balance; ὄλεθρος ἡμῖν, 'settles down upon us,' Ξ 99.

ἐπι-ρρέω (σρέω): *flow upon*, B 754; met., *stream on*, Λ 724. (Il.)

ἐπι-ρρήσσω: only ipf. iter. ἐπιρρήσσεσκον, *drove to*, *pushed home*, Ω 454, 456. (Il.)

ἐπι-ρρῑπτω (ϝρίπτω), aor. ἐπέρρῑψαν: *fling upon* or *at*, ε 310†.

ἐπί-ρροθος (cf. ἐπιτάρροθος): *helper*. (Il.)

ἐπι-ρρώομαι: see ῥώομαι, ipf. ἐπερρώοντο, *plied their toil* at the mills, υ 107; aor. ἐπερρώσαντο, *flowed down*; χαῖται, A 529.

ἐπι-σείω, ἐπισσείω: *shake* or *brandish over* or *against*; τινί, Δ 167, O 230. (Il.)

ἐπι-σεύω, ἐπισσεύω, aor. 1 ἐπέσσευε, part. ἐπισσεύᾱς, mid. ipf. ἐπεσσεύοντο, perf. w. pres. signif. ἐπέσσυμαι, part. ἐπεσσύμενος, plup. ἐπέσσυτο, ἐπεσσύμεθα: I. act., *set upon*, *incite* or *send against*; κῆτός τινι, ε 421, ξ 399; met., κακά, ὀνείρατα, σ 256, τ 129, υ 87.—II. mid., *rush on* or *at*, *hasten on*, *speed to*, w. dat. of person, esp. in hostile sense; w. gen. of thing aimed at, τείχεος, M 388, Π 511, cf. χ 310; acc., δέμνια, ζ 20; also foll. by inf.; met., θῡμὸς ἐπέσσυται, 'is so moved,' A 173.

ἐπί-σκοπος (σκοπέω): *look-out*, *watch*, *spy* against, in hostile sense w. dat., Τρώεσσι, νήεσσι, K 38, 342; otherwise w. gen., θ 163; *guardian*, X 255, Ω 729.

ἐπι-σκύζομαι, aor. opt. ἐπισκύσσαιτο: *be indignant* or *wroth at*; τινί, I 370, η 306.

ἐπι-σκύνιον: *skin over the brows* (supercilium), knitted in frowning, P 136†.

ἐπι-σμυγερῶς: *miserably*, *sadly*, γ 195, δ 672. (Od.)

ἐπί-σπαστος (σπάω): *drawn on* himself, σ 73. (Od.)

ἐπισπεῖν: see ἐφέπω.

ἐπι-σπέρχω: *urge on*, χ 451, Ψ 430; intr., *drive fast*, of storms, ε 304.

ἐπισπέσθαι, ἐπισπών: see ἐφέπω.

ἐπισσείω, ἐπισσεύω: see ἐπισείω, ἐπισεύω.

ἐπίσσωτρον: *tire* of a wheel. (Il.)

ἐπι-σταδόν (ἵστημι): adv., *stepping up to*; *standing*, i. e. on the spot, π 453.

ἐπίσταμαι, ipf. ἐπίστατο, fut. ἐπιστήσονται: *know how*, *understand*, w. inf., B 611; often the part. in the sense of *skilled in*, w. gen., φ 406, abs., Σ 599; w. dat., O 282; of 'knowing' a fact, δ 730.

ἐπισταμένως (ἐπίσταμαι): *skilfully*.

ἐπι-στάτης: *one who stands by* or *over*; σὸς ἐπιστάτης, 'thy petitioner,' meaning a beggar, ρ 455†.

ἐπι-στενάχομαι: *groan besides*, Δ 154†.

ἐπι-στεφής, ές (στέφω): *brimful*.

ἐπι-στέφομαι (στέφω), aor. ἐπεστέψαντο: *fill to the brim* for oneself.

ἐπιστήμων: *knowing*, *sagacious*, π 374†.

ἐπίστιον: *dock-yard* or *boat-house*, a place for keeping ships, ζ 365†.

ἐπι-στοναχέω: only aor., ἐπεστονάχησε, the billows *roared* as they closed *upon* her, Ω 79†.

ἐπι-στρέφω, aor. part. ἐπιστρέψᾱς: *turn towards*, sc. μίν, Γ 370†.

ἐπι-στροφάδην: *turning in every direction*, *on every side*.

ἐπί-στροφος (ἐπιστρέφομαι): *conversant with* (ἀνθρώπων), through wanderings, α 177†.

Ἐπίστροφος: (1) son of Iphitus, leader of the Phocians, B 517.—(2) leader of the Halizonians, B 856.—(3) son of Evēnus, slain by Achilles at the sack of Lyrnessus, B 692.

ἐπι-στρωφάω (frequentative of ἐπιστρέφω): *haunt*; πόληας, ρ 486†.

Ἐπίστωρ: a Trojan, slain by Patroclus, Π 695†.

ἐπι-σφύριον (σφυρόν): anything *at the ankle*, pl., *ankle-clasps* fastening the greaves, or perhaps, *ankle-guards*, Γ 331. (Il.) (See cut on next page.)

ἐπι-σχερώ (σχερός): adv., *in a row*, *close together*, Ψ 125. (Il.)

ἐπι-σχεσίη (ἐπέχω): μῦθον ποιήσασθαι ἐπισχεσίην, give a *direction* to one's statements, φ 71†.

ἐπί-σχεσις (ἐπέχω): *restraint*, foll. by inf., ρ 451†.

ἐπ-ίσχω (parallel form of ἐπέχω): *direct to* or *at*; ἵππους, P 465†.

ἐπι-τάρροθος (cf. ἐπίρροθος): *helper*. (Il. and ω 182.)

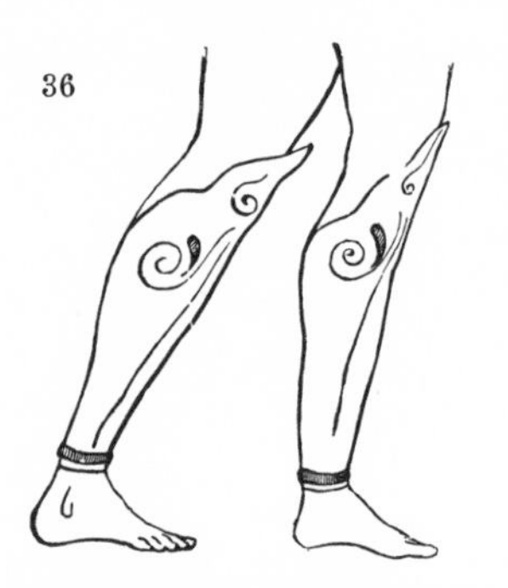
36

ἐπι-τέλλω, aor. ἐπέτειλα, imp. ἐπίτειλον, inf. ἐπιτεῖλαι, part. ἐπιτείλᾱς, mid. aor. ἐπετείλατο, part. ἐπιτειλαμένῳ: act. and mid., *enjoin, lay* command or order *upon, charge,* τινί (τι), and w. foll. inf.; συνθεσίᾱς, E 320; μῦθον, Λ 840; ἀέθλους, λ 622; ὧδ' ἐπέτελλε, μὴ πρὶν πημανέειν, 'thus charged me,' 'gave me this assurance,' Ω 781. ἐπῑτέλλω, ψ 361.

ἐπι-τέρπομαι: *take pleasure in,* ξ 228†.

ἐπιτέτραπται, ἐπιτετράφαται: see ἐπιτρέπω.

ἐπι-τηδές: *sufficiently, as are needed,* A 142, ο 28.

ἐπι-τίθημι, fut. ἐπιθήσω, aor. ἐπέθηκα, imp. ἐπίθες, opt. ἐπιθείη, 2 pl. -θεῖτε: *put* or *place to* or *upon, add,* H 364; of putting food on the table, α 140; a veil on the head, ε 314; the cover on a quiver, ι 314; a stone against a doorway, ι 243; and regularly of 'closing' doors (cf. 'pull the door *to*'), Ξ 169, χ 157, cf. E 751, Θ 395, λ 525; metaph., θωήν, 'impose' a penalty, β 192; μύθῳ τέλος, 'give fulfilment,' T 107.

ἐπι-τῑμήτωρ: *avenger, protector,* ι 270†.

ἐπι-τλῆναι, imp. ἐπιτλήτω: *be patient (at),* Ψ 591; μύθοισιν, 'hearken patiently to,' T 220.

ἐπι-τολμάω, imp. ἐπιτολμάτω, aor. ἐπετόλμησε: *hold out, endure,* abs., ρ 238, w. inf., α 353.

ἐπί-τονος (τείνω): *back-stay* of a mast, μ 423†. (See cut, representing a Phoenician war-ship.)

ἐπι-τοξάζομαι: *bend the bow upon, shoot at;* τινί, Γ 79†.

ἐπι-τραπέω: *commit, intrust to,* K 421†.

ἐπι-τρέπω, aor. 1 ἐπέτρεψα, aor. 2 ἐπέτραπον, imp. 2 pl. ἐπιτράφεθ', mid. aor. 2 ἐπετραπόμην, pass. perf. ἐπιτέτραμμαι, 3 pl. ἐπιτετράφαται: act., *turn* or *give over to, commit, intrust,* pass., B 25, E 750; of 'leaving' the victory to another, Φ 473; intr., 'give up,' 'give in to,' γήραϊ, K 79; mid. (met.), *be inclined,* θῡμός, ι 12.

ἐπι-τρέχω, aor. 1 part. ἐπιθρέξαντος, aor. 2 ἐπέδραμον, perf. ἐπιδέδρομα: *run up, run upon,* often in hostile sense, ξ 30; of horses putting forth their speed, 'ran *on*,' Ψ 418, 447; the chariot rolling close *on* (behind) the horses, Ψ 504; a spear impinging upon a shield, N 409; λευκὴ δ' ἐπιδέδρομεν αἴγλη, *runs over* all, ζ 45; ἀχλύς, υ 357.

ἐπι-τροχάδην: *glibly, fluently,* Γ 213, σ 26.

ἐπι-φέρω, fut. ἐποίσει, aor. 1 inf. ἐπενεῖκαι: *bear upon,* only in unfavorable sense, χεῖρα, χεῖρας, *lay* hands *upon,* A 89, π 438; 'touch,' T 261.

ἐπι-φθονέω: *begrudge, refuse, deny,* λ 149†.

ἐπι-φλέγω: *burn, consume;* ὕλην, νεκρόν, B 455, Ψ 52. (Il.)

ἐπι-φράζομαι, aor. 1 2 sing. ἐπεφράσω, 3 ἐπεφράσατο, subj. ἐπιφράσσετ', opt. ἐπιφρασσαίμεθα, 3 pl. -αίατο, pass. aor. ἐπεφράσθης: *consider, mark, devise,* ο 444; joined w. νοεῖν (Odysseus weeps), Ἀλκίνοος δέ μιν οἶος ἐπεφράσατ' ἠδ' ἐνόησεν, 'remarked' and noted the fact, θ 94, 533, E 665; οἷον δὴ τὸν μῦθον ἐπεφράσθης ἀγορεῦσαι, 'didst take it into thy head' to say, ε 183.

ἐπι-φρονέουσα: part., *sagaciously,* τ 385†.

ἐπι-φροσύνη: *thoughtfulness, sagacity;* pl. ἀνελέσθαι, assume *discretion,* τ 22. (Od.)

37

ἐπί-φρων: *thoughtful, sagacious, discreet;* βουλή, μῆτις, γ 128, τ 326. (Od.)

ἐπι-χειρέω (χείρ): *put hand to, apply oneself to;* δείπνῳ, σίτῳ, ω 386 and 395.

ἐπιχεῦαι: see ἐπιχέω.

ἐπι-χέω, aor. 1 ἐπέχευε, inf. ἐπιχεῦαι, mid. aor. 1 ἐπεχεύατο, aor. 2 ἐπέχυντο: *pour upon, heap up,* mid. (aor. 1), for oneself; not of liquids only, but of earth, leaves, etc.; πολλὴν δ' ἐπεχεύατο ὕλην, for wattling, ε 257; χύσιν φύλλων, for a bed, ε 487; mid., aor. 2, intr. (metaph.) τοὶ δ' ἐπέχυντο, *poured in,* O 654, Π 295.

ἐπι-χθόνιος (χθών): *upon the earth, earthly,* epith. of men, mortals, as opp. to gods; subst., *dwellers upon earth,* Ω 220, ρ 115.

ἐπι-χράω, aor. 2 ἐπέχραον: *assail;* τινί, Π 352, 356; fig., of the suitors 'besetting' Penelope with their wooing, β 50.

ἐπι-χρίω, aor. part. ἐπιχρίσᾶσα: *besmear, anoint,* mid., oneself, σ 179. (Od.)

ἐπι-ψαύω: *touch upon;* met., πραπίδεσσιν, 'have perception,' θ 547†.

ἐπι-ωγαί, pl.; *places of shelter against* wind and wave, *roadstead,* ε 404†.

ἐπιών: see ἔπειμι 2.

ἔπλε: see πέλω.

ἔπλεο, ἔπλευ, ἔπλετο: see πέλομαι.

ἔπληντο: see πελάζω.

ἐποίσει: see ἐπιφέρω.

ἐπ-οίχομαι, ipf. ἐπῴχετο: *go up to, go against,* w. acc. of person or of thing; ἐποιχόμενον στίχας ἀνδρῶν, i. e. to marshall them, O 279, Π 155; οὐρῆας μὲν πρῶτον ἐπῴχετο, 'attacked,' A 50; ἐπῴχετο κῆλα θεοῖο, 'sped' to their mark, A 383; ἐποιχομένη πόσιν εὗρεν, had 'gone abroad' to find a husband, ζ 282; ἔργον ἐποίχεσθαι, δόρπον, α 358, ν 34; ἱστὸν ἐποιχομένη, 'plying' the loom, i. e. going up and down before it, A 31.

ἕπομαι: see ἕπω.

ἐπ-όμνῡμι, ἐπομνύω, ipf. ἐπώμνυον, aor. ἐπώμοσα: *take oath, swear upon* some matter, ο 437; ἐπίορκον, 'swear a vain oath,' K 332.

ἐπ-ομφάλιος (ὀμφαλός): βάλεν σάκος ἐπομφάλιον, *on the boss,* H 267†.

ἐπ-οπίζομαι (ὄπις): *stand in awe of, reverence,* ε 146†.

ἐπ-οπτάω: *broil over* a fire, μ 363†.

ἐπ-οπτεύω, ipf. iter. ἐποπτεύεσκε: *oversee, superintend,* π 140†.

ἐπ-ορέγω: only mid. aor. part., ἐπορεξάμενος, *reaching out after, lunging at,* E 335†.

ἐπ-όρνῡμι, ἐπορνύω, ipf. ἐπώρνυε, aor. 1 ἐπῶρσα, mid. aor. 2 ἐπῶρτο: act., *rouse against, arouse, send upon,* mid., *rise against;* ἄγρει μάν οἱ ἔπορσον Ἀθηναίην, E 765; (Ζεύς) ὅς μοι ἐπῶρσε μένος, Υ 93; τῇ τις θεὸς ὕπνον ἐπῶρσεν, χ 429; mid. (the river Scamander), ἐπῶρτ' Ἀχιλῆι κυκώμενος, Φ 324.

ἐπ-ορούω, aor. ἐπόρουσα: *rush upon, hasten to;* τινί, usually in hostile sense, but not always, E 793; w. acc., ἅρμα, P 481; met., ὕπνος, 'came swiftly upon,' ψ 343.

ἔπος (root Ϝεπ., cf. v o x), pl. ἔπεα: *word, words,* rather with reference to the feeling and ethical intent of the speaker than to form or subject-matter (ῥῆμα, μῦθος); κακόν, ἐσθλόν, μείλιχον, ἅλιον, ὑπερφίαλον ἔπος, Ω 767, A 108, ο 374, Σ 324, δ 503; pl., ἔπεσιν καὶ χερσὶν ἀρήξειν, A 77; δώροισίν τ' ἀγανοῖσιν ἔπεσσί τε μειλιχίοισιν, I 113; so of the bard, ἔπε' ἱμερόεντα, ρ 519, θ 91; phrases, ποῖόν σε Ϝέπος φύγεν ἕρκος ὀδόντων, ἔπος τ' ἔφατ' ἔκ τ' ὀνόμαζεν, εὐχόμενος ἔπος ηὔδᾱ, ἔπεα πτερόεντα προσηύδᾱ. ἔπος, ἔπεα are best literally translated; if paraphrased, 'command,' 'threat,' are admissible, not 'tale,' 'message,' or the like.

ἐπ-οτρύνω, aor. ἐπώτρῡνα: *urge on, move, prompt, impel,* τινά, and w. inf., rarely τινί (most of the apparent instances of the dat. depend on some other word), O 258, κ 531; joined with κελεύω, ἄνωγα, β 422, K 130; often θῡμὸς ἐποτρύνει, Z 439; in bad sense, 'stirred me up,' θ 185; of things, πόλεμόν τινι, ἀγγελίᾱς πολίεσσι, χ 152, ω 335; mid., ἐποτρῡνώμεθα πομπήν, 'be quick with our escort,' θ 31 (cf. act., 30).

ἐπ-ουράνιος (οὐρανός): *in heaven, heavenly,* epithet of the gods (opp. ἐπιχθόνιος).

ἐπ-οχέομαι, fut. -ήσεται: *be carried*

upon, ride upon, ἵπποις (in the sense of *chariot*), P 449. (Il.)

ἐπόψομαι: see ἐφοράω.

ἔπραθον: see πέρθω.

ἑπτά: *seven*.

ἑπτα-βόειος (βοείη): *of seven folds of hide;* σάκος, H 220 ff. (Il.)

ἑπτα-έτης (ϝέτος): only neut., ἑπτάετες, *seven years*. (Od.)

ἑπτα-πόδης (πούς): *seven feet long*, O 729†.

Ἑπτάπορος: a river in Mysia, flowing from Mt. Ida, M 20.

ἑπτά-πυλος (πύλη): *seven-gated*, epith. of Boeotian Thebes, Δ 406.

ἔπταρον: see πταίρω.

ἔπτατο: see πέτομαι.

ἔπταχα: *in seven parts*, ξ 434†.

ἕπω, ipf. ἕπον, mid. **ἕπομαι,** imp. ἕπεο, ἕπευ, ipf. εἱπόμην, ἑπόμην, fut. ἕψομαι, aor. ἑσπόμην, imp. σπεῖο, ἑσπέσθω, part. ἑσπόμενος: *move about, be busy.* — I. act., ἀμφ' Ὀδυσῆα Τρῶες ἕπον, 'moved around Odysseus,' Λ 43; ἄλλοι δ' ἐπὶ ἔργον ἕποιεν, 'be busy with their work,' ξ 195; trans., περικαλλέα τεύχε' ἕποντα, 'occupied with,' Z 321; οὐ μὲν δὴ τόδε μεῖζον ἔπει κακόν, a greater evil that 'approaches,' μ 209 (v. l. ἔπι).—II. mid., once like act., ἀμφὶ δ' ἄρ' αὐτὸν Τρῶες ἕπονθ', 'moved around him,' Λ 474 (cf. 483); usually *go along with, accompany, follow*, κέκλετο θεράποντας ἅμα σπέσθαι ἑοῖ αὐτῷ, δ 38; σοὶ δ' ἄλοχον σπέσθαι, χ 324; τούτου γ' ἑσπομένοιο, 'if *he* should go too,' K 246; ἕπεο προτέρω, 'come along in,' Σ 387; ὣς εἰπὼν ἡγεῖθ', ἣ δ' ἕσπετο, *followed*, α 125; also w. adverbs, μετά, σύν, ἐπί, Ψ 133, κ 436, Δ 63 (met.); often of things, ὅσσα ἔοικε φίλης ἐπὶ παιδὸς ἕπεσθαι, 'go along with,' i. e. be given as dowry, α 278; οἵη ἐμὴ δύναμις καὶ χεῖρες ἕπονται, 'answer to' my strength, υ 237; γούνατα, Δ 314; in hostile sense only in Il., Λ 154, 165, etc.

ἐπ-ώνυμος (ὄνομα): *by a name* given for some reason ('s u r name,' cf. ἐπίκλησις), I 562; ὄνομα ἐπώνυμον, of a *significant* name, η 54, τ 409.

ἐπῶρτο: see ἐπόρνῡμι.

ἐπ-ώχατο, plup. pass. 3 pl. from ἐπέχω: *were shut*, M 340†.

ἔρα-ζε: *upon the ground*, with πίπτω and χέω, χ 20, M 156.

ἔραμαι, ἐράομαι, ipf. 2 pl. ἐράασθε, aor. ἠρασάμην, ἐρά(σ)σατο: *be* (aor. *become*) *enamoured of, in love with;* fig., πολέμου, φῡλοπίδος, I 64, Π 208.

ἐραννός (ἔραμαι): *lovely, charming*, epith. of places, I 531, η 18.

ἔρανος: *picnic*, α 226. (Od.)

ἐράσσατο: see ἔραμαι.

ἐρατεινός (ἐρατός): *lovely, charming;* epith. of places and of things; twice of persons, δ 13 and (in a litotes, much like ποθεινός) ι 230.

ἐρατίζω (ἔραμαι): only part., *craving;* κρειῶν, Λ 551, P 660.

ἐρατός (ἔραμαι): *lovely*, neut. pl., Γ 64†.

ἐργάζομαι (ϝέργον), ipf. **εἰργάζετο,** ἐργάζοντο: *work, do, perform;* κέλευσε δὲ ϝεργάζεσθαι, bade his bellows *be at work*, Σ 469; ἔργα ἐργάζεσθαι, υ 72; ἐναίσιμα, 'do what is right,' ρ 321; χρῡσὸν εἰργάζετο, *wrought*, γ 435.

ἔργαθεν, ἐέργαθεν (ϝέργω), ipf. or aor.: *sundered, cut off;* τὶ ἀπό τινος, E 147. (Il.)

ἔργον (ϝέργον): *work, deed, act, thing;* μέγα ἔργον, usually in bad sense (f a c i n u s), γ 261, but not always, K 282; collectively, and pl., ἔργον ἐποίχεσθαι, ἐπὶ ἔργα τρέπεσθαι, νῦν ἔπλετο ϝέργον ἅπᾱσιν, 'something for all to do,' M 271; with specifying adj., πολεμήια, θαλάσσια ἔργα, ἔργα γάμοιο, B 614, E 429; esp. of husbandry, οὔτε βοῶν οὔτ' ἀνδρῶν φαίνετο ϝέργα (b o u m q u e h o m i n u m q u e l a b o r e s), κ 98, and simply ἔργα, *fields*, Ἰθάκης εὐδειέλου ἔργ' ἀφίκοντο, ξ 343, B 751; of the results of labor (κρητήρ) ἔργον Ἡφαίστοιο, δ 617; (πέπλοι) ἔργα γυναικῶν, Z 289; also in the sense of 'accomplishments,' θ 245, etc.; ὅπως ἔσται τάδε ϝέργα, these 'matters,' 'affairs.'

ἔργω, ἐέργω, εἴργω, ἔργνῡμι (ϝεργ.), ipf. ἔεργε, ἐέργνῡ, aor. 3 pl. ἔρξαν, pass. perf. ἔεργμαι, 3 pl. ἐέρχαται, plup. 3 pl. ἔρχατο, ἐέρχατο, aor. part. acc. ἐρχθέντα: *shut off* by barrier or enclosure, ἐντὸς ἐέργειν, *shut in*, B 617, etc.; of simply 'enclosing,' διακεκριμέναι δὲ ἕκασται | ἔρχατο, the young animals were severally 'penned,' ι 221, ξ 73; ἐρχθέντ' ἐν ποταμῷ, 'shut up,' Φ 282; also of 'crowding,' 'pressing closely,' Π 395; mostly w. specifying adv. (as ἐντός above), ζυγὸν ἀμφὶς ἐέργει (βόε), 'holds apart,' N 706; so ἐκτός, μ 219; κατά, κ 238; the gen. may follow even the simple verb, ὡς ὅτε μήτηρ | παιδὸς ἐέργῃ μυῖαν, 'keeps a fly away from her child,' Δ 131; ἐεργμέναι, E 89; better reading ἐερμέναι.

ἔρδω (root Ϝεργ.), ipf. iter. ἔρδεσκες, fut. ἔρξω, aor. ἔρξα, perf. ἔοργα, plup. ἐώργειν: *do*, esp. *do sacrifice*, *sacrifice*; ἑκατόμβᾱς, A 315, η 202; ἱρὰ θεοῖς, Λ 207; w. two accusatives, or w. dat., ὅ με πρότερος κάκ' ἔοργεν, Γ 351; πολλὰ κάκ' ἀνθρώποισιν ἐώργει, ξ 289, Ξ 261; ἔρξον ὅπως ἐθέλεις, 'do as thou wilt,' ν 145; defiantly, ἔρδ'· ἀτὰρ οὔ τοι πάντες ἐπαινέομεν, 'go on and *do!*' Δ 29.

ἐρεβεννός (Ἔρεβος): *black* (a t e r), *gloomy*; νύξ, ἀήρ, νέφεα, E 659, 864, X 309. (Il.)

ἐρέβινθος: *chick-pea*, N 589.

Ἔρεβος, gen. Ἐρέβευς, Ἐρέβεσφι: *Erebus*, the realm of nether darkness, Θ 368, Π 327, κ 528, μ 81.—**Ἔρεβόσδε**, *to Erebus*, υ 356.

ἐρεείνω, ipf. ἐρέεινε, mid. ἐρεείνετο: *ask*, abs., Γ 191, η 31; τινά (τι), Z 176, α 220; ἀμφί τινι, ω 262; mid., with μύθῳ, ρ 305.

ἐρεθίζω = ἐρέθω, A 32, Ω 560.

ἐρέθω (cf. ἔρις): *irritate*, *provoke*, A 519, Γ 414; ὀδύναι, μελεδῶναι, 'disquiet,' 'worry,' δ 813, τ 517.

ἐρείδω, pass. perf. ἐρήρεισμαι, 3 pl. ἐρηρέδαται, plup. 3 sing. ἠρήρειστο, 3 pl. ἐρηρέδατο, aor. ἐρείσθη, mid. aor. ἐρείσατο, part. ἐρεισάμενος: I. act., *lean* one thing against another, usually with some notion of weight or violence, *support*, *press* or *force down*; δόρυ πρὸς τεῖχος ἐρείσᾱς, X 112; θρόνον πρὸς κίονα, θ 66; ἀσπὶς ἀσπίδ' ἔρειδε, 'bore hard on,' N 131; ἐρείδοντες βελέεσσιν, 'pressing him hard,' Π 108; pass., ἐπὶ μελίης ἐρεισθείς, 'supported,' 'supporting himself,' 'leaning' upon the lance, X 225; θρόνοι περὶ τοῖχον ἐρηρέδατο, 'set firmly,' η 95; λᾶε ἐρηρέδαται, 'planted,' Ψ 329; ὕπτιος οὖδει ἐρείσθη, 'forced heavily to the ground,' H 145; οὔδεϊ δέ σφιν | χαῖται ἐρηρέδαται, their manes 'rest upon' the ground), Ψ 284; διὰ θώρηκος ἠρήρειστο, 'forced through,' Γ 358.—II. mid., *lean* or *support oneself firmly*; ἐρείσατο χειρὶ γαίης, 'upon the ground with his hand,' E 309; ἐρεισάμενος, 'planting himself firmly,' M 457; of wrestlers, Ψ 735.

ἐρείκω, aor. 2 ἤρικε, pass. pres. part. ἐρεικόμενος: act. (aor. 2), intr., *broke*, P 295; pass., ἐρεικόμενος περὶ δουρί, *transfixed*, N 441. (Il.)

ἔρειο: see ἔρομαι.

ἐρείομεν: see ἐρέω.

ἐρείπω, ipf. ἔρειπε, aor. 2 ἤριπε, ἔριπε, subj. ἐρίπῃσι, part. -ών, -οῦσα, pass. plup. ἐρέριπτο: act. (exc. aor. 2), *throw down*, *overthrow*; τεῖχος, ἐπάλξεις, M 258, O 356, 361; pass., Ξ 15; intr., aor. 2, *fall down*, *tumble*, E 47, 75, χ 296; ἔστη γνὺξ ἐριπών, held himself up, 'sinking on his knee,' E 309.

Ἐρεμβοί: a fabulous people, δ 84†.

ἐρεμνός = ἐρεβεννός. ἐρεμνὴ γαῖα = Ἔρεβος, ω 106.

ἔρεξα: see ῥέζω.

ἐρέομαι: see ἐρέω.

ἐρέπτομαι, only part. ἐρεπτόμενοι: *bite off*, *crop*, usually of animals, B 776, Φ 204, τ 553; of men 'plucking' and eating of the lotus, ι 97.

ἐρέριπτο: see ἐρείπω.

ἐρέσσω: *row*, I 361, ι 490.

ἐρέτης: pl., *rowers*, *oarsmen*, A 142.

Ἐρετμεύς ('Oarman'): a Phaeacian, θ 112.

ἐρετμόν: *oar*. (Od. and A 435.) (The cut, from an antique vase, repre-

38

sents a different way of working the oars from that of the Homeric age; see cut No 120.)

ἐρεύγομαι, aor. 2 ἤρυγε: *belch*, *belch forth*, intr., ι 374; trans., Π 162; of the sea, partly with reference to sound, *bellow*, P 265, E 403, 438; and aor. 2 of animals, Υ 403, 404, 406.

Ἐρευθαλίων: a noble Arcadian, slain by Nestor in a war of the Pylians with the Arcadians, H 136.

ἐρεύθω, aor. inf. ἐρεῦσαι: *redden, dye* with blood, Λ 394, Σ 329. (Il.)

ἐρευνάω: *track, trace, scent out* or *seek*, χ 180.

ἐρέφω, aor. ἔρεψα: *roof over*, Ω 450, ψ 193; specific for generic, 'built,' A 39.

'Ερεχθεύς: *Erechtheus*, a national hero of the Athenians, B 547, η 81.

ἐρέχθω (cf. ἐρείκω): *rack;* metaph., θυμόν, ε 83; pass., of a ship, *be buffeted about*, ἀνέμοισι, Ψ 317.

ἐρέω = ἐρῶ, see εἴρω 1.

ἐρέω, part. ἐρέων, subj. ἐρείομεν, opt. ἐρέοιμεν, mid. ἐρέομαι, ipf. ἐρέοντο, subj. ἐρέωμαι, inf. ἐρέεσθαι: *ask*, τινά, and abs.; ἔκ (adv.) τ' ἐρέοντο, 'made inquiry,' I 671.

ἐρῆμος (Att. ἔρημος): *deserted, desolate*, E 140.

ἐρηρέδαται: see ἐρείδω.

ἐρητύω (ἐρύω), aor. iter. ἐρητύσασκε, opt. ἐρητύσειε, pass. aor. 3 pl. ἐρήτυθεν: *hold back, restrain, control;* φάλαγγας, λᾱόν, Λ 567, Σ 503; pass. B 99, 211; met., θυμόν, A 192, pass., I 635; mid. as dep., O 723, elsewhere subjective and not easily distinguished from the pass., I 462.

ἐρι-: intensive prefix, like ἀρι-.

ἐρι-αύχην, ενος: *with high-arching neck*, epith. of steeds, Λ 159, K 305. (Il.)

ἐρι-βρεμέτης, εω (βρέμω): *loud-thundering*, N 624†.

ἐρι-βῶλαξ, ακος, and **ἐρίβωλος**: *with large clods*, i. e. with rich soil, *fertile*, epith. of lands. (Il. and ν 235, ε 34.)

ἐρί-γδουπος and **ἐρίδουπος** (γδοῦπος): *loud-thundering, resounding;* epith. of Zeus, also of the seashore, the feet of horses, and the portico of a palace, E 672, Υ 50, Λ 152, Ω 323.

ἐριδαίνω (ἔρις), mid. aor. 1 inf. ἐρῑδήσασθαι: *contend, dispute, strive, vie with;* τινί, ἀντία τινός, α 79; ἕνεκα, περί τινος, β 206, σ 403; abs., ποσσίν, 'in running,' Ψ 792; fig., of winds, Π 765.

ἐριδμαίνω (ἔρις): *irritate, stir up*, Π 260†.

ἐρίδουπος: see ἐρίγδουπος.

ἐρίζω, ipf. iter. ἐρίζεσκον, aor. subj. ἐρίσωσιν, opt. ἐρίσειε, -αν, mid. aor. subj. ἐρίσσεται: = ἐριδαίνω, θ 225, E 172.

ἐρί-ηρος (root ἀρ), pl. **ἐρίηρες**: *trusty, faithful;* epith. of ἑταῖροι (sing., Δ 266), Γ 47, ι 100; of ἀοιδός, α 346, θ 62, 471.

ἐρι-θηλής, ές (θάλλω): *blooming, luxuriant*, E 90. (Il.)

ἔρῑθος: pl., *reapers*, Σ 550, 560.

ἐρι-κῡδής, ές (κῦδος): *glorious, famous;* epith. of gods, also of things, δῶρα θεῶν, ἥβη, δαίς, Γ 65, Λ 225, γ 66.

ἐρί-μῡκος (μῡκάομαι): *loud-bellowing*, epith. of cattle, ο 235.

ἐρῑνεός: *wild fig-tree*, μ 103; in the Iliad a particular tree near the sources of the Scamander, Z 433.

ἐρῑνόν = ἐρῑνεός, the reading of Aristarchus in ε 281†.

'Ερῑνύς, ύος, acc. pl., 'Ερῑνῦς, -ύας: the *Erinnys*, pl., the *Erinnyes* (F u r i a e), goddesses who fulfil curses and avenge crimes, I 571. (See cut.)

39

ἔριον, εἴριον: *wool*, δ 124, M 434, pl., Γ 388, etc.

ἐρι-ούνης and **ἐριούνιος** (ὀνίνημι): *helpful*, the *Helper*, epith. of Hermes; subst., Ω 440.

ἔρις, acc. ἔριδα and ἔριν: *strife, contention, rivalry*, A 8, H 210; ἔριδα προφέρουσαι, 'putting forth rivalry,' 'vying with one another' in speed, ζ 92; ἔριδά τινι προφέρεσθαι ἀέθλων, 'challenge one to a contest for prizes,' θ 210; ἐξ ἔριδος, 'in rivalry,' Θ 111, δ 343.—Personified, Ἔρις, *Discord*, Λ 73. Ἔρῐς, Δ 440.

ἐρι-σθενής, έος (σθένος): *most mighty, all-powerful*, epith. of Zeus, T 355, θ 289.

ἔρισμα (ἐρίζω): *matter* or *cause of strife*, Δ 38†.

ἐρι-στάφυλος (σταφυλή): *large-clustered*, οἶνος, ι 111, 358.

ἐρί-τῑμος (τῑμή): *highly-prized, precious*, B 447. (Il.)

ἔριφος: *kid*, pl., ι 220.

Ἐριφῦλη: *Eriphȳle*, the wife of Amphiarāus, λ 326†.

Ἐριχθόνιος: son of Dardanus, and father of Tros, Υ 219, 230.

Ἐριῶπις: wife of Oïleus, N 697.

ἑρκεῖος (ἕρκος): *of the enclosure, of the court* (αὐλή), epith. of Zeus as *household* god, having his altar in the court, χ 335†. (See plate III., at end of volume.)

ἑρκίον (ἕρκος): *wall* or *hedge* of the court-yard; αὐλῆς, I 476, σ 102.

ἕρκος, εος (ϝέργω): *hedge, wall*, then the *enclosure* itself, i. e. the court, Ω 306, pl., θ 57, etc.; *bulwark, defence* against, ἀκόντων, βελέων, Δ 137, E 316; said of persons, ἕρκος πολέμοιο, ἕρκος Ἀχαιῶν, A 284, Γ 229 (cf. πύργος); ἕρκος ὀδόντων (the 'fence of the teeth'), used in connections where we should always say 'lips.'

1. ἕρμα (εἴρω 2, root σερ): only pl., ἕρματα, *pendants, ear-rings*, probably strings of beads. (See cuts, the one on the left an Athenian tetradrachm, that on the right a Sicilian decadrachm.)

2. ἕρμα, ατος: *prop;* pl., of the supports placed under ships when drawn up on shore, A 486; met., of persons, ἕρμα πόληος, 'prop and stay,' 'pillar' of the state, Π 549; of an arrow, μελαινέων ἕρμ' ὀδυνάων, 'bearer of black pains,' by some referred to ἕρμα 1, Δ 117.

Ἕρμαιος: *of Hermes*, λόφος, a hill in the island of Ithaca, a spur of Mt. Neion, π 471†.

Ἑρμῆς, Ἑρμείᾱς, gen. Ἑρμαίᾱο and Ἑρμείω, dat. Ἑρμῇ and Ἑρμέᾳ, acc. Ἑρμῆν and Ἑρμείᾱν, voc. Ἑρμείᾱ: *Hermes* (Mercurius), son of Zeus and Maia, ξ 435; messenger of the gods, guide of mortals (of Priam, Ω 457), and conductor of the shades of the dead; his winged sandals and magic wand, ε 44 ff. Epithets, ἀκάκητα, ἐριούνιος, ἐύσκοπος, σῶκος, χρῡσόρραπις, διάκτορος, Ἀργεϊφόντης.

Ἑρμιόνη: *Hermione*. — (1) the daughter of Menelāus and Helen, δ 14.—(2) name of a city in Argolis, B 560.

ἑρμίς, ῖνος (ἕρμα 2): pl., *bed-posts*, θ 278 and ψ 198.

Ἕρμος: a river in Phrygia and Mysia, Υ 392.

ἔρνος, εος: *shoot, scion, young tree*, P 53; ἔρνεϊ ϝῖσος, of young persons, Σ 56, ξ 175, cf. ζ 163.

ἔρξω: see ἔρδω.

ἔρομαι, assumed pres. for aor. subj. ἐρώμεθα, opt. ἔροιτο, imp. ἐρεῖο, inf. ἐρέσθαι: *ask*, α 135, γ 243.

ἔρος: see ἔρως.

ἑρπετόν (ἕρπω): *creeping thing;* ὅσσ' ἐπὶ γαῖαν ἑρπετὰ γίγνονται, i. e. all the 'creatures that move' upon the earth, δ 418†. Cf. the 2d example under ἕρπω.

ἑρπύζω: parallel form of ἕρπω. ἑρπύζων, 'dragging himself,' the effect of grief or of old age, Ψ 225, ν 220, α 193.

ἕρπω (cf. s e r p o), ipf. εἷρπον, ἕρπε: *creep, crawl; ῥῑνοί*, a prodigy, μ 395; specific for generic, ὅσσα τε γαῖαν ἔπι πνείει τε καὶ ἕρπει, 'breathes and crawls,' i. e. lives and moves, P 448, σ 131; ἥμενος ἢ ἕρπων, an alliterative saying, 'sitting or stirring,' intended to suit any possible attitude or condition, ρ 158.

ἐρράδαται: see ῥαίνω.

ἔρρῑγα: see ῥῑγέω.

ἔρρω (ϝέρρω): *go* with pain or difficulty, δ 367; of the lame Hephaestus, Σ 421; esp. imp. as imprecation, ἔρρε, ἔρρετε, *begone!* Θ 164, κ 72, 75, Ω 239; ἐρρέτω, 'off with him!' ε 139; 'let him go to Perdition!' I 377; similarly the part., ἐνθάδε ϝέρρων, 'coming hither, to my ruin,' Θ 239, I 364.

ἔρση, ἐέρση (ἐϝέρση): pl., *dew-drops*, Λ 53 (in a prodigy); of new-born lambs, ι 222.

ἐρσήεις, εσσα, **ἐερσήεις** (Ϝέρση): *dewy, fresh*, Ξ 348, Ω 419, 757.

ἐρύγμηλος (ἐρυγεῖν): *bellowing*, Σ 580†.

ἐρυγών: see ἐρεύγομαι.

ἐρυθαίνομαι (ἐρυθρός): only ipf., *was reddened*, Κ 484, Φ 21. (Il.)

Ἐρυθῖνοι: a place in Paphlagonia, Β 855.

Ἐρύθραι: *Erythrae*, in Boeotia, Β 499.

ἐρυθρός: *red, ruddy*; οἶνος, νέκταρ, χαλκός, ι 163, Τ 38, Ι 365.

ἐρῡκακέειν, ἐρύκακον: see ἐρύκω.

ἐρῡκανάω, ἐρῡκάνω: parallel forms of ἐρύκω, α 199, κ 429 (v. l. ἐρύκακε).

ἐρύκω, ipf. ἔρῡκε, fut. ἐρύξω, aor. 1 ἔρῡξα, aor. 2 ἠρύκακε, ἐρύκακε: *hold back, restrain, detain*, τινά τινος, and abs.; καί κέν μιν τρεῖς μῆνας ἀπόπροθεν οἶκος ἐρύκοι, 'keep him at a distance,' ρ 408; met., μένος, Θ 178; θῡμόν, Λ 105; ἕτερος δέ με θῡμὸς ἔρῡκεν, ι 302; mid., *tarry*, Ψ 443, ρ 17; like act., Μ 285.

Ἐρύλāος: a Trojan, slain by Patroclus, Π 411†.

ἔρυμα (ἐρύομαι): *a protection*; χροός, Δ 137†.

Ἐρύμανθος: *Erymanthus*, a mountain in Arcadia, ζ 103†.

Ἐρύμᾱς: (1) a Trojan, slain by Idomeneus, Π 435.—(2) a Lycian, slain by Patroclus, Π 415.

ἐρύομαι, εἰρύομαι (Ϝερ.), ipf. ἐρύετο, fut. 3 sing. ἐρύσσεται, 3 pl. εἰρύσσονται, aor. 2 sing. εἰρύσαο, 3 sing. εἰρύσατο, ἐρύσσατο, ἐρύσατο, opt. εἰρύσσαιτο, ἐρύσαιτο, 2 pl. εἰρύσσαισθε, inf. εἰρύσσασθαι, also from **εἴρυμαι, ἔρυμαι,** 3 pl. εἰρύαται, inf. ἔρυσθαι, εἴρυσθαι, ipf. 2 sing. ἔρῡσο, 3 sing. ἔρῡτο, εἴρῡτο, 3 pl. εἴρυντο, εἰρύατο: *shield, protect, preserve*; ὅσσον τ' ἠὲ δύω ἠὲ τρεῖς ἄνδρας ἔρυσθαι, enough leaves to 'cover' two or three men, ε 484; (βουλή) ἥ τίς κεν ἐρύσσεται ἠδὲ σαώσει | Ἀργείους καὶ νῆας, Κ 44; ἔπος εἰρύσσασθαι, 'observe' the command, Α 22; οὐ σύ γε βουλᾶς | εἰρύσαο Κρονίωνος, Φ 230; φρεσὶν εἰρύσσαιτο, 'keep' the secret, π 459; πὰρ νηΐ τε μένειν καὶ νῆα Ϝέρυσθαι, 'watch' the ship, κ 444; so 'watch for,' 'lie in wait for,' π 463, ψ 82; from the sense of protecting comes that of 'warding off,' 'defending against,' ἣ δ' (ἀσπίς) οὐκ ἔγχος ἔρῡτο, Ε 538, Δ 186, Β 859; χόλον, 'keep down,' Ω 584.

ἐρυσ-άρματες (ἐρύω, ἅρμα), pl.: *chariot-drawing*, steeds, Ο 354. (Il.)

ἐρυσί-πτολις (ἐρύω): *city-rescuing, city-protecting*, epith. of Athēna, Ζ 305†.

ἐρύω (Ϝερύω), fut. ἐρύουσι, aor. εἴρυ(σ)σε, ἔρυσε, mid. εἰρυόμεσθα, inf. ἐρύεσθαι (or fut.), fut. 2 sing. ἐρύσσεαι, inf. ἐρύσσεσθαι and ἐρύεσθαι, aor. εἰρυσάμην, -ύ(σ)σατο, perf. 3 pl. εἰρύαται, part. εἰρῡμέναι, plup. εἴρυτο, 3 pl. εἴρυντο and εἰρύατο: *draw, drag*, mid., *draw for oneself* or *to oneself, rescue*, esp. the fallen in battle, νέκυν, νεκρόν; act., of drawing an arrow from the wound, Ε 110; a mantle down over the head, θ 85; drawing the bow, Ο 464; ships into the sea, Α 141; pulling flesh off the bones, ξ 134; battlements from a wall, Μ 258; pass., Δ 248, Ξ 75, ζ 265; mid., of drawing one's sword or dagger, Γ 271; one's ships into the sea, Ξ 79; drawing off meat from the spits (to eat it yourself), Α 466, and other subjective actions; *draw to oneself, rescue*, Ε 456, Ρ 161, Ξ 422, Σ 152.

ἔρχαται, ἔρχατο: see ἔργω.

ἐρχατάω (Ϝέργω): only ipf. pass., ἐρχατόωντο, *were penned up*, ξ 15†.

ἐρχθείς: see ἔργω.

ἔρχομαι, fut. ἐλεύσομαι, aor. ἦλθον and ἤλυθον, perf. εἰλήλουθα, εἰλήλουθμεν, part. εἰληλουθώς and ἐληλυθώς, plup. εἰληλούθει: *come, go*; the word needs no special illustration, as there is nothing peculiar in its numerous applications. The part. ἐλθών is often employed for amplification, οὐ δύναμαι . . μάχεσθαι | ἐλθὼν δυσμενέεσσιν, 'to go and fight,' Π 521.

ἔρῳ: see ἔρως.

ἐρῳδιός: *heron*, Κ 274†.

ἐρωέω (ἐρωή), fut. ἐρωήσει, aor. ἠρώησα: (1) *flow*, Α 303, π 441.—(2) *recede, fall away*; (νέφος) οὔ ποτ' ἐρωεῖ, μ 75; μηδέ τ' ἐρώει, 'rest not,' Β 179; αἳ δ' (the horses) ἠρώησαν ὀπίσσω, 'fell back,' Ψ 433; w. gen., πολέμοιο, χάρμης, Ν 776, Ξ 101; once trans., τῷ κε καὶ ἐσσύμενόν περ ἐρωήσαιτ' ἀπὸ νηῶν, 'drive him away,' Ν 57.

ἐρωή (cf. ῥέω, ῥώομαι): (1) *rush*,

sweep, force in motion, Γ 62; **ὅσον τ' ἐπὶ δουρὸς ἐρωὴ | γίγνεται**, a spear's 'throw,' Ο 358, Ψ 529.—(2) *cessation;* πολέμου, Π 302, Ρ 761.

ἔρως, ἔρος, dat. ἔρῳ, acc. ἔρον: *love;* θεᾶς, γυναικός, 'for' a goddess, a woman, Ξ 315; fig., of things, γόου, Ω 227; often **πόσιος καὶ ἐδητύος**, 'appetite,' see ἵημι.

ἐρωτάω: see εἰρωτάω.

ἐσ-: for words compounded with ἐς, see under εἰσ-.

ἐσᾶλτο: see εἰσάλλομαι.

ἔσβη: see σβέννῡμι.

ἐσδύσεαι: see εἰσδύνω.

ἐσέδρακον: see εἰσδέρκομαι.

ἐσελεύσομαι: see εἰσέρχομαι.

ἐσεμάσσατο: see εἰσμαίομαι.

ἐσέχυντο: see εἰσχέω.

ἐσήλατο: see εἰσάλλομαι.

ἔσθην: see ἕννῡμι.

ἐσθής, ῆτος (Ϝεσθ.): *clothing, clothes,* α 165, ζ 74; 'bedding,' ψ 290. (Od.)

ἐσθίω, ἔσθω, inf. ἐσθέμεναι, ipf. ἤσθιον, ἦσθε, aor. ἔφαγον, inf. φαγέμεν, φαγέειν, for fut. and perf., see ἔδω: *eat,* said of both men and animals; fig., 'consume,' 'devour,' β 75; πῦρ, Ψ 182; pass., οἶκος, δ 318.

ἐσθλός: a poetic synonym of ἀγαθός, q. v.; examples are numerous in every application of the meaning *good,* opp. **κακός, ἄλλοτε μέν τε κακῷ ὅ γε κύρεται, ἄλλοτε δ' ἐσθλῷ**, Ω 530.

ἔσθος, έος (Ϝέσθος): *garment,* Ω 94†.

ἔσθω: see ἐσθίω.

ἐσιδεῖν: see εἰσεῖδον.

ἐσῑέμεναι: see εἰσίημι.

ἔσκον: see εἰμί.

ἐσόψομαι: see εἰσοράω.

ἑσπέριος (Ϝέσπερος): *in the evening,* Φ 560, ι 336; *of the West,* θ 29.

ἕσπερος (Ϝέσπ., cf. v e s p e r): *of* or *at evening;* ἀστήρ, 'evening star,' Χ 318; usually subst., *evening,* α 422 f.; pl., **ἕσπερα,** the *evening* hours, ρ 191.

ἕσπετε, defective imp.: *relate,* only in the formula ἕσπετε νῦν μοι Μοῦσαι, Β 484, Λ 218, Ξ 508, Π 112.

ἑσπόμην: see ἕπω.

ἕσσα, ἕσσαι, ἑσσάμενος: see ἕννῡμι.

ἐσσεῖται, ἐσσί: see εἰμί.

ἐσσεύοντο: see σεύω.

ἔσσο: see εἰμί.

ἕσσο: see ἕννῡμι.

ἔσσυμαι, ἐσσύμενος: see σεύω.

ἐσσυμένως (σεύω): *hastily.*

ἑστάμεν(αι), ἕσταμεν, ἕσταν, ἕστασαν, ἕστασαν, ἑστεώς, -αώς, ἕστηκα, ἑστήκειν: see ἵστημι.

ἕστωρ, ορος: *bolt* at the end of the pole of a chariot, *yoke-pin,* Ω 272†. (See cut; cf. also No. 46.)

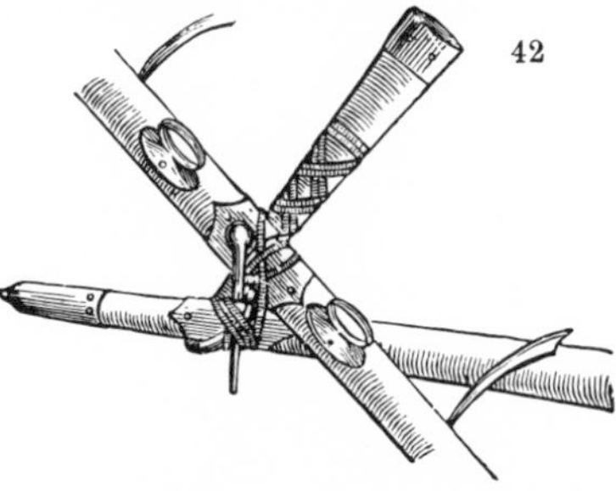

42

ἔσχ' = ἔσκε in β 346, see εἰμί.—For ἔσχε, see ἔχω.

ἐσχάρη, gen. and dat. ἐσχαρόφιν: *hearth, fire-place;* πυρός, of watch-fires, Κ 418. (According to some, 'portable' hearths are to be understood in certain passages, e. g., ε 59, ζ 305, υ 123. Portable fire-basins were doubtless common in the time of Homer as now in the Orient. See cut No. 83; cf. also the Pompeian warming-pan and water-warmer represented in the adjoining cut.)

43

ἐσχατιή (ἔσχατος): *border, edge, remotest part;* λιμένος, νήσου, β 391, ε 238; Φθίης, πολέμοιο, Ι 484, Λ 524; without gen., ἐσχατιῇ, *at the remotest estate,* ξ 104.

ἔσχατος (ἐξ): *furthest, remotest, extremest, last,* only of place; of the Aethiopians, ἔσχατοι ἀνδρῶν, α 23, cf. 24; ἔσχατοι ἄλλων, 'outside of the others,' Κ 434; neut. pl. as adv., **ἔσχατα,** *at the outside, at the ends,* Θ 225, Λ 8.

ἐσχατόων, -όωσα, defective part.: *at the border, at the end;* δηίων ἐσχατόων, 'a straggler,' K 206; of 'frontier' towns, B 508, 616.

ἔσχεθον, ἔσχον, ἔσχετο: see ἔχω.

ἔσω: see εἴσω.

ἑταίρη, ἑτάρη: *companion, attendant,* Δ 441; usually fig., I 2, ρ 271.

ἑταιρίζω, ἑταρίζω; aor. inf. ἑταιρίσσαι, mid. aor. opt. ἑταρίσσαιτο: act., *be companion to, attend,* Ω 335; mid., causative, *take as one's companion,* N 456. (Il.)

ἑταῖρος, ἕταρος: *companion, comrade;* fig., of a wind, ἐσθλὸς ἑταῖρος, λ 7, cf. ἑταίρη; as adj., w. ἀνήρ, λᾱοί, P 466, N 710.

ἐτεθήπεα: see θαπ-.

Ἐτεοκλήειος: *of Eteocles* (the son of Oedipus, king of Thebes); βίη Ἐτεοκληείη, periphrasis for the name of the man (see βίη), Δ 386.

Ἐτεόκρητες (ἐτεός, Κρής): *true* (primitive) *Cretans,* τ 176†.

ἐτεός: *true, real;* νεικεῖν πόλλ' ἐτεά τε καὶ οὐχί, 'reproaches true and untrue,' Υ 255; elsewhere only **ἐτεόν,** *the truth* or *truly;* εἰ δή ῥ' ἐτεόν γε καὶ ἀτρεκέως ἀγορεύεις, O 53, and freq. εἰ ἐτεόν γε (sc. ἐστί), Ξ 125, γ 122.

ἑτερ-αλκής, ές (ἕτερος, ἀλκή): νίκη, *lending strength to the other party,* i. e. to the party previously inferior, H 26, Θ 171, Π 362; in more general sense, *decisive,* χ 236; δῆμος, *able to change the fortune of the fight,* O 738.

ἑτερ-ήμερος (ἡμέρη): *on alternate days,* pl., Λ 303†.

ἕτερος: *the other* or *one* of two (a l t e r); pl., ἕτεροι, *one* or *the other party,* Υ 210; ἕτερα ἅρματα, chariot 'of the other party,' Δ 306; freq. ἕτερος μὲν . . ἕτερος δέ, also w. article, or replaced in one member by ἄλλος, Ξ 272, Φ 164, I 913; ἑτέρῃ χειρί, or simply ἑτέρῃ or ἑτέρηφι, Π 734; with reference to more than two, like ἄλλος, Φ 437, η 124, ρ 266.

ἐτέρσετο: see τερσαίνω.

ἑτέρωθεν: *from* or *on the other side.*

ἑτέρωθι: *on the other side, elsewhere.*

ἑτέρως: *otherwise,* α 234†.

ἑτέρωσε: *in the other direction,* Δ 492, τ 470; *to one side,* Θ 306, 308; *in another direction, away,* Ψ 231, π 179.

ἐτέταλτο: plup. pass. from τέλλω. See ἐπιτέλλω.

ἐτετεύχατο: see τεύχω.

ἔτετμον, defective aor., 3 sing. ἔτετμε, τέτμε, subj. 2 sing. τέτμῃς: *find, reach,* Z 374, ο 15; fig. ὅν γῆρας ἔτετμεν, α 218.

ἐτέτυκτο: see τεύχω.

Ἐτεωνεύς: son of Boethous, a companion-at-arms of Menelāus, δ 22.

Ἐτεωνός: a town in Boeotia, B 497†.

ἔτης (Ϝέτης), pl. **ἔται**: *friends, retainers,* distinguished from near relatives, δ 3, Z 239, I 464.

ἐτήτυμος (cf. ἔτυμος, ἐτεός): *true, truthful, real;* ἄγγελος, νόστος, μῦθος, X 438, γ 241, ψ 62; freq. neut. as adv., **ἐτήτυμον,** *actually, really,* A 558, Σ 128.

ἔτι: *still, yet.*—I. temporal, πάλαι ἠδ' ἔτι καὶ νῦν, *still* to this day, I 105; often w. neg., οὐδ' ἄρ' ἔτι δϜὴν | ἦν, he lived 'not much longer,' 'not long thereafter,' Z 139; and idiomatically, οὐ γὰρ ἔτι Τροίην αἱρήσομεν, we shall not take Troy 'any more,' i. e. we can no longer *hope* to take the city, B 141.—II. denoting addition, ἄλλος, ἕτερος ἔτι, *yet* another, H 364, ξ 325; ἔτι μᾶλλον, μᾶλλον ἔτι, α 322.

ἔτλην: see τλῆναι.

ἑτοιμάζω, aor. imp. ἑτοιμασάτω, -άσατε, mid. aor. ἑτοιμάσαντο: *make ready, prepare,* A 118, ν 184.

ἑτοῖμος: *ready, at hand;* μῆτις, 'feasible,' I 425; 'actual,' 'actually,' Ξ 53, θ 384; πότμος, 'certain,' Σ 96.

ἔτορον: see τορέω.

ἔτος, εος (Ϝέτος, cf. v e t u s): *year.* See ἐνιαυτός.

ἔτραπον: see τρέπω.

ἐτράφην, ἔτραφον: see τρέφω.

ἔτυμος, pl. ἔτυμα, and **ἔτυμον** = ἐτήτυμος, ἐτήτυμον, τ 203, 567, ψ 26.

ἐτώσιος (Ϝετ.): *fruitless, vain;* ἔγχος, βέλεα, δῶρα, ἄχθος, Γ 368, Ω 283, Σ 104.

εὖ, ἐύ (neut. of ἐύς): *well,* answering in meaning as adv. to the adjectives ἀγαθός and καλός; hence 'rightly,' 'finely,' 'carefully,' etc., esp. 'happily,' 'prosperously,' εὖ ζώειν, εὖ οἴκαδ' ἱκέσθαι, ρ 423, A 19, γ 188, 190; εὖ ἔρδειν τινά, i. e. ἀγαθὰ ἔρδειν, E 650; used to strengthen other words, εὖ μάλα, εὖ πάντες, 'quite all,' κ 452, σ 260.

εὖ: see οὖ.

εὐ-αγγέλιον: *reward for good tidings*, ξ 152, 166.

εὔαδε: see ἁνδάνω.

Εὐαιμονίδης: *son of Euaemon*, Eurypylus, E 76, H 167. (Il.)

Εὐαίμων: son of Ormenus, and father of Eurypylus, B 736, E 79.

εὐ-ανθής, ές (ἄνθος): *luxuriant, abundant*, λ 320†.

Εὐάνθης: the father of Maron, ι 197†.

Εὔβοια: *Euboea*, the island separated from Boeotia by the Eurīpus, named by Homer as the home of the Abantes, B 536, γ 174, η 321.

εὔ-βοτος (βόσκω): *with fine cattle*, ο 406†.

εὖγμα, ατος (εὔχομαι): *boast*, pl., χ 249†.

εὔ-γναμπτος, ἐύγ. (γνάμπτω): *gracefully bent*, σ 294†.

εὐ-δείελος: (if from δείλη) *westering, sunny*; (if from δέελος, δῆλος) *clearly* or *far seen*; epith. of islands, esp. Ithaca, β 167. (Od.)

εὐ-δικίη (δίκη): *fair justice*, pl., τ 111†.

εὔ-δμητος, ἐύδ. (δέμω): *well-built*.

εὕδω, ipf. εὗδον, iter. εὕδεσκε: *sleep, lie down to sleep*, β 397; fig., of death, Ξ 482; of the wind, E 524.

Εὔδωρος: son of Hermes and Polymēle, a leader of the Myrmidons, Π 186, 179.

εὐ-ειδής, ές (Ϝεῖδος): *beautiful*, Γ 48†.

εὐ-εργεσίη (Ϝέργον): *well-doing, kindness*, χ 235, 374†.

εὐ-εργής, ές: *well-made, well-wrought*; pl., εὐεργέα, *good deeds, benefactions*, χ 319.

εὐ-εργός: *doing right, good*, λ 434. (Od.)

εὐ-ερκής, ές (ἕρκος): *well-fenced, well-enclosed*; αὐλή, I 472; θύραι, 'well hung,' ρ 267 (v. l. εὐεργέες).

εὔ-ζυγος, ἐύζ. (ζυγόν): *well-yoked*, of a ship, i. e. 'well-beamed,' or according to others, 'well-benched,' ν 116, ρ 288.

ἐύ-ζωνος, οιο, ους (ζώνη): *beautifully girdled*, the girdle giving a graceful appearance to the garment, Z 467, A 429. (Il.) (See cut No. 44.)

εὐ-ηγενής, ές (= εὐγενής): *well* or *nobly born*, Λ 427. (Il.)

εὐ-ηγεσίη (ἡγέομαι): *good government*, τ 114† (v. l. εὐεργεσίης).

εὐ-ήκης, ες (ἀκή): *well-pointed, sharp*, X 319†.

Εὐηνίνη: *daughter of Evēnus*, Marpessa, I 557†.

Εὐηνορίδης: *son of Evēnor*, Leiocritus, β 242. (Od.)

Εὐηνός: (1) son of Selepius, B 693. —(2) father of Marpessa,

εὐ-ήνωρ, ορος (ἀνήρ): *manly* or 'inspiring manliness,' χαλκός, οἶνος, ν 19, δ 622. (Od.)

εὐ-ήρης, ες (root ἀρ): *well-fitted, handy*, of oars, λ 121. (Od.)

ἐύ-θριξ, τριχος: *well-maned*, 'with flowing mane,' Ψ 13.

ἐύ-θρονος: *well-throned*, 'with beautiful throne,' Ἠώς, Θ 565. (Od.)

εὐθύς: see ἰθύς.

εὔ-θυμος: *well-disposed, kindly*, ξ 63†.

Εὔιππος: a Lycian, slain by Patroclus, Π 417†.

εὐ-καμπής, ές (κάμπτω): *well-bent, curved*, sickle, key, φ 6. (Od.)

εὐ-κέατος (κεάζω): *easily cleft* or *split, fissile*, ε 60†.

εὔκηλος (Ϝέκηλος, ἐϜκ.) = **ἕκηλος**, A 554, γ 263.

εὐ-κλεής, ές, εὐκλειής (κλέος), acc. pl. εὐκλεῖας: *glorious, renowned*, K 281, φ 331.—Adv., **εὐκλεῶς, εὐκλειῶς**, *gloriously*, X 110.

ἐυ-κλείη: *good reputation, fame*, Θ 285, ξ 402.

ἐυ-κλήῖς, ῖδος (κληίω): *close-shutting*, Ω 318†.

ἐυ-κνήμῖς, ῖδος: *well-greaved*, epith. of Ἀχαιοί, and in the Od. also of ἑταῖροι. (See cut under ἀμφίβροτος.)

εὐ-κόσμως: *well arranged* or *disposed*, φ 123†.

ἐυ-κτίμενος, 'ύκτιτος (κτίζω): *well-built, well-appointed, well-tilled*, B 501, Φ 77, ι 130, ω 336.

εὐκτός (εὔχομαι): *prayed-for, wished-for*; neut. pl., 'occasion for triumph,' Ξ 98†.

εὔ-κυκλος: *well-rounded, well-rimmed* (Il.), *well-wheeled*, ζ 58.

εὐ-λείμων: *with fair meadows, abounding in meadows*, δ 607†.

εὐλή (cf. Ϝείλω): *worm, maggot*. (Il.)

εὔληρα, pl.: *reins*, Ψ 481.

Εὔμαιος: *Eumaeus*, the faithful swine-herd of Odysseus, ξ 17–190, χ 267; son of Ctesius, king of the island of Syria; the story of his life, ο 400 ff.

εὐ-μενέτης = **εὐμενής**, ζ 185 (opp. *δυσμενής*, 184).

Εὐμήδης: father of Dolon, a Trojan herald, Κ 314, 412.

εὔ-μηλος: *abounding in sheep*, ο 406†.

Εὔμηλος: *Eumēlus*, son of Admētus and Alcestis, Ψ 288. (Il.)

ἐυ-μμελίης, gen. *ίω* (*μελίη*): *good at the ashen lance, good at the spear*, epith. of Priam and others. (Il. and γ 400.)

εὐνάζω and **εὐνάω** (*εὐνή*), fut. *εὐνάσω*, aor. *εὔνησε*, mid. pres. inf. *εὐνάζεσθαι*, pass. aor. inf. *εὐνηθῆναι*: *put in a place to lie, place in ambush*, δ 408, 440; mid. and pass., *lie down* to sleep or rest, Γ 441, υ 1; fig., of winds, ε 384.

εὐναιετάων, -άωσα: see *ναιετάω*.

εὐναιόμενος: see *ναίω*.

εὐνή, gen. *εὐνῆφι*: (1) *place to lie, bed, couch;* said of an army, Κ 408; of the 'lair' of wild animals, Λ 115; esp. typical of love and marriage, *φιλότητι καὶ εὐνῇ, οὐκ ἀποφώλιοι εὐναὶ | ἀθανάτων*, λ 249. —(2) pl., **εὐναί**, *mooring-stones*, which served as *anchors*, having cables (*πρυμνήσια*) attached to them, and being cast into the water or upon the shore, Α 436, 476.

εὐνῆθεν: *from his couch*, υ 124†.

Εὔνηος: son of Jason, and king of Lemnos, Η 468. (Il.)

εὔ-ννητος (*νέω*): *well-woven*, Σ 596.

εὐνῆφι(ν): see *εὐνή*.

εὖνις, *ιος*: *reft, bereft*, Χ 44, ι 524.

εὐ-νομίη (*νόμος*): *good order, obedience to laws*, ρ 487†.

ἐύ-ξεστος and **ἐύξοος** (*ξέω*), gen. *εὐξου*: *well-scraped, well-planed, polished;* in act. sense, *σκέπαρνον ἐύξοον*, ε 237.

εὔ-ορμος: *affording good moorage* or *anchorage*, Φ 23. (Od.)

εὐ-πατέρεια: daughter *of a noble father*, epith. of Helen and Tyro, Ζ 292, λ 235.

Εὐπείθης: father of the suitor Antinous, slain by Laertes, ω 523.

εὔ-πεπλος: *with beautiful mantle, beautifully robed*, Ε 424, ζ 49.

εὐ-πηγής and **ἐύπηκτος** (*πήγνῡμι*): *well* or *firmly joined, well built*, φ 334†, Β 661, ψ 41.

ἐύ-πλειος: *well filled*, ρ 467†.

ἐυ-πλεκής and **ἐύ-πλεκτος** (*πλέκω*): *well plaited.*

εὐ-πλοίη (*πλέω*): *prosperous voyage*, Ι 362†.

ἐυ-πλοκαμῖς, *ῖδος*, and **ἐυ-πλόκαμος** (*πλόκαμος*): *with beautiful tresses, fair-tressed*, epithet of goddesses and of women, ε 125, β 119. (See cut.)

ἐυ-πλυνής, *ές* (*πλύνω*): *well-washed.* (Od.)

εὐ-ποίητος: *well-made, well-wrought.*

εὔ-πρηστος (*πρήθω*): *well* or *strongly burning* or *blowing*, Σ 471†.

εὔ-πρυμνος (*πρυμνή*): of ships, *with well-built* or *decorated sterns*, Δ 248†.

εὔ-πυργος: *well towered* or *walled*, Η 71†.

εὔ-πωλος (*πῶλος*): *abounding in horses, with fine horses*, epith. of Ilium, Ε 551, β 18.

εὐράξ (*εὖρος*): *on one side, sidewise*, Λ 251, Ο 541.

εὑρίσκω, aor. 2 *εὗρον*, mid. pres. imp. *εὕρεο*, aor. ind. *εὕρετο*: *find, find out, discover*, mid., for oneself; of 'thinking up' a name for a child, τ 403; 'bringing (trouble) on oneself,' φ 304.

Εὖρος: *Eurus*, the south-east wind, stormy, Β 145, Π 765; but warm enough to melt the snow, τ 206.

εὖρος, εος (εὐρύς): *breadth, width*, λ 312†.

ἐυ-ρραφής, ές (ῥάπτω): *well-sewed*, β 354, 380.

ἐυ-ρρεής, gen. ἐυρρεῖος, **ἐυ-ρρείτης**, ᾱο: *fair-flowing*, epith. of rivers.

ἐύ-ρροος = ἐυρρεής, ἐυρρείτης.

εὐρυ-άγυια: *wide-streeted*, epith. of cities.

Εὐρυάδης: a suitor of Penelope, slain by Telemachus, χ 267†.

Εὐρύαλος: *Euryalus*.—(1) an Argive, son of Mecisteus, Ζ 20, Ψ 677.—(2) a Phaeacian, θ 115, 396.

Εὐρυβάτης: *Eurybates*.—(1) a herald of Agamemnon, Α 320.—(2) a herald of Odysseus, Β 184, τ 247.

Εὐρυδάμᾱς: *Eurydamas*.—(1) a Trojan, the father of Abas and Polyīdus, Ε 149.—(2) a suitor of Penelope, slain by Odysseus, χ 283.

Εὐρυδίκη: *Eurydice*, the wife of Nestor, γ 452.

Εὐρύκλεια: *Euryclēa*, the nurse of Odysseus, and faithful housekeeper in his palace, τ 357, β 361.

εὐρυ-κρείων: *wide-ruling*, epith. of Poseidon and of Agamemnon, Λ 751, Α 102.

Εὐρύλοχος: a cousin and companion of Odysseus, κ 232, λ 23, μ 195. 339. (Od.)

Εὐρύμαχος: son of Polybus, a suitor of Penelope, slain by Odysseus, α 399, χ 82. (Od.)

Εὐρυμέδουσα: an attendant of queen Arēte, η 8†.

Εὐρυμέδων: *Eurymedon*.—(1) son of Ptolemaeus, and charioteer of Agamemnon, Δ 228.—(2) a servant of Nestor, Θ 114, Λ 620.—(3) king of the Giants, father of Periboea, η 58.

εὐρυ-μέτωπος: *broad-browed*.

Εὐρυμίδης: *son of Eurymus*, Telemus, a seer among the Cyclōpes, ι 509†.

Εὐρυνόμη: *Eurynome*.—(1) an Oceanid, Σ 398†.—(2) stewardess of Penelope, ρ 495, τ 97.

Εὐρύνομος: an Ithacan, the son of Aegyptius, β 22. (Od.)

εὐρύνω (εὐρύς), aor. 1 **εὔρῡνα**: *widen, enlarge*, θ 260†.

εὐρυ-όδεια (ὁδός): *wide-wayed*, i. e. 'wide-wandered,' epith. of the earth as field of human travel, always χθονὸς εὐρυοδείης.

εὐρύ-οπα, nom., acc., and voc.: (if from ὄψ) *wide (far) thundering*; (if from ὤψ) *wide (far) seeing*, Ε 265, Π 241, Α 498.

εὐρύ-πορος (πόρος): *wide-traversed*, epith. of the sea (cf. εὐρυόδεια), always θαλάσσης εὐρυπόροιο. (Od.)

εὐρυ-πυλής, ες (πύλη): *wide-gated*, εὐρυπυλὲς Ἄιδος δῶ.

Εὐρύπυλος: *Eurypylus*.—(1) son of Euaemon, from Thessaly, Β 736, Ε 76, Ζ 36, Λ 580, 809.—(2) son of Poseidon and Astypalaea, from the island of Cos, Β 677.—(3) son of Telephus, slain by Neoptolemus, λ 520.

εὐρυ-ρέεθρος and **εὐρυρέων**; *broad-flowing*, Φ 141†, Β 849. (Il.)

εὐρύς, εῖα, ύ, gen. -έος, -είης, acc. εὐρέα and εὐρύν: *broad, wide*; comp., **εὐρύτερος**, Γ 194, Ψ 427; adv., εὐρὺ ῥέειν, Ε 545.

εὐρυ-σθενής, ές (σθένος): *widely powerful, with far-reaching might*, epith. of Poseidon, ν 140. (Il.)

Εὐρυσθεύς: *Eurystheus*, son of Sthenelus, and king of Mycēnae; by a trick of Hera upon Zeus, Eurystheus was born to power over Heracles, and imposed upon him the celebrated labors, Τ 103 ff., 123 ff., θ 363, λ 620.

Εὐρυτίδης: son of *Eurytus*, Iphitus, guest-friend of Odysseus, φ 14, 37. (Od.)

Εὐρυτίων: a Centaur, φ 295†.

Εὔρυτος (εὖ, ἐρύω, 'Drawer of the Bow'): *Eurytus*.—(1) son of Actor (or of Poseidon) and Molione, brother of Cteatus (see **Ἀκτορίων**), with his brother an ally of Augēas against Nestor and the Pylians, Β 621, Λ 709 ff.—(2) son of Melaneus and Stratonice, king of Oechalia, father of Iole and Iphitus. A celebrated archer, he challenged Apollo to a contest, and was slain by the god, θ 204 ff. Odysseus received the bow of Eurytus from his son Iphitus, φ 32 ff.

εὐρυ-φυής, ές (φύω): *wide-growing*, i. e. with its rows of kernels far apart, epith. of barley, δ 604†.

εὐρύ-χορος: (if from χορός) *with broad dancing-places* or *lawns*; (if from χῶρος) *spacious;* epith. of lands and cities.

εὐρώεις, εσσα (εὐρώς): *mouldy, dank,* epith. of Hades.

ἐύς, ἐύ, and **ἠύς, ἠύ,** gen. ἐῆος, acc. ἐύν, ἠύν, pl. gen. ἐάων: synonym of ἀγαθός and καλός, the neut. forms of the sing. mostly adverbial, see εὖ. ἐὺς παῖς, υἱός, θεράπων, Βίᾶς, παιδὸς ἐῆος, esp. in Il.; also μένος ἠύ, 'noble ardor,' β 271, etc.; ἠύς τε μέγας τε, Β 653.—gen. pl. ἐάων, *of good things, blessings,* Ω 528; θεοὶ δωτῆρες ἐάων, θ 325.

εὖσα: see εὔω.

ἐύ-σκαρθμος (σκαίρω): *lightly bounding,* Ν 31†.

ἐύ-σκοπος: (1) *well-aiming,* epith. of Artemis, the huntress, λ 198.—(2) *sharp-seeing,* of Hermes, Ω 24, etc.

ἐύ-σσελμος (σέλμα): *with good deck, well-decked,* of ships, Β 170, β 390. (The Homeric ships were decked only at bow and stern.)

Ἐύσσωρος: a Thracian, the father of Acamas, Ζ 8†.

εὐ-σταθής (ἵστημι): *well-based, firm-standing;* μέγαρον, θάλαμος, Σ 374, ψ 178.

ἐυ-στέφανος (στεφάνη): *with beautiful head-band,* epith. of goddesses and women, Φ 511, σ 193, β 120; fig., of Thebes, *with noble wall,* Τ 99.

ἐύ-στρεπτος, ἐυστρεφής, ἐύστροφος (στρέφω): *well-twisted.*

εὖτε: (1) *when, at the time when,* foll. by the same constructions as other relative words (see ἄν, κέν). εὖτε is always employed 'asyndetically,' i. e. without a connecting particle, and is freq. followed by a demonstrative temporal word in the apodosis, ἔνθα, τῆμος δή, καὶ τότε δή, ἔπειτα, etc.; εὖτ' ἀστὴρ ὑπερέσχε φαάντατος . . τῆμος δὴ νήσῳ προσεπίλνατο ποντοπόρος νηῦς, ν 93; the clause introduced by εὖτε may, however, follow its apodosis, τλῆ δ' Ἀίδης . . ὠκὺν ὀιστόν . . εὖτέ μιν ωὑτὸς ἀνὴρ . . ὀδύνῃσιν ἔδωκεν, Ε 396.—(2) *as, even as,* introducing a simile, Γ 10, Τ 386 (where some write ηὖτε, for ἠύτε).

εὐ-τείχεος, metapl. acc. sing. εὐτείχεα: *well-walled, well-fortified,* Α 129, Π 57.

ἐύ-τμητος (τέμνω): *well-cut,* of straps, Ψ 684. (Il.)

ἐυ-τρεφής, ές (τρέφω): *well-nourished, fat,* ι 425. (Od.)

Εὔτρησις: a village in Boeotia, Β 502.

ἐύ-τρητος (τιτράω): *well pierced,* Ξ 182†.

ἐύτριχας: see εὔθριξ.

ἐύ-τροχος (τροχός): *well-wheeled,* Θ 438.

εὔ-τυκτος (τεύχω): *well-wrought,* Γ 336, δ 123.

εὐ-φημέω (εὔφημος): *observe a holy silence,* i. e. avoid ill-omened words by not speaking at all, Ι 171†.

Εὔφημος: son of Troezēnus, and leader of the Ciconians, Β 846†.

Εὐφήτης: ruler over Ephyra in Elis, Ο 532†.

Εὔφορβος: *Euphorbus,* a Trojan, the son of Panthous; after wounding Patroclus, he is slain by Menelāus, Π 806, Ρ 59.

ἐυ-φραδέως (φράζομαι): *thoughtfully, wisely,* τ 352†.

εὐ-φραίνω (φρήν), fut. εὐφρανέω, aor. εὔφρηνα: *cheer, gladden,* mid., *take one's pleasure,* β 311.

ἐυ-φρονέων: *well meaning and well judging, with good and wise intent,* always ἐυφρονέων ἀγορήσατο καὶ μετέειπεν.

ἐυ-φροσύνη: *mirth, gladness.*

ἐύ-φρων: *glad, cheerful;* in act. sense, οἶνος, Γ 246.

ἐυ-φυής, ές (φύω): *well-grown, shapely,* Φ 243, Δ 147. (Il.)

εὔ-χαλκος: *of fine bronze, well mounted with bronze,* Υ 322.

εὐχετάομαι (εὔχομαι), opt. εὐχετοῴμην: *pray* or *offer obeisance,* τινί, *boast;* εὐχετόωντο θεῶν Διὶ Νέστορί τ' ἀνδρῶν, Λ 761, θ 467; ὑπέρβιον, αὔτως εὐχετάασθαι, Ρ 19, Υ 348; τίνες ἔμμεναι εὐχετόωνται, α 172 (see εὔχομαι).

εὐχή: *prayer, vow,* pl., κ 526†.

Εὐχήνωρ: son of Polyīdus, Ν 663.

εὔχομαι, imp. εὔχεο and εὔχου, ipf. εὐχόμην, aor. εὐξάμην: (1) *pray, vow;* then *solemnly declare* and *wish;* εὔχετο πάντ' ἀποδοῦναι, 'asseverated,' Σ 499; εὐξάμενός τι ἔπος ἐρέω . . εἴθ' ὣς ἡβώοιμι, ξ 463, 468, Ξ 484; usually, however, of praying to the gods.—(2) *avow, avouch oneself, boast;* ἡμεῖς τοι πατέρων μέγ' ἀμείνονες εὐχόμεθ' εἶναι,

Δ 405; usually of just pride, but not always, N 447.

εὖχος (εὔχομαι, *boast*): *glory*, esp. of war and victory, freq. διδόναι εὖχός τινι, εὖχος ἀρέσθαι, E 285, ι 317, H 203.

εὐ-χροής, ές (χρώς): *bright-colored*, ξ 24†.

εὐχωλή (εὔχομαι): (1) *prayer, vow*, ν 357, A 65.—(2) *boast, exultation, shout of triumph*, Δ 450, Θ 229, B 160; 'my pride,' X 433.

εὕω, aor. εὗσα: *singe*, bristles of swine, I 468, β 300; the eyelids of Polyphēmus, ι 379.

εὐ-ώδης, ες (ὄζω, ὄδωδα): *sweet-smelling, fragrant*.

εὐ-ῶπις, ιδος (ὤψ): *fair-faced*. (Od.)

ἔφαγον: see φαγεῖν.

ἐφ-άλλομαι, aor. 2 ἐπᾶλτο, part. ἐπάλμενος and ἐπιάλμενος: *leap* or *spring upon* or *at*; ἵππων, H 15; and freq. in hostile sense, τινί, N 643; in friendly sense, abs., ω 320.

ἔφ-αλος (ἅλς): situated *on the sea*, epith. of maritime cities, B 538, 584. (Il.)

ἔφαν: see φημί.

ἐφ-ανδάνω, ἐπιανδάνω (ϝανδάνω). *be pleasing* or *acceptable to, please*.

ἐφάνη: see φαίνω.

ἐφ-άπτω, pass. perf. ἐφῆπται, plup. ἐφῆπτο, mid. aor. subj ἐφάψεαι: act., *attach to*, pass. (metaph.), *be hung over, hang over, impend; τινί*, B 15, Z 241; mid., *touch*, ε 348.

ἐφ-αρμόζω, aor. opt. ἐφαρμόσσειε: intr., *fit, suit*, T 385†.

ἐφ-έζομαι, ipf. ἐφέζετο: *sit upon* or *by*, Φ 506, ρ 334.

ἐφέηκα, ἐφείην: see ἐφίημι.

ἐφ-εῖσα, defective aor., inf. ἐφέσσαι, mid. aor. imp. ἔφεσσαι, part. ἐφεσσάμενος, fut. inf. ἐφέσσεσθαι: *cause to sit upon* or *by, set*, mid., for oneself; of putting on board ship, ν 274; mid., w. gen. (νηός), ο 277; τινί τι, I 455, π 443.

ἐφ-έλκω, *drag to* or *after*, pass., Ψ 696; mid. (met.), *draw to oneself, attract*, π 294.

ἐφ-έννῡμι: see ἐπιέννῡμι.

ἐφ-έπω, ipf. ἔφεπε, iter. ἐφέπεσκον, fut. ἐφέψεις, aor. ἐπέσπον, opt. ἐπίσποι, inf. ἐπισπεῖν, mid. aor. inf. ἐπισπέσθαι, part. -όμενος: I. act., *follow up, pursue*, and seemingly causative, Πατρόκλῳ ἔφεπε κρατερώνυχας ἵππους, 'urge on against,' Π 724; ὡς τοὺς Ἀτρείδης ἔφεπε, 'followed up,' 'pursued,' Λ 177; (κυνηγέται) κορυφὰς ὀρέων ἐφέποντες, 'pushing to,' ι 121; ὑσμίνης στόμα, 'move over,' Υ 359, Λ 496; freq. met., θάνατον καὶ πότμον ἐπισπεῖν, 'meet' one's fate; so οἶτον, ὀλέθριον or αἴσιμον ἦμαρ, γ 134, T 294, Φ 100.—II. mid., *follow close; τινί*, N 495; ποσίν, 'in running,' Ξ 521; met., ἐπισπόμενοι μένει σφῷ, θεοῦ ὀμφῇ, ξ 262, γ 215.

ἐφέσσαι, ἔφεσσαι, ἐφέσσεσθαι, ἐφεσσάμενος: see ἐφεῖσα.

ἐφ-έστιος (ἑστίᾱ): *at* or *to the hearth, at* one's own *hearth* or *home*, γ 234, ψ 55; ἐφέστιοι ὅσσοι ἔᾱσιν, i. e. all the *native* Trojans, B 125; (ἐμέ) ἐφέστιον ἤγαγε δαίμων, 'to her hearth,' η 248.

ἐφ-ετμή (ἐφίημι): *command, behest*, mostly in pl. (Il. and δ 353).

ἐφ-ευρίσκω, aor. ἐφεύρομεν, opt. ἐφεύροι: *come upon and find, surprise*, freq. w. part.

ἐφ-εψιάομαι: *mock, make sport of, τινί*. (Od.)

ἔφ-ημαι: *sit upon* or *at*. (Od.)

ἐφ-ημέριος: *the day through*, δ 223; ἐφημέρια φρονεῖν, thoughts 'but for the day,' i. e. no thought for the morrow, φ 85

ἐφ-ημοσύνη (ἐφίημι) = ἐφετμη.

ἔφησθα: see φημί.

ἔφθην: see φθάνω.

ἐφθίαθ': see φθίω.

Ἐφιάλτης: *Ephialtes*, the giant, son of Alōeus, and brother of Otus, E 385, λ 308.

ἐφ-ιζάνω: *sit upon* or *at*; δείπνῳ, K 578; met., ὕπνος ἐπὶ βλεφάροισιν, K 26.

ἐφ-ίζω, ipf. iter. ἐφίζεσκε: *sit upon*. (Od.)

ἐφ-ίημι, part. ἐφῑείς, ipf. ἐφῑει, fut. ἐφήσεις, aor. ἐφῆκα, ἐφέηκα, subj. ἐφείω, opt. ἐφείην, imp. ἔφες, mid. pres. part. ἐφῑέμενος: *let go at* or *upon*.—I. act., of 'sending' one person to another, Ω 117; 'letting fly' missiles at anything, βέλεά τινι, A 51, Φ 170; 'laying (violent hands) upon' one, A 567, α 254; met., of 'inciting' a person to some action, w. inf., χαλεπῆναι, ἀεῖσαι, Σ

108, ξ 464; also of 'bringing' or 'imposing' troubles, etc., upon one, πότμον, ἄεθλον, κήδεά τινι, Δ 396, τ 576, Α 445.—II. mid., *enjoin upon, command*; τινί (τι), Ψ 82, Ω 300, ν 7.

ἐφ-ικνέομαι: only aor. ἐφίκοντο (ἀλλήλων), *fell upon* each other, Ν 613†.

ἐφίληθεν: see φιλέω.

ἐφ-ίστημι, perf. 3 pl. ἐφέστᾶσι, inf. ἐφεστάμεν(αι), part. gen. ἐφεσταότος, plup. ἐφεστήκει, 3 pl. ἐφέστασαν, aor. 2 ἐπέστη, mid. ipf. ἐφίστατο: perf. and mid., *stand upon, by*, or *at*, aor. 2, *come up to, draw near*, w. dat., or a prep. and its case, Ζ 373, Ψ 201, Κ 124, Λ 644; in hostile sense, 'set upon,' Ο 703; fig., Κῆρες ἐφεστᾶσιν θανάτοιο, Μ 326.

ἐφ-όλκαιον (ἕλκω): *rudder*, ξ 350†.

ἐφ-ομαρτέω: *follow close upon*. (Il.)

ἐφ-οπλίζω, fut. -οπλίσσουσι, aor. ἐφόπλι(σ)σα, mid. aor. subj. ἐφοπλισόμεσθα: *equip, get ready*, mid., for oneself, νῆα, ἄμαξαν, δαῖτα, δόρπα, β 295, ζ 37, Θ 503, Ι 66.

ἐφ-οράω, fut. ἐπόψομαι, ἐπιόψομαι, aor. ἐπεῖδον: *look upon, behold, watch over*; (Ζεύς) ἀνθρώπους ἐφορᾷ καὶ τίνυται ὅς κεν ἁμάρτῃ, ν 214; also 'go to see' (visere), η 324, ψ 19, and 'look up' (in order to choose), here the form ἐπιόψομαι, Ι 167, β 294; fig., 'live to see,' κακά, Χ 61.

ἐφ-ορμάω, aor. ἐφώρμησα, pass. ἐφωρμήθην: act., *set a-going against, arouse against*; πόλεμόν τινι, ἀνέμους, Γ 165, η 272; mid. and pass., *rush upon, be impelled, be eager*; ἐνὶ δίφρῳ | ἔγχει ἐφορμᾶσθαι, Ρ 465; w. acc., ὀρνίθων πετεηνῶν αἰετὸς αἴθων | ἔθνος ἐφορμᾶται, Ο 691, Υ 461; εἴ οἱ θῡμὸς ἐφορμᾶται γαμέεσθαι, α 275.

ἐφ-ορμή: *way to speed to* (from the interior to the ὁδὸς ἐς λαύρην), χ 130†.

ἐφ-υβρίζω: only part., *insultingly*, Ι 368†.

ἔφ-υδρος (ὕδωρ): *wet, rainy*, ξ 458†.

ἐφ-ύπερθε(ν): *above*.

Ἐφύρη: *Ephyra*.—(1) the ancient name of Corinth, Ζ 152, 210.—(2) a Pelasgic city in Northern Elis, the residence of Augēas, Β 659, Ο 531, Λ 739, α 259, β 328.

Ἔφυροι: the inhabitants of Crannon in Thessaly, which formerly bore the name of Ephyra, Ν 301.

ἔχαδον: see χανδάνω.

ἔχεαν, ἔχεε: see χέω.

ἐχέ-θῡμος: *restraining passion*; οὐκ ἐχέθῡμος, *incontinent*, θ 320†.

Ἐχεκλῆς: a Myrmidon, the son of Actor, Π 189.

Ἔχεκλος: (1) a son of Agēnor, slain by Achilles, Υ 474†.—(2) a Trojan, slain by Patroclus, Π 694†.

Ἐχέμμων: a son of Priam, slain by Diomed, Ε 160†.

Ἐχένηος: an aged Phaeacian, λ 342.

ἐχε-πευκής, ές (cf. πικρός): *having a sharp point, sharp*, ὀιστός. (Il.)

Ἐχέπωλος: (1) a descendant of Anchīses, dwelling in Sicyon, Ψ 296.—(2) a Trojan, the son of Thalysius, slain by Antilochus, Δ 458.

ἔχεσκον: see ἔχω.

Ἔχετος: a barbarous king in Epīrus, φ 308. (Od.)

ἔχευα, ἐχευάμην: see χέω.

ἐχέ-φρων: *thoughtful, prudent*. (Od.)

Ἐχέφρων: a son of Nestor, γ 413.

ἔχησθα: see ἔχω.

ἐχθαίρω (ἔχθος), aor. ἤχθηρα: *hate*, opp. φιλεῖν, δ 692.

ἔχθιστος (sup. of ἐχθρός): *most hateful, most odious*. (Il.)

ἐχθο-δοπέω: only aor. inf. ἐχθοδοπῆσαι, *to enter into hostilities against*, τινί, Α 518†.

ἔχθομαι, inf. ἔχθεσθαι, ipf. ἤχθετο: *be hated, odious*. (Od.)

ἔχθος, εος: *hate, enmity, wrath*.

ἐχθρός: *hateful, odious*.

Ἐχῖναι: νῆσοι, name of a group of islands in the Ionian Sea, near Dulichium, Β 625.

Ἐχίος: (1) the father of Mecisteus, Θ 333.—(2) a Lycian, slain by Patroclus, Π 416.—(3) a Lycian, slain by Polītes, Ο 339.

ἔχμα (ἔχω), pl. **ἔχματα**: *props, supports, bearers*; νηῶν, πύργων, Ξ 410, Μ 260; of the earth under a mass of rock, πέτρης, Ν 139; also of the mud or rubbish from a canal, *holding back* the flow of water, Φ 259.

ἔχω, subj. 2 sing. ἔχῃσθα, ipf. εἶχον, ἔχον, iter. ἔχεσκον, fut. ἕξω, σχήσω, aor. ἔσχον, inf. σχέμεν, mid. fut. ἕξεται, σχήσεσθε, aor. ἐσχόμην, imp. σχέο, parallel forms of aor. act. ἔσχεθον, σχεθέειν: *hold, have.*—I. act. (and pass.) —(1) trans., *hold*, in the hands, A 14; or in any way or direction, hence 'wear,' N 163, Ψ 136, Π 763, τ 225; 'hold up,' 'support,' α 53; 'hold back,' 'stop,' Δ 302, M 456; and similarly of holding something to a course, 'guide,' 'steer,' a ship, horses, ι 279, N 326; met., of holding watch, holding under one's protection, I 1, Ω 730; also *have, keep*, esp. 'have to wife,' δ 569; as one's abode, 'inhabit,' E 890; under one's authority, β 22; and w. inf., 'be able,' Π 110, μ 433. Pass., H 102.—(2) intrans., *hold* still, or in some position, ἕξω, ὡς λίθος, τ 494; also of motion, direction, ἔγχος ἔσχε δι' ὤμου, simply giving verbal force to the prep. διά, N 520; freq. w. an adv., ῥίζαι ἑκὰς εἶχον, were 'far reaching,' μ 435; εὖ ἔχει, 'it is well,' ω 245; answering to the trans. use w. νῆα, ἵππους, but without object, 'steer,' 'drive,' γ 182, Ψ 401; and similarly where no object can be thought of, ἐπὶ δ' αὐτῷ πάντες ἔχωμεν, 'have at him,' χ 75.—II. mid., *hold* something for oneself, or of one's own, *hold fast, hold still, cease from, hold on* to something (τινός); ἄντα παρειάων σχομένη λιπαρὰ κρήδεμνα, 'before her cheeks,' α 334, Υ 262; ἔχεο κρατερῶς, Π 501; τῷ προσφὺς ἐχόμην ὡς νυκτερίς, μ 433; ἔσχετο φωνή, 'stuck,' 'stopped,' P 696, Φ 345; w. gen., B 98; metaph., 'depend on,' σέο ἕξεται, I 102, ζ 197, λ 346.

ἐψιάομαι: *make merry*, ρ 530; μολπῇ καὶ φόρμιγγι, φ 429.

ἐῶ, ἐῷ: see ἐάω.

ἔωθα: see ἔθω.

ἐῴκει: see ἔοικα.

ἐώλπει: see ἔλπω.

ἕωμεν: unintelligible word in T 402†. (According to most of the ancient grammarians it is equiv. to ἄδην ἔχωμεν, πληρωθῶμεν, κορεσθῶμεν.)

ἐών: see εἰμί.

ἐῳνοχόει: see οἰνοχοέω.

ἐώργει: see ἔρδω.

ἕως, εἵως, εἷος: (1) *as long as, until;* foll. by the usual constructions with rel. words (see ἄν, κέν). A clause introduced by ἕως often denotes purpose, δ 800, ι 376.—(2) like τέως, *for a while*, usually with μέν, β 148, etc. —ἕως, to be read with 'synizesis,' except β 78.

ἕωσι: see εἰμί.

ἐῶσι: see ἐάω.

Ἑωσ-φόρος: *morning star* (**Lucifer**), Ψ 226†.

Z.

ζα- (διά): intensive prefix, like δα-.

ζαής, ές (ἄημι), acc. ζαῆν: *strongly blowing, tempestuous.*

ζά-θεος, 3: *most divine, sacred*, of localities favored by the gods. (Il.)

ζά-κοτος (κότος): *surly, morose*, Γ 220†.

Ζάκυνθος: *Zacynthus* (now Zante), an island in the realm of Odysseus, south of Same, α 246, B 634. A short syllable is not necessarily lengthened by position before the initial Z of this word, ι 124, α 246; cf. Ζέλεια.

ζα-τρεφής, ές (τρέφω): *highly fed, fat, sleek.*

ζα-φλεγής, ές (φλέγω): *strongly burning*, met., *full of fire*, Φ 465†.

ζα-χρηής (χράω): *raging, impetuous.* (Il.)

ζάω: see ζώω.

ζειαί: a coarse kind of barley, *spelt*, [δ 41, 604.

ζεί-δωρος: *grain-giving.*

Ζέλεια: a town at the foot of Mt. Ida. A short syllable is not necessarily lengthened by position before the initial Z of this word, B 824; cf. Ζάκυνθος. (Il.)

ζέσσεν: see ζέω.

ζεύγλη: *yoke-cushion*, between neck and yoke. (Il.) (See cut No. 72, also 45, letter *d*.)

ζεύγνῡμι, ζευγνύω, inf. ζευγνύμεν (ζευγνῡμεν, Π 145), aor. ἔζευξα, ζεῦξε, pass. perf. part. ἐζευγμέναι: *yoke, yoke up, yoke together,* mid., for oneself; ἵππους, βόας, also w. ὑπ' ὄχεσφιν, ὑπ' ἀπήνῃ, etc., Υ 495, Ψ 130, ζ 73, ο 46, γ 492; abs., Ω 281.

ζεῦγος, εος: pl., *a pair, yoke* of draught animals, Σ 543†.

Ζεῦς (Διεύς, root διϝ), gen. Διός, dat. Διί, acc. Δία, voc. Ζεῦ, also gen. Ζηνός, dat. Ζηνί, acc. Ζῆν(α): *Zeus* (Diespiter, Juppiter; cf. Ζεῦ πάτερ, Γ 320), the son of Cronos and the father of gods and men, god of the lightning, the clouds and weather, of time itself, hence ὑψίζυγος, αἰθέρι ναίων, Διὸς ὄμβρος, Διὸς ἐνιαυτοί, εὐρύοπα, ἐρίγδουπος πόσις Ἥρης, αἰγίοχος, ὑψιβρεμέτης, νεφεληγερέτα, κελαινεφής, στεροπηγερέτα, τερψικέραυνος, ἀστεροπητής, ἀργικέραυνος, ἐριβρεμέτης. Zeus is the sender of portents, and the shaper of destiny, πανομφαῖος, Διὸς τάλαντα, etc.; he is the protector of kings, of suppliants, of house and court, and he presides over the fulfilment of oaths, διοτρεφεῖς, διογενεῖς βασιλῆες, Ζεὺς ξείνιος, ἱκετήσιος, ἑρκεῖος. The original meaning of the root of the word is the *brightness of the sky,* afterwards personified; cf. δῖος, Lat. sub divo.

ζεφυρίη: the *western breeze,* η 119†. (The first syllable long in the verse.)

ζέφυρος (ζόφος): the *west wind,* rough and violent, ε 295, μ 289, 408; and the swiftest of the winds, Τ 415; bringing snow and rain, τ 202, ξ 458; only in fable-land soft and balmy, η 119, δ 567; personified, Π 150, Ψ 200.

ζέω, ipf. ζέε, aor. ζέσσε: *boil, seethe;* λέβης ζεῖ, the kettle boils, Φ 362.

Ζῆθος: *Zethus,* son of Zeus and Antiope, brother of Amphīon, with whom he founded Thebes, λ 262; the husband of Aëdon, and father of Itylus, τ 523.

ζηλήμων (ζῆλος): *jealous, grudging,* ε 118†.

Ζήν, Ζηνός: see Ζεύς.

ζητέω: *seek,* Ξ 258†.

ζόφος (cf. κνέφας, γνόφος, δνόφος): (1) *gloom, darkness,* esp. of the nether world, and for the realm of shadows itself, Ο 191.—(2) *evening,* the *Occident,* the *West,* ι 26, μ 81.

ζυγό-δεσμον: *yoke-band,* a cord or strap for fastening the yoke to the pole, Ω 270. (See cut under ζυγόν, *b;* and cut No. 42.)

ζυγόν (ζεύγνῡμι), gen. ζυγόφιν: (1) *yoke* or cross-bar by means of which beasts of draught were attached to whatever was to be drawn. (See adjacent cut, combined from several an-

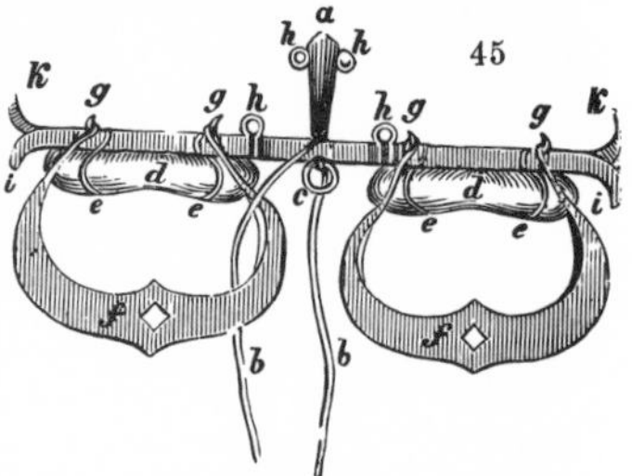

tique representations.) *a,* ὀμφαλός; *b,* ζυγόδεσμον; *c,* κρίκος; *d,* ζεῦγλαι; *e,* straps to fasten the ζεῦγλαι; *f,* λέπαδνα; *g* and *h,* οἴηκες, points of attachment for the collars, and rings through which the reins pass; *i,* ζυγόν; *k,* projections to hold, e. g., the reins of the παρήορος ἵππος. (Cf. also the Assyrian yoke on the chariot on board a ship, represented in the adjoining cut.)—(2) *cross-bar* of a lyre

(see φόρμιγξ), to which the strings were attached, Ι 187.—(3) pl., ζυγά, *rowers' benches, thwarts* of a ship (see cut No. 32, under ἔδαφος).

ζω-άγρια, pl. (ζωός, ἀγρέω): *reward for saving life,* Σ 407, θ 462.

1. ζωγρέω (ζωός, ἀγρέω): *take alive,* i. e. grant quarter and not slay, Κ 378†.

2. **ζωγρέω** (ζωή, ἐγείρω): *revive, reanimate;* θυμόν, Ε 698†.

ζωή (ζάω): *means of life, substance,* ξ 208, π 429. (Od.)

ζῶμα (ζώννυμι): (1) *apron* of leather or of felt, extending from the flank to the upper part of the thigh, and serving to protect the part of the body left exposed between the cuirass and the greaves (see cut under Ἀχιλλεύς, also cut No. 12, the figure of Aenēas). —(2) *broad girdle* around the waist of boxers, like that of the tumbler in the adjoining cut, Ψ 683.

Tumbler. Athēne with owl.

ζώνη: *girdle* of a woman (see cut No. 48, also Nos. 44 and 61); then for *waist*, Β 479, Λ 234.

ζώννυμι, aor. part. ζώσαντες, mid. pres. subj. ζώννυνται, ipf. ζώννυτο, iter. ζωννύσκετο, aor. ζώσατο, imp. ζῶσαι, part. ζωσαμένω: act., *gird* another, σ 76, mid.; *gird oneself, gird on,* w. acc. or dat. of the belt used, Ε 857, Κ 78; abs., Λ 15, σ 30.

ζωός, ζώς, acc. ζών: *alive, living,* Ε 887, Π 445.

ζωρός, comp. **ζωρότερος**: *lively, fiery,* of wine; ζωρότερον κέραιε, i. e. mix it stronger, pour in less water, Ι 203†.

ζωστήρ, ῆρος (ζώννυμι): (1) warrior's *body-girdle,* of leather strengthened with metal plates, which covered the lower part of the θώρηξ, and the upper part of the μίτρη and of the ζῶμα (see cuts Nos. 3 and 79). (Il.) —(2) *girdle* worn over the tunic, ξ 72. (See cut No. 73.)

ζῶστρον = ζώνη, ζ 38†.

ζώω, inf. ζώειν, ζωέμεναι, part. ζώοντος and ζῶντος, ipf. ἔζωον: *live;* freq. joined with ὁρᾶν φάος ἠελίοιο, δ 833; with ἔστιν, ω 263; ῥεῖα ζώοντες, of the gods and their untroubled existence.

H.

ἤ, ἠέ: *or, than, whether.*—(1) disjunctive, *or,* and in correlation, *either . . or,* ὅππως κε μνηστῆρας . . κτείνῃς ἠὲ δόλῳ ἢ ἀμφαδόν, α 296.—(2) comparative, *than.*—(3) interrogative, (*a*) rarely in a single indirect question, *whether,* Θ 111, ν 415 (v. l. εἰ).—(*b*) freq. in double questions, direct or indirect (*whether*) . . *or* (Att. πότερον . . ἤ), the accentuation of the second particle according to the ancient grammarians being **ἦ** (**ἠε**). The first member is introduced either by ἤ (ἠέ), or by some other particle, or stands without any particle; θεός νύ τις ἦ βροτός ἐσσι; ζ 149. οὐδέ τι οἶδα, ζώει ὅ γ' ἦ τέθνηκε, λ 464. Τυδείδην δ' οὐκ ἂν γνοίης ποτέροισι μετείη, | ἠὲ μετὰ Τρώεσσιν ὁμιλέοι ἦ μετ' Ἀχαιοῖς, Ε 86. With εἰ in first clause, π 33.

ἦ: see (1) εἰμί.—(2) ἠμί.

ἦ: *in truth, surely, verily.*—(1) particle of asseveration, always standing at the beginning of its clause except in the phrase ἐπεὶ ἦ (sometimes written ἐπειή). Freq. in combination with other particles, ἦ δή, ἦ μάλα (δή), ἦ θήν, ἦ τε, ἦ τοι (q. v.), and esp. ἦ μήν (μέν), which may be retained even in indirect quotation, καί μοι ὄμοσσον | ἦ μέν μοι . . ἀρήξειν (representing in the direct form, ἦ μέν σοι ἀρήξω, 'I solemnly declare that I will defend thee'), A 77, Ξ 275.—(2) the same particle may introduce a direct question, esp. a specific question following a general one, always, however, with the expression of some feeling; τίπτ' αὖτ' . . εἰλήλουθας; ἦ ἵνα ὕβριν ἴδῃ Ἀγαμέμνονος, '*is it* that thou may'st behold, etc.?' A 203, Γ 400, Υ 17; Ζεῦ πάτερ, ἦ ῥά τις ἔστι βροτῶν, κτλ., '*pray*, lives there a man, etc.?' H 446.

ἥ: see ὅς.

ἧ: regarded by some as an adv. in the phrase ἣ θέμις ἐστίν, *as is right.* See ὅς.

ᾗ: *where* (*whither*), *as;* dat. fem. of the rel. pron., used as adv., M 389, O 46, I 310.

ἦα: see εἰμί.

ᾖα: see ἤια.

ἠβαιός (Att. βαιός): *little, slight,* usually w. neg., οὐδ' οἱ ἔνι φρένες, οὐδ' ἠβαιαί, 'not the least,' Ξ 141, φ 288, σ 355.—Adv., **ἠβαιόν,** *a little,* ι 462, elsewhere w. neg.

ἡβάω, opt. ἡβώοιμι, ἡβῷμι, part. ἡβῶν, ἡβώοντα, etc., aor. ἥβησα: *be* (aor. *arrive*) *at one's prime, have youthful vigor;* fig., of a vine, 'luxuriant,' ε 69.

ἥβη: *youth;* ἥβης μέτρον, 'youthful prime,' A 225, λ 317; youthful strength or vigor, Π 857, θ 181.

Ἥβη: *Hebe,* daughter of Zeus and Hera, spouse of Heracles, λ 603. In the Iliad she always appears as a goddess performing some manual service for other divinities, Δ 2, E 722, 905.

ἡβῷμι, ἡβώοιμι: see ἡβάω.

ἠγάασθε: see ἄγαμαι.

ἤγαγον, ἠγαγόμην: see ἄγω.

ἠγάθεος: *highly divine, sacred,* of localities, Z 133, δ 702. Cf. ζάθεος.

ἤγειρα: see (1) ἀγείρω.—(2) ἐγείρω.

ἠγάσσατο: see ἄγαμαι.

ἡγεμονεύω (ἡγεμών), fut. **-εύσω**: *be leader, lead the way* (w. dat.), *command* an army (w. gen.), (Il.); τοῖσι γέρων ὁδὸν ἡγεμόνευεν, ω 225; ὕδατι ῥόον, Φ 258; ἑτέρης (στιχός), Π 179 (dat. B 816).

ἡγεμών, όνος: *guide, leader, commander.* (Il. and κ 505, ο 310.)

ἡγέομαι (ἄγω), fut. **-ήσομαι,** aor. -ησάμην: *go before, lead the way, guide, lead;* opp. ἕπομαι, α 125; πρόσθεν ἡγεῖσθαι, Ω 696; ὁδόν, κ 263; w. acc. of the place led to, ἄστεα, ο 82; met., w. gen., ὀρχηθμοῖο, ψ 134; w. gen. of persons commanded, B 567, 620, 851.

ἠγερέθομαι (ἀγείρω): *assemble.*

ἤγερθεν: see ἀγείρω.

ἠγηλάζω: parallel form of ἡγέομαι, w. acc., ρ 217; μόρον, λ 618. (Od.)

ἡγήτωρ, ορος (ἡγέομαι): *leader, chief;* freq. ἡγήτορες ἠδὲ μέδοντες, w. ἄνδρες, Π 495.

ἠγοράασθε, ἠγορόωντο: see ἀγοράομαι.

ἠδέ: *and;* combined, ἠδὲ . . καὶ . . ἠδέ, τ' ἠδέ, τὲ . . ἠδέ, τὲ . . ἠδὲ καί, O 663, B 206, α 12, E 822; ἠδὲ καί, 'and also,' A 334, etc.; freq. correl. to ἠμέν, also to μέν.

ᾔδεα, ᾔδη: see εἴδω (II.).

ἤδη: *already, now* (i a m); ἤδη ποτὲ ἤλυθε, 'once before,' Γ 205; ἐπὶ νῆα κατελεύσομαι ἤδη, 'at once,' α 303; freq. ἤδη νῦν, A 456, O 110, Π 844.

ἥδομαι (ἡδύς): only aor. ἥσατο, *was delighted,* ι 353†.

ἦδος, εος: *joy, enjoyment;* δαιτός, A 576, σ 404; ἡμέων ἔσσεται ἦδος, 'joy of us,' i. e. from us, A 318; 'profit,' 'advantage,' Σ 80, ω 95. Always w. neg. expressed or implied.

ἡδυ-επής (ϝέπος): *sweet-speaking,* A 248†.

ἡδύ-ποτος (πίνω): *sweet to drink.* (Od.)

ἡδύς, εῖα, ύ (σϝηδύς), sup. **ἥδιστος**: *sweet, pleasant;* adv., **ἡδύ, κνώσσειν,** γελᾶν, δ 809, B 270.

ἠέ (**ἦε**): see ἤ.

ἦε: see εἰμί.

ἠείδειν, ἠείδη, ἠείδης: see εἴδω (II.)

ἠέλιος: the *sun;* of rising, ἀνιέναι, ἀνορούειν, γ 1; ἀνανεῖσθαι, κ 192; στείχειν πρὸς οὐρανόν, λ 17; noon, μέσον οὐρανὸν ἀμφιβαίνειν, Θ 68; afternoon, μετανίσσειν βουλυτόνδε, Π 779; ἂψ ἐπὶ γαῖαν προτρέπεσθαι, λ 18; setting, δύειν, ἐπιδύειν, καταδύειν, ἐμπίπτειν Ὠκεανῷ, Θ 485; of shining, ἐπιλάμπειν, ἀκτῖσι βάλλειν, ἐπιδέρκεσθαι ἀκτίνεσσιν, also φάος ἠελίοιο, often as typical of life, λ 93, Σ 11, 61, δ 540; αὐγή, αἴγλη, μένος, Ψ 190, κ 160; epithets, ἀκάμᾱς, λαμπρός, λευκός, παμφανόων, φαεσίμβροτος. Expressions for east and west, ν 240, M 239, κ 191.—**Ἠέλιος, Ἥλιος** (θ 271).

Helius, the sun-god, son of Hyperion, μ 176, α 8; father of Circe, and of Phaethūsa and Lampetie, κ 138, μ 133; propitiated by sacrifice, Γ 104, Τ 197; oath by the sun, Τ 259; the kine of Helius, μ 128, 322, τ 276, ψ 329.

ἦεν: see εἰμί.

ἠέπερ: see ἤπερ.

ἠερέθομαι (ἀείρω): *flutter, float*, Φ 12; φρένες, 'are unstable,' Γ 108.

Ἠερίβοια: *Eriboea*, the second wife of Alōeus, step-mother of Otus and Ephialtes, Ε 389.

ἠέριος: adj., *at early morn*, always used predicatively, Α 497, ι 52.

ἠερο-ειδής, ές (εἶδος): *misty, murky, gray*; πόντος, σπέος, πέτρη, Ψ 744, μ 80, 233; ὅσσον δ' ἠεροειδὲς ἀνὴρ ἴδεν ὀφθαλμοῖσιν, sees 'into the dim distance,' 'through the haze,' Ε 770.

ἠερόεις, εσσα, εν (ἀήρ): *cloudy, gloomy*, mostly with reference to the nether world, Θ 13, Ο 191, υ 64.

ἠέρος: see ἀήρ.

ἠερο-φοῖτις (φοιτάω): *walking in darkness*; Ἐρῑνύς, Ι 571. (Il.)

ἠερό-φωνος: *loud-voiced*; (if from ἀείρω) 'raising the voice,' (if from ἀήρ) 'sending the voice abroad.'

Ἠετίων: *Eëtion*.—(1) king of Thebe in the Troad, the father of Andromache, Ζ 396, Α 366.—(2) an Imbrian, a guest-friend of Priam, Φ 43.—(3) a Trojan, Ρ 590.

ἤην: see εἰμί.

ἠθεῖος (ἔθος, ἦθος): *familiar, beloved, dear*; usually the voc., ἠθεῖε, also ἠθείη κεφαλή, 'dear heart' we should say, Ψ 94; ἀλλά μιν ἠθεῖον καλέω, 'dear master,' ξ 147.

ἦθος (Ϝῆθος), pl. **ἤθεα**: *accustomed places, haunts*, Ζ 511; of 'pens,' ξ 411.

ἦϊα, ἦα: (1) *provisions, food*, Ν 103. (Od.)—(2) gen. ἠίων θημῶνα, heap *of chaff*, ε 368†.

ἦιε: see εἶμι.

ἠίθεος: *unmarried youth, bachelor*; παρθένος ἠίθεός τε, Σ 593, λ 38.

ἤικτο: see ἔοικα.

ἤϊξε: see ἀίσσω.

ἠιόεις, εσσα: doubtful word, *with changing banks*, Ε 36†. (The above interpretation assumes a derivation from ἠιών, some rivers like the Scamander, in warm countries, with their sources in neighboring mountains, have in consequence of rains a broad rugged bed out of proportion to the ordinary size of the stream, and banks ragged and often high.)

ἤιον: see εἶμι.

Ἠιόνες: name of a sea-port in Argolis, Β 561†.

Ἠιονεύς: (1) father of the Thracian king Rhesus, Κ 435.—(2) a Greek, slain by Hector, Η 11.

ἤιος: epithet of Apollo in the apostrophe, ἤιε Φοῖβε, Ο 365, Υ 152; perhaps 'far-darting' (ἵημι).

ἤισαν: see εἶμι.

ἠΐχθη: see ἀίσσω.

ἠιών, όνος: *sea-bank, shore*, Μ 31, ζ 138.

ἦκα (Ϝῆκα): *gently, softly, slightly*, Υ 440, Σ 596, υ 301.

ἧκα: see ἵημι.

ἤκαχε: see ἀκαχίζω.

ἠκέσσατο: see ἀκέομαι.

ἤ-κεστος (κεντέω): *ungoaded*, hence *untamed*, Ζ 94. (Il.)

ἥκιστος (Ϝῆκα): *slowest, most sluggish*, Ψ 531†.

ἥκω: *am come*, Ε 478, ν 325.

ἠλάκατα, pl.: *wool*, or *woollen thread* on the distaff; στρωφῶσα, στροφαλίζετε, 'ply the distaff,' σ 315. (Od.) (See the first of the cuts below.)

ἠλᾰκάτη: *spindle*, Ζ 491. (Od.) (See the cuts, representing distaff and spindles.)

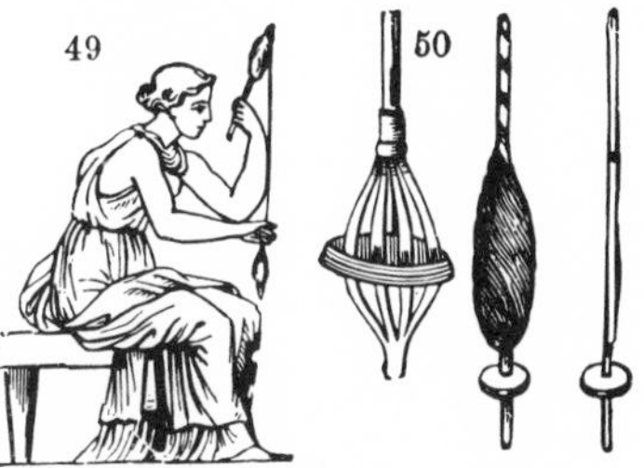

ἤλασα, ἠλασάμεσθα: see ἐλαύνω.

ἠλασκάζω (ἠλάσκω): *wander about*; trans., ἐμὸν μένος, 'try to escape' by dodging, ι 457.

ἠλάσκω (ἀλάομαι): *prowl about, swarm about*, Μ 104, Β 470.

ἠλᾶτο: see ἀλάομαι.

ἤλδανε: see ἀλδαίνω.

ἠλέ: see ἠλεός.

Ἠλεῖοι: the *Elēans*, inhabitants of Elis, Λ 671†.

ἤλεκτρον: *amber*, δ 73. (Od.)

ἠλέκτωρ: *beaming* (*sun*), with and without Ὑπερίων, Τ 398, Ζ 513. (Il.)

ἠλεός, ἠλός: *crazed, infatuated*, with φρένας, Ο 128, β 243; in active sense, οἶνος, ξ 464.

ἠλήλατο: see ἐλαύνω.

ἠλίβατος: *towering, lofty*, ι 243, Ο 273.

ἤλιθα (ἅλις): *sufficiently*, always ἤλιθα πολλή(ν), 'very much' (satis multum), Λ 677, ε 483.

ἡλικίη (ἧλιξ): *time of life, age*, for concrete, *mates, fellows*, Π 808. (Il.)

ἧλιξ, ικος: pl., *equal in age*, σ 373†.

ἥλιος: see ἠέλιος.

Ἦλις, ιδος: *Elis* a division of the Peloponnēsus on the west coast, inhabited in the north by Epeians, in the south by Achaeans, Β 316, δ 635.

ἤλιτε: see ἀλιταίνω.

ἠλιτό-μηνος (ἀλιτεῖν, μήν): *untimely born*, Τ 118†.

ἥλκησε: see ἑλκέω.

ἧλος: pl., *nails, studs*, only used for ornamentation, Α 246, Λ 29, 633. (Il.)

ἤλυθον: see ἔρχομαι.

Ἠλύσιον πεδίον: *the Elysian fields*, the abode of the blest, δ 563 ff.

ἦλφον: see ἀλφάνω.

ἥλω: see ἁλίσκομαι.

ἠλώμην: see ἀλάομαι.

Ἠλώνη: a city in Phthiōtis, Β 739†.

ἧμα, ατος (ἵημι): *throw; ἥμασιν ἄριστος*, best 'at javelin-throwing,' Ψ 891†.

Ἠμαθίη: *Emathia*, the ancient name of Macedonia, Ξ 226†.

ἠμαθόεις (ἄμαθος): *sandy*, epithet of Pylos.

ἧμαι, ἧσ(αι), ἧσται, ἥμεθα, ἧσθε, ἕαται and εἵαται, imp. ἧσο, inf. ἧσθαι, part. ἥμενος, ipf. ἥμην, ἧστο, ἥσθην, ἥμεθα, ἧντο and ἕατο and εἵατο: *sit*; often w. a part. to denote some condition of mind or body, ἧστο ὀδῡρόμενος, θαυμάζων, ὀλιγηπελέων, etc.; and, in general, the verb may denote a settled condition of any sort, 'stay,' 'keep,' ἑκὰς ἥμεθα πατρίδος αἴης, Ο 740, Ω 542; σῑγῇ, ἀκέουσα, σιωπῇ ἧσο, Δ 412.

ἦμαρ, ατος: *day;* divided by Homer into ἠώς, μέσον ἦμαρ, and δείλη, Φ 111, η 288; ἦμαρ χειμέριον, ὀπωρῑνόν, also αἴσιμον, μόρσιμον ἦμαρ, νηλεὲς ἦμαρ, νόστιμον ἦμαρ, δούλιον and ἐλεύθερον ἦμαρ, mostly poetic periphrases for the noun implied in the adj.; ἤματα πάντα, ἐπ' ἤματι (see ἐπί), πᾶν, πρόπαν ἦμαρ, freq. formula ἤματι τῷ ὅτε.

ἠμάτιος: *by day*, β 104; *daily*, Ι 72.

ἤμβροτον: see ἁμαρτάνω.

ἡμεῖς and ἄμμες, gen. ἡμέ͜ων and ἡμείων, dat. ἡμῖν and encl. ἧμιν, also ἄμμι(ν), acc. ἄμμε, ἡμέ͜ας (encl. ἧμας, π 372): *we, us*.

ἠμέν: always in correlation, usually with ἠδέ, *both* . . (*and*), *as well* . . (*as*), Β 789, ξ 193; also correl. to δέ, καί, or τέ, Μ 428, Ο 664, θ 575.

ἡμέρη, pl. ἡμέραι: *day;* other forms than the nom. are supplied by ἦμαρ.

ἡμερίς (ἥμερος): cultivated (not wild) *vine*, ε 69†.

ἥμερος: *tame, domesticated*, ο 162†.

ἡμέτερος (ἡμεῖς): *our, ours;* ἐφ' ἡμέτερα νέεσθαι, Ι 619; adv., ἡμέτερόνδε, *homeward, home*.

ἠμί: only ipf., ἦ (dixit), at the beginning of the verse, and regularly foll. by καί and a verb expressing action; ἦ ῥα, καὶ ἐκ χειρὸς χεῖρα σπάσατ' Ἀντινόοιο, 'he spoke,' and drew his hand away, β 321, Γ 355; in slightly different combination, σ 356, Ζ 390.

ἡμι-: *half-* (semi-), in composition.

ἡμι-δαής (δαίω): *half-burnt*, Π 294†.

ἡμί-θεος: *demi-god*, pl., Μ 23†.

ἡμι-όνειος: *of mules;* ἄμαξα, ζυγόν, *mule*-wagon, *mule*-yoke, ζ 62, Ω 268.

ἡμί-ονος (ὄνος): *mule;* the name designates the hybrid, cf. οὐρεύς.—As adj., Ψ 266.

ἡμι-πέλεκκον (πέλεκυς): *half-axe, one-edged axe*. (Il.)

ἥμισυς, σεια, συ: *half;* sing. only neut. as subst., Ζ 193, Ι 579, 580; pl., ἡμίσεες λᾱοί, Φ 7, γ 155, 157; gen. ἡμίσεων πλείους, ω 464.

ἡμι-τάλαντον: *half a talent, half a pound* (gold), Ψ 751, 796.

ἡμι-τελής: *half-finished*, Β 701†.

ἦμος: *when, at the time when*, always at the beginning of a verse, exc. μ 439; followed in the apod. by τῆμος, δὴ τότε, δή, καὶ τότ' ἔπειτα.

ἠμύω, aor. ἤμυσα: *nod, bow, droop;* with κάρη or καρήατι, Θ 308, Τ 405; of a field of grain, ἐπί (adv.) τ' ἠμύει ἀσταχύεσσιν, 'nods its heads to the breeze,' B 148; fig. of cities, 'sink to earth,' B 373, Δ 290.

ἥμων, ονος (ἵημι): *darter; ἥμονες ἄνδρες*, 'javelin men,' Ψ 886†.

ἤν (εἰ, ἄν): *if;* for constructions see εἰ, ἄν, κέν. Sometimes called 'interrogative,' 'in case that,' α 282, and often. For ἤνπερ, ἤν που, ἤν πως, see the several particles.

ἠναίνετο: see ἀναίνομαι.

ἤνεικα, ἠνείκατο: see φέρω.

ἠνεμόεις, εσσα, εν (ἄνεμος): *windy, breezy, airy,* of towns, trees, and mountain-tops.

ἡνία, pl.: *reins;* often adorned with gold or ivory, σῑγαλόεντα, E 226.

ἡνίκα: *when, at the time when,* χ 198†.

Ἡνιοπεύς: son of Thebaeus, a charioteer of Hector, slain by Diomed, Θ 120†.

ἡνιοχεύς, ῆος=ἡνίοχος. (Il.)

ἡνιοχεύω: *be charioteer, hold the reins, drive.*

ἡνί-οχος (ἡνία, ἔχω): *holding the reins,* θεράπων, E 580; *charioteer.* The charioteer usually stood at the left of the πρόμαχος. (Among the Assyrians, as shown by the cut, the warrior, armed with a bow, had also a second attendant as shield-bearer with himself on the chariot. The Egyptian monuments represent only one warrior or triumphing king upon the war-chariot.)

ἠνίπαπε: see ἐνίπτω.

ἦνις, ιος, acc. pl. ἤνῑς: *a year old, yearling;* thus the word was understood by the ancients.

ἦνον: see ἄνω.

Ἠνοπίδης: *son of Enops,* Satnius, Ξ 444†.

ἠνορέη (ἀνήρ), dat. ἠνορέηφι: *manliness, manly courage, prowess.*

ἦνοψ, οπος (Ϝῆνοψ): *bright, gleaming,* χαλκός.

Ἦνοψ: (1) a Mysian, the father of Satnius and Thestor, Ξ 445.—(2) father of Clytomēdes, from Aetolia, Ψ 634.

ἤνπερ: see ἤν and πέρ.

ἤντεον: see ἀντάω.

ἧντο: see ἧμαι.

ἤνυτο: see ἀνύω.

ἠνώγεα, ἠνώγει: see ἄνωγα.

ἧξε: see ἄγνῡμι.

ἠοῖος (ἠώς): fem. ἠοίη, as subst., *morning, dawn,* δ 447; adj., *eastern* (opp. ἑσπέριοι), *Oriental,* ἄνθρωποι, θ 29.

ἦος: see ἕως.

ἧπαρ, ατος: *liver.*

ἤπαφε: see ἀπαφίσκω.

ἠπεδανός: *feeble, weakly.*

ἤπειρος: *land* (terra firma), as opp. to the sea, A 485, ε 56; *mainland,* as opp. to the islands, B 635, ω 378;

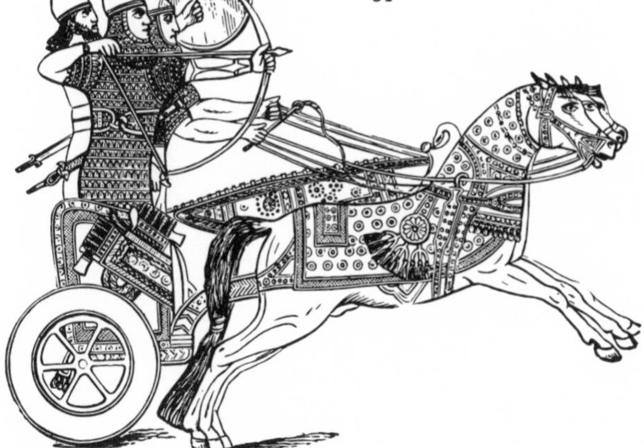

51

designating inland as opp. to coast, ι 49. — **ἤπειρόνδε**: *landwards, toward the land, inland.*

ἤπερ, ἠέπερ: see ἤ, ἠέ.

ᾗπερ: see ὅσπερ.

ἠπεροπεύς, ῆος, and **ἠπεροπευτής**, *deceiver, seducer*, λ 364†, Γ 39 and Ν 769.

ἠπεροπεύω: *talk with intent to deceive, cajole, seduce.*

ἠπιό-δωρος: *kindly giving, bountiful*, Ζ 251†.

ἤπιος: *mild;* of persons, remedies, Δ 218, counsels, Δ 361.

ἠπύτα (for ἠπύτης, ἠπύω): *loud-calling, loud-voiced*, Η 384†.

Ἠπυτίδης: *son of Epytus*, Periphas, a Trojan, Ρ 324†.

ἠπύω: *call afar, hail*, τινά, ι 399, κ 83; 'resound,' 'pipe,' of the lyre, and wind, ρ 271, Ξ 399.

ἦρα (ϝῆρα): only with φέρειν, *favor, gratify, humor*, θυμῷ, 'the impulse,' Ξ 132; also w. ἐπί, μητρὶ φίλῃ ἐπὶ ϝῆρα φέρων, Α 572, 578.

Ἡρᾱκλείδης: *son of Heracles.*—(1) Tlepolemus, Β 653.—(2) Thessalus, Β 679.

Ἡρᾱκλέης, gen. Ἡρᾱκλῆος: *Heracles*, son of Zeus and Alcmēna, Τ 98; his celebrated labors, Θ 362, λ 623, φ 26; he destroys the Troy of Laomedon, and conquers Pylos, Υ 145, Ε 642, Λ 689 ff., cf. Ε 392, 397; his death, and his shade, Σ 117, λ 601. Heracles was celebrated in song as a national hero before the time of Homer, λ 602, 267. Epithets, θεῖος, θρασυμέμνων, κρατερόφρων, καρτερόθῡμος.

Ἡρᾱκλήειος: *of Heracles*, only in the periphrasis βίη Ἡρᾱκληείη (see βίη).

ἤραρε: ἀραρίσκω.

ἤρατο: see ἄρνυμαι.

ἠρᾶτο: see ἀράω.

Ἥρη: *Hera*, daughter of Cronus and Rhea, sister and spouse of Zeus, see Ξ 201 ff. The perpetual jarring of Zeus and Hera in Olympus, described with humor in the Iliad, but as too serious to be trivial, Α 568, Ο 14 ff. Hera is the friend of the Greeks and enemy of the Trojans. Her children, Ares, Hephaestus, Hebe, Eilithyia; favorite haunts, Argos, Mycēnae, Sparta, Δ 51 f. Epithets, Ἀργείη, Βοῶπις πότνια, πρέσβα θεά, Διὸς κυδρὴ παράκοιτις, ἠύκομος, λευκώλενος, χρῡσόθρονος, χρῡσοπέδῑλος, besides many uncomplimentary titles applied to her by Zeus.

ἠρήρει: see ἀραρίσκω.

ἠρήρειστο: see ἐρείδω.

ἦρι: *at early morn.*

ἠρι-γένεια: *early born*, epith. of ἠώς. As subst. = Eos, *child of dawn*, χ 197.

ἤρικε: see ἐρείκω.

ἠρίον: *sepulchral mound*, Ψ 126†.

ἤριπε: see ἐρείπω.

ἤρυγε: see ἐρεύγομαι.

ἠρῶ: see ἀράω.

ἠρώησαν: see ἐρωέω.

ἥρως, gen. ἥρωος and ἥρῶος, dat. ἥρῳι and ἥρῳ, acc. ἥρω(α): *hero, warrior;* a title of honor for the free and brave; alone as subst., Α 4, Κ 179; in address, Υ 104, Κ 416; w. Δαναοί, Ἀχαιοί, likewise with single names, Δ 200, β 15, Φ 163; joined w. θεράποντες Ἄρηος, Β 110; γέρων, η 155. Never = demigod.

ἧσαι: see ἧμαι.

ἥσατο: see ἥδομαι.

ἧσειν: see ἵημι.

ἦσθα: see εἰμί.

ἤσκειν: see ἀσκέω.

ἧσο: see ἧμαι.

ἥσσων, ἧσσον, ονος: *inferior.* — Neut. as adv., *less.*

ἧσται: see ἧμαι.

ἤστην: see εἰμί.

ἡσυχίη: *peace, quiet*, σ 22†.

ἡσύχιος: *in quiet*, Φ 598†.

ᾐσχυμμένος: see αἰσχύνω.

ἠτε, ἤ τε: *or*, Τ 148; *than*, π 216; usu. in correlation, ἤτε . . ἤτε, *whether . . or, either . . or* (sive . . sive).

ἦτε, ἦ τε: see ἦ.

ᾐτιάασθε, ᾐτιόωντο: see αἰτιάομαι.

ἤτοι (ἤ τοι): *verily, to be sure*, particle of asseveration (see ἤ), and antithesis, not always to be translated; in correlation ἤτοι . . αὐτάρ differs from μὲν . . δέ only in so far as disyllabic and initial words must necessarily have more weight than monosyllabic and postpositive ones. As αὐτάρ, q. v., often correlates to μέν, so ἤτοι may be followed by δέ, Α 68, and often. Freq. ἀλλ' ἤτοι, also ἤτοι μέν, Α 140, 211, Π 451.

ἦτορ, ορος: *heart*, B 490, K 93; always fig., as typical of life, or thought, or feeling; ἐν δέ τέ οἱ κραδίῃ στένει ἄλκιμον ἦτορ, Υ 169.

ἠυ-γένειος (γένειον): *strong-bearded;* epith. of the lion, O 275, δ 456.

ηὔδā: see αὐδάω.

ἠύ-κομος (κόμη): *fair-haired*, epith. of goddesses and women. (Il. and μ 389).

ἠύς: see ἐύς.

ἦυσε: see αὔω.

ἠύτε: *as*, *like*, *as when*, Δ 277, A 359, B 87.

Ἥφαιστος: *Hephaestus* (Vulcanus), the son of Zeus and Hera, the god of fire and of arts which need the aid of fire: in the Iliad married to Charis, Σ 382 ff., but in the Odyssey to Aphrodīte, θ 266 ff. His works are the houses of the gods on Olympus, the armor of Achilles, the sceptre and aegis of Zeus, etc. Epithets, ἀμφιγυήεις, κυλλοποδίων, χαλκεύς, κλυτοτέχνης, κλυτόεργος, κλυτόμητις, πολύφρων, περίκλυτος, πολύμητις. The name Ἥφαιστος is used by personification for the element which he represents, B 426, cf. I 468.

ἧφι (σϝῆφι)=ᾗ, see ὅς, ἑός.

ἠχή (ϝηχή): resounding, echoing *noise*, *roar;* of voices (compared to the waves), wind, B 209, Π 769; freq. ἠχῇ θεσπεσίῃ, γ 150.

ἠχήεις, εσσα, εν (ϝηχή): *sounding*, *echoing*, *roaring*, δ 72, A 157.

ἤχθετο: see (1) ἄχθομαι.—(2) ἔχθομαι.

ἧχι: *where*.

ἠῶθεν (ἠώς): *in the morning*, Λ 555, α 372; *to-morrow morning*, Σ 136, T 320, α 372.

ἠῶθι: always with πρό (q. v.), *early in the morning*, Λ 50.

ἠώς, ἠοῦς, ἠοῖ, ἠῶ: *dawn*, *morning*, Φ 111; for *day*, Ω 31; *east*, ι 26.—**Ἠώς,** *Eos* (Aurora), consort of Tithōnus, cf., however, ε 121, ο 250. Mother of Memnon, δ 188; her abode, μ 3, Λ 1, T 1, χ 197. Epithets, ἠριγένεια, ῥοδοδάκτυλος, δῖα, ἐύθρονος, κροκόπεπλος, χρῡσόθρονος.

Θ.

θαάσσω, inf. -έμεν, ipf. θάασσε: *sit*. (Il. and γ 336.)

θαιρός: *hinge*, pl., M 459†. (See cuts from Egyptian originals; also under ἐπιβλής, No. 35.)

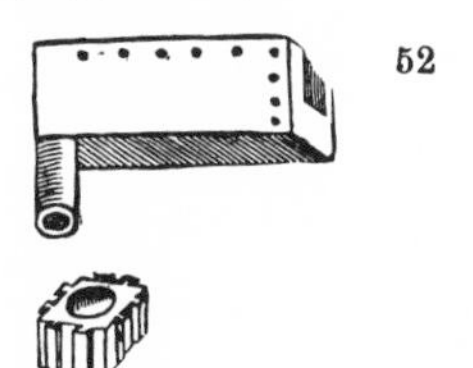

52

θαλάμη: *bed*, *hole*, of an animal, ε 432†.

θαλαμη-πόλος (πέλομαι): *chambermaid*. (Od.)

θάλαμος: the rear portion of the house, hence any *room*, *chamber* therein; e. g. women's chamber, δ 121; room for weapons, τ 17; store-room, β 337; bedchamber, Γ 423.—**θάλαμόνδε,** *to the chamber*. (See table III., at end of volume.)

θάλασσα: *the sea*.

θαλάσσιος: *of the sea;* θαλάσσια ϝέργα, 'business on the sea,' navigation, fishing, B 614, ε 67.

θάλεα, pl.: *good cheer*, X 504†.

θαλέθω: parallel form of θάλλω, ψ 191; fig., ζ 63; ἀλοιφῇ, 'teeming,' 'loaded' with fat, I 467, Ψ 32.

θάλεια: fem. adj., δαίς, *bounteous*, *plentiful* repast.

Θάλεια ('Bloomer'): a Nereid, Σ 39†.

θαλερός (θάλλω): *swelling*, *blooming;* with reference to growth, μηρώ, χαίτη, 'lusty,' 'thick,' O 113, P 439; the freshness of youth, παράκοιτις, γάμος, Γ 53, ζ 66; 'rich' fat, θ 476;

'big,' 'bursting,' tear, sobs, B 266, κ 457; the 'full,' 'swelling' voice, δ 705.

θαλίη: *abundance, prosperity;* pl., *good cheer*, λ 603.

θαλλός: collectively, *twigs* for fodder, ρ 224†.

θάλλω, perf. part. τεθηλώς, τεθαλυῖα, plup. τεθήλει: *swell, teem, bloom; σταφυλῇσιν*, ε 69; φύλλοισι, μ 103; ἀλοιφῇ, I 208; freq. the part. as adj. w. ἀλωή, ὀπώρη, ἐέρση, etc. Cf. θαλερός.

θάλος: *scion*, only metaph., X 87, ζ 157.

θαλπιάω (θάλπος): *be warm*, part., τ 319†.

Θάλπιος: son of Eurytus, a leader of the Epeians, B 620†.

θάλπω: *warm, warm up.* (Od.)

θαλπωρή: *warming*, met., *comfort.*

θαλύσια, pl. (θάλλω): *offering of first fruits, harvest offering*, I 534†.

Θαλυσιάδης: *son of Thalysius*, Echepōlus, Δ 458†.

θάμα: *frequently, often.*

θαμβέω (root θαπ), aor. θάμβησα: *be astonished* or *wonder at, gaze upon with wonder*, β 155, Ω 483.

θάμβος, ευς: *wonder, astonishment.*

θαμέες, θαμειαί (θάμα), dat. θαμέσι, θαμειαῖς, acc. θαμέας: *frequent, thick;* σταυροὶ πυκνοὶ καὶ θαμέες, 'thick set and numerous,' ξ 12.

θαμίζω: *come* or *go* or *do frequently, resort to;* w. part. **οὔ τι κομιζόμενός** γε θάμιζεν = οὐ θάμα ἐκομίζετο.

θάμνος: *thicket, bush;* of the leaves and branches of an olive-tree, ψ 190.

Θάμυρις: *Thamyris*, a Thracian bard vanquished and blinded by the Muses, B 595†.

θάνατος: *death;* θάνατόνδε, *to death*, Π 693.—Personified, *Death*, twin-brother of Sleep, Ξ 231.

θανέειν: see θνήσκω.

1. θάομαι, aor. opt. 3 pl. θησαίατο: *admire*, σ 191†.

2. θάομαι, inf. θῆσθαι, aor. θήσατο: *suck*, Ω 58; *milk*, δ 89.

θαπ- or **ταφ-,** perf. w. pres. signif. τέθηπα, part. -πώς, ότες, ότας, plup. ἐτεθήπεα, aor. 2 part. ταφών: *wonder, be amazed at, be dazed*, Δ 243.

θάπτω, aor. θάψαν, pass. plup. ἐτέθαπτο: *inter, bury.*

θαρσαλέος (θάρσος), comp. **-εώτερον**: *courageous, daring, bold;* in bad sense, ρ 449.—Adv., **θαρσαλέως.**

θαρσέω (θάρσος), aor. θάρσησε, perf. τεθαρσήκᾱσι: *be bold, confident, full of courage*, aor., *take courage*, A 92, γ 76; w. acc. of specification, θ 197.

θάρσος, εος: *courage, confidence, boldness, audacity.*

θάρσυνος: *confident, relying upon* (τινί), N 823.

θαρσύνω, ipf. iter. θαρσύνεσκε, aor. θάρσῡνα: *encourage.*

θάσσων: see ταχύς.

θαῦμα: a *wonder, marvel;* θαῦμα ϝιδέσθαι, E 725, ζ 306; *wonder, amazement*, θαῦμά μ' ἔχει, κ 326.

θαυμάζω, ipf. iter. θαυμάζεσκον, fut. θαυμάσσεται, aor. subj. θαυμάσωσι: *wonder, admire.*

θαυμαίνω, fut. part. θαυμανέοντες = θαυμάζω, θ 108†.

Θαυμακίη: a town in Magnesia, under the rule of Philoctētes, B 716†.

θεᾱ́, θεᾶς, dat. pl. θεαῖς, θεῇς, θεῇσιν: *goddess.*

θέαινα = θεᾱ́, only pl.

Θεᾱνώ: *Theāno*, daughter of Cisseus, and wife of Antēnor, a priestess of Athēna in Troy, Z 302.

θέειον and **θήιον** (Att. θεῖον): *sulphur*, used for fumigation and purification, hence called κακῶν ἄκος, χ 481; 'sulphurous fumes,' μ 417.

θεειόω (Att. θειόω): *fumigate* with sulphur, mid., ψ 50.

θεῖεν: see τίθημι.

θειλόπεδον: *drying-place*, a sunny spot in the vineyard where grapes were dried, η 123†.

θεῖμεν, θεῖναι: see τίθημι.

θείνω, inf. θεινέμεν(αι), subj. θείνῃ, aor. ἔθεινε, θεῖνε, part. θείνᾱς, pass. pres. part. θεινόμενος: *strike.*

θείομεν: see τίθημι.

θεῖος (θεός): *of the gods, god-like, sacred;* of anything belonging or related to, given or sent by, the gods, γένος (the Chimaera), Z 180; ὄνειρος, B 22; also of things consecrated to them or under their protection, χορός, θ 264; κῆρυξ, Δ 192; ἀοιδός, α 336; then of persons, θεῖοι βασιλῆες, δ 691; and even of things excellent in a high degree, ποτόν, β 341; δόμος, δ 43.

θείω: see (1) θέω.—(2) τίθημι.

θέλγω, ipf. θέλγε, iter. θέλγεσκε, fut

θέλξω, aor. ἔθελξα, pass. pres. opt. θέλγοιτο, aor. 3 pl. ἔθελχθεν: *charm, enchant;* Hermes with his magic wand, ἀνδρῶν ὄμματα θέλγει, 'charms' their eyes, 'entrances,' puts them to sleep, Ω 343, ε 47; so Poseidon casts a blindness upon Alcathous, θέλξας ὄσσε φαεινά, N 435; usually in a bad sense, of 'bewitching,' 'beguiling,' νόον, θυμόν, M 255, O 322; ἐπέεσσιν, ψεύδεσσι, δόλῳ, γ 264, Φ 276, 604; of love, pass., σ 612; rarely in good sense, ρ 514, 521.

θελκτήριον (θέλγω): any means of charming or winning, *spell, charm;* attributed to the girdle of Aphrodīte, ἔνθα τέ οἱ θελκτήρια πάντα τέτυκτο, Ξ 215; of songs, θελκτήρια βροτῶν (obj. gen.), α 337; and of the Trojan Horse, a winsome offering to the gods, θ 509.

θέμεθλα and **θεμείλια** (τίθημι), pl.: *foundations, base;* 'roots,' 'bed,' στομάχοιο, ὀφθαλμοῖο, P 47, Ξ 493.

θέμεν(αι): see τίθημι.

θέμις, θέμιστος (τίθημι): old (established) *law, right* by custom or usage; ἣ θέμις ἐστίν, 'as is right'; ἣ θέμις ἀνθρώπων πέλει, 'the old way' of mankind, I 134.—Pl., **θέμιστες,** *ordinances, decrees, prerogatives;* Διός, π 403, cf. A 238; κρίνειν, Π 387; τελεῖν, as 'dues,' 'tribute,' I 156, 298.—Personified, *Themis,* β 68, Υ 4, O 87, 93.

θεμιστεύω (θέμις): *be judge for* or *over, judge;* τινί, λ 569; τινός, ι 114.

θεμόω: only aor., θέμωσε, *caused,* w. inf., ι 486 and 542.

-θεν: a suffix forming an ablatival genitive; of place, Τροίηθεν, οἴκοθεν, ἄλλοθεν, 'from Troy,' 'from home,' 'from elsewhere,' and with prepositions, ἀπὸ Τροίηθεν, ι 38; ἐξ ἁλόθεν, Φ 335; less often of persons, Διόθεν, θεόθεν, 'from Zeus,' 'from a god.'

θέναρ, αρος: *flat of the hand,* E 339†.

θέο: see τίθημι.

θεό-δμητος (δέμω): *god-built,* Θ 519†.

θεο-ειδής, ές (ϝεῖδος): *god-like, beautiful as the gods.*

θεο-είκελος (ϝείκελος): *like the gods, god-like,* of persons.

θεόθεν: *from a god, from God,* π 447†.

Θεοκλύμενος: a seer in Ithaca, ο 256, υ 350.

θεο-προπέω: *prophesy,* only part.

θεο-προπίη and **θεοπρόπιον** (Il.): *prophecy, oracle.*

θεο-πρόπος: one who reveals and interprets the will of the gods, *seer, prophet;* as adj., N 70.

θεός, gen. and dat. pl. θεόφιν: *god* (or *goddess*); of individual divinities, and collectively, *the deity, God,* σὺν θεῷ, ἄνευ θεοῦ, etc. Forms of the pl. are often to be read with synizesis, e. g. θεοῖσιν, ξ 251.

θεουδής (θεός, δϝέος): *god-fearing, pious.* (Od.)

θεραπεύω (θεράπων): *be servant to, serve, defer to,* ipf., ν 265†.

θεράπων, οντος: *attendant, comrade at arms* (esquire, not servant), cf. λ 255, B 110, δ 23.

θερέω: see θέρω.

θερμαίνω, aor. subj. θερμήνῃ: *warm, heat;* pass., *get hot,* ι 376.

θερμός: *warm, hot.*

θέρμω, imp. θέρμετε: = θερμαίνω, pass., Ψ 381.

θέρος, ευς: *warm season, summer* (opp. ὀπώρη, *late summer*), μ 76.

Θερσίλοχος: (1) a Trojan, P 216. —(2) a Paeonian, slain by Achilles, Φ 209.

Θερσίτης: *Thersītes,* the ugliest Greek before Troy, and a brawler (as his name indicates), B 212 ff.

θέρω, pass. pres. inf. θέρεσθαι, aor. ἐθέρην, subj. θερέω, mid. fut. part. θερσόμενος: *warm, be warm, warm oneself;* πυρός, 'by the fire,' ρ 23; 'burn,' πυρός, 'with fire,' Z 331, Λ 667.

θές: see τίθημι.

θέσκελος (θεός): *supernatural,* fig., *wondrous;* ἔργα, λ 374, 610.—Adv., **θέσκελον,** *wonderfully,* Ψ 107.

θεσμός (τίθημι): *site, place,* ψ 296†.

Θέσπεια: a town in Boeotia, B 498†.

θεσπέσιος (θεός, root σεπ, ἔσπετε): *divinely uttered* or *uttering* (θεσπεσίῃ, 'by divine decree,' B 367), *divine;* ἀοιδή, B 600; Σειρῆνες, 'heavenly-singing,' μ 158; βηλός, 'of heaven,' A 591; then of anything *prodigious, vast, wondrous, mighty,* a storm, clamor, panic, etc.—Adv., **θεσπεσίως,** O 637.

θεσπι-δαής, ές (δαίω 1): *prodigiously* or *fiercely blazing,* πῦρ. (Il. and δ 418).

θέσπις, ιος (cf. θεσπέσιος): *inspired, divine;* ἀοιδή, ἀοιδός, α 328, θ 498, ρ 385.

Θεσπρωτοί: the *Thesprotians,* a tribe dwelling about Dodōna in Epīrus, π 427; their king Pheidon, ξ 316. (Od.)

Θεσσαλός: a son of Heracles, father of Pheidippus and Antiphus, B 679†.

Θεστορίδης: *son of Thestor.*—(1) Calchas, the seer, A 69.—(2) Alcmāon, M 394.

Θέστωρ: (1) the father of Calchas.—(2) father of Alcmāon.—(3) son of Enops, slain by Patroclus, Π 401†.

θέσ-φατος (θεός, φημί): *declared* or *decreed by God,* Θ 477, δ 561; *divine* (miraculous), ἀήρ, η 143; as subst., θέσφατον, *decree of heaven, fate, oracle.*

Θέτις: *Thetis,* a Nereid, married to Peleus, and the mother of Achilles, Σ 431 ff., Ω 62, cf. A 502 ff., 397 ff. Epithets, ἁλοσύδνη, ἀργυρόπεζα, ἠύκομος, καλλιπλόκαμος, τανύπεπλος.

θέω, θείω, inf. θείειν, ipf. ἔθεε, θέε, ἔθει, iter. θέεσκον, fut. 2 sing. θεύσεαι, inf. θεύσεσθαι: *run;* often the part. joined to other verbs, ἦλθε θέων, etc.; said of ships, the potter's wheel, Σ 601; a vein, N 547; and otherwise figuratively.

θεώτερος: *divine, for the gods,* i. e. rather than for men, of the *two* entrances (cf. θηλύτερος), πύλαι, ν 111†.

Θῆβαι, ῶν, and **Θήβη**: *Thebes* or *Thebē.*—(1) the city in Boeotia, founded by Cadmus and fortified by Amphīon and Zethus, epithets ἑπτάπυλος, ἐυστέφανος, πολυήρατος.—(2) Egyptian Thebes, on the Nile, called ἑκατόμπυλαι, I 381, δ 126.—(3) a city in the Troad, at the foot of Mt. Placus, the residence of king Eetion, A 366, Z 397.

Θήβᾱσδε: *to Thebes,* Ψ 679.

Θηβαῖος: (1) *a Theban.*—(2) name of the father of Eniopeus, Θ 120.

θήγω, mid. aor. imp. θηξάσθω: *whet, sharpen,* mid., something of one's own, B 382.

θηέομαι (Att. θεάομαι), opt. 2 sing. θηοῖο, ipf. θηεῖτο, ἐθηεύμεθα, θηεῦντο, aor. 2 sing. θηήσαο, opt. θηήσαιο: *gaze at, behold* with admiration or delight; joined with θαμβεῖν, θαυμάζειν, Ψ 728, θ 265.

θήης: see τίθημι.

θηητήρ (θηέομαι): *beholder,* i. e. *fancier;* τόξων, φ 397†.

θήιον: see θέειον.

θήλεας: see θῆλυς.

θηλέω = θάλλω, w. gen. of fulness, ε 73†.

θῆλυς, θήλεια, θῆλυ (also w. two endings): *female;* ἀυτή, i. e. of women's voices, ζ 122; ἐέρση, with the thought of 'nourishing,' ε 467; comp., θηλύτερος, *weaker* (of the two sexes), *weak,* Θ 520, θ 324.

θημών, ωνος: *heap,* ε 368†.

θήν: *doubtless, surely now,* enclitic particle, much like δή or δήπου in prose; combined, ἦ θην, οὔ θην (δή), οὐ μέν θην, ἐπεί θην, καὶ γάρ θην, γ 352, π 91, Φ 568.

θηοῖο: see θηέομαι.

θήρ, θηρός: *wild beast,* ε 473.

θηρευτής (θηρεύω): *hunts(man), hunting*-dog, only with ἀνδράσιν and κύνεσσιν. (Il.)

θηρεύω (θήρ): *hunt,* part., τ 465†.

θήρη (θήρ): *hunting, chase, game.*

θηρητήρ, ῆρος, and **θηρήτωρ,** ορος (θηράω): *hunter;* also as adj., M 170, Φ 252; in φ 397 the better reading is θηητήρ.

θηρίον: *wild animal, beast; μέγα* θηρίον, of a stag, κ 171.

θής, θητός: *hired laborer, day laborer,* pl., δ 644†.

θησαίατο: see θάομαι 1.

θήσατο: see θάομαι 2.

Θησεύς: *Theseus,* national hero of Athens and Attica, A 265.

θῆσθαι: see θάομαι 2.

θητεύω (θής), inf. θητευέμεν, aor. θητεύσαμεν: *be a day laborer, work for hire.*

-θι (cf. Lat. -bi): a suffix denoting the place *in which,* e. g. ἀγρόθι, ἄλλοθι. Of time in ἠῶθι.

θίς, θινός: *heap,* μ 45; then of the sandy shore, *strand.*

Θίσβη: a town in Boeotia, B 502†.

θλάω, aor. ἔθλασε, θλάσσε: *crush, bruise.*

θλίβω: *press, squeeze;* only mid. fut., θλίψεται ὤμους, 'will rub his shoulders,' ρ 221†.

θνήσκω, ipf. θνῆσκον, fut. inf. θανέεσθαι, aor. ἔθανον, θάνον, inf. θανέειν, perf. τέθνηκα, 3 pl. τεθνᾶσι, opt. τεθναίην, imp. τέθναθι, -άτω, inf. τεθνάμεν(αι), part. τεθνηώς, τεθνηκυῖα, τεθνηῶτος and τεθνηότος, dat. τεθνεῶτι: *die, be killed,* perf. *be dead.*

θνητός: *mortal;* subst., θνητοί, opp. ἀθάνατοι.

Θόας: (1) son of Andraemon, king of Pleuron and Calydon in Aetolia, Β 638, Δ 527.—(2) king in Lemnos, son of Dionȳsus and Ariadne, Ξ 230.—(3) a Trojan, slain by Menelāus, Π 311.

Θόη: a Nereid, Σ 40†.

θοινάω: only aor. pass. inf., θοινηθῆναι, *to be entertained* at the feast, δ 36†.

θόλος, οιο: *rotunda,* a building of circular form, with vaulted roof, in the court-yard of Odysseus's palace. (See plate III., *k.*)

θοός (θέω): *swift, quick;* of night, 'swift-descending,' because night in the countries of the Mediterranean follows the setting of the sun more speedily than with us (cf. β 388); θοαὶ νῆσοι, islands 'swiftly flitting by' and sinking in the horizon, ο 299.—Adv., **θοῶς.**

θοόω, aor ἐθόωσα: *make pointed, bring to a point,* ι 327†.

θόρε: see θρώσκω.

θοῦρος and **θοῦρις,** ιδος (θρώσκω): *impetuous, rushing.*

θόωκος: see θῶκος.

Θόων: (1) a Phaeacian, θ 113.—(2) son of Phaenops, a Trojan, slain by Diomed, Ε 152.—(3) a Trojan slain by Odysseus, Λ 422.—(4) a Trojan, comrade of Asius, slain by Antilochus, Μ 140, Ν 545.

Θόωσα: a nymph, the daughter of Phorcys, and mother of Polyphēmus.

Θοώτης: the herald of Menestheus, Μ 342.

Θράσιος: a Paeonian, slain by Achilles, Φ 210.

θράσος = θάρσος, Ξ 416†.

Θρασύδημος: see Θρασύμηλος.

θρασυ-κάρδιος: *stout-hearted.* (Il.)

θρασυ-μέμνων, ονος: *bravely steadfast* (if from μίμνω), epith. of Heracles, Ε 639 and λ 267.

Θρασυμήδης: a son of Nestor, Π 321, Κ 255.

Θρασύμηλος: charioteer of Sarpēdon, Π 463†.

θρασύς, εῖα, ύ: *bold, daring, confident.*

θρέξασκον: see τρέχω.

θρέπτρα (= θρεπτήρια, τρέφω): *return for rearing;* οὐδὲ τοκεῦσιν θρέπτρα φίλοις ἀπέδωκεν, 'nor did he recompense his parents for their tender care' (since his life was cut short), Δ 478 and Ρ 302.

θρέψα: see τρέφω.

Θρηίκιος: *Thracian;* πόντος, the northern part of the Aegēan, Ψ 230; Σάμος, *Samothrace,* Ν 13.

Θρῆιξ, ικος, **Θρῇξ**: *inhabitant of Thrace, Thracian;* allies of the Trojans.

Θρῄκη: *Thrace,* a region of northern Greece, beyond the Penēus, traversed by the river Axius, and inhabited by the Ciconians and Paeonians, Β 845, Υ 485, Λ 222.—**Θρῄκηθεν,** *from Thrace.*—**Θρῄκηνδε**: *to Thrace.*

θρηνέω: *chant* or *sing a dirge,* ω 61; ἀοιδήν, 'were raising the funeral song,' Ω 722.

θρῆνος: *dirge,* Ω 721.

θρῆνυς, υος: *footstool,* either as in cut No. 105, from an Assyrian original, attached to the chair, or as usual standing free; also for the feet of rowers, or of the helmsman, in a ship, Ο 729.

Θρῇξ: see Θρῆιξ.

θριγκός: *coping, cornice,* pl., *battlements,* ρ 267. (Od.)

θριγκόω: only aor. ἐθρίγκωσεν, *crowned the top* of the wall, to make it impassable, with bramble-bushes, ξ 10†.

Θρινακίη: a fabulous island, the pasture of the kine of Helius, μ 135; identified by the ancients with Sicily.

θρίξ, τριχός, dat. pl. θριξί: *hair, hairs,* of animals as well as men; hence of wool, Γ 273; and bristles, Τ 254.

θρόνον, pl. **θρόνα**: *flowers,* in woven work, Χ 441†.

Θρόνιον: a town of the Locrians, Β 533†.

θρόνος: *arm-chair,* with high back and foot-stool; cushions were laid upon the seat, and over both seat and back rugs were spread. (See cut, under ἄμπυξ. Cf. also Nos. 105, 106, where two chairs, from Assyrian and Greek originals, are represented.)

θρόος: *speech, tongue*, Δ 437†.

θρῡλίσσω, aor. pass. θρῡλίχθη: *crush*, Ψ 396†.

θρύον: *rush*, collectively, *rushes*, Φ 351†.

Θρύον and **Θρυόεσσα** ('Rushton'): a town in Elis, on the Alphēus, Β 592, Λ 711.

θρώσκω, ipf. θρῶσκον, aor. ἔθορον, θόρον, part. θορών: *spring, leap up*, freq. in hostile sense with ἐπί or ἐν, Θ 252, Ε 161; also fig., of arrows, plants, lots, etc.

θρωσμός (θρώσκω): πεδίοιο, *rise* or *elevation* of the plain of the Scamander, Κ 160. (Il.)

θυγάτηρ, gen. θῠγατέρος and θυγατρός: *daughter*.

θυέεσσιν: see θύος.

θύελλα (θύω): *blast, gust, squall*; πυρὸς ὀλοοῖο, from volcanic islands, μ 68, 202, 219; figuratively assumed as the agency causing the sudden disappearance of lost persons (cf. ἅρπυια), υ 63, δ 515.

Θυέστης: *Thyestes*, the brother of Atreus, and father of Aegisthus, δ 517, Β 107.

Θυεστιάδης: *son of Thyestes*, Aegisthus, δ 518.

θυήεις (θύος): *smoking with incense, fragrant*.

θυηλή (θύω): the part of the victim to be burned, *sacrificial offering*, pl., Ι 220†.

θῡμ-αλγής, ες (ἄλγος): *heart-grieving, distressing*.

θῡμ-ᾱρής, ές: *pleasing to the heart, dear, welcome*.

Θυμβραῖος: a Trojan, slain by Diomed, Λ 320†.

Θύμβρη: a region or a plain bordering on the Thymbrius, a branch of the Scamander, Κ 430†.

θυμ-ηγερέω (ἀγείρω): *collect* or *rally the life* in one, *recover*, η 283†.

θῡμ-ηδής, ές (ἦδος): *delighting the heart, agreeable*, π 389†.

θυμ-ηρής, ές = θῡμᾱρής, 'to suit the feelings,' κ 362†.

θυμο-βόρος (βιβρώσκω): *heart-gnawing*, ἔρις. (Il.)

θῡμο-δακής, ές (δάκνω): *heart-stinging, cutting*, θ 185†.

Θυμοίτης: a Trojan chief, Γ 146†.

θῡμο-λέων, οντος: *lion-hearted*, Ε 639.

θῡμο-ραϊστής, ες (ῥαίω): *life-destroying*. (Il.)

θῡμός (θύω): *heart, soul, life*, the seat of emotion, reason, and of the vital principle itself; an extremely common and highly characteristic word in Homer, often employed where no equivalent is called for in modern speech. Of life, θῡμὸν ἀφελέσθαι, ὀλέσαι, θῡμὸν ἀποπνείειν, ἐγείρειν, θῡμὸν ἀπὸ μελέων δῦναι δόμον Ἄιδος εἴσω, Η 131; emotion, χόλος ἔμπεσε θῡμῷ, θῡμὸν ὀρίνειν, ἐκ θῡμοῦ φιλέειν, θῡμῷ χαίρειν, ἀπὸ θῡμοῦ | μᾶλλον ἐμοὶ ἔσεαι, 'further from my heart,' Α 562; desire, appetite, πλήσασθαι, τέρπειν θῡμόν, θῡμὸς ἀνώγει, κέλεται, κατὰ θῡμόν, 'to one's wish,' Α 136; thoughts, disposition, θῡμὸν πείθειν, φράζεσθαι θῡμῷ, ἕνα θῡμὸν ἔχειν, ἐν θυμῷ βαλέσθαι, 'lay to heart'; κατὰ φρένα καὶ κατὰ θῡμόν, 'in mind and soul.'

θυμο-φθόρος (φθείρω): *life-destroying, deadly*; σήματα, 'of fatal import,' Ζ 169; φάρμακα, β 329; 'inhuman,' τ 323; 'heart-wasting,' ἄχος, κάματος, δ 716, κ 363.

θύνω (θύω), ipf. θῦνον: *rush along, charge*. (Il. and ω 449.)

θυόεις, εν (θύος): *odorous*, Ο 153†.

θύον: a tree with fragrant wood, *arbor-vitae*, ε 60†.

θύος, εος: pl., *burnt-offerings*.

θυο-σκόος: *prophet*, drawing omens from the smoke of burnt-offerings, Ω 221, φ 145.

θυόω (θύος) = θύω, only pass. perf. part., τεθυωμένον, *fragrant*, Ξ 172†.

θύραζε: *to the door, forth, out*, Ε 694, ε 410.

θυρα-ωρός (root Ϝορ, ὁράω): *door-watching*, of watch-dogs, Χ 69†.

θυρεός (θύρη): *door-stone*, placed by Polyphēmus at the mouth of his den, ι 240.

θύρετρα, pl.: *wings of a door, door*, Β 415; αὐλῆς, near to the στόμα λαύρης, χ 137 (see plate III., ο).

θύρη: *door, gate, folding-doors, entrance*, ν 370; ἐπὶ θύρῃσι, 'at the court' (cf. 'Sublime Porte,' of the Sultan, and Xenophon's *βασιλέως θύραι*).

θύρηθι: *out of doors*, out of the sea, ξ 352 (cf. *θύραζε*, ε 410).

θύρηφι = *θύρηθι*.

θυσανόεις, εσσα (*θύσανος*): *tasselled, many-tasselled*, of the aegis. (Il.)

θύσανος: pl., *tufts, tassels, fringe*. (Il.)

θύσθλα (*θύω*), pl.: the *thyrsi*, wands and other sacred implements used in the worship of Dionȳsus, Z 134†. (See cuts.)

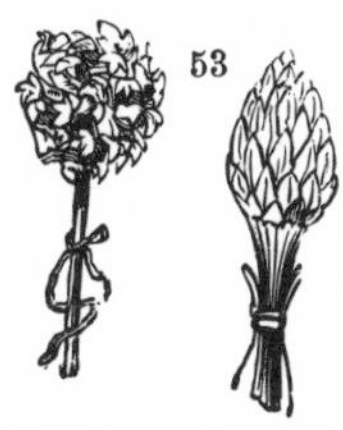

53

θῦω: *rage;* of men, and of winds, waves, torrents, 'surging,' Φ 234; *δάπεδον δ' ἅπαν αἵματι θῦεν*, 'reeked,' 'swam' with blood, λ 420.

θύω, part. *θύοντα*, but ipf. *θῦε*, aor. *ἔθῡσα*: *offer* as *burnt* offering, ξ 446, ο 260. (See cut.)

54

θυ-ώδης (*θύος*): *fragrant*. (Od.)

θωή (*τίθημι*): *penalty*, β 192, N 669.

θῶκος and **θόωκος** (Att. *θᾶκος*) *seat*, β 14; *assembly*, β 26.—**θῶκόνδε,** *to the assembly*.

Θῶν: *Thon*, a noble Egyptian, δ 228†.

θωρηκτής (*θωρήσσω*): *cuirassed, well-cuirassed*. (Il.)

θώρηξ, ηκος: *breast-plate, cuirass, corselet*, Λ 19 ff. It was usually of bronze, consisting of two plates, *γύαλα*. (See adjacent cut, also cut No. 33.) The cuirass fitted closely to the body, and was cut square off at the waist; the shoulder-pieces (see cut) were drawn down by small

55

chains and fastened to buttons in front; the metal plates were united by clasps (see cut No. 19); the upper part of the thighs was protected by the *μίτρη*, worn over the apron, *ζῶμα*, of leather or felt, and by its metal flaps, *πτέρυγες* (Nos. 12, 33, 79), or plates (Nos. 3 and 33); over the *θώρηξ, μίτρη*, and *ζῶμα* was bound the *ζωστήρ* (No. 3), below which projected the lower end of the *χιτών* (Nos. 3, 19, 33; cf. *λινοθώρηξ* and *χιτών*).

θωρήσσω, aor. *θώρηξε*, subj. *θωρήξομεν*, mid. fut. *θωρήξομαι*, pass. ipf. 3 du. *θωρήσσεσθον*, aor. *θωρήχθησαν*: *arm with cuirass*, mid., *arm oneself* for battle.

θώς, *θωός*: *jackal*. (Il.)

I.

ἴα, ἰῆς: see *ἴος*.

ἰά: see *ἰός*.

ἰαίνω, aor. *ἴηνα*, pass. *ἰάνθη* (ῑ when with augment): *warm, soften* by warming, μ 175; met., *warm, melt, move* the heart to compassion, cheer, etc., ο 379; often thus in pass., *θῡμός, κῆρ*, Ψ 598, χ 59; *μέτωπον ἰάνθη*, 'brightened,' Ο 103; also w. acc. of specification, *θῡμόν, φρένας*, ψ 47, ω 382; w. dat., τ 537.

Ἴαιρα: a Nereid, Σ 42†.

ἰάλλω, aor. *ἴηλα*, inf. *ἰῆλαι*: *send*, mostly implying quick motion toward some definite point; freq. *ἐπ' ὀνείατα χεῖρας ἰάλλειν*, 'apply' the hands to viands, Ι 91, etc.; *ἑτάροις ἐπὶ* (adv.) *χεῖρας ἴαλλεν*, 'flung out' his arms to them, ι 288; *ὀιστὸν ἀπὸ νευρῆφιν ἴαλλεν* | *Ἕκτορος ἀντικρύ*, Θ 300; *ἐπὶ* (adv.) *δεσμὸν ἴηλον*, 'whip' on a knot, θ 443, cf. 497; met., *ἀτῑμίῃσιν ἰάλλειν*, 'assail' as with missiles, ν 142.

Ἰάλμενος: a son of Ares, leader of Boeotians, Β 512, Ι 82.

Ἰαμενός: a Trojan chief, Μ 139†.

Ἰάνασσα, Ἰάνειρα: Nereids, Σ 47†.

ἰάνθη: see *ἰαίνω*.

ἰάομαι, ipf. *ἰᾶτο*, fut. *ἰήσεται*, aor. *ἰησάμην*: *heal, cure*, Μ 2, ι 525.

Ἰάονες: *Ionians*, Ν 685†.

Ἰάπετος: a Titan, Θ 479†.

ἰάπτω: only *μὴ κλαίουσα κατὰ* (adv.) *χρόα καλὸν ἰάπτῃ(ς)*, *harm* by smiting, β 376, δ 749.

Ἰάρδανος: the river *Iardanus*.—(1) in Crete, γ 292.—(2) in Elis, near Pheiae, Η 135.

ἴᾶσι: see *εἶμι*.

Ἰασίδης: *son of Iasus*.—(1) Amphīon, λ 283.—(2) Dmetor, ρ 443.

Ἰασίων: a mortal beloved by Demeter, and slain by the thunderbolt of Zeus, ε 125†.

Ἴασον Ἄργος: *Iasian* Argos, meaning the Peloponnēsus, the origin of the epithet being unknown, σ 246†.

Ἴασος: (1) son of Sphelus, a leader of the Athenians, slain by Aenēas, Ο 332.—(2) the father of Amphīon.—(3) the father of Dmetor.

ἰαύω (cf. *ἄϝεσα*), ipf. *ἴαυον*, iter. *ἰαύεσκον*, aor. inf. *ἰαῦσαι*: *sleep, rest, lie*; *πολλᾶς μὲν ἀύπνους νύκτας ἴαυον*, Ι 325, 470, τ 340.

ἰαχή (*ϝιαχή*): loud, sharp *cry, shriek*; of men in battle, Δ 456; the shades in the nether world, λ 43; hunters, Ο 275.

ἰάχω (*ϝιάχω*), ipf. *ἴαχον* (ῑ when with augment): *cry* loud and sharply, *shriek, scream*; of applause, the cry of battle, of wounded men, Ψ 766, Δ 506, Ε 343, etc.; of Circe, threatened with Odysseus's sword, κ 323; of a child, Ζ 468; transferred to inanimate objects, the 'twanging' of the bow-string, Δ 125; the 'blare' of the trumpet, Σ 219; 'hissing' of hot iron in water, ι 392; 'crackling' of fire, Ψ 216; but the Eng. words do not involve a personification like the Greek.

Ἰαωλκός: *Iolcus*, a town in Thessaly on the Pagasaean gulf, λ 256, Β 712.

ἰγνύη (*γόνυ*): *hollow of the knee*, Ν 212†.

Ἰδαῖος: *of Mt. Ida, Idaean*, epith. of the mountains belonging to the range, Θ 170, Υ 189; also of Zeus, whose grove and altar were upon Gargaron, Π 605, Ω 291.

Ἰδαιος: *Idaeus*.—(1) a herald of the Trojans, charioteer to Priam.—(2) a Trojan, the son of Dares, Ε 11.

ἰδέ = *ἠδέ, and*.

ἴδε, ἰδέειν, ἴδεσκε: see *εἴδω* (I.).

ἰδέω: see *εἴδω* (II.).

Ἴδη: *Ida*, a mountain range, rich in springs, ravines, forest, and game, extending from Phrygia, through Mysia, toward the Hellespont, and subsiding into the plain near Troy, Β 821, Λ 183; its summit, *Γάργαρον*.—**Ἴδηθεν**, *from Ida*.

ἴδηαι: see *εἴδω* (I.).

Ἴδης: a famous archer, the father of Cleopatra, Ι 558†.

ἴδιος: *private*, opp. *δήμιος*, γ 82 and δ 314.

ἰδίω = *ἱδρόω*, only ipf., υ 204†.

ἴδμεν(αι): see *εἴδω* (II.).

ἰδνόω, pass. aor. ἰδνώθη, part. -θείς: *bend* backward, *double up*, pass. as mid., β 266, θ 375.

ἰδοίατο: see εἴδω (I.).

Ἰδομενεύς: *Idomeneus*, son of Deucalion, grandson of Minos, king in Crete, Δ 265, M 117, B 645; his son Arsilochus, ν 259; comrade-at-arms, Meriones, Ψ 113.

ἰδρείη (ϝιδρ.): *knowledge, skill.* (Il.)

ἴδρις (ϝιδρ.): *knowing, skilled, skilful*, w. inf., η 108. (Od.)

ἰδρόω (ἱδρώς), part. ἱδρώοντα, etc., fem. pl. ἱδρῶσαι, fut. ἱδρώσει, aor. ἵδρωσα: *sweat.*

ἱδρύω (root ἑδ), aor. ἵδρῡσα, pass. ἱδρύνθην: *cause* or *bid to be seated*, B 191; pass., *take seats, be seated*, Γ 78.

ἱδρώς, dat. -ῷ, acc. -ῶ (σϝιδρ.): *sweat.*

ἰδυῖα: see εἴδω (II.).

ἴδω, ἴδωμι: see εἴδω (I.).

ἴε, ἴεν: see εἶμι.

ἵει: see ἵημι.

ἰείη: see εἶμι.

ἵεμαι: see ἵημι.

ἵενται, ἵεσθε: more correct reading, ἵενται, ἵεσθε, see ἵημι.

ἱερεύς, ἱρεύς, ῆος: *priest*, in charge of the sacrifices to some special god, also *soothsayer*, A 23.

ἱερεύω, ἱρεύω, ipf. iter. ἱρεύεσκον, fut. inf. ἱερεύσειν, aor. ἱέρευσα, pass. plup. ἱέρευτο, mid. aor. inf. ἱρεύσασθαι: *sacrifice*, esp. by killing the victim, *offer*, then, in general, *slaughter*, Z 174; ξείνῳ, 'in honor of the guest,' ξ 414; mid., subjective, τ 198.

ἱερήιον: *victim*, animal for sacrifice or slaughter, ξ 94.

ἱερόν, ἱρόν, neut. of ἱερός as subst.: *sacrifice, victim*, α 61, A 147.

ἱερός, ἱρός: (1) *strong, powerful;* ἴς, μένος, φυλάκων τέλος, πυλαωροί, στρατός, β 409, η 167, K 56, Ω 681, ω 81; ἰχθύς, 'lively,' Π 407.—(2) *sacred, hallowed.*

ἱζάνω (ἵζω): *sit;* trans., *cause* or *bid to be seated*, Ψ 258.

ἵζω (root ἑδ), ipf. ἵζον, iter. ἵζεσκε: *take a seat, sit down, sit still, rest;* βουλήν, 'hold a council,' 'session,' B 53; mid., like act., of an ambuscade, Σ 522.

ἴηλα, ἰῆλαι: see ἰάλλω.

Ἰηλῡσός: a town in Rhodes, B 656†.

ἵημι, ἵησι, 3 pl. ἱεῖσι, inf. ἱέμεναι, part. ἱέντες, ἱεῖσαι, imp. ἵει, ipf. ἵει, 3 pl. ἵεν, fut. ἥσω, aor. ἧκα, ἕηκα, 3 pl. ἧκαν and ἕσαν, subj. ἥσιν, opt. εἵην, inf. εἷναι, mid. pres. ἵεται, imp. ἵεσθε, part. ἱέμενος, ipf. ἵετο, ἵεντο, aor. 3 pl. ἕντο: *let go*, i. e. set in motion of any sort.—I. act., *send*, ἄγγελόν τινι, Σ 182; *put* to anything, as harness, Π 152; *throw, let fly*, μετὰ (adv.) δ' ἰὸν ἕηκεν, 'in among them,' A 48; so 'let fall' anything, as tears, a sword from the hand, 'let down' the hair, 'let on' water, M 25, and of the river itself 'rolling' its waters (thus, intrans., λ 239, η 130); metaph., of 'dismissing,' i. e. by satisfying, a desire, ἔρον, N 638; 'inspiring' one with force, E 125; 'laying' misfortune on one, K 71. The applications of the word are very numerous, but always distinct if the fundamental signification be held in mind. The ground-meaning, as may be seen from the examples, usually gets a specific turn from the context, esp. by means of adverbs (ἐν, ἐξ, κατά, μετά, etc.).—II. mid., *set oneself in motion* at something (τινός), ἱέμενος ποταμοῖο ῥοάων, 'giving thyself a direction' toward Oceanus, κ 529; so 'press on,' 'hasten,' N 707, M 274; met., with and without θῡμῷ, 'strive after' (τινός), 'be eager,' Ψ 371; θῡμός, Θ 301; freq. phrase, ἐπεὶ πόσιος καὶ ἐδητύος ἐξ ἔρον ἕντο, had dismissed 'from themselves,' A 469, α 150.

ἰήνατε: see ἰαίνω.

ἰήσασθε: see ἰάομαι.

ἴῃσι: see εἶμι.

Ἰησονίδης: *son of Iēson* (Jason), Euneus, H 468, 471, Ψ 747.

Ἰήσων: *Iēson* (Jason), the leader of the Argonauts, μ 72.

ἰητήρ, ῆρος, = ἰητρός.

ἰητρός (ἰάομαι): *healer, surgeon, physician;* with ἀνήρ, Λ 514.

ἰθαι-γένης (ἰθύς): *born in lawful wedlock, legitimate*, ξ 203†.

Ἰθαιμένης: a Lycian, Π 586†.

Ἰθάκη *Ithaca.*—(1) the native island of Odysseus, with **Mts.** Neritus, Neius, and Corax, and the harbor Reithrum. Epithets, ἀμφίαλος, εὐδείελος, ἐυκτιμένη, κραναή, παιπαλόεσσα, τρηχεῖα.—(2) the city, at the foot of **Mt.** Neius, γ 81, cf. π 322. —**Ἰθάκηνδε,** *to Ithaca.* —**Ἰθακήσιος**: *inhabitant of Ithaca, Ithacan.*

῎Ιθακος: the eponymous hero of the island of Ithaca, ρ 207†.

ἴθι, imp. of εἶμι: *come! go!* employed as an interjection, freq. with ἄγε.

ἴθμα, ατος: *step, gait,* pl., E 778†.

ἰθύντατα: see ἰθύς.

ἰθύνω (ἰθύς), aor. ἴθῡνα, subj. ἰθύνομεν. *make straight, straighten,* ἐπὶ στάθμην, 'to the line,' ε 245; pass., ἵππω δ' ἰθυνθήτην, 'placed themselves in line' with the pole of the chariot, Π 475; *guide* a ship, chariot, etc., and, of missiles, *aim, direct,* E 290, P 632, mid., 'his arrow,' χ 8.

ἰθυ-πτίων, ωνος (πέτομαι): *straight-flying,* μελίη, Φ 169†.

ἰθύς, εῖα, ύ: *straight;* τέτραπτο πρὸς ἰθύ οἱ, 'straight opposite him,' Ξ 403; usually metaph., *straight, right, just,* Ψ 580; sup., **ἰθύντατα,** *most fairly,* Σ 508.—As adv., **ἰθύς, ἰθύ,** *straight at, straight for,* τινός, E 849; also with prepositions, and abs., Υ 99, γ 10; ἰθὺς φέρειν, μάχεσθαι, φρονεῖν, 'turn the mind straight on,' 'be bent on battle,' N 135, cf. Λ 95.

ἰθύς, ύος: *straight course,* ἀν' ἰθύν, 'straight up,' 'straight on,' Φ 303, θ 377; hence 'attack,' 'tendency,' 'disposition,' Z 69, δ 434, π 304.

ἰθύω, aor. ἴθῡσα: *go straight forward, advance, attack,* of warriors, a lion, M 48; w. gen., **νεός,** O 693; w. inf., 'strive,' λ 591.

Ἰθώμη: a town in Thessaly, B 729†.

ἱκάνω (ἵκω), mid. ἱκάνομαι: *come to, arrive at, reach,* w. acc. of person or thing attained to, less often with prep., A 431; freq. of supplication, γούναθ' ἱκάνω, ε 449; met., 'come upon,' 'come home to,' ὕπνος, θέσφατα, K 96, ι 507, etc. Often with perf. signif., 'am come to,' I 197, ζ 119.

Ἰκάριος: *Icarius,* the brother of Tyndareus, and father of Penelope, α 276, 329, δ 797.

Ἰκάριος πόντος: the *Icarian* Sea, S.W. of Asia Minor, B 145†.

ἴκελος (ϝικ.), *like, resembling.*

Ἱκετᾱονίδης: *son of Hicetāon,* Melanippus, O 546†.

Ἱκετάων: (1) a son of Laomedon, and brother of Priam, Γ 147, Υ 238.—(2) the father of Melanippus, O 576.

ἱκετεύω (ἱκέτης), aor. ἱκέτευσα: *approach as suppliant, supplicate,* **τινά,** also w. praep. (Od. and Π 574).

ἱκέτης (ἵκω): *suppliant,* for protection of any sort, but esp. one in search of purification from homicide (cf. Tlepolemus, Lycophron, Patroclus), ι 269, Φ 75.

ἱκετήσιος: *of suppliants, protector of suppliants,* epith. of Zeus, ν 213†.

ἵκηαι: see ἱκνέομαι.

Ἰκμάλιος a joiner in Ithaca, τ 57†.

ἰκμάς, άδος: *moisture,* P 392†.

ἴκμενος: *fair* wind (οὖρος), a wind 'that follows fast' (secundus). (Od.)

ἱκνέομαι (ἵκω), part. ἱκνεύμεναι, ipf. ἱκνεύμεσθα, fut. ἵξομαι, aor. ἱκόμην, 2 sing. ἶκευ (ῑ when with augment): *come to, arrive at, reach,* w. acc., also with praep.; 'return,' when the context gives this sense, ψ 151; esp. 'approach as suppliant,' 'supplicate,' Ξ 260, X 123, ι 267; met., ποθή, κάματος, σέβας, τί σε φρένας ἵκετο πένθος; A 362.

ἴκρια, ἰκριόφιν, pl.: *deck-beams, deck,* which in the Homeric ship was partial, only fore and aft (see plate IV., at end of volume); also *ribs* of a ship. (See cut No. 32.)

ἵκω, subj. ἵκωμι, ipf. ἶκε, aor. **ἶξον:** *come (to), reach;* ἵκω is the stem-form answering to ἱκάνω and ἱκνέομαι, and has the same applications and constructions as those verbs; **πινυτὴ φρένας** ἵκει, 'informs,' υ 228.

ἰλαδόν (ϝίλη): adv., *in troops,* B 93†.

ἵλᾱος: *appeased,* hence *propitious, gracious, kind.* (Il.)

ἱλάσκομαι and **ἱλάομαι** (B 550), ipf. ἱλάσκοντο, aor. subj. (or fut.) ἱλάσσομαι, ἱλασόμεσθα, part. ἱλασσάμενοι: *reconcile to oneself, appease, propitiate.*

Ἰλήιος (ϝῑλ.): *of Ilus,* **πεδίον,** so named, according to the scholiast, from the tomb of Ilus, Φ 558†.

ἵλημι, imp. ἵληθι, perf. subj. ἱλήκῃσι, opt. ἱλήκοι: *be propitious, gracious,* γ 380. (Od.)

Ἰλιόθεν (ϝῑλ.): *from Ilium.*

Ἰλιόθι (ϝῑλ.): always with **πρό,** *before Ilium.*

Ἴλιος (ϝίλιος) and Ἴλιον (O 71): *Ilium,* a name for Troy derived from that of its founder Ilus; epithets, λιπεινή, αἰπύ, ἐρατεινή, εὐτείχεος, ἠνεμόεσσα, ἱερή, ὀφρυόεσσα. In wider signification, for the region about Troy, Α 71, τ 182. In Ο 66, Φ 104, Χ 6, the true form of the gen. is Ἰλίοο, as the scansion shows (cf. Αἴολος).

²Ἰλιόφι = ²Ἰλίου, Φ 295.

ἰλλάς, άδος (εἴλω): pl., *twisted cords,* Ν 572†.

Ἶλος: *Ilus.*—(1) son of Tros, and father of Laomedon, Λ 166, Υ 232; his tomb, Κ 415, Λ 372.—(2) son of Mermeros of Ephyra, α 259.

ἰλύς, ὕος: *mud, slime,* Φ 318†.

ἱμάς, αντος: leather *strap* or *thong.*—(1) in connection with the chariot, (a) *straps* in which the chariot-box was hung, or perhaps more likely the network of plaited straps enclosing the body of the chariot, Ε 727; (b) the *reins,* Ψ 324, 363; (c) the *halter,* Θ 544.—(2) the *chin-strap* of a helmet, Γ 371.—(3) the *cestus* of boxers, see πυγμάχοι.—(4) the *leash* or *latch-string* by which doors were fastened. See adjacent cut, in four divisions:

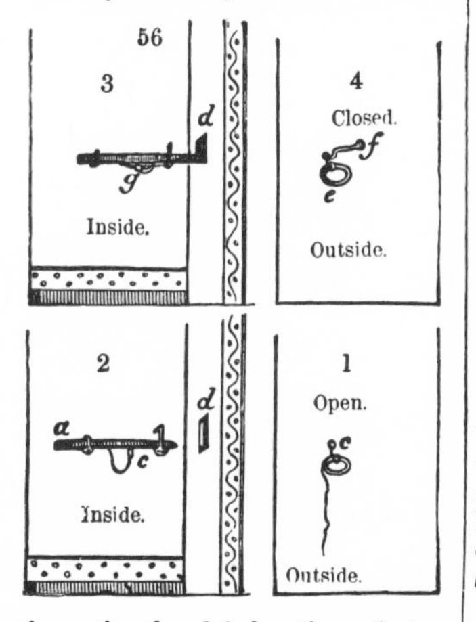

above, the closed, below the unfastened door; on the left, as seen from the inner side, on the right as seen from the outside. To close the door from the outside, the string, hanging loosely in fig. 1, was pulled until it drew the bolt from the position of fig. 2 to that of fig. 3, when it was made fast by a knot to the ring, κορώνη, *e*, fig. 4. To open from the outside, the string was first untied, and then the κληΐς, not unlike a hook (fig. 4, *f*), was introduced through the key-hole, *c*, and by means of a crook (*g*, fig. 3) at the end of it the bolt was pushed back from the position of fig. 3 to that of fig. 2, and the door opened, α 442.—(5) for a *bed-cord,* ψ 201.—(6) the magic *girdle* of Aphrodīte, Ξ 214, 219.—(7) a *thong to make a drill revolve,* ι 385. (See cut No. 121.)

ἱμάσθλη: *lash, whip.*

ἱμάσσω, aor. ἵμασε, subj. ἱμάσσω: *lash, scourge, beat,* Ε 589, Β 782, Ο 17.

Ἰμβρασίδης: *son of Imbrasus,* Piroüs, Δ 520†.

Ἴμβριος: (1) *inhabitant of Imbros, Imbrian,* Φ 43.—(2) the son of Mentor, son-in-law of Priam, slain by Teucer, Ν 171, 197.

Ἴμβρος: *Imbros,* an island on the coast of Thrace, with capital city of the same name, Ξ 281, Ν 33.

ἱμείρω (ἵμερος), mid. ἱμείρεται, ἱμειρόμενος, aor. opt. ἱμείραιτο, subj. ἱμείρεται: *long for, yearn for,* τινός, and w. inf., κ 431, Ξ 163.

ἴμεν(αι): see εἶμι.

ἱμερόεις, εσσα, εν (ἵμερος): *passionate, fond, lovely;* γόος, ἔργα γάμοιο, ἀοιδή, κ 398, Ε 429, α 421.—Adv., **ἱμερόεν** κιθάριζε, *charmingly,* Σ 570.

ἵμερος: *longing, passion, love;* freq. w. obj. gen.; w. two genitives, πατρὸς ἵμερος γόοιο, 'yearning after tears, to weep for his father,' Ω 507, δ 113.

ἱμερτός (ἱμείρω): *lovely,* Β 751†.

ἴμμεναι: see εἶμι.

ἵνα: (1) adv., *where;* this meaning being the primary one, is to be assumed in preference to signif. (2), when the sense admits, e. g. Ω 382. Apparently demonstrative, *there,* in Κ 127.—(2) conj., *in order that, that;* rarely with κέ, μ 156.

ἰνδάλλομαι (root Ϝιδ): *be seen, appear,* w. part., Ρ 213; ὥς μοι ἰνδάλλεται ἦτορ, impers., 'as floats before me in recollection' (ἦτορ like κατὰ θυμόν), τ 224.

ἶνεσι: see ἴς.

ἰνίον (Ϝῖν.): bone of the *back of the head.* (Il.)

Ἰνώ: *Ino*, see Λευκοθέᾱ.

ἴξαλος: doubtful word, *spry*, epith. of the wild goat, Δ 105†.

Ἰξῑόνιος: ἄλοχος Ἰξιονίη, wife *of Ixīon*, Ξ 317†.

ἶξον: see ἵκω.

ἰξύς, dat. ἰξυῖ: *waist*. (Od.)

ἰο-δνεφής, ές (ϝίον, δνόφος): *violet-dark*, *dark-hued*, εἶρος. (Od.)

ἰο-δόκος (ἰός, δέχομαι): *arrow-receiving*, quiver.

ἰο-ειδής, ές (ϝίον, ϝεῖδος): *violet-colored*, *deep blue*, epith. of the sea.

ἰόεις, εσσα (ϝίον) = ἰοειδής, of iron, Ψ 850†.

ἰό-μωρος (ϝιομ.): doubtful word, a disparaging epithet applied to the Greeks, Ἀργεῖοι ἰόμωροι, *boasters*. (Il.)

ἴον (ϝίον): collectively, *violets*, ε 72†.

ἰονθάς, άδος (ϝιονθ.): *shaggy*, ξ 50†.

ἰός, pl. ἰοί (ἰά, Υ 68): *arrow*.

ἴος, ἴα, ἴον (= εἷς, μία, ἕν), gen. ἰῆς, dat. ἰῷ, ἰῇ: *one;* as subst. τὴν ἴαν, 'one portion.' (Il. and ξ 435.)

ἰότης, ητος: *will*, mostly θεῶν ἰότητι, η 214, etc.; μνηστήρων ἰότητι, 'according to their wish,' σ 234.

ἴουλος (οὖλος): *first growth of beard*, *down*, λ 319†.

ἰο-χέαιρα (χέω): *pouring arrows*, *archeress*, epith. of Artemis, both as adj. and subst.

ἱππάζομαι: *drive* one's horses, Ψ 426†.

Ἱππασίδης: *son of Hippasus*.—(1) Apisāon, P 348.—(2) Hypsēnor, N 411.—(3) Charops, Λ 426.—(4) Socus, Λ 431.

ἵππειος: *of horses*, *horse-;* λόφος, *horse-hair* plume.

ἱππεύς, ῆος, pl. ἱππῆες: *chariot-man*, whether as warrior fighting from the chariot, or as competitor in a chariot-race, Δ 297, Ψ 262.

ἱππ-ηλάσιος (ἐλαύνω): *for driving chariots;* ἱππηλασίη ὁδός, H 340 and 439.

ἱππ-ηλάτα (ἐλαύνω), for -άτης: *driver of steeds*, *chariot-fighter*, *knight*.

ἱππ-ήλατος: *passable with chariots*, *adapted to driving horses*. (Od.)

Ἱππ-ημολγοί (ἀμέλγω): the *Hippemolgi*, 'mare-milkers,' a Scythian tribe, N 5.

ἱππιο-χαίτης (χαίτη): *of horse-hair;* λόφος, Z 469†.

ἱππιο-χάρμης (χάρμη): *fighter from a chariot*, Ω 257, λ 259.

ἱππό-βοτος (βόσκω): *horse-nourishing*, *horse-breeding*, esp. as epith. of Argos, B 287.

Ἱπποδάμᾱς: a Trojan, slain by Achilles, Υ 401.

Ἱπποδάμεια: *Hippodamīa*.—(1) a daughter of Anchīses, N 429.—(2) an attendant of Penelope, σ 182.—(3) the wife of Pirithoüs, B 742.

ἱππό-δαμος (δαμάζω): *horse-taming*, epith. of the Trojans, and of individual heroes. (Il. and γ 17, 181.)

Ἱππόδαμος: a Trojan, slain by Odysseus, Λ 335†.

ἱππο-δάσεια (δασύς, εῖα): *with thick horse-hair* plume, epith. of the helmet. (Il. and χ 111, 145.)

ἱππό-δρομος: *course for chariots*, Ψ 330.

ἱππόθεν: *from the* (wooden) *horse*, θ 515, λ 531.

Ἱππόθοος: (1) a son of Priam, Ω 251.—(2) a leader of the Pelasgians, slain by Ajax, P 289.

ἱππο-κέλευθος: *making way with the chariot*, *swift-driving*, epith. of Patroclus. (Il.)

ἱππό-κομος (κόμη): *decked with horse-hair*.

ἱππο-κορυστής (κορύσσω): *chariot-equipped*, *chariot-fighter*, epith. of the Maeonians and Paeonians, and of individual heroes, B 1, Ω 677.

Ἱπποκόων: a cousin of Rhesus, K 518†.

Ἱππόλοχος: (1) son of Antimachus, slain by Agamemnon, Λ 122.—(2) a Lycian, son of Bellerophon, the father of Glaucus, Z 206.

ἱππό-μαχος: *fighting from horses* (chariots), K 431†.

Ἱππόμαχος: a Trojan, the son of Antimachus, slain by Leonteus, M 189†.

Ἱππόνοος: a Greek, slain by Hector, Λ 303†.

ἱππό-πολος (πολεύω): *horse-managing*, *horse-training*, Thracians, N 4 and Ξ 227.

ἵππος: *horse* or *mare;* ἄρσενες ἵπποι, 'stallions,' ν 81; θήλεες ἵπποι, ἵπποι θήλειαι, E 269, Λ 681; the Homeric Greeks did not ride horseback, but employed chariots; hence **ἵπποι**, oftener **ἵππω,** *span, chariot,* alone or w. ἅρμα, M 120; freq. ἵπποισιν καὶ ὄχεσφιν, M 114, 119; ἐξ or ἀφ' ἵππων ἀποβῆναι, Γ 265, E 13; of chariotmen as opposed to infantry, ξ 267, B 554, Π 167, Σ 153.

ἱπποσύνη: *horsemanship,* i. e. chariot-fighting. (Il. and ω 40.)

ἱππότα, for -ότης: *horseman, knight,* esp. as epith. of Nestor, B 336, 628.

Ἱπποτάδης: *son of Hippotes,* Aeolus, κ 36†.

Ἱπποτίων: an Ascanian, slain by Meriones, N 792, Ξ 514.

ἵππ-ουρις, ιος (οὐρά): *with horsetail* plume, epith. of the helmet. (Il. and χ 124.)

ἵπτομαι, fut. ἴψεται, aor. 2 sing. ἴψαο: *smite, chastise, afflict;* said of gods and kings, A 454, B 193.

ἱρεύς: see ἱερεύς.

ἱρεύσασθαι: see ἱερεύω.

Ἱρή: a town in Messēne, under the sway of Agamemnon, I 150, 292.

ἴρηξ, ηκος: *hawk* or *falcon;* typical of swiftness, O 237.

ἶρις (Ϝῖρις), dat. pl. ἴρισσιν: *rainbow,* Λ 27, P 547.—Personified, **Ἶρις,** ιδος, acc. **Ἶριν,** voc. **Ἶρι,** *Iris,* messenger of the gods in the Iliad. To men she usually appears under the assumed form of some mortal.

ἱρόν, ἱρός: see ἱερόν, ἱερός.

Ἶρος (Ϝῖρις): *Irus,* a nickname of Arnaeus the beggar, given to him by the suitors of Penelope, because he went on errands, σ 5 follg.

ἴς (Ϝίς, cf. v i s), acc. ἶνα, pl. ἶνες, dat. ἴνεσι: (1) *sinew,* collectively, P 522, elsewhere pl.—(2) *strength, force,* literally and fig.; freq. with gen. as periphrasis for the person, κρατερὴ ἲς Ὀδυσῆος, i. e. the mighty strong Odysseus himself, Ψ 720 and Φ 356.

ἰσάζω (Ϝῖσος), part. ἰσάζουσα, mid. aor. iter. ἰσάσκετο: *make equal, balance,* M 435; mid., *deem oneself equal, vie with,* Ω 607.

ἴσαν: see (1) εἶμι.—(2) εἴδω (II.).

Ἴσανδρος: *Isander,* son of Bellerophon, slain by Ares, Z 197, 203.

ἴσᾱσι: see εἴδω (II.).

ἰσάσκετο: see ἰσάζω.

ἴσθι: see εἴδω (II.).

ἴσθμιον: *necklace,* σ 300†. (See cuts Nos. 2, 40, 41 and 93.)

ἴσκε: defective ipf., perhaps from the same root as ἔσπετε, *said, spoke,* τ 203, χ 31.

Ἴσμαρος: a city of the Ciconians, ι 40.

ἰσό-θεος (Ϝῖσος): *equal to the gods, godlike;* always ἰσόθεος φώς. (Il., and of Telemachus, α 324, υ 124.)

ἰσό-μορος (Ϝῖσος): *of equal lot, a peer,* O 209†.

ἰσό-πεδον (Ϝῖσος): *level ground,* N 142†.

ἶσος (Ϝῖσος, Att. ἴσος), **ἴση, ἶσον**: *equal* in size, weight, or number, also *like;* freq. ἴση as subst., μή τίς μοι ἀτεμβόμενος κίοι ἴσης, *of an equal share* in the feast, ι 42, Λ 705, M 423; also **ἶσα** as subst, 'reparation,' β 203.—Adv., **ἶσον, ἶσα,** *equally, on equal terms,* I 616; also κατὰ Ϝῖσα, ἐπὶ Ϝῖσα, 'equally balanced,' 'undecided, Λ 336, M 436, O 413.

Ἶσος: a natural son of Priam, slain by Agamemnon, Λ 101†.

ἰσο-φαρίζω (Ϝῖσος, φέρω): *deem oneself equal, vie with, rival,* in anything (τί), Z 101, I 390. (Il.)

ἰσο-φόρος: *bearing alike, equally strong,* σ 373†.

ἰσόω (Ϝῖσος), mid. aor. opt. ἰσωσαίμην: mid., *compare oneself,* η 212†.

ἵστημι, ἱστᾶσι, imp. ἵστη, inf. ἱστάμεναι, ipf. iter. ἵστασκε, 3 pl. ἵστασαν, fut. inf. στήσειν, aor. 1 ἔστησα, στῆσα, aor. 2 ἔστην, στῆν, 3 pl. ἔστησαν, ἔσταν, στάν, iter. στάσκε, subj. στήῃς, στήῃ, 1 pl. στέωμεν, στείομεν, perf. ἕστηκα, du. ἕστατον, 2 pl. ἕστητε, 3 pl. ἑστᾶσι, subj. ἑστήκῃ, imp. ἕσταθι, ἕστατε, inf. ἑστάμεν(αι), part. ἑσταότος, etc., also ἑστεῶτα, etc., plup. 1 pl. ἕσταμεν.—Mid. (and pass.), ἵσταμαι, imp. ἵστασο, ipf. ἵστατο, fut. στήσομαι, aor. 1 στήσαντο, στήσασθαι, -σάμενος, aor. pass. ἐστάθη: I. trans. (pres., ipf., fut., and aor. 1 act.), *set* in place, *set on foot, cause to stand, rise,* or *stop;* of marshalling soldiers, στίχας, λᾱόν, B 525, Z 433; causing clouds, waves, to rise, μ 405, Φ 313; bringing horses to a standstill, ships to anchor, E 368, γ 182; metaph., 'excite,' 'rouse,' battle, strife, λ 314, π 292; *weigh,* T 247, X 350, Ω 232.—Mid. aor. 1 is causative, *set up* or *set on foot* for oneself, or something of one's own, κρητῆρα, ἱστόν, met., μάχην, Z

528, Α 480, ι 54. —II. intrans. (pass., fut. mid., aor. 2 and perf. and plup. act.), *place oneself, come to a stand, rise,* perf. and plup., *stand;* κῦμα ἵσταται, Φ 240; ὀφθαλμοὶ ὡσεὶ κέρα ἕστασαν, 'were fixed,' τ 211; στῆ δ' ὀρθός, ὀρθαὶ τρίχες ἔσταν, Ω 359; met., νεῖκος ἵσταται, ἕβδομος ἐστήκει μείς, 'had set in,' Τ 117; μὴν ἱστάμενος, 'beginning of the month,' ξ 162, τ 307; of spring, τ 519; aor. pass., ὁ δ' ἐστάθη ἠύτε πέτρη, ρ 463.

Ἱστίαια: a city in Euboea, Β 537†.

ἱστίη (Att. ἑστία): *hearth.* (Od.)

ἱστίον (ἱστός): *sail.* (See cut, from an ancient coin bearing the inscription ΝΙΚΟΜΗΔΙΩΝ. ΔΙΣ. ΝΕΩΚΟΡΩΝ.)

57

ἱστο-δόκη (δέχομαι): *mast-receiver, mast-crutch,* a saw-horse shaped support on the after-deck to receive the mast when lowered, Α 434†. (Plate IV.)

ἱστο-πέδη: *mast-stay, mast-block,* a thwart or transverse beam with a depression into which the mast fitted, which was by this means, as well as by the ἐπίτονοι, prevented from falling forward, μ 51. (See cut, letter *b*.)

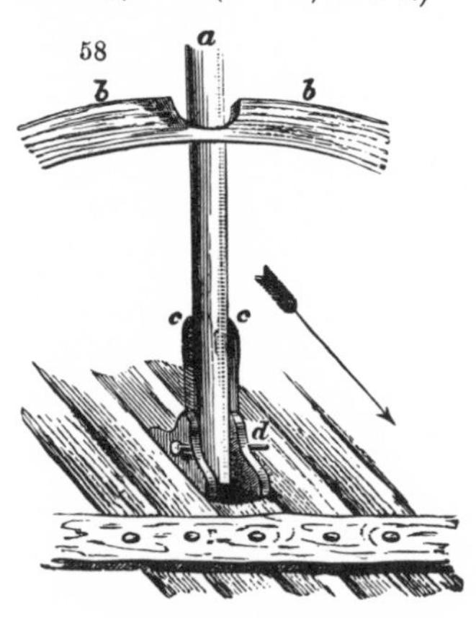

58

ἱστός (ἵστημι): *anything that stands.* —(1) *mast,* in the middle of the ship, held in place by the μεσόδμη, ἱστοπέδη, πρότονοι, ἐπίτονοι. During stay in port the mast was unstepped and laid back upon the ἱστοδόκη (cf. preceding cut, and Nos. 60, 84). —(2) *weaver's beam, loom.* The frame of the loom was not placed, as in modern handlooms, in a horizontal position, but stood upright, as appears in the cut,

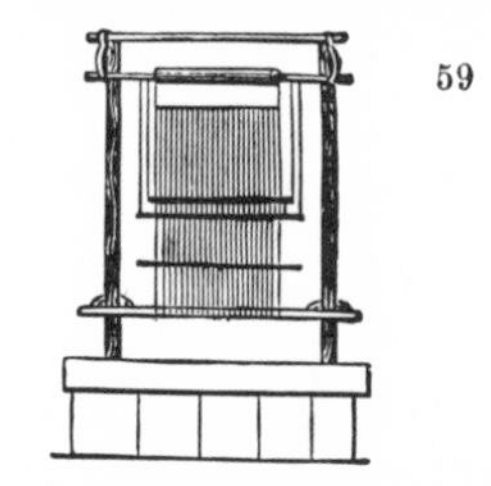

59

representing an ancient Egyptian loom. The threads of the warp hung perpendicularly down, and were drawn tight by weights at their lower ends. To set up the beam and so begin the web is (ἱστὸν) στήσασθαι. In weaving, the weaver passed from one side to the other before the loom (ἐποίχεσθαι), as he carried the shuttle (κανών), on which was wound the thread of the woof, through the warp, and then drove the woof home with a blow of the κερκίς.—(3) *warp,* and in general, *web, woven stuff.*

ἴστω: see εἴδω (II.).

ἴστωρ, ορος (root ϝιδ): *one who knows, judge,* Σ 501, Φ 486.

ἰσχαλέος (ἰσχνός): *dry, withered,* τ 233†.

ἰσχανάω, ἰσχάνω (ἴσχω), ipf. iter. ἰσχανάασκον: *hold, restrain, detain,* Ρ 747, ο 346; intrans., w. gen., or inf., *hold to, crave, desire,* Ρ 572, Ψ 300, θ 288; mid., *restrain oneself, delay,* Μ 38, Τ 234, η 161.

ἰσχίον (cf. ἰξύς): *hip-joint,* Ε 306; then the parts about the *hips, loins, flanks.*

ἴσχω (σισέχω, root σεχ, ἔχω), inf. ἰσχέμεναι, mid. ipf. ἴσχετο: *hold* in the simplest sense, then *hold* back, *check, restrain,* τινός, 'from' something, Ε 90; mid., *restrain oneself, stop, desist* from (τινός), χ 367, ω 54.

ἰτέη (Ϝιτέη): *willow*, Φ 350 and κ 510.

ἴτην: see εἶμι.

Ἴτυλος: *Itylus* (in the tragic poets *Itus*), son of Aēdon, slain by her through mistake, and lamented in her plaintive notes, of which the name is an imitation, τ 522†.

Ἰτυμονεύς: son of Hypirochus in Elis, slain by Nestor, Λ 672†.

ἴτυς (Ϝίτυς): *felloe* of a wheel. (Il.)

ἴτω: see εἶμι.

Ἴτων: a town in Thessaly, Β 696†.

ἰυγμός: *cry of joy, jubilant outcry*, Σ 572†.

ἰύζω: *cry out, scream* with intent to scare something away, ο 162 and Ρ 66.

Ἰφεύς (Ϝιφ.): a Trojan, slain by Patroclus, Π 417†.

Ἰφθίμη: daughter of Icarius, the sister of Penelope and wife of Eumēlus, δ 797†.

ἴφθιμος: doubtful word, *mighty, strong, goodly*, the latter interpretation to suit the epith. as applied to women, ἄλοχος, θυγάτηρ, Πηρώ, Ε 415, ο 364, λ 287.

ἶφι (Ϝίς): *with might*, ἀνάσσειν, etc.; *by violence*, κτάμενος, Γ 375.

Ἰφιάνασσα: *Iphianassa*, daughter of Agamemnon, Ι 145 and 287.

Ἰφιδάμας: son of Antēnor and Theāno, Λ 21 ff.

Ἰφικλήειος: *of Iphiclus*, βίη Ἰφικληείη, i. e. the mighty Iphiclus himself (see βίη), λ 290, 296.

Ἴφικλος: son of Phylacus, father of Podarces and Protesilāüs, Β 705, Ν 698, Ψ 636, λ 289 ff.

Ἰφιμέδεια: wife of Alōeus, and mother of Otus and Ephialtes, λ 305.

Ἰφίνοος: son of Dexius, slain by Glaucus, Η 14†.

ἴφιος: *strong, fat, goodly*, only ἴφια μῆλα.

Ἶφις: from Scyros, a slave of Patroclus, Ι 667†.

Ἰφιτίδης: *son of Iphitus*, Archeptolemus, Θ 128†.

Ἰφιτίων: son of Otrynteus, slain by Achilles, Υ 382.

Ἴφιτος (Ϝιφ.): *Iphitus*.—(1) son of Eurytus, an Argonaut, guest-friend of Odysseus, slain by Heracles, φ 14–37.—(2) son of Nautolus, an Argonaut, from Phocis, father of Schedius and Epistrophus, Β 518, Ρ 306.—(3) father of Archeptolemus.

ἰχθυάω, ipf. iter. ἰχθυάασκον: *catch fish, fish*, μ 95 and δ 368.

ἰχθυόεις, only -όεντι, -όεντα: *abounding in fish, fishy*.

ἰχθῦς, ύος, acc. pl. ἰχθύας, ἰχθῦς, *fish*.

ἴχνιον = ἴχνος.

ἴχνος, εος: *foot-step, track, trace*, ρ 317†.

ἰχώρ, acc. ἰχῶ: *ichor*, attributed to the gods in place of blood, see Ε 339–342.

ἴψ, ἰπός: *worm* that eats into horn or wood, *borer*, φ 395.

ἴψαο, ἴψεται: see ἴπτομαι.

ἰωγή: *shelter*; βορέω, 'from' the wind, ξ 533†. Cf. ἐπιωγαί.

ἰωή: *sound* of a voice, Κ 139; *tone* of a lyre, ρ 261; *whistling* of the wind, Δ 276, Λ 308.

ἰωκή, acc. ἰῶκα (διώκω): *pursuit, attack, battle-tumult*. Personified, Ε 740. (Il.)

ἰωχμός = ἰωκή, Θ 89 and 158.

K.

κ' = (1) κέ.—(2) καί.

κάββαλε: see καταβάλλω.

κάγ: see κατά.

Καβησόθεν: *from Cabēsus*, a city in Thrace, or, according to others, in Asia Minor, Ν 363†.

κάγχανος: *dry*, Φ 364, σ 308.

καγχαλάω, 3 pl. καγχαλόωσι, part. καγχαλόων: *laugh aloud* or *exultingly*.

κάδ: see κατά.

καδδραθέτην: see καταδαρθάνω.

καδδῦσαι: see καταδύω.

Καδμεῖοι, Καδμείωνες: the *Cadmeians*, *Thebans*, Δ 391, 385.

Κάδμος: *Cadmus*, the founder of Thebes, father of Ino, ε 333†.

Κάειρα, fem. of Κάρ: *of Caria*, *Carian*, Δ 142†.

καήμεναι: see καίω.

καθ-αιρέω, fut. καθαιρήσουσι, aor. καθείλομεν, subj. καθέλῃσι, part. καθελοῦσα: *take down*, ἱστία, ζυγὸν ἀπὸ πασσαλόφι, ι 149, Ω 268; of closing the eyes of the dead, Λ 453, ω 296; fig., μοῖρα θανάτοιο, *bring low*, *overcome*, β 100, γ 238.

καθαίρω (καθαρός), aor. (ἐ)κάθηρα, imp. κάθηρον, inf. -ῆραι, part. -ήραντες: *cleanse*, *clean*; 'make fair,' σ 192; w. acc., *wash off* or *away*, Ξ 171, ζ 93; with two accusatives, Π 667.

καθ-άλλομαι: *rush down*, of a storm, Λ 298†.

καθ-άπαξ: *once for all*, φ 349†.

καθ-άπτομαι, -άπτεσθαι, -όμενος, ipf. καθάπτετο: only fig., *accost*, *address*, and in unfavorable sense, *upbraid*, *chide*, *reprove*, σ 415, Ο 127, β 240, γ 345.

καθαρός: *clean*, *fair*, *clear*; of an open space, Θ 491; fig., of an honorable death, χ 462.

καθ-έζομαι, subj. καθεζώμεσθα, part. -όμενος, ipf. καθέζετο: *sit down*; of a public session, α 372; πρόχνυ καθεζομένη, 'kneeling down,' Ι 570; of a bird, 'perched,' τ 520; 'staying,' ζ 295.

καθέηκα: see καθίημι.

καθείατο: see κάθημαι.

καθ-εῖσα (εἶσα): *cause* or *bid to sit down*, Σ 389; *set*, *place*, *establish*, δ 524, Ξ 204.

καθέξει: see κατέχω.

καθ-εύδω, imp. καθεῦδε: *lie down to sleep*, *sleep*. (Od. and Α 611.)

καθ-εψιάομαι: *make sport of*; τινός, τ 372†.

κάθ-ημαι, imp. κάθησο, ipf. καθῆστο, 3 pl. καθείατο: *sit*, esp. of sitting quiet or inactive, 'remaining' anywhere, Ω 403, Β 191, Α 565, γ 186.

κάθηρα: see καθαίρω.

καθ-ιδρύω: *bid to sit down*, υ 257†.

καθ-ιζάνω: *take seat*; θῶκόνδε, ε 3†.

καθ-ίζω, ipf. καθῖζον, aor. 3 pl. κάθισαν, imp. κάθισον, part. καθίσσᾱς, καθίσᾱσα: intrans., *sit*; trans., *cause to sit*, *place*, *convoke*, β 69.

καθ-ίημι, imp. καθίετε, aor. καθέηκα, 1 pl. κάθεμεν, 3 pl. κάθεσαν: *let go down*, *let down*; of lowering sails, ι 72; pouring wine down the throat, Ω 642.

καθ-ικνέομαι, aor. καθῑκόμην: *reach*, *touch*, α 342, Ξ 104.

καθ-ίστημι, imp. καθίστᾱ, aor. 1 imp. κατάστησον, inf. -στῆσαι: *set down*; νῆα, 'bring to anchor,' μ 185; so of bringing one to his destination, ν 274.

καθ-οράω, mid. part. καθορώμενος: *look down upon*, Λ 337, Ν 4.

καθ-ύπερθε(ν): *from above*, *above*, *over*; whether the word expressly denotes 'northward' is doubtful, Ω 545, γ 170, ο 404.

καί: *and*, *also*, *too*, *even*; the purely copulative use needs no illustration, but the word is idiomatically employed in many ways that call for insight and feeling rather than translation; (Νέστωρ) ἀνόρουσε, λιγὺς Πυλίων ἀγορητής, | τοῦ καὶ ἀπὸ γλώσσης μέλιτος γλυκίων ῥέεν αὐδή, 'even from whose tongue, etc.' (comparing γλυκίων with λιγύς), Α 249; this comparing καί may appear in both members of the statement, δότε δὴ καὶ τόνδε γενέσθαι | παῖδ' ἐμόν, ὡς καὶ ἐγώ περ, ἀριπρεπέα Τρώεσσι, Ζ 476; καί introducing an apodosis institutes a comparison between dependent clause and main clause, Α 478. καί appears in Greek often where we employ a disjunctive word, ἕνα καὶ δύο, 'one or two,' Β 346. Combined w. other particles, καὶ εἰ, εἰ καί (see εἰ), καὶ δέ (δέ the connective), καὶ δή, καὶ μήν, καί ῥα, καί τε, καὶ . . πέρ (see πέρ), etc. καί sometimes suffers elision, κ' ἔτι, Ψ 526; freq. in crasis, χἠμεῖς (καὶ ἡμεῖς), κἀγώ, etc.

Καινεΐδης: *son of Caeneus*, Corōnus, Β 746†.

Καινεύς: a king of the Lapithae, Α 264†.

καίνυμαι, ipf. ἐκαίνυτο, perf. 2 sing. κέκασσαι, 3 κέκασται, inf. κεκάσθαι, plup. (ἐ)κέκαστο: *excel*, w. acc., ἐκαίνυτο φῦλ' ἀνθρώπων | νῆα κυβερνῆσαι, γ 282; ἐγχείῃ δ' ἐκέκαστο Πανέλληνας καὶ Ἀχαιούς, Β 530; mostly w. dat. of the thing and prep. governing the person, ἐν Δαναοῖσι, μετὰ δμωῇσι, πᾶσαν ἐπ' αἶαν, δ 725, τ 82, ω 509; gen. of person, Ω 546; ἐπί with dat. of thing, Υ 35.

καίριος (καιρός): *in the right place*, a *fatal* place for a wound, Θ 84, Δ 185. (Il.)

καιροσέων or **καιροσσέων**: gen. pl. fem. from an adj. καιρόεις, *with many loops* (καῖροι) or thrums to which the threads of the warp were attached; κ. ὀθονέων, from the *fine-woven* linen, η 107†.

καίω, inf. καιέμεν, ipf. καῖον, aor. ἔκηα, opt. 3 sing. κήαι, 3 pl. κήαιεν, subj. 1 pl. κήομεν, inf. κῆαι, imp. κῆον, part. κήαντες, pass. pres. καίεται, ipf. 2 sing. καίεο, aor. (ἐ)κάη, inf. καήμεναι, mid. aor. κήαντο, part. κηάμενος: *burn*, *consume*, mid., for oneself, Ι 88, 234, π 2; pass., *burn*, *burn up*.

κάκ: see κατά.

κακίζομαι: *play the coward*, Ω 214†.

κακκεῖαι, -ῆαι: see κατακαίω.

κακκείοντες: see κατακείω.

κακο-είμων, ονος (ϝεῖμα): *ill-clad*, σ 41.

κακο-εργίη (ϝέργον): *ill-doing*, χ 374†.

κακο-εργός: *evil-doing*, *rascally*, σ 54†.

Κακο-ΐλιος (ϝίλιος): *sad Ilium*, *Ilium of evil name*, τ 260, 597, ψ 19.

κακο-μήχανος (μηχανή): *contriving evil*, *malicious*, π 418.

κακό-ξεινος: *having sorry guests*, comp., υ 376†.

κακο-ρραφίη (ῥάπτω): *evil device*, *maliciousness*, μ 26.

κακός, comp. κακώτερος, κακίων, sup. κάκιστος: *bad*, opp. ἀγαθός, ἐσθλός. The variety of applications is as great as that of the opp. words, hence 'cowardly,' 'ugly,' 'poor,' 'vile,' 'sorry,' 'useless,' 'destructive,' 'miserable,' 'unlucky,' 'ill-boding,' etc. Not often of persons morally bad, λ 384. As subst., **κακόν, κακά**, *evil*, *pest*, *ills* of all sorts, Ε 831, μ 118, λ 482.—Adv., **κακῶς**.

κακό-τεχνος (τέχνη): *devised in evil*; δόλος, Ο 14†.

κακότης, ητος: *evil*, *wickedness*, *cowardice*; also 'hardship,' 'misery,' ρ 318, and esp. the ills suffered in war or battle, e. g. Λ 382.

κακο-φραδής, ές (φράζομαι): *ill judging*, *perverse*, Ψ 483†.

κακόω, imp. κάκου, aor. ἐκάκωσα: *bring to evil* or *trouble*, *maltreat*, *disfigure*, ζ 137; κεκακωμένοι, 'in a sad plight,' Λ 689; μηδὲ γέροντα κάκου κεκακωμένον, 'afflict the afflicted,' δ 754.

κάκτανε: see κατακτείνω.

κακώτερος: see κακός.

καλάμη (cf. κάλαμος, calamus): *reed*, *stalk*, Τ 222 (straw as opp. to kernel); fig., as relic of former bloom, 'by looking on the poor husk that remains I fancy thou canst perceive' what I once was, ξ 214.

καλαῦροψ, οπος: *shepherd's staff*, Ψ 845†.

καλέω, καλέει and καλεῖ, etc., inf. καλήμεναι, part. καλεῦντες, ipf. (ἐ)κάλει, iter. καλέεσκον, aor. (ἐ)κάλεσσα, part. καλέ(σ)σᾶς, pass. καλέονται, ipf. καλεῦντο, iter. καλέσκετο, perf. κέκλημαι, plup. 3 pl. κεκλήατο, fut. perf. 2 sing. κεκλήσῃ, mid. aor. (ἐ)καλέσσατο, καλέσαντο: *call* by name, *call* together, *summon*, *invite*, mid., to or for oneself; w. cognate acc., τινὰ ἐπώνυμον or ἐπίκλησιν καλεῖν, call a person 'by a name,' Ι 562, Σ 487; freq. pass., esp. perf., 'be called,' 'pass for,' often only a poetic amplification of εἶναι, αἲ γὰρ ἐμοὶ τοιόσδε πόσις κεκλημένος εἴη, ζ 244; often of inviting to dinner, see λ 185–187; mid., Ω 193, φ 380.

Καλήσιος: companion of Axylus, slain by Diomed, Ζ 18†.

Καλητορίδης: *son of Calētor*, *Aphareus*, Ν 541†.

καλήτωρ, ορος: *crier*, Ω 577†.

Καλήτωρ: (1) son of Clytius, cousin of Hector, slain by Ajax, Ο 419.—(2) the father of Aphareus.

καλλείπω: see καταλείπω.

Καλλιάνασσα and **Καλλιάνειρα**: Nereids, Σ 46, 44†.

Καλλίαρος: a town in Locris, Β 531†.

καλλί-γυναιξ, only acc. καλλιγύναικα: *with beautiful women*, epith. of Hellas, Achaea, Sparta.

καλλί-ζωνος: *with beautiful girdles.* (See cut No. 44.)

καλλί-θριξ, καλλίτριχος: of horses, *with beautiful manes*; sheep, *fair-fleeced.*

Καλλικολώνη: *Fair-mount*, near Ilium, Υ 53, 151.

καλλί-κομος (κόμη): *with beautiful hair*, cf. ἠύκομος.

καλλι-κρήδεμνος (κρήδεμνον): *with beautiful head-bands*, pl., δ 623†.

κάλλιμος = κᾱλός. (Od.)

κάλλιον: see κᾱλός.

καλλι-πάρῃος (παρειᾱ́): *fair-cheeked.*

κάλλιπε, -πέειν: see καταλείπω.

καλλι-πλόκαμος: *with beautiful locks* of hair, cf. ἐυπλοκαμίς. (See cut No. 44.)

καλλι-ρέεθρος: *beautifully-flowing.* (Od.)

καλλί-ρροος: *beautifully-flowing, fair-flowing.*

κάλλιστος: see κᾱλός.

καλλί-σφυρος (σφυρᾱ́): *fair-ankled.*

κάλλιφ' = κάλλιπε, see **καταλείπω.**

καλλί-χορος: *with beautiful dancing-lawns*, λ 581†.

κάλλος, εος: *beauty;* κάλλος ἀμβρόσιον, apparently conceived as an unguent, σ 192.

κᾱλός, comp. καλλίων, κάλλιον, nom. pl. καλλίονες, sup. κάλλιστος: *beautiful, fair;* sometimes figuratively, λιμήν, ἄνεμος, ζ 263, ξ 253; met., *fine, well, proper*, only neut. in Homer, κᾱλὸν εἰπεῖν, κᾱλὰ ἀγορεύειν, κᾱλόν ἐστί τινι. — Adv., **κᾱλόν, κᾱλά, καλῶς,** Θ 400, β 63.

κάλος (Att. κάλως): pl., *ropes, halyards;* passing through a hole at the top of the mast, then made fast at the bottom, and serving to hoist and lower the yard. (See cut.)

κάλπις: *water-jar, urn*, η 20†. (See cut, from a picture on an ancient vase.)

Καλύδναι νῆσοι: the *Calydnian* islands, near Cos, Β 677†.

Καλυδών: *Calydon*, a city in Aetolia, Ι 530, Ν 217, Β 640.

κάλυμμα (καλύπτω): *veil*, Ω 93†. (See cuts Nos. 2, 44, 62, 70.)

κάλυξ, υκος: pl., women's ornaments, perhaps cup-shaped *ear-rings*, Σ 401†. (See cut No. 8.)

καλύπτρη: *veil.* (Cf. cut, and Nos. 2, 44, 70.)

καλύπτω, fut. -ψω, aor. (ἐ)κάλυψα, pass. perf. part. κεκαλυμμένος, plup. κεκάλυπτο, aor. part. καλυφθείς, mid. aor. καλύψατο: *cover, veil, hide*, mid., oneself or some part of oneself; τινί, 'with' something, but sometimes w. acc. of the thing used to cover with, τόσσην οἱ ἄσιν καθύπερθε καλύψω, Φ 321, Ε 315; fig., of darkness, sorrow, war, death, Ρ 243, Λ 250, ω 315; mid., θ 92, κ 179.

Καλυψώ (the 'Concealer,' O c c u l i n a): *Calypso*, a goddess, daughter of Atlas, dwelling in the isle of Ogygia, where she detains Odysseus for seven years, until commanded by Zeus to dismiss him, ε 28, η 259, 265; epithets, δολόεσσα, δεινὴ θεός, ἐυπλόκαμος, αὐδήεσσα, ἠύκομος, νύμφη πότνια.

Κάλχᾱς, αντος: *Calchas*, the son of Thestor, renowned seer of the Greeks before Troy, A 69–72, B 300. (Il.)

κάμ: see κατά.

κάμαξ, ακος: *vine-pole, vine-prop*, pl., Σ 563†.

κάματος (κάμνω): *fatigue, weariness, toil;* 'fruit of our labor,' ξ 417.

κάμβαλε: see καταβάλλω.

κάμε: see κάμνω.

Κάμειρος: a town on the west coast of Rhodes, B 656†.

καμῑνώ, οῦς: γρηὶ καμῑνοῖ ϝῖσος, like an old *oven*-woman, *bake*-woman (of a clattering tongue, as in Eng. 'fish-woman'), σ 27†.

καμμίξᾱς: see καταμίγνῡμι.

καμ-μονίη (καταμένω): *steadfastness, endurance* (meaning the *victory* won thereby), X 257, Ψ 661.

κάμ-μορος (κατάμορος): 'given over to fate,' hence, *ill-starred, hapless.*

κάμνω, fut. καμεῖται, aor. 2 ἔκαμον, κάμε, subj. κάμῃσι, perf. κέκμηκα, part. κεκμηώς, -ηῶτα, -ηότας, mid. aor. ἐκάμοντο, καμόμεσθα: I. intr., *grow weary*, frequently w. acc. of specification, γυῖα, ὦμον, χεῖρα, also w. thing as subj., πόδες, ὄσσε, μ 232; w. part., Δ 244, H 5; euphem., καμόντες, the *dead*, those who have finished their toil, λ 476.—II. trans. (aor. act.), *wrought* with toil, μίτρη, τὴν χαλκῆες κάμον ἄνδρες, Δ 187; also with τεύχων; aor. mid., 'won by toil,' Σ 341; 'worked up for oneself,' 'tilled,' ι 130.

κάμπτω, fut. inf. -ψειν, aor. ἔκαμψα: *bend*, Δ 486; 'into a lyre,' Ω 274; freq. γόνυ, with weariness.

καμπύλος (κάμπτω): *bent, curved.*

καναχέω: only aor., *rang*, τ 469†.

καναχή: *ringing* of bronze, *rattling* of a mule-wagon, ζ 82; 'gnashing' of teeth, T 365.

καναχίζω: only ipf., *rattled*, M 36; *re-echoed*, κ 399.

κάνεον, κάνειον: *tray, basket*, for bread and meat, and for sacrificial barley, α 147, ρ 343.

καννεύσᾱς: see κατανεύω.

κανών, όνος: (1) *shuttle* or *spool*, by which the thread of the woof was drawn through the thread of the warp, Ψ 761.—(2) *handle* on the interior of a shield, grasped by the left hand, Θ 193, N 407. (Il.) (See cuts Nos. 12, 16, 79; rudely represented in the adjacent cut.)

63

κάπ: see κατά.

Καπανεύς: *Capaneus*, one of the Seven against Thebes, the father of Sthenelus, E 319.

Καπανηιάδης and **Καπανήιος**, υἱός: *son of Capaneus*, Sthenelus, E 109, 108.

κάπετος: *ditch, grave*, Σ 564, Ω 797. (Il.)

κάπη, pl. dat. κάπῃσι: *crib, manger*, δ 40, Θ 434.

καπνίζω (καπνός): only aor., *lighted fires*, B 399†.

καπνός: *smoke;* in μ 202 of a cloud of spray from violently agitated water.

κάππεσον: see καταπίπτω.

κάπριος (κάπρος): *wild boar*, with and without σῦς, M 42, P 282.

κάπρος: *wild boar, boar*, T 197.

Κάπυς: *Capys*, son of Assaracus, and father of Anchīses, Υ 239†.

καπύω: only aor., ἀπὸ (adv.) δὲ ψῡχὴν ἐκάπυσσεν, *breathed forth* (in a swoon), X 467†.

κάρ: see κατά.

κάρ (κάρη): only ἐπὶ κάρ, *headlong*, Π 392†.

Κάρ, pl. **Κᾶρες**: the *Carians*, inhabitants of Caria in Asia Minor, B 867. (Il.)

καρός, defect. gen.: doubtful word, only τίω σέ μιν ἐν καρὸς αἴσῃ, 'the value of a straw,' 'not a *whit*,' I 378.

Καρδαμύλη: a town in Messēne, under the sway of Agamemnon, I 150†.

καρδίη, κραδίη: *heart*, as an organ

of the body, K 94, N 282, 442; then as seat of life, courage, emotion, reason, A 225, I 646, K 244, δ 548, 260.

κάρη (Att. *κάρα*), gen. *κάρητος*, *καρήατος*, *κρᾶτός*, *κράατος*, dat. similarly, acc. *κάρη*, *κρᾶτα*, pl. *καρήατα*, *κρᾶτα*, *κράατα*, dat. *κρᾶσί*, *κράτεσφι*: *head*, of men or animals; also of a poppy, mountain-peaks, the head of a harbor, Θ 306, Υ 5, ι 140. For **κρῆθεν**, see *κατάκρηθεν*.

καρη-κομόωντες: *long-haired;* epith. of the Achaeans, who cut their hair only in mourning or on taking a vow, Ψ 146, 151, while slaves and Orientals habitually shaved their heads.

κάρηνον (*κάρη*): only pl., *heads*, also *summits* (*ὀρέων*), and of towers, battlements, B 117.

Κάρησος: a river rising in Mt. Ida, M 20†.

καρκαίρω: *quake*, ipf., Υ 157†.

καρπάλιμος (cf. *κραιπνός*): *swift*. —Adv., **καρπαλίμως**, *swiftly*, *speedily*, *quickly*.

1. καρπός: *fruit* of tree, field, or vine, Γ 246.

2. καρπός: *wrist*, always *ἐπὶ καρπῷ*, and with *χείρ*, E 458, σ 258, Σ 594.

καρρέζουσα: see *καταρρέζω*.

καρτερό-θῦμος: *strong-hearted*. (Il.)

καρτερός: see *κρατερός*.

κάρτιστος: *strongest*, *mightiest*; neut., *φυγέειν κάρτιστον ἀπ' αὐτῆς* (sc. *ἐστί*), *best*, i. e. 'the better part of valor,' μ 120.

κάρτος: see *κράτος*.

καρτύνω: only aor. mid., *ἐκαρτύναντο φάλαγγας*, *strengthened their* ranks. (Il.)

Κάρυστος: a town at the southern extremity of Euboea, B 539†.

καρφαλέος: *dry;* of sound (cf. *αὖον*), N 409. (Il. and ε 369.)

κάρφω, fut. *κάρψω*, aor. *κάρψε*: *parch*, *shrivel up*, ν 398 and 430.

καρχαλέος: *rough* with thirst (*δίψῃ*), of the throat, *dry*, Φ 541†.

καρχαρ-όδους, *όδοντος*: *sharp-toothed*, epith. of dogs. (Il.)

κασι-γνήτη (*κάσις*, *γίγνομαι*): *sister* (of the same mother).

κασί-γνητος (*κάσις*, *γίγνομαι*): *brother;* of a cousin, O 545, Π 456.

Κάσος: an island near Cos, B 676†.

Κασσάνδρη: *Cassandra*, daughter of Priam, the prophetess, carried to Greece as captive by Agamemnon, and slain by Clytaemnestra, N 366, Ω 699, λ 422.

κασσίτερος: *tin;* used to ornament weapons and chariots.

Κασσιάνειρα: the mother of Gorgythion, Θ 305†.

καστορνῦσα: see *καταστορέννῡμι*.

Κάστωρ: *Castor*.—(1) son of Zeus and Leda, brother of Polydeuces and Helen, famed for horsemanship (*ἱππόδαμος*), as participant in the hunt of the Calydonian boar, and in the Argonautic expedition, Γ 237, λ 299 ff.—(2) son of Hylacus, ξ 204.

κάσχεθε: see **κατέχω**.

κατά, before γ sometimes *κάγ*, before δ *κάδ*, before μ *κάμ*, before π and φ *κάπ*, before ρ *κάρ*, or written as one word, e. g. *καγγόνυ*, *καδδύναμιν*: *down*. —**I.** adv., *down*, *utterly* (here belong all examples of 'tmesis' so-called); *κατὰ δάκρυ χέουσα*, fig., *κατὰ δ' ὅρκια πάτησαν*, 'under foot,' Δ 157; *κατὰ δ' ἅρματα ἄξω*, break 'to pieces;' *κατὰ ταῦρον ἐδηδώς*, having *devoured*, stronger than 'eaten,' through the force of *κατά*, P 542; *Πηλῆά γ' ὀίομαι ἢ κατὰ πάμπαν* | *τεθνάμεν*, to be dead and *gone*, cf. *καταθνήσκω*, T 334; the appropriate case of a subst. may specify the relation of the adv., *κατὰ δὲ νότιος ῥέεν ἱδρὼς* | *ὤμων καὶ κεφαλῆς* (local gen.), Λ 811.—**II.** prep., (a) w. gen., *down*, *down from*, *down over*, *κατ' οὐρανοῦ εἰλήλουθεν*, η 199; *κατ' ὀφθαλμοῦ κέχυτ' ἀχλύς*, E 696; *ἀμβροσίην καὶ νέκταρ ἐρυθρὸν* | *στάξε κατὰ ῥῑνῶν*, 'down through,' 'in through,' T 39; *κατ' ἄκρης*, 'from top to bottom,' 'utterly.'—(b) w. acc., *down*, *down through*, *down into*, *κατὰ τεῖχος ἔβησαν*, N 737; of motion not so vaguely as *ἀνά*, 'up and down,' but usually rather with reference to some definite end or purpose, *δοιὼ δὲ κυβιστητῆρε κατ' αὐτοὺς . . ἐδίνευον κατὰ μέσσους*, 'among them . . down the centre,' δ 18; *ναίειν κατὰ πόλιν*, in particular places *throughout* the city, B 130; so, *κατὰ γαῖαν*, *κατὰ πόντον*, and simply local, *κατὰ στῆθος*, *in* the breast, met., *κατὰ θῡμόν*, 'in the heart;' transferred from the physical or local sense to other relations, distributive. *according* *to*, *by*, κατὰ σφέας, 'by themselves;' fitness, κατὰ θῡμόν, *according to* one's wish; κατὰ κόσμον, κατ' αἶσαν, κρομύοιο λοπὸν κάτα, 'after the semblance' of an onion-skin, τ 233; purpose, κατὰ πρῆξιν, 'on business'; κατὰ δαῖτα, 'for a banquet,' A 424.

κατα-βαίνω, aor. 2 κατέβην, 3 pl. -έβησαν, κατέβαν, subj. -βείομεν, imp. κατάβηθι, inf. -βῆναι, -βήμεναι, mid. aor. κατεβήσετο, imp. καταβήσεο, subj. καταβήσεται: *step down*, *descend*, τινός, 'from,' οὐρανόθεν, ζ 281; εἴς τι, ἐπί τι, and sometimes w. acc. of end of motion without prep., κατεβήσετο θάλαμον, β 337; then apparently trans., κλῖμακα, ἐφόλκαιον, 'down-stairs,' 'down the rudder,' α 330, ξ 350; ὑπερώια, as acc. of the place *from* which (as if the verb meant to *leave*), σ 206, ψ 85.

κατα-βάλλω, ipf. κατέβαλλε, aor. sync. κάββαλε (κάμβαλε): *cast* or *throw down*, O 357, ζ 172; then merely 'put down,' 'let fall,' I 206, E 343, Θ 249; (κυών) οὔατα κάββαλεν, 'dropped' his ears, ρ 302†.

κατα-βλώσκω: *come down*, *go through*, π 466†.

κατα-βρόχω: *swallow*, aor. δ 222†.

κατα-γηράσκω and **κατα-γηράω**: *grow old*.

κατ-αγῑνέω(ἄγω): *carry down*, κ 104†.

κατ-άγνῡμι, fut. κατάξω, aor. κατέαξα, κατῆξα: *shatter*.

κατ-άγω, aor. κατήγαγε, inf. καταξέμεν, mid. ipf. κατήγετο, κατάγοντο, aor. -ηγαγόμεσθα: *lead* or *bring down*, *bring* to some definite place, ἵππους, ἐπὶ νῆας, E 26; τινὰ Κρήτηνδε, 'drove' to Crete, τ 186; mid., of sailing, *bring to land* or *port*, *put in* (opp. ἀνάγεσθαι), γ 10, 178, κ 140.

κατα-δάπτω, aor. κατέδαψαν: *tear*, *devour*; ἦτορ καταδάπτεται, π 92.

κατα-δαρθάνω, aor. κατέδραθον, du. sync. καδδραθέτην: *fall asleep*, *sleep*.

κατα-δέρκομαι: *look down upon*, λ 16†.

κατα-δεύω: *drench*, *wet*, I 490†.

κατα-δέω, ipf. κατέδει, aor. κατέδησε: *bind down*, *bind fast*, *confine*.

κατα-δημο-βορέω (δημοβόρος): *devour in common*, aor., Σ 301†.

καταδράθω: see καταδαρθάνω.

κατα-δύω, aor. 2 κατέδῡν, inf. καταδῦναι, -δύμεναι, part. -δύς, nom. pl. fem. sync. καδδῦσαι, mid. fut. καταδῡσόμεθα, aor. κατεδύσετο: *go down into*, *enter*; εἰς 'Αΐδāο δόμους, κ 174; κατά, T 25. and often w. acc., δόμον, πόλιν, ὅμῑλον, etc.; of the sun, *set*; apparently trans., τεύχεα, *put on*, Z 504, μ 228.

καταειμένος, καταείνυσαν: see καταέννῡμι.

καταείσατο: see κάτειμι.

κατα-έννῡμι (Fέννῡμι), ipf. καταείνυσαν, pass. perf. part. καταειμένος: *clothe*, *cover*, Ψ 135; fig., ὕλῃ, ν 351.

κατ-αζαίνω, aor. iter. καταζήνασκε: *make dry*, *dry up*, λ 587†.

κατα-θάπτω, aor. inf. καταθάψαι: *inter*, *bury*. (Il.) [θημι.

καταθείομαι, -θείομεν: see κατατί-

κατα-θέλγω, aor. κατέθελξε: *subdue by charming*, *charm*, *enchant*, κ 213†.

κατα-θνήσκω, aor. 2 sync. κάτθανε, perf. κατατεθνήκᾱσι, opt. -τεθναίη, part. -τεθνηῶτος, etc., fem. -τεθνηυίης: *go down to death*, *die*, perf., *be dead and gone*; ψῡχαὶ νεκύων κατατεθνηώτων, shades of the 'departed dead,' λ 37.

κατα-θνητός: *mortal*.

κατα-θύμιος (θῡμός): *in* or *upon the mind* or *heart*, K 383, P 201, X 392.

καται-βατός: *to be descended*, *passable*, ν 110†.

κατ-αικίζω, pass. perf. κατῄκισται: *disfigure*, *soil*, π 290 and τ 9.

κατ-αισχύνω: *disgrace*, *dishonor*.

κατα-ΐσχω: see κατίσχω.

καταῖτυξ, υγος, *leather helmet* or *skull-cap*, K 258†. (See cut No. 115.)

κατα-καίριος (καιρός): *mortal*, with τέλος (like τέλος θανάτοιο), Λ 439†.

κατα-καίω, inf. -καιέμεν, aor. 1 κατέκηα, subj. -κήομεν, inf. sync. κακκῆαι (-κεῖαι): *burn up*, *consume*.

κατά-κειμαι, 3 pl. κατακείαται, ipf. κατέκειτο: *lie down*, *lie*, *remain* in any settled condition; met., *rest*; as pass. of κατατίθημι, *be set down*, Ω 527.

κατα-κείρω: *shear down*, hence *waste*, *consume*. (Od.)

κατα-κείω, subj. κατακείομεν, part. sync. κακκείοντες: *lie down*; as desiderative, part. w. ἔβαν, went *to lie down*, *to sleep*, A 606, α 424.

κατακῆαι, -κηέμεν, -κήομεν: see κατακαίω.

κατα-κλάω, ipf. κατέκλων: *break down*, *break off*; pass., fig., κατεκλάσθη φίλον ἦτορ, my heart *broke*, 'gave way.'

κατα-κλίνω, aor. part. -κλίνᾱς: *lean* or *lay down;* δόρυ ἐπὶ γαίῃ, κ 165†.

Κατακλῶθες: see Κλῶθες.

κατα-κοιμάω, only aor. pass. κατεκοιμήθην: pass., *lie down to sleep, sleep, lie.* (Il.)

κατακοιρανέω: see κοιρανέω.

κατα-κοσμέω, mid. aor. subj. κατακοσμήσησθε: *put in order,* χ 440; 'fitted,' Δ 118.

κατά-κρηθεν (κάρη): *from top to bottom, utterly.*

κατάκρης = κατάκρηθεν, see ἄκρη.

κατα-κρύπτω, fut. inf. -ύψειν, aor. part. κατακρύψᾱς: *hide, conceal; αὐτόν,* 'himself,' δ 427; 'make no concealment,' η 205.

κατα-κτείνω, fut. κατακτενεῖ, 3 pl. κτανέουσι, aor. 1 opt. κατακτείνειε, aor. 2 κατέκτανον, imp. κάτακτανε, κάκτανε, also κατέκταν, inf. -κτάμεν(αι), part. -κτᾱ́ς, pass. aor. 3 pl. κατέκταθεν, mid. fut. κατακτανέεσθε, aor. part. κατακτάμενος: *kill, slay;* mid. w. pass. signif., Ξ 481, π 106.

κατα-κύπτω, aor. κατέκυψε: *bend down the head, bow down.* (Il.)

1. κατα-λέγω, fut. -λέξω, aor. κατέλεξα. *enumerate, recount,* τ 497, π 235; then *narrate, relate,* with εὖ, ἀτρεκέως, ἐν μοίρῃ, I 115, T 186.

2. κατα-λέγω (root λεχ), mid. fut. καταλέξεται, aor. κατελέξατο, imp. κατάλεξαι, aor. 2 κατέλεκτο, inf. καταλέχθαι, part. καταλέγμενος: mid., *lay oneself down, lie down* to sleep or rest, *lie.*

κατα-λείβω: only pass. part. *trickling down,* Σ 109†.

κατα-λείπω, καλλείπω, aor. 2 κάλλιπον (κάλλιφ', Z 223, K 338), inf. -έειν: *leave behind, leave* in the lurch, *abandon,* Φ 414, X 383, Ω 383; 'give over,' ἕλωρ γενέσθαι, P 151, γ 271, ε 344.

κατα-λήθομαι: *forget entirely.*

καταλοφάδεια (λόφος): adv., 'down over the neck'; φέρων, carrying the animal *crosswise over his back* (the feet being tied together and held under the chin of the bearer), κ 169†.

κατα-λύω, aor. κατέλῡσε, subj. -λύσομεν: *loose* (unharness), δ 28; fig., *undo,* 'destroy,' B 117, I 24.

κατα-μάρπτω, aor. subj. καταμάρψῃ: *overtake.*

κατ-αμάω: only aor. mid. καταμήσατο, had *heaped upon himself,* Ω 165†.

κατ-αμύσσω: only aor. mid., καταμύξατο χεῖρα, has *scratched her* hand, E 425†.

κατα-νεύω, part. κατᾱνεύων (ι 490), fut. -νεύσομαι, aor. κατένευσα, part. sync. καννεύσᾱς: *nod down* (forward), *nod* to, to give a sign, regularly of *assent* (opp. ἀνανεύω); κεφαλῇ or κρᾱτί, A 527; joined with ὑπέσχετο, ὑπέστην, B 112, ν 133, Δ 267; *grant* (τινί τι), νῑκήν, κῦδος, also w. inf., K 393, δ 6.

κατ-άνομαι (ἄνω): pass., *be used up, wasted.* (Od.)

κάτ-αντα (κατάντης): adv., *downhill,* Ψ 116†.

κατάντηστιν: see ἄντηστις.

καταντικρύ: see ἀντικρύ.

κατά-παυμα (παύω): *rest from, alleviation; τινός,* P 38†.

κατα-παύω, fut. -σω, aor. κατέπαυσα, subj. -παύσομεν: *put an end to, quell;* of persons and w. gen. of separation, *silence, stop* in anything (ἀγηνορίης, ἀφροσυνᾱ́ων), X 457, ω 457; ironically of killing, Π 618.

κατα-πέσσω, aor. subj. καταπέψῃ: *digest,* fig., χόλον (as we say 'swallow' one's anger), A 81†.

καταπέφνων: see κατέπεφνον.

κατα-πήγνῡμι, aor. κατέπηξα, mid. aor. sync. κατέπηκτο: *stick fast, plant,* mid. intrans., Λ 378.

κατα-πίπτω, aor. sync. κάππεσον: *fall down;* fig., παραὶ ποσὶ κάππεσε θῡμός, i. e. their courage utterly forsook them, O 280.

κατα-πλέω: *sail down, put in* (to shore from the high sea), ipf., ι 142†.

κατα-πλήσσω: only aor. pass., κατεπλήγη, *was struck with dismay* (ἦτορ, acc. of specification), Γ 31†.

κατα-πρηνής, ές: 'down-turned forward,' only w. χείρ, the *flat* of the hand.

κατα-πτήσσω, aor. 1 part. καταπτήξᾱς, aor. 2 κατέπτην, 3 du. καταπτήτην: *crouch down, cower* with fear, Θ 136.

κατα-πτώσσω = καταπτήσσω. (Il.)

κατα-πῡ́θομαι (πῡ́θω): *become rotten, rot away,* Ψ 328†.

κατ-ᾱράομαι: *utter imprecations, invoke upon* (τινί τι); followed by inf. denoting the substance of the prayer, I 454.

κατᾱ-ρῑγηλός (Ϝρῖγος): *horrible*, ξ 226†.

κατα-ρρέζω, καταρέζω, part. καρρέζουσα, aor. κατέρεξε: *stroke, caress.*

κατα-ρρέω, part. neut. καταρρέον: *flow down.*

κατ-άρχομαι: only ipf., in ritualistic sense, χέρνιβά τ' οὐλοχύτᾱς τε, *began the sacred* hand-washing and sprinkling of barley meal, γ 445†.

κατα-σβέννῡμι, aor. κατέσβεσε: *extinguish, quench*, Φ 381†.

κατα-σεύομαι: only aor. 2, κατέσσυτο, *rushed down*, Φ 382†.

κατα-σκιάω: *overshadow*, ipf., μ 436†.

κατα-στορέννῡμι and **καταστόρνῡμι,** part. sync. κᾶστορνῦσα, aor. κατεστόρεσα: *spread down, spread out upon*, ρ 32; then of 'covering over,' Ω 798.

κατα-στυγέω: only aor., κατέστυγε, *was horror-struck*, P 694†.

κατασχεθεῖν: see κατέχω.

κατα-τήκω, aor. κατέτηξε: *melt down, melt*; pass. intrans.; fig., 'pine away,' κατατήκομαι ἦτορ (acc. of specification), τ 136.

κατα-τίθημι, fut. -θήσω, aor. κατέθηκα, pl. κάτθεμεν, κάτθεσαν, imp. κάτθετε, subj. καταθείομεν, inf. -θεῖναι, κατθέμεν, part. du. καταθέντε, mid. aor. 2 κατθέμεθα, κατθέσθην, subj. καταθείομαι, part. κατθέμενοι: *put* or *lay down, put away*, mid., for oneself; of setting one ashore or at any other place of destination, π 230, Π 683; spreading a bed, τ 317; proposing as a prize in a contest, Ψ 267; laying the dead on the bier, ω 190, 44; depositing things for safe keeping, etc.

κατα-τρῡ́χω: *wear* or *waste away, exhaust, consume.*

καταῦθι, καταυτόθι: see αὖθι and αὐτόθι.

κατα-φέρω: only fut., κατοίσεται, *will bring* me *down* to the grave, X 425†.

κατα-φθίω, fut. -φθίσει, mid. aor. κατέφθιτο, inf. καταφθίσθαι, part. -φθίμενος: *destroy*, mid., *perish, pass away, die*; νεκύεσσι καταφθιμένοισιν (κατά because they have passed *down* to Hades, cf. καταθνήσκω), λ 491.

κατα-φλέγω, fut. -ξω: *burn up, consume*; πυρί, X 512†.

κατα-φῡλαδόν (φῦλον): *in tribes, in clans*, B 668†.

κατα-χέω, aor. κατέχευα, inf. καταχεῦαι, mid. aor. 3 pl. κατέχυντο: *pour down, shower down, shed over* (τινί τι); not of fluids only, but variously, of letting fall a garment, E 734; throwing down wands, Z 134; levelling a wall, H 461; and often metaph., χάριν, πλοῦτον, ὀνείδεα, β 12, B 670, ξ 38; mid., ὅπλα εἰς ἄντλον, 'fell in a heap,' μ 411.

κατα-χθόνιος: *subterranean, nether*, Ζεύς (= Hades), I 457†.

κατέαξα: see κατάγνῡμι.

κατέδει: see καταδέω.

κατ-έδω, fut. κατέδονται: *eat up, devour*; fig., οἶκον, θῡμόν, β 237, Z 202.

κατ-είβω (= καταλείβω): *let flow down, shed*; mid., *flow apace, trickle down*, fig., αἰών, 'ebb away,' ε 152.

κάτ-ειμι (εἶμι), κάτεισι, inf. κατίμεν, ipf. κατήιε, mid. aor. καταείσατο: *go* or *come down*, in some definite direction, as back home, into port, etc.; fig., of a river, 'flow down,' Λ 492; a ship, π 472; a spear, Λ 358.

κατέκταθεν: see κατακτείνω.

κατεναίρω, mid. aor. κατενήρατο: *slay*, λ 519†.

κατ-εναντίον: *down against, go to meet*; τινί, Φ 567†.

κατ-ένωπα: *in the face of, turned toward*, O 320†.

κατεπάλμενος: see κατεφάλλομαι.

κατέπαλτο: see ἐκκαταπάλλω.

κατ-έπεφνον, subj. καταπέφνῃ, part. (w. irreg. accent) καταπέφνων: *kill, slay.*

κατ-ερείπω, aor. κατήριπεν, perf. κατερήριπεν: aor. and perf., intr., *fall down, be prostrated*, fig., 'fall away,' 'come to nought,' E 92. (Il.)

κατ-ερητύω: *hold back, restrain.*

κατ-ερῡκάνω and **κατερῡ́κω**: *hold back, hinder, detain*, pass., α 197.

κατ-ερύω, aor. κατείρυσε, pass. perf. κατείρυσται, κατειρύσθαι: *draw down, launch* a vessel.

κατ-έρχομαι, fut. κατελεύσομαι, aor. κατήλυθον, inf. κατελθέμεν: *come* or *go down, come* in some definite direction, as from country to town, home, from high sea to harbor, etc.; πέτρη, 'descending,' ι 484.

κατέσσυτο: see κατασεύομαι.

κατ-ευνάζω and **κατευνάω,** aor. opt. κατευνήσαιμι, aor. pass. 3 pl. κατεύνασθεν, part. κατευνηθέντα: *put to bed, lull to sleep*, pass., *lie down, sleep.*

κατ-εφ-άλλομαι: only aor. part., **κατεπάλμενος,** *springing down to* the attack, Λ 94†.

κατ-έχω, fut. καθέξει, aor. 2 κατέσχον, pass. κατέχονται, ipf. κατείχετο, -έχοντο, mid. aor. κατέσχετο, part. κατασχομένη, aor. 2, parallel forms, **κατέσχεθον,** sync. κάσχεθε: I. act., *hold down*, ω 242; *hold fast, keep back*, Λ 702, ο 200; *occupy*, 'fill,' Π 79; fig., of the earth holding down (within its depths) the buried dead, πρὶν καί τινα γαῖα καθέξει, Π 629, Γ 243; of the heavens held (obscured) by night, the moon by clouds, ν 269, ι 145.—II. mid., *hold down upon* or *cover oneself* or a part of oneself, Γ 419, τ 361; *stop, tarry*, γ 284.

κατ-ηπιάω (ἤπιος): *alleviate, assuage*, pass., Ε 417†.

κατ-ηρεφής, ές (ἐρέφω): *covered over, vaulted, overhanging.*

κατήριπε: see κατερείπω.

κατ-ηφείη (κατηφής): *humiliation, shame.* (Il.)

κατ-ηφέω, aor. κατήφησαν, part. -φήσᾱς: *be humiliated, confounded*, π 342, Χ 293.

κατ-ηφής, ές: *humiliated, disgraced*, ω 432†.

κατ-ηφών, όνος = κατηφείη, abstract for concrete, *disgraces*, Ω 253†.

κάτθανε: see καταθνήσκω.

κατθάψαι: see καταθάπτω.

κατθέμεν, κάτθεμεν, κάτθετε, κάτθεσαν: see κατατίθημι.

κατίμεν: see κατιέναι.

κατ-ίσχω and **καταΐσχω,** inf. κατισχέμεν(αι), pass. καταΐσχεται: *hold down, occupy*, ι 122; *hold back*, Ψ 321; *hold* to a course, *steer*, νῆα, λ 456; mid., *keep* for oneself, Β 233.

κατ-οίσεται: see καταφέρω.

κατ-όπισθε(ν): *in the rear, behind;* w. gen., μ 148; of time, *in the future, afterwards.*

κάτω (κατά): *down, downward*, Ρ 136 and ψ 91.

κατ-ωμάδιος (ὦμος): *(down) from (over) the shoulder*, of the discus so hurled, Ψ 431†. (See cut No. 30.)

κατ-ωμαδόν (ὦμος): *(down) from (over) the shoulder*, of the whip as used by the driver, or 'down on the shoulders' of the horses. (Il.)

κατ-ῶρυξ, υχος (ὀρύσσω): *dug in, buried* or *firmly set in the earth.* (Od.)

Καύκωνες: the *Caucomans.*—(1) in Paphlagonia, Κ 429.—(2) in Elis, γ 366.

καυλός: *spear-shaft*, part next the point, Π 115; also *sword-hilt*, Π 338.

καῦμα, ατος (καίω): *burning heat*, Ε 865†.

καύστειρα (καίω), fem. adj.: *hot, raging*, μάχη. (Il.)

Καΰστριος: the *Caÿster*, a river in Ionia, emptying into the sea near Ephesus, Β 461.

καὐτός = καὶ αὐτός.

καφ-: only perf. part., **κεκαφηότα,** *gasping out*, θῡμόν, Ε 698 and ε 468.

κέ, κέν: enclitic modal adv. indicating a condition; essentially equivalent to ἄν, but of more frequent occurrence, esp. in affirmative sentences, and sometimes found in combination with ἄν, Λ 187, Ν 127, Ω 437, ε 361, ζ 259, ι 334. Homer uses κέν, like ἄν, with the fut. indic. and w. the subj. in independent sentences, καί κέ τις ὧδ' ἐρέει, 'thus many a one will be like to say,' Δ 176; ἐγὼ δέ κ' ἄγω Βρῑσηΐδα, 'just as certainly will I,' etc., Α 184. With inf., Χ 110. See ἄν.

Κεάδης: *son of Ceas*, Troezenius, Β 847.

κεάζω, aor. (ἐ)κέασσε, κέασε, opt. κεάσαιμι, inf. κεάσσαι, pass. perf. part. κεκεασμένα, aor. κεάσθη: *split, cleave;* of lightning, *shiver*, ε 132, η 250.

κέαται: see κεῖμαι.

Κεβριόνης: a son of Priam, charioteer of Hector, slain by Patroclus, Θ 318, Π 738.

κεδάννῡμι (parallel form of σκεδάννῡμι, employed for metrical convenience), aor. ἐκέδασσε, pass. aor. 3 pl. ἐκέδασθεν, κεδασθείς: *disperse, scatter;* γεφῡ́ρᾱς, 'burst the dikes,' Ε 88.

κεδνός (root καδ, κήδω), sup. κεδνότατος: *careful, true, good, excellent;* a poetic synonym of ἀγαθός, ἐσθλός, used mostly of persons; κεδνὰ Ϝιδυῖα, 'careful-minded,' α 428.

κεδρινός: *of cedar*, Ω 192†.

κέδρος: *cedar*, of the tree and of the wood, ε 60†.

κειάμενος, κείαντες: see *καίω*.

κείαται, κείατο: see *κεῖμαι*.

κεῖθεν (κεῖνος): *thence, then*, Ο 234.

κεῖθι: *there*.

κεῖμαι, κεῖσαι, κεῖται, 3 pl. κεῖνται, κέαται, κείαται, subj. κῆται, imp. κεῖσο, κείσθω, inf. κεῖσθαι, part. κείμενος, ipf. (ἐ)κείμην, 3 pl. κέατο, κείατο, iter. 3 sing. κέσκετο, fut. κείσομαι: *lie, be placed* or *situated*, of both persons and things, and often virtually a pass. to τίθημι, as κεῖται ἄεθλα, prizes 'are offered,' Ψ 273; freq. where we say 'stand,' δίφρος, θρῆνυς, ρ 331, 410; fig., πένθος ἐπὶ φρεσὶ κεῖται, ω 423; ταῦτα θεῶν ἐν γούνασι κεῖται, 'rest' in their disposal; see γόνυ.

κειμήλιον (κεῖμαι): *treasure, heirloom;* of 'landed property,' β 75.

κεῖνος, κείνη, κεῖνο: see ἐκεῖνος.

κεινός: see κενός.

κείρω, fut. inf. κερέειν, aor. 1 ἔκερσα, κέρσε, mid. part. κειρόμενος, ipf. κείροντο, aor. inf. κείρασθαι: *shear, shear off, cut down;* κόμην, δοῦρα, τένοντε, Ψ 146, Ω 450, Κ 546; then 'consume,' 'waste,' κτήματα, βίοτον, β 312, 143; fig., μάχης ἐπὶ (adv.) μήδεα κείρει, 'cuts short,' Ο 467; mid., *cut* off one's own hair (as an offering to the dead), Ψ 46, δ 198.

κεῖσε (κεῖνος): *thither, there;* 'thus far,' Ψ 461.

1. **κείω, κέω**, inf. κειέμεν, part. κείων, κέων, a future with desiderative force: *wish to sleep;* freq. the part. w. verb of motion, βὰν κείοντες, ὄρσο κέων, η 342.

2. **κείω**, stem form of κεάζω: *split*, part., ξ 425†.

κεκαδήσει, -δησόμεθα: see κήδω.

κεκάδοντο, κεκαδών: see χάζομαι.

κέκασμαι: see καίνυμαι.

κεκαφηώς: see καφ-.

κέκλετο: see κέλομαι.

κέκληγα: see κλάζω.

κεκλήατο: see καλέω.

κεκλήσῃ: see καλέω.

κεκλόμενος: see κέλομαι.

κέκλυθι, κέκλυτε: see κλύω.

κέκμηκας, κεκμηώς: see κάμνω.

κεκοπώς: see κόπτω.

κεκόρημαι, κεκορηότε: see κορέννυμι.

κεκορυθμένος: see κορύσσω.

κεκοτηώς: see κοτέω.

κεκράανται, κεκράαντο: see κεράννυμι.

κεκρύφαλος: *net* to confine the hair, Χ 469†. (See cut No. 41.)

κεκύθωσι: see κεύθω.

κελαδεινός: *sounding, ringing, clanging, echoing;* Ζέφυρος, Ψ 208; elsewhere, κελαδεινή, epithet of Artemis as huntress (leader of the pack), as subst., Φ 511.

κελαδέω: *sound* applause, *shout* in applause, aor. (Il.)

κέλαδος: *clang, echo, clamor*, of the hunt or the combat, and otherwise, σ 402.

κελάδων, οντος: part., *sounding*, Φ 16†.

Κελάδων: a stream in Elis, Η 133†.

κελαι-νεφής, ές (κελαινός, νέφος): as epith. of Zeus, god *of the dark clouds*, subst., ν 147; of blood, *dark*.

κελαινός: *dark, black;* of the skin, blood, night, wave, storm, the earth, Π 384.

κελαρύζω: *gurgle*, of flowing water; of blood, Λ 813.

κέλευθος, pl. κέλευθοι, oftener κέλευθα: *path, way;* ἀνέμων λαιψηρὰ κέλευθα, κελεύθους, ε 383; ὑγρά, ἰχθυόεντα κέλευθα, of the paths of air and of the sea; of a journey, κ 539; κέλευθον πρήσσειν, τιθέναι, θέσθαι, γεφῦροῦν, of making a way over a ditch, Ο 357; νυκτός τε καὶ ἤματος κέλευθοι, 'outgoings of night and day,' κ 86; met., θεῶν ἀπόεικε κελεύθου, 'cease from walking heavenly ways,' Γ 406.

κελευτιάω (frequentative of κελεύω), part. -τιόων: *urge* or *cheer on*, 'animate,' Μ 265. (Il.)

κελεύω (root κελ), ipf. (ἐ)κέλευον, fut. inf. κελευσέμεναι: *urge*, μάστῑγι, Ψ 642; then *command, bid, request*, τινί τι, or w. inf., π 136, Β 50; freq. w. acc. and inf.; w. two accusatives in the formula ὄφρ' εἴπω τά με θῡμὸς ἐνὶ στήθεσσι κελεύει, Η 68.

κέλης, ητος (root κελ, cf. celer): *racer, courser*, w. ἵππος, *race-horse*, ε 371†.

κελητίζω (κέλης): *ride race-horses*, ἵπποισι, of professional fancy riding, Ο 679†.

κέλλω, aor. ἔκελσα: *beach* a ship (νῆα); also intr., κελσάσῃσι δὲ νηυσί, the ships 'having run on the beach,' we, etc., ι 149.

κέλομαι (root κελ), κέλεαι, fut. κελήσεται, aor. 2 redupl. (ἐ)κέκλετο, part. κεκλόμενος: *command, urge on, exhort, call to* (τινί or τινά, Z 66, Σ 391); fig., the wax was softened, ἐπεὶ κέλετο μεγάλη Ϝὶς | ἠελίου, μ 175.

κέλσαι: see κέλλω.

κεμάς, άδος: a two-year old *deer*, K 361†.

κέν: see κέ.

κενε-αυχής, ές (αὐχέω): *emptily* or *idly boasting*, Θ 230†.

κενεός: see κενός.

κενεών, ῶνος (κενεός): the empty space of the body, part between the hips and ribs, *waist, small of the back*, χ 295; acc. of specification, E 284; elsewhere w. ἐς.

κενός, κενεός, κεινός: *empty;* met., *vain, idle*, εὔγματα, χ 249.

κένσαι: see κεντέω.

Κένταυρος: a *Centaur*, e. g. Eurytion, φ 295. In Homer the Centaurs were a wild Thessalian tribe, A 268.

κεντέω, aor. inf. κένσαι: *goaded on;* ἵππον, Ψ 337†.

κεντρ-ηνεκής, ές: *goaded on.* (Il.)

κέντρον (κεντέω): *goad.* (Il.)

κέντωρ, ορος: *goader;* κέντορες ἵππων, epith. of Cadmaeans and Trojans. (Il.)

κέονται: see κεῖμαι.

κεράασθε: see κεράννῡμι.

κεραΐζω (cf. κείρω), inf. κεραϊζέμεν: *lay waste, destroy;* also *kill*, B 861.

κεραίω, κεράω: see κεράννῡμι.

κεραμεύς, ῆος: *potter*, Σ 601†.

κέραμος: anything of *earthen* ware, *pot* or *jar*, such as are sometimes found half buried in the earth (see cut), Γ 469; in E 387, χαλκέῳ ἐν κεράμῳ, serving as a dungeon (cf. the pit into which Joseph was thrown by his brethren).

64

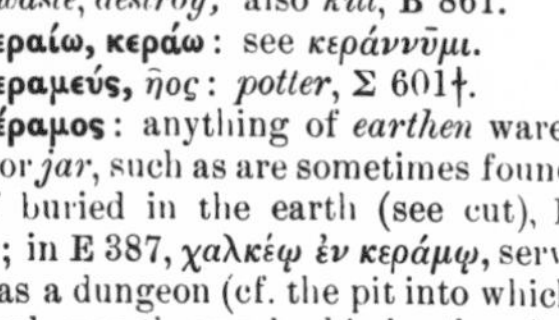

κεράννῡμι, κεράω, κεραίω (cf. also κιρνάω and κίρνημι), aor. κέρασσε, part. fem. κεράσᾱσα, mid. pres. subj. κέρωνται, imp. κεράασθε, κερᾶσθε, ipf. κερόωντο, κερῶντο, aor. κεράσσατο, pass. perf. κεκρᾱ́αντai, plup. -αντο: *mix, prepare by mixing*, mid., for oneself, *have mixed;* esp. of tempering wine with water, also of preparing water for a bath, κ 362; of alloy, or similar work in metal, χρυσῷ δ' ἐπὶ χείλεα κεκρᾱ́ανται, 'plated' with gold, δ 132.

κεραο-ξόος (κέρας, ξέω): *horn-polishing, worker in horn*, τέκτων, Δ 110†.

κεραός: *horned.*

κέρας, κέραος, dat. κέραι (κέρᾳ), pl. κέρᾱ (but shortened before a vowel), κεράων, dat. κέρασι, κεράεσσι: *horn;* bows were made of horn, Δ 109 ff., φ 395; hence said for 'bow,' Λ 385; a sheath of horn was used to encase a fishing-line, to prevent the hook from being bitten off, Ω 81; with a play upon the word κραίνω, τ 566.

κεραυνός: *thunderbolt, lightning.*

κεράω: see κεράννυμι.

κερδαλέος (κέρδος): *profitable, advantageous;* hence *cunning, sly*, ζ 148, θ 548, ν 291.

κερδαλεό-φρων: *with mind bent on gain, greedy-minded*, A 149; *crafty-minded*, Δ 339.

κερδίων, κέρδιον: *more profitable, more advantageous*, 'better,' σ 166.—Sup. **κέρδιστος**, the *slyest*, Z 153†.

κέρδος, εος: *gain, profit; shrewd counsel*, esp. pl., Ψ 515; κέρδεα ἐπίστασθαι, εἰδέναι, to be 'versed in cunning arts,' Ψ 322; νωμᾶν ἐνὶ φρεσί, 'devise clever counsels,' σ 216; in bad sense, β 88, ψ 217.

κερδοσύνη: *craft;* only dat. as adv., *cunningly, craftily.*

κερκίς, ίδος: *rod* (in later times 'comb'), by a blow from which the threads of the woof were driven home into the warp, and the web made firm and close, ε 62. (See cut No. 59.)

κέρσᾱς: see κείρω.

κερ-τομέω (κέρτομος), ipf. (ἐ)κερτόμεον: *taunt, tease*, Π 261.

κερτομίη: *taunt*, only pl.

κερτόμιος (cf. κείρω): *taunting, cutting*, ἔπεα, Δ 6; also as subst., κερτόμια (=κερτομίαι), A 539, ι 474.

κερῶνται, κερόωντο: see κεράννῡμι.

κέσκετο: see κεῖμαι.

κεστός (κεντέω): of needle-work, *embroidered* (girdle of Aphrodite), Ξ 214†.

κευθάνω = κεύθω, Γ 453†.

κευθμός: *lair*, pl., N 28†.

κευθμών, ῶνος: *hiding-place, cranny*, ν 367; of the sties of swine, κ 283.

κεῦθος, εος, = κευθμός, κευθμών, only pl., ὑπὸ κεύθεσι γαίης, 'in the depths of the earth beneath,' of Hades, X 482, ω 204.

κεύθω, fut. -σω, aor. 2 κύθε, subj. redupl. κεκύθω, perf. κέκευθα: *hold concealed, hide, cover;* esp. of death, κύθε γαῖα, γ 16; pass., 'Αιδι κεύθωμαι, Ψ 244; met., νόῳ, ἐνὶ φρεσίν, etc.; with two accusatives, γ 187, ψ 273.

κεφαλή, κεφαλῆφι: *head;* typical of life, Δ 162, β 237, P 242; several expressions have no equivalent in Eng., φίλη, ἠθείη κεφαλή (c a r u m c a p u t), terms of endearment; as the source of voice, Λ 462, Π 76.

Κεφαλλῆνες: the *Cephallenians*, collective designation of the subjects of Odysseus on islands and mainland, B 631, ξ 100, υ 187, ω 355, 378, 429.

κέχανδα: see χανδάνω.

κεχαρησέμεν, κεχαρήσεται, κεχαρηώς, κεχαροίατο, κεχάροντο: see χαίρω.

κεχηνώς: see χαίνω.

κεχαρισμένος: see χαρίζομαι.

κεχόλωμαι: see χολόω.

κεχρημένος: see χράομαι.

κέχυμαι: see χέω.

κέω: see κείω.

κῆαι, κήαι, κηάμενος: see καίω.

κήδειος, κήδεος (κῆδος): of any object of solicitude, *dear;* esp. of those who claim burial service, T 294 and Ψ 160.

κηδεμών, όνος: one solicitous, *near friend, mourner*, only pl. (Il.)

κήδιστος, a sup. to κήδειος: *dearest.*

κῆδος, εος: *care, trouble*, esp. for deceased friends, *mourning*, Δ 270; pl. κήδεα, *sorrows.*

κήδω, ipf. iter. κήδεσκον, fut. part. κηδήσοντες, mid. ipf. iter. κηδέσκετο, fut. κεκαδησόμεθα: *trouble, distress*, E 404, Φ 369, Ω 240, 542, ι 402; pass. and mid., *be concerned, care for*, τινός, H 204, A 196, ξ 146.

κῆεν: see καίω.

κηκίω (κίω): *gush forth*, ε 455†.

κήλεος, κήλειος (καίω): *blazing;* πῦρ, O 744.

κηληθμός (κηλέω): *charm;* κηληθμῷ δ' ἔσχοντο, they were *spell-bound*, λ 334 and ν 2.

κῆλον: pl., *shafts, missiles* of the gods; of snow, M 280. (Il.)

κήξ: (sea-)*gull*, ι 479†.

κήομεν: see καίω.

κῆπος: *garden.*

Κῆρ, Κηρός (κείρω): the *angel of death*, any form of death personified, hence κῆρες θανάτοιο, *fates* of death, μυρίαι, M 326, ξ 207, B 302. Immediately upon the birth, the *Moira* or *Aisa* was determined for the life, and the κῆρ for the death (cf. I 411, where the choice of a twofold destiny is offered to Achilles; the passage also shows that the Κῆρ impels to destruction, cf. κηρεσσιφόρητος). When the time of death for the special favorites of Zeus approaches, he weighs the fortunes of combatants, e. g. Patroclus and Sarpēdon, Achilles and Hector. (See cut, representing Hermes discharging this function.) Freq. joined

65

w. θάνατος, β 283; φόνος, δ 273, β 165; hence w. adj. μέλαινα, Φ 66; like θάνατος, Π 687; often = death, Λ 360, 362, E 652, I 411; symbol of hate, A 228.

κῆρ, κῆρος: *heart*, Π 481; then in wider signification, as the seat of understanding, will, and emotion, thus answering approximately to Eng. 'heart'; hence (ἐν)φρεσίν, ἐνὶ στήθεσσιν, ἐν θυμῷ, Z 523, 'within me'; (περὶ) κῆρι, 'at heart exceedingly,' 'most heartily,' ε 36; κηρόθι μᾶλλον, 'still more in heart,' ρ 458; also used periphrastically like μένος, βίη, etc., B 851, cf. A 395.

κηρεσσι-φόρητος: *borne on by* their *fates* to death, Θ 527†.

Κήρινθος: a town in Euboea, N. E. from Chalcis, B 538†.

κηρόθι: see κῆρ.

κηρός: *wax.* (Od.)

κήρῡξ, ῡκος: *herald.* The heralds convoked the popular assembly, kept order at trials, bore as sign of their office a staff (see cut, from an archaic relief, No. 114), which they handed over to him who had the right to speak. They served also as messengers of the chiefs and as their assistants in sacrifice. Epithets, θεῖοι, Διὸς ἄγγελοι, Διὶ φίλοι. κήρυκι Ἠπυτίδῃ, P 324.

κηρῡ́σσω: *proclaim as herald, summon, order,* πόλεμόνδε, ἀγορήνδε. 'In the office of herald,' P 325.

κῆται: see κεῖμαι.

Κήτειοι: a Mysian tribe, followers of Eurypylus, λ 521†.

κῆτος, εος: *sea-monster,* e. g. sharks and seals, Υ 147, δ 446.

κητώεις, εσσα (κῆτος): *full of ravines,* epith. of Lacedaemon, B 581, δ 1.

Κηφῑσίς, ίδος: λίμνη, name of a lake in Boeotia, later Copāis, E 709†.

Κηφῑσός: a river in Phocis.

κηώδης: *sweet-smelling, fragrant,* Z 483†.

κηώεις = κηώδης.

κίδναμαι (κίδνημι = σκεδάννῡμι): Ἠώς, *be diffused.*

κιθαρίζω: *play on the cithara, play;* φόρμιγγι, Σ 570†. (See cut, representing a Greek woman.)

66

κίθαρις: *cithara, lyre;* for κιθαριστύς, N 731.

κιθαριστύς: *cithara-playing.* (See cut.)

67

κικλήσκω (καλέω): *call* by name, *call, summon,* mid., to oneself, I 569, K 300.

Κίκονες: the *Ciconians,* a Thracian tribe, B 846, ι 39 ff.

κῖκυς: *force,* λ 393†.

Κίλικες: the *Cilicians,* a tribe of Greater Phrygia, dwelling under two leaders, in Hypoplacian Thebe and in Lyrnessus, Z 397, 415.

Κίλλα: *Cilla,* a town in the Troad, A 38, 452.

Κιμμέριοι: the *Cimmerians,* a fabulous people dwelling at the entrance of Hades, λ 14†.

κῑνέω (κίω), aor. κίνησα, pass. κῑνήθη, 3 pl. ἐκίνηθεν: *move, set in motion, disturb, stir,* pass. intr., *move,* A 47.

κίνυμαι, part. κῑνύμενος = κῑνέομαι, *move on, march.*

Κινύρης: a ruler in Cyprus, Λ 20†.

κινυρός: *whimpering, wailing,* P 5†.

Κίρκη: *Circe,* the enchantress, daughter of Helius, sister of Aeētes, dwelling in the isle of Aeaea, κ 230 ff.

κίρκος: a *hawk* or *falcon* that flies in circles, ἴρηξ, ν 87; Ἀπόλλωνος ἄγγελος, ο 526.

κιρνάω, κίρνημι (parallel form of κεράννῡμι), part. κιρνᾱ́ς, ipf. ἐκίρνᾱ: *mix.*

Κισσηΐς: *daughter of Cisses,* Theāno, Z 299†.

Κισσῆς: a ruler in Thrace, the father of Theāno, Λ 223†.

κισσύβιον: *cup* or *bowl,* originally of ivy-wood, for drinking or for mixing, ι 346, ξ 78, π 52. (Od.)

κίστη: *box, chest,* ζ 76†.

κιχάνω, κίχημι, κιχᾱ́νομαι, fut. κιχήσομαι, pres. subj. κιχείω, inf. κιχῆναι, κιχήμεναι, ipf. 2 sing. κίχεις, -εν. -ήτην, aor. κιχήσατο, aor. 2 ἔκιχε, κίχον: *overtake, come upon, find*, freq. w. part., A 26, B 18.

κίχλη: *thrush*, pl., χ 468†.

κίω, opt. κίοι, κιοίτην, κίοιτε, part. κιών, -οῦσα, ipf. ἔκιον, κίον: *go, go away*, usually of persons, rarely of things, Z 422, ο 149, π 177; the part. κιών is often employed for amplification, κ 156, ω 491.

κίων, ονος: *pillar*, very often of those that support the beams of a house. (See plate III. at end of vol., F and G.)

κλαγγή (κλάζω): *scream*, properly of birds, λ 605; of animals, as the squealing of pigs, ξ 412; and of the loud cry of warriors, B 100; the sharp twang of a bowstring, A 49.

κλαγγηδόν: adv., *with cries*, B 463†.

κλάζω, aor. ἔκλαγξα, perf. part., w. pres. signif., κεκληγώς, pl. κεκλήγοντες: *scream*, properly of birds, Π 429; then of animals, ξ 30; applied also to warriors and to men under other circumstances, E 591, μ 256, B 222; to things, as arrows, the wind, etc., A 46, P 88, μ 408. The verb may be translated according to the context in the several passages, but its original and proper application shows its force. Cf. κλαγγή.

κλαίω, ipf. κλαῖον, iter. κλαίεσκε, fut. κλαύσομαι, aor. κλαῦσε: *weep, cry;* freq. of lamenting the dead (as natural or as formal ceremonial utterance), hence used transitively, T 300, α 263.

κλαυθμός (κλαίω): *weeping.*

κλαῦσε: see κλαίω.

κλάω, aor. κλάσε, pass. ἐκλάσθη: *break, break off*, pass. intrans., Λ 584.

κλεηδών, όνος, and **κληηδών** (κλέος): *rumor, tidings*, δ 317; then of something heard as favorable *omen*, β 35, σ 117, υ 120.

κλειτός (κλέος): *celebrated, famous*, epith. of persons and of things; esp. ἐπίκουροι, ἑκατόμβη, Γ 451, A 447. (Il. and ζ 54.)

Κλεῖτος: (1) a Greek, the son of Mantius, ο 249.—(2) a Trojan, the son of Pisēnor, companion of Polydamas, slain by Teucer, O 445.

1. κλείω, κλέω (root κλυ, κλύω), pass. κλέομαι, ipf. 2 sing. (ἐ)κλεο: *celebrate, make famous;* pass., Ω 202, ν 299.

2. κλείω: see κληΐω.

Κλεόβουλος: a Trojan, slain by the lesser Ajax, Π 330†.

Κλεοπάτρη: the wife of Meleāger, identical w. Ἀλκυόνη, I 556†.

κλέος (root κλυ, κλύω), pl. κλέᾱ (shortened before a vowel): *rumor, tidings, glory;* σόν, ἐμὸν κλέος, 'news of thee,' 'of me,' ν 415; κλέος πρὸς Τρώων, 'an honor to thee before the Trojans,' X 415; ἀνδρῶν κλέᾱ, *glorious deeds* (l a u d e s), I 189.

κλέπτης: *thief*, Γ 11†.

κλεπτοσύνη: *thieving, trickery*, τ 396†.

κλέπτω, aor. ἔκλεψα: *steal;* then *deceive*, νόον τινός, Ξ 217; μὴ κλέπτε νόῳ, 'do not hide things in thy heart,' A 132.

Κλεωναί: a town in Argolis, B 570†.

κλήδην (καλέω): *by name*, I 11†.

κληηδών: see κλεηδών.

κλήθρη: *alder*, ε 64 and 239.

κληΐς, ῖδος (Att. κλείς): (1) *bolt, bar* (see cuts Nos. 29 and 35, both from Egyptian originals); cut No. 56, in four compartments, shows above the open, below the closed door: on the left as seen from within; on the right from without. *c, g, f*, mark the place of the key-hole, through which the thong (ἱμάς, α 442) ran, and the key was passed by which the bolt was first lifted (as is seen at *g*), ἀνέκοψεν, and then pushed back, ἀπῶσαν. The adjoining cut (No. 68), from a Greek sepulchral monument, as well as No. 29, presupposes double bolts, and above on the right we see the key as it is applied, and below on the other half of the door the loosened thong. These bolts of double doors are also called ἐπιβλής, ὀχῆες. κρυπτῇ, with hidden, concealed bolt.—(2) *key*, better described as *hook*, M 456. (See cut No. 56, *f, g.*)—(3) *collar-bone.*—(4) curved *tongue* of a buckle, σ 294. (See cut No. 97.)—(5) pl., *thole-pins, rowlocks*, ἐπὶ κληῖσι, to which the oars were made fast by a thong, and round which they played, see cuts Nos. 120 and 32; for later, different arrangements, see cuts Nos. 38, 60, and the

68

Assyrian war-ship, cut No. 37. ἐπὶ κληῖσι, translate, *at the oars.*

κληϊστός: *that may be closed*, β 344†.

κληΐω (Att. κλείω), aor. (ἐ)κλήῖσε, inf. κληῖσαι: *shut; ὀχῆας*, 'draw forward' the bolts closing the door, by means of the thong. (See cut No. 56.)

κλῆρος: (1) *lot*, a stone or potsherd, on which each man scratched his mark, Η 175. The lots were then shaken in a helmet, and he whose lot first sprang forth was thereby selected for the matter in hand.—(2) *paternal estate*, ξ 64.

κλητός (καλέω): *called, chosen, invited*, Ι 165, ρ 386.

κλῖμαξ, ακος (κλίνω): *stair-way, ladder.* (Od.)

κλιντήρ, ῆρος: *couch, sofa.* (See cut.)

69

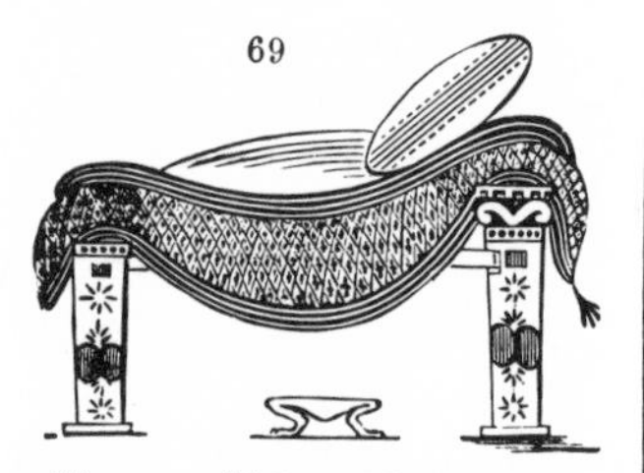

κλίνω, aor. ἔκλῖνα, κλῖναν, pass. aor. (ἐ)κλίνθη, ἐκλίθη, perf. 3 pl. κεκλίαται, κεκλιμένος, plup. κέκλιτο, mid. aor. part. κλῖνάμενος: I. act., *make to slope* or *incline, lean* one thing against another, τινί τι, or πρός τι, Λ 593, χ 121; of turning away the eyes, Γ 427; turning the tide of battle (μάχην, inclinare pugnam), Ξ 510, and esp. *put to flight*, Ε 37, ι 59.—II. pass., *bend oneself, sink* or *lie down; ἐκλίνθη καὶ ἀλεύατο κῆρα, ἑτέρωσ' ἐκλίνθη κάρη, κλίνθη κεκμηώς*, Γ 360, Ν 543, Ψ 232; *be supported, lean against*, τινί, Λ 371, ζ 307, mid., ρ 340.

κλισίη (κλίνω), dat. κλισίηφι: *hut* or *lodge* of shepherds, Σ 589, ξ 45, ο 301, π 1; *barrack* (not exactly 'tent') of warriors, Λ 448 ff; often in pl.; also *couch* or *easy-chair*, δ 123, τ 55. (See cut No. 73.)

κλισίηθεν: *from the hut, from the barrack.*

κλισίηνδε: *to the hut, to the barrack.*

κλίσιον (κλίνω): *an adjoining building* for servants, etc., ω 208†.

κλισμός (κλίνω): *reclining chair, easy-chair*, α 145. (Cf. adjoining cut, or Nos. 105, 106.

70

κλῖτύς, pl. acc. κλῖτῦς: *slope, hill-side.*

κλονέω, κλονέει, pass. κλονέονται, ipf. κλονέοντο: *put to rout, drive in confusion*, pass., *be driven* or *rush* *wildly about;* fig., of wind, driving clouds or flame, Ψ 213, Υ 492; pass., Δ 302, Φ 528. (Il.)

Κλονίος: leader of the Boeotians, slain by Agēnor, B 495, O 340.

κλόνος: *tumult;* ἐγχειάων, 'press of spears,' E 167. (Il.)

κλόπιος: *deceitful,* ν 295†.

κλοτοπεύω: doubtful word, *be wasting words* or *making fine speeches,* T 149†.

κλύδων, ωνος (κλύζω): *surge, billow,* μ 421†.

κλύζω, ipf. iter. κλύζεσκον: of waves, *plash, dash,* Ψ 61; aor. pass., 'was dashed high,' 'rose in foam,' Λ 392, ι 484, 541.

κλῦθι: see κλύω.

Κλυμένη: (1) a Nereid, Σ 47.—(2) an attendant of Helen, Γ 144. —(3) daughter of Minyas or Iphis, mother of Iphiclus, λ 326.

Κλύμενος: king of the Minyans in Orchomenus, father of Eurydice, mortally wounded at Thebes, γ 452.

Κλυταιμνήστρη: daughter of Tyndareus, sister of Helen, and wife of Agamemnon. She was slain at the same time that her paramour Aegisthus was killed by Orestes, A 113, γ 266, 310, λ 439. (See cut No. 33.)

Κλυτίδης: *son of Clytius.*—(1) Dolops.—(2) Piraeus.

Κλύτιος: (1) a son of Laomedon, brother of Priam, and father of Calētor, O 419, 427, Γ 147, Υ 238. —(2) father of Piraeus in Ithaca, π 327.—(3) a Greek, the father of Dolops.

κλυτό-εργος (ϝέργον): *maker of famous works,* θ 345.

Κλυτομήδης: son of Enops of Aetolia, beaten by Nestor in a boxing-match, Ψ 634†.

Κλυτόνηος: son of Alcinous, θ 119, 123.

κλυτό-πωλος: *with famous steeds,* epithet of Hades, E 654 ff. Probably said with reference to the rape of Proserpine. (Il.)

κλυτός, 2 and 3 (κλύω): *illustrious, glorious,* epith. of gods and men; then of things, *famous, fine,* ἄλσος, μῆλα, ἔργα, etc.; ὄνομα, ι 364, cf. τ 183.

κλυτο-τέχνης: *famous in art, renowned artificer,* epithet of Hephaestus.

κλυτό-τοξος: *with glorious bow, illustrious archer,* epith. of Apollo.

κλύω, ipf.. w. aor. signif., ἔκλυον, κλύον, ἔκλυε, aor. 2 imp. κλῦθι, κλῦτε, redupl. κέκλυθι, κέκλυτε: *hear,* esp. *hear willingly, hearken to* prayer or entreaty; hence very often the imp., κλῦθί μευ, ἀργυρότοξε, κέκλυτέ μευ μῦθων, A 37, κ 189; also implying obedience, τοῦ μάλα μὲν κλύον ἠδ' ἐπίθοντο, H 379, γ 477; w. participle, ἔκλυον αὐδήσαντος, K 47; freq. w. acc. of thing heard.

Κλῶθες: the 'Spinsters,' i. e. the *Fates,* η 197†.

κλωμακόεις, εσσα: *rock-terraced, rocky,* B 729†.

κνάω, ipf. (or aor.) κνῆ: *grate* (cheese), Λ 639†.

κνέφας (cf. γνόφος, δνόφος): *darkness, dusk,* of the first part of the night.

κνῆ: see κνάω.

κνήμη: the part of the leg between knee and ankle, *shin.*

κνημίς, ῖδος (κνήμη): *greave.* The greaves were metal plates, lined with some soft material, bent around the shin-bone under the knee, and fastened by clasps at the ankle (see cut No. 36), thus only in the Iliad. In the Odyssey, ω 229, the word signifies *leather leggins.*

κνημός: only pl., *mountain-valleys* (saltus).

κνῆστις, dat. κνήστῑ (κνάω): *grater,* or knife for grating, Λ 640†.

κνίση: the *steam* or *savor* of burnt offerings, originally *fat,* esp. that of the caul or diaphragm, in which the thighs of the victim were wrapped. It was then laid upon the fire and burned, together with pieces of flesh piled upon it, A 460.

κνισήεις, εν: *redolent of savory viands,* κ 10†.

κνυζηθμός (κνύζω): *whimpering,* of dogs, π 163†.

κνυζόω, fut. -ώσω, aor. κνύζωσε: *render dim* or *lustreless,* ν 401 and 433.

κνώδαλον: *wild animal,* ρ 317†.

Κνωσός: *Cnosus,* the principal city in Crete, B 646, Σ 591, τ 178.

κνώσσω: *slumber,* δ 809†.

κοῖλος (cf. cavus): *hollow;* often of places between mountains, ὁδός, Λακεδαίμων, Ψ 419, δ 1; λιμήν, 'deep-embosomed,' i. e. extending far into the land, κ 92.

κοιμάω (cf. κεῖμαι), aor. (ἐ)κοίμησα, mid. ipf. κοιμᾶτο, κοιμῶντο, aor. (ἐ)κοιμήσατο, pass. aor. (ἐ)κοιμήθην: act., *put to bed* or *to rest*, γ 397, δ 336; *lull to sleep*, τινὰ ὕπνῳ, μ 372; fig. of winds, μ 281; mid. and pass., *lie down to sleep* or *to rest* (esp. w. reference to the comfort or discomfort of the resting-place), *sleep;* fig. of the sleep of death, Λ 241.

κοιρανέω (κοίρανος): *be lord* or *ruler*, *rule*, ἀνά, κατά, διά τινας, whether in war or peace; of the suitors of Penelope, 'playing the lord,' 'lording it,' ν 377.

κοίρανος (cf. κῦρος): *lord*, *ruler*, *master*, σ 106.

Κοίρανος: (1) a Lycian, slain by Odysseus, Ε 677.—(2) from Lyctus in Crete, charioteer of Meriones, slain by Hector, Ρ 611, 614.

κοίτη (κεῖμαι): *bed*, τ 341†.

κοῖτος: *night's rest*, *sleep*, then *resting-place*, χ 470.

κολεόν, κουλεόν: *sheath* or *scabbard* of a sword, made of metal, and decorated with ivory, Λ 30 ff., Γ 272.

κολλήεις (κολλάω): ξυστὰ ναύμαχα κολλήεντα, ship-spears *united* with rings, Ο 389†.

κολλητός (κολλάω): *joined*, well-*compacted* or 'shod,' with bands or otherwise, δίφρος, σανίδες, Τ 395, Ι 593, ψ 194.

κόλλοψ, οπος: *peg* of a lyre, round which the string was fastened, φ 407†.

κολοιός: *jack-daw*. (Il.)

κόλος: *docked*, *pointless*, Π 117†.

κολοσυρτός: *noisy rout*, of the hunt, Μ 147 and Ν 472.

κολούω (κόλος): *cut short*, *curtail*, only fig., Υ 370, θ 211, κ 340.

κόλπος: *bosom*, also of the *fold* of the garment about neck and breast, Ι 570; fig. of the sea, θαλάσσης, ἁλός.

κολῳάω (κολῳός), ipf. ἐκολῴā: *bawl*, Β 212†.

κολώνη: *hill*. (Il.)

κολῳός: *noisy wrangling*, *racket*, Α 575†.

κομάω (κόμη): only part., *wearing long hair;* κάρη κομόωντες Ἀχαιοί, 'long-haired Achaeans;' Ἄβαντες ὄπιθεν κομόωντες, i. e. shorn in front, Β 542; ἐθείρῃσι, 'with long manes,' Θ 42.

κομέω, κομέουσι, ipf. ἐκόμει, κομείτην, iter. κομέεσκε: *take care of*, *tend*, by affording food, bed, clothing, bath, λ 250; of animals, ρ 310, 319.

κόμη: *hair* of the head, with reference to comeliness, pl., *locks*, ζ 231; then *foliage*, ψ 195.

κομιδή: *care*, *attendance*, bestowed on persons, horses, garden, ω 245, 247.

κομίζω (κομέω), fut. κομιῶ, aor. κόμισσα, (ἐ)κόμισε, mid. aor. (ἐ)κομίσσατο, κομίσαντο: I. act. (1) *wait upon*, *attend*, *care for*, esp. *entertain* as guest, κ 73, ρ 113, cf. 111; of feeling (τινά τινι), υ 69; pass., θ 451.—(2) *take* or *bring away* to be cared for, *fetch*, *convey*, Β 183, Γ 378, Λ 738, Ν 196, Ψ 699, ν 68.—II. mid., *take to one's care*, *entertain* hospitably, *take* or *convey home* or *to oneself*, Ε 359, Θ 284, ξ 316, Α 594, ζ 268; of carrying off a spear in one's body, Χ 286.

κομπέω: *clash*, Μ 151†.

κόμπος: *clashing;* 'stamping' of feet, θ 380; 'gnashing' of the tusks of a wild boar, Λ 417, Μ 149.

κοναβέω, aor. κονάβησα: *resound*, *ring*, of echoing and of metallic objects, πήληξ, νῆες, δῶμα. (Il. and ρ 542.)

κοναβίζω = κοναβέω. (Il.)

κόναβος: *din*, κ 122†.

κονίη: *dust*, *sand*, *ashes*, λ 600, Ψ 502, η 153.

κόνις, ιος, dat. κόνῑ=κονίῃ.

κονίσαλος: *dust-cloud*, *dust-whirl*. (Il.)

κονίω, fut. κονίσουσι, aor. ἐκόνῑσα, pass. perf. part. κεκονῑμένος, plup. κεκόνῑτο: *make dust* or *make dusty*, *cover with dust;* pass., Χ 405, Φ 541; intr., κονίοντες πεδίοιο, 'scampering' over the plain in a cloud of dust.

κοντός: *punting-pole*, *pole*, ι 487†.

Κοπρεύς: the father of Periphētes, herald of Eurystheus, Ο 639†.

κοπρέω: only fut. part. κοπρήσοντες, *for manuring* the fields, ρ 299†.

κόπρος: *dung*, *manure*, Ω 164; then 'farm-yard,' 'cow-yard,' Σ 575.

κόπτω, aor. κόψε, perf. part. κεκοπώς, mid. aor. κόψατο: *knock*, *smite*, *hammer*, Σ 379, θ 274, mid., oneself or a part of oneself, Χ 33.

Κόρακος πέτρη: *Raven's* Rock, in Ithaca, ν 408†.

κορέννῡμι, fut. κορέω, aor. ἐκόρεσα, pass. perf. κεκόρημαι, part., act. w. pass. signif., κεκορηώς, aor. pass. (ἐ)κορέσθην, aor. mid. (ἐ)κορέ(σ)σατο: *sate, satisfy*, τινά τινι, Θ 379; mid., *satisfy oneself*, τινός; met., *have enough of, be tired of*, w. gen. or participle, υ 59.

κορέω, aor. imp. κορήσατε: *sweep, sweep out*, υ 149†.

κόρη: see κούρη.

κορθύομαι (κόρυς): *rise to a head, tower up*, I 7†.

Κόρινθος: *Corinth*, B 570; anciently named Ephyra.—**Κορινθόθι,** *at Corinth*, N 664.

κορμός (κείρω): *log, trunk* of a tree, ψ 196†.

κόρος: *satiety, surfeit*, τινός.

κόρση (κάρη): *temple.* (Il.)

κορυθ-ᾶϊξ (ἀίσσω): *helmet-shaking, with waving plume*, X 132†.

κορυθ-αίολος: *with glancing helm;* epith., esp. of Hector and Ares. (Il.)

κόρυμβος, pl. κόρυμβα (cf. κόρυς, κάρη): pl., the *heads, bow-ends* of a vessel, cf. ἄφλαστα, I 241†. (See cut No. 38.)

κορύνη: *battle-mace*, club of iron. (Il.)

κορυνήτης: *club-brandisher.* (Il.)

κόρυς (cf. κάρη), acc. κόρυθα and κόρυν: *helmet;* epithets, βριαρή, δαιδαλέη, ἱπποδάσεια, ἱππόκομος, λαμπομένη, λαμπρή, παναίθη, τετράφαλος, φαεινή, χαλκήρεος, χαλκοπάργος. (See cuts under these adjectives.)

κορύσσω, mid. aor. part. κορυσσάμενος, pass. perf. part. κεκορυθμένος: *arm* the head *with the helmet;* then, in general, *arm, equip*, mid., *arm oneself;* of weapons, κεκορυθμένα χαλκῷ, with *head* of bronze, bronze-shod, Γ 18, Π 802; met., πόλεμον, κῦμα (cf. κορθύομαι), Φ 306, Δ 424.

κορυστής, du. κορυστᾶ: *helmeted*, hence *armed, equipped* for battle. (Il.)

κορυφή (cf. κόρυς, κάρη): *crest, summit.* (Il. and ι 121.)

κορυφόω, mid. κορυφοῦται: mid., *rise with towering crest;* κῦμα (cf. κορθύομαι), Δ 426†.

Κορώνεια: *Coronēa*, a city in Boeotia, south of lake Copāis, B 503†.

κορώνη: anything *crooked* or *curved.* —(1) the *ring* on a door, α 441. (See cuts Nos. 68 and 56.)—(2) the *curved end* of the bow over which the loop of the bow-string was brought. (See cut No. 34.)—(3) *sea-crow cormorant*, ε 66.

κορωνίς, ίδος (κορώνη): *curved*, epith. of ships; always νηυσὶ (or νήεσσι) κορωνίσιν. (See cuts Nos. 38, 87, 88.)

Κόρωνος: son of Caeneus, father of Leonteus, king of the Lapithae, B 746†.

κοσμέω (κόσμος), aor. ἐκόσμησα, pass. aor. 3 pl. κόσμηθεν, mid. aor. part. κοσμησάμενος: *arrange, order*, esp. *marshall* troops, mid., one's own men, B 806; of preparing a meal, η 13.

κοσμητός: *well laid out*, η 127†.

κοσμήτωρ, ορος: *marshaller*, in Il. always κοσμήτορε λᾱῶν, of the Atrīdae and the Dioscūri; sing., σ 152.

κόσμος: *order, arrangement*, then *ornaments* (of women), *trappings* (of horses); of building or construction, ἵππου (the wooden), θ 492; freq. κόσμῳ, and (εὖ) κατὰ κόσμον, both literally and figuratively, 'duly,' 'becomingly,' θ 489; also οὐ κατὰ κόσμον, υ 181.

κοτέω, κοτέομαι, perf. part. κεκοτηώς, mid. aor. κοτέσσατο: *be angry* with, τινί, also w. causal gen., Δ 168.

κοτήεις: *wrathful*, E 191†.

κότος: *grudge, rancor, wrath.*

κοτύλη: *little cup, hip-joint*, E 306.

κοτυληδών, όνος, dat. pl. κοτυληδονόφιν: pl., *suckers* at the ends of the tentaculae of a polypus, ε 433†.

κοτυλ-ήρυτος (ἀρύω): *that may be caught in cups, streaming*, Ψ 34†.

κουλεόν: see κολεόν.

κούρη: *young girl, daughter;* also of young married women, Z 247.

κούρητες (κοῦρος), pl.: *youths*, usually *princes.*

Κουρῆτες: the *Curētes*, a tribe in Aetolia, afterward expelled by the Aetolians; their siege of Calydon, I 529–599.

κουρίδιος: doubtful word, *regular, wedded*, epith. of ἄλοχος, πόσις, λέχος, as opposed to irregular connections; δῶμα, house *of the husband*, or *princely* house, τ 580; as subst. (= πόσις), ο 22.

κουρίζω: only part., *when a young man*, χ 185†.

κουρίξ: adv., *by the hair*, χ 188†.

κοῦρος: *youth, boy*, esp. of noble rank, so when applied to the attendants at sacrifices and banquets, as these were regularly the sons of princely houses, A 470, *α* 148; also implying vigorous youth, ability to bear arms, P 726; *son*, *τ* 523.

κουρότερος: *younger;* as subst., Δ 316. [ι 27†.

κουρο-τρόφος: *nourisher of youths,*

κοῦφος: *light, agile;* adv., **κοῦφα,** *quickly,* N 158; **κουφότερον,** *with lighter heart,* θ 201.

Κόων: son of Antēnor, slain by Agamemnon, Λ 248–260, T 53.

Κόωνδε: see Κῶς.

κράατα, κράατι, κράατος: see *κάρη*.

κραδαίνω = *κραδάω*, only mid. part., *quivering.* (Il.)

κραδάω, part. *κραδάων*: *brandish.*

κραδίη: *heart.*

κραίνω, κραιαίνω, *κραίνουσι*, ipf. *ἐκραίαινε*, aor. imp. *κρήηνον, κρῆνον*, inf. *κρηῆναι, κρῆναι*, mid. fut. inf. *κρανέεσθαι* (for *κεκράανται, -ντο*, see *κεράννῡμι*): *accomplish, fulfil, bring to pass;* fut. mid. as pass., I 626; 'bear sway,' θ 391.

κραιπνός, comp. *κραιπνότερος*: *rapid, quick;* fig., *hasty*, *νόος*, Ψ 590.—Adv., **κραιπνῶς,** also *κραιπνά*, E 223.

Κρανάη: name of an island, Γ 445.

κραναός: *rocky*, epith. of Ithaca.

κρανέεσθαι: see *κραίνω*.

κράνεια: *cornel-tree*, Π 767, *κ* 242.

κρᾱνίον (*κρᾶνον*): upper part of the *skull*, Θ 84†.

Κράπαθος (later *Κάρπαθος*): an island near Rhodes, B 676.

κρᾶτα, κρᾱτί: see *κάρη*.

κραται-γύαλος: *with strong breastplates*, T 361†. (See cut No. 55.)

κραταιΐς: *overpowering force*, 'weight' we should say, i. e. the force of gravitation, in the stone of Sisyphus, λ 597.—Personified, **Κραταιΐς,** *Crataeis*, the mother of Scylla, *μ* 124.

κραταιός: *powerful, mighty;* Μοῖρα, *θήρ* (lion), Λ 119.

κραταί-πεδος (*πέδον*): *with strong* (*hard*) *footing* or *surface*, *ψ* 46†.

κρατερός, καρτερός, *κρατερῆφι*: *strong, powerful, mighty*, of persons and things, and sometimes in bad sense, *μῦθος*, 'stern,' A 25.—Adv., **κρατερῶς.**

κρατερό-φρων: *stout-hearted, dauntless.*

κρατερ-ῶνυξ (*ὄνυξ*): *strong-hoofed, strong-clawed.*

κρᾰτεσφι: see *κάρη*.

κρατευταί: explained by Aristarchus as *head-stones*, on which the spits were rested in roasting meat; cf. our 'fire-dogs,' 'andirons.' Possibly the shape was like the horns (*κέρας*) on the altar in cut No. 95. I 214†.

κρατέω (*κράτος*): *be superior* in might, *have power, rule over, τινός*, sometimes *τισίν* (among), λ 485, *π* 265; *κρατέων*, 'with might.'

κράτος, κάρτος, *εος*: superior *strength, might, power*, then *mastery, victory*, *α* 359, *φ* 280.

κρᾱτύς: see *κάρη*.

κρατύς = *κρατερός*, epith. of Hermes.

κρέας, *ατος*, pl. *κρέα* and *κρέατα*, gen. *κρεῶν* and *κρειῶν*, dat. *κρέασιν*: *flesh, meat*, pl., pieces of dressed *meat; κρέα*, *ι* 347.

κρεῖον (*κρέας*): *meat-tray, dresser*, I 206†.

κρείσσων, *ον*: *stronger, superior* in strength or might, *better;* w. inf., *φ* 345.

Κρειοντιάδης: *son of Creon*, Lycomēdes, T 240†.

κρείων, *ουσα*, properly part.: *ruling, ruler; εὐρὺ κρείων*, 'ruling far and wide,' title esp. of Agamemnon, as generalissimo of the Greek forces; also of Zeus and Poseidon; more freely applied, *δ* 22.

Κρείων: *Creon.*—(1) a king of Thebes, the father of Megara, λ 269.—(2) father of Lycomēdes.

κρεμάννῡμι, κρέμαμαι, fut. *κρεμόω*, aor. *κρέμασε*, mid. ipf. (*ἐ*)*κρέμω*: *hang, hang up*, mid. intrans., O 18.

κρεῶν: see *κρέας*.

κρήγυος: *good, useful, helpful*, A 106†.

κρήδεμνον (*κάρη, δέω*): *head-band;* in women's attire, a short veil, as seen in the cut, *α* 334; also of the 'battlements' of cities, *ν* 388; 'lid' of a wine-jar, *γ* 392. (See cut No. 64.)

κρηῆναι: see *κραίνω*.

κρῆθεν: see *κατάκρηθεν*.

Κρηθεύς: *Cretheus*, of Iolcus, the husband of Tyro, λ 237, 258.

Κρήθων: son of Diocles, slain by Aenēas, E 542, 549.

κρημνός (*κρέμαμαι*): *steep*, overhanging *bank*, often of the gullied banks of the Scamander, Φ 26, 175.

κρηναῖος (*κρήνη*): *of the fount*, *νύμφαι*, *fountain*-nymphs, ρ 240†.

κρήνη: *fount*, *spring*; *κρήνηνδε*, *to the spring*, υ 154. (Cf. cut No. 61.)

Κρής, pl. **Κρῆτες**: the *Cretans*, *inhabitants of Crete*.

Κρήτη, also pl. Κρῆται: *Crete*; epithets, *ἑκατόμπολις*, *εὐρεῖα*, τ 172, 175.—**Κρήτηνδε**, *to Crete*, τ 186; **Κρήτηθεν**, *from Crete*, Γ 233.

κρητήρ, ῆρος (*κεράννῡμι*): *mixing-bowl*, *wassail-bowl*, in which wine and water were mingled, to be distributed in cups; two parts of wine to three of water was a common mixture; *κρητῆρα μίσγεσθαι*, *στήσασθαι*, 'set up,' place at hand. The wassail-bowl was usually placed near the hearth, and often on a tripod (esp. when several *κρητῆρες* were in use at the banquet); the contents were poured into the cups (*δέπαα*) by means of a filler (*πρόχοος*, pitcher), γ 339. Cut No. 7 shows (1) the *ἀμφιφορεύς*, from which the wine was poured into the upper, smaller mixing-bowl, on which the *πρόχοος* stands. The second mixing-bowl served to contain the water, and then the contents of both bowls may be imagined as mixed in the largest bowl, which stands upon the tripod, and from which the diluted wine was distributed. (Cf. cut No. 26.)

κρῖ = *κριθή*.

κρίζω, aor. 2 *κρίκε*: *creak*, said of the yoke under a strain, Π 470.

κριθή, only pl. *κριθαί*: *barley*, *barley-corn*.

κρίκε: see *κρίζω*.

κρίκος (*κίρκος*): *yoke-ring*, Ω 272†. (See adjoining cut, from the antique; still clearer are cuts Nos. 42, 45.)

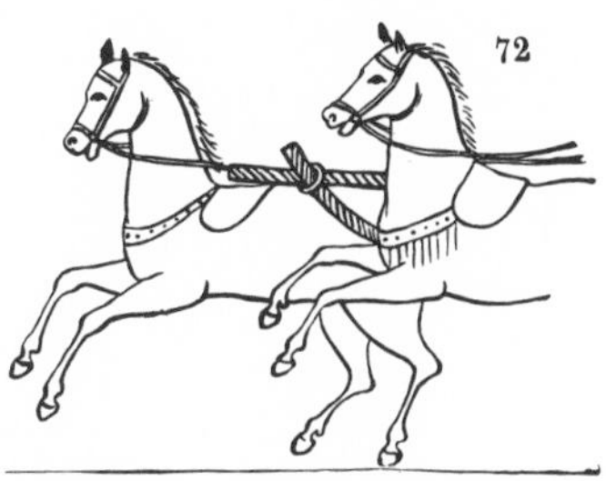
72

κρίνω, imp. *κρῖνε*, pass. perf. part. *κεκριμένος*, aor. *κρινθέντες*, mid. aor. *ἐκρίνατο*, subj. *κρίνωνται*, inf. *κρίνασθαι*, part. *κρῑνάμενος*: I. act., *separate*, *καρπόν τε καὶ ἄχνᾱς*, E 501; hence of arranging troops, B 446; then *select*, Z 188; freq. the pass., N 129, ν 182; *decide* (c e r n e r e), *νεῖκος*, *θέμιστας*, σ 264, Π 387; *οὖρος κεκριμένος*, a 'decided' wind, Ξ 19.—II. mid., *select* or *choose for oneself*; δ 408, θ 36; *get* a contest *decided*, 'measure oneself' in battle, *κρίνεσθαι Ἄρηι* (d e c e r n e r e p r o e l i o), B 385; abs. ω 507, cf. π 269; of 'interpreting' dreams, E 150.

κριός: *ram*. (Od.)

Κρῖσα: a town in Phocis, near Delphi, termed *ζαθέη*, B 520.

κριτός (*κρίνω*): *chosen*, H 434 and θ 258.

κροαίνω (*κρούω*): *gallop*. (Il.)

Κροῖσμος: a Trojan, slain by Meges, O 523†.

κροκό-πεπλος: *with saffron-colored mantle*, *saffron-robed*; epith. of Eos. (Il.)

κρόκος: *saffron*, Ξ 348†.

Κροκύλεια: an island or a village belonging to Ithaca, B 633†.

κρόμυον: *onion*.

Κρονίδης: *son of Cronus*, Zeus, often used alone without *Ζεύς*, Δ 5.

Κρονίων = Κρονίδης.

Κρόνος: *Cronus* (S a t u r n u s), the father of Zeus, Poseidon, Hades, Hera, Demēter, and Hestia; overthrown with the Titans, Θ 415, 479, 383, E 721.

κρόσσαι (cf. *κόρση*, *κάρη*): *πύργων*, *walls* or *breasting* of the towers, between foundations and battlements, M 258, 444.

κροταλίζω (*κρόταλον*): *rattle*; *ὄχεα κροτάλιζον*, 'drew the rattling chariots,' Λ 160†.

κρόταφος (cf. *κόρση*, *κάρη*): *temples* of the head, Δ 502, Υ 397; usually pl.

κροτέω (*κρότος*) = *κροταλίζω*, O 453†.

Κρουνοί: 'Springs,' a place in Elis, ο 295†.

κρουνός: *source*, *spring*. (Il.)

κρύβδα, κρύβδην: *secretly.*

κρυερός (κρύος): *chilling, dread.*

κρυόεις = κρυερός. (Il.)

κρυπτάδιος: *secret;* κρυπτάδια φρονέοντα δικαζέμεν, 'harbor secret counsels,' A 542.

κρυπτός: *concealed, secret,* Ξ 168†.

κρύπτω, ipf. iter. κρύπτασκε, fut. κρύψω, aor. ἔκρυψα, pass. aor. κρύφθη, perf. part. κεκρυμμένος: *hide, conceal,* sometimes implying protection, τινὰ σάκεϊ, κεφαλὰς κορύθεσσι, cf. καλύπτω; pass., κρύφθη ὑπ ἀσπίδι, 'hid himself,' N 405; met., 'keep secret,' ἔπος τινί, λ 443.

κρύσταλλος: *clear ice, ice,* ξ 477 and X 152.

κρυφηδόν: *secretly,* ξ 330 and τ 299.

Κρῶμνα: a locality in Paphlagonia, B 855†.

κτάμεν(αι): see κτείνω.

κτάομαι, aor. 2 sing. ἐκτήσω, perf. inf. ἐκτῆσθαι: *acquire,* perf. *possess,* I 402; of acquiring for another than oneself, υ 265.

κτέαρ, dat. pl. κτεάτεσσι: pl., *possessions, property.*

κτεατίζω, aor. κτεάτισσα=κτάομαι.

Κτέατος: son of Actor and Molione, B 621.

κτείνω, ipf. κτεῖνον, iter. κτείνεσκε, fut. κτενέει, part. κτανέοντα, aor. ἔκτεινα, κτεῖνε, aor. 2 ἔκτανον, κτάνον, also ἔκτα, ἔκταμεν, ἔκταν, subj. κτέωμεν, inf. κτάμεναι, pass. pres. inf. κτείνεσθαι, aor. 3 pl. ἔκταθεν, aor. 2 mid., w. pass. signif., κτάσθαι, κτάμενος: *kill, slay,* esp. in battle; rarely of animals, O 587, μ 379, τ 543; pass., E 465; aor. mid. as pass., O 558.

κτέρας = κτέαρ, K 216 and Ω 235.

κτέρεα, pl.: possessions burned in honor of the dead upon the funeral-pyre, hence *funeral honors, obsequies* (extremi honores), always with κτερεΐζειν.

κτερίζω, κτερεΐζω, inf. κτερεϊζέμεν, fut. κτεριῶ, aor. opt. κτερίσειε, inf. κτερεΐξαι: *bury with solemn honors;* ἀέθλοις, 'celebrate one's funeral with games,' Ψ 646; ἐπὶ (adv.) κτερέα κτερεΐξαι, 'bestow funeral honors upon' one, α 291, Ω 38.

κτῆμα (κτάομαι): *possession, property,* sing., ο 19; elsewhere pl., in the Iliad mostly of *treasures,* H 350, I 382.

Κτήσιος: the father of Eumaeus, ο 414†.

Κτήσιππος: son of Polytherses, from Same, one of the suitors of Penelope, slain by Philoetius, υ 288, χ 279, 285.

κτῆσις, ιος (κτάομαι): *property.*

κτητός: *that may be acquired,* I 407†.

κτίδεος (ἰκτίς): *of weasel-skin;* κυνέη, K 335 and 458.

κτίζω, aor. ἔκτισα, κτίσσε: *settle, found,* a city or land.

κτίλος: *ram,* Γ 196 and N 492.

Κτιμένη: daughter of Laertes, sister of Odysseus, settled in marriage in Same, ο 363.

κτυπέω, aor. ἔκτυπε: *crash, thunder;* of falling trees, the bolts of Zeus.

κτύπος: any loud noise such as a *crash, thunder;* of the stamping of the feet of men, or the hoofs of horses, the tumult of battle, and the bolts of Zeus, π 6, K 532, M 338.

κύαμος: *bean,* pl., N 589†.

κυάνεος (κύανος): *of steel,* Σ 564, then *steel-blue, dark blue, dark;* of the brows of Zeus, A 528; the hair of Hector, X 402; a serpent, Λ 26; earth or sand, μ 243; and esp. νεφέλη, νέφος, even in metaphor, Π 66, Δ 282.

κυανό-πεζα: *with steel-blue feet,* τράπεζα, Λ 629†.

κυανό-πρῳρος and **κυανο-πρῴρειος** (πρῴρᾱ): *dark-prowed, dark-bowed,* epith. of ships.

κύανος: probably blue *steel,* Λ 24, 35, and η 87.

κυανο-χαίτης and **κυανο-χαῖτα**: the *dark-haired,* epith. of Poseidon, also as subst.; *dark-maned,* ἵππος, Υ 224.

κυαν-ῶπις, ιδος: *dark-eyed,* μ 60†.

κυβερνάω, aor. inf. κυβερνῆσαι: *steer,* νῆα, γ 283†.

κυβερνήτης, εω, and **κυβερνητήρ,** ῆρος: *helmsman, pilot.* (Od.)

κυβιστάω (κύβη, *head,* found only in glossaries), ipf. κυβίστων: *turn somersaults, tumble,* Π 745, 749; of fishes, Φ 354.

κυβιστητήρ, ῆρος: *tumbler; diver,* Π 750.

κῡδαίνω (κῦδος), aor. κύδηνε, inf. κυδῆναι: *glorify, ennoble;* θυμόν, *rejoice,* trans., ξ 438.

κῡδάλιμος (κῦδος): *glorious, noble,*

epith. of persons, and of κῆρ, as typical of the person.

κῡδάνω: *glorify, exalt;* intrans., *exult*, Υ 42.

κῡδι-άνειρα: *man-ennobling*, ἀγορή, μάχη. (Il.)

κῡδιάω, part. κῡδιόων: *triumph, be proud.* (Il.)

κύδιστος: *most glorious.*

κυδοιμέω, aor. κυδοίμησαν: *rush tumultuously, spread confusion;* trans., *throw into confusion*, Ο 136.

κυδοιμός: *uproar, confusion, din* or *mêlée of battle;* personified, Ε 593, Σ 535.

κῦδος, εος: *glory, majesty, might;* of persons, in address, μέγα κῦδος Ἀχαιῶν, 'pride of the Greeks,' Nestor and Odysseus, Κ 87, ι 673.

κυδρός: *glorious, illustrious,* always κυδρὴ παράκοιτις.

Κύδωνες: the *Cydonians*, a tribe in the northwest of Crete, γ 292, τ 176.

κυέω: *conceive, carry* in the womb; of a mare with mule foal, Ψ 266.

κύθε: see κεύθω.

Κυθέρεια: *Cytherēa*, epithet of Aphrodite, from the island of Cythēra.

Κύθηρα, pl.: *Cythēra*, an island off the coast of Laconia, S.W. of the promontory of Malēa, where the worship of Aphrodite had been introduced by an early Phoenician colony, ι 81, Ο 432. — **Κυθηρόθεν,** *from Cythēra*, Ο 538. —Adj. **Κυθήριος,** *of Cythēra*, Κ 268, Ο 431.

κυκάω, part. κυκόωντι, ipf. ἐκύκᾱ, aor. κύκησε, pass. κυκήθην: *stir up, stir in, mix up;* met., only pass., *be stirred up*, 'panic-stricken,' Υ 489; of waves and the sea, *foam up, be in commotion*, Φ 235, μ 238.

κυκεών, acc. κυκεῶ: a *mixed drink*, compounded of barley meal, grated cheese, and wine, Λ 624; Circe adds also honey, κ 290, 234.

κυκλέω: *wheel away, carry forth*, of corpses, Η 332†.

κύκλος, pl. κύκλοι and κύκλα: *ring, circle;* δόλιος, employed by hunters for capturing game, δ 792; ἱερός, the solemn circle of a tribunal, etc., Σ 504; *wheel*, Ψ 340, pl., τὰ κύκλα, Ε 722, Σ 375; of the *rings* on the outside of a shield, or the *layers* which, lying one above the other and gradually diminishing in size toward the boss, made up the whole disc, Λ 33, Υ 280.

κυκλόσε: *in a circle*, Δ 212 and Ρ 392.

κυκλο-τερής, ές (τείρω): *circular*, ρ 209; stretch or draw 'into a circle,' Δ 124.

Κύκλωψ, pl. **Κύκλωπες**: *Cyclops*, pl., the *Cyclōpes;* sing., Polyphēmus, whose single eye was blinded by Odysseus, ι 428. The Cyclōpes are in Homer a lawless race of giants, dwelling without towns, social ties, or religion, ι 166.

κύκνος: *swan.*

κυλίνδω, part. neut. κυλίνδον, pass. ipf. (ἐ)κυλίνδετο, aor. κυλίσθη: *roll;* Βορέης κῦμα, ε 296; fig., πῆμά τινι, Ρ 688; pass., *be rolled, roll*, of a stone, λ 598; of persons in violent demonstrations of grief, Χ 414, δ 541; met., Λ 347, θ 81.

Κυλλήνη: *Cyllēne*, a mountain-chain in northern Arcadia, Β 603.

Κυλλήνιος: *Cyllenian.* —(1) epith. of Hermes, from his birthplace, Mt. Cyllēne in Arcadia, ω 24. —(2) an inhabitant of the town Cyllēne in Elis, Ο 518.

κυλλο-ποδίων, voc. -πόδῑον (κυλλός, πούς): *crook-footed*, epith. of Hephaestus. (Il.)

κῦμα (κύω): *wave, billow;* κατὰ κῦμα, 'with the current,' β 429.

κῡμαίνω: only part., πόντον κῡμαίνοντα, *billowy* deep. (Od.)

κύμβαχος: *head foremost*, Ε 586; as subst., *crown* or *top* of a helmet, the part in which the plume is fixed, Ο 536. (See cuts Nos. 16 and 17.)

κύμινδις: *night-hawk*, called in the older language χαλκίς, Ξ 291.

Κῡμο-δόκη and **Κυμοθόη**: Nereids, Σ 39, 41†.

κυνά-μυια: *dog-fly*, an abusive epithet applied by Ares to Athēna, Φ 394.

κυνέη: properly 'dog-skin,' a soldier's *cap*, generally of leather, ταυρείη, Κ 257; κτιδέη, Κ 335; also mounted with metal, χαλκήρης, χαλκοπάρῃος, and πάγχαλκος, *helmet*, σ 378; the κυνέη αἴγειη was a goat-skin cap for country wear (like that of the oarsmen in cut No. 38), ω 231; Ἄιδος, the cap of Hades, rendered the wearer invisible, Ε 845.

κύνεος: *dog-like*, i. e. *shameless*, I 373†.

κυνέω, ipf. κύνεον, κύνει, aor. ἔκυσα, κύ(σ)σε, inf. κύσσαι: *kiss*; κύσσε δέ μιν κεφαλήν τε καὶ ἄμφω φάεα καλὰ | χεῖράς τ' ἀμφοτέρας (this shows the range of the word), π 15, cf. ρ 39; ἄρουραν, his native soil, ν 354.

κυν-ηγέτης (κύων, ἡγέομαι): literally *leader of dogs*, i. e. *hunter*, pl., ι 120†.

κυνο-ραιστής (ῥαίω): literally *dog-breaker* (cf. 'house-breaker'), i. e. *flea*, pl., ρ 300†.

Κῦνος: a harbor-town of Locris, B 531†.

κύντερος, comp., sup. κύντατος: *more* (*most*) *dog like*, i. e. *shameless*, *impudent*, *audacious*, K 503.

κυν-ώπης, voc. κυνῶπα, and **κυν-ῶπις**, ιδος: literally *dog-faced*, i. e. *impudent*, *shameless*.

Κυπαρισσήεις: a town in Elis, B 593†.

κυπαρίσσινος: *of cypress wood*, ρ 340†.

κυπάρισσος: *cypress*, evergreen, ε 64†.

κύπειρον: *fragrant marsh-grass*, perhaps 'galingal,' used as food for horses, δ 603.

κύπελλον: drinking-*cup*, *goblet*, Ω 305, cf. 285, I 670.

Κύπρις: *Cypris*, epith. of Aphrodīte, from the island of Cyprus, E 330.

Κύπρος: the island of *Cyprus*, δ 83.—**Κυπρονδε**, *to Cyprus*, Λ 21.

κύπτω, aor. opt. κύψει(ε), part. κύψᾱς: *bend the head*, *bow down*. (Il. and λ 585.)

κυρέω, **κῦρω**, ipf. κῦρε, aor. inf. κυρῆσαι, part. κύρσᾱς, mid. pres. κῦρεται: *chance upon*, *encounter*, ipf. *try to hit*, *aim*, Ψ 281; w. ἐπί or dat. merely, Ω 530; of colliding in the race, Ψ 428. Cf. τυγχάνω.

κύρμα (κυρέω): what one chances upon, hence *prey*, *booty*; usually with ἕλωρ, E 488.

κύρσᾱς: see κυρέω.

κυρτός: *curved*, *rounded*, *arched*. (Il.)

κυρτόω: *make curved*; κῦμα κυρτωθέν, 'arched,' λ 244†.

κύστις: *bladder*. (Il.)

Κύτωρος: a town in Paphlagonia, B 853.

κῡφός (κύπτω): *bowed*, *bent*, β 16†.

Κύφος: a town in Perrhaebia in Thessaly, B 748†.

κύω: see κυέω and κυνέω.

κύων, κυνός, acc. κύνα, voc. κύον, pl. dat. κύνεσσι: *dog*, *bitch*; κύνες θηρευταί, τραπεζῆες, 'hunting' and 'lap-dogs,' Ἀίδᾱο, i. e. Cerberus, Θ 368, λ 623; 'sea-dog,' perhaps seal, μ 96; dog of Orīon, Sirius, X 29; as symbol of shamelessness, applied to women and others, N 623; λυσσητήρ, 'raging hound,' Θ 299.

κῶας, pl. κώεα, dat. κώεσιν: *fleece*, serving for seat or bedding, π 47. I 661, γ 38.

κώδεια: *poppy-head*, Ξ 499†.

κωκῡτός (κωκύω): *wailing*. As proper name **Κωκῡτός**, *Cocȳtus*, river of the nether world, κ 514.

κωκύω, aor. κώκῡσ(ε), part. κωκύσᾱσα: *wail*, always of women's voices; sometimes trans., 'bewail,' τινά, ω 295.

κώληψ, ηπος: *bend* or *hollow of the knee*, Ψ 726†.

κῶμα (κοιμάω): *deep sleep*.

Κῶπαι: a town on lake Copāis in Boeotia, B 502†.

κώπη: *handle* of sword or oar, *hilt*, *oar*; of a key, φ 7. (See cut No. 68.)

κωπήεις: *hilted*.

κώρυκος: leather *knapsack* or *wallet*. (Od.)

Κῶς: the island of *Cos*, B 677.—**Κόωνδε**, *to Cos*, O 28.

κωφός (κόπτω): *blunted*, Λ 390; 'dull-sounding,' of a wave before it breaks, Ξ 16; κωφὴ γαῖα, *dull*, 'senseless' dust, of a dead body, Ω 54.

Λ.

λᾶας, λᾶος, dat. λᾶι, acc. λᾶαν, du. λᾶε, pl. gen. λάων, dat. λάεσσι: *stone.*

Λάας: a town in Laconia, B 585†.

λαβρ-αγόρης (λάβρος): *reckless talker,* Ψ 479†.

λαβρεύομαι: *talk rashly,* Ψ 474 and 478.

λάβρος, sup. λαβρότατος: *rapid, rushing.*

λαγχάνω, aor. ἔλαχον, λάχεν, redupl. subj. λελάχητε, perf. λέλογχεν: *obtain by lot* or by destiny, *obtain, receive;* abs., H 171; reversing the usual relation, Κὴρ λάχε γεινόμενον, 'won me to her power at my birth,' Ψ 79; w. part. gen., Ω 76, ε 311; causative, 'put in possession of,' 'honor with,' θανόντα πυρός, only with redupl. aor., H. 80, etc.; intrans., 'fall by lot,' ι 160.

λαγωός (Att. λαγώς): *hare.*

Λαέρκης: (1) son of Aemon, father of Alcimedon, a Myrmidon, Π 197.—(2) a goldsmith in Pylos, γ 425.

Λᾱέρτης: *Laertes,* son of Arcīsius, and father of Odysseus, king in Ithaca, α 430, ω 206, 270, δ 111, 555, χ 185, ω 219 ff.

Λᾱερτιάδης: *son of Laertes,* Odysseus.

λάζομαι (=λαμβάνω), opt. 3 pl. λαζοίατο, ipf. (ἐ)λάζετο: *take;* γαῖαν ὀδάξ, 'bite the dust,' B 418; μῦθον πάλιν, 'caught back again' the words (of joy which were on his lips), ν 254.

λαθι-κηδής, ές (κῆδος): *causing to forget care,* 'banishing care,' X 83†.

λάθρῃ: *secretly, unbeknown,* τινός, 'to one'; 'imperceptibly,' T 165.

λᾶϊγξ, ιγγος: *pebble.* (Od.)

λαῖλαψ, απος: *tempest* of wind and rain, *hurricane.*

λαιμός: *throat, gullet.* (Il.)

λᾱΐνεος and **λάϊνος** (λᾶας): *of stone, stony;* τεῖχος, in the interpolated passage, M 177.

λαισήιον: light *shield* or *target;* λαισήια πτερόεντα, perhaps so called on account of the 'fluttering' apron of untanned leather (λάσιος) hanging from the shield. (See adjoining cut and esp. No. 79.)

73

Λαιστρῡγόνιος: *Laestrygonian,* κ 82, ψ 318.

Λαιστρῡγών, pl. **Λαιστρῡγόνες**: *Laestrȳgon,* the *Laestrȳgons,* a tribe of savage giants, κ 106, 119, 199.

λαῖτμα: the great *gulf* or *abyss* of the sea, usually w. ἁλός or θαλάσσης. (Od. and T 267.)

λαῖφος, εος: *shabby, tattered garment,* ν 399 and υ 206.

λαιψηρός: *nimble, swift;* adv., λαιψηρὰ ἐνώμᾱ, 'plied nimbly,' O 269.

λάκε: see λάσκω.

Λακεδαίμων: *Lacedaemon,* the district whose capital was Sparta; epithets, δῖα, γ 326; ἐρατεινή, Γ 239; εὐρύχορος, ν 414; κοίλη, κητώεσσα, δ 1.

λακτίζω: *kick* with the heel, of the mortally wounded, struggling convulsively, σ 99 and χ 88.

λαμβάνω, only aor. 2 act. and mid., ἔλλαβ(ε), ἐλλάβετ(ο), inf. redupl. λελαβέσθαι: *take, receive,* mid., *take hold of;* freq. w. part. gen.; sometimes of 'seizing,' 'taking captive,' λ 4, Λ 114; in friendly sense, 'take in,' η 255; met., of feelings, χόλος, πένθος, τρόμος, etc.

Λάμος: the king of the Laestrȳgons, κ 81†.

λαμπετάω = λάμπω.

Λαμπετίδης: *son of Lampus*, Dolops, Ο 526†.

Λαμπετίη: a nymph, daughter of Helius, μ 132, 375.

Λάμπος: (1) son of Laomedon, father of the Trojan Dolops, Γ 147, Ο 526.—(2) name of one of the steeds of Eos, ψ 246.—(3) one of Hector's horses, Θ 185.

λαμπρός, sup. λαμπρότατος: *bright, brilliant, shining*. (Il. and τ 234.)

λαμπτήρ, ῆρος: *fire-pan, light-stand, cresset*, to hold blazing pine splinters for illuminating, σ 307, τ 63. (See cuts, after bronze originals from Pompeii.)

λάμπω, ipf. ἔλαμπ(ε), λάμφ': *shine, gleam, be radiant* or *brilliant*.

λανθάνω, λήθω, ipf. (ἐ)λάνθανον, ἔληθον, λῆθεν, iter. λήθεσκε, fut. λήσω, aor. 2 ἔλαθον, λάθον, subj. redupl. λελάθῃ, mid. λήθομαι, ipf. λανθανόμην, aor. 2 λάθετο, redupl. λελάθοντο, opt. 3 pl. λαθοίατο, imp. redupl. λελαθέσθω, perf. λέλασται, part. λελασμένος: I. act., *escape the notice of*, τινά, the obj. of the Greek verb usually appearing as the subj. in Eng., οὐδέ σε λήθω, 'nor dost thou ever *fail to mark* me,' Α 561, ρ 305; the thing that one does when somebody else fails to mark him is regularly expressed by the part., ἄλλον πού τινα μᾶλλον Ἀχαιῶν χαλκοχιτώνων | λήθω μαρνάμενος, σὲ δὲ ϝίδμεναι αὐτὸν ὀίω, 'another perchance is likely enough to *overlook my prowess*, but you know it right well,' Ν 272. The learner cannot afford to be careless about the above meaning and construction. Sometimes w. ὅτι or ὅπως, ὅτε, Ρ 626. The redupl. aor. is causative, *make to forget; τινά τινος*, Ο 60.—II. mid., *forget; τινός*, Δ 127, γ 224.

λάξ: adv., *with the heel*, with ποδί, Κ 158, ο 45.

Λαό-γονος: (1) a Trojan, the son of Onētor, slain by Meriones, Π 604.—(2) a Trojan, the son of Bias, slain by Achilles, Υ 460.

Λᾱόδαμας: (1) son of Antēnor, slain by Ajax, Ο 516.—(2) a Phaeacian, son of Alcinous, θ 119, 132, η 170, θ 117, 141.

Λᾱοδάμεια: daughter of Bellerophon, and mother of Sarpēdon, Ζ 198.

Λᾱοδίκη: *Laodice*.—(1) a daughter of Agamemnon, Ι 145, 287.—(2) a daughter of Priam, wife of Helicāon, Γ 124, Ζ 252.

Λᾱόδοκος: (1) a son of Antēnor, Δ 87.—(2) a comrade of Antilochus, Ρ 699.

Λαοθόη: daughter of Altes, mother of Lycāon, Φ 85, Χ 48.

Λᾱομεδοντιάδης: *son* or *descendant of Laomedon*.—(1) Priam, Γ 250.—(2) Lampus, Ο 527.

Λᾱομέδων: *Laomedon*, son of Ilus and father of Priam. He had promised his daughter Hesione to Heracles, on condition of her being delivered from the sea-monster sent by Poseidon to ravage the Troad, but proving false to his agreement was slain by Heracles, Ε 638 ff., 269, Ζ 23, Υ 237, Φ 443.

λᾱός, pl. λᾱοί: *people, host*, esp.

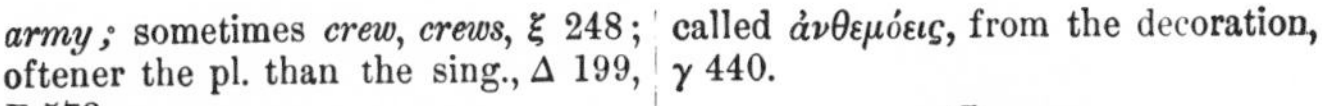

army; sometimes *crew, crews,* ξ 248; oftener the pl. than the sing., Δ 199, E 573.

λᾱο-σσόος (σεύω): *driving the people on* (to combat), *rousing the people;* epith. of Ares, Eris, Athēne (Apollo, Amphiarāus), N 128, χ 210.

λᾱο-φόρος: ὁδός, *public way,* O 682†.

λαπάρη: the soft part of the body between hips and ribs, *flank, loins.* (Il.)

Λαπίθαι: the *Lapithae,* a warlike tribe dwelling by Mts. Olympus and Pelion in Thessaly, M 128, 181, φ 297.

λάπτω, fut. part. λάψοντες: *lap up* with the tongue, Π 161†.

Λάρῑσα: a town in Asia Minor, near Cyme, B 841, P 301.

λάρναξ, ακος: *chest,* Σ 413; *vase* or *urn,* Ω 795.

λάρος: a sea bird, *cormorant,* with ὄρνῑς, ε 51†.

λᾱρός, sup. λᾱρώτατος: *rich, fine, well-relished,* P 572.

λάσιος: *hairy, shaggy,* epith. of στῆθος, also κῆρ, as sign of manly strength and spirit; of sheep, *woolly,* ι 433.

λάσκω, aor. 2 λάκε, perf. part. w. pres. signif. λεληκώς, λελακυῖα: *give voice,* of animals, Scylla (as dog), a falcon, X 141; of things, *sound,* χαλκός, ἀσπίς, ὀστέα. (Il. and μ 85.)

λαυκανίη: *throat, gullet.* (Il.)

λαύρη: *lane, side-passage* between the house (of Odysseus) and the outer wall of the court, χ 128, 137. (See plate III., *o, n.*)

λαφύσσω: *gulp down, swallow.* (Il.)

λάχε: see λαγχάνω.

λάχεια: *with good soil* for digging, *fertile,* νῆσος, ι 116 and κ 509.

λάχνη: *woolly hair, down,* K 134; *sparse hair* or *beard,* B 219, λ 320.

λαχνήεις: *hairy, shaggy.* (Il.)

λάχνος = λάχνη, *wool,* ι 445†.

λάω, part. λάων, ipf. λάε: doubtful word, 'bury the teeth in,' of a dog strangling a fawn, τ 229 f.

λέβης, ητος: *kettle, caldron,* for warming water or for boiling food over fire, Φ 362; in the Odyssey usually, *basin, wash-basin,* held under the hands or feet while water was poured from a pitcher over them, τ 386; called ἀνθεμόεις, from the decoration, γ 440.

76

λέγω, ipf. ἔλεγ', λέγε, λέγομεν, fut. part. λέξοντες, aor. ἔλεξεν, imp. λέξον, mid. pres. subj. λεγώμεθα, ipf. λέγοντο, fut. λέξομαι, aor. λέξατο, aor. 2 ἐλέγμην, ἔλεκτο, λέκτο, imp. λέξο, λέξεο, pass. aor. ἐλέχθην. The above forms are common to two distinct roots λεγ, *gather,* and λεχ, *lay.* — I. root λεγ, *gather, collect,* Ψ 239, K 755, σ 359, ω 72, 224; *count,* δ 452; pass., Γ 188; then *enumerate, recount, tell, relate,* B 222, ε 5, λ 374; mid., *collect for oneself, count oneself in, select,* Θ 507, 547, ι 335, B 125; λέκτο ἀριθμόν, *counted over* the number (for himself), δ 451; also *talk over* (with one another), μηκέτι ταῦτα λεγώμεθα, γ 240.—II. root λεχ, act. aor. 1, *lay, put to bed* or *to rest,* Ω 635; met., Ξ 252; mid., fut. and aor. 1 and 2, *lay oneself down, lie down* to sleep, *lie,* δ 413, 453, Δ 131, Θ 519, I 67.

λειαίνω (λεῖος), fut. λειανέω, aor. 3 pl. λείηναν, part. λειήνᾱς: *make smooth, smooth, level off,* θ 260.

λείβω, ipf. λεῖβε, aor. inf. λεῖψαι: *pour* (*in drops*), *shed,* δάκρυα often; also esp., *pour a libation,* (οἶνον) τινί, or *drink-offering;* abs., Ω 285. (See cut No. 77 on next page; cf. also Nos. 21 and 95.)

λειμών, ῶνος: *meadow, mead;* λειμωνόθεν, *from the meadow,* Ω 451.

λεῖος (l ē v i s): *smooth, even, level;* πετράων, 'free from rocks,' ε 443.

λείπω, ipf. λεῖπ(ε), fut. λείψω, aor. 2 ἔλιπον, λίπον, perf. λέλοιπεν, mid. ipf. λείπετ(ο), aor. 2 λιπόμην, pass. perf. λέλειπται, plup. λελείμμην, fut. perf. λελείψεται, aor. 3 pl. λίπεν: *leave, forsake;* ἔλιπον ἰοί ἄνακτα, arrows 'failed' him, χ 119, cf. ξ 213; pass. and aor. mid., *be left, remain, survive,* M 14; w. gen., *be left behind* one, as in running,

Ψ 523, 529; λελειμμένος οἰῶν, 'remaining behind' the other sheep, ι 448; λίπεν ἅρματ' ἀνάκτων, 'had been forsaken by' their masters, Π 507.

λειριόεις, εσσα (λείριον): *lily-like, lily-white,* Ν 830; ὄψ, 'delicate,' Γ 152. (Il.)

Λειώδης: son of Oenops, a suitor of Penelope and the soothsayer of the suitors; he shares their fate, φ 144, χ 310.

Λειώκριτος: (1) son of Arisbas, slain by Aenēas, Ρ 344.—(2) son of Euēnor, a suitor of Penelope, slain by Telemachus, β 242, χ 294.

λείουσι: see λέων.

λεϊστός: see ληϊστός.

λέκτο: see λέγω.

Λεκτόν: a promontory on the Trojan coast, opposite Lesbos, Ξ 284.

λέκτρον (root λεχ): *bed,* freq. the pl.; λέκτρονδε, θ 292.

λελαβέσθαι, λελάβῃσι: see λαμβάνω.

λελάθῃ, λελάθοντο: see λανθάνω.

λελακυῖα: see λάσκω.

λέλασμαι: see λανθάνω.

λελάχητε, λελάχωσι: see λαγχάνω.

Λέλεγες: a piratical tribe on the south and west coast of Asia Minor, Κ 429, Φ 86.

λεληκώς: see λάσκω.

λελίημαι: only part., λελιημένος, as adj., *eager, desirous;* w. ὄφρα, Δ 465, Ε 690. Cf. λιλαίομαι. (Il.)

λέλογχα: see λαγχάνω.

λέξεο, λέξο: see λέγω.

Λεοντεύς: a Lapith, the son of Corōnus, a suitor of Helen, Β 745, Ψ 841.

λέπαδνον, pl. λέπαδνα: *breast-collar,* a strap passing around the breast of the horses, and made fast to the yoke, Ε 730. (See *g* in cut No. 78 below, also cut No. 45, *f*.)

λεπταλέος (λεπτός): *fine, delicate,* Σ 571†.

λεπτός (λέπω), sup. λεπτότατος: *peeled, husked,* Υ 497; then *thin, fine, narrow, delicate.*

λέπω, aor. ἔλεψεν: *peel, strip off;* φύλλα, Α 236†.

Λέσβος: *Lesbos,* the island opposite the gulf of Adramyttium, γ 169, Ω 544. —**Λεσβόθεν,** *from Lesbos,* Ι 664.— **Λεσβίς,** ἴδος: *Lesbian* woman, Ι 129, 271.

λέσχη: *inn, tavern,* σ 329†.

λευγαλέος (cf. λυγρός, λοιγός): *mournful, miserable.*—Adv., **λευγαλέως,** Ν 732.

λευκαίνω: *make white,* with foam, μ 172†.

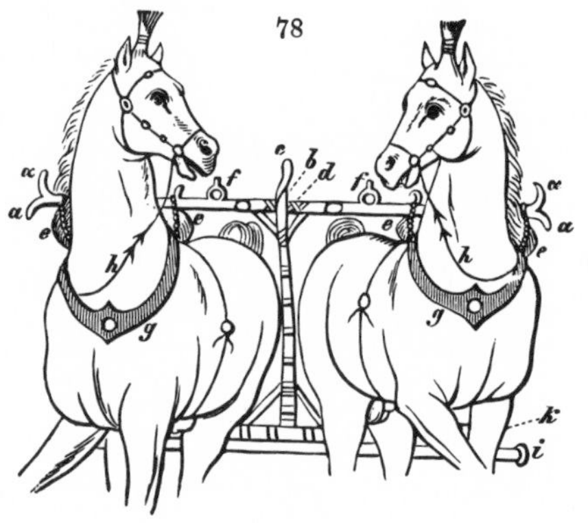

Λευκάς: πέτρη, 'White rock,' at the entrance of the nether world, on the border of Oceanus, ω 11†.

λεύκ-ασπις, ιδος: *with white shield, white-shielded,* Χ 294†.

Λευκοθέη: *Leucothea,* a sea-goddess, once Ino, the daughter of Cadmus, ε 334, 461.

λευκός: *clear,* i. e. transparent or full of light, as water, the surface of water, or the radiance of the sky, ε 70, κ 94, ζ 45; then *white,* as snow, milk, bones, barley, Κ 437, ι 246, α 161, Υ 496.

Λεῦκος: a companion of Odysseus, Δ 491†.

λευκ-ώλενος (ὠλένη, *elbow, forearm*): *white-armed;* epithet of goddesses and women according to the metrical convenience of their names; ἀμφίπολος, δμωαί, σ 198, τ 60.

λευρός: *level,* η 123†.

λεύσσω (cf. λευκός, l u x), ipf. λεῦσσε: *see, behold.*

λεχε-ποίης (λέχος, ποίη): *with grassy bed* (of a river); *grassy* (of towns), Δ 383, Β 697.

λέχος, εος (root λεχ, λέγω): *bed, bedstead,* also pl. in both senses; typical in connubial relations, λέχος ἀντιᾶν, πορσύνειν, Α 31, γ 403; funeral-couch, *bier,* ω 44, ψ 165; λέχοσδε, *to the bed,* Γ 447.

λέων, οντος, dat. pl. λείουσι and λέουσι: *lion;* fig., where we should expect 'lioness,' Φ 483.

λήγω, inf. ληγέμεναι, ipf. λῆγ', fut. λήξω, aor. 3 pl. λῆξαν: *leave off, cease,* w. gen. or w. part., Ζ 107, Φ 224; trans., *abate,* μένος, Ν 424; χεῖρας φόνοιο, 'stay' my hands from slaughter, χ 63.

Λήδη: *Leda,* the wife of Tyndareus, mother by Zeus of Helen, Castor, and Polydeuces, and of Clytaemnestra by Tyndareus, λ 298, 300.

ληθάνω: *cause to forget,* τινός, η 221†.

λήθη: *forgetfulness, oblivion,* Β 33†.

Λῆθος: son of Teutamus, and father of Hippothous, Β 843, Ρ 288.

λήθω: see λανθάνω.

ληιάς, άδος: *captive,* Υ 193†.

ληι-βότειρα (λήιον, βόσκω): *crop-eating, crop-destroying,* σ 29†.

ληίζομαι, fut. ληίσσομαι, aor. ληίσσατο: *carry off as booty.*

λήιον: *crop, grain* still standing in the field, *field of grain.*

ληίς, ίδος: *booty, prey.*

ληιστήρ, ῆρος (ληίζομαι): *buccaneer, rover,* pl. (Od.)

ληιστός: *to be plundered* or *taken by plundering,* see ἑλετός.

ληίστωρ, ορος = ληιστήρ, Ο 427†.

ληῖτις, ιδος: *booty-bringing, giver of booty,* epith. of Athēna, Κ 460†.

Λήιτος: son of Alectryon, a leader of the Boeotians, Β 494, Ν 91, Ρ 601, Ζ 35.

λήκυθος: *oil-flask,* ζ 79 and 215.

Λῆμνος: *Lemnos,* the island west of the Troad, with probably in Homer's time a city of the same name, Ξ 230, 281; called ἠγαθέη, as sacred to Hephaestus (also to the Cabīri) on account of its volcano, Moschylus; now Stalimene [(ἐ)ς τὴ(ν) Λῆμνον].

λήσω: see λανθάνω.

Λητώ: *Leto* (L a t o n a), mother of Apollo and Artemis, λ 580, Α 9; epith., ἐρικῦδής, ἠύκομος, καλλιπάρῃος.

λιάζομαι, part. λιαζόμενον, ipf. λιάζετο, aor. pass. (ἐ)λιάσθην: *turn aside, withdraw;* κῦμα, 'parted,' Ω 96; εἴδωλον, 'vanished,' δ 838; also *sink down, droop;* προτὶ γαίῃ πτερά, Υ 420, Ψ 879.

λιαρός: *warm, lukewarm;* αἷμα, ὕδωρ, Λ 477, ω 45; then *mild, gentle,* ε 268, Ξ 164.

Λιβύη: *Libya,* west of Egypt, δ 85, ξ 295.

λίγα (λιγύς): adv., *clear, loudly,* ἀείδειν, κωκύειν.

λιγαίνω (λιγύς): *cry with clear, loud voice,* Λ 685†.

λίγγω, aor. λίγξε: *twang,* Δ 125†.

λίγδην: adv., *grazing;* βάλλειν χεῖρα, χ 278†.

λιγέως: see λιγύς.

λιγυ-πνείων, οντος: *loudly blowing, whistling,* δ 567†.

λιγυρός (λιγύς): *clear-toned, whistling, piping;* ἀοιδή, μάστιξ, πνοιαί, μ 44, Λ 532, Ε 526.

λιγύς, λιγεῖα, λιγύ: *clear* and *loud* of tone, said of singers, the harp, an orator, 'clear-voiced,' 'clear-toned,' ω 62, Ι 186, Α 248; of the wind, 'piping,' 'whistling,' γ 176, Ν 334.—Adv., **λιγέως,** ἀγορεύειν, φῦσᾶν, κλαίειν, Γ 214, Ψ 218, κ 201.

λιγύ-φθογγος: *loud-voiced, clear-voiced.*

λιγύ-φωνος: *with loud, clear note,* of a falcon, T 350†.

λίζω: see λίγγω.

λῑην: *too, excessively, greatly, very;* μή τι λίην προκαλίζεο, provoke me not 'too far,' σ 20; οὐδέ τι λίην οὕτω νώνυμός ἐστι, not so *very* unrenowned, ν 238, cf. ο 405; often καὶ λίην at the beginning of a statement, 'most certainly,' 'ay, by all means,' etc.

λίθαξ, ακος: *stony, hard,* ε 415†.

λιθάς, άδος, dat. pl. λιθάδεσσι = λίθος. (Od.)

λίθεος: *of stone.*

λίθος, usually m.: *stone, rock;* fig. as symbol of firmness, or of harshness, τ 494, Δ 510.

λικμάω (λικμός), part. gen. plur. λικμώντων: *winnow,* E 500†.

λικμητήρ, ῆρος: *winnower,* who threw the grain with his winnowing-shovel against the wind, thus separating it from the chaff, N 590†.

λικριφίς: adv., *sideways, to one side,* Ξ 463 and τ 451.

Λικύμνιος: brother of Alcmēna, slain by Tlepolemus, B 663†.

Λίλαια: a town in Phocis, at the source of the Cephissus, B 523†.

λιλαίομαι, ipf. λιλαίετο: *desire, be desirous of* or *eager for,* τινός, ν 31; freq. w. inf.; with the inf. omitted, λ 223; metaph., of the lance, λιλαιομένη χροὸς ἆσαι. Cf. λελίημαι.

λιμήν, ένος (cf. λείβω, λίμνη): *harbor;* pl. also in signif. of *inlets, bays,* Ψ 745, ν 96, δ 846.

λίμνη (cf. λείβω, λιμήν): *lake, pond,* even of a swamp or a marsh, Φ 317; also of the sea, γ 1.

Λιμνώρεια ('Harbor Ward'): a Nereid, Σ 41†.

λῑμός: *hunger, famine.*

Λίνδος: a town in Rhodes, B 656†.

λινο-θώρηξ: *with linen cuirass,* B 529. (As represented in adjoining cut, No. 79; cf. also No. 12.)

λίνον: *flax,* then anything made of it, *thread, yarn,* esp. *fishing-line,* Π 408; of a fisher's net, E 487; linen cloth, *linen,* I 681; fig., of the thread of destiny, Υ 128, Ω 210, η 198. (See cuts under ἠλακάτη.)

79

λίνος: *lay of Linus,* the *Linus-song,* an ancient popular melody, Σ 570†.

λίπα: adv., always λίπ' ἐλαίῳ, *richly* with olive oil; but if the word is really an old dat., then *with* olive *oil,* ἐλαίῳ being adj.

λιπαρο-κρήδεμνος: *with shining head-band,* Σ 382†.

λιπαρο-πλόκαμος: *with shining locks* or *braids,* T 126†.

λιπαρός (λίπα): *sleek, shining* with ointment, ο 332; *shining* (nitidus), B 44; then fig., *rich, comfortable,* θέμιστες, γῆρας, I 156, λ 136.—Adv., **λιπαρῶς,** fig., δ 210.

λιπόω: *be sleek,* v. l., τ 72†.

1. **λίς,** acc. λῖν: *lion,* Λ 239, 480.

2. **λίς** (λισσός): *smooth, sheer,* πέτρη, μ 64 and 79.

3. **λῑς,** dat. λῑτί, acc. λῖτα: *linen* cloth, used as cover for a seat, κ 353; or for a chariot when not in use, Θ 441; also as shroud for the dead, Σ 352; and to cover a cinerary urn, Ψ 254.

λίσσομαι (λιτή), ipf. (ἐ)(λ)λίσσετο, iter. λισσέσκετο, aor. 1 ἐλλισάμην, imp. λίσαι, aor. 2 ἐλιτόμην, inf. λιτέσθαι: *pray, beseech* with prayer; abs., X 91, β 68, and τινὰ εὐχῇσι, εὐχωλῇσι λιτῇσί τε, Ζηνός, 'in the name of Zeus'; πρός, ὑπέρ τινος, γούνων (λαβών, ἁψάμενος), etc.; foll. by inf., sometimes ὅπως or ἵνα, γ 19, 237, θ 344; with two accusatives, β 210, cf. δ 347.

λισσός: *smooth, sheer,* πέτρη. (Od.)

λιστρεύω (λίστρον): *dig about*, ω 227†.

λίστρον: *hoe* or *scraper*, used in cleaning the floor of a hall, χ 455†.

λῖτα: see λίς 3.

λιτανεύω (λιτή), ipf. ἐλλιτάνευε, λιτάνευε, fut. λιτανεύσομεν, aor. ἐλλιτάνευσα: *pray, implore*, abs., and w. acc., η 145, I 581.

λιτή: *prayer*. Plur. personified in an allegory, I. 502 ff.

λῖτί: see λίς 3.

λό': see λούω.

λοβός: *lobe* of the ear, pl. Ξ 182†.

λόγος (λέγω): *tale, story*, as entertaining recital, with enumeration of details, pl., O 393 and α 56. [λούω.

λόε, λοέσσαι, λοεσσάμενος: see

λοετρόν (λοϝετρόν, λούω): *bathing, bath*, pl., Ὠκεανοῖο, 'in Ocean,' ε 275.

λοετρο-χοός (χέω): *pouring* (containing) *water for the bath*, τρίπος, tripod with water-kettle, Σ 346, θ 435; subst., *bath-maid*, υ 297.

λοέω: see λούω.

λοιβή (λείβω): *libation*.

λοίγιος (λοιγός): *destructive, ruinous, deadly*; as subst., Φ 533, Ψ 310.

λοιγός: *destruction, ruin, death*, by sickness (pestilence) or war. (Il.)

λοιμός: *pestilence*, A 61 and 97.

λοισθήιος (λοῖσθος): *for the last* in the race, only of prizes, ἄεθλον; and as subst. λοισθήια (cf. πρωτεῖα, δευτερεῖα), *prize for the last*, Ψ 751. (Il.)

λοῖσθος (λοιπός): *last*, Ψ 536†.

Λοκροί: the *Locrians*, a tribe occupying one of the divisions of Hellas, and dwelling on the Eurīpus, on both sides of Mt. Cnemis, B 527, 535, N 686.

λοπός (λέπω): *peel, skin*, τ 233†.

λούω, λοέω (cf. lavo), ipf. λοῦον, λό' (λόϝε), aor. λοῦσ(εν), subj. λούσῃ, imp. λόεσον, λούσατε, inf. λοέ(σ)σαι, part. λοέσᾱσα, mid. pres. inf. λούεσθαι, λοῦσθαι, fut. λοέσσομαι, aor. λοέσσατο, λούσαντο, etc., pass. perf. part. λελουμένος: *bathe, wash*, mid., *bathe, get washed*, Z 508; fig., of the rising of Sirius, λελουμένος Ὠκεανοῖο, 'after his bath in Ocean,' E 6.

λοφιή (λόφος): the *bristly ridge* or *comb* of a wild boar's back, τ 446†.

λόφος: (1) *crest* or *plume* of a helmet, usually of horse-hair, E 743. (See adjoining cuts, and Nos. 3, 11, 12, 16, 17, 35, 73, 116, 122.)—(2) *back of the neck* of animals or of men, Ψ 508, K 573.—(3) *hill, ridge*. (Od.)

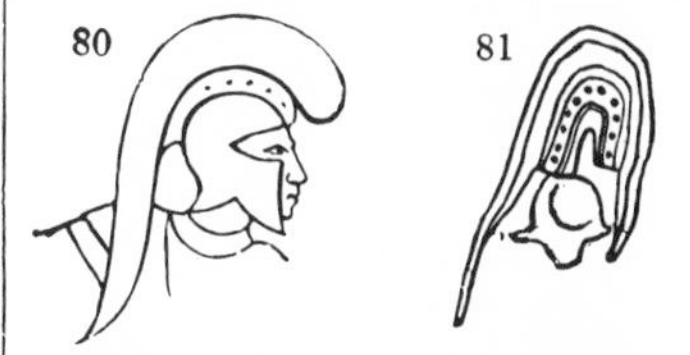

λοχάω (λόχος), aor. inf. λοχῆσαι, mid. fut. λοχήσομαι, aor. part. λοχησάμενος: act. and mid., *lie in ambush, lie in wait for, waylay*, τινά, ν 425.

λόχμη (root λεχ): *lair* of a wild beast, *thicket, jungle*, τ 439†.

λόχος (root λεχ): place of *ambush*, act of *lying in wait*; said of the Trojan horse, Σ 513, δ 277; also of the party forming the *ambuscade*, Θ 522; and of any armed company, υ 49; λόχος γέροντος, 'means of entrapping' the old man of the sea, δ 395.—**λόχονδε**: *upon an ambuscade, into the ambush*, A 227, ξ 217.

λύγος: *willow-twig, osier, withe*.

λυγρός (cf. λευγαλέος): *sad, mournful, miserable*; in apparently active sense, φάρμακα, σήματα, etc., δ 230, Z 168; also fig., and in derogatory sense, 'sorry,' εἵματα, π 457; so of persons, N 119.—Adv., **λυγρῶς**.

λῦθεν: see λύω.

λύθρον: properly pollution, then *gore* (or blood mixed with dust), with and without αἷμα.

λυκά-βᾱς, αντος (root λυκ, lux, βαίνω): *year*, ξ 161 and τ 306.

Λύκαστος: a town in the southern part of Crete, B 647.

Λυκάων: (1) a Lycian, the father of Pandarus, E 197, 95. — (2) son of Priam and Laothoe, slain by Achilles, Φ 144 ff.

λυκέη: *wolf-skin*, K 459†.

λυκη-γενής, έος (root λυκ, lux): *light-born*, epith. of Apollo as sun-god, Δ 101, 119.

Λυκίη: *Lycia*. — (1) a division of Asia Minor, B 877.—(2) a district on the river Aesēpus, its chief town Zeleia, B 824, E 173.—**Λυκίηθεν**, *from*

Lycia, E 105.—**Λυκίηνδε,** *to Lycia*, Z 168.

Λύκιοι : the *Lycians*, inhabitants of Lycia (1). Led by Glaucus and by Sarpēdon, H 13, E 647, Ξ 426, Π 490.

Λυκομήδης : son of Creon in Boeotia, P 346, T 240.

Λυκόοργος (Λυκοϝ.) : *Lycurgus.*—(1) son of Dryas, king of the Edonians in Thrace, banishes from his land the worship of Dionȳsus (Bacchus), Z 134.—(2) an Arcadian, slays Arithous, H 142–148.

λύκος (ϝλύκος): *wolf;* symbol of bloodthirstiness, Δ 471, Λ 72.

Λυκοφόντης : a Trojan, slain by Teucer, Θ 275.

Λυκόφρων : son of Mastor, from Cythēra, a companion of Ajax, O 430.

Λύκτος : a city in Crete, east of Cnosus, B 647, P 611.

Λύκων : a Trojan, slain by Peneleüs, Π 335, 337.

λῦμα, pl. λύματα : anything washed away, *defilement*, Ξ 171; in symbolical and ritualistic sense, *offerings of purification*, A 314.

λυπρός : *sorry, poor*, ν 243†.

Λυρνη(σ)σός : *Lyrnessus*, a town in Mysia, under the sway of Hypoplacian Thebes, B 690, T 60, Υ 92, 191.

Λύσανδρος : a Trojan, slain by Ajax, Λ 491†.

λῦσι-μελής, ές (λύω, μέλος): *relaxing the limbs*, ὕπνος, υ 57 (with a play upon the word in v. 56).

λύσις, ιος (λύω): *loosing, ransoming*, Ω 655; θανάτου, 'deliverance' from death, ι 421.

λύσσα : martial *rage.* (Il.)

λυσσητήρ, ῆρος: one who rages, *raging*, w. κύων, Θ 299†.

λυσσώδης (εἶδος): *raging*, N 53†.

λύχνος : *light, lamp*, τ 34†.

λύω, ipf. ἔλυον, λύε, fut. λύσω, aor. ἔλῦσα, λῦσεν, mid. aor. ἐλύσαο, inf. λύσασθαι, aor. 2, w. pass. signif., λύτο, λύντο, pass. perf. λέλυμαι, opt. λελῦτο, aor. λύθη, 3 pl. λύθεν: I. act., *loose, loosen, set free*, of undoing garments, ropes, Δ 215, λ 245, β 415; unharnessing horses, δ 35; of freeing from bonds or captivity (said of the captor), A 20; pass., of anything giving way, coming apart, B 135, χ 186; fig., in senses answering to those enumerated, τινὰ κακότητος, 'deliver' from misery; ἀγορήν, 'dismiss'; so λύτο δ' ἀγών; and with reference to emotion, or fainting, death, λύτο γούνατα καὶ φίλον ἦτορ, 'gave way,' 'sank,' 'quaked' (sometimes the act., υ 118); of sleep 'relaxing' the limbs, or 'dissolving' cares, δ 794, Ψ 62; of 'undoing' (destroying) cities, B 118.—III. mid., *loose* or *undo oneself*, ι 463, or something of one's own, *get loosed* or *released, ransom;* λυσόμενος θύγατρα, said of the father, A 13; cf. the act., v. 20.

λωβάομαι (λώβη), aor. imp. λωβήσασθε, opt. λωβήσαιο: *maltreat, outrage;* w. cognate acc. and obj. τινὰ λώβην, *do despite*, N 623.

λωβεύω : *mock*, ψ 15 and 26.

λώβη : *outrage, insult ;* σοὶ λώβη, 'shame upon thee,' if, etc., Σ 180; of a person, 'object of ignominy,' Γ 42.

λωβητήρ, ῆρος: one who outrages or insults, *slanderer, scoundrel*, B 275, Λ 385. (Il.)

λωβητός : *maltreated, outraged*, Ω 531†.

λώϊον, λωΐτερον : *better, preferable;* 'more liberally,' ρ 417.

λώπη (λέπω): *mantle*, ν 224†.

λωτοῦντα (λωτός), either a part., or adj., for λωτόεντα: *full of lotus*, 'clovery,' πεδία, M 283†.

λωτός : *lotus.*—(1) a species of clover, δ 603, Ξ 348.—(2) the tree and fruit enjoyed by the Lotus-eaters, ι 91 ff. Said to be a plant with fruit the size of olives, in taste resembling dates, still prized in Tunis and Tripoli under the name of *Jujube.*

Λωτοφάγοι : the *Lotus-eaters*, ι 84 ff.

λωφάω, fut. λωφήσει, aor. opt. λωφήσειε: *rest from, cease from, retire*, ι 460, Φ 292.

M.

μ': usually for *μέ*, sometimes for *μοί*, Z 165, κ 19, etc.

μά: *by*, in oaths, w. acc. of the divinity or of the witness invoked; mostly neg., w. *οὐ*, A 86; sometimes, w. *ναί*, affirmative, A 234.

Μάγνητες: a Thessalian tribe, sprung from Aeolus, B 756.

μαζός: *nipple*, *pap*, then mother's *breast*.

μαῖα (cf. *μήτηρ*): voc., used esp. in addressing the old nurse, 'good mother,' 'aunty,' υ 129, ψ 11.

Μαιάς, *ἄδος*: *Maia*, daughter of Atlas, and mother of Hermes, ξ 435†.

Μαίανδρος: the *Maeander*, the river of many windings that flows into the sea near Milētus, B 869†.

Μαιμαλίδης: *son of Maemalus*, Pisander, Π 194†.

μαιμάω, *μαιμώωσι*, part. *μαιμώωσα*, aor. *μαίμησα*: *strive* or *desire madly*, *rage*; fig., *αἰχμή*, E 661.

μαινάς, *ἄδος* (*μαίνομαι*): *madwoman*, X 460†.

μαίνομαι, ipf. *μαίνετο*: *be mad*, *rave*, *rage*, Z 132, σ 406; often of the frenzy of battle, E 185, λ 537; fig., of the hand, weapons, fire, Π 75, Θ 111, O 606.

μαίομαι, inf. *μαίεσθαι*, part. *μαιομένη*: *seek for*, *explore*, ξ 356, ν 367; *μάσσεται*, 'will find' a wife for me (*γὲ μάσσεται*, Aristarchus' reading for vulg. *γαμέσσεται*), I 394.

Μαῖρα: (1) a Nereid, Σ 48.—(2) an attendant of Artemis, mother of Locrus, λ 326.

Μαίων: son of Haemon in Thebes, Δ 394, 398.

μάκαρ, *αρος*, sup. *μακάρτατος*: *blessed*, *blest*, of gods, A 339, and without *θεοί*, κ 299; of men, *blissful*, *happy*, through wealth or otherwise, λ 483, α 217.

Μάκαρ: son of Aeolus, ruling in Lesbos, Ω 544†.

μακαρίζω: *pronounce happy*. (Od.)

μακεδνός (cf. *μακρός*): *tall*, η 106†.

μάκελλα: *mattock*, Φ 259†.

μακρός, comp. *μακρότερος* and **μᾶσσον**, sup. *μακρότατος*: *long*, *tall*, of space and of time (*κέλευθος*, *ἤματα*), and of things that are high or deep (*οὔρεα*, *δένδρα*, *φρείατα*, Φ 197); freq. adv., **μακρόν**, **μακρά**, *far*, *afar*, *βοᾶν*, *ἀῦτεῖν*; *μακρὰ βιβάς*, 'with long strides.'

μακών: see *μηκάομαι*.

μάλα, comp. *μᾶλλον*, sup. *μάλιστα*: (1) positive, *μάλα*, *very*, *quite*, *right*, modifying adjectives and other adverbs, and sometimes placed after its word, *ἦρι μάλ'*, I 360; occasionally with substantives, *μάλα χρεώ*, I 197, σ 370; also with verbs (*μάλα πολεμίζειν*, 'with might and main'), and esp. to strengthen an assertion as a whole, *certainly*, *verily*, Γ 204. *μάλα* admits of much variety in translating in connection with its several usages.—(2) comp., **μᾶλλον**, *more*, *all the more*, ε 284; 'more willingly,' 'more gladly,' E 231, α 351.—(3) sup., **μάλιστα**, *most*, *especially*, *far*, *by far*, with adjectives forming a superlative, Z 433; and even with superlatives themselves, B 57 f., Ω 334.

μαλακός, comp. *μαλακώτερος*: *soft*, and metaph., *mild*, *gentle*; *θάνατος*, *ὕπνος*, K 2, σ 202, X 373.—Adv., **μαλακῶς**.

Μάλεια: *Malea*, southern promontory of the Peloponnesus, ι 80, τ 187, γ 287.

μαλερός: *powerful*, *destroying*, epith. of fire. (Il.)

μαλθακός = *μαλακός*, fig. *effeminate*, *cowardly*, P 588†.

μάλιστα, **μᾶλλον**: see *μάλα*.

μάν (= *μήν*): *verily*, *truly*, *indeed*; *ἄγρει μάν*, 'come now!' *ἦ μάν*, *οὐ μάν*, *μὴ μάν*, E 765, B 370, Δ 512, Θ 512.

μανθάνω, only aor. *μάθον*, *ἔμμαθες*: *learn*, *come to know*, *τὶ*, and w. inf., Z 444.

μαντεύομαι (*μάντις*), ipf. *μαντεύετο*, fut. *μαντεύσομαι*: *declare oracles*, *divine*, *prophesy*, β 170.

μαντήιον: *oracle, prophecy*, pl., μ 272†.

Μαντινέη: a city in Arcadia, B 607†.

Μάντιος: son of Melampus, and brother of Antiphates, ο 242, 249.

μάντις, ιος (μάντηος, κ 493): *seer, prophet*, expounder of omens, which were drawn from the flight of birds, from dreams, and from sacrifices. Seers celebrated by Homer are Tiresias, Calchas, Melampus, Theoclymenus.

μαντοσύνη: the art or gift of *divination, prophecy*; pl., B 832.

μάομαι: see μαίομαι.

Μαραθών (μάραθον, 'fennel'): a village in Attica, η 80†.

μαραίνομαι, ipf. ἐμαραίνετο, aor. ἐμαράνθη: of fire, *die gradually away*.

μαργαίνω (μάργος): *rage madly* or *wildly*, E 882†.

μάργος: *mad, raving, raging*. (Od.)

Μάρις: a Lycian, son of Amisodarus, Π 319.

μαρμαίρω: *sparkle, flash, glitter*.

μαρμάρεος: *flashing, glittering*. (Il.)

μάρμαρος: doubtful word, *crushing*; πέτρος, Π 735; as subst., *block of stone*, M 380, ι 499.

μαρμαρυγή (μαρμαρύσσω = μαρμαίρω): the quick *twinkling* of dancers' feet, pl., θ 265†.

μάρναμαι, opt. μαρνοίμεθα, inf. μάρνασθαι, ipf. ἐμαρνάσθην: *fight*; also *contend, wrangle*, A 257.

Μάρπησσα: daughter of Euēnus, and wife of Idas, who recovered her after she had been carried off by Apollo, I 557 ff.

μάρπτω, ipf. ἔμαρπτε, μάρπτε, fut. μάρψω, aor. ἔμαρψα: *seize, lay hold of, overtake*; of reaching or touching with the feet, Ξ 228; inflicting a stroke (κεραυνός), Θ 405, 419; fig., of sleep, age, υ 56, ω 390.

μαρτυρίη: *testimony*, pl., λ 325†.

μάρτυρος: *witness*.

Μάρων: son of Euanthes, priest of Apollo in Ismarus, ι 197†.

μάσασθαι: see μαίομαι.

Μάσης: a town in Argolis, near Hermione, B 562†.

μάσσεται: see μαίομαι. Cf. ἐπιμαίομαι.

μᾶσσον: see μακρός.

μάσταξ, ακος (μαστάζω, *chew*): *mouth*; a *mouthful* of food, I 324.

μαστίζω: *use the* μάστῑξ, *lash, whip*.

μάστῑξ, ῑγος, and **μάστις**, dat. μάστῑ, acc. μάστῑγα, μάστιν: *whip, scourge*; fig., Διὸς μάστῑγι, M 37, N 812.

μαστίω = μαστίζω, mid., Υ 171.

Μαστορίδης: *son of Mastor*.—(1) Halitherses in Ithaca, β 158, ω 452.—(2) Lycophron, O 438, 430.

ματάω (μάτην), aor. ἐμάτησεν, subj. du. ματήσετον: *do in vain, fail*, Π 474; then *be idle, delay, linger*.

ματεύω, fut. ματεύσομεν: *seek*, Ξ 110†.

ματίη (μάτην): *fruitless toil*, κ 79†.

μάχαιρα: *dagger, knife* for sacrificing, broad and short in shape. (Il.) (See the cut, and No. 109.)

Μαχάων: *Machāon*, one of the sons of Asclepius, ruler in Tricca and Ithōme in Thessaly, distinguished in the art of healing, Λ 512, 613, Δ 200, B 732; wounded by Hector, Λ 506, 598, 651.

μαχειόμενος, μαχεούμενον: see μάχομαι.

μάχη: *fight, battle, combat*; μάχην μάχεσθαι, τίθεσθαι, στήσασθαι, ὀρνύμεν, ἐγείρειν, ὀτρῡ́νειν, ἀρτῡ́νειν, συμφέρεσθαι: of single combat, H 263 and Λ 255; for the field of battle, E 355.

μαχήμων: *warlike*, M 247†.

μαχητής: *fighter, warrior*.

μαχητός: *that may be vanquished*, μ 119†.

μαχλοσύνη (μάχλος): *lust, indulgence*, Ω 30†.

μάχομαι, μαχέομαι, opt. μαχέοιτο, -οίατο (A 272, 344), part. μαχειόμενος, μαχεούμενος, ipf. (ἐ)μαχόμην, iter. μαχέσκετο, fut. *μαχήσομαι, μαχέσσομαι, μαχεῖται, μαχέονται*, aor. inf. *μαχήσασθαι, μαχέσασθαι*: *fight, contend*, usually in war, including single combat, but sometimes of friendly contest, Ψ 621; and of wrangling, quarrelling with words, etc., A 304, E 875, I 32.

μάψ, μαψιδίως: *rashly* (temere), *in vain*, B 120; *wantonly*, E 759, γ 138, cf. P 120, N 627, B 214.

Μεγάδης: *son of Megas*, Perimus, Π 695†.

μεγά-θῡμος: *great-hearted, high-hearted, high-spirited*, epith. of nations, Athēna, a bull.

form prostrate upon the earth, Π 776, Σ 26, ω 40.

Μεγαπένθης ('Mournful,' from the deserted father): *Megapenthes*, son of Menelāus by a slave, ο 100, 103, δ 11.

Μεγάρη: *Megara*, daughter of Creon in Thebes, wife of Heracles, λ 269†.

μέγαρον (*μέγας*): properly *large room*.—(1) the men's *dining-hall*, the chief room of the Homeric house. The roof was supported by columns, the light entered through the doors, the smoke escaped by an opening overhead and through loop-holes (*ὀπαῖα*) just under the roof. The cut, combined from different ancient representations, is designed to show the back part of the *μέγαρον* in the house of Odysseus, cf. plate III. for ground-plan.—(2) the *women's apartment*, behind the one just described, see plate III. G. Pl., τ 16.—(3) the *housekeeper's apartment* in the upper story (*ὑπερώιον*), β 94.—(4) a *sleeping-apartment*, λ 374.—(5) in wider signif., in pl., *house*, A 396.

μεγαίρω (*μέγας*), aor. *μέγηρε*, subj. *μεγήρῃς*: properly, to regard something as too great, *grudge, begrudge*, hence, *refuse, object*; with acc.; also part. gen., N 563; and foll. by inf., γ 55.

μεγα-κήτης, ες (*κῆτος*): *with great gulf* or *hollow*; *δελφίν*, 'voracious,' Φ 22; *νηῦς*, 'wide-bellied,' Θ 222; *πόντος*, 'wide-yawning,' γ 158.

μεγαλ-ήτωρ (*ἦτορ*): *great-hearted, proud*.

μεγαλίζομαι: *exalt oneself, be proud*. (Il. and ψ 174.)

μεγάλως: see *μέγας*.

μεγαλωστί: *μέγας μεγαλωστί*, 'great in his (thy) greatness,' of a stately

μέγας, μεγάλη, μέγα, comp. **μείζων**, sup. **μέγιστος**: *great, large*, of persons, *tall* (*κᾱλός τε μέγας τε, κᾱλή τε μεγάλη τε*, Φ 108, ο 418); of things with reference to any kind of dimension, and also to power, loudness, etc., *ἄνεμος*, ἰαχή, ὀρυμαγδός; in unfavorable sense, μέγα ἔργον (facinus), so μέγα ἔπος, μέγα φρονεῖν, εἰπεῖν, 'be proud,' 'boast,' γ 261, χ 288.—Adv., **μεγάλως,** also μέγα, μεγάλα, *greatly, exceedingly, aloud,* etc.

μέγεθος, εος: *stature, height;* see μέγας, third definition.

Μέγης: son of Phyleus and of the sister of Odysseus, chief of the inhabitants of Dulichium and the Echinades, Ε 69, Ν 692, Ο 520, 535, Β 627, Τ 239.

μέγιστος: see μέγας.

μεδέων: *ruling, bearing sway,* only of Zeus. (Il.)

Μεδεών: a town in Boeotia, Β 501†.

μέδομαι, fut. μεδήσομαι: *be mindful of, bethink oneself of;* δόρποιο, κοίτου, ἀλκῆς, Σ 245, Δ 418; also *devise,* κακά τινι, Δ 21, Θ 458.

μέδων, οντος (μέδομαι): ἁλός, *ruler* of the sea, α 72; pl., ἡγήτορες ἠδὲ μέδοντες, *counsellors.*

Μέδων: (1) son of Oïleus, step-brother of Ajax, from Phylace, chief of the warriors from Methōne in Phthia, Ν 693, 695 ff., Β 727; slain by Aenēas, Ο 332.—(2) a Lycian, Ρ 216.—(3) a herald in Ithaca, δ 677, ρ 172, χ 357, 361, ω 439.

μεθ-αιρέω: only aor. iter. μεθέλεσκε, *would* reach *after* and *catch,* i. e. 'on the fly,' θ 376.

μεθ-άλλομαι: only aor. part., μετάλμενος, *springing after* or *upon* a person or thing, *overtaking.* (Il.)

μεθείω: see μεθίημι.

μεθέλεσκε: see μεθαιρέω.

μεθέμεν: see μεθίημι.

μεθ-έπω, ipf. μέθεπε, aor. 2 part. μετασπών, mid. μετασπόμενος: *move after, follow after, follow up;* trans., w. two accusatives, ἵππους Τυδείδην, *turn* the steeds *after* Tydīdes, Ε 329; of 'visiting' a place, α 175; mid., Ν 567.

μέθ-ημαι: only part., μεθήμενος, *sitting among,* α 118†.

μεθ-ημοσύνη: *remissness,* Ν 108 and 121.

μεθ-ήμων (μεθίημι): *remiss, careless.*

μεθ-ίημι, μεθίεις, μεθίει (-ιεῖς, ιεῖ), inf. μεθιέμεν(αι), subj. μεθιῇσι (-ίῃσι), ipf. μεθίεις, μεθίει (-ίης, -ίη), 3 pl. μέθιεν, μεθίεσαν, fut. μεθήσω, aor. μεθέηκα, μεθῆκεν, subj. μεθείω, μεθείῃ, μεθήῃ, μεθῶμεν, inf. μεθέμεν, μεθεῖναι: *let go after* or *among.*—(1) trans., of letting a person go away, or go free, ο 212, Κ 449; letting a thing go (ἐς ποταμόν), ε 460; *give up, give over,* Γ 414, Ξ 364, and w. inf., Ρ 418; metaph., in the above senses, μεθέμεν χόλον, 'dismiss,' Ο 138; εἴ με μεθείη ῥῖγος, ε 471.—(2) intrans., *relax effort, be remiss,* abs., Ζ 523, δ 372; w. gen., *desist from, neglect, cease,* φ 377, Λ 841; w. part. or inf., ω 48, Ν 234.

μεθ-ίστημι, fut. μεταστήσω, mid. ipf. μεθίστατο: *substitute,* i. e. *exchange,* δ 612; mid., *stand over among,* 'retire' *among,* Ε 514.

μεθ-ομῑλέω: *associate with, have dealings with,* ipf., Α 269†.

μεθ-ορμάομαι: only aor. part., μεθορμηθείς, *starting after,* 'making a dash after.'

μέθυ, υος (cf. 'mead'): *strong drink, wine.*

μεθύω (μέθυ): *be drunken,* fig., *soaked,* ρ 390.

μειδάω (root σμι), **μειδιάω,** part. μειδιόων, -όωσα, aor. μείδησα: *smile.*

μείζων: see μέγας.

μείλανι: see μέλας.

μείλια: *soothing gifts, gifts of reconciliation,* Ι 147 and 289.

μείλιγμα, ατος (μειλίσσω): *that which soothes,* μειλίγματα θυμοῦ, things to appease the appetite, *tid-bits,* κ 217†.

μείλινος: see μέλινος.

μειλίσσω, inf. μειλισσέμεν, mid. imp. μειλίσσεο: *appease* the dead with fire (πυρός, cf. constr. w. λαγχάνειν), Η 410; mid., 'extenuate,' γ 96 ('try to make it pleasant' for me).

μειλιχίη: *mildness,* i. e. 'feebleness,' πολέμοιο, Ο 741†.

μειλίχιος and **μείλιχος**: *mild, pleasant, gentle, winsome,* θ 172.

μείρομαι (root μερ, μορ), ipf. 2 sing. μείρεο, perf. ἔμμορε, pass. plup. εἵμαρτο: *cause to be divided, receive as a portion,* ipf. w. acc., Ι 616; perf. w. gen., *share,* Α 278, Ο 189, ε 335; pass., εἵμαρτο, *it was ordained, decreed by fate,* Φ 281, ε 312, ω 34.

μείς, μήν, μηνός: *month,* Τ 117.

μείων: see μῑκρός.

μελαγ-χροιής, ές: *dark-skinned, swarthy,* 'bronzed,' π 175†.

μέλαθρον, μελαθρόφι: *beam*, cross-beam of a house, supporting rafters and roof; these beams passed through the wall and projected externally, hence ἐπὶ προὔχοντι μελάθρῳ, τ 544; then *roof* (tectum), and in wider sense *dwelling, mansion*, Ι 640.

μελαίνω (μέλᾱς): only mid., *become dark, grow dark*, of blood-stains, and of the glebe under the plough, Ε 354 and Ζ 548.

Μελάμπους: *Melampus*, son of Amythāon, a famous seer in Pylus. Undertaking to fetch from Phylace in Thessaly the cattle of Iphiclus, and thus to win the hand of Pero for his brother Bias, he was taken captive, as he had himself predicted, and held prisoner for one year, when in consequence of good counsel given by him he was set free by Iphiclus, gained his end, and settled in Argos, λ 287 ff., ο 225 ff.

μελάν-δετος (δέω): *black-bound* or *mounted*, i. e. with dark hilt or scabbard, Ο 713†.

Μελανεύς: father of Amphimedon in Ithaca, ω 103.

Μελανθεύς or **Μελάνθιος:** *Melanthius*, son of Dolius, goat-herd on the estate of Odysseus, of insolent disposition, ρ 212, υ 173, φ 181, χ 135 ff., 182.

Μελάνθιος: (1) see Μελανθεύς.—(2) a Trojan, slain by Eurypylus, Ζ 36.

Μελανθώ: *Melantho*, sister of Melanthius (1), and of the same stripe, σ 321, τ 65.

Μελάνιππος: (1) an Achaean chief, Τ 240.—(2) a Trojan, son of Hicetāon, slain by Antiochus, Ο 547–582.—(3) a Trojan, slain by Teucer, Θ 276.—(4) a Trojan, slain by Patroclus, Π 695.

μελανό-χροος and **μελανό-χρως,** οος: *dark-skinned, black*, τ 246 and Ν 589.

μελάν-υδρος: *of dark water*, κρήνη.

μελάνω: *grow black, darken*, Η 64† (v. l. μελανεῖ).

μέλᾱς, μέλαινα, μέλαν, dat. μείλανι, comp. μελάντερος: *dark, black*, in the general and extensive meaning of these words, opp. λευκός, Γ 103; said of dust, steel, blood, wine, water, grapes, ships, clouds, evening, night, death. — As subst., μέλαν δρυός, i. e. the 'heart-wood,' which is always the darkest, ξ 12.

Μέλᾱς: son of Portheus, Ξ 117†.

μέλδομαι (root σμελδ): *melt;* **λέβης** κνίσην μελδόμενος, 'filled with melting fat,' Φ 363†.

Μελέαγρος (ᾧ μέλει ἄγρα): *Meleāger*, son of Oeneus and Althaea, husband of Cleopatra, the slayer of the Calydonian boar. A quarrel arose between the Curētes of Pleuron and the Aetolians for the head and skin of the boar. The Aetolians had the upper hand until Meleāger withdrew from the struggle in consequence of the curses of his mother. But he was afterwards induced by his wife to enter the conflict again, and he drove the Curētes vanquished into Acarnania, Ι 543 ff., Β 642.

μελέδημα, ατος (μέλω): *care, anxiety*, only pl.

μελεδών, ῶνος (μέλω) = **μελέδημα, τ** 517† (v. l. μελεδῶναι).

μέλει: see μέλω.

μελεϊστί (μέλος): adv., *limb-meal, limb by limb*, Ω 409, ι 291, σ 339.

μέλεος: *fruitless, idle, unrewarded*, neut. as adv., *in vain*, Π 336.

μέλι, ιτος: *honey;* used even as a drink, mixed with wine; burned upon the funeral-pyre, Ψ 170, ω 68; mixed with milk in drink-offerings, μελίκρητον. Figuratively, **Α** 249, Σ 109.

Μελίβοια: a town in Magnesia, **Β** 717†.

μελί-γηρυς: *honey-toned, sweet-voiced*, μ 187†.

μελίη: the *ash*-tree, Ν 178, Π 767; then of the *shaft* of the lance, *lance*, freq. w. Πηλιάς, 'from Mt. Pelion'; other epithets, εὔχαλκος, χαλκογλώχῑν.

μελι-ηδής, ές: *honey-sweet;* fig., ὕπνος, νόστος, θῡμός.

μελί-κρητον (κεράννῡμι): *honey-mixture, honey-drink*, a potion compounded of milk and honey for libation to the shades of the nether world, κ 519, λ 27.

μέλινος, μείλινος (μελίη): *ashen.*

μέλισσα (μέλι): *bee.*

Μελίτη: a Nereid, Σ 42†.

μελί-φρων: *honey-minded, honey-like, sweet.*

μέλλω, ipf. ἔμελλον, μέλλε: *be going* or *about* to do something, foll. by fut. inf., sometimes pres., rarely aor., Ψ

773; μέλλω never means to intend, although intention is of course sometimes implied, τῇ γὰρ ἔμελλε διεξίμεναι πεδίονδε, 'for by that gate he was going to pass out,' Z 393; by destiny as it were, of something that was or was not *meant* to happen, Κύκλωψ, οὐκ ἄρ' ἔμελλες ἀνάλκιδος ἀνδρὸς ἑταίρους | ἔδμεναι, 'you were not going to eat the comrades of a man unable to defend himself after all,' i. e. he was no coward whose companions you undertook to eat, and therefore it was not *meant* that you should eat them with impunity, ι 475, and often similarly. Virtually the same is the usage that calls for *must* in paraphrasing, οὕτω που Διὶ μέλλει ὑπερμενέϊ φίλον εἶναι, such methinks 'must' be the will of Zeus; τὰ δὲ μέλλετ' ἀκουέμεν, ye 'must' have heard, B 116, Ξ 125, δ 94, α 232; μέλλει μέν πού τις καὶ φίλτερον ἄλλον ὀλέσσαι, 'may well' have lost, Ω 46.

μέλος, εος: *limb, member*, only pl.

μέλπηθρον: *plaything*, pl. *sport;* κυνῶν, κυσίν, N 233, P 255. (Il.)

μέλπω: act., *celebrate with dance and song*, A 474; mid., *play* (and sing), φορμίζων, on the lyre, δ 17, ν 27; *dance and sing*, ἐν χορῷ, Π 182; fig., μέλπεσθαι Ἄρηι, H 241.

μέλω, μέλει, μέλουσι, imp. μελέτω, μελόντων, inf. μελέμεν, ipf. ἔμελε, μέλε, fut. μελήσει, inf. μελησέμεν, perf. μέμηλεν, subj. μεμήλῃ, part. μεμηλώς, plup. μεμήλει, mid. pres. imp. μελέσθω, fut. μελήσεται, perf. μέμβλεται, plup. μέμβλετο: *be an object of care or interest;* πᾶσι δόλοισι | ἀνθρώποισι μέλω, i. e. my wiles give me a world-wide 'renown,' ι 20; cf. Ἀργὼ πᾶσι μέλουσα, i. e. the Argo 'all-renowned,' μ 70; mostly only the 3d pers., μέλει μοί τις or τὶ, 'I care for,' 'am concerned with' or 'in' somebody or something, he, she, or it 'interests me,' 'rests' or 'weighs upon my mind'; μελήσουσί μοι ἵπποι, 'I will take care of the horses,' E 228; ἀνὴρ ᾧ τόσσα μέμηλεν, who has so many 'responsibilities,' B 25; perf. part. μεμηλώς, 'interested' or 'engaged in,' 'intent on,' τινός, E 708, N 297; mid., A 523, T 343, Φ 516, χ 12.

μέμαα, perf. w. pres. signif., du. μέματον, pl. μέμαμεν, μέματε, μεμάᾱσι, imp. μεμάτω, part. μεμαώς, μεμαυῖα, μεμαῶτος, μεμᾱότες, μεμᾱότε, plup. μέμασαν: *be eagerly desirous, press on hotly, go impetuously at;* ἐπί τινι, Θ 327, X 326, abs. Φ 174; foll. by inf., even the fut., B 544, ω 395; freq. the part., as adj. (or adv.), *hotly desirous* or *eager*.

μεμακυῖα: see μηκάομαι.

μέμβλωκα: see βλώσκω.

μέμβλεται, μέμβλετο: see μέλω.

μεμηκώς: see μηκάομαι.

μέμηλα: see μέλω.

μεμνέῳτο, μεμνώμεθα: see μιμνήσκω.

Μέμνων: *Memnon*, son of Eos and Tithōnus, came to the aid of Priam after the death of Hector, and slew Antilochus, λ 522, cf. δ 188.

μέμονα, μέμονας, μέμονεν, perf. w. pres. signif.: *have in mind, be minded, be impelled* or *prompted*, w. inf., sometimes the fut., H 36, ο 521; μέμονεν δ' ὅ γε ἶσα θεοῖσι (cf. φρονέειν ἶσα), 'vies with the gods,' Φ 315; δίχθα κραδίη μέμονε, 'yearns with a twofold wish,' in hesitation, Π 435.

μέμῡκα: see μῡκάομαι.

μέν (μήν): (1) the same as μήν, *in truth, indeed, certainly*, H 89, A 267, γ 351; sometimes might be written μήν, as the scansion shows, H 389, X 482; freq. to emphasize a pronoun or another particle, and of course not always translatable, τοῦ μέν, ἢ μέν, καὶ μέν, οὐ μέν, οὐδὲ μὲν οὐδέ, ζ 13, B 703.—(2) in correlation, μέν without losing the force above described calls attention to what follows, the following statement being introduced by δέ, αὐτάρ, or some other adversative word. μέν in correlation may sometimes be translated *to be sure* (q u i d e m), *although*, but oftener does not admit of translation. It should be remembered that μέν is never a connective, that it always looks *forward*, never backward. Its combinations with other particles are various.

μενεαίνω, inf. μενεαινέμεν, ipf. μενεαίνομεν, aor. μενεήναμεν: *eagerly desire*, w. inf., sometimes fut., Φ 176 and φ 125; also *be angered, strive, contend*, Π 491, α 20, T 58.

μενε-δήιος (μένω): *withstanding the enemy, steadfast, brave*, M 247 and N 228.

Μενέλᾱος: *Menelāus*, son of Atreus and brother of Agamemnon, the successful suitor of Helen. King in Lacedaemon, a brave and spirited warrior, but not of the warlike temperament that distinguishes others of the Greeks before Troy above him, P 18 ff. After the war he wanders eight years before reaching home, δ 82 ff. Epithets, ἀρήιος, ἀρηίφιλος, διοτρεφής, δουρικλειτός, κυδάλιμος, ξανθός.

μενε-πτόλεμος (μένω): *steadfast in battle.* (Il.)

Μενεσθεύς: *Menestheus*, son of Peteos, leader of the Athenians, renowned as a chariot-fighter, B 552, M 331, N 195, O 331.

Μενέσθης: a Greek, slain by Hector, E 609†.

Μενέσθιος: (1) son of Areïthous, slain by Paris, H 9.—(2) a Myrmidon, son of Spercheius, Π 173.

μενε-χάρμης and **μενέ-χαρμος** (μένω, χάρμη): *steadfast* or *stanch in battle.* (Il.)

μενο-εικής, ες (μένος, ϝείκω): *suiting the spirit*, i. e. *grateful*, *satisfying;* usually said with reference to quantity, *plenty of*, so pl. μενοεικέα, ξ 232; and w. πολλά, I 227.

μενοινάω, μενοινέω, μενοινώω, subj. μενοινάᾳ, μενοινήῃσι, aor. 1 ἐμενοίνησα: *have in mind, ponder* (M 59), *intend, devise;* φρεσί, μετὰ φρεσί, ἐνὶ θῡμῷ, ὁδόν, νόστον, κακά τινι, λ 532.

Μενοιτιάδης: *son of Menoetius*, Patroclus, Π 554, Σ 93, I 211.

Μενοίτιος: *Menoetius*, son of Actor and father of Patroclus, an Argonaut, Λ 765, Π 14, Ψ 85 ff.

μένος, εος: *impulse, will, spirit, might, courage*, martial *fury, rage* (noble or otherwise), pl. μένεα πνείοντες, 'breathing might,' B 536. A very characteristic Homeric word, with a wide range of application; joined w. θῡμός, ἀλκή, θάρσος, ψῡχή, χεῖρες, γυῖα, and w. gen. of names as periphrases for the person, Ξ 418, η 167; said of things as well as men and animals, wind, fire, the sun, etc.

Μέντης: (1) leader of the Ciconians, P 73.—(2) son of Anchialus, king of the Taphians, under whose form Athena visits Telemachus, α 105, 180

μέντοι: *indeed, to be sure, however;* see μέν and τοί.

Μέντωρ: *Mentor.*—(1) an Ithacan, the son of Alcimus, a near friend of Odysseus, to whom Odysseus intrusts the oversight of his household during his absence. Under the form of Mentor, Athēna guides Telemachus on his travels in search of his father, and helps him to baffle the suitors; in other words she makes herself his *mentor*, β 225, 243, γ 22, 340, χ 206, 208, ω 446.—(2) father of Imbrius, under whose form Apollo incites Hector to battle, N 171.

μένω and **μίμνω**, ipf. iter. μένεσκον, fut. μενέω, aor. ἔμεινα, μεῖνα: *remain, wait*, and trans., *await, withstand*, π 367, Z 126; foll. by inf., O 599; εἰσόκε, I 45; freq. of standing one's ground in battle or elsewhere, Λ 317, κ 83; also w. obj., δόρυ, ἔγχος, etc.

Μένων: a Trojan, slain by Leonteus, M 193†.

Μερμερίδης: *son of Mermesus*, Ilus, α 259†.

μέρμερος: *memorable, signal; μέρμερα ἔργα*, also μέρμερα as subst. (Il.)

Μέρμερος: a Mysian, slain by Antilochus, Ξ 513†.

μερμηρίζω, aor. μερμήριξα: *ponder, wonder, reflect*, trans., *think over*, α 427; freq. w. δίχα, διάνδιχα, of a mind hesitating between two resolves, A 189, π 73; foll. by ἤ (ἢ . . ἤ), also ὡς, ὅπως, and by inf., ω 235; 'imagine,' π 256, 261.

μέρμῑς, ῑθος: *cord*, κ 23†.

μέροψ, οπος: probably *mortal*, μέροπες ἄνθρωποι, μερόπεσσι βροτοῖσιν, Σ 288, B 285.

Μέροψ: a seer and ruler in Percōte on the Hellespont, father of Adrastus and Amphīus, B 831, Λ 329.

μέρομαι: see μείρομαι.

μεσαι-πόλιος (μέσος, πολιός): *half-gray, grizzled*, N 361†.

Μεσαύλιος: a servant of Eumaeus, ξ 449, 455.

μεσηγῡ(ς), μεσσηγῡ(ς): *in the middle*, Λ 573, Ψ 521; *meantime*, η 195; elsewhere w. gen., *between, betwixt*, Z 4, χ 341.

μεσήεις (μέσος): *middling*, M 269†.

Μέσθλης: son of Talaemenes, leader of the Maeonians, B 864, P 216.

μεσόδμη (δέμω): properly something *mid-built*.—(1) *mast-block*, represented in the cut (see *a*) as a metal shoe in which the mast was firmly fastened so as to be turned backward on the pivot (*c*) to a horizontal position, until it rested upon the ἱστοδόκη, β 424. See also plate IV., where the μεσόδμη is somewhat differently represented as a three-

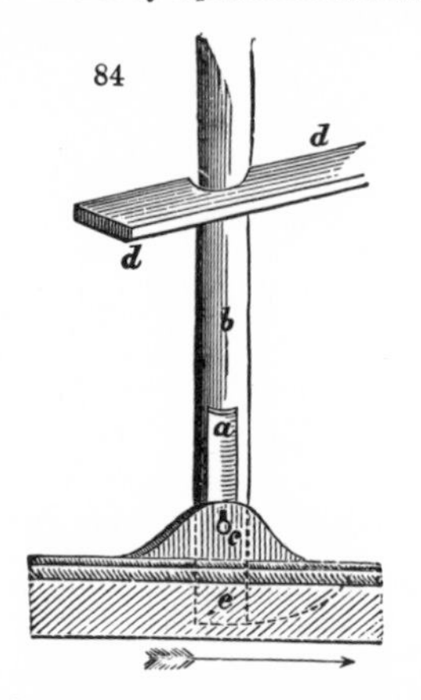

sided trough or mast-box.—(2) μεσόδμαι, small spaces or *niches*, opening into the μέγαρον of the house, and enclosed on three sides, behind by the outside wall, and on either side by the low walls which served as foundations of the columns, τ 37. (See plate III., *r*, and cut No. 83.)

μέσος, μέσσος: *in the middle of*; μέσσῃ ἁλί, *in mid-sea*, δ 844; ἥμενοι ἐν μέσσοισι, 'in the midst of them,' δ 281; of time, μέσον ἦμαρ; as subst., **μέσον**, *the middle*; ἐς μέσον τιθέναι, 'offer for competition,' as prize, Ψ 794; ἐς μέσον ἀμφοτέροις δικάζειν, 'impartially,' Ψ 574; as adv., **μέσον**, *in the middle*, M 167, ξ 300.

μέσσατος (sup. to μέσος): *in the very middle*, Θ 223 and Λ 6.

μέσσ-αυλος: mid-court, *court, farmyard*, P 112; *cattle-yard*, Λ 548.

Μέσση: a harbor-town near Taenarum in Laconia, B 582†.

μεσσηγύς: see μεσηγύς.

Μεσσηίς: a spring in Thessalian Hellas, Z 457†.

Μεσσήνη: a district about Pherae in what was afterward Messenia, φ 15.

Μεσσήνιοι: the *Messenians*, inhabitants of Messēne, φ 18.

μεσσο-παγής, ές (πήγνυμι): *fixed up to the middle*; ἔθηκεν ἔγχος, drove the spear *half its length firm* into the bank, Φ 172 (v. l. μεσσοπαλές, 'vibrating to the middle').

μέσφα (=Att. μέχρι): *till, until*, w. gen., Θ 508†.

μετά: *amid, among, after*.—I. adv. (here belong all instances of 'tmesis'), μετὰ δ' ἰὸν ἕηκεν, let fly an arrow *among* them (the ships), A 48, σ 2; πρῶτος ἐγώ, μετὰ δ' ὔμμες, *afterward*, φ 231, and so of time, ο 400: denoting *change* of position, μετὰ δ' ἄστρα βεβήκει, 'had passed over the meridian'; μετὰ δ' ἐτράπετ', 'turned around'; μετὰ νῶτα βαλών, μ 312, A 199, Θ 94. The relation of the adv. may be specified by a case of a subst., thus showing the transition to the true prepositional use, μετὰ καὶ τόδε τοῖσι γενέσθω, 'let this be added to those and be *among* them,' ε 224.—II. prep., (1) w. gen., *along with*; μετ' ἄλλων λέξο ἑταίρων, μάχεσθαι μετά τινος, 'in league with,' κ 320, N 700.—(2) w. dat., *amid, among, between, in*; μετὰ χερσὶν ἔχειν, 'in the hands,' Λ 184, γ 281; μετὰ γένυσσι, ποσσί, 'between,' Λ 416, T 110; μετὰ πνοιῇς ἀνέμοιο πέτεσθαι, i. e. as fast as the winds, β 148; Οὖτιν ἐγὼ πύματον ἔδομαι μετὰ οἷς ἑτάροισιν, the last 'among' his mates, the position of honor in being eaten, ι 369.—(3) w. acc., denoting motion, *among, towards, to, after*, μετ' Αἰθιοπῆας ἔβη, μετὰ μῶλον Ἄρηος, σφαῖραν ἔρριψε μετ' ἀμφίπολον, βῆναι μετά τινα, A 423, H 147, ζ 115, E 152, and sometimes of course in a hostile sense; so fig., βάλλειν τινὰ μετ' ἔριδας, 'plunge in,' 'involve in,' B 376; sometimes only position, without motion, is denoted, B 143; of succession, *after, next to*, whether locally or of rank and worth, μετὰ κτίλον ἕσπετο μῆλα, N 492; κάλλιστος ἀνὴρ μετὰ Πηλείωνα, B 674; then of time, purpose, conformity, or adaptation, μετὰ Πάτροκλόν γε θανόντα, 'after the death of P.'; πλεῖν μετὰ χαλκόν, 'after,' i. e. to get bronze; μετὰ σὸν κῆρ, 'after,' i. e. to suit thy heart, Ω 575, α 184, O

52, Σ 552, β 406, Λ 227.—μέτα = μέτεστι, φ 93.

μετα-βαίνω, aor. imp. μετάβηθι: *pass over* to a new subject, θ 492†.

μετα-βουλεύω: only aor. μετεβούλευσαν, have *changed* their *purpose* (cf. μεταφράζομαι), ε 286†.

μετ-άγγελος: *messenger between* two parties (internuntius, internuntia). Also written as two words, O 144 and Ψ 199.

μετα-δαίνυμαι, fut. μεταδαίσεται, aor. subj. μεταδαίσομαι: *feast with, have a share in the feast*, ἱρῶν, Ψ 207.

μετα-δήμιος (δῆμος): *among the people, in the community*, ν 46; *at home*, θ 293.

μετα-δόρπιος (δόρπος): *during supper*, δ 194† (cf. 213, 218).

μετα-δρομάδην: adv., *running after*, E 80†.

μετα-ΐζω: *sit among*, Π 362†.

μετ-ᾱΐσσω, aor. part. μεταΐξᾱς: *dart* or *spring after*.

μετα-κιάθω, only ipf. μετεκίαθον: *go after, pursue, pass over to, traverse*, Λ 714.

μετα-κλαίω, fut. inf. μετακλαύσεσθαι: *weep afterward, lament hereafter*, Λ 764†.

μετα-κλίνω: only pass. aor. part. πολέμοιο μετακλινθέντος, should the tide of battle *turn the other way*, Λ 509†.

μετα-λήγω, aor. opt. μεταλλήξειε, part. -λλήξαντι: *cease from*. (Il.)

μεταλλάω, μεταλλῶ, -ᾷς, -ᾷ, imp. μετάλλᾱ, aor. μετάλλησαν, inf. -ῆσαι: *search after, investigate, inquire about, question*; τὶ or τινά, also τινά τι or ἀμφί τινι, ρ 554; coupled w. verbs of similar meaning, A 550, γ 69, ψ 99, η 243.

μεταλλήγω: see μεταλήγω.

μετάλμενος: see μεθάλλομαι.

μετα-μάζιος: *between the paps*, μαζοί, E 19†.

μετα-μῑ́γνῡμι and **μετα-μίσγω,** fut. μεταμίξομεν: *mix among, intersperse, place in the midst*, σ 310; 'we will merge thy possessions with those of Odysseus' (for subsequent division among us), χ 221.

μεταμώνιος: *vain, fruitless*, only neut. pl. (v. l. μεταμώλια).

μετα-νάστης (ναίω): *new-comer, interloper, immigrant*. (Il.)

μετα-νίσσομαι: *pass over* (the meridian), of the sun, only w. βουλῡτόνδε.

μεταξύ: *between*, A 156†.

μετα-παύομαι: *cease* or *rest between whiles*, P 373.

μετα-παυσωλή: *pause between, rest, respite*, T 201†.

μετα-πρεπής, ές (πρέπω): *conspicuous among*, τισίν, Σ 370†.

μετα-πρέπω: *be conspicuous* or *prominent among*, τισίν.

μετα-σεύομαι, ipf. μετεσσεύοντο, aor. μετέσσυτο: *rush* or *hurry after*, τινά, Ψ 389.

μετασπόμενος, μετασπών: see μεθέπω.

μέτασσαι (μετά): of lambs, 'middlings,' i. e. *yearlings, summer-lambs*, those born in the second of the three bearings of the year, ι 221, see δ 86.

μετασσεύομαι: see μετασεύομαι.

μετα-στένω: *lament afterwards, rue*, δ 261†.

μετα-στοιχί (στοῖχος): *in a line, in a row*, side by side, Ψ 358 and 757.

μετα-στρέφω, fut. μεταστρέψεις, aor. subj. -ψῃ, opt. -ψειε, pass. aor. part. μεταστρεφθείς: *turn about* or *away, change*, fig., ἦτορ ἐκ χόλου, νόον, K 107, O 52; 'cause a reverse of fortune,' β 67; intr., O 203; so the aor. pass., Λ 447, 595.

μετα-τίθημι, aor. μετέθηκεν: *cause among*, σ 402†.

μετα-τρέπομαι: *turn oneself towards*, met., *regard, consider*, τινός, always w. neg.

μετα-τροπαλίζομαι (τρέπω): *turn about* to look behind (in flight), Υ 190†.

μετ-αυδάω, ipf. μετηύδων, μετηύδᾱ: *speak among*, ἔπεα τισί. See αὐδάω.

μετά-φημι, ipf. μετέφη: *speak among* or *to*, τισί, also w. acc., B 795. See φημί.

μετα-φράζομαι, fut. μεταφρασόμεσθα: *consider afterward* or *by and by*, A 140†.

μετά-φρενον (φρένες): the part behind the diaphragm, upper part of the *back*; also pl., M 428.

μετα-φωνέω (φωνή): *speak among, make one's voice heard among*, κ 67 (sc. τοῖσι).

μετέᾱσι: see μέτειμι 1.

1. μέτ-ειμι (εἰμί), subj. μετείω, μετέω,

inf. *μετεῖναι, μετέμμεναι*, fut. *μετέσσομαι*: *be among* (*τισίν*), *intervene*, B 386.

2. μέτ-ειμι (*εἶμι*), *μέτεισιν*, mid. aor. part. *μετεισάμενος*: *go among, go after, go* or *march forth*; *πόλεμόνδε*, N 298.

μετ-εῖπον, μετέειπον: *spoke among* or *to, τισί*. See *εἶπον*.

μετεισάμενος: see *μέτειμι* 2.

μετείω, μετέμμεναι: see *μέτειμι* 1.

μετ-έπειτα: *afterward.*

μετ-έρχομαι, part. *μετερχόμενος*, fut. *μετελεύσομαι*, aor. 2 opt. *μετέλθοι*, imp. *μέτελθε*, part. *μετελθών*: *come* or *go among* (*τισί*), *to*, or *after* (*τινά* or *τὶ*); of seeking or pursuing, Z 280, Φ 422; *πατρὸς κλέος*, γ 83; of 'attending to' or 'caring for' something, *ἔργα, ἔργα γάμοιο*, π 314, ε 429.

μετέσσυτο: see *μετασεύομαι*.

μετέω: see *μέτειμι* 1.

μετ-ήορος (*ἀείρω*, the later *μετέωρος*): *raised aloft, into the air*, Θ 26, Ψ 369.

μετ-οίχομαι, imp. *μετοίχεο*, part. *μετοιχόμενος*, ipf. *μετῴχετο*: *go away with* or *after*, in friendly or hostile sense, τ 24, θ 47, E 148.

μετ-οκλάζω: *keep changing the position* (from one knee to the other), N 281†.

μετ-όπισθε(ν): *behind, in the rear*, toward the west, ν 241; *afterwards*, λ 382; w. gen., ι 539.

μετ-οχλίζω, aor. opt. *μετοχλίσσειε*: *pry* or *push back* or *away*.

μετρέω, aor. part. *μετρήσαντες*: *measure*, fig. *πέλαγος*, of traversing its extent, γ 179†.

μέτρον: *measure, measuring-rod*, M 422; then of any vessel and its contents, H 471; *ὅρμου μέτρον*, of the proper point for mooring, ν 101; *μέτρα κελεύθου*, periphrasis for *κέλευθος, κέλευθα*; fig., *ἥβης*, 'full measure,' 'prime.'

μετ-ώπιον: *on the forehead*, Λ 95 and Π 739.

μέτ-ωπον (*ὤψ*): *forehead*, also *front* of a helmet, Π 70.

μεῦ: see *ἐγώ*.

μέχρι(s): *as far as, τινός. τέο μέχρις*; *how long?* Ω 128.

μή: *not, lest.*—(1) adv., *not*, differing from *οὐκ* in expressing a negation *subjectively*. *μή* is the regular neg. particle with the inf., in conditions and cond. rel. clauses, in prohibitions and exhortations, in wishes, and in final clauses introduced by *ἵνα, ὡς*, etc. *μή σε παρὰ νηυσὶ κιχείω*, 'let me not catch thee near the ships!' A 26; *ἴστω νῦν Ζεὺς . . μὴ μὲν τοῖς ἵπποισιν ἀνὴρ ἐποχήσεται ἄλλος* (*μή*, and not *οὐ*, because the statement is in sense dependent on *ἴστω*, though grammatically the ind. is allowed to stand instead of being changed to the inf.), K 330, cf. O 41.—(2) conj., *that not, lest* (n e), introducing final clauses and object clauses after verbs of fearing, *ἀπόστιχε, μή τι νοήσῃ* | *Ἥρη*, 'in order that Hera may not take note of anything,' A 522; *δείδω μὴ δὴ πάντα θεᾶ νημερτέα Ϝεῖπεν*, 'lest all the goddess said was true,' ε 300.—*μή* is combined variously with other particles, *μὴ δή, μὴ μάν, μή που, μή ποτε, μή πως*, etc. It is joined to interrogative words only when the question expects a negative answer, *ἦ μή* (n u m), ι 405, 406, ζ 200.

μηδέ: *but not, and not, nor, not even, not at all*; *μηδέ* always introduces an additional negation, after some negative idea has already been expressed or implied. It is never a correlative word; if more than one *μηδέ* occurs at the beginning of successive clauses, the first *μηδέ* refers to some previous negative idea just as much as the second one or the third one does; *μηδέ τις . . οἶος μεμάτω μάχεσθαι, μηδ' ἀναχωρείτω*, Δ 303; here the first *μηδέ* means *and not, nor*, the direct quotation being regarded as a continuation of what precedes in the indirect form. Usually *μηδέ* at the beginning of a sentence means *not even* or *not at all.* For the difference between *μηδέ* and *οὐδέ*, see *μή*. See also *οὐδέ, fin.*

μηδέν: *nothing*, Σ 500†.

Μηδεσικάστη: a natural daughter of Priam, wife of Imbrius, N 173†.

μήδομαι, fut. *μήσεαι*, aor. *μήσαο*, (*ἐ*)*μήσατο*: *take counsel for oneself*, B 360; *devise* (*τινί τι*), esp. in bad sense; *decide upon* (*τι*), γ 160.

1. μῆδος, *εος*: only pl., *μήδεα, plans, counsels.*

2. μῆδος, *εος*: pl., *privy parts.* (Od.)

Μηθώνη: a city in Magnesia, the home of Philoctētes, B 716.

μηκάομαι, aor. part. *μακών*, perf., w. pres. signif., *μεμηκώς*, *μεμακυῖαι*, ipf., formed on perf. stem., (ἐ)*μέμηκον*: of sheep, *bleat;* of wounded animals, or game hard-pressed, *cry*, *shriek*, K 362; once of a man, σ 98.

μηκάς, ἄδος (μηκάομαι): *bleating* (of goats).

μηκ-έτι: *no longer*, *no more.*

Μηκιστεύς: (1) son of Talaus, brother of Adrastus, and father of Euryalus, B 566, Ψ 678.—(2) son of Echius, companion of Antilochus, slain by Polydamas, O 339, Θ 333, N 422.

Μηκιστηϊάδης: *son of Mecisteus*, Euryalus, Z 28.

μήκιστος: *tallest;* as adv., *μήκιστα*, *finally*, ε 299.

μῆκος: *length*, *lofty stature*, υ 71.

μήκων, ωνος: *poppy*, Θ 306†.

μηλέη (μῆλον): *apple-tree.* (Od.)

μηλο-βοτήρ, ῆρος: *shepherd*, pl., Σ 529†.

1. μῆλον: *apple* (m ā l u m).

2. μῆλον: *sheep* or *goat*, μ 301, ξ 305; mostly pl., *μῆλα*, *small cattle*, *flocks.*

μῆλοψ, οπος: probably *shining*, η 104†.

μήν: asseverative particle, *indeed*, *in truth*, *verily*, cf. *μάν* and *μέν* (2). *μήν* regularly stands in combination with another particle (*καὶ μήν*, *ἦ μήν*, *οὐ μήν*), or with an imperative like ἄγε, A 302.

μήν, μηνός: see *μείς.*

μήνη: *moon*, Ψ 455 and T 374.

μηνιθμός (μηνίω): *wrath.* (Π)

μήνῑμα, ατος: *cause of wrath.*

μῆνις, ιος: *wrath*, i. e. enduring anger, usually of gods, A 75, γ 135; but also of the wrath of Achilles.

μηνίω, aor. part. *μηνίσᾱς*: *be wroth*, abs., and w. dat. of pers., also causal gen. of thing. *μήνῑεν*, B 769.

Μῄονες: the *Maeonians*, i. e. the Lydians, B 864, K 431.

Μῃονίη: *Maeonia*, ancient name of Lydia, Γ 401.

Μῃονίς, ίδος: *Maeonian* woman, Δ 142.

μήποτε, μήπου, μήπω, μήπως: see *μή* and *ποτέ*, *πού*, *πώ*, *πώς.*

μῆρα: see *μηρίον.*

μήρινθος (μηρύω): *cord.* (Ψ)

μηρίον: only pl., *μηρία* and *μῆρα*, pieces of meat from the thighs (*μηροί*) of victims, *thigh-pieces*, which were burned upon the altar, wrapped in a double layer of fat, A 40, γ 456.

Μηριόνης: *Meriones* or *Merion*, the son of Molus, a Cretan, charioteer of Idomeneus, N 246, 249, 528, 566, 650, K 270, H 166, Ξ 514, Π 342, 603.

μηρός: *ham*, upper part of the *thigh; μηρὼ πλήσσεσθαι*, to 'smite the thighs,' a gesture indicative of surprise or other excitement, M 162, Π 125; of victims, *μηροὺς ἐξέταμον*, i. e. cut out the *μηρία* from the *μηροί*, A 460, μ 360.

μηρύομαι, aor. *μηρῡ́σαντο*: *draw up*, *furl* by brailing up; *ἱστία*, μ 170†. (See cut No. 5, an Egyptian representation of a Phoenician ship.)

μήστωρ, ωρος (μήδομαι): *counsellor*, *deviser; ὕπατος μήστωρ*, Zeus, Θ 22; *θεόφιν μ. ἀτάλαντος*, of heroes with reference to their wisdom, γ 110, 409; w. ref. to prowess, *ἀϋτῆς*, *φόβοιο*, 'raiser' of the battle-cry, 'author' of flight, Δ 328, Z 97.

Μήστωρ: a son of Priam, Ω 257†.

μήτε (μή τε): regularly correlative, *μήτε . . μήτε*, *neither . . nor*, (*not*) *either . . or*, dividing a single neg. statement. *μήτε . . τε*, N 230. For the difference between *μήτε* and *οὔτε*, see *μή.*

μήτηρ, *μητέρος* and *μητρός*: *mother;* epithets, *πότνια*, *αἰδοίη*, *κεδνή*; fig., *μήτηρ μήλων*, *θηρῶν*, of regions abounding in sheep, game, etc., B 696, ο 226.

μήτι: see *μήτις.*

μήτῑ: see *μῆτις.*

μητιάω (μῆτις), 3 pl. *μητιόωσι*, part. *μητιόωσα*, *μητιόωντες*, mid. pres. *μητιάασθε*, ipf. *μητιόωντο*: *deliberate*, *conclude*, *devise*, abs., and w. acc., *βουλᾱ́ς*, *νόστον*, *κακά τινι*, Υ 153, ζ 14; mid., *debate with oneself*, *consider*, X 174, M 17.

μητίετα (μητίομαι), nom., for -*της*: *counselling*, 'all-wise,' epith. of Zeus.

μητιόεις, pl. -*εντα* (μῆτις): *full of device*, *helpful*, *φάρμακα*, δ 227†.

μητίομαι (μῆτις), fut. *μητίσομαι*, aor. subj. *μητίσομαι*, opt. *μητῑσαίμην*, inf. *μητίσασθαι*: *devise*, *perpetrate* upon, *τινί τι*, and *τινά τι*, σ 27.

μητιόωσα, μητιόωσι: see *μητιάω.*

μῆτις, ιος, dat. *μήτῑ*: *counsel*, *wis-*

dom, B 169, ψ 125; concretely, *plan*, *device*, μῆτιν ὑφαίνειν, τεκταίνεσθαι, H 324, δ 678.

μήτις, μήτι (μή τις, μή τι): *no one*, *not anything*, adv., μήτι, *not at all*, *by no means;* for the difference between μήτις and οὔτις, see μή. In ι 410, εἰ μὲν δή μήτις σε βιάζεται, μήτις shows that the other Cyclōpes understood Polyphēmus to say οὔτις in v. 408 instead of Οὖτις (he said 'Noman,' but they thought he said *no man*).

μητρο-πάτωρ: *mother's father*, *maternal grandfather*, Λ 224†.

μητρυιή: *step-mother*. (Il.)

μητρώιος: *of a mother*, *maternal*, δῶμα, τ 410†.

μήτρως, ωος: *maternal uncle*. (Il.)

μηχανάω, μηχανάομαι (μηχανή), part. μηχανόωντας, ind. 3 pl. μηχανόωνται, opt. μηχανόῳτο, ipf. μηχανόωντο: *contrive*, *set at work*, *perpetrate*, freq. in unfavorable sense.

μῆχος, εος: *help*, *remedy*.

Μήων: see Μῄονες.

μία: see εἷς.

μιαίνω, aor. subj. μιήνῃ, pass. pres. inf. μιαίνεσθαι, ipf. ἐμιαίνετο, aor. 3 pl. ἐμίανθεν: *dye*, *stain*, *soil*. (Il.)

μιαι-φόνος: *blood-stained*, epith. of Ares. (Il.)

μιαρός: *stained* (with blood), Ω 420†.

μιγάζομαι = μίγνυμαι, part., θ 271†.

μίγδα: *promiscuously*, *together*, Θ 437, ω 77.

μίγνῡμι and **μίσγω**, inf. μισγέμεναι, aor. inf. μῖξαι, mid. ipf. iter. μισγέσκετο, ἐμισγέσκοντο, fut. μίξεσθαι, μισγήσεσθαι, aor. 2 ἔμῖκτο, μῖκτο, pass. perf. part. μεμῖγμένος, ἐμέμῖκτο, aor. 3 pl. ἔμῖχθεν, aor. 2 ἐμίγην, μίγη, 3 pl. μίγεν: I. act., *mix*, *mingle;* οἶνον καὶ ὕδωρ, α 110; pass., ἄλεσσι μεμῖγμένον εἶδαρ, λ 123; φάρμακα, δ 230; met., of bringing together, or one thing in contact with another, χεῖρας τε μένος τε (m a n u s c o n s e r e r e), O 510; ἄνδρας κακότητι καὶ ἄλγεσι, υ 203; γλῶσσ' ἐμέμῖκτο, Δ 438, cf. τ 175.—II. mid., *mingle*, *come in contact* with something, B 475, ε 517, K 457; freq. of intercourse, *have relations with*, friendly or hostile, ω 314, E 143, and esp. of sexual union, in various phrases; ἣν ἐμίγης, 'that you had' (cognate acc.), O 33.

Μίδεια: a town in Boeotia on Lake Copāis, B 507†.

μῑκρός, comp. **μείων**: *small*, *little;* of stature, δέμας, E 801, γ 296; comp. (Il.)

μῖκτο: see μίγνῡμι.

Μίλητος: *Milētus*.—(1) an Ionian city in Caria, B 868.—(2) in Crete, mother-city of the foregoing, B 647.

μιλτο-πάρῃος (μίλτος, 'vermilion'): *red-cheeked*, epith. of ships painted red, B 637, ι 125.

Μίμᾱς: a promontory in Asia Minor, opposite Chios, γ 172†.

μιμνάζω (μίμνω): *remain*, B 392 and K 549.

μιμνήσκω and **μνάομαι**, act. pres. imp. μίμνησκ', fut. μνήσω, aor. ἔμνησας, subj. μνήσῃ, part. μνήσᾱσα, mid. μιμνήσκομαι, part. μνωομένω, ipf. μνώοντο, fut. μνήσομαι, aor. ἐμνήσατο, μνήσαντο, imp. μνῆσαι, perf. μέμνημαι, μέμνηαι and μέμνῃ, subj. μεμνώμεθα, opt. μεμνῄμην, μεμνέῳτο, fut. perf. μεμνήσομαι, inf. -εσθαι, pass. aor. inf. μνησθῆναι: act., *remind*, τινά (τινος), μ 38, A 407; mid., *call to mind*, *remember*, and in words, *mention*, τινός, also τινά or τὶ, περί τινος, η 192; φύγαδε, 'think on flight,' Π 697; the perf. has pres. signif., 'remember,' implying solicitude, mindfulness, σ 267.

μίμνω: see μένω.

μίν: enclitic personal pronoun, acc. sing., *him*, *her*, *it;* it is sing., as always, in ρ 268, κ 212, M 585; *αὐτόν μιν* together form a reflexive, δ 244, not elsewhere.

Μινύειος, Μινυήιος: *Minyeian*, belonging to the ancient stock of the Minyae in Orchomenus, λ 284 and B 511.

Μινυήιος: a river in Elis, Λ 722.

μινύθω, ipf. iter. μινύθεσκον: trans., *lessen*, *diminish*, O 492, ξ 17; intr., *decrease*, *fall* or *waste away*, δ 467, μ 46.

μίνυνθα: *for a little*, *a little while*.

μινυνθάδιος, comp. -διώτερος: *lasting but a little while*, *brief*, X 54, O 612.

μινυρίζω, ipf. μινύριζον: *whimper*, *whine*, *moan*, E 889 and δ 719.

Μίνως: *Minos*, son of Zeus and Eurōpa, father of Deucalion and Ariadne, ruler of Crete, and after his death a ruler in the nether world. λ 322, 568 ff.

μισγ-άγκεια (ἄγκος): *meeting of mountain glens, basin*, Δ 453†.

μισγω: see μίγνῡμι.

μῑσέω, aor. μίσησε: *hate*, 'the thought was abominable to him that, etc.,' Ρ 272†.

μισθός: *pay, wages*, also pl.

μιστύλλω: *cut in bits* or *small pieces*, preparatory to roasting the meat on spits, Α 465.

μίτος: *thread* of the warp, *warp*, Ψ 762†. (See cuts Nos. 59, 123.)

μίτρη: a *band* or *girdle* round the waist and abdomen, below the στατὸς θώρηξ, the exterior of metal plates, the interior lined with wool (see cut No. 33), shorter than the ζῶμα, which covered it, while over both and the θώρηξ passed the ζωστήρ. (See cut No. 3.)

μῑχθείς: see μίγνῡμι.

1. **μνάομαι**: see μιμνήσκω.

2. **μνάομαι**, 2 sing. μνᾱᾳ, μνῶνται, inf. μνάασθαι, μνᾶσθαι, part. μνώμενος, ipf. μνώμεθα, μνώοντο, iter. μνάσκετο: *woo, court, win* by wooing; γυναῖκα, ἄκοιτιν, δάμαρτα, ω 125; abs., π 77, τ 529.

μνῆμα, ατος (μιμνήσκω): *memorial*.

μνημοσύνη (μνήμων): *remembrance*, w. γενέσθω, a periphr. for a pass. of μέμνημαι, Θ 181†.

μνήμων (μιμνήσκω): *mindful, remembering*, 'bent on,' τινός, θ 163.

μνῆσαι, μνησάσκετο: see μιμνήσκω.

Μνῆσος: a Paeonian, slain by Achilles, Φ 210†.

μνηστεύω (μνηστός), aor. part. μνηστεύσαντες: *woo*, δ 684 and σ 277.

μνηστήρ, ῆρος (μνάομαι 2): only pl., *suitors*, of whom Penelope had 108, and they had 10 servants, π 247.

μνῆστις (μιμνήσκω): *remembrance*, ν 280†.

μνηστός, only fem. μνηστή: *wooed* and won, *wedded*, ἄλοχος. Opp. παλλακίς, δουρικτήτη, etc., Ζ 246, α 36.

μνηστύς, υος: *wooing, courting*. (Od.)

μνωόμενος, μνώμενος, μνώοντο: see μιμνήσκω.

μογέω (μόγος), aor. (ἐ)μόγησα: *toil, labor, suffer*, in the last sense often w. acc., ἄλγεα, πολλά, β 343, Ψ 607; freq. the part. w. another verb, 'hardly,' λ 636; ἐξ ἔργων μογέοντες, 'weary after their work,' ω 388.

μόγῑς: *with toil, scarcely*.

μόγος: *toil*, Δ 27†.

μογοσ-τόκος (τίκτω): *travail-producing*, epith. of the Eilithyiae. (Il.)

μόθος: *tumult* of battle, of war-chariots (ἵππιον). (Il.)

μοῖρα (μείρομαι): *part, portion, share*, in booty, of the feast, etc., Κ 252, Ο 195, δ 97; οὐδ' αἰδοῦς μοῖραν, 'not a particle,' ν 171; significant of a *proper* share, hence ἐν μοίρῃ, κατὰ (παρὰ) μοῖραν, 'properly,' 'duly,' 'rightly,' etc.; then of one's *lot, fortune, fate, doom*; μοῖρα βιότοιο, θανάτου, Δ 170, β 100; w. acc. and inf., εἰ μοῖρα (sc. ἐστί) δαμῆναι πάντας ὁμῶς, Ρ 421.—Personified, Μοῖρα, *Fate*; pl., Ω 49, cf. η 197.

μοιρη-γενής, voc. -ές: *child of destiny, Fortune's child*, Γ 182†.

μοιχ-άγρια (μοιχός, ἄγρη): the fine imposed upon one taken in adultery, θ 332†.

μολεῖν: see βλώσκω.

μόλιβος: *lead*, Λ 237†.

Μολίων: (1) *son of Molione*, the wife of Actor, dual **Μολίονε**, see Ἀκτορίωνε.—(2) a Trojan, companion of Thymbraeus, slain by Odysseus, Λ 322.

μολοβρός: *glutton, gormandizer*, ρ 219 and σ 26.

Μόλος: father of Meriones, Κ 269, Ν 249.

μολοῦσα, μολών: see βλώσκω.

μολπή (μέλπω): *play*, entertainment with music and dancing, ζ 101, Α 472; *music, singing* and *dancing*, Σ 572.

μολύβδαινα: *lead* attached to a fishing-line, *sinker*, Ω 80†.

μονόω, μουνόω, aor. μούνωσε, pass. part. μονωθείς, μουνωθέντα: *make lone* or *single*, so propagate a race that there shall always be but one solitary heir, π 117; pass. part., *left alone*.

μόριμος (μόρος) = μόρσιμος, Υ 302†.

μορμύρω: only part., of water, *murmuring, dashing*; ἀφρῷ, Ε 599, Σ 403.

μορόεις, εσσα, εν: doubtful word, *mulberry-colored, dark-hued*.

μόρος (μείρομαι, cf. mors): *lot, fate, doom*; ὑπὲρ μόρον, Φ 517, α 34; esp. in bad sense, κακός, αἰνὸς μόρος,

Σ 465; hence *death* (abstract noun answering to the adj. βροτός).

μόρσιμος (μόρος): *fated*, ordained by fate, w. inf., T 417, E 674; of persons, *destined* to death, *doomed*, X 13; to marriage, π 392; μόρσιμον ἦμαρ, 'day of death,' O 613.

Μόρυς: a Mysian, the son of Hippotion, slain by Meriones, N 792, Ξ 514.

μορύσσω: only pass. perf. part., μεμορυγμένα (-χμένα), *stained*, ν 435†.

μορφή: *form*, fig., *grace*: ἐπέων, λ 367, θ 170. (Od.)

μόρφνος: a species of eagle, *swamp-eagle*, Ω 316†.

μόσχος: as adj. w. λύγοισι, *young*, *tender*, *pliant*, Λ 105†.

Μούλιος: (1) an Epeian, slain by Nestor, Λ 739.—(2) a Trojan, slain by Patroclus, Π 696.—(3) a Trojan, slain by Achilles, Υ 472.—(4) a native of Dulichium, herald of Amphinomus, σ 423.

μούναξ: *singly*. (Od.)

μοῦνος (Att. μόνος): *alone*, 'single,' 'desolate,' 'forsaken,' β 365, κ 157.

Μοῦσα, pl. **Μοῦσαι**: *Muse*, the *Muses*, nine in number, daughters of Zeus and Mnemosyne, θ 488, B 598, ω 60; they sing for the gods, and inspire the bard, A 604, A 1, α 1, B 484.

μοχθέω (μόχθος), fut. inf. μοχθήσειν: *toil*, *suffer*, 'be worn with suffering,' K 106†.

μοχθίζω = μοχθέω, B 723†.

μοχλέω: *pry* or *heave up* (with levers, μοχλοί), M 259†.

μοχλός: *lever*, *crow*, *hand-spike* (not roller), ε 261; in ι, of a stake.

Μύγδων: a king of Phrygia, Γ 186†.

μυδαλέος: *wet*, *dripping* (with blood), Λ 54†.

Μύδων: (1) son of Atymnius, charioteer of Pylaemenes, slain by Antilochus, E 580.—(2) a Paeonian, slain by Achilles, Φ 209.

μυελόεις, εσσα, εν (μυελός): *full of marrow*, *marrowy*, ι 293†.

μυελός: *marrow;* fig., of nourishing food, μυελὸς ἀνδρῶν, β 290.

μυθέομαι (μῦθος), 2 sing. μυθέαι and μυθεῖαι, ipf. iter. μυθέσκοντο, fut. μυθήσομαι, aor. μυθησάμην: *speak* or *talk of*, *describe*, *explain*, *relate*, strictly with reference to the subject-matter of discourse (see μῦθος), ἕκαστα, πάντα κατὰ θυμόν, νημερτέα, μῆνιν Ἀπόλλωνος, ν 191, I 645, Z 382, A 74; w. pred. adj., πόλιν πολύχρυσον, 'spoke of it as rich in gold,' Σ 289.

μυθο-λογεύω: *relate*. (Od.)

μῦθος: *speech* with reference to the subject-matter, like the later λόγος, hence to be paraphrased in Eng. by various more specific words, 'conversation,' 'recital,' 'subject,' 'request,' 'counsel,' 'command,' etc., δ 214, 597, ο 196, A 545.

μυῖα: *fly*, house-fly or horse-fly; as symbol of audacity, P 570. (Il.)

Μυκάλη: *Mycale*, a promontory in Asia Minor, opposite Samos, B 869†.

Μυκαλησσός: a town in Boeotia, B 498†.

μυκάομαι, part. μυκώμεναι, aor. 2 μύκον, μύκε, perf. part. μεμυκώς, plup. ἐμεμύκει: *low*, *bellow*, of cattle; of the river-god Scamander, μεμυκὼς ἠύτε ταῦρος, Φ 237; then of things, as of gates 'groaning,' a shield 'resounding,' M 460, Υ 260.

μυκηθμός: *lowing*, *bellowing*, Σ 575 and μ 265.

Μυκήνη: *Mycēne*, daughter of Inachus, β 120; eponymous heroine of the city **Μυκήνη** or **Μυκῆναι**, *Mycēnae*, the residence of Agamemnon.—**Μυκήνηθεν**, *from Mycēnae*. — **Μυκηναῖος**, *of Mycēnae*.

μύκον: see μυκάομαι.

μύλαξ, ακος: *mill-stone*, then of any large round *stone*, pl., M 161†.

μύλη: *mill*, hand-mill. (Od.) (Probably similar to the Roman hand-mills found in Switzerland, and represented in the cut.)

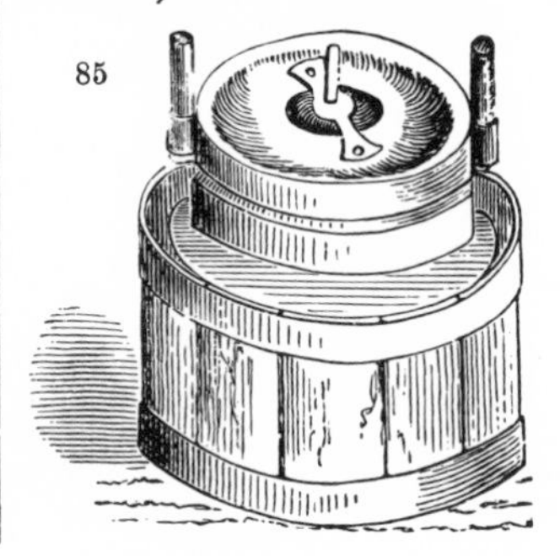
85

μυλή-φατος (*φένω*): *crushed in a mill, ground*, β 355†.

μυλο-ειδής, ές (εἶδος): *like a millstone*, Η 270†.

μύνη: *excuse*, pl., φ 111†.

Μύνης: son of Evēnus, slain by Achilles, Β 692 and Τ 296.

μυρῖκη: *tamarisk*. (Il.)

μυρίκινος: *of tamarisk*, ὄζος, 'tamarisk-shoot,' Ζ 39†.

Μυρίνη: an Amazon, whose funeral-mound was called 'Thorn-hill,' Βατίεια, Β 814†.

μῡρίος: *countless*, 'myriad,' often in pl., μάλα μῡρίοι, 'infinite in number,' ο 556, etc.; μῡρίον, w. gen., 'a vast quantity,' Φ 320.

Μυρμιδόνες: the *Myrmidons*, a Thracian tribe in Phthiōtis, the followers of Achilles; their chief centres were Phthia and Hellas, Π 269, Β 684, Α 180, λ 495.

μύρομαι, ipf. *μύρονθ'*: *flow, dissolve in tears, weep, lament*.

Μύρσινος: a village in Elis, later τὸ Μυρτούντιον, Β 616†.

Μῡσοί: (1) a tribe on the Danube, Ν 5.—(2) kindred with the foregoing, the *Mysians* of Asia Minor, occupying territory from the river Aesēpus to Mt. Olympus, Β 858, Κ 430, Ξ 512, Ω 278.

μυχμός (*μύζω*): *moaning*, ω 416†.

μυχοίτατος, sup. formed from the locative of *μυχός*: *inmost* (in the men's hall), *farthest away* (from the rest and from the entrance), φ 146†.

μυχόνδε: *to the inmost part*, χ 270†.

μυχός: *inmost* or *farthest part, corner*, of house, hall, harbor, cave, etc. Freq. μυχῷ w. gen., 'in the farthest corner,' Ζ 152, γ 263.

μύω, aor. 3 pl. *μύσαν*, perf. *μέμῡκεν*: *close*, said of the eyes, wounds, Ω 637, 420. (Il.)

μυών, ῶνος: *mass of muscle, muscles*, Π 315, 324. (Il.)

μῶλος: *toil and moil* of battle, freq. w. Ἄρηος, Η 147, Ρ 397.

μῶλυ: *moly*, an herb given by Hermes to Odysseus to afford protection against the spells of Circe, κ 305†, described v. 304.

μωμάομαι, fut. *μωμήσονται*: *censure, reproach*, Γ 412†.

μωμεύω = *μωμάομαι*, ζ 274†.

μῶμος: *blame, censure; μῶμον ἀνάψαι*, 'set a brand of shame upon us,' β 86†.

μῶνυξ, υχος: according to the ancients, *single-hoofed, solid-hoofed* (μόνος, ὄνυξ), epith. of horses (as opp. to the cloven-footed cattle). (Il. and ο 46.)

N.

ν: *νῦ ἐφελκυστικόν*, or nu euphonic, affixed to the pl. case-ending **-σι**, to εἴκοσι, -φι, νόσφι, κέ, and to forms of the verb ending in **-ε** and **-ι** of the 3d person.

ναί (cf. n a e): *yea, verily*, always affirmative; w. μά, Α 234.

ναιετάω (*ναίω*), part. *ναιετάων*, *-άωσα*, ipf. iter. *ναιετάασκον*: *dwell, inhabit*, Γ 387; and of localities, *be situated, be inhabited*, often w. εὖ, so of houses, etc., 'comfortable,' Β 648, β 400; significant of the very *existence* of a place, α 404; trans., Β 539, Ρ 172, ι 21.

ναίω, inf. *ναιέμεν*, ipf. iter. *ναίεσκον*, aor. *νάσσα*, pass. aor. *νάσθη*, mid. pres. part. (εὖ) *ναιόμενος*: *dwell, inhabit, be situated*, Β 626; the aor. is causative, *καί κέ οἱ Ἄργεϊ νάσσα πόλιν*, 'would have assigned him a town to dwell in,' δ 174; pass., *νάσθη, settled in*, Ξ 119.

νάκη: *hairy skin; αἰγός*, ξ 530†.

νάπη: *forest glen, woody dell*, Θ 558 and Π 300.

ναρκάω: only aor., *νάρκησε, was palsied*, Ο 328†.

νάσθη, νάσσα: see *ναίω*.

νάσσω: only aor. *ἔναξε, stamped down; γαῖαν*, φ 122†.

Νάστης: son of Nomion, leader of the Carians, slain by Achilles, B 867 ff.

Ναυβολίδης: *son of Naubolus.*—(1) Iphitus, B 518.—(2) a Phaeacian, θ 116.

ναύ-λοχος (root λεχ): *for ships to lie in*, 'safe for ships,' of harbors, δ 846 and κ 141.

ναύ-μαχος: *for naval combat*; ξυστά, O 389 and 677.

ναῦς: see νηῦς.

Ναυσίθοος: a son of Poseidon, the father of Alcinous, colonizes the Phaeacians in Scheria, η 56 ff.

Ναυσικάā: *Nausicaa*, the Phaeacian princess, daughter of Alcinous and Arēte, ζ 17 ff., η 12, θ 457, 464.

ναυσι-κλειτός: *renowned for ships*, ζ 22†.

ναυσι-κλυτός = ναυσικλειτός, pl., epith. of the Phaeacians and the Phoenicians, o 415.

Ναυτεύς: a Phaeacian, θ 112†.

ναύτης: *seaman, sailor*, only pl.

ναυτιλίη: *seamanship*, θ 253†.

ναυτίλλομαι: *sail*, δ 672 and ξ 246.

ναῦφι(ν): see νηῦς.

νάω, ναίω (σνάϝω), ipf. ναῖον (v. l. νᾶον): *flow*; ὀρῷ, 'ran over' with whey, ι 222.

Νέαιρα: a nymph, the mother of Lampetie and Phaethūsa by Helius, μ 133†.

νεαρός (νέος): *youthful*, B 289†.

νέατος, νείατος (νέος): *newest*, but always of position, *extremest, last, lowest*, Z 295, o 108; apparently, 'topmost,' Ξ 466.

νεβρός: *fawn*; as symbol of timorousness, Δ 243.

νέες, νέεσσι: see νηῦς.

νέηαι: see νέομαι.

νεη-γενής, ές: *new-born*, δ 336 and ρ 127.

νε-ηκής, ές (ἀκή): *freshly whetted*, N 391 and Π 484.

νέ-ηλυς (ἤλυθον): *newly come*, K 434 and 558.

νεηνίης (Att. νεāνίāς): *young* (man), *youth*, always w. ἀνήρ. (Od.)

νεῆνις, ιδος: *maiden*.

νεῖαι: see νέομαι.

νείαιρα (νέος, cf. νέατος): *lower*; γαστήρ, the lower part of the belly, abdomen, E 539. (Il.)

νείατος: see νέατος.

νεικέω, νεικείω (νεῖκος), **νεικῶσι**, subj. νεικείῃ(σι), inf. νεικείειν, part. νεικείων, ipf. νείκειον, iter. νεικείεσκε, fut. νεικέσω, aor. (ἐ)νείκε(σ)σα: *strive, quarrel*; ἔριδας καὶ νείκεα ἀλλήλοις, 'contend in railing and strife,' Y 252; *upbraid, reprove*, opp. αἰνεῖν, K 249, Ω 29; μάλα, 'angrily'; ἄντην, 'outright,' ρ 239.

νεῖκος, εος: *contention, strife, quarrel*, esp. in words; *dispute, dissension*, often pl.; at law, Σ 497, μ 440; also of war and battle, πολέμοιο, φῡλόπιδος, ἔριδος, N 271, P 384, Y 140; *reproof, taunt*, I 448, H 95.

νεῖμα: see νέμω.

νειόθεν (νέος): *from below*; ἐκ κραδίης, 'from the depths of his heart,' K 10†.

νειόθι (νέος): *below*; λίμνης, 'down in the depths of the sea,' Φ 317†.

νειός (νέος): sc. γῆ, *new land, fallow land*, newly ploughed after having lain fallow; thrice ploughed, after such rest, in Σ 541, ε 137.

νεῖται: see νέομαι.

νείφω: see νίφω.

νεκάς, άδος (νέκῡς): *heap of slain*, E 886†.

νεκρός: *dead body, corpse*; with τεθνηῶτα, μ 10; also νεκρῶν κατατεθνηώτων, see καταθνήσκω. Said of the inhabitants of the nether world, *the dead*, Ψ 51, λ 34.

νέκταρ, αρος: *nectar*, the drink of the gods, as ambrosia is their food, A 598, Δ 3, applied as a preservative against decay, T 38. Why the lexicons say that νέκταρ means wine when the Cyclops speaks of a 'sample of nectar and ambrosia,' we do not know, ι 359.

νεκτάρεος: *nectar-like, fragrant as nectar*. (Il.)

νέκῡς, υος = νεκρός.

νεμέθομαι = νέμομαι, *feed*, Λ 635†.

νεμεσάω, νεμεσσάω (νέμεσις), fut. νεμεσήσω, aor. νεμέσησα, mid. fut. νεμεσήσομαι, pass. aor. 3 pl. νεμέσσηθεν: *be indignant* or justly *angry* with one (at anything), τινί (τι), *take it ill*, ζ 286, Ψ 494; also w. part., or οὕνεκα, φ 169, ψ 213; mid., like active, also *shrink from, be ashamed*, w. inf., δ 158.

νεμεσητός, νεμεσσητός: *causing indignation, reprehensible, wrong*, usually neut. as pred., Γ 310; w. neg., 'no wonder,' I 523, χ 59, *to be dreaded*, Λ 649.

νεμεσίζομαι (νέμεσις), ipf. νεμεσίζετο: *be angry* with one (for something), τινί (τι), E 757; *be ashamed*, foll. by acc. and inf., P 254; *dread, fear*, θεούς, α 263.

νέμεσις, dat. νεμέσσῖ (-ει), (νέμω, 'dispensation'): just *indignation, anger, censure*; οὐ νέμεσις, 'no wonder,' Γ 156; ἐν φρεσὶ θέσθε αἰδῶ καὶ νέμεσιν, self-respect and a 'regard for men's indignant blame,' N 122, Z 351.

νεμεσσάω, νεμεσσητός: see νεμεσάω, νεμεσητός.

νεμέσσει, νεμέσσῖ see νέμεσις.

νέμος, εος (νέμεσθαι, cf. nemus): *wood-pasture, glade*, Λ 480†.

νέμω, aor. ἔνειμα, νεῖμεν, imp. νεῖμον: I. act., *dispense, divide, assign*, μοίρᾱς, κρέα, etc.; τινί τι, Γ 274, ζ 188, then *pasture* or *tend flocks*, ι 233; pass., *be consumed* (cf. the mid.), πυρί, B 780.—II. mid., *have to oneself, possess, enjoy*, πατρώια, τέμενος, υ 336, M 313; *inhabit*, β 167; then *feed (upon)*, esp. of flocks and herds, *graze*, E 777, ν 407, ι 449.

νένιπται: see νίζω.

νεο-αρδής, ές (ἄρδω): *freshly watered*, Φ 346†.

νεο-γῑλός: *new-born, young*; σκύλαξ, μ 86†.

νεό-δαρτος (δέρω): *newly-flayed*. (Od.)

νεο-θηλής, ές (θάλλω): *fresh-sprouting*, Ξ 347†.

νεοίη: *youthfulness*, youthful thoughtlessness, Ψ 604†.

νέομαι, νεῦμαι, νεῖαι, νεῖται, subj. 2 sing. νέηαι, inf. νεῖσθαι, ipf. νεόμην, νέοντο pres., usually w. fut. signif., *go* or *come* somewhere (as specified), esp. *return*, abs., β 238, λ 114, μ 188.

νέον: see νέος.

νεο-πενθής, ές: *new to sorrow*, λ 39†.

νεό-πλυτος (πλῡ́νω): *newly washed*, ζ 64†

νεό-πριστος (πρίω): *fresh-sawn*, θ 404†

Νεοπτόλεμος: *Neoptolemus*, the son of Achilles, reared in Scyros, conducts the Myrmidons home from Troy, and weds Hermione, the daughter of Menelāus, T 327, γ 189, δ 5, λ 520.

νέος, comp. **νεώτερος**: *new, fresh, young*; opp. παλαιός, δ 720, θ 58; as subst., τ 433, I 36, θ 202; adv., **νέον,** *just now, lately*, π 181, 199.

νεός: see νηῦς.

νεό-σμηκτος (σμάω): *freshly polished*, N 342†.

νεοσσός (νέος): *young (bird), fledgling*. (Il.)

νεό-στροφος (στρέφω): *newly twisted*; νευρή, O 469†.

νεό-τευκτος (τεύχω): *newly wrought*, Φ 592†.

νεο-τευχής, ές (τεύχω): *newly made*, E 194†.

νεότης, ητος (νέος): *youth*. (Il.)

νε-ούτατος (οὐτάω): *lately wounded*. (Il.)

νέ-ποδες (νέω): 'swim-footed,' *web-footed*, δ 404†. According to a modern interpretation (and an Alexandrian usage) the word = nepotes, 'offspring.'

νέρθε(ν) (ἔνερθεν, ἔνερος): *below, under*, w. gen., λ 302.

Νεστόρεος: *of Nestor*.

Νεστορίδαι, the *sons of Nestor*, Antilochus and Thrasymēdes, Π 317.

Νεστορίδης: *son of Nestor*.—(1) Antilochus, Z 33, O 589, Ψ 353.—(2) Pisistratus, γ 482, δ 71, 155, etc.

Νέστωρ: *Nestor*, the aged king of Pylos, son of Neleus and Chloris, was ruling over the 3d generation of men when he joined the expedition against Troy, A 247 ff. His youthful exploits, Δ 319, Λ 669 ff., A 262 ff., Ψ 630 ff. In the Odyssey he is at home again in Pylos, γ 17, cf. 412 ff.

νεῦμαι: see νέομαι.

νευρή: sinew, only as *bow-string*.

νεῦρον: *sinew, tendon*; as bowstring, Δ 122; also for a cord to bind the arrow-head to the shaft, Δ 151.

νευστάζω (νεύω): *keep nodding, nod* κεφαλῇ, bending down the head, σ 154; ὄφρυσι, of giving a sign, μ 194.

νεύω (cf. nuo), fut. νεύσω, aor. νεῦσα: *nod*, often of giving assent or a promise, Θ 246; freq. said of the helmet and its plume, Γ 337, χ 124; κεφαλάς, 'let their heads hang down,' σ 237.

νεφέλη: *cloud*; fig., of death, grief, Υ 417, P 591, ω 315.

νεφελ-ηγερέτα (ἀγείρω), nom. for -της: *cloud-gathering*, the *cloud-compeller*, Zeus.

νέφος, εος: *cloud*, often in pl., O 388; fig., νέφος θανάτοιο, Π 350, δ 180; also of dense numbers, Τρώων, πολέμοιο, Π 66, P 243.

1. **νέω** (σνέϜω), ipf. ἔννεον: *swim*.

2. **νέω** (cf. n e o), mid. aor. νήσαντο: *spin*, η 198†.

νη-: inseparable neg. prefix.

νῆα, νηάδε: see νηῦς.

νηγάτεος: doubtful word, *new-made*, B 43 and Ξ 185.

νήγρετος (νη-, ἐγείρω): *sound*, *deep* sleep; neut., as adv., εὕδειν, *without waking*. (Od.)

νήδυια (νηδύς), pl.: *bowels*, P 524†.

νήδυμος: doubtful word, epith. of sleep, *sweet*, *balmy*.

νηδύς, ύος: *belly*, *stomach*; 'womb,' Ω 496.

νῆες, νήεσσι: see νηῦς.

νηέω (Att. νέω), ipf. νήεον, νήει, aor. νήησα, mid. aor. inf. νηήσασθαι, imp. -άσθω: *heap* or *pile up*; also *load*, *fill with cargo*; νῆας, I 359; mid., one's own ship, I 137, 279.

Νηιάς, άδος: *Naiad*, water-nymph, pl. (Od.)

Νήιον: Mt. *Neium*, in Ithaca, α 186†.

νήιος (νηῦς): *for ships*; δόρυ νήιον, *ship-timber*, also without δόρυ, N 391, Π 484.

Νηίς, ίδος = Νηιάς. (Il.)

νῆις, ιδος (νη-, root Ϝιδ): *unknowing*, *unpractised in*; τινός, θ 79; abs., *inexperienced*, H 198.

νη-κερδής, ές (κέρδος): *profitless*, *useless*.

νηκουστέω (ἀκούω), aor. νηκούστησα: *fail to hearken*, *disobey*, w. gen., Υ 14†.

νηλεής, νηλής (νη-, ἔλεος): *pitiless*, *ruthless*, *relentless*; of persons, and often fig., θυμός, ἦτορ, δεσμός, νηλεὲς ἦμαρ, 'day of death'; ὕπνος, of a sleep productive of disastrous consequences, μ 372.

Νηλείδης = Νηληιάδης, Ψ 652.

νήλειτις, ιδος (νη-, ἀλιταίνω): *guiltless*, *innocent*. V. l. νηλῖτεῖς. (Od.)

Νηλεύς: *Neleus*, son of Poseidon and Tyro, husband of Chloris, and father of Pero and Nestor, λ 254, 281, ο 233; driven from Iolcus in Thessaly by his brother Pelias, he wanders to Messenia and founds Pylos, γ 4; all of his sons except Nestor were slain in a war with Heracles, Λ 692.

Νηληιάδης: *son of Neleus*, Nestor.

Νηλήιος: *of Neleus*, *Neleian*.

νηλής: see νηλεής.

νηλῖτής, νηλιτεῖς: see νήλειτις.

νῆμα, ατος (νέω 2): *that which is spun*, *yarn*. (Od.)

νημερτής, ές (ἁμαρτάνω): *unerring*, *infallible*; freq., νημερτές, νημερτέα εἰπεῖν, *truthfully*, *truly*, γ 19, δ 314.—Adv., **νημερτέως,** ε 98, τ 296.

Νημερτής: a Nereid, Σ 46†.

νηνεμίη (νήνεμος): *windless calm*, E 523; as adj. (or appositive), w. γαλήνη, ε 392, μ 169.

νήνεμος (νη-, ἄνεμος): *windless*, *breathless*; αἰθήρ, Θ 556†.

νηός (ναίω): dwelling of a god, *temple*, *fane*. (For an idea of the interior of the c e l l a of a temple, cf. cut under βωμός, with statue of Aphrodite and altar.)

νηός: see νηῦς.

νη-πενθής, ές (πένθος): 'without sorrow,' *soothing sorrow*; **φάρμακον**, an Egyptian magic drug,' δ 221†.

νηπιάᾱς: see νηπιέη.

νηπιαχεύω: *play like a child*, part., X 502†.

νηπίαχος = νήπιος. (Il.)

νηπιέη (νήπιος), acc. pl. **νηπιάᾱς**: *infancy*, *childhood*, *helplessness of childhood*, I 491; pl., *childish thoughts*.

νήπιος: epith. of little children or young animals, 'infant,' 'helpless,' **νήπια τέκνα**, I 440, B 311, Λ 113; often fig., indicating the blind unconsciousness on the part of men that suggests an analogy between the relation of men to higher powers and that of infants to adults, 'helpless,' 'unwitting,' and sometimes disparagingly, 'simple,' 'childish,' Λ 561, X 445.

νή-ποινος (ποινή): *without compensation*, *unavenged*; adv., **νήποινον**, *with impunity*, α 160.

νηπύτιος = νήπιος. (Il.)

Νηρηίς, ίδος: *Nereid*, i. e. daughter of Nereus, who is himself not named by Homer, but is only called ἅλιος γέρων, Λ 538; pl., Σ 38, 49, 52.

Νήρικος: originally a promontory

on the coast of Acarnania, later converted into the island of Leucas; subjugated by Laertes, ω 377†.

Νήριτον: Mt. *Neritum*, in Ithaca, ν 351, B 632, ι 22.

Νήριτος: an Ithacan, ρ 207†.

νήριτος: see εἰκοσινήριτος.

Νησαίη: a Nereid, Σ 40†.

νῆσος (νέω 1): *island.*

νῆστις, ιος (νη-, ἔδω): *not eating, without food, fasting.*

νητός (νέω, νηέω): *piled up*, β 338†.

νηῦς (νέω 1), gen. νηός and νεός, dat. νηί, acc. νῆα and νέα, pl. νῆες, νέες, gen. νηῶν, νεῶν, ναῦφιν, dat. νηυσί, νήεσσι, νέεσσιν, ναῦφιν, acc. νῆας, νέας: *ship, vessel.* The parts of a ship, as named in Homer (see cut under ἔδαφος), are as follows: of the hull, τρόπις, πρῴρη, πρύμνη, ἐπηγκενίδες, πηδάλιον, οἰήια, ἱστός, ἱστοπέδη, ἱστοδόκη, ζυγά, κληῖδες, τροπός. Of the rigging, ἱστία, πείσματα, πόδες, ἐπίτονος, πρότονος. Oar, ἐρετμός, κώπη. Homer mentions ships of burden, φορτίδες, ι 323; otherwise ships of war are meant. Pl., νῆες, *the ships*, often in the Iliad of the *camp* of the Greeks, which included νῆες and **κλισίαι**, B 688. (See plate IV., at end of volume.)—**νῆάδε,** *to the ship*, ν 19.

νήχω (σνήχω) and **νήχομαι,** inf. νηχέμεναι, part. νηχόμενος, ipf. νῆχον, fut. νήξομαι: *swim.* (Od.)

νίζω, imp. νίζ(ε), ipf. νίζον, fut. νίψω, aor. νίψα, mid. ipf. νίζετο, aor. νιψάμην, pass. perf. νένιπται: *wash, wash off*, mid., oneself or a part of oneself; w. two accusatives, νίψαι τινὰ πόδας, τ 376; mid., χρόα ἅλμην, 'the brine from his person,' ζ 224; ἁλός, 'with water from the sea,' β 261; pass., Ω 419.

νῑκάω, ipf. (ἐ)νίκων, iter. νῑκάσκομεν, fut. νῑκήσω, aor. (ἐ)νίκησα, pass. aor. part. νῑκηθείς: *be victorious* or *victor*, and trans., *conquer, vanquish*, in games, battle, or legal dispute (w. cognate acc., λ 545), of 'surpassing' or 'excelling' in anything (**τινί**), and of things, 'prevail,' A 576, κ 46.

νίκη: *victory*, in battle or before the tribunal, λ 544.

Νιόβη: *Niobe*, daughter of Tantalus and wife of Amphīon, king of Thebes. Her six sons were slain by the arrows of Apollo, and her six daughters by the arrows of Artemis, because she had presumed to compare her children with those of Leto. Niobe in grief was changed into stone, a legend that connects itself with a natural conformation in the rock of Mt. Sipylus, which resembles a woman in a sitting posture, Ω 602, 606.

νίπτω: see νίζω.

Νῑρεύς: *Nireus*, son of Charopus and Aglaïa, of Syme, the handsomest of the Greeks before Troy, next to Achilles, B 671 ff.

Νῖσα: a village on Mt. Helicon in Boeotia, B 508†.

Νῖσος: son of Arētus, father of Amphinomus of Dulichium, π 395, σ 127, 413.

νίσσομαι, fut. νίσομαι, ipf. νίσσοντο = νέομαι.

Νίσῡρος: a small island, one of the Sporades, B 676†.

νιφάς, άδος (σν.): *snow-flake, snow*, mostly pl.; w. χιόνος, M 278. (Il.)

νιφετός (σν.): *snow-storm, snows*, K 7 and δ 566.

νιφόεις, εσσα, εν (σν.): *snowy, snow-clad*, epith. of mountains.

νίφω (σν.), inf. νῑφέμεν: *snow*, M 280†. (V. l. νειφέμεν.)

νίψα, νιψάμενος: see νίζω.

νοέω (νόος), imp. νόει, fut. νοήσω, aor. (ἐ)νόησα, mid. νοήσατο: *think, be thoughtful* or *sensible, have in mind, intend, be* (aor. *become*) *aware, perceive;* **οὕτω νῦν καὶ ἐγὼ νοέω,** 'I think so too,' δ 148; **τοῦτό γ' ἐναίσιμον οὐκ ἐνόησεν,** 'that was not a right thought of hers,' η 299; **νοῆσαι ἅμα πρόσσω καὶ ὀπίσσω,** 'to direct his mind forward and backward,' 'take thought at once of the present and the future,' A 343; **μητρὶ ἐγὼ παράφημι, καὶ αὐτῇ περ νοεούσῃ,** 'though she has a good mind of her own,' A 577; **καὶ μᾶλλον νοέω φρεσὶ τῑμήσασθαι,** 'I mean to prize thee still more,' X 235; freq. **ὀξὺ νοῆσαι,** of 'keenly noting' an occurrence, often w. part., B 391, Γ 21, 30; common transitional phrase, **ἄλλ(ο) ἐνόησεν,** 'had another idea,' 'thought again,' 'passed to a new plan.' Mid., 'thought to,' w. inf., only K 501. Cf. νόος.

νόημα, ατος (νοέω): *thought, idea,*

plan, *mind* (more concrete than *νόος*), *υ* 82; as symbol of swiftness, *νέες ὠκεῖαι ὡς εἰ πτερὸν ἠὲ νόημα*, *η* 36.

νοήμων, *ονος*: *thoughtful*, *discreet*. (Od.)

Νοήμων: (1) a Lycian, slain by Odysseus, E 678.—(2) son of Phronius in Ithaca, *δ* 630, *β* 386.—(3) a Pylian, Ψ 612.

νόθος: *illegitimate* or *natural* son, opp. *γνήσιος*, Λ 102, 490; daughter (*νόθη*), N 173.

νομεύς, *ῆος* (*νέμω*): *shepherd;* w. *ἄνδρες*, P 65.

νομεύω, ipf. *ἐνόμευε*: *pasture*, *μῆλα*. (Od.)

Νομίων: father of Nastes and Amphimacus of Caria, B 871†.

νομός (*νέμω*): *pasture;* fig., *ἐπέων*, 'range,' Υ 249.

νόος: *mind*, *understanding*, *thought;* *οὐ γάρ τις νόον ἄλλον ἀμείνονα τοῦδε νοήσει*, | *οἷον ἐγὼ νοέω*, a better 'view' than mine,' I 104. The word is somewhat flexible in its application, but needs no special illustration. Cf. *νοέω*.

νόσος: see *νοῦσος*.

νοστέω (*νόστος*), fut. *νοστήσω*, aor. *νόστησα*: *return*, often with the implication of a happy escape, K 247, P 239, *κεῖσέ με νοστήσαντα*, 'when I came there on my way home,' *δ* 619; *ο* 119.

νόστιμος (*νόστος*): *νόστιμον ἦμαρ*, day *of return;* of a person, destined *to return*, *υ* 333, *δ* 806.

νόστος (*νέομαι*): *return*, *return home;* *νόστου γαίης Φαιήκων*, a *reaching* the land of the Phaeacians (*γαίης*, obj. gen.), without the notion of 'returning,' except in so far as a man who had been swimming as long as Odysseus had to swim would feel as if he had got *back* somewhere when he touched dry land, *ε* 344.

νόσφ(ιν): *apart*, *away*, *aloof from*, *except*, w. gen., A 349, B 346.

νοσφίζομαι, aor. *νοσφισάμην*, pass. aor. part. *νοσφισθείς*: *depart from* (*τινός*), *hold aloof from*, 'disregard,' B 81, Ω 222; w. acc., *abandon*. (Od.)

νοτίη: *moisture*, pl., *rain*, *showers*, Θ 307†.

νότιος: *moist*, *wet:* neut. as subst., *water* of a harbor, *δ* 785.

Νότος: *south* (*west*) *wind*, bringing rain, B 145, *γ* 295; *ἀργεστής*, Λ 306, Φ 334; *πρὸς Νότου*, *from the South*, *ν* 111.

νοῦς: see *νόος*.

νοῦσος: *sickness*, *illness*, *disease*.

νύ(ν): *now*, enclitic particle, perhaps sometimes temporal, but as a rule differing from the temporal *νῦν* as the logical and temporal uses of 'now' differ in Eng. The context in each case must decide whether the word admits of paraphrasing or not. Often *τί νυ*; and *οὔ νυ*.

νυκτερίς, *ίδος* (*νύξ*): *bat*, *μ* 433 and *ω* 6.

νύμφη, voc. *νύμφα* (cf. n u b o): *bride*, *lady;* after as well as at the time of marriage, I 560, λ 447, Γ 130, *δ* 743.

Νύμφη: *nymph*, goddess of secondary rank, as the Naiads, mountain nymphs, etc., Z 420, *ζ* 123; offerings were made to them, *ρ* 211, *μ* 318; Calypso and Circe are termed nymphs, *ε* 153, *κ* 543.

νύμφιος (*νύμφη*): *newly-married*, *η* 65 and Ψ 223.

νῦν: *now*, freq. *νῦν δή*, *νῦν αὖ*, and esp. *νῦν δέ*, 'as it is,' 'as it was,' contrasting the real state of the case with a supposed one, A 417. In the uses that are not strictly temporal *νῦν* differs from *νύν* only in form (quantity), not in meaning, K 175.

νύξ, *νυκτός*, acc. *νύκτα*, *νύχθ'*: *night*, fig., of death, E 310. — Personified, **Νύξ**, *Night*, Ξ 259.

νυός: *daughter-in-law* or *sister-in-law*, Γ 49.

Νυσήιον: *Nysaeum*, the region about Nysa, where the god Dionȳsus was reared, Z 133†.

νύσσα: *turning-post* (m e t a), in the hippodrome, Ψ 332; elsewhere, *starting-point* or *line*.

νύσσω, part. *νύσσων*, *-οντες*, pass. pres. part. *νυσσομένων*: *prick*, *pierce*. (Il. and ξ 485.)

νῶ: see *νῶι*.

νωθής, *ές*: *lazy*, *sluggish*, Λ 559†.

νῶι (cf. n o s), nom. dual, gen. and dat. *νῶιν*, acc. *νῶι* and *νῶ*: *we two*, *both of us*.

νωίτερος: *of us two*, *of us both*, O 39 and *μ* 185.

νωλεμές: *continually*, *unceasingly*, Ξ 58; usually with *αἰεί*.

νωλεμέως: *unceasingly, firmly*, Δ 428.

νωμάω (νέμω), aor. νώμησα: *deal out, distribute*, Α 471, γ 340; *handle, wield, control*; ἔγχος, σκῆπτρον, πόδα νηός, Ε 594, Γ 218, κ 32; *ply* the limbs, πόδας καὶ γούνατα, Κ 358; met., 'revolve' (versare), νόον, κέρδεα, ν 255, σ 216.

νώνυμος and **νώνυμνος** (νη-, ὄνομα): *nameless, inglorious*.

νῶροψ, οπος: epithet of χαλκός, *shining, glittering*. (Il. and ω 467, 500.)

νῶτον: *back*, of meat, *back-piece, chine*, Ι 207, pl., Η 321; fig., εὐρέα νῶτα θαλάσσης.

νωχελίη: *sloth, sluggishness*, Τ 411†.

Ξ.

ξαίνω (cf. ξέω): *comb* or *card* wool, χ 423†.

ξανθός: *reddish-yellow, blond* or *auburn* (flavus); of horses, *sorrel* or *cream-colored*, Λ 680.

Ξάνθος: *Xanthus*. — (1) son of Phaenops, a Trojan, slain by Diomed, Ε 152.—(2) name of one of the horses of Achilles (see ξανθός), Π 149. — (3) name of one of Hector's horses, Θ 185. — (4) another name of the river Scamander, and, personified, the river-god, Υ 40, 74, Φ 146. —(5) a river in Lycia, flowing from Mt. Taurus into the Mediterranean, Β 877.

ξεινήιον: *token of guest-friendship*, or *hospitality*, a *present* given in honor of this relation, Κ 269, Ζ 218, or *entertainment*, Σ 408; ironically, ι 370; as adj., w. δῶρα, ω 273.

86

ξεινίζω: *entertain* (a stranger or guest-friend), Γ 207, γ 355.

ξείνιος and **ξένιος**: pertaining to hospitality or guest-friendship, Ζεύς, *protector of guests* (strangers), Ν 625, ι 271; τράπεζα, *hospitable* board, ξ 158; neut. as subst. = ξεινήιον, pl., sc. δῶρα.

ξεινο-δόκος (δέχομαι): *guest-receiving, hospitable*; as subst., *host*, σ 64.

ξεῖνος: *strange, foreign*, Ω 302, η 32; ξεῖνε πάτερ, 'sir stranger'; *stranger, guest, guest-friend*; the relation of guest-friend existed from the time when ξεινήια were exchanged as tokens and pledges; hence πατρώιος ξεῖνος, 'hereditary friend,' Ζ 215.

ξεινοσύνη: *hospitality*, φ 35†.

ξενίη: *hospitality*, *entertainment* as guest, *guest-friendship*. (Od.)

ξένιος: see ξείνιος.

ξερός: *dry*; ξερὸν ἠπείροιο, 'dry land,' ε 402†.

ξέσσε: see ξέω.

ξεστός (ξέω): *scraped*, *hewn* smooth, *polished*; of wood, stone, horn, etc.

ξέω, aor. ἔξεσε, ξέσσε: *scrape*, *hew* smooth, *polish*; ἀπὸ (adv.) δ' ἔξεσε χεῖρα, 'cut clean off,' Ε 81.

ξηραίνω: only pass. aor., ἐξηράνθη, *was dried up*. (Il.)

ξίφος, εος: *sword*. The ξίφος had a two-edged blade, joined to the hilt (κώπη) by bands of dark metal (μελάνδετον). It was worn in a sheath (κουλεόν), suspended by a baldric (τελαμών) that passed over the shoulder. (See cut on preceding page.)

ξύλον (ξύω): mostly pl., *wood*, not standing, but cut; sing., *trunk* of a tree, Ψ 327.

ξύλοχος: *thicket*, *jungle*.

ξυμ- and **ξυν-**: the former is used in compounds of βάλλω and πᾶς, the latter in comp. w. ἀγείρω, ἄγνυμι, ἄγω, δέω, ἐλαύνω, ἔσεσθαι, ἔχω, ἰέναι, ἰέναι, and in ξύνεσις and ξυνοχή. See under συμ-, συν-.

ξυν-εείκοσι: *twenty together*, ξ 98†.

ξυνέηκε, ξυνέηχ': see συνίημι.

ξυνήιος (ξῡνός): *common*, *as common property*.

ξυνίει, ξύνιον: see συνίημι.

ξυνιόντος, ξύνισαν: see σύνειμι.

ξῡνός (= κοινός): *common*; Ἐνῡάλιος, 'even-handed,' 'shifting,' Σ 309.

ξυρόν (ξύω): *razor*; proverb 'on the razor's edge,' see ἀκμή, Κ 173†.

ξυστόν (ξύω): the polished *shaft* of a spear, *spear*; ναύμαχον, 'ship-pike,' Ο 388, 677.

ξύω (cf. ξέω), ipf. ξῦον, aor. ἔξῦσε: *shave*, *scrape* smooth, *smooth*, Ξ 179.

O.

ο: 'prothetic,' as in ὄβριμος, ὀμίχλη, ὄνομα; 'copulative,' as in ὄπατρος, οἰέτης.

ὁ, ἡ, τό, epic forms, gen. τοῖο, du. τοῖιν, pl. τοί, ταί, gen. τάων, dat. τοῖσι, τῇς(ι): (1) as demonstrative pronoun, *that*, *those*, often merely an emphatic *he*, *she*, *it*, pl. *they*, *them*; οὐδὲ παλαιῶν (γυναικῶν), | τάων αἳ πάρος ἦσαν, 'those ancient,' β 119; the emphatic after-position being common when the word is adjectival, cf. Ε 320, 332; the pron. is often foll. by a name in apposition, αὐτὰρ ὃ μήνιε . . Ἀχιλλεύς, '*he*, namely Achilles,' Α 488; ἣ δ' ἕσπετο Παλλὰς Ἀθήνη, α 125; freq. ὃ μὲν . . ὃ δέ, τὸ μὲν . . τὸ δέ, etc., *the one* . . *the other*, *this* . . *that*, etc. The word should be accented when used as a demonstrative.—(2) as definite article, *the*, a use denied by some to Homer, but the sense imperatively demands the later weakened force in many passages, and does not admit the stronger, Αἴας δ' ὁ μέγας, Π 358; αἰὲν ἀποκτείνων τὸν ὀπίστατον, Θ 342; τά τ' ἐόντα τά τ' ἐσσόμενα, Α 70, and oftenest w. adjectives.—(3) as relative pronoun, *who*, *which*, esp., but not exclusively, the forms beginning with τ. The masc. sing. as rel. occurs, Π 835, Φ 59, 230, α 254, β 262, δ 777; πατρὸς, ὅ σ' ἔτρεφε τυτθὸν ἐόντα, λ 67. τέ is often appended to the word when used relatively, ταί τε, ὅ τε, μ 40.—For ὅ γε, see ὅγε.

ὅ: neuter, see ὅς.

ὄαρ, αρος, dat. pl. ὥρεσσιν: *wife*. (Il.)

ὀαρίζω, inf. ὀαριζέμεναι, ipf. ὀάριζε: *converse familiarly*, *chat*. (Il.)

ὀαριστής (ὀαρίζω): *bosom friend*, τ 179†.

ὀαριστύς, ύος (ὀαρίζω): *familiar converse*; πάρφασις, 'fond beguilement,' Ξ 216; iron., πολέμου, προμάχων, Ρ 228, Ν 291.

ὀβελός: *spit*. (See cuts under πεμπώβολον.)

ὀβριμο-εργός (*ϝέργον*): *worker of grave* or *monstrous deeds*, Ε 403 and Χ 418.

ὀβριμο-πάτρη: *daughter of a mighty father*, Athēna.

ὄβριμος (*βρίθω*): *heavy, ponderous; ἄχθος, θυρεόν*, ι 233, 241; then of persons, *stout, mighty*, Ο 112, Τ 408.

ὀγδόατος and **ὄγδοος**: *eighth*.

ὀγδώκοντα: *eighty*.

ὅγε, ἥγε, τόγε (*ὅ γε*, etc.): the demonstr. *ὅ, ἥ, τό* intensified, and yet often employed where we should not only expect no emphasis, but not even any pronoun at all, as in the second of two alternatives, Γ 409, Μ 240, β 327. *ὅ γε* serves, however, to keep before the mind a person once mentioned (and perhaps returned to after an interruption), thus usually the very opp. of *ὁ δέ*, which introduces a new person in antithesis.

ὄγκιον (*ὄγκος*): *basket* or *box* to hold arrow-heads or other things of iron, φ 61†.

ὄγκος: *barb* of an arrow, pl. (Il.)

ὄγμος (*ἄγω*): *furrow*, also *swath* made by the mower or reaper, Σ 552, 557.

Ὀγχηστός: *Onchestus*, a town on Lake Copāis in Boeotia, with a grove of Poseidon, Β 506.

ὄγχνη: *pear-tree, pear*. (Od.)

ὁδαῖος (*ὁδός*): *belonging to a journey*, pl. **ὁδαῖα,** *freight, cargo*, θ 163 and ο 445.

ὀδάξ (*δάκνω*): adv., *with the teeth, biting; λάζεσθαι, ἑλεῖν, γαῖαν, οὖδας*, 'bite the dust,' Χ 17; *ὀδὰξ ἐν χείλεσι φύντο*, 'bit their lips,' in vexation, α 381.

ὅδε, ἥδε, τόδε, pl. dat. *τοῖσδε* and *τοίσδεσ(σ)ι*: demonstr. pron., *this* here, 'he, she, it *here*,' pointing out a person or thing that is either actually (locally) present, or is a subject of present consideration or interest; hence the word is often 'deictic,' i. e. appropriately accompanied by a gesture, *καί ποτέ τις εἴπῃσιν . . Ἕκτορος ἥδε γυνή*, see, 'this' is the wife of Hector, Ζ 460; *νηῦς μοι ἥδ' ἕστηκεν ἐπ' ἀγροῦ*, is stationed 'here,' just outside the town, α 185; *ἡμεῖς οἵδε*, 'we here,' α 76; freq. referring to what follows, Α 41, ο 211; and sometimes anticipating a relative, Β 346.

ὁδεύω (*ὁδός*): *travel, go*, Λ 569†.

Ὀδίος: (1) leader of the Halizonians, slain by Agamemnon, Β 856, Ε 39.—(2) a herald of the Greeks, Ι 170.

ὁδίτης (*ὁδός*): *traveller, wayfarer*; w. *ἄνθρωπος*, Π 263, ν 123.

ὀδμή (root *ὀδ*): *smell, fragrance*.

ὁδοι-πόριον: *reward for* the *journey*, ο 506†.

ὁδοί-πορος: *travelling*, as subst., *wayfarer*, Ω 375†.

ὁδός, οὐδός: *way, path, road, journey*, ρ 196; even by sea, β 273; *πρὸ ὁδοῦ γενέσθαι*, 'progress on one's way,' Δ 382.

ὀδούς, *ὀδόντος*: *tooth*.

ὀδύνη: *pain*, sometimes of the mind; sing., *Ἡρᾱκλῆος*, 'for Heracles,' Ο 25; elsewhere pl.

ὀδυνή-φατος (*φένω*)· *pain-killing, relieving pain*. (Il.)

ὀδύρομαι, aor. part. *ὀδῡράμενος*: *grieve, lament;* abs., or w. causal gen., or trans., *τινά* or *τί*, α 243, ε 153.

Ὀδυσήιος: *of Odysseus*, σ 353.

Ὀδυσσεύς, Ὀδυσεύς, gen. *Ὀδυσσῆος. Ὀδυσῆος. Ὀδυσεῦς*, ω 398; dat. *Ὀδυσῆι, Ὀδυσεῖ*, acc. *Ὀδυσσῆα, Ὀδυσσέα, Ὀδυσῆ*, τ 136: *Odysseus* (Ulysses, Ulixes), son of Laertes and Anticlēa, resident in the island of Ithaca and king of the Cephallenians, who inhabited Ithaca, Same, Zacynthus, Aegilops, Crocyleia, and a strip of the opposite mainland. Odysseus is the hero of the Odyssey, but figures very prominently in the Iliad also. He inherited his *craft* from his maternal grandfather Autolycus, see τ 394 ff. Homer indicates the origin of Odysseus' name in τ 406 ff., and plays upon the name also in α 62.

ὀδύσσομαι, aor. *ὠδύσαο, -ατο, ὀδύσαντο*, part. *ὀδυσσάμενος*, perf. *ὀδώδυσται*: *be incensed with, hate, τινί*, mostly of gods; w. reciprocal meaning, τ 407; pass., ε 423.

ὀδώδει: see *ὄζω*.

ὀδώδυσται: see *ὀδύσσομαι*.

ὄεσσι: see *ὄις*.

ὄζος: *shoot, twig;* fig., *Ἄρηος*, 'scion of Ares,' Β 540, 745.

ὄζω (root *ὀδ*), plup. *ὀδώδει*: *be fragrant* or *redolent; ὀδμὴ ὀδώδει*, 'was exhaled,' ε 60 and ι 210.

ὅθεν (*ὅς*): *whence;* with pers. antecedent when place or source is meant, γ 319.

ὄθ(ι) (ὅς): *where, there where;* ὅθι περ, 'even where,' ξ 532.

ὄθομαι, ὄθεται, ipf. ὄθετ(ο): always w. neg., not to *heed, trouble oneself* or *care about*, τινός, also abs., and w. inf. or part., E 403.

ὀθόνη: only pl., *fine linen, linen garments*, Σ 595.

Ὀθρυονεύς: an ally of the Trojans from Cabēsus, N 363, 370, 374, 772.

οἷ: see οὗ.

οἷα: see οἷος.

οἴγνῡμι, aor. ᾤιξε, ᾦξε, ᾤιξαν, part. οἴξᾱσα, pass. ipf. ὠίγνυντο: *open* doors or gates, *broach* wine, γ 392.

οἶδα, οἶδας, οἶδε: see εἴδω, II.

οἰδάνω (οἰδέω): *cause to swell*, met., νόον (with rage), I 554; pass., also met., *swell*, I 646.

οἰδέω, ipf. ᾤδεε: *swell, be swollen*, ε 455†.

Οἰδιπόδης: *Oedipus*, king of Thebes, son of Laius and Epicaste, and father of Eteocles, Polynīces, and Antigone, Ψ 679, λ 271.

οἶδμα, ατος: *swell* of the sea, *billow*, Φ 234 and Ψ 230.

οἰέτης (ὀϝέτης, ϝέτος): *of equal age*, pl., B 765†.

ὀϊζῡρός, comp. -ώτερος, sup. -ώτατος: *full of woe, wretched*, P 446, ε 105.

ὀϊζύς, ύος (οἴ, 'alas!'): *woe, misery*.

ὀϊζύω, ipf. ὀίζυε, ὀϊζύομεν, aor. part. ὀϊζύσᾱς: *suffer woe, be miserable, suffer;* κακά, Ξ 89.

οἰήιον: *tiller*, then *helm, rudder*, ι 483; usually pl., because a Homeric ship had two rudders or steering-oars, μ 218. (See foll. cuts and No. 60.)

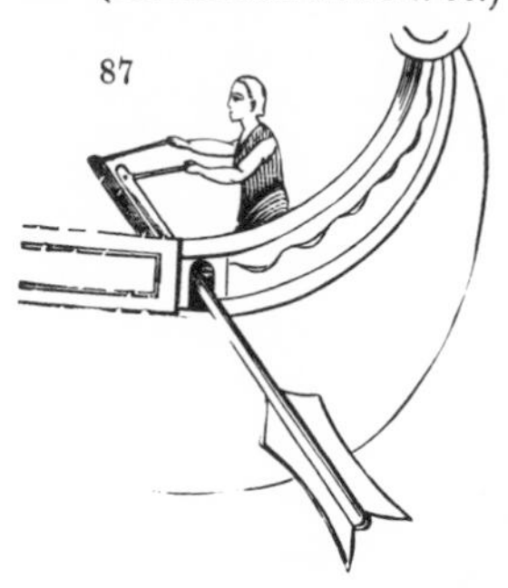

οἴηξ, ηκος: pl., *yoke-rings*, through which the reins passed, Ω 269†. (Cf. cuts Nos. 45 *h*, 10, 78 *f*.)

οἴκαδε (old acc. ϝοῖκα): adv., *homeward, home*.

οἰκεύς, ῆος (ϝοῖκος): *inmate* of a house, then *servant*, mostly pl., δ 245, ξ 4.

οἰκέω (ϝοῖκος), ipf. ᾤκεον, ᾤκει, pass. pres. opt. οἰκέοιτο, aor. 3 pl., ᾤκηθεν: *dwell, inhabit;* aor. pass., 'were settled,' 'came to dwell,' B 668.

οἰκίον, pl. **οἰκία** (ϝοῖκος, dim. in form only): only pl., *abode, habitation;* of the nest of a bird, bees, etc., M 167, 221, Π 261.

Οἰκλείης: *Oecles*, son of Antiphates and father of Amphiarāus, ο 244.

οἰκόθεν: *from the house, from home*, 'from one's own store' or 'possessions,' H 364.

οἴκοθι and **οἴκοι**: *at home*.

οἰκόνδε: *home, homeward, into the house, to the women's apartment*, α 360, φ 354.

οἶκος (ϝοῖκος, cf. v i c u s): *house* as *home*, including the family, and other inmates and belongings, β 45, 48; said of the tent of Achilles, the cave of Polyphemus, Ω 471, 572; the *women's apartment*, α 356, cf. 360.

οἰκτείρω (οἶκτος), aor. ᾤκτειρε: *pity*. (Il.)

οἴκτιστος: see οἰκτρός.

οἶκτος (οἴ, 'alas!'): exclamation of pity, *pity, compassion*.

οἰκτρός (οἶκτος), comp. -ότερος, sup. -ότατος and οἴκτιστος: *pitiable, pitiful, miserable;* adv., **οἰκτρά, οἴκτιστα,** *pitifully, most miserably*, κ 409, χ 472.

οἰκ-ωφελίη (ϝοῖκος, ὀφέλλω): *bettering one's estate, thrift*, ξ 223†.

Ὀϊλεύς: *Oïleus*.—(1) king of Locris, father of the lesser Ajax and of Medon, N 697, O 333, B 727, see Αἴᾱς.—(1) charioteer of Biēnor, slain by Agamemnon, Λ 93.

Ὀϊλιάδης: *son of Oïleus*, Ajax, M 365, N 712, Ξ 446, Π 330, Ψ 759.

οἶμα, ατος (οἴσω, φέρω): *spring, swoop*. (Il.)

οἰμάω (οἶμα), aor. *οἴμησε*: *dart upon, swoop after*, X 308, 140, ω 538.

οἴμη: *song, lay*. (Od.)

οἶμος: *course, stripe, band*, pl., Λ 24†.

οἰμωγή (οἰμώζω): *cry of grief, lamentation*.

οἰμώζω (οἴμοι, 'woe me!'), aor. *ᾤμωξα*, part. *οἰμώξᾱς*: *cry out in grief* (or pain), *lament*, ἐλεεινά, σμερδαλέον, μέγα.

Οἰνείδης: *son of Oeneus*, Tydeus, E 813, K 497.

Οἰνεύς (ϝοιν.): *Oeneus*, son of Portheus, king of Calydon in Aetolia, the husband of Althaea, and father of Tydeus and Meleāger, a guest-friend of Bellerophon. The Calydonian boar was sent upon his territory through the anger of Artemis, B 641, Z 216, I 535, Ξ 117.

οἰνίζομαι (ϝοῖνος), ipf. *οἰνίζοντο*: *supply oneself with wine*. (Il.)

οἰνο-βαρείων (βαρύς), part.: *heavy with wine*. (Od.)

οἰνο-βαρής, voc. **-ές** = foregoing, 'wine-bibber,' A 225†.

Οἰνόμαος: (1) an Aetolian, slain by Hector, E 706.—(2) a Trojan, M 140, N 506.

οἰνό-πεδος (πέδον): consisting of wine-land, *wine-yielding*; subst., **οἰνόπεδον**, *vineyard*, I 579.

Οἰνοπίδης: *son of Oenops*, Helenus, E 707†.

οἰνο-πληθής: *abounding in wine*, ο 406†.

οἰνο-ποτάζω: *quaff wine*.

οἰνο-ποτήρ, ῆρος: *wine-drinker*, θ 456†.

οἶνος (ϝοῖνος, cf. v i n u m): *wine*. It was regularly mixed with water before drinking, see κρητήρ, ἀμφιφορεύς, ἀσκός, πίθος, πρόχοος, νέμειν. Epithets, αἶθοψ, ἐρυθρός, μελιηδής, μελίφρων, ἡδύς, ἡδύποτος, εὐήνωρ. γερούσιος οἶνος, typical of the dignity of the council of elders. Places famed for the quality of wine produced were Epidaurus, Phrygia, Pedasus, Arne, Histiaea, Lemnos, Thrace, Pramne, and the land of the Ciconians.

οἰνο-χοέω and **οἰνοχοεύω**, ipf. *ᾠνοχόει* (*οἰνοχόει*), *ἐῳνοχόει*, aor. inf. *οἰνοχοῆσαι*: *be cup-bearer, pour wine*, nectar, Δ 3.

οἰνο-χόος (χέω): *wine-pourer, cupbearer*.

οἶνοψ, οπος: *winy, wine-colored*, epithet of the sea and of cattle, ν 32.

Οἶνοψ: an Ithacan, the father of Liōdes, φ 144†.

οἰνόω: only pass. aor. part., *οἰνωθέντες*, *overcome by wine, drunken*, π 292 and τ 11.

οἴξᾱσα: see οἴγνῡμι.

οἷο: see ὅς 2.

οἰόθεν: adv., used for an emphatic doubling, *οἰόθεν οἶος*, *all alone* (cf. *αἰνόθεν αἰνῶς*). (Il.)

οἴομαι: see *ὀΐω*.

οἰο-πόλος (πέλομαι): *lonely*.

οἶος: *alone*; *μι' οἴη*, *δύ' οἴω*, *δύο οἴους*, γ 424; *οἶος ἄνευθε* or *ἀπό τινος*, X 39, ι 192; 'alone of its kind,' i. e. best, Ω 499.

οἷος, οἵη, οἷον: relative word, (such) *as, of what sort* (q u a l i s), with antecedent *τοῖος* expressed or implied. It may be causal in effect, also exclamatory, *αἵματος εἰς ἀγαθοῖο, φίλον τέκος, οἷ' ἀγορεύεις*, 'such words you speak,' = *ὅτι τοῖα*, δ 611; *οἷον δή νυ θεοὺς βροτοὶ αἰτιόωνται*, 'how mortals do, etc.!' α 32; foll. by inf., as implying capability, *οἷος ἐκεῖνος ἔην βουλευέμεν*, 'such a man was he to plan,' ξ 491; freq. the neut. **οἷον, οἷα**, as adv., *as, how, what* (sort), etc. *οἷα τε* in comparisons, *οἷον δή* exclamatory and causal, ι 128, λ 429.

οἰός and **ὄιος**: see *ὄϊς*.

οἰο-χίτων, ωνος: *with tunic only*, ξ 489†.

οἰόω (οἶος), pass. aor. *οἰώθη*: *leave alone, abandon*. (Il.)

ὄϊς (ὄϝις, cf. o v i s), gen. *ὄϊος, οἰός*, acc. *ὄϊν*, pl. *ὄϊες* (*οἴιες*, ι 425), gen. *ὀΐων, οἰῶν*, dat. *οἴεσι, ὀΐεσσι, ὄεσσι*, acc. *ὄϊς*: *sheep*; with *ἀρνειός, ἄρσην, θήλεια*.

ὀΐσατο: see *ὀΐω*.

οἴσετε: see φέρω.
οἶσθα: see εἴδω, II.
ὀισθείς: see ὀίω.
ὀιστεύω (ὀιστός), aor. imp. ὀίστευσον, part. ὀιστεύσᾱς: *discharge an arrow, shoot arrows; τόξῳ*, μ 84. (The foll. cuts, from Assyrian reliefs, illustrate the manner of drawing the bow and holding the arrow. See also cut under πῶμα.)

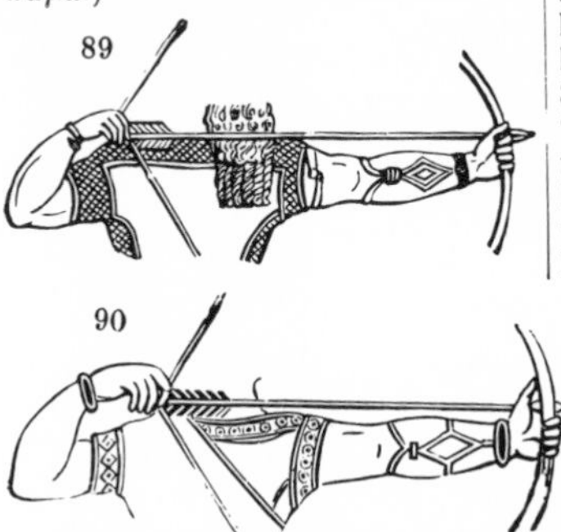
89
90

ὀιστός (οἴσω, φέρω): *arrow*. Made of wood, or a reed, with barbed metal point, the lower end feathered and notched (γλυφίδες), or with projections, enabling the fingers to take a firm hold on the arrow in drawing. Poisoned arrows are mentioned only exceptionally, α 261, Δ 213.
οἶστρος: *gadfly*, χ 300†.
οἰσύινος: *of willow, willow*, ε 256†.
οἴσω: see φέρω.
οἶτος: *fate*, mostly in bad sense, and usually with **κακός**. Without **κακός**, I 563, Ω 388, θ 489, 578.
Οἴτυλος: a town on the coast of Laconia, B 585†.
Οἰχαλίη: a town on the river Peneius, the home of Eurytus, B 730.—**Οἰχαλίηθεν**: *from Oechalia*, B 596.—**Οἰχαλιεύς**: the *Oechalian*, Eurytus, B 596, θ 224.
οἰχνέω (οἴχομαι), **οἰχνεῦσιν**, ipf. iter. οἴχνεσκον: *go* or *come* (frequently), E 790, O 640, γ 322.
οἴχομαι, ipf. ᾠχόμην: *go, depart*, and freq. w. perf. signif., ἤδη . . οἴχεται εἰς ἅλα δῖαν, *is gone*, O 223, E 472; so the part., Ὀδυσσῆος πόθος οἰχομένοιο, the 'absent,' perhaps the 'departed' Odysseus, ξ 144. The verb is common with a supplementary part., the more specific part of the predication being contained in this participle, ᾤχετ' ἀποπτάμενος, 'sped on wings away,' flew *away*, B 71.
ὀίω, οἴω, ὀίομαι, οἴομαι, opt. οἴοιτο, ipf. ὠίετο, aor. ὀίσατο, pass. aor. ὠίσθην, part. ὀισθείς: verb of subjective view or opinion, *think, believe, fancy*, regularly foll. by inf.; often iron. or in litotes, ὀίω, *methinks*, θ 180, N 263; likewise parenthetically (o p i n o r), π 309; sometimes to be paraphrased, 'suspect,' or when the reference is to the future, 'expect'; implying apprehension, τ 390. γόον δ' ὠίετο θῡμός, was 'bent on,' or 'engrossed with' lamentation, κ 248; once impers., like δοκεῖ, τ 312.
οἰωνιστής: (bird) *seer;* as adj., N 70.
οἰωνο-πόλος (πολέω): *versed in* omens drawn from *birds, seer*, pl., A 69 and Z 76.
οἰωνός (cf. a v i s): *bird* of prey, bird of *omen;* εἷς οἰωνὸς ἄριστος, ἀμῡνεσθαι περὶ πάτρης, N 243. (Said by Hector. A fine example of an early protest for free-thought.)
ὀκνέω, ὀκνείω, ipf. ὤκνεον: *shrink* from doing something, *hesitate* through some sort of dread, E 255 and Υ 155.
ὄκνος: *shrinking, hesitancy* through dread. (Il.)
ὀκριάω (ὄκρις, ἄκρος): only pass. ipf. ὀκριόωντο, met., *were becoming incensed, furious*, σ 33†.
ὀκριόεις, εσσα, εν (ὄκρις, ἄκρος): *having sharp points, jagged, rugged.*
ὀκρυόεις, εσσα, εν (κρύος): *chilling, horrible*, I 64 and Z 344.
ὀκτά-κνημος (κνήμη): *eight-spoked*, of wheels, E 723†. (See cut, from a

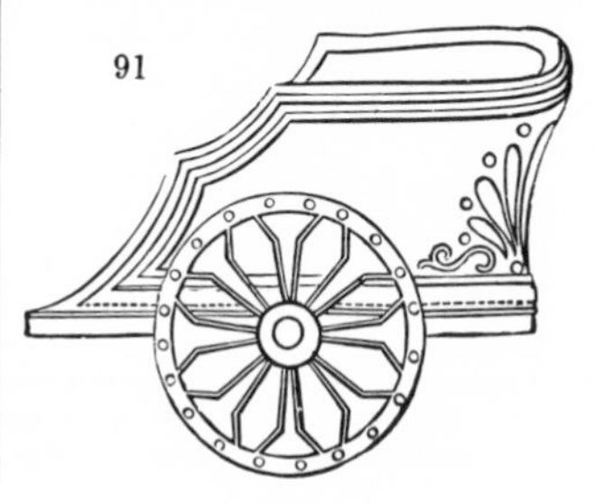
91

painting on a Panathenaic amphora found at Volsci.)

ὀκτώ: *eight.*

ὀκτω-και-δέκατος: *eighteenth.*

ὀλβιο-δαίμων: *blessed by the deity,* Γ 182†.

ὄλβιος (ὄλβος): *happy, blessed,* esp. with riches, σ 138; (δῶρα) ὄλβια ποιήσειαν, 'may they bless' them, ν 42; pl., ὄλβια, *blessings.*

ὄλβος: *happiness, fortune, riches.*

ὀλέεσθαι, ὀλέεσκε: see ὄλλῡμι.

ὀλέθριος: ὀλέθριον ἦμαρ: day *of destruction,* Τ 294 and 409.

ὄλεθρος (ὄλλῡμι): *destruction, ruin, death;* αἰπύς, λυγρός, ἀδευκής, οἴκτιστος.

ὀλεῖται: see ὄλλῡμι.

ὀλέκω, ipf. iter. ὀλέκεσκεν, pass. ὀλέκοντο: = ὄλλῡμι.

ὀλέσαι, ὀλέσᾱς, ὀλέσσαι, ὀλέσσᾱς, ὀλέσθαι: see ὄλλῡμι.

ὀλετήρ, ῆρος: *destroyer,* Σ 114†.

ὀλιγη-πελέω: *be weak, faint, swooning,* only part.

ὀλιγη-πελίη: *weakness, faintness,* ε 468.

ὀλίγιστος: see ὀλίγος.

ὀλιγο-δρανέω: only part., *able to do little, feeble.* (Il.)

ὀλίγος, sup. ὀλίγιστος: *little, small;* of a 'short' time (ὀλίγος χρόνος), a 'thin' voice (ὀλίγῃ ὀπί), a 'feebly-flowing' spring (πίδακος ὀλίγης), 'little' fishes (ὀλίγοι ἰχθύες). Neut. as adv., **ὀλίγον,** *a little,* also **ὀλίγου,** *almost,* ξ 37. Sup., Τ 223, 'scanty shall be the reaping.'

ὀλίζονες: see ὑπολίζονες.

Ὀλιζών: a town in Magnesia in Thessaly, Β 717†.

ὀλισθάνω, aor. 2 ὄλισθε: *slip, slip and fall, fall.* (Il.)

ὄλλῡμι, part. ὀλλύς, -ύντα, pl. fem. ὀλλῦσαι, ipf. iter. ὀλέεσκε, fut. ὀλέσω, ὀλέσσεις, aor. ὤλεσα, ὄλεσ(σ)ε, inf. ὀλέ(σ)σαι, part. ὀλέ(σ)σᾱς, part. ὄλωλα, plup. ὀλώλει, mid. pres. part. ὀλλύμενοι, fut. ὀλεῖται, inf. ὀλέεσθαι, aor. 2 ὤλεο, ὄλοντο, inf. ὀλέσθαι (see οὐλόμενος): act., *lose, destroy,* mid., *be lost, perish;* perf. and plup. mid. in sense, Ω 729, Κ 187.

ὅλμος: *smooth round stone, quoit,* Λ 147†.

ὀλοιός = ὀλοός, Α 342, Χ 5.

ὀλολυγή: *outcry* of women's voices, Ζ 301†.

ὀλολύζω, aor. ὀλόλυξα: *cry out aloud,* only of women, either with jubilant voice or in lamentation, χ 408, 411, δ 767.

ὀλόμην: see ὄλλῡμι.

ὀλοοί-τροχος (Ϝολ., cf. volvo): *rolling stone, round rock,* Ν 137†.

ὀλοός (ὄλλῡμι), comp. -ώτερος, sup. -ώτατος: *destroying, destructive, deadly.*

Ὀλοοσσών: a town on the river Eurōtas in Thessaly, situated on white cliffs, Β 739†.

ὀλοό-φρων: *destructive-minded, baleful.*

ὀλοφυδνός: *doleful, pitiful.*

ὀλοφῡ́ρομαι, aor. ὀλοφῡράμην: *lament, mourn, bewail, commiserate;* freq. abs., esp. in part., also w. gen. of the person mourned for, Θ 33; and trans., τινά, Ω 328, κ 157, τ 522; w. inf., 'bewail that thou must be brave before the suitors,' χ 232.

ὀλοφώιος: *pernicious, baleful;* ὀλοφώια εἰδώς = ὀλοόφρων, δ 460. (Od.)

Ὀλυμπιάς, pl. **Ὀλυμπιάδες**: *Olympian,* epith. of the Muses, Β 491†.

Ὀλύμπιος: *Olympian,* dwelling on Olympus, epith. of the gods and their homes, and as subst. = Zeus, *the Olympian.*

Ὄλυμπος, Οὔλυμπος: *Olympus,* a mountain in Thessaly, not less than nine thousand feet in height, penetrating with snow-capped peaks through the clouds to the sky, and conceived by Homer as the abode of the gods. Epithets, ἀγάννιφος, αἰγλήεις, αἰπύς, μακρός, πολύπτυχος.

ὄλῡραι, pl.: a kind of grain similar to *barley,* Ε 196 and Θ 564.

ὄλωλα: see ὄλλῡμι.

ὁμαδέω (ὅμαδος): only aor. ὁμάδησαν, they *raised a din.* (Od.)

ὅμαδος (ὁμός): *din,* properly of many voices together. (Il. and κ 556.)

ὁμαλός (ὁμός): *even, smooth,* ι 327†.

ὁμ-αρτέω (ὁμός, root ἀρ), part. ὁμαρτέων, aor. opt. ὁμαρτήσειεν, part. ὁμαρτήσᾱς: *accompany* or *attend, keep pace with, meet, encounter,* Ω 438, ν 87, Μ 400.

ὁμαρτῇ: see ἁμαρτῇ.

ὀμβριμοπάτρη, ὄμβριμος: see ὀβριμ.

ὄμβρος (cf. imber): *rain, rainstorm;* also of a heavy fall of snow, M 286.

ὀμεῖται: see ὄμνῡμι.

ὁμ-ηγερής, ές (ὁμός, ἀγείρω): *assembled together.*

ὁμ-ηγυρίζομαι, aor. inf. ὁμηγυρίσασθαι: *assemble, convoke,* π 376†.

ὁμ-ήγυρις: *assembly,* Υ 142†.

ὁμ-ηλικίη: *equal age,* Υ 465; for the concrete, *person of like age, mate, companion.*

ὁμ-ῆλιξ, ικος: *of like age; τινός,* 'with' one, τ 358.

ὁμ-ηρέω (root ἀρ), aor. ὡμήρησε: *meet,* π 468†.

ὁμῑλαδόν: adv., *in crowds.* (Il.)

ὁμῑλέω, ipf. ὡμίλευν, ὁμίλεον, ὁμίλει, aor. ὡμίλησα: *be in a throng, throng about, associate with, τινί,* so μετά, ἐνί, παρά τισι, περί τινα, Π 641, 644; of meeting in battle, Λ 523, α 265.

ὅμῑλος: *throng, crowd;* in the Iliad freq. of the crowd and tumult of battle, E 553, K 499. [N 336. (Il.)

ὀμίχλη: *mist, cloud ;* fig., of dust,

ὄμμα, ατος (root ὀπ, cf. oculus): *eye,* only pl.

ὄμνῡμι, ὀμνύω, imp. ὄμνυθι, ὀμνυέτω, ipf. ὤμνυε, fut. ὀμοῦμαι, -εῖται, aor. ὤμοσα, ὄμο(σ)σα: *take oath, swear;* ὅρκον (τινί, or πρός τινα), Γ 279, ξ 331; foll. by inf., also w. acc. of the person or thing in whose name, or *by* whom or which, the oath is taken, Ξ 271, O 40.

ὁμο-γάστριος (γαστήρ): κασίγνητος, *own* brother, by the same mother. (Il.)

ὁμόθεν: *from the same place* (root), ε 477†.

ὁμοῖος, ὁμοίιος: *like, similar, equal;* τὸν ὁμοῖον, 'his peer,' Π 53; prov., τὸν ὁμοῖον ἄγει θεὸς ὡς τὸν ὁμοῖον, 'birds of a feather,' ρ 218; as epith. of πόλεμος (ὁμοιίου πολέμοιο), θάνατος, etc., *common, impartial,* levelling all alike, ω 543.

ὁμοιόω: *make like;* ὁμοιωθήμεναι, 'to liken,' 'compare oneself,' A 187, γ 120.

ὁμοκλέω and **ὁμοκλάω** (ὁμοκλή), ipf. ὁμόκλεον, ὁμόκλᾱ, aor. ὁμόκλησα, iter. ὁμοκλήσασκε: *shout together, call out to, command* sharply; abs., and w. dat., Ω 248; w. (acc. and) inf., ω 173, Π 714.

ὁμο-κλή (ὁμός, καλέω): *call of many together,* loud, sharp *call* or *command.*

ὁμο-κλητήρ, ῆρος: *one who shouts* or *calls* loudly and sharply, M 273 and Ψ 452.

ὀμόργνῡμι, ipf. ὀμόργνῡ, mid. ὠμόργνυντο, aor. part. ὀμορξάμενος: *wipe, wipe away,* mid., one's own tears, etc., Σ 124.

ὁμός (cf. ἅμα): *like, common.*

ὀμόσᾱς: see ὄμνῡμι.

ὁμόσε: *to the place, together,* M 24 and N 337.

ὁμο-στιχάω (στείχω): *march along with, keep pace with,* O 635†.

ὁμό-τῑμος: *like-honored, entitled to equal honor,* O 186†.

ὁμοῦ: *in the same place* with, *together, at once, alike.*

ὁμο-φρονέω: *be like-minded, of one mind.* (Od.)

ὁμο-φροσύνη: *harmony* of mind, *congeniality.* (Od.)

ὁμό-φρων: *like-minded, harmonious, congenial,* X 263†.

ὁμόω: only pass. aor. inf., ὁμωθῆναι, *to be united;* φιλότητι, Ξ 209†.

ὀμφαλόεις, εσσα, εν: furnished with an ὀμφαλός or ὀμφαλοί, *bossy, studded,* epith. of shield, yoke. (Il.)

ὀμφαλός (cf. umbilicus): *navel,* Δ 525, Φ 180; fig., θαλάσσης, α 50; then (1) of a shield, *boss,* the projection in the centre ending in a button or point; pl., *studs,* serving as ornaments, Λ 34.—(2) of a yoke, *knob,* or pin, on the centre (see cut No. 45 *a*), Ω 273. The Assyrians had the same (see cut No. 51), while the Egyptians ornamented the ends of the yoke with a ball of brass. (See cut No. 92 on next page.)

ὄμφαξ, ακος: pl., *unripe grapes,* η 125†.

ὀμφή: divine or prophetic *voice,* conveyed by a dream or through omens of birds, etc. See πανομφαῖος.

ὁμ-ώνυμος (ὄνομα): *having the same name,* P 720†.

ὁμῶς (ὁμός): *together, alike, likewise, equally as, just as.*

ὅμως (ὁμός): *yet,* M 393†.

ὄναρ: *dream, vision;* opp. ὕπαρ, 'reality,' τ 547, υ 90.

ὄνειαρ, ατος (ὀνίνημι): anything that is helpful, *help, relief, refresh-*

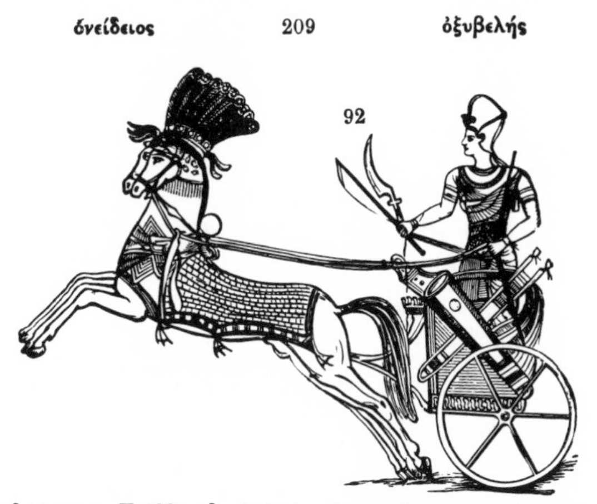
92

ment; of a person, X 433; pl., *ὀνείατα, viands,* once of *treasures,* Ω 367.

ὀνείδειος (ὄνειδος): *reproachful;* μῦθος, ἔπεα, and without ἔπος, X 497.

ὀνειδίζω (ὄνειδος), aor. ὀνείδισας, imp. ὀνείδισον: *reproach,* 'cast in one's teeth,' τινί τι, I 34, σ 380.

ὄνειδος, εος: *reproach,* often pl., ὀνείδεα μυθεῖσθαι, λέγειν, προφέρειν, βάζειν, κατ' ὀνείδεα χεῦαί τινι, 'overwhelm one with reproach,' χ 463; then *matter of reproach, disgrace,* Π 489.

ὀνείρατα: see ὄνειρος.

ὀνείρειος: ἐν ὀνειρείῃσι πύλῃσιν, at the gates *of dreams,* δ 809†.

ὀνειρο-πόλος (πέλω): *versed in dreams, interpreter of dreams.*

ὄνειρος, ὄνειρον, pl. ὄνειροι and **ὀνείρατα**: *dream;* personified, B 6, Π 22; as a people dwelling hard by the way to the nether world, ω 12; a dream-allegory, τ 562, cf. δ 809†.

ὀνήμενος, ὄνησα: see ὀνίνημι.

ὄνησις (ὀνίνημι): *benefit, luck, prosperity,* φ 402†.

Ὀνητορίδης: *son of Onētor,* Phrontis, γ 282.

Ὀνήτωρ: a Trojan, father of Laogonus, Π 604†.

ὄνθος: *dung.* (Ψ)

ὀνίνημι, fut. ὀνήσω, aor. ὤνησα, ὄνησα, mid. fut. ὀνήσομαι, aor. 2 imp. ὄνησο, part. ὀνήμενος: act., *benefit, help* (τινά), mid., *derive benefit* or *advantage* from, *enjoy,* τινός, Π 31; ἐσθλός μοι δοκεῖ εἶναι, ὀνήμενος, 'bless him!' β 33.

ὄνομα, οὔνομα, ατος (for ὄ-γνομα, γνῶναι, cf. nomen): *name;* for 'fame,' 'glory,' ν 248, ω 93.

ὀνομάζω, ipf. ὀνόμαζον, aor. ὠνόμασα: *call* or *address by name* (X 415, K 68), *name, mention;* the phrase ἔπος τ' ἔφατ' ἔκ (adv.) τ' ὀνόμαζεν (and 'familiarly addressed' him) is always followed either by the name of the person addressed or by some substantial equivalent for the name.

ὄνομαι, ὄνοσαι, ὄνονται, opt. ὄνοιτο, fut. ὀνόσσομαι, aor. 1 ὠνοσάμην, ὀνόσασθ(ε), -ντ(ο), part. ὀνοσσάμενος, aor. 2 ὤνατο, P 25: *find fault with, scorn,* τινά or τί, usually w. neg. expressed or implied, Δ 539, P 399; once w. gen., κακότητος, 'esteem lightly,' ε 379.

ὀνομαίνω (parallel form to ὀνομάζω), aor. ὀνόμηνας: *call by name, name, name over, mention;* in the sense of 'appointing' or 'constituting,' Ψ 90.

ὀνομα-κλήδην: adv., *calling the name, by name.*

ὀνομά-κλυτος: *of famous name, renowned,* X 51†.

ὀνομαστός: *to be named,* w. neg., of a name not to be uttered for the ill-omen it contains. (Od.)

ὄνος: *ass,* Λ 558†.

ὀνόσασθε, ὀνοσσάμενος, ὀνόσσεσθαι: see ὄνομαι.

ὀνοστός (ὄνομαι): w. neg., not *to be despised,* not *contemptible,* I 164†.

ὄνυξ, υχος: pl., *claws, talons,* of the eagle.

ὀξυ-βελής, ές (βέλος): *sharp-pointed,* Δ 126†.

ὀξυ-όεις, -εσσα, εν: *sharp-pointed.*

ὀξύς, εῖα, ύ, sup. ὀξύτατος: *sharp*, of weapons and other implements, crags, hill-tops, ε 411, μ 74; metaph., of light, pains, sounds, etc., 'keen,' 'piercing,' Ρ 372, λ 208; 'fierce' Ares, Λ 836; neut. as adv., **ὀξύ** and **ὀξέα**, met. as above, προϊδεῖν, νοεῖν, βοᾶν, ε 393, Γ 374, Ρ 89.

ὅο and **ὅου**: see ὅς 1.

ὀπάζω (cf. ἕπω), fut. ὀπάσσω, aor. ὤπασα, ὄπα(σ)σα, mid. pres. part. ὀπαζόμενος, fut. ὀπάσσεαι, aor. ὀπάσσατο, part. ὀπασσάμενος: I. act., *join as companion* (*guide, escort*), τινά τινι (ἅμα, μετά), *cause to follow* or *accompany*, Ν 416, ο 310, Ω 153, 461, κ 204; then of things, *bestow, lend, confer;* κῦδός τινι, χάριν καὶ κῦδος ἔργοις, γ 57, ο 320, w. inf., Ψ 151; also *follow hard upon, press upon.* τινά, Θ 341; fig., γῆρας, Δ 321; pass., Λ 493.—II. mid., *take with one* (as companion, guide, escort), τινά, Κ 238, Τ 238, κ 59.

ὀπαῖος (ὀπή): *with an opening;* neut. pl. as subst., ἀν' ὀπαῖα (v. l. ἀνοπαῖα, q. v.), through the *loop-holes*, i. e. between the rafters under the eaves, α 320†. These spaces were in later times closed, and termed specifically μετόπαι. (See cut No. 83.)

ὄ-πατρος: *of the same father*, Λ 257 and Μ 371.

ὀπάων, ονος (cf. ἕπω, ὀπάζω): *attendant*, 'armor-bearer,' 'esquire.' (Il.)

ὅπερ: see ὅσπερ.

ὅπῃ, ὅππῃ: adv. of place or manner, *where* (whither), *as*, κ 190, Μ 48, θ 45.

ὀπηδέω (ὀπηδός, ὀπάζω), ipf. ὀπήδει: *accompany, attend, follow*, τινί (ἅμα τινί); said of things as well as persons, τόξα, ἀρετή, τιμή, Ε 216, θ 237, Ρ 251.

ὀπίζομαι (ὄπις), ipf. ὀπίζεο, ὠπίζετο: *have regard to* with awe, *reverence, dread;* Διὸς μῆνιν, μητρὸς ἐφετμήν, τινά, ξ 283, Σ 216, Χ 332.

ὄπιθεν: see ὄπισθεν.

ὀπιπτεύω and **ὀπιπεύω** (root ὀπ), aor. part. -εύσᾱς: *peer after, watch* (timorously, or in lurking for one), Δ 371, Η 243; γυναῖκας, *ogle*, τ 67 (cf. παρθενοπίπης).

ὄπις, acc. ὄπιδα and ὄπιν (root ὀπ): *jealous and vengeful regard, divine vengeance*, always w. θεῶν exc. ξ 82, 88. (Od. and Π 388.)

ὄπισθε(ν), ὄπιθε(ν): *from behind, behind, afterward, hereafter;* w. gen., Ν 536.

ὀπί(σ)σω: *backward, behind, hereafter, in*(to) *the future.*

ὀπίστατος: *hindmost*, Θ 432 and Λ 178.

Ὀπίτης: a Greek, slain by Hector, Λ 301†.

ὁπλέω (= ὁπλίζω): only ipf., ὥπλεον (ὅπλεον), *were getting ready*, ζ 73†.

ὁπλή: *hoof*, pl., Λ 536 and Υ 501.

ὁπλίζω (ὅπλον), aor. ὥπλισσε, imp. ὥπλισσον, inf. ὁπλίσαι, mid. aor. ὁπλί(σ)σατο: *equip, make ready*, as a chariot, a ship for sailing, *prepare* a meal; mid., *equip* or *arm oneself, prepare for oneself*, ξ 526, π 453; aor. pass., ὅπλισθεν γυναῖκες, 'arrayed themselves' for the dance, ψ 143.

ὅπλον: mostly pl., ὅπλα, *implements, arms* (*armor*), *rigging* of a ship, Σ 409, γ 433, κ 254, β 390; sing., *rope, cable*, φ 390, ξ 346.

ὅπλομαι: *prepare*, inf. (Il.)

ὁπλότερος comp., sup. **ὁπλοτάτη**: *younger, youngest;* γενεῇ, γενεῆφιν, Β 707, Ι 58; sup., γ 465, η 58, λ 283, ο 364.

Ὀπόεις: *Opūs*, a city in Locris, the home of Menoetius, father of Patroclus, Ψ 85, Σ 326, Β 531.

ὁποῖος, ὁπποῖος: indirect interrog., *of what sort*, α 171; ὁποῖ' ἄσσα (ὁποῖά τινα), 'about what sort' of garments, τ 218; also rel., like οἷος, correl. to τοῖος, Υ 250, ρ 421.

ὀπός: *sap* of the wild fig-tree, used for curdling milk, Ε 902†.

ὀπός: see ὄψ.

ὁπόσος, ὁπόσσος, ὁππόσος: *how great, how much, how many.*

ὁπότε, ὁππότε: *whenever, when;* w. the same constructions as other rel. words, see ἄν, κέν.

ὅπου: *where.* (Od.)

ὁππόθεν: *whence.* (Od.)

ὅπποθ(ι): *where.*

ὁππόσε: *whithersoever*, ξ 139†.

ὁππότερος: *whichever* (of two).

ὁπποτέρωθεν: *from* or *on which side* (of two), Ξ 59†.

ὀπταλέος (ὀπτός): *roasted.*

ὀπτάω (ὀπτός), ipf. ὤπτων (ὤπτων),

aor. ὤπτησα, ὄπτησα, pass. aor. inf. ὀπτηθῆναι: *roast* on the spit; w. part. gen., κρεῶν, ο 98.

ὀπτήρ, ῆρος (root ὀπ): *scout, spy,* pl., ξ 261 and ρ 430.

ὀπτός (root πεπ, πέσσω): *roasted, broiled.* (Od.)

ὀπυίω, inf. ὀπυιέμεν(αι), ipf. ὤπυιε, ὄπυιε, pass. part. ὀπυιομένη: *wed, take to wife;* part., *married,* act. of man, pass. of woman, ζ 63, Θ 304.

ὄπωπα: see ὁράω.

ὀπωπή (ὄπωπα): *sight,* power of *vision,* ι 512; ἤντησας ὀπωπῆς, 'hast met the view,' 'thine eyes have seen,' γ 97.

ὀπώρη (ὥρη): *late summer* (or early autumn), *harvest-tide;* the season extended from the rising of Sirius (end of July) to the setting of the Pleiades, thus corresponding nearly to our 'dog-days,' τεθαλυῖα, 'luxuriant,' 'exuberant,' fruit-time, λ 192.

ὀπωρῖνός: *of late summer;* ἀστήρ, Sirius, E 5.

ὅπως, ὅππως: *how, in order that, as.*—(1) indirect interrog., οὐδέ τί πω σάφα ϝίδμεν ὅπως ἔσται τάδε ϝέργα, 'how these things will be,' B 250; then implying purpose, φράζεο νῦν ὅππως κε πόλιν καὶ ϝάστυ σαώσεις, 'how you are to save,' P 144; and purely final, λίσσεσθαι δέ μιν αὐτός, ὅπως νημερτέα ϝείπῃ, 'that he speak the truth,' γ 19.—(2) rel., *as;* ἔρξον ὅπως ἐθέλεις, Δ 37; θαύμαζεν δ' ὁ γεραιός, ὅπως ἴδεν ὀφθαλμοῖσιν, γ 373; causal, δ 109.

ὁράω, ὁρόω (root ϝορ), ipf. ὅρα, ὁρῶμεν, mid. ὁρῶμαι, 2 sing. ὅρηαι, ipf. ὁρᾶτο, ὁρῶντο (from root ὀπ, perf. ὄπωπα, plup. ὀπώπει, mid. fut. ὄψεαι, ὄψει, 2 pl. [or aor. imp.] ὄψεσθε; from root ϝιδ, see εἴδω I.): act. and mid., *see, behold, look on;* freq. phrases, (ἐν) ὀφθαλμοῖσιν ὁρᾶν, ὁρᾶσθαι, ὁρᾶν φάος ἠελίοιο (= ζῆν).

ὄργυια (ὀρέγω): distance spanned by the outstretched arms, *fathom.*

ὀρέγνῡμι, ὀρέγω, part. ὀρέγων, ὀρεγνύς, fut. ὀρέξω, aor. ὤρεξα, mid. pres. inf. ὀρέγεσθαι, aor. ὠρέξατ(ο), ὀρέξατ(ο), perf. 3 pl. ὀρωρέχαται, plup. 3 pl. ὀρωρέχατο: *reach, extend,* mid., *stretch out* oneself, or one's own hands, etc., *reach for,* τινός, sometimes τὶ, Π 314, 322, Ψ 805; of 'reaching and giving' something, Ω 102; and metaph., ὁπποτέροισι πατὴρ Ζεὺς κῦδος ὀρέξῃ, 'may bestow,' E 33; mid., of trying to hit, 'lunging' at one with the spear, Δ 307; of horses 'laying themselves out,' to exert their speed (perf. and plup.), Π 834; so δράκοντες, 'outstretched,' Λ 26.

ὀρεκτός (ὀρέγω): *extended, thrust out,* B 543†.

ὀρέομαι = ὄρνυμαι, only ipf., ὀρέοντο, *rushed forth,* B 398 and Ψ 212.

Ὀρέσβιος: a Boeotian from Hyle, slain by Hector, E 707†.

ὀρεσί-τροφος: *mountain-bred.*

ὀρεσ-κῷος (κεῖμαι): *having mountain-lairs,* A 268 and ι 155.

ὀρέστερος (ὄρος, cf. ἀγρότερος): *of the mountains, mountain-,* dragon, wolves, X 93, κ 212.

Ὀρέστης: *Orestes.*—(1) the son of Agamemnon, who having been reared at Athens returns to Mycēnae and slays Aegisthus, after the latter had reigned eight years. Clytaemnestra was slain at the same time. (See cut under ἕδρη, from a painting on an ancient Greek vase.) The murder of Agamemnon was thus avenged, and the throne restored to its rightful heir, γ 306, λ 461, α 30, 40, 298, δ 546, I 142, 284.—(2) a Greek slain by Hector, E 705.—(3) a Trojan, slain by Leonteus, M 139, 193.

ὀρεστιάς, άδος: *mountain-nymph,* pl., Z 420†.

ὄρεσφι: see ὄρος.

ὀρεχθέω: doubtful word, *bellow* in last agonies, *rattle in the throat,* Ψ 30†.

ὄρθαι: see ὄρνῡμι.

Ὀρθαῖος: a Trojan, N 791†.

Ὄρθη: a town in Thessaly, B 739†.

ὄρθιος: of the voice, *high;* adv., ὄρθια, 'with shrill voice,' Λ 11†.

ὀρθό-κραιρος (κέρας), only gen. pl. fem. ὀρθοκραιράων: *straight-horned, high-horned;* βοῶν, μ 348, Θ 231; then of ships, either with reference to the pointed bow and stern, or perhaps to the yards (κεραίᾱ).

ὀρθός: *upright, erect.*

ὀρθόω, aor. ὤρθωσε, pass. aor. part. ὀρθωθείς: *raise up* straight, pass., *rise up.* (Il.)

ὀρίνω (parallel form of ὄρνῡμι), aor.

ὤρῑνα, ὄρῑνα, pass. ipf. ὠρίνετο, aor. ὠρίνθην, ὀρίνθη: *stir, rouse, arouse, move*, wind, waves, etc.; metaph., of anger and other passions, θῡμόν τινι, Ω 467, pass. σ 75, γόον, κῆρ, ἦτορ; ὀρινθέντες κατὰ δῶμα, 'stirred with dismay,' χ 23.

ὅρκιον (ὅρκος): (1) *oath*, Δ 158, elsewhere pl.—(2) pledges of the covenant, hence *victims*, Γ 245, 269.—(3) the *covenant* or *treaty* itself; ὅρκια πιστὰ ταμεῖν (f o e d u s f e r i r e), because victims were slaughtered as a part of the ceremony, B 124, Γ 73, ω 483.

ὅρκος: (1) that by which one swears, *witness* of an oath, for the gods the Styx; for men Zeus, Earth, the Erinnyes, etc., B 755, O 38, Γ 276 ff., T 258 ff., ξ 394; Achilles swears by his sceptre, A 234.—(2) *oath;* ἑλέσθαι τινός or τινί, 'take an oath from one,' X 119, δ 746; ὅρκος θεῶν, 'by the gods,' cf. Υ 313; γερούσιος ὅρκος, X 119; ὅρκῳ πιστωθῆναι, ο 436.

ὁρμαθός (ὅρμος): *chain, cluster* of bats hanging together, ω 8†.

ὁρμαίνω (ὁρμάω), ipf. ὥρμαινε, aor. ὥρμηνε: *turn over* in the mind, *debate, ponder;* κατὰ φρένα καὶ κατὰ θῡμόν, ἀνὰ θῡμόν (ἐνὶ) φρεσίν, K 4, γ 169; foll. by acc., πόλεμον, πλόον, χαλεπὰ ἀλλήλοις, γ 151; and by ὅπως, ἤ .. ἤ, etc., Ξ 20, Φ 137.

ὁρμάω (ὁρμή), aor. ὥρμησα, mid. ipf. ὡρμᾶτο, aor. ὡρμήσατο, subj. ὁρμήσωνται, pass. aor. ὡρμήθην, ὁρμηθήτην: I. act., *set in motion, impel, move;* πόλεμον, τινὰ ἐς πόλεμον, σ 376, Z 338; pass. (met.), ὁρμηθεὶς θεοῦ, 'inspired of heaven,' θ 499; intrans., *start, rush;* τινός, 'at one,' Δ 335; w. inf., Φ 265 (cf. X 194), N 64.—II. mid., *be moved, set out, start, rush*, esp. in hostile sense, *charge upon;* ἔγχεϊ, ξιφέεσσι, E 855, P 530; τινός, 'at one,' Ξ 488; freq. w. inf., and met., ἦτορ ὡρμᾶτο πολεμίζειν, Φ 572.

Ὀρμενίδης: *son of Ormenus.*—(1) Amyntor, I 448.—(2) Ctesius, ο 414.

Ὀρμένιον: a town in Magnesia, B 734†.

Ὅρμενος: (1) a Trojan slain by Teucer, Θ 274.—(2) a Trojan slain by Polypoetes, M 187.—(3) and (4), see Ὀρμενίδης.

ὅρμενος: see ὄρνῡμι.

ὁρμή: *start, impetus, rush, attack, effort;* of things as well as persons, κύματος, πυρός, ἐς ὁρμὴν ἔγχεος ἐλθεῖν, within the 'cast' of a spear, E 118; 'departure,' β 403; ἐμὴν ὁρμήν, 'prompting from me,' K 123.

ὅρμημα, ατος (ὁρμάω): pl., met., *struggles*, i. e. agonies and sorrows, B 356†.

ὁρμίζω, aor. ὡρμίσαμεν, subj. ὁρμίσσομεν: *bring to anchor, moor*, νῆα.

1. ὅρμος: *anchorage, mooring-place.*

2. ὅρμος (root σερ, εἴρω): *necklace.* (See cut, also Nos. 40, 41.)

93

Ὀρνειαί: *Orneae*, a town in Argolis, B 571†.

ὄρνεον: *bird*, N 64†.

ὄρνῑς, ῑθος, pl. dat. ὀρνίθεσσι: *bird*, freq. w. specific name added, ὄρνῑσιν ἐοικότες αἰγυπιοῖσιν, H 59, ε 51; then like οἰωνός, bird of *omen*, Ω 219.

ὄρνῡμι, ὀρνύω, inf. ὀρνύμεν(αι), ipf. ὤρνυον, fut. ὄρσομεν, part. ὄρσουσα, aor. ὦρσα, iter. ὄρσασκε, aor. 2 ὤρορε(ν), perf. ὄρωρεν, subj. ὀρώρῃ, plup. ὀρώρει (see also ὄρομαι), ὠρώρει, mid. ὄρνυμαι, ὄρνυται, ipf. ὤρνυτο, fut. ὀρεῖται, aor. ὤρετο, ὦρτο, ὄροντο, subj. ὄρηται, opt. ὄροιτο, imp. ὄρσο, ὄρσεο, ὄρσευ, inf. ὄρθαι, part. ὄρμενος, perf. ὀρώρεται, subj. ὀρώρηται: I. trans. (act., exc. perf.), *arouse, awake, excite;* λᾱούς, αἶγας, νεβρὸν ἐξ εὐνῆς, O 475, ι 154, X 190; freq. of the mind, E 105, δ 712; w. inf., M 142, ψ 222, γόον, φόβον, σθένος, B 451; so of things, ἄνεμον, κύματα, etc. — II. intrans. (mid., and perf.), *rouse oneself, arise, spring up*, w. inf., β 397, part., θ 342; in hostile sense, χαλκῷ, Γ 349; freq. of 'beginning' to do something, M 279, θ 539; εἰσόκε μοι φίλα γούνατ' ὀρώρῃ, 'have strength to move.'

ὀροθύνω, aor. imp. ὀρόθῡνον = ὄρνῡμι, ἐναύλους, 'cause all the river-beds to swell,' Φ 312.

ὄρομαι (root Ϝορ, ὁράω), ὄρονται, ipf. ὄροντο, plup. ὀρώρει: *keep watch* or *ward*, ἐπὶ (adv., 'over') δ' ἀνὴρ ἐσθλὸς ὀρώρει, Ψ 112, ξ 104, γ 471.

ὄρος, οὖρος, εος, pl. dat. ὄρεσφι: *mountain.*

ὀρός: *whey*, ι 222 and ρ 225.

ὀρούω (ὄρνῡμι), aor. ὄρουσα: *rush, spring;* of persons and things, αἰχμή, ἄνεμοι δ' ἐκ ('forth') πάντες ὄρουσαν, ἐκ κλήρος ὄρουσεν, Γ 325.

ὀροφή (ἐρέφω): *roof, ceiling*, χ 298†.

ὄροφος (ἐρέφω): *reeds* for thatching, Ω 451†.

ὁρόω: see ὁράω.

ὅρπηξ, ηκος: *shoot, sapling*, pl., Φ 38†.

ὄρσ', ὄρσεο, ὄρσευ, ὀρσᾶς, ὄρσασκε: see ὄρνῡμι.

'Ορσίλοχος: *Orsilochus.*—(1) son of Alpheius, E 547, = 'Ορτίλοχος, father of Diocles, γ 489, ο 187, cf. φ 16.—(2) son of Diocles from Pherae, grandson of the foregoing, E 549.—(3) a Trojan, slain by Teucer, Θ 274.—(4) a fabled son of Idomeneus, ν 260.

ὀρσο-θύρη (ὄρρος): *back door*, in the side wall of the men's hall (μέγαρον) of the house of Odysseus, leading into the passage (λαύρη), χ 126, 132, 333. (See cut No. 83, and plate III., *h*, at end of vol.)

'Ορτίλοχος: see 'Ορσίλοχος (1).

'Ορτυγίη (ὄρτυξ): *Ortygia* ('Quail-land'), a fabulous place, ο 404, ε 123.

ὀρυκτός (ὀρύσσω): *dug.* (Il.)

ὀρυμαγδός: loud *noise, din, crash;* often of crowds of men, esp. in battle, ω 70, B 810, P 740, ι 133; also of trees felled, wood thrown down, a torrent, stones, Π 633, ι 235, Φ 256, 313.

ὀρύσσω, inf. ὀρύσσειν, aor. ὄρυξα: *dig, dig up*, κ 305.

ὀρφανικός: *bereft, orphaned, fatherless;* ἦμαρ, 'day of orphanhood,' the day that makes one an orphan, X 490.

ὀρφανός: *bereft, orphaned;* ὀρφαναί, as 'orphans,' υ 68†.

ὀρφναῖος (ὄρφνη, ἔρεβος): *dark, gloomy, murky*, νύξ. (Il. and ι 143.)

ὄρχαμος (ἄρχω): the first of a row, *leader, chief;* always w. ἀνδρῶν or λᾱῶν, said of heroes, and of Eumaeus and Philoetius, ξ 22, υ 185.

ὄρχατος (ὄρχος): trees planted in rows, *orchard.* (The resemblance between the Eng. and Greek words is accidental.)

ὀρχέομαι, ipf. du. ὠρχείσθην, 3 pl. ὠρχεῦντο, aor. inf. ὀρχήσασθαι: *dance.*

ὀρχηθμός: *dancing*, choral *dance.*

ὀρχηστήρ, ῆρος, and **ὀρχηστής**: *dancer.*

ὀρχηστύς, ύος, dat. -υῖ: *dancing, dance.*

'Ορχομενός: *Orchomenus.*—(1) Μινύειος, *Minyian*, a very ancient city on Lake Copāis in Boeotia, seat of the treasure-house of Minyas, B 511, λ 284.—(2) a city in Arcadia, B 605.

ὄρχος: *row* of vines, η 127 and ω 341.

ὄρωρε, ὀρώρεται: see ὄρνῡμι.

ὀρώρει: see (1) ὄρνῡμι.—(2) ὄρομαι.

ὀρωρέχαται, ὀρωρέχατο: see ὀρέγνῡμι.

1. ὅς, ἥ, ὅ, gen. ὅου (ὅο), B 325, α 70, ἕης, pl. dat. ᾗσ(ιν): demonstrative and relative pronoun.—(1) dem., *he, this, that;* ὅς (as antecedent to ὅντινα), Z 59; ὅ, M 344; and so both forms elsewhere.—(2) rel., *who, that, which.* The rel. pron. in Homer is either definite or conditional (see ἄν, κέν), and exhibits in the main the same peculiarities as regards position, agreement (attraction, assimilation), and syntactical construction as in prose. To express purpose it is not foll. by the fut. ind. as in Att., but by the subj., with or without κέ, or by a potential optative, Γ 287, ο 311, A 64.—**ὅ,** conj., like quod (ὅτι), *that*, Σ 197, δ 206, etc.

2. ὅς, ἥ, ὅν (σϜός, cf. suus), gen. οἷο (Ϝοῖο), dat. ᾗφι, X 107, see ἑός: poss. pron. of the third person, *own*, (*his*) *own*, (*her*) *own;* placed before or after the subst., with or without article, θυγατέρα σϜήν, τὰ Ϝὰ κῆλα, M

280; the word is not always directly reflexive, α 218, ι 369, etc. Some passages in which ὅς appears to be of the 1st or 2d pers. are doubtful as regards the text.

ὁσίη: *divine* or *natural right*, οὐχ ὁσίη, w. inf. (non fas est), 'it is contrary to divine law.' (Od.)

ὅσος, ὅσσος: *how great, how much*, pl. *how many*, w. τόσσος expressed or implied as antec., (*as great*) *as*, (*as much*) *as*, pl. (*as many*) *as* (quantus, quot); very often the appropriate form of πᾶς precedes (or is implied) as antecedent, Τρώων ὅσσοι ἄριστοι, *all* the bravest of the Trojans, M 13, B 125, λ 388, etc.—Neut. as adv., **ὅσον, ὅσσον**, ὅσον ἔπι, ὅσσον τ' ἔπι, *as far as*, B 616, Ψ 251; ὅσον ἐς Σκαιὰς πύλᾱς, '*only* as far as,' I 354; so ὅσον τε, 'about,' ι 322; w. comp. and sup., 'by how much,' 'how far,' I 160, A 516.

ὅσπερ (**ὅπερ**, H 114), **ἥπερ, ὅπερ**: *just who* (*which*), *who* (*which*) *however*, B 286; adv., **ᾗπερ**, *just where* (*whither*), *just as.* See πέρ.

ὄσσα (root Ϝεπ, cf. vox): *rumor.*—Personified, **Ὄσσα**, daughter of Zeus, B 93, ω 413.

Ὄσσα: *Ossa*, a mountain in Thessaly, λ 315.

ὅσσα: see ὅσος.

ὁσσάκι: *as often as.*

ὁσσάτιος: *how great*, E 758†.

ὄσσε (root ὀπ, cf. oculus), du.: the (two) *eyes*, with attributes in du. or pl., and verb in all three numbers.

ὄσσομαι (ὄσσε), ipf. ὄσσετο, ὄσσοντο: *see*, esp. in spirit, 'with the mind's eye,' *forebode*, υ 81, κ 374, Σ 224; causative, *give to foresee, forebode, threaten*, β 112, Ξ 17.

ὅσσος: see ὅσος.

ὅστε (**ὅ τε**, μ 40, etc.), **ἥτε, ὅ τε**: rel. pron., rarely to be distinguished in translating from the simple word. See τέ.

ὀστέον, pl. gen. and dat. ὀστεόφιν: *bone.*

ὅστις, ἥτις, ὅ τι (**ὅ ττι**), gen. οὗτινος, ἧστινος, and ὅτ τεο, ὅ(τ)τευ, dat. ὅτεῳ, acc. ὅτινα, pl. neut. ὅτινα, ἅσσα, gen. ὅτεων, dat. ὀτέοισι, acc. ὅτινας: *who*(*so*)*ever*, *which*(*so*)*ever*, *what*(*so*)*ever*, both relative and indirect interrogative; ξεῖνος ὅδ', οὐκ οἶδ' ὅστις, 'unknown to me,' θ 28. See ὅτι.

ὅτ': = (1) ὅτε.—(2) ὅ τε, i. e. ὅτι τε. Never = ὅτι, which does not suffer elision.

ὅταν: = ὅτ' ἄν, see ὅτε and ἄν.

ὅ τε: see ὅστε.

ὅτε: *when, since.*—(1) temporal, w. the same constructions as other relative words, see ἄν, κέν. Freq. in similes, ὡς δ' ὅτε, ὡς δ' ὅτ' ἄν, and without verb, ὡς ὅτε, *just like;* there is nothing peculiar in such a usage.—(2) less often causal, A 244.

ὀτέ: regularly found in correlation, ὀτὲ μὲν . . ὀτὲ δέ, *now . . now;* ἄλλοτε (μέν or δέ) may replace one of the terms, *now* (*at one time*) . . *at another*, Υ 49, Λ 566.

ὀτέοισι, ὅτευ, ὅτεῳ: see ὅστις.

ὅτι, ὅττι (neut. of ὅστις): (1) conj., *that because* (quod).—(2) adv., strengthening superlatives, ὅττι τάχιστα, *as quickly as possible*, Δ 193.

ὅ τι, ὅ ττι: see ὅστις.

ὀτραλέως (cf. ὀτρηρός): *busily, nimbly, quickly.*

Ὀτρεύς: son of Dymas, king of Phrygia, Γ 186†.

ὀτρηρός (cf. ὀτραλέως): *busy, nimble, ready.*

ὅ-τριχες (θρίξ), pl.: with *like hair, like-colored*, B 765†.

Ὀτρυντείδης: *son of Otrynteus*, Iphition, Υ 383, 389.

Ὀτρυντεύς: king of Hydē, Υ 384.

ὀτρυντύς, ύος (ὀτρύνω): *encouragement.* (Il.)

ὀτρύνω, inf. ὀτρῡνέμεν, ipf. iter. ὀτρύνεσκον, fut. ὀτρυνέω, aor. ὤτρῡνα, subj. ὀτρύνῃσι, inf. ὀτρῦναι: *urge on, send forth, hasten, speed, encourage*, mid., *make haste*, mostly foll. by inf., in both act. and mid., κ 425; the obj. is usually a person, rarely animals or things, ἵππους, κύνας, ὁδόν τινι, β 253.

ὅττι: see ὅτι.

ὅ ττι: see ὅστις.

οὐ, οὐχί, οὐκί (q. v.), before vowels οὐκ, or, if aspirated, οὐχ: *not, no*, the adv. of objective negation, see μή. οὐ may be used w. the inf. in indirect discourse, P 174; in a condition, when the neg. applies to a single word or phrase and not to the whole clause.

εἰ δέ τοι οὐ δώσει, 'shall *fail to grant*,' Ω 296. οὐ (like n o n n e) is found in questions that expect an affirmative answer. **οὔτι,** 'not a whit,' 'not at all,' 'by no means,' so *οὐ πάμπαν, οὐ πάγχυ*, etc. οὐ may be doubled for emphasis, γ 27 f.

οὗ (σϝ., cf. s u i), dat. **οἷ,** acc. **ἕ,** other forms, gen. *εὗ, εἷο, ἕο, ἕθεν*, dat. *ἑοῖ*, acc. *ἑέ*: (1) simple personal pron. of 3d pers., (*of, to*) *him, her*, rarely *it*, A 236; in this sense enclitic, except *ἑέ*. —(2) reflexive pron., not enclitic, (*of, to*) *himself, herself* (*itself*), η 217; usually with *αὐτῷ, αὐτῇ, αὐτόν, αὐτήν*, δ 38, Ξ 162.

οὔασι, οὔατα: see *οὖς*.

οὖδας, εος: *ground, earth, floor*, ψ 46; *ἄσπετον οὖδας*, see *ἄσπετος*. *ὀδὰξ ἑλεῖν*, see *ὀδάξ*.—**οὖδάσδε,** *to the ground*.

οὐδέ: (*but not*), *and not, nor, not even;* never a correlative word, but always (except when meaning 'but not') adding a new negation after a previous one expressed or implied; if *οὐδέ* occurs at the beginning of several successive clauses, the first one refers to some previous negation just as much as the 2d or the 3d, **Τηλέμαχ', οὐδ'** *ὄπιθεν κακὸς ἔσσεαι οὐδ' ἀνοήμων*, *not even* in the future, i. e. even as not in the past, β 270. *οὐδὲ γὰρ οὐδέ*, doubled for emphasis, *no, not at all*, E 22, etc. (When the meaning is 'but not,' it would be well to write *οὐ δέ* separately, as this usage is essentially different from the other one. See *μηδέ*.)

οὐδείς, οὐδέν: *no one, nothing*, in Homer only the neut. as adv., and the dat. masc., *τὸ ὃν μένος οὐδενὶ εἴκων*, X 459, λ 515.

οὐδενόσ-ωρος (*ὥρᾱ*): *not to be regarded, worthy of no notice*, Θ 178†.

οὐδέπῃ: *in no way, by no means*.

οὐδέποτε: *never*.

οὐδέπω: *not yet, not at all*.

οὐδετέρωσε: *in neither direction*, Ξ 18†.

1. οὐδός: *threshold;* fig., *γήραος*, 'threshold of old age,' a poetic periphrasis for old age itself (of course not meaning the 'beginning' of old age), ο 246, 348.

2. οὐδός: see *ὁδός*.

οὖθαρ, ατος: *udder*, met., *ἀρούρης*, of fat land, I 141.

οὐκ: see *οὐ*.

Οὐκαλέγων: *Ucalegon*, a Trojan elder, Γ 148†.

οὐκ-έτι: *no longer, no more*.

οὐκί: = *οὐκ*, only *καὶ οὐκί* at the close of a verse and a sentence.

οὐλαί: *barley-corns*, roasted, mixed with salt and sprinkled between the horns of the victim to be sacrificed, γ 441†.

οὐλαμός (*εἴλω*): *ἀνδρῶν*, dense *throng, crowd* of men. (Il.)

οὖλε (cf. *οὖλος* 1): imp. (s a l v e), *hail!* ω 402†.

οὐλή: *scar*. (Od.)

οὔλιος (*οὖλος* 3): *baleful, deadly*, Λ 62†.

οὐλο-κάρηνος (*οὖλος* 2): *with thick, curly hair*, τ 246†.

οὐλόμενος (*ὄλλῡμι*): *accursed, cursed*, properly designating that upon which the imprecation *ὄλοιο* has been pronounced.

1. οὖλος (Att. *ὅλος*): *whole*, ρ 343 and ω 118.

2. οὖλος: *thick, woolly, woollen;* of fabrics and of hair; fig., of the cry of many voices; neut. as adv., **οὖλον,** *loudly, incessantly*, P 756.

3. οὖλος (*ὀλοός, ὄλλῡμι*): *destructive, murderous*, E 461; *baneful* Dream, B 6, 8.

οὐλό-χυται (*οὐλαί, χέω*): *sprinkled barley*, poured or scattered from baskets, δ 761; *οὐλοχύτᾱς κατάρχεσθαι*, to begin the solemn rites by sprinkling the barley between the horns of the victim, γ 445, A 458.

Οὔλυμπος: see *Ὄλυμπος*.

οὑμός = *ὁ ἐμός*, Θ 360†.

οὖν: inferential or resumptive particle, *now, then*, in Homer regularly found in connection with some other particle, *γὰρ οὖν, ἐπεὶ οὖν, ὡς οὖν, μὲν οὖν*, and as in the 1st or 2d of a pair of correlative clauses, *οὔτ' οὖν . . οὔτε*, α 414; *εἴ γ' οὖν ἕτερός γε φύγῃσιν*, if 'for that matter,' etc., E 258. The various shades of meaning assumed by *οὖν* must be learned from the context of the passages in which it occurs.

οὕνεκα (*οὗ ἕνεκα*): (1) *wherefore*, (q u a m o b r e m), corresponding to **τοὔ-**

νεκα, Γ 403.—(2) *because*, **A** 11, **δ** 569. —(3) *that*, like ὅτι. (Od.)

οὔνεσθε: v. l. for ὀνόσασθε, see ὄνομαι.

οὔνομα: see ὄνομα.

οὔπερ: *not at all.*

οὔπῃ: *nowhere, in no way.*

οὔποθε: *nowhere.*

οὔποτε: *never.*

οὔπω: *not yet, by no means.*

οὔπως: *nohow, on no terms.*

οὖρα: see οὖρον.

οὐραῖος (οὐρή): *of the tail;* **τρίχες**, Ψ 520†.

οὐρανίων, ωνος: *heavenly;* as subst., Οὐρανίωνες, the *Celestials*, i. e. the gods, E 373, 898.

οὐρανόθεν: *from heaven;* also with ἐξ and ἀπό, Θ 19, Φ 199.

οὐρανόθι: *in the heavens* (see πρό), Γ 3†.

οὐρανο-μήκης (μῆκος): *high as heaven*, ε 239†.

οὐρανός: *heaven*, i. e. the skies, above and beyond the **αἰθήρ**, **B** 458; and penetrated by the peaks of Mt. Olympus, the home of the gods, hence (θεοὶ ἀθανατοὶ) τοὶ οὐρανὸν εὐρὺν ἔχουσιν, α 67, etc. The epithets χάλκεος, σιδήρεος, etc., are figurative, **P** 425, ο 329.

οὔρεα: see ὄρος.

οὐρεύς, ῆος (ὄρος): *mule*, as mountain animal, cf. **ἡμίονος**. [For οὖρος 3, in **K** 84.] (Il.)

οὐρή: *tail.*

οὐρίαχος: *butt end* of a spear. (Il.) (See cut under ἀμφίγυος.)

οὖρον (cf. ὄρνυμι): *range, stretch;* of the extent of a discus-throw (cf. δίσκουρα), Ψ 431, and of a furrow's length, as ploughed by mules, **K** 351, θ 124.

1. οὖρος: *fair wind* (secundus ventus), ἴκμενος, **κάλλιμος, ἀπήμων**, **λιγύς**, Διὸς οὖρος.

2. οὖρος (Att. ὅρος): *land-mark, boundary.* (Il.)

3. οὖρος (root Ϝορ, ὁράω): *guard, watch, warder;* often of Nestor, οὖρος Ἀχαιῶν.

4. οὖρος: see ὄρος.

οὐρός (ὀρύσσω): *ditch, channel*, serving as ways for ships in drawing them down into the sea, **B** 153†.

οὖς, gen. οὔατος, pl. dat. ὠσίν: *ear;* ἀπ' οὔατος, 'far from the ear,' i. e. unheard, Σ 272, X 445; of the *handles* of a tankard, Λ 633.

οὐτάζω, οὐτάω, οὔτημι, imp. οὔταε, ipf. οὔταζον, aor. οὔτασα, οὔτησα, iter. οὐτήσασκε, aor. 2 οὖτα, iter. οὔτασκε, inf. οὐτάμεν(αι), pass. ipf. οὐτάζοντο, perf. οὔτασται, part. οὐτασμένος and, with irreg. accent, οὐτάμενος: *stab, wound* by cutting or thrusting (αὐτοσχεδίην, αὐτοσχεδόν), thus opp. to βάλλειν, hit with a missile, Λ 659, 826; ἕλκος, 'inflict' a wound, **E** 361; hence οὐταμένη ὠτειλή, Ξ 518, **P** 86.

οὔτε: negative particle, regularly correlative, **οὔτε . . οὔτε**, *neither . . nor*, (*not*) *either . . or*, dividing a negation already expressed or implied; but the correlation is often irregular as a different word (**τέ, καί, δέ**) replaces one or the other οὔτε, e. g. **Z** 450, θ 563, Ω 156, **H** 433.

οὐτήσασκε: see οὐτάζω.

οὔτι: see οὔτις.

οὐτιδανός: *good-for-nothing, worthless*, only of persons.

οὔτις, οὔτι: *no one, not anything;* the neut. as adv., *not at all, by no means.*

Οὖτις: *Noman*, a feigned name assumed by Odysseus to delude the Cyclōpes. (ι)

οὔτοι: *certainly not.*

οὗτος, αὕτη, τοῦτο: demonstrative pronoun, *this*, (*he*), sometimes however to be translated *that*, as when it anticipates a following relative, ζ 201 f. Sometimes deictic and local, 'here' like ὅδε, K 82, 341, Λ 612. The article, required with οὗτος in prose, occurs in Homer once, **τοῦτον τὸν ἄναλτον**, σ 114.

οὕτω(ς): *this way, thus, so*, adv. answering to the usage of **οὗτος**. In wishes, 'so surely (as),' N 825.

οὐχ, οὐχί: see οὐ.

ὀφείλω, ὀφέλλω, ipf. ὄφειλον, ὤφελλον, ὄφελλον, aor. 2 ὄφελον, ὤφελες, pass. ὀφείλεται, ipf. ὀφείλετο: *owe, ought;* **χρεῖος** ὄφειλον, 'they were owing' a debt; pass. χρεῖος ὀφείλεταί μοι, 'is due' me, Λ 688, 686, γ 367; then of obligation (ipf. and aor. 2), **τῑμήν πέρ μοι** ὄφελλεν Ὀλύμπιος ἐγγυαλίξαι, honor at all events 'he ought to have bestowed' upon me, **A** 353;

hence the use in wishes impossible of realization (past or present), explained in the grammars, αἴθ' ὄφελες παρὰ νηυσὶν ἀδάκρυτος καὶ ἀπήμων | ἧσθαι, 'would that thou wert sitting, etc.,' A 415.

'Οφελέστης: (1) a Trojan, slain by Teucer, Θ 274.—(2) a Paeonian, slain by Achilles, Φ 210.

1. ὀφέλλω: see ὀφείλω.

2. ὀφέλλω, ipf. ὤφελλον, ὄφελλε(ν), aor. opt. ὀφέλλειεν, pass. ipf. ὀφέλλετο: *augment, increase;* οἶκον, οἶκος, ὀφέλλετο, in riches, ο 21, ξ 233; μῦθον, 'multiply words,' Π 631.

ὄφελος, εος: *advantage, profit;* w. neg., 'no good,' X 513. (Il.)

'Οφέλτιος: (1) a Greek, slain by Hector, Λ 302.—(2) a Trojan, slain by Euryalus, Z 20.

ὀφθαλμός (root ὀπ, cf. o c u l u s): *eye;* freq., (ἐν) ὀφθαλμοῖσιν ὁρᾶσθαι, 'see with one's eyes'; ἐς ὀφθαλμοὺς ἐλθεῖν, 'into one's sight,' Ω 204.

ὄφις, ιος: *snake, serpent,* M 208†.

ὄφρα: *while, until, in order that.*—(1) temporal; once as adv., *for a while, some time;* ὄφρα μέν, O 547; elsewhere conj., *as long as, while,* freq. w. correl. τόφρα, Δ 220; then *until,* with ref. to the past or the fut., and with the appropriate constructions, E 557, A 82.—(2) final conj., *in order that, that,* A 147, α 85, ω 334.

ὀφρυόεις, εσσα, εν (ὀφρύς): *with beetling brows, beetling,* X 411†.

ὀφρύς, ύος, pl. acc. ὀφρῦς: *brow,* I 620; fig., of a hill, Υ 151.

ὄχα (cf. ἔξοχα): *by far,* always ὄχ' ἄριστος.

ὄχεσφι: see ὄχος.

ὀχετ-ηγός (ἄγω): *laying out a ditch,* Φ 257†.

ὀχεύς, ῆος (ἔχω): *holder;* the chin-strap of a helmet, Γ 372; clasps on a belt, Δ 132; bolt of a door, M 121. (See cut No. 29.)

ὀχέω (root Ϝεχ, cf. v e h o), ipf. iter. ὀχέεσκον, pass. pr. inf. ὀχέεσθαι, ipf. ὀχεῖτο, mid. fut. ὀχήσονται, aor. ὀχήσατο: *bear, endure,* μόρον, ἄτην; fig., νηπιάας ὀχέειν, 'put up with,' 'be willing to exhibit,' α 297; pass. and mid., *be borne, ride, sail,* P 77, ε 54.

'Οχήσιος: an Aetolian, father of Periphas, E 843.

ὀχθέω, aor. ὤχθησαν: *be moved* with indignation, grief, anger, *be vexed,* A 570, O 101; usually the part., ὀχθήσας.

ὄχθη (ἔχω): *bank* of a river, the sea, a trench, O 356; mostly pl., sing., Φ 17, 171 f.

ὀχλέω (ὀχλός): only pass., ὀχλεῦνται, *are swept away,* Φ 261†.

ὀχλίζω (ὀχλός): only aor. opt., ὀχλίσσειαν, *would heave* from its place, *raise,* M 448, ι 242.

1. ὄχος, εος (root Ϝεχ, cf. v e h o), pl. dat. ὀχέεσσιν and ὄχεσφιν: only pl., *car, chariot.*

2. ὄχος (ἔχω): only pl., νηῶν ὄχοι, *places of shelter* for ships, ε 404†.

ὄψ, ὀπός (Ϝόψ, root Ϝεπ): *voice,* properly the human voice with its varied expressiveness; then applied to the cicada, lambs, Γ 152, Δ 435.

ὀψέ (cf. ὄπισθε): *late, long afterward, in the evening,* Δ 161, Φ 232, ε 272.

ὀψείω (ὄψομαι): only part., ὀψείοντες, *desiring to see,* Ξ 37.

ὀψί-γονος: *late-born, born afterward, posterity.*

ὄψιμος: *late,* B 325†.

ὄψις, ιος (root ὀπ): power of *sight;* ὄψεϊ ἰδεῖν, 'with one's eyes,' Υ 205, ψ 94; *appearance, looks,* Z 468, Ω 632.

ὀψι-τέλεστος: *late-fulfilled,* B 325†.

ὄψομαι: see ὁράω.

ὄψον (ἕψω): properly *that which is cooked* (boiled), said of anything that is eaten with bread, *relish, sauce,* of an onion as a relish with wine, Λ 630; of meat, γ 480.

Π.

πάγεν, πάγη: see πήγνῡμι.

πάγος (πήγνῡμι): pl., *cliffs*, ε 405 and 411.

παγ-χάλκεος and **πάγχαλκος**: *all of bronze*; fig., of a man, Υ 102.

παγ-χρῡ́σεος: *all of gold*, Β 448†.

πάγχυ: *altogether, entirely*; w. μάλα, λίην, Ξ 143, ξ 367, δ 825.

πάθε, παθέειν: see πάσχω.

παιδνός (παῖς): *of childish age, a lad*, φ 21 and ω 338.

παιδο-φόνος: *slayer of one's children*, Ω 506†.

παίζω (παῖς), ipf. παίζομεν, aor. imp. παίσατε: *play* (as a child); of dancing, θ 251; a game at ball, ζ 100.

Παιήων, ονος: *Paean*, the physician of the gods, Ε 401, 899; from him the Egyptian physicians traced their descent, δ 232.

παιήων, ονος: *paean*, song of triumph or thanksgiving (addressed to Apollo), Α 473, Χ 391.

Παίων, ονος: *Paeonian*, pl. the Paeonians, a tribe in Macedonia and Thrace, on the river Axius, allies of the Trojans, Κ 428, Π 287, 291, Φ 155.

Παιονίδης: *son of Paeon*, Agastrophus, Λ 339, 368.

Παιονίη: *Paeonia* (see Παίων), Ρ 350, Φ 154.

παιπαλόεις, εσσα, εν: doubtful word, *rugged, rough*, epith. of mountains and roads.

παῖς or **πάϊς**, παιδός, voc. πάϊ: *child*, boy or girl, hence sometimes *son, daughter*; as adj., Φ 282.

Παισός: a town on the Propontis (see Ἀπαισός), Ε 612.

παιφάσσω: only part., παιφάσσουσα, *darting gleams*, 'like lightning,' Β 450†.

πάλαι: *long ago, long, all along*.

παλαι-γενής, ές: *ancient-born, full of years*.

παλαιός, comp. παλαίτερος a d -ότερος: *ancient, old, aged*.

παλαισμοσύνη (παλαίω): *wrestling, wrestling-match*.

παλαιστής (παλαίω): *wrestler*, pl., θ 246†.

παλαί-φατος (φημί): *uttered long ago*; θέσφατα, ι 507, ν 172; δρυός, 'of ancient fable,' τ 163.

παλαίω (πάλη), fut. παλαίσεις, aor. ἐπάλαισεν: *wrestle*.

παλάμη: *palm* of the hand, *hand*.

παλάσσω (cf. πάλλω), fut. inf. παλαξέμεν, pass. perf. part. πεπαλαγμένος, plup. πεπάλακτο, also mid., perf. imp. πεπάλαχθε, inf. πεπαλάχθαι (or -ασθε, -άσθαι): *sprinkle*, hence *stain, defile*; αἵματι, ἱδρῷ, ν 395, χ 402, 184; mid. (perf. w. pres. signif.), 'select among themselves by lot,' the lots being *shaken* in a helmet, Η 171 and ι 331.

πάλη: *wrestling*, Ψ 635 and θ 206.

παλίλ-λογος (πάλιν, λέγω): *gathered together again*, Α 126†.

παλιμ-πετής, ές (πίπτω): neut. as adv., (falling) *back again, back*, Π 395, ε 27.

παλιμ-πλάζομαι (πλάζω), aor. part. παλιμπλαγχθείς: *be driven vainly* (drifting) *back*, ν 5, Α 59.

πάλιν: *back again, back, again*; πάλιν ποίησε γέροντα, made him an old man 'again' (as he had been before), π 456; also of contradiction, πάλιν ἐρέει, Ι 56; of taking back a word, speech, Δ 357, ν 254; joined w. αὖτις, ἄψ, ὀπίσσω.

παλιν-άγρετος (ἀγρέω = αἱρέω): *to be taken back, revocable*, Α 526†.

παλιν-όρμενος: *rushing back*, Λ 326†. Better written as two words.

παλίν-ορσος (ὄρνῡμι): *springing back, recoiling*, Γ 33†.

παλίν-τιτος (τίνω): *paid back, avenged*; ἔργα, 'works of retribution,' α 379 and β 144.

παλίν-τονος (τείνω): *stretched* or *bending back*, 'elastic,' epith. of the bow.

παλιρρόθιος (ῥόθος): *surging back, refluent*, ε 430 and ι 485.

παλίωξις (ἴωξις, διώκω): *pursuit back again, rally*. (Il.)

παλλακίς, *ίδος*: *concubine.*

Παλλάς, *άδος*: *Pallas* Athena, an epithet explained by the ancients as from *πάλλω*, i. e. she who 'brandishes,' the spear and the aegis.

πάλλω, aor. 1 *πῆλε*, inf. *πῆλαι*, mid. aor. 2 *πάλτο*, pass. pres. *πάλλεται*, part. *παλλόμενος*: act. *brandish, swing, shake* lots (*κλήρους*), Γ 316, 324, and without *κλήρους*, Η 181, Ψ 353; mid., *brandish* or *hurl* for oneself, *cast lot* for oneself (or, of several, among one another), Ο 191, Ω 400; *ἐν ἀσπίδος ἄντυγι πάλτο*, 'struck,' 'stumbled' against the rim, Ο 645; fig., of the heart, 'throb,' 'palpitate,' Χ 452, 461.

Παλμύς: a Trojan chief, Ν 792.

πάλτο: see *πάλλω*.

παλύνω, ipf. (*ἐ*)*πάλῡνε*, aor. part. *παλῡ́νᾱς*: *strew, sprinkle; ἄλφιτα, ἀλφίτου ἀκτῇ τι*, ξ 429; of snow, Κ 7.

παμ-μέλᾱς, *αινα, αν*: *all black, jet black.* (Od.)

Πάμμων: a son of Priam, Ω 250†.

πάμπαν: *altogether, entirely;* with neg., *not at all*, 'by no means.'

παμ-ποίκιλος: *all variegated, embroidered all over*, Ζ 289 and ο 105.

πάμ-πρωτος: *very first, first of all;* adv., **πάμπρωτον** (Od.), **πάμπρωτα** (Il.)

παμφαίνω (redup. from *φαίνω*), subj. *παμφαίνῃσι*, ipf. *πάμφαινον*: *shine* or *gleam brightly; στήθεσι*, 'with white shining breasts' (bare), Λ 100.

παμφανόων, *ωσα*: variant form of present partic. from *παμφαίνω*, q. v.

πάν-αγρος (*ἀγρέω* = *αἱρέω*): *all-taking, all-catching*, Ε 487†.

πάν-αιθος (*αἴθω*): *all-glowing, burnished*, Ξ 372†.

παν-αίολος: *all-gleaming, glancing.* (Il.)

παν-άπαλος: *all-tender, delicate*, ν 223.

παν-ά-ποτμος: *all-hapless*, Ω 255 and 493.

παν-άργυρος: *all of silver, solid silver*, ι 203 and ω 275.

παν-αφ-ῆλιξ, *ικος*: *deprived of all playmates*, Χ 490†.

Παν-αχαιοί: *all the Achaeans*, 'the Pan-achaean host.'

παν-α-ώριος (*ὥρη*): *all-untimely*, 'to die an untimely death,' Ω 540†.

παν-δαμάτωρ: *all-subduing*, Ω 5 and ι 373.

Πανδάρεος: *Pandareüs*, a friend of Tantalus, father of Aëdon and other daughters, τ 518, υ 66.

Πάνδαρος: *Pandarus*, the Lycian archer, who by an arrow-shot violates the truce between Trojans and Greeks, and is afterwards slain by Diomed, Β 827, Δ 88, Ε 168, 171, 294, 795.

παν-δήμιος: *belonging to all the people (the town), public, common*, σ 1†.

Πανδίων: a Greek, Μ 372†.

Πάνδοκος: a Trojan, wounded by Ajax, Λ 490†.

Παν-έλληνες: the *Panhellēnes*, the united Greeks, Β 530.

παν-ῆμαρ: adv., *all day long*, ν 31†.

παν-ημέριος: *all day long, from morn till eve.*

Πανθοΐδης: *son of Panthoüs.*—(1) Euphorbus, Ρ 70.—(2) Polydamas, Ξ 454.

Πάνθοος: *Panthous*, son of Othrys, father of Euphorbus and Polydamas, a priest of Apollo at Delphi, afterward a priest and an elder at Troy, Γ 146, Ρ 9, 23, 40, 59, Ο 522.

παν-θῡμαδόν: *all in wrath, in full wrath*, σ 33†.

παν-νύχιος and **πάννυχος**: *all night long, the night through.*

παν-ομφαῖος (*ὀμφή*): *author of all omens, all-disclosing*, Θ 250†.

Πανοπεύς: (1) a Greek, the father Epeius, Ψ 665.—(2) a city in Phocis, on the Cephissus, Β 520, Ρ 307, λ 581.

Πανόπη: a Nereid, Σ 45†.

πάν-ορμος: *offering moorage at all points*, 'convenient for landing,' ν 195†.

παν-όψιος (*ὄψις*): *before the eyes of all*, Φ 397†.

παν-συδίῃ (*σεύω*): *with all haste.*

πάντῃ or **πάντη**: *on all sides, in all directions.*

πάντοθεν: *from every side.*

παντοῖος: *of all sorts, of every kind;* 'in various guise,' ρ 486.

πάντοσε: *on every side, in every direction; πάντοσ' ἐίσην*, denoting a circular form.

πάντως: *by all means*, and w. neg. 'by no means.'

παν-υπέρτατος: *quite the highest*,

i. e. above or farther off than the rest, ι 25†.

παν-ύστατος: *the very last.*

παππάζω: *say papa, call one father,* E 408†.

πάππας, voc. πάππα: *papa, father,* ζ 57†.

παπταίνω, du. παπταίνετον, aor. πάπτηνε, part. παπτήνᾱς: *peer around, look about* cautiously, *look* in quest of something, N 551, ρ 330, Λ 546, Δ 200; δεινόν, 'glancing terribly about him,' λ 608.

πάρ: (1) an abbreviated form of παρά before certain consonants.—(2) for πάρεστι or πάρεισι, I 43, A 174, γ 325.

παρά, παραί, πάρ: *beside, by.* — I. adv. (here belong all instances of the so-called 'tmesis'), written πάρα ('anastrophe') when placed after the verb it modifies, or when the verb is not expressed; ἐτίθει πάρα πᾶσαν ἐδωδήν, placed food 'beside' (we should say 'before') him, ε 196; πάρ ῥ' ἄκυλον βάλεν, threw 'down,' we should say, κ 242; παρά μ' ἤπαφε δαίμων, deceived and led me 'astray' (cf. our 'beside oneself'), ξ 488. The relation of the adv. may be made more specific by the addition of an appropriate case of a subst. in the same sentence, thus showing the transition to the true prepositional usage, πὰρ δ' ἴσαν Ὠκεανοῦ ῥοάς (acc. of extent of space), ω 11. — II. prep. (1) w. gen., *from beside, from;* φάσγανον παρὰ μηροῦ ἐρύσσασθαι, παρά τινος ἔρχεσθαι, often 'from one's house,' Φ 444; then to denote the giver, author, ζ 290, Λ 795.—(2) w. dat., of rest or position beside, but also where a certain amount of motion is meant, as with verbs of placing, sitting, falling, θεῖναι, πεσεῖν παρά τινι, N 617, ο 285; then of possession, keeping, πὰρ κεινοῖσιν ἐμὸν γέρας, 'in their hands,' λ 175. — (3) w. acc., *to the side of, unto, along by, beyond,* implying motion, though sometimes very faintly, A 463; τύψε κατὰ κληῖδα παρ' αὐχένα, motion implied in the mere act of striking, Φ 117; βῆναι παρὰ θῖνα, 'along the shore'; στῆναι παρά τινα, 'come and stand by one'; then the thought of over-passing, over-stepping, transgressing, πὰρ δύναμιν, παρὰ μοῖραν, 'contrary to right,' ξ 509.—As a prep. also πάρα is written with anastrophe when standing after its case, unless there is elision, σ 315.—In composition παρά has the meanings above given, but that of winning over (persuading from one side to the other), leading 'astray,' 'amiss' (also in good sense) by words, etc., is particularly to be noted.

παρα-βαίνω: only perf. part. παρβεβαώς, -ῶτε, *standing by* one in the chariot. (Il.)

παρα-βάλλομαι: only part. (fig.) *risking, staking,* I 322†.

παρα-βάσκω, ipf. παρέβασκε: *stand beside* one in the chariot (as παραιβάτης, q. v.), Λ 104†.

παρα-βλήδην: *with comparisons, insinuatingly,* Δ 6.

παρα-βλώσκω, perf. παρμέμβλωκε: *go (with help) to the side of,* Δ 11 and Ω 73.

παρα-βλώψ, ωπος (παραβλέπω): *looking askance,* I 503†.

παρα-γίγνομαι: *be present at,* ipf., ρ 173†.

παρα-δαρθάνω, aor. 2 παρέδραθον, inf. παραδραθέειν: *sleep beside, lie with.*

παρα-δέχομαι, aor. παρεδέξατο: *receive from,* or 'at the hands of,' Z 178†.

παραδραθέειν: see παραδαρθάνω.

παραδραμέτην: see παρατρέχω.

παρα-δράω, 3 pl. παραδρώωσι: *perform in the service of;* τινί, ο 324†.

παρα-δύω, aor. inf. παραδύμεναι: *slip past, steal past,* Ψ 416†.

παρ-αείδω: *sing beside* or *before;* τινί, χ 348†.

παρ-αείρω: only aor. pass., παρηέρθη, *hung down,* Π 341†.

παραι-βάτης (βαίνω): *one who stands beside* the charioteer and fights, 'chariot-fighter,' pl., Ψ 132†.

παραιπεπίθησι, -θών: see παραπείθω.

παρ-αίσιος (αἶσα): *unlucky, adverse,* Δ 381†.

παρ-ᾱΐσσω, part. παρᾱΐσσοντος, aor. παρήϊξεν: *dart by, spring by.* (Il.)

παραιφάμενος: see παράφημι.

παραί-φασις: *persuasion, encouragement,* Λ 793 and O 404.

παρακάββαλε: see the foll. word

παρα-κατα-βάλλω, aor. 2 παρακάββαλον: *throw down beside* one, 'lay in one's reach,' Ψ 167 and 683.

παρα-κατα-λέγομαι, aor. 2 παρκατέλεκτο: *lie down beside;* τινί, I 565†.

παρά-κειμαι, ipf. παρέκειτο, iter. παρεκέσκετο: *lie by* or *near, be placed* or *stand by* or *before,* φ 416, ξ 521; met., ὑμῖν παράκειται, 'ye have the choice,' χ 65.

παρα-κλιδόν (κλίνω): adv., *turning to one side, evasively,* δ 348 and ρ 139.

παρα-κλίνω, aor. part. παρακλίνᾱς: *incline to one side, turn aside,* Ψ 424, υ 301.

παρα-κοίτης: *bed-fellow, spouse, husband,* Z 430 and Θ 156.

παρά-κοιτις, dat. παρακοιτῑ: *wife.*

παρα-κρεμάννῡμι, aor. part. παρακρεμάσᾱς: *let hang by the side* or *down,* N 597†.

παρα-λέγομαι, aor. παρελέξατο, subj. παραλέξομαι: *lie down to sleep beside, lie with.*

παρ-αμείβομαι, aor. part. παραμειψάμενος: *pass by, drive past;* τινά, ζ 310†.

παρα-μένω, παρμένω, inf. παρμενέμεν, aor. 1 παρέμεινε: *remain with, stay by, hold out.* (Il.)

παρα-μίμνω: = παραμένω. (Od.)

παρα-μῡθέομαι (μῦθος), aor. opt. παραμυθησαίμην: *exhort, encourage;* τινί, and w. inf. (Il.)

παρα-νηέω, intens. ipf. παρενήνεεν: *heap up,* α 147 and π 51.

παρα-νήχομαι, fut. παρανήξομαι: *swim along near* the shore, ε 417†.

πάρ-αντα (ἄντα): *sideways,* Ψ 116†.

παρ-απαφίσκω, aor. 2 παρήπαφεν: *deceive, cheat, beguile,* w. inf., Ξ 360†.

παρα-πείθω, παραιπείθω, aor. 1 παρέπεισε, aor. 2 redup. subj. παραιπεπίθῃσι, part. -θοῦσα, sync. παρπεπιθών: *win over* by persuasion, *gain over, coax, wheedle,* H 120; w. inf., χ 213.

παρα-πέμπω, aor. παρέπεμψε: *send past, guide past,* μ 72†.

παρα-πλάζω, aor. παρέπλαγξε, part. fem. παραπλάγξᾱσα, pass. aor. παρεπλάγχθη: *cause to drift past, drive by* or *away from,* ι 81, τ 187; pass., *swerve away* from the mark, O 464; met., *confuse, perplex,* υ 346.

παρα-πλήξ, ῆγος (πλήσσω): *beaten on the side* by waves, hence *shelving, sloping;* ἠιόνες, ε 418, 440.

παρα-πλώω, aor. 2 παρέπλω: *sail by,* μ 69†.

παρα-πνέω, aor. subj. παραπνεύσῃ: *blow out by the side, breathe off, escape,* κ 24†.

παρα-ρρητός (ῥηθῆναι): *to be prevailed upon, placable;* neut. pl. as subst., *words of persuasion,* N 726.

παρα-σταδόν, adv., *standing by, going up to.* (Od.)

παρα-σφάλλω, aor. 1 παρέσφηλεν: *cause to glance away,* ὀιστόν, Θ 311†.

παρα-σχέμεν: see παρέχω.

παρα-τεκταίνομαι, aor. opt. παρατεκτηναίμην: *alter* in building, *make over,* Ξ 54; ἔπος, *invent,* 'fix up a story,' ξ 131.

παρα-τίθημι, παρτιθεῖ, fut. παραθήσομεν, aor. παρέθηκα, 3 pl. πάρθεσαν, subj. παραθείω, opt. παραθεῖεν, imp. παράθες, mid. aor. 2 opt. παραθείμην, part. παρθέμενοι: *place* or *set by* or *before* one, esp. food and drink; then in general, *afford, give;* δύναμιν, ξείνιά τινι, Λ 779; mid., *set before oneself, have set before one;* fig., put up as a stake, wager, *risk, stake;* κεφαλάς, ψῡχάς, β 237, γ 74.

παρα-τρέπω, aor. part. παρατρέψᾱς: *turn aside.* (Il.)

παρα-τρέχω, aor. 2 παρέδραμον, παραδραμέτην, opt. παραδράμοι: *run by, outrun, overtake,* Ψ 636.

παρα-τρέω, aor. παρέτρεσσαν: *spring to one side, shy,* E 295†.

παρα-τροπέω (= παρατρέπω): met., *mislead,* δ 465†.

παρα-τρωπάω (τρέπω): fig., *change in purpose, move, propitiate.* θεοὺς θύεσσι, I 500†.

παρα-τυγχάνω: *chance to be at hand,* Λ 74†.

παρ-αυδάω, imp. παραύδᾱ, aor. part. παραυδήσᾱς: *try to win over by address, persuade, urge:* θάνατόν τινι, 'speak consolingly of,' 'extenuate,' λ 488. (Od.)

παρ-αυτόθι: *in that very place,* M 302†.

παρα-φεύγω, aor. inf. παρφυγέειν: *flee past, slip by,* μ 99†.

παρά-φημι, mid. aor. inf. παρφάσθαι, part. παρφάμενος, παραιφάμενος, *ad-*

vise, A 577; mid., *mislead*, *delude*, *appease*, Ω 771.

παρα-φθάνω, aor. 2 opt. παραφθαίησι, part. παραφθάς, mid. παραφθάμενος: *overtake*, *pass by*. (Il.)

παρβεβαώς: see παραβαίνω.

παρδαλέη: *leopard-skin*, Γ 17 and K 29.

πάρδαλις: see πόρδαλις.

παρ-έζομαι, imp. παρέζεο, part. -όμενος, ipf. παρέζετο: *sit by*, *take a seat near* or *by*, τινί.

παρειαί, pl.: *cheeks;* of eagles, β 153.

παρείθη: see παρίημι.

1. πάρ-ειμι (εἰμί), πάρεστι, πάρεστε, παρέᾱσι, opt. παρείη, inf. παρεῖναι, παρέμμεναι, part. παρεών, ipf. παρῆσθα, παρῆν, πάρεσαν, fut. παρέσσομαι, -έσσεται, πάρεσται: *be present*, *at hand*, *ready*, e. g., to help one (τινί); also 'stay with' one, and of things, μάχῃ, ἐν δαίτῃσι, K 217; w. a thing as subject, εἴ μοι δύναμίς γε παρείη, 'were at my command,' β 62; παρεόντων, 'of her store,' α 140.

2. πάρ-ειμι (εἶμι), part. παριών, παριοῦσι: *go* or *pass by*.

παρ-εῖπον, def. aor. 2, subj. παρείπῃ, part. πᾱρειπών, -οῦσα: *persuade*, *win over*.

παρ-έκ, παρέξ: *along past*, *close by*, ε 439, Λ 486; met., εἰπεῖν, ἀγορεύειν, *away from* the point, *evasively;* 'different from this,' ξ 168; as prep., w. gen., *outside of;* w. acc., *beyond*, *away from*, *along beyond*, μ 276; **παρὲκ νόον,** 'contrary to reason,' 'foolishly,' Υ 133, K 391; παρὲξ Ἀχιλῆα, 'without the knowledge of Achilles,' Ω 434.

παρεκέσκετο: see παράκειμαι.

παρ-εκ-προ-φεύγω, aor. subj. -φύγῃσιν: fig., *elude the grasp*, Ψ 314†.

παρ-ελαύνω, fut. παρελάσσεις, aor. παρέλασσε, -ήλασαν: *drive by*, *sail by;* τινὰ ἵπποισιν, νηί, Ψ 638, μ 186, 197.

παρ-έλκω, imp. παρέλκετε, mid. ipf. παρέλκετο: *draw along*, fig., *prolong*, *put off*, φ 111; mid., *draw aside to oneself*, *get hold of*, σ 282.

παρέμμεναι: see πάρειμι 1.

παρενήνεεν: see παρανηέω.

παρέξ: see παρέκ.

παρ-εξ-ελαύνω, -ελάω, inf. παρεξελάᾱν, aor. subj. παρεξελάσῃσθα: *drive* or *row past* (νῆα), and intrans., μ 109.

παρ-εξ-έρχομαι, aor. inf. παρεξελθεῖν, part. -οῦσα: *come* or *go* (*out*) *by*, *slip by*, κ 573; fig., *elude*, ε 104, 138.

παρέπλω: see παραπλώω.

παρ-έρχομαι, fut. παρελεύσεαι, aor. παρῆλθε, inf. παρελθέμεν: *come* or *go by*, *pass by*, *outstrip*, θ 230; fig., *evade*, *overreach*, A 132.

πάρεσαν: see πάρειμι 1.

παρ-ευνάζομαι: *lie beside*, χ 37†.

παρ-έχω, fut. παρέξω, aor. 2 παρέσχον, παρέσχεθον, subj. παράσχῃ, inf. παρασχεῖν, παρασχέμεν: *hold* or *hand to*, *hold ready*, Σ 556; *supply*, *furnish*, *provide*, δῶρα, σῖτον, ἀρετήν; also with a thing as subject, θάλασσα δὲ πᾱρέχει (i. e. παρ(σ)έχει) ἰχθῦς, τ 113; w. inf., δ 89.

παρηέρθη: see παραείρω.

παρήιον (παρειά): *cheek*, *jaw; cheek-piece* of a bridle, Δ 142.

παρήλασε: see παρελαύνω.

πάρ-ημαι, part. παρήμενος: *sit down at* or *near*, *remain* or *dwell near*, ν 407; implying annoyance, I 311.

παρ-ηορίη: gear of the παρήορος or extra horse, his *head-gear*, bridle and reins (represented in plate I. as hanging from the ζυγόν), Θ 87, Π 152.

παρ-ήορος (ἀείρω): *hanging* or *floating beside; stretched out*, *sprawling*, H 156; met., *flighty*, *foolish*, Ψ 603; esp. παρήορος (ἵππος), a third or extra horse, harnessed by the side of the pair drawing the chariot, but not attached to the yoke, and serving to take the place of either of the others in case of need, Π 471, 474. (Plate I. represents the παρήορος in the background as he is led to his place. See also the adj. cut, the first horse.)

94

παρήπαφε: see παραπαφίσκω.

παρθέμενος: see παρατίθημι.

παρθενική = παρθένος.

παρθένιος: adj., *virgin*, **ζώνη,** λ 245; as subst., *virgin's child*, born out of wedlock, Π 180.

Παρθένιος: a river in Paphlagonia, B 854†.

παρθεν-οπίπης, voc. -ῖπα (ὀπιπτεύω): *ogler of girls*, Λ 385†.

παρθένος: *virgin, maiden.*

πάρθεσαν· see παρατίθημι.

παρ-ιαύω· *sleep by*, I 336†.

παρ-ίζω, ipf. παρῖζεν: *sit down by*, δ 311†.

παρ-ίημι: *let go by the side*, only aor. pass., παρείθη, *hung down*, Ψ 868†.

Πάρις: *Paris*, son of Priam, who by the help of Aphrodīte carried off Helen from Sparta and thus brought on the war with Troy, Ω 28 ff. The name Paris is supposed to mean 'Fighter' (rendered in the Greek Ἀλέξανδρος), and he is represented by Homer as not without warlike prowess, though naturally uxorious and averse to fighting, Γ 39 ff, Z 350.

παρ-ίστημι, aor. 2 παρέστην, subj. du. παρστήετον, opt. παρσταίη, part. παρστάς, perf. παρέστηκε, inf. παρεστάμεναι, plup. 3 pl. παρέστασαν, mid. pres. παρίσταμαι, imp. παρίστασο, ipf. παρίστατο, fut. inf. παραστήσεσθαι: only intrans. forms in Homer (aor 2 and mid.), *come and stand by* or *near* (esp. the part. παραστάς), *come up to, draw near*, (perf.) *stand by* or *near;* the approach may be with either friendly or hostile intent, and the subj. may be a thing (lit. or fig.), νῆες, θάνατος, μοῖρα, H 467, Π 853, ω 28.

παρ-ίσχω (parallel form of παρέχω), inf. παρισχέμεν: *hold by* or *ready, offer;* τινί τι, Δ 229, I 638.

παρκατέλεκτο: see παρακαταλέγομαι.

παρμέμβλωκε: see παραβλώσκω.

παρμένω: see παραμένω.

Παρνησός: *Parnassus*, the double-peaked mountain in Phocis, north of the ravine in which lies Delphi, τ 394, φ 220, ω 332.

πάροιθ(εν): *in front*, Υ 437; *heretofore, beforehand*, Ψ 20; τὸ πάροιθεν, α 322; w. gen., 'in the presence of,' 'before,' A 360, O 154.

παροίτερος: one *in front*, pl., Ψ 459, 480.

παρ-οίχομαι, ipf. παρῴχετο, perf. παρῴχηκε: *pass by*, Δ 272, K 252.

πάρος: *before, formerly;* Τυδεΐδαο πάρος, 'in advance of,' Θ 254; correl., οὐ πάρος . . πρίν γε, E 218; freq. w. τό, and foll. by πέρ, γέ.

παρπεπιθών: see παραπείθω.

Παρρασίη: a town in Arcadia, B 608†.

παρσταίην, παρστάς, παρστήετον: see παρίστημι.

παρτιθεῖ: see παρατίθημι.

παρφάμενος, παρφάσθαι: see παράφημι.

πάρ-φασις (παράφημι): *persuasion, allurement*, Ξ 317†.

παρφυγέειν: see παραφεύγω.

παρῴχηκα: see παροίχομαι.

πᾶς, πᾶσα, πᾶν, pl. gen. fem. πᾱσέων, πᾱσάων, dat. πάντεσσι: sing., *every* (*one*), Π 265, ν 313; pl., *all*, ἐννέα πάντες, nine 'in all,' H 161, θ 258; *whole, entire*, B 809, ρ 549; *all sorts, all kinds*, in pl., A 5, etc.—Neut. pl. as adv., **πάντα**, *in all respects*, in the Iliad mostly in comparisons, but in the Odyssey only so in ω 446; *all over*, π 21, ρ 480.

Πᾱσιθέη: the name of one of the Graces, Ξ 276.

πᾱσι-μέλουσα: 'world-renowned,' μ 70. Better written in two words, see μέλω.

πάσσαλος, gen. πασσαλόφιν· wooden nail or pin, *peg*, used to hang things upon, as the harp, Ω 268, α 440, θ 67, 105.

πάσσασθαι: see πατέομαι.

πάσσω, ipf. ἔπασσε, πάσσε: *strew, sprinkle;* fig., of weaving, ἐν (adv.) δὲ θρόνα ποικίλ' ἔπασσεν, 'worked in,' X 441.

πάσσων: see παχύς.

πασσυδίη: see πανσυδίη.

πάσχω, fut. πείσομαι, aor. 2 ἔπαθον, πάθον, inf. παθέειν, perf. πέπονθα, 2 pl. πέποσθε, part. fem. πεπαθυῖα, plup. ἐπεπόνθει: the verb of passivity, meaning to be affected in any way, in Homer regularly in a bad sense, *suffer*, κακόν, κακά, πήματα, ἄλγεα θῡμῷ, so κακῶς, 'be maltreated,' π 275; μή τ πάθω, 'lest anything should happen to me' (euphem. for μὴ θάνω); τί παθών, 'by what mischance'; οὐλὴν ὅ ττι πάθοι, 'how he came by it,' τ 464; τί πάθω; 'what am I to do?' Λ 404, ε 465; the same in participle Λ 313; cf. ω 106.

πάταγος: any loud sound of things

striking together, *crash* of falling trees, *chattering* of teeth, *dashing* of waves, *din* of combat, Π 769, Ν 283, Φ 9, 387.

πατάσσω: *beat*; κραδίη, θυμός, Ν 282, Η 216, cf. Ψ 370.

πατέομαι, aor. (ἐ)πα(σ)σάμην, plup. πεπάσμην: *taste, eat, partake of, enjoy*, usually τινός, acc. σπλάγχνα, ἀκτήν, Α 464, Φ 76.

πατέω: *tread*; fig., κατὰ (adv.) δ' ὅρκια πάτησαν, 'trampled under foot,' Δ 157†.

πατήρ, gen. πατρός and πατέρος, pl. gen. πατέρων and πατρῶν: *father*; pl. πατέρες, *forefathers*, Δ 405, θ 245.

πάτος: *treading, step*, ι 119; meaning 'the society' of men, Ζ 602; *trodden way, path*, Υ 137.

πάτρη (πατήρ): *native country, native land, home*, Ν 354.

πατρίς, ίδος: *of one's fathers, native*; γαῖα, ἄρουρα, α 407; as subst. = πάτρη.

πατρο-κασίγνητος: *father's brother, uncle*. (Od. and Φ 469.)

Πάτροκλος, also gen. Πατροκλῆος, acc. -κλῆα, voc. Πατρόκλεις: *Patroclus*, son of Menoetius of Opus, the bosom friend of Achilles. He had fled as a youth to Peleus on account of an involuntary homicide, Α 765 ff. Wearing Achilles' armor at the head of the Myrmidons, he repulsed the Trojans from the ships, but was slain by Hector, and his death was the means of bringing Achilles again into the battle-field, Π. The funeral games in honor of Patroclus, Ψ.

πατρο-φονεύς, ῆος: *murderer of a father*. (Od.)

πατρο-φόνος: *murderer of a father, parricide*, Ι 461†.

πατρώιος: *from one's father, paternal, hereditary*; neut. pl. as subst., *patrimony*, π 388, χ 61.

παῦρος, comp. παυρότερος: *little, feeble*; pl., *few*, opp. πολλοί, Ι 333.

παυσωλή: *cessation, rest*, Β 386†.

παύω, inf. παυέμεναι, ipf. iter. παύεσκον, fut. part. παύσουσα, aor. ἔπαυσα, παῦσε, mid. παύομαι, ipf. iter. παυέσκετο, aor. ἐπαύσατο, perf. πέπαυμαι, plup. ἐπέπαυτο: *cause to cease* or *leave off, stop* (τινά τινος), mid., *cease, stop, leave off, rest from* (τινός), also w. part., Λ 506; inf., Λ 442.

Παφλαγών, pl. Παφλαγόνες: *Paphlagonian*, inhabitant of the district south of the Euxine, and bounded by the rivers Halys and Parthenius, and by Phrygia, Β 851, Ε 577, Ν 656, 661.

παφλάζω: only part., *bubbling, foaming*, Ν 798†.

Πάφος: *Paphos*, a city in Cyprus, θ 363†.

πάχετος = παχύς. (Od.)

πάχιστος: see παχύς.

πάχνη (πήγνυμι): *hoar frost*, ξ 476†

παχνόω: *congeal*, only pass. (fig.) παχνοῦται, 'is chilled with dread,' Ρ 112†.

πάχος, εος: *thickness*, ι 324†.

παχύς, εῖα, ύ (πήγνυμι), comp. **πάσσων,** sup. **πάχιστος**: *thick, stout*, as of a thick jet of blood, χ 18; or to indicate strength or fulness, so with χείρ. Usually of men, but of Athēna, Penelope, Φ 403, φ 6.

πεδάω (πέδη), πεδάᾳ, ipf. iter. πεδάασκον, aor. (ἐ)πέδησε, inf. πεδῆσαι: *fetter, bind fast*, ψ 17, ν 168; often fig., *constrain, detain, entangle*; θεοῦ κατὰ (adv.) μοῖρα πέδησεν, λ 292; ἀπὸ πατρίδος αἴης, ψ 353; w. inf., Χ 5, γ 269, σ 155.

πέδη (πούς): *fetter*, pl., Ν 36†.

πέδῑλον: *sandal*, only pl.; the gods wear golden sandals that bear them over land and sea, Ω 340.

πεδίον (πέδον): *plain*; the freq. gen. πεδίοιο with verbs of motion is local, *on, over*, or *through the plain*.

πεδίονδε: *to the plain, earthward* (opp. οὐρανόθεν), Θ 21.

πεδόθεν: *from the ground*; fig., 'to thy very heart,' ν 295†.

πέδονδε: *to the ground, earthward*.

πέζα (πούς): a metallic *end-piece* or *cap* (*shoe*) at the end of a chariot-pole, Ω 272†. (See cut No. 42.)

πεζός: *on foot*, pl. *foot*-forces, opp. ἱππῆες or ἵπποι, Θ 59, ρ 436; *on land*, opp. ἐν νηί, Ω 438, λ 58.

πείθω, ipf. ἔπειθον, πεῖθε, fut. inf. πεισέμεν, aor. inf. πεῖσαι, aor. 2 red. πέπιθον, fut. πεπιθήσω, mid. opt. 3 pl. πειθοίατο, ipf. (ἐ)πείθετο, fut. πείσομαι, aor. 2 (ἐ)πιθόμην, red. opt. πεπίθοιτο, perf. πέποιθα, subj. πεποίθω, plup. πεποίθει, 1 pl. ἐπέπιθμεν: I. act., *make to believe, convince, persuade, prevail* *upon*, τινά, φρένας τινός or τινί, and w. inf.; the persuasion may be for better or for worse, 'talk over,' A 132; 'mollify,' A 100.—II. (1) mid., allow oneself to *be prevailed upon, obey, mind;* μύθῳ, τινὶ μύθοις, Ψ 157; τεράεσσι, Δ 408; ἅ τιν' οὐ πείσεσθαι ὀΐω, 'wherein methinks many a one will not comply,' A 289.—(2) perf., **πέποιθα** and plup., *put trust in, depend upon;* τινί, ἀλκί, etc., κ 335, π 98.

πείκετε: see πέκω.

πεινάω, inf. πεινήμεναι, part. πεινάων: *be hungry, hunger after;* τινός, υ 137.

πείνη: *hunger, famine*, ο 407†.

πειράζω (πειράω): *make trial of, test;* τινός, π 319.

Πειραΐδης: *son of Piraeus*, Ptolemaeus, Δ 228†.

Πείραιος: *Piraeus*, a comrade of Telemachus, son of Clytius, ο 544, ρ 55.

πειραίνω, aor. part. πειρήνᾱς, pass. perf. 3 sing. πεπείρανται: (1) *bring to an end, accomplish*, pass., μ 37.—(2) *bind to*, χ 175, 192.

πεῖραρ, ατος: (1) pl. πείρατα, *ends, limits;* γαίης καὶ πόντοιο, Θ 478; τέχνης, 'tools,' 'implements,' which bring to completion, γ 433; 'chief points' in each matter, Ψ 350; sing., *decision*, Σ 501, cf. ψ 248.—(2) *cord, rope;* fig., ὀλέθρου πείρατα, 'snares' or 'cords' of destruction, cf. Psalm xviii. 5, 2 Sam. xxii. 6; οἰζύος, 'net' of woe, ε 289; so πολέμοιο, νίκης, N 358.

πειράω (πεῖρα), inf. πειρᾶν, fut. πειρήσω, mid. 2 sing. πειρᾷ, πειρᾶται, ipf. (ἐ)πειρώμην, fut. πειρήσομαι, aor. (ἐ)πειρησάμην, perf. πεπείρημαι: *make trial of, test, put to proof* (τινός), *try, attempt*, abs. and w. inf., also w. εἰ, ὡς, or ὅπως, mid., the same subjectively; in hostile sense, *attack*, M 301, ζ 134; rarely w. acc., Σ 601, δ 119, ω 238.

πειρητίζω (πειράω): *make trial of, test, sound;* τινός, ο 304; 'measure one's strength' in contest, H 235; w. acc., M 47.

Πειρίθοος: *Pirithous*, son of Ixīon (or Zeus) and Dia, king of the Lapithae, a friend of Theseus; at his wedding with Hippodamīa arose the quarrel between the Centaurs and the Lapithae, M 129, 182, φ 298, Ξ 318, A 263.

πείρινς, acc. πείρινθα: *wagon-box* or *body*, perhaps of wicker-work, ο 131.

Πείροος: *son of Imbrasus*, a chief of the Thracians, slain by Thoas, Δ 520, 525.

πείρω, ipf. ἔπειρον, πεῖρε, pass. perf. part. πεπαρμένος, plup. πέπαρτο: *pierce through, pierce, transfix*, Π 405; of piercing meat with spits (κρέα ὀβελοῖσιν), and pass., ἥλοισι πεπαρμένος, 'studded,' A 246; fig., ὀδύνῃσι, E 399; also fig., κέλευθον, κύματα, 'cleave' one's way, 'plow' the waves, β 434, θ 183.

πεῖσα (πείθω): *obedience*, 'subjection,' υ 23†.

Πείσανδρος: *Pisander*.—(1) a Trojan, son of Antimachus, slain by Agamemnon, Λ 122, 143. —(2) a Trojan, slain by Menelāus, N 601-619.—(3) a Greek, son of Maemalus, a chief of the Myrmidons, Π 193. —(4) a suitor of Penelope, son of Polyctor, slain by Philoetius, σ 299, χ 268.

Πεισηνορίδης: *son of Pisēnor*, Ops, α 429, β 347, υ 148.

Πεισήνωρ: (1) father of Clitus, O 445.—(2) father of Ops.—(3) a herald in Ithaca, β 38.

Πεισίστρατος: *Pisistratus*, the youngest son of Nestor, Telemachus's companion on his journey to Pherae and Sparta, γ 36, δ 155, ο 46, 48, 131, 166.

πεῖσμα, ατος: *rope, cable*, esp. the stern-cable or hawser used to make the ship fast to land, ζ 269, κ 96, ν 77; also a cord plaited of willow withes, κ 167. (Od.)

πείσομαι: see (1) πάσχω.—(2) πείθω.

πέκω, πείκω, imp. πείκετε, mid. aor. part. πεξαμένη: *comb* or *card* wool; mid., *comb one's own* hair, Ξ 176.

πέλαγος, εος: the open, high *sea;* pl., ἁλὸς ἐν πελάγεσσιν, 'in the briny deep,' ε 335.

Πελάγων: (1) a chief of the Pylians, Δ 295. —(2) an attendant of Sarpēdon, E 695.

πελάζω (πέλας), aor. (ἐ)πέλα(σ)σα, imp. du. πελάσσετον, mid. aor. 1 opt. 3 pl. πελασαίατο, aor. 2 ἐπλήμην, πλῆτο, ἔπληντο, πλῆντο, pass. perf. πεπλημένος, aor. 3 pl. πέλασθεν: *bring near, make to approach* (τινί τινα or τὶ);

mid. (aor. 2) and pass., *draw near, approach*, (τινί); of bringing the mast down into the mast-crutch, A 434; fig., τινὰ ὀδύνῃσι, E 766; aor. mid., causative, *bring near*, P 341.

πέλας: *near, hard by;* w. gen., ο 257. (Od.)

Πελασγικός: *Pelasgic*, epithet of Zeus in Dodōna, Π 233; see also Ἄργος.

Πελασγός, pl. Πελασγοί: *Pelasgian*, the Pelasgians, the early population of Greece, first mentioned in the region about Dodōna; then in Thessaly, B 840; Boeotia, Attica, and the Peloponnēsus, P 288; Homer mentions other Pelasgians from Cyme, on the side of the Trojans, K 429; and still others in Crete, τ 177.

πέλεθρον: *plethron*, a measure of surface 100 ft. square, about ¼ of an acre.

πέλεια: *wild dove, wild pigeon.*

πελειάς, άδος: = πέλεια, only pl. (Il.)

πελεκάω, aor. πελέκκησεν: *hew*, shape with an axe, ε 244†.

πέλεκκος: *axe-helve*, N 612†.

πέλεκυς, εος, pl. dat. πελέκεσσι: *axe* or *hatchet*, for felling trees, Ψ 114, P 520; double-edged, ε 234, see ἡμιπέλεκκα. A sacrificial instrument in γ 449. In the contest with the bow of Odysseus the 'axes' were either axheads without the handles, arranged in line, or iron blocks resembling axes, made for the purpose of target-shooting, τ 573.

πελεμίζω, aor. inf. πελεμίξαι, pass. ipf. πελεμίζετο, aor. πελεμίχθη: *shake, brandish, make to quiver* or *quake;* σάκος, ὕλην, τόξον, φ 125; pass., *quake, quiver*, Θ 443; esp. and often in aor., *be forced back*, Δ 535.

πελέσκεο, πέλευ: see πέλω.

Πελίης: *Pelias*, son of Poseidon and Tyro, king of Iolcus, drove his brother Neleus into exile, and forced Jason, the son of his other brother Aeson, into the Argonautic expedition, λ 254. Pelias was the father of Alcestis, B 715.

πέλλα: *milk-pail, milk-bowl*, Π 642†.

Πελλήνη: a town in Achaea, B 574†.

Πέλοψ: *Pelops*, son of Tantalus, father of Atreus and Thyestes, gained with his wife Hippodamīa, the daughter of Oenomaus, the throne of Elis, B 104 ff.

πέλω, πέλει, ipf. πέλεν, aor. ἔπλε, and **πέλομαι**, imp. πέλευ, ipf. πέλοντο, iter. 2 sing. πελέσκεο, aor. ἔπλεο, ἔπλευ, ἔπλετο: a poetic synonym of εἶναι, γίγνεσθαι, perhaps originally containing some idea of motion (v e r s a r i), but in Homer simply *to be*, Γ 3, M 271, ν 60, E 729; the aor. has pres. signif. (like ἔφυ in Attic), εἰ δή ῥ' ἐθέλεις καί τοι φίλον ἔπλετο θυμῷ, 'and it pleases thee,' Ξ 337, ν 145, etc.

πέλωρ: *monster;* the Cyclops, ι 428; Scylla, μ 87; Hephaestus, Σ 410.

πελώριος: *monstrous, huge;* Ares, Polyphēmus, Hector, etc.; also of things, ἔγχος, λᾶας, θαῦμα, ι 190.

πέλωρον = πέλωρ, also pl.

πέλωρος = πελώριος.

πεμπάζομαι (πέντε), aor. subj. πεμπάσσεται: *reckon up* on the five fingers, δ 412†.

πεμπταῖος: *on the fifth day*, pl., ξ 257†.

πέμπτος: *fifth.*

πέμπω, fut. πέμψω, aor. ἔπεμψα, πέμψεν: *send, dismiss, send* or *convey home, escort;* the last meaning constitutes a characteristic difference between the Greek verb and the Eng. 'send,' A 390, λ 626; freq. of the Phaeacians in Od.

πεμπ-ώβολον (πέντε, ὀβελός): *five-tined fork*, used at sacrificial burnings, A 463. (Cf. cut No. 95, combined from several ancient representations.)

πενθερός: *father-in-law*, θ 582 and Z 170.

πενθέω, πενθείω, du. πενθείετον, inf. πενθήμεναι, aor. inf. πενθῆσαι: *mourn, mourn for;* τινά, Ψ 283; γαστέρι, 'by fasting,' T 225.

πένθος, εος: *mourning, grief.*

πενίη: *poverty*, ξ 157†.

πενιχρός: *poor, needy*, γ 348†.

πένομαι, ipf. (ἐ)πένοντο: *labor, be at work* or *busy upon* (περί τι), *prepare* (τί), δ 624, ξ 251.

πεντα-έτηρος (Ϝέτος): *five years old.*

πεντα-ετής (Ϝέτος): only neut. as adv., πενταετές, *five years long*, γ 115†.

πένταχα: *in five divisions*, M 87†.

95

πέντε: *five.*

πεντήκοντα: *fifty.*

πεντηκοντό-γυος: *of fifty acres*, I 579†.

πεντηκόσιοι: *five hundred*, γ 7†.

πεπαθυῖα: see πάσχω.

πεπάλαγμαι: see παλάσσω.

πεπάλασθε, πεπαλάσθαι: see παλάσσω.

πεπαρμένος: see πείρω.

πεπάσμην: see πατέομαι.

πεπερημένος: see περάω.

πέπηγε: see πήγνῡμι.

πεπιθεῖν, πέπιθμεν, πεπιθήσω: see πείθω.

πέπληγον, πεπληγώς: see πλήσσω.

πεπλημένος: see πελάζω.

πέπλος: *robe*, used as a cover for a chariot, E 194; for chairs, η 96; for funeral-urns, Ω 796; and esp. of a woman's over-garment, E 315, Z 90, σ 292. (See adjoining cut, and No. 2.)

96

πεπνῡμένος: see πνέω.

πέποιθα: see πείθω.

πέπονθα, πέποσθε: see πάσχω.

πεποτήαται: see ποτάομαι.

πεπρωμένος, πέπρωτο: see πορ-.

πέπταμαι: see πετάννῡμι.

πεπτεῶτα: see πίπτω.

πεπτηώς: see πτήσσω.

πεπύθοιτο, πέπυσμαι: see πυνθάνομαι.

πέπων, ονος, voc. πέπον (πέσσω): cooked by the sun, *ripe, mellow;* in Homer only fig., (1) as term of endearment, *dear, pet*, Z 35, P 120, ι 447.—(2) in bad sense, *coward, weakling*, B 235, N 120.

πέρ: enclitic particle, giving emphasis or prominence to an idea, usually to what immediately precedes it, *very, at least, even, just*, etc. ἐπεί μ' ἔτεκές γε μινυνθάδιόν περ ἐόντα, 'for a very short life,' A 352, 416, Γ 201; here belongs the use with participles denoting opposition (concession), so **καίπερ**, where πέρ itself of course does not mean 'although,' but the logical relation of the part. is emphasized, οὔ τι δυνήσεαι ἀχνύμενός περ | χραισμεῖν, 'however distressed,' 'distressed tho' you be,' i. e. though *very* distressed, A 241. πέρ is freq. appended to other particles, conditional, temporal, etc., and to all relative words, ὡς ἔσεταί περ (ὥσπερ), 'just as,' τ 312; ἔνθα περ, εἴ περ, 'that is if'; ἐπεί περ, see ὅσπερ.

περάᾱν: see περάω.

Περαιβοί: the *Perrhaebians*, a Pelasgian tribe about Dodōna and the river Titaresius, B 749†.

περαιόω: only aor. pass. part., **περαιωθέντες**, *crossing over*, ω 437†.

περάτη: *farthest border, horizon*, implying the west side, ψ 243†.

1. περάω (πέρας, 'end'), 3 pl. περόωσι, inf. περάᾱν, part. περῶντα, ipf. πέραον, iter. περάασκε, fut. inf. περησέμεναι, aor. ἐπέρησα, πέρησε, inf. περῆσαι: go from one end to the other, *pass through, penetrate, traverse;* τὶ, διά τινος, also ἐπὶ πόντον, etc., B 613, δ 709.

2. περάω (πέρην, πιπρᾱ́σκω), inf. περάᾱν, aor. ἐπέρασσα, πέρασαν, pass. perf. πεπερημένος: *export for sale, sell;* ἐς Λῆμνον, **κατ' ἀλλοθρόους ἀνθρώπους**, Φ 40, ο 453.

Πέργαμος: *Pergamus*, the citadel of Ilium, Δ 508, E 446, Z 512, H 21.

Περγασίδης: *son of Pergasus*, Deïcoön, E 535†.

πέρην: *on the other side, beyond, opposite;* τινός, B 626, 535.

περησέμεναι: see περάω 1.

πέρθω, fut. inf. πέρσειν, aor. ἔπερσα, πέρσε, aor. 2 ἔπραθον, pass. pres. part. περθομένη, ipf. πέρθετο, mid. (w. pass. signif.), fut. πέρσεται, aor. 2 inf. πέρθαι: *sack, plunder, lay waste*, regularly of cities, ἄστεα, πόλιν, Β 660; pass., Π 708, Ω 729.

περί: *around*, see ἀμφί.—I. adv. (including the so-called 'tmesis').—(1) *around, all round;* περὶ γάρ ῥά ἑ χαλκὸς ἔλεψεν | φύλλα τε καὶ φλοιόν, i. e. the leaves and bark that *encircled* it, Α 236; so of throwing a cloak about one, standing around in crowds, being enveloped by the shades of night, Γ 384, Κ 201.—(2) *over and above* others, *in an extraordinary degree, very;* περί τοι μένος, 'thou hast exceeding strength,' μ 279; περὶ μὲν θείειν ταχύν, Π 186; τὸν περὶ Μοῦσα φίλησε, 'above others,' 'extraordinarily,' θ 63.—A subst. in the appropriate case may specify the relation of the adv., περὶ δὲ ζώνην βάλετ' ἰξυῖ (dat. of place), ε 231; ἥ σε περὶ Ζεὺς ἀνθρώπων ἤχθηρε (partitive gen.), τ 363, in the phrase περὶ κῆρι, περὶ θυμῷ, περί is adv., and the dat. local.—II. prep., (1) w. gen., rare of place, περὶ τρόπιος βεβαώς, i. e. bestriding it, ε 130, 68; usually met., *about, for, in behalf of*, of the obj. of contention or the thing defended, μάχεσθαι περὶ νηός, ἀμύνεσθαι περὶ νηῶν, Π 1, Μ 142; then with verbs of saying, inquiring, *about, concerning, of* (d e), μνήσασθαι περὶ πομπῆς, η 191; rarely causal, περὶ ἔριδος μάρνασθαι, Η 301; denoting superiority, *above*, περὶ πάντων ἔμμεναι ἄλλων, Α 287; so with adjectives, περὶ πάντων κρατερός, ὀιζυρός.—(2) w. dat., local, *around, on*, as of something transfixed on a spit or a weapon, περὶ δουρὶ πεπαρμένη, Φ 577; so of clothing on the person, περὶ χροῒ εἵματα ἔχειν, χαλκὸς περὶ στήθεσσι, κνίση ἑλισσομένη περὶ καπνῷ, curling 'around in' the smoke, Α 317; then sometimes w. verbs of contending, like the gen., *about, for*, β 245, ρ 471, Π 568, and w. a verb of fearing, Κ 240. Often the dat. is to be explained independently, περί being adverbial, see above (I).—(3) w. acc., local implying motion, στῆσαι (τὶ) περὶ βωμόν, φυλάσσειν περὶ μῆλα, and esp. of sounds, fumes floating around, coming over the senses, stealing over one, περὶ δέ σφεας ἤλυθ' ἰωή, Κύκλωπα περὶ φρένας ἤλυθεν οἶνος, 'went to his head,' we should say, ρ 261, ι 362; met., of that in which one is interested, πονεῖν περί τι, 'about,' 'over,' 'with,' Ω 444, δ 624.

πέρι: (1) = περίεστι, Κ 244, μ 279.—(2) thus written by 'anastrophe' for περί, when the prep. follows its case.

περι-άγνῡμι (Ϝάγνυμι): only pass., and fig., (ὄψ) περιάγνυται, *breaks around, spreads around*, Π 78†.

περι-βαίνω, aor. 2 περίβη, -ησαν, inf. περιβῆναι, part. -βάς: *go around* (as to bestride) or *in front of* a fallen man, to *protect* the body, as animals stand over and protect their young, τινός, Ε 21, also τινί, Ρ 80, 313.

περι-βάλλω, aor. 2 περιέβαλον: *throw about* or *around;* πεῖσμά τινος, χ 466; met., *excel, surpass*, Ψ 276, ο 17; mid., of putting on armor, ψ 148.

Περίβοια: *Periboea*.—(1) daughter of Acessamenus, mother of Pelagon, Φ 142.—(2) daughter of Eurymedon, mother of Nausithous by Poseidon, η 57.

περι-γίγνομαι: *be superior, surpass;* τινός, Ψ 318, θ 102.

περι-γλαγής, ές (γλάγος): *filled with milk*, Π 642†.

περι-γνάμπτω: *double* a cape, in nautical sense, part., ι 80†.

περι-δείδω, aor. περίδϜεισα, part. περιδϜείσᾱς, perf. περιδείδια: *fear for, be afraid for;* τινός, also τινί, and w. μή, Ρ 240, 242, Ο 123.

περι-δέξιος: *ambidextrous*, skilful in both hands, or *very skilful, expert*, Φ 163†.

περι-δίδωμι, only mid. fut., and aor. subj. 1 du. περιδώμεθον: mid., *stake, wager*, w. gen. of the thing risked, Ψ 485; ἐμέθεν περιδώσομαι αὐτῆς, 'will stake my life,' ψ 78.

περι-δῑνέω: only pass. aor. du., περιδινηθήτην, *ran round and round*, Χ 165†.

περίδραμον: see περιτρέχω.

περί-δρομος: *running round, round, circular;* κολώνη, αὐλή, that can be run around, hence 'detached,' 'alone,' Β 812, ξ 7.

περι-δρύπτω: only pass. aor., περιδρύφθη, *had the skin all torn off* from his elbows, Ψ 395†.

περι-δύω: only aor. 1 περίδῡσε, *stripped off*, Λ 100†.

περιδώμεθον: see περιδίδωμι.

περί-ειμι (εἰμί): *be superior*, *excel* one in something; τινός τι, σ 248, τ 326.

περι-έχω, mid. aor. 2 περισχόμην, imp. περίσχεο: mid., *surround to protect*, w. gen., Α 393; acc., ι 199.

περιήδη: see περίοιδα.

Περιήρης: the father of Borus, Π 177†.

περι-ηχέω: only aor., περιήχησεν, *rang all over*, Η 267†.

περιίδμεναι: see περίοιδα.

περι-ίστημι, aor. 2 περίστησαν, subj. περιστήωσι, opt. περισταῖεν, pass. ipf. περιίστατο, aor. περιστάθη: only intrans. forms, *station oneself about*, *rise and stand around*, w. acc.

περι-καλλής, ές: *very beautiful*, often of things, rarely of persons, Ε 389, Π 85, λ 281.

περί-κειμαι, ipf. περίκειτο: *lie* or *be placed* (pass. of περιτίθημι) *around*, as a covering, φ 54; in embrace, Τ 4; fig., *remain over; οὐδέ τί μοι περίκειται*, 'I have won nothing by it,' Ι 321.

περι-κήδομαι, ipf. περικήδετο: *care greatly for*, *take good care of; τινός*, γ 219, ξ 527.

περί-κηλος: *very dry*, *well seasoned*, ε 240 and σ 309.

Περικλύμενος: son of Neleus and Pero, λ 286†.

περι-κλυτός: *highly renowned* or *famous*.

περι-κτείνω: *kill round about*, pass., Δ 538 and Μ 245.

περι-κτίονες (κτίζω), pl.: *dwellers around*, *neighbors*.

περι-κτίται = περικτίονες, λ 288.

περι-μαιμάω: only part. περιμαιμώωσα, *feeling* or *groping about for*, w. acc., μ 95†.

περι-μάρναμαι, ipf. 2 sing. περιμάρναο: *fight for; τινός*, Π 497†.

περί-μετρος: *beyond measure*, *exceedingly large*. (Od.)

Περιμήδης: (1) a companion of Odysseus, λ 23, μ 195.—(2) father of Schedius, Ο 515.

περι-μήκετος = περιμήκης.

περι-μήκης (μῆκος), neut. περίμηκες: *very long*, *very tall* or *high*.

περι-μηχανάομαι, 3 pl. -νόωνται, ipf. -νόωντο: *cunningly devise; τινί*, 'against one,' ξ 340 and η 200.

Περίμος: a Trojan, son of Meges, slain by Patroclus, Π 695†.

περι-ναιετάω, 3 pl. -άουσι: of persons, *dwell about*, β 66; of places, *be inhabited*, *lie round about*, δ 177.

περι-ναιέτης: *neighbor*, pl., Ω 488†.

περί-ξεστος: *polished on every side*, μ 79†.

περί-οιδα (Ϝοῖδα), περίοιδε, inf. περιίδμεναι, plup. περιήδη: *know* or *be skilled above* others, *understand* or *know better; τινός τινι* or τὶ, and with inf., Ν 728, γ 244, Κ 247.

περι-πέλομαι (πέλω), aor. part. περιπλόμενος: *be* or *go around*, *surround*, Σ 220; *revolve* (ἐνιαυτοί).

περι-πευκής, ές: *very sharp*, Λ 845†.

περι-πλέκω, pass. aor. περιπλέχθην: pass., *embrace; τινί*, ξ 313 and ψ 33.

περι-πληθής, ές: *very full*, *populous*, ο 405†.

περιπλόμενος: see περιπέλομαι.

περι-πρό: *around and before*, Λ 180 and Π 699.

περι-προ-χέω: only pass. aor. part., περιπροχυθείς, *pouring in a flood over*, Ξ 316†.

περι-ρρέω (σρέω), ipf. περίρρεε: *stream around*, w. acc., ι 388†.

περι-ρρηδής, ές: *tumbling across; τραπέζῃ*, χ 84†.

περί-ρρυτος (σρέω): *flowed around*, *sea-girt*, τ 173†.

περι-σαίνω, περισσαίνω: wag the tail about one, *fawn upon; τινά* (οὐρῇσιν), 'with their tails,' i. e. wagging them, κ 215. (Od.)

περι-σείω, περισσείω: only pass., *be tossed about*, *float in the air*, Τ 382 and Χ 315.

περι-σθενέω (σθένος): only part., *exulting in* his *might*, χ 368†.

περί-σκεπτος: (if from σκέπτομαι) *conspicuous* from *every side*, or (if from σκέπω) *covered*, *shut in* on all sides. (Od.)

περισσαίνω, περισσείω: see περισαίνω, περισείω.

περι-σταδόν: *standing around*, *drawing near from every side*, Ν 551†

περιστάθη: see *περιίστημι.*

περι-στείχω, aor. *περίστειξας*: *walk around,* δ 277†.

περι-στέλλω, aor. part. *περιστείλᾱς*: *enwrap,* as in funeral clothes, ω 293†.

περι-στεναχίζομαι: *moan, ring,* or *echo around; ποσσίν,* 'with the tread of feet,' ψ 146, κ 10.

περι-στένω (*στενός*): *make narrow* or *close all round,* only pass., 'be stuffed full.' Π 163†.

περι-στέφω: *set closely around, surround,* ε 303; pass., fig., his words are not 'crowned' with grace, θ 175.

περίστησαν: see *περιίστημι.*

περι-στρέφω, aor. part. *περιστρέψᾱς*: *whirl around.*

περίσχεο: see *περιέχω.*

περι-τάμνομαι (*τάμνω, τέμνω*): *cut off* for oneself, *intercept,* of driving away cattle as booty. (Od.)

περι-τέλλομαι: *roll around, revolve, recur.*

περι-τίθημι, aor. opt. *περιθεῖεν*: *place around;* fig., *δύναμίν τινι,* 'bestow,' 'invest with,' γ 205†.

περι-τρέφω: *make thick around;* pass., of milk, *curdle,* Ε 903; of ice, *congeal,* 'form around,' ξ 477.

περι-τρέχω, aor. *περίδραμον*: *run up from every side,* Λ 676†.

περι-τρομέομαι: *quiver* (*around*) with fear, σ 77†.

περι-τροπέω: only part., intrans., *revolving,* Β 295; *turning often about,* ι 465.

περί-τροχος: *round,* Ψ 455†.

περι-φαίνομαι: only part., *visible from every side,* Ν 179; as subst., a *conspicuous* (*place*), ε 476.

Περίφᾱς: (1) an Aetolian, son of Ochesius, slain by Ares, Ε 842, 847.—(2) a Trojan herald, the son of Epytus, Ρ 323.

Περιφήτης: (1) a Mysian, slain by Teucer, Ξ 515.—(2) a Greek from Mycēnae, the son of Copreus, slain by Hector, Ο 638.

περι-φραδέως: *circumspectly, carefully.*

περι-φράζομαι: *consider on all sides* or *carefully,* α 76†.

περί-φρων, ον: *very thoughtful* or *prudent.*

περι-φύω, aor. 2 inf. *περιφῦναι,* part. *περιφύς*: aor. 2, *grow around, embrace, τινί.* (Od.)

περι-χέω, aor. 1 *περιχεύῃ* (*περίχευα*), mid. aor. 1 subj. *περιχεύεται*: *pour* or *shed around* or *over,* mid. for oneself, ζ 232, ψ 159; fig., *χάριν τινί,* ψ 162.

περι-χώομαι, aor. *περιχώσατο*: *be very wroth; τινὶ τινος* (causal gen.), Ι 449, Ξ 266.

περι-ωπή (root *ὀπ*): *look-out place.*

περι-ώσιος (*περιούσιος, περίειμι*): *beyond measure, exceeding great;* neut. as adv., **περιώσιον,** exceedingly, *too greatly.*

περκνός: *dappled,* as specific name of a kind of eagle, Ω 316†.

Περκώσιος: *of Percōte.*

Περκώτη: a town in the Troad, Λ 229, Ο 548, Β 835.

πέρνημι (parallel form of *περάω* 2), part. *περνᾱ́ς,* ipf. iter. *πέρνασκε,* pass. pres. part. *περνάμενα*: *sell.* (Il.)

περονάω (*περόνη*), aor. *περόνησε,* mid. ipf. *περονᾶτο,* aor. *περονήσατο*: *pierce, transfix;* mid., *fasten* with a buckle about one, Κ 133, Ξ 180. (Il.)

περόνη (*πείρω*): *brooch-pin, buckle, clasp,* Ε 425, σ 293. (See the cut, which though of modern form is from an ancient original.)

περόωσι: see *περάω* 1.

πέρσα: see *πέρθω.*

Περσεύς: *Perseus.*—(1) the son of Zeus and Danaë, daughter of king Acrisius of Argos, Ξ 320.—(2) a son of Nestor, γ 414, 444.

Περσεφόνεια: *Persephone* (Proserpina), daughter of Zeus and Dēmēter, wife of Hades and queen of the nether world, often termed *ἐπαινή* in Homer, Ι 457, κ 494, 509, λ 213, 217.

Πέρση: daughter of Oceanus, wife of Helius, mother of Aeētes and Circe, κ 139†.

Περσηιάδης: *descendant of Perseus,* Sthenelus, Τ 116†.

πεσέειν, πεσέεσθαι: see *πίπτω.*

πεσσός: only pl., *draughts, checkers,* the game played with them, the nature of which is unknown. (The following cut represents an Egyptian game of this character.)

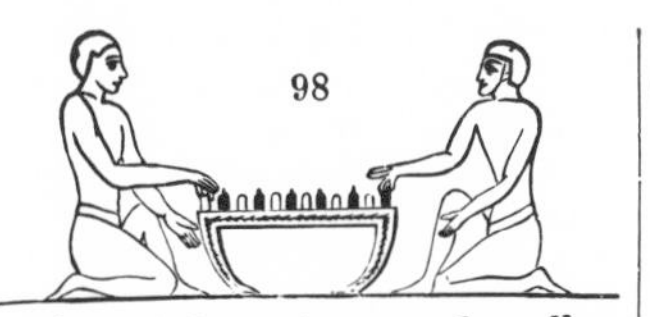
98

πέσσω, inf. πεσσέμεν: *make mellow, ripen*, η 119; fig., *digest*, then met., χόλον, 'brood over,' 'coddle,' Δ 513, I 565; κήδεα, 'swallow,' Ω 617, 639; γέρᾱ, 'enjoy,' B 237; βέλος, 'chew on,' 'nurse' the wound, Θ 513.

πεσών: see πίπτω.

πέταλον: *leaf*, mostly pl.

πετάννῡμι, aor. πέτα(σ)σα, pass. perf. πέπταμαι, part. πεπταμένος, plup. πέπτατο, aor. πετάσθην: *spread out, spread wide;* as of sails, the arms (in supplication, or as a sign of joy), A 480, Ξ 495, ω 397; of doors, *open* wide, often in perf. pass., fig., αἴθρη, αὐγή, θῡμόν, ζ 45, P 371, σ 160.

πετεηνός (πέτομαι): *flying, winged, fledged*, π 218; as subst., **πετεηνά,** *flying things, birds.*

Πετεών: a village in Boeotia, B 500†.

Πετεώς, ῶο: son of Orneus, father of Menestheus, Δ 338, M 355.

πέτομαι, aor. ἔπτατο, subj. πτῆται, part. πταμένη: *fly*, of birds and insects; then often fig., of gods and men running, horses, missiles, snow and hail, E 99, O 170; the oars 'fly' from the hands of the rowers as they drop them, μ 203; at death the life 'flies' from the body, Ψ 880, Π 469.

πετραῖος: *of a rock, inhabiting a rock*, μ 231†.

πέτρη: *rock, cliff, reef*, N 137, γ 293, κ 4; symbol of firmness, of hard-heartedness, O 618, Π 35.

πετρήεις, εσσα, εν: *rocky.*

πέτρος: *piece of rock, stone.* (Il.)

πεύθομαι: see πυνθάνομαι.

πευκάλιμος: *prudent, sagacious*, φρένες. (Il.)

πευκεδανός: *destructive*, K 8†.

πεύκη: *pine, fir.* (Il.)

πεύσομαι: see πυνθάνομαι.

πέφανται: see (1) φαίνω.—(2) φεν-.

πεφάσθαι: see φεν-.

πεφασμένος: see φαίνω.

πεφήσομαι: see (1) φαίνω.—(2) φεν-.

πεφιδέσθαι, πεφιδήσομαι: see φείδομαι.

πέφνον: see φεν-.

πέφραδον, πεφραδέειν: see φράζω.

πέφρῑκα: see φρίσσω.

πεφύᾱσι: see φύω.

πεφυγμένος, πεφυζότες: see φεύγω.

πεφυλαγμένος: see φυλάσσω.

πεφυυῖα: see φύω.

πέφυρμαι: see φύρω.

πῇ or **πῆ**: interrogative adv., *whither? in what way? how?*

πή or **πῄ**: enclitic adv., *anywhere, somewhere, in any way.*

πηγεσί-μαλλος (πήγνῡμι): *thick-fleeced*, Γ 197†.

πηγή: only pl., *sources.*

πήγνῡμι (cf. p a n g o, p a x), fut. πήξεις, aor. ἔπηξα, πῆξε, perf. πέπηγε, plup. (ἐ)πεπήγει, pass. aor. ἐπάγην, πάγη, 3 pl. πάγεν, aor. 1 3 pl. πῆχθεν: *fix*, both in the sense *make stiff* or *compact*, and *plant firmly;* of fixing or sticking a spear ἔν τινι, an oar upon a mound (ἐπὶ τύμβῳ), impaling a head (ἀνὰ σκολόπεσσι), Δ 460, λ 77, Σ 177; hence *build*, νῆας, B 664; mid., for oneself, ε 163; fig., 'fix' the eyes upon the ground, Γ 217; pass., and perf. act., *stiffen, stick fast, stick in*, X 453, N 442.

πηγός (πήγνῡμι): *stout, thick, tough*, I 124; κῦμα, *big* wave, ε 388.

πηγυλίς, ίδος (πήγνῡμι): *frosty, ice-cold*, ξ 476†.

Πήδαιον: a place in Troy, N 172†.

Πήδαιος: son of Antēnor and Theāno, slain by Meges, E 69†.

πηδάλιον (πηδόν): steering-oar or *rudder*, γ 281, ε 255. (Strictly, the word probably denotes the handle or

99

bar connecting the two rudders, and serving to move them. See cuts Nos. 87, 88, and cf. Nos. 37, 38, 60. The adjoining cuts represent the rudders of Egyptian ships; in the first cut both rudders are depicted as on one side of the vessel.)

Πήδασος: (1) a town of the Leleges in the Troad, on the Satnioeis, destroyed by Achilles, Ζ 35, Υ 92, Φ 87.—(2) a town in the realm of Agamemnon, Ι 152, 294.

Πήδασος: (1) a Trojan, the son of Bucolion, slain by Euryalus, Ζ 21.—(2) name of a horse of Achilles, Π 152, 467.

πηδάω, ipf. *ἐπήδᾱ*, aor. *ἐπήδησα*: *jump, bound, leap.* (Il.)

πηδόν: *oar-blade.* (Od.)

πηκτός (*πήγνῡμι*): *compact, firm.*

πῆλαι, πῆλε: see *πάλλω.*

Πηλεγών: son of the river-god Axius, and father of Asteropaeus, Φ 141, 152, 159.

Πηλείδης and **Πηληϊάδης**: *son of Peleus*, Achilles.

Πηλείων=*Πηλείδης*.—**Πηλείωνάδε**, *to Peleus' son*, Ω 338†.

Πηλεύς: *Peleus*, son of Aeacus, fled from his native island Aegīna to Phthia, and married Antigone, daughter of Eurytion, king of the Myrmidons. His daughter by this marriage, Polydōra is mentioned, Π 175 ff. He afterwards married the Nereid Thetis, who became the mother of Achilles, Ι 147, 252, 289, Σ 87, Ω 61, Φ 188.

Πηλήιος: *of Peleus*, Σ 60.

Πηληιάδης: see *Πηλείδης.*

πήληξ, *ηκος*: *helmet.* (Il.)

Πηλιάς, *άδος*: *Pelian*, i. e. from Mt. Pelion, epithet of the ashen spear (*μελίη*), a gift of the Centaur Chiron to Peleus, Υ 277, Π 143. (Il.)

Πήλιον: *Pelion*, a mountain in Thessaly, Β 757, Π 144, λ 316.

πῆμα, *ατος* (*πάσχω*): *suffering, woe, harm;* common periphrasis, *πῆμα κακοῖο*, also *δύης πῆμα*, ξ 338; of persons, *bane, nuisance*, ρ 446.

πημαίνω, fut. *πημανέει*, inf. *-έειν*, aor. 1 opt. *πημήνειαν*, pass. aor. *πημάνθη*, inf. *-ῆναι*: *harm, hurt; ὑπὲρ ὅρκια*, 'work mischief' by violating the oaths, Γ 299; pass., θ 563.

Πηνειός: *Penēus*, a river in Thessaly, flowing through the vale of Tempe into the Thermaic gulf, Β 752, 757.

Πηνέλεως: a leader of the Boeotians, Β 494, Ξ 496, 487, 489, Π 340, Ρ 597.

Πηνελόπεια: *Penelope*, the daughter of Icarius, and wife of Odysseus, α 329, etc.

πηνίον: *thread of the woof*, passed from one side to the other, in and out through the upright threads of the warp, before which the weaver stood, Ψ 762†.

πηός: *brother-in-law.*

Πηρείη: a region in Thessaly, Β 766†.

πήρη: *knapsack*, beggar's *wallet.* (Od.)

πηρός: *lame, mutilated; blind* in Β 599†.

Πηρώ: *Pero*, daughter of Neleus and Chloris, sister of Nestor, and wife of Bias, λ 287†.

πῆχυς, *εος*: *elbow*, then *fore-arm, arm*, Φ 166, ρ 38. Also *centre-piece* of a bow, joining the arms (horns) of the weapon, being the part grasped by the left hand in shooting, Λ 375, φ 419. (For the manner of holding, see cuts Nos. 104, Heracles; 127, Paris; 63, 89, 90, Assyrians.)

πῖαρ (*πῖϝαρ, πίων*): *fat*, Α 550; fig., *fatness*, of land, ι 135.

πῖδαξ, *ακος*: *spring, fount*, Π 825†.

πῑδήεις, *εσσα, εν*: *rich in springs*, Λ 183†.

Πīδύτης: a Trojan from Percōte, slain by Odysseus, Z 30†.

πίε, πιέειν: see πίνω.

πιέζω, ipf. ἐπίεζον, πίεζε, pass. aor. part. πιεσθείς: *squeeze, press, pinch;* fig., ἐν δεσμοῖς, 'load with fetters,' μ 164; pass., θ 336.

πίειρα: see πίων.

Πīερίη: *Pieria*, a region in Macedonia, on the borders of Thessaly, by the sea, near Mt. Olympus, Ξ 226, 250.

πιθέσθαι: see πείθω.

πιθέω, assumed pres. for the foll. forms, fut. πιθήσεις, aor. part. πιθήσᾱς (for πεπιθήσω see πείθω): *obey*, φ 369; *rely on*, part.

πίθος: large earthen *jar*, for wine or oil, ψ 305, β 340. (Sometimes half buried in the earth, as seen in cut No. 64.)

πικρό-γαμος: *having a bitter marriage;* pl., of the suitors of Penelope, ironically meaning that they would not live to be married at all. (Od.)

πικρός: *sharp;* ὀιστός, βέλεμνα, X 206; then of taste and smell, *bitter, pungent*, Λ 846, δ 406; and met., of feelings, 'bitter,' 'hateful,' ρ 448.

πίλναμαι (parallel form to πελάζω), πίλναται, ipf. πίλνατο: *draw near, near, approach*, T 93, Ψ 368.

πῖλος: *felt*, K 265†.

πιμπλάνω = πίμπλημι, only mid., πιμπλάνεται, *is filled*, with wrath, I 679†.

πίμπλημι, 3 pl. πιμπλᾶσι, aor. πλῆσε, opt. πλήσειαν, part. πλήσᾱσα, mid. ipf. πίμπλαντο, aor. opt. 3 pl. πλησαίατο, aor. 2 πλῆτο, -ντο, pass. aor. 3 pl. πλῆσθεν: *make full, fill*, τινά (τὶ) τινος, less often τινί, Π 374; mid. (aor. 1), *fill* for oneself, δέπας οἴνοιο, I 224; fig., θῡμόν, *satisfy*, ρ 603; pass. and aor. 2 mid., *be filled, get full, fill up*, A 104, θ 57.

πίναξ, ακος: *board*, ship's timbers, planks, μ 67; *tablet*, Z 169; wooden plate or *trencher* for meat, α 141.

πινύσσω (πινυτός, πνέω), ipf. ἐπίνυσσε: *make shrewd*, 'sharpen the wits,' Ξ 249†.

πινυτή: *prudence, understanding.*

πινυτός (πινύσσω, πνέω): *prudent, discreet.* (Od.)

πίνω, inf. πῑνέμεναι, ipf. iter. πίνεσκε, fut. part. πῑόμενος, aor. 2 ἔπιον, πίον, subj. 2 sing. πίῃσθα, opt. πίοιμι, imp. πίε, inf. πιεῖν, πιέειν, πῖέμεν, part. πιών, -οῦσα, pass. pres. πίνεται, ipf. πίνετο: *drink;* κρητῆρας, κύπελλα, *drain, quaff*, Θ 232, Δ 346; also w. dat. of the cup, ξ 112; freq. w. part. gen. of the drink.

πίομαι: see πίνω.

πῑότατος: see πίων.

πίπτω (root πετ, for πιπέτω), ipf. ἔπῑπτον, πῖπτε, fut. πεσέονται, inf. πεσέεσθαι, aor. 2 πέσον, inf. πεσέειν, perf. part. πεπτεῶτα: *fall;* fig., ἐκ θῡμοῦ τινί, out of one's favor, Ψ 595; freq. of falling in battle, and from the pass. sense of being killed, w. ὑπό ('at the hands of') τινος, also ὑπό τινι, Z 453, P 428; in hostile sense, *fall* upon, ἐν νηυσί, Λ 311; upon each other (σύν, adv.), H 256; fig. (ἐν, adv.), Φ 385; of the wind 'falling,' 'abating,' 'subsiding,' ξ 475, ρ 202.

πῖσος, εος (πίνω): *meadow, dell.*

πίσσα: *pitch.*

πιστός, sup. πιστότατος: *trusty, faithful;* w. inf., Π 147; neut. pl. as subst., πιστὰ γυναιξίν, 'faith,' 'confidence,' in, λ 456.

πιστόω, mid. aor. (ἐ)πιστώσαντο, pass. aor. subj. du. πιστωθῆτον, inf. -ῆναι: mid., *bind oneself* or *each other mutually* by oath, pledges, Z 283; pass., *be pledged, trust*, φ 218.

πίσυνος (πείθω): *trusting in, relying upon*, τινί.

πίσυρες (Aeolic for τέσσαρες): *four.*

Πιτθεύς: son of Pelops, king in Troezen, father of Aethra, Γ 144†.

πιτνάω and **πίτνημι** (parallel forms to πετάννῡμι), part. πιτνάς, ipf. πίτνᾱ, pass. ipf. πίτναντο: *spread out, extend;* mid., 'float,' flutter,' X 402.

Πιτύεια: a town in Mysia, B 829†.

πίτυς, υος: *pine* or *fir.*

πῑφαύσκω, πῑφαύσκομαι (πι-φάϝ-σκω, φάος): *make to shine, make manifest, make known;* in the physical sense, φλόγα, κῆλα, Φ 333, M 280; then met., ἔπος, ἔπεα, φῶτα, K 202, ο 518.

πίων, ονος, fem. **πίειρα**, sup. πῑότατος: *fat, fertile, rich*, I 577, E 512.

Πλαγκταί (πλάζω): πέτραι, the *Planctae*, or Clashing Rocks, against which everything that approached was dashed to pieces, μ 61, ψ 327.

πλαγκτός (πλάζω): *crazy*, or, according to others, *vagabond*, φ 363†.

πλαγκτοσύνη: *roving*, *roaming*, ο 343†.

πλάγχθη: see πλάζω.

πλάζω (cf. πλήσσω), aor. πλάγξε, mid. fut. πλάγξομαι, pass. aor. πλάγχθη, part. πλαγχθείς: I. act., *strike*, Φ 269; esp., *strike* or *drive back*, *cause to drift; ῥόον, τινὰ ἀπὸ πατρίδος*, P 751, α 75, ω 307; met., of the mind, 'make to wander,' 'confuse,' β 396.—II. mid. and pass., *be driven*, *drift*, *wander;* 'be struck away,' 'rebound,' Λ 351.

Πλάκος: a mountain above the city of Thebe, in Mysia, Z 396, 425, X 479.

πλανάομαι, πλανόωνται: *rove*, Ψ 321†.

Πλάταια: *Plataea*, a town in Boeotia, B 504†.

πλατάνιστος: *plane-tree*, not unlike our maple, B 307.

πλατύς, εῖα, ύ: *broad*, *wide; αἰπόλια αἰγῶν*, 'wide-roaming,' because goats do not keep close together in the herd as sheep do in the flock, B 274, ξ 101, 103.

πλέες: see πλείων.

πλεῖος, πλέος, comp. πλειότερος: *full.*

πλεῖστος (sup. of πολύς): *most*, *a great many.*—Adv., **πλεῖστον**, *most*, *especially.*

πλείω: see πλέω.

πλείων, πλεῖον, and **πλέων, πλέον** (comp. of πολύς), pl. nom. πλέονες (Hdt. πλεῦνες), σ 247, πλείους, πλέες, dat. πλείοσιν, πλεόνεσσιν, acc. πλέας: *more*, *greater*, *the greater part.*

πλεκτός (πλέκω): *braided*, *twisted.*

πλέκω, aor. ἔπλεξε, mid. aor. part. πλεξάμενος: *plait*, *twist.*

πλευρή: only pl., *side*, *ribs*, *flank.*

πλευρόν = πλευρή, pl., Δ 468†.

Πλευρών: *Pleuron*, a town in Aetolia, B 639, N 217, Ξ 116.—**Πλευρώνιος**: inhabitant *of Pleuron*, Ψ 635.

πλέω, πλείω (πλέϝω), inf. πλείειν, part. πλέων (α 183), πλείοντες, ipf. ἔπλεον, πλέεν, fut. πλεύσεσθε: *sail;* as if trans., ὑγρὰ κέλευθα, γ 71.

πλέων, πλέον: see πλείων.

πληγή (πλήσσω): *blow*, *stroke*, from a stick, a whip, a thong, O 17, δ 244; **Διός**, the lightning-stroke, Ξ 414.

πλῆθ' = πλῆτο, see πίμπλημι.

πλῆθος, εος (πλήθω): *multitude*, *mass* of men. (Il.)

πληθύς, ύος = πλῆθος, esp. of the masses, the commons, as opp. to the chiefs, B 143, 278.

πλήθω, ipf. πλῆθε: *be* or *become full*, w. gen.; said of rivers 'swelling,' the full moon, Π 389, Σ 484.

Πληιάδες: the *Pleiads*, the 'Seven Sisters' in the constellation Taurus, ε 272, μ 62.

πληκτίζομαι (πλήσσω): *contend with*, inf., Φ 499†.

πλήμνη (πλήθω): *hub* or *nave* of a wheel. (Il.)

πλημυρίς, ίδος: *rise of the sea*, *swell*, *flood*, ι 486†.

πλήν: *except*, w. gen., θ 207†.

πλῆντο: see (1) πίμπλημι.—(2) πελάζω.

πλῆξα: see πλήσσω.

πλήξ-ιππος: *lasher of horses.* (Il.)

πλησίος (πέλας): *near*, *neighboring to*, τινός, sometimes τινί, β 149; as subst., *neighbor*, B 271, κ 35.—Adv., **πλησίον**, *near*, *hard by.*

πλησ-ίστιος (ἱστίον): *filling the sail*, λ 7 and μ 149.

πλήσσω, aor. πλῆξα, aor. 2 redup. (ἐ)πέπληγον, inf. πεπληγέμεν, perf. πέπληγα, part. -γώς, -γυῖα, mid. aor. part. πληξάμενος, aor. 2 πεπλήγετο, -οντο, pass. aor. πλήγη, πληγείς: *strike*, *smite;* mid., subjectively, Π 125; χορὸν ποσίν, in dancing, θ 264; of the bolt struck (shot) by the key, φ 50; freq. of wounding, Λ 240, Π 332; metaph., ἐκ γάρ με πλήσσουσι, 'distract,' σ 231, N 394.

πλῆτο: see (1) πίμπλημι.—(2) πελάζω.

πλίσσομαι: only ipf., *strode out*, ζ 318†.

πλόκαμος (πλέκω): *lock* of hair, pl., Ξ 176†.

πλόος (πλέω): *voyage*, γ 169†.

πλοῦτος (πλέος, πλήθω): *wealth*, *riches.*

πλοχμός = πλόκαμος, pl., P 52†.

πλυνός (πλύνω): *washing-pit*, pl., tanks or basins in the earth, lined with stone.

πλύνω, part. πλυνούσῃ, ipf. iter. πλύνεσκον, fut. part. πλυνέουσα, aor. 3 pl. πλῦναν, part. -ᾶσα: *wash*, *clean*, *cleanse.*

πλωτός: *floating*, κ 3†.

πλώω (πλώϝω, parallel form to πλέω), ipf. πλῶον: *swim, float.*

πνεύμων, ονος: *lung.* (Il.)

πνέω, πνείω (πνέϝω), πνέει, πνείει, aor. subj. πνεύσῃ, mid. perf. 2 sing. πέπνῦσαι, inf. πεπνῦσθαι, part. πεπνῦμένος, plup. 2 sing. πέπνῦσο: (1) *breathe*, sometimes synonymous with *live*, P 447, σ 131; of the wind and air, odors, δ 446; fig., μένεα πνείοντες, 'breathing might'; ἐν (adv.) δὲ θεὸς πνεύσῃ μένος ἀμφοτέροιιν, 'inspire,' T 159.—(2) the perf. mid. comes to mean, *be prudent, discreet*, Ω 377, κ 495; esp. freq. the part. πεπνῦμένος, *sensible.*

πνοιή (πνέω): *breathing, breath;* freq. of the air, winds, esp. the pl., πνοιαὶ λιγυραί, *blasts*, E 526; of fire, Φ 355.

Ποδαλείριος: *Podalirius*, son of Asclepius, and brother of Machāon, B 732, Λ 833.

ποδά-νιπτρον (νίπτω): *water for washing the feet*, τ 343 and 504.

Ποδάργη: name of a Harpy, the dam of Achilles' horses, Π 150, T 400.

Πόδαργος: name of a horse of Hector, and of one of Menelāus, Θ 185, Ψ 295.

ποδ-άρκης (ἀρκέω): strong of foot, *swift-footed.* (Il.)

Ποδάρκης: son of Iphiclus, brother of Protesilāus, chief of the contingent from Phylace and Pyrasus, B 704, N 693.

ποδ-ηνεκής, ές (ἠνεκής, φέρω): *extending to the feet.* (Il.)

ποδ-ήνεμος (ἄνεμος): *wind-swift*, epith. of Iris. (Il.)

Ποδῆς: son of Eëtion, slain by Menelāus, P 575, 590.

ποδ-ώκεια: *swiftness of foot*, pl., B 792†.

ποδ-ώκης, ες (ὠκύς): *swift of foot, fleet-footed.*

ποθέεσκε: see ποθέω.

πόθεν: interrog. adv., *whence?* Of origin and parentage, τίς πόθεν εἶς ἀνδρῶν; Φ 150, α 170.

ποθέν: enclitic indef. adv., *from somewhere*, ω 149; freq. w. εἰ.

ποθέω, inf. ποθήμεναι, part. ποθέων, -ουσα, ipf. πόθεον, πόθει, iter. ποθέεσκε, aor. πόθεσαν, inf. ποθέσαι: *miss* one that is absent, *yearn for, desire*, β 375, λ 196.

ποθή: *missing, yearning for, desire, lack*, κ 505.

πόθι: interrog. adv., *where?* (Od.)

ποθί: enclitic indef. adv., *somewhere, anywhere; somehow;* so esp. w. αἴ κε, 'if in any case,' 'if at all,' etc., α 379, β 144.

πόθος = ποθή, σὸς πόθος, 'yearning for thee,' λ 202.

Ποιάντιος: υἱός, son *of Poeas*, Philoctētes, γ 190†.

ποιέω, imp. πόιει, ipf. (ἐ)ποίει, ποίεον, aor. (ἐ)ποίησα, fut. inf. ποιησέμεν, mid. pres. ποιεῖται, ipf. ποιεύμην, fut. ποιήσομαι, aor. ποιήσατο, pass. perf. πεποίηται: I. act., *make*, i. e. construct, build, δῶμά τινι, σάκος ταύρων, A 608, H 222; as an artist, Σ 490; then met., *make, cause, do*, of actions and results, ποιῆσαί τινα βασιλῆα, λᾱοὺς λίθους, 'change to stones,' Ω 611; w. prep., νόημα ἐνὶ φρεσί, 'cause,' 'put' in one's thoughts, N 55; and w. inf., σὲ ἱκέσθαι ἐς οἶκον, ψ 258.—II. mid., *make* (construct) *for oneself;* οἰκία, σχεδίην, M 168, ε 251; less literally, ἀγορήν, 'bring about,' θ 2; κλέος αὐτῇ, 'procure,' 'win,' β 126; ῥήτρην, of binding oneself by an agreement, ξ 393; w. two accusatives, τινά ἄλοχον, 'make her his' wife, Γ 409.

ποίη: *grass.*

ποιήεις, εσσα, εν: *grassy.*

ποιητός: (well) *made* or *built*, with and without εὖ.

ποικίλλω (ποικίλος): only ipf., ποίκιλλε, *wrought with skill*, Σ 590†.

ποίκιλμα, ατος (ποικίλλω): any variegated work, *broidery*, Z 294 and ο 107. (The cut represents a woman embroidering.)

101

ποικιλο-μήτης (μῆτις): *with versatile mind, fertile in device, inventive, cunning.*

ποικίλος: *variegated, motley, spotted,* as the leopard or a fawn, Κ 30, τ 228; also of stuffs embroidered in various colors, and of metal or wood artistically wrought, Ε 735, σ 293, Χ 441, Δ 226, Κ 501.

ποιμαίνω, ipf. iter. ποιμαίνεσκε, mid. ipf. ποιμαίνοντο: act., *tend* as a shepherd, Ζ 25, ι 188; mid. or pass., *be tended, pasture, feed.*

ποιμήν, ένος (πῶυ): *shepherd;* fig., λᾱῶν, 'shepherd of the people,' said of rulers.

ποίμνη: *flock,* pl., ι 122†.

ποιμνήιος: *of the flock;* σταθμός, 'sheep-fold,' Β 470†.

ποινή (cf. p o e n a): price paid for purification or *expiation, satisfaction, penalty,* w. gen. of the person whose death is atoned for by the quittance, Ι 633; also w. gen. of a thing, *price,* Γ 290, Ε 266, Ρ 217.

ποῖος: interrog. adj. pron., *of what sort?* (q u a l i s). Freq. rather exclamatory than interrogative, as in the phrase, ποῖόν σε ϝέπος φύγεν ἕρκος ὀδόντων; 'what a speech!'

ποιπνύω (redup. from πνέω), part. ποιπνύων, ipf. ποίπνυον, aor. part. ποιπνύσᾱς: *puff, pant,* 'bestir oneself,' 'make haste,' Θ 219, υ 149.

πόκος (πέκω): shorn *wool, fleece,* Μ 451†.

πολέες: see πολύς.

πολεμήιος: *of* or *pertaining to war* or *battle, warlike.*

πολεμίζω, πτολεμίζω, fut. -ίξομεν: *fight, war;* πόλεμον, Β 121; 'to fight with,' Σ 258.

πολεμιστής, πτολεμιστής: *warrior.* (Il. and ω 499.)

πόλεμος, πτόλεμος: *fighting, war, battle.*—**π(τ)όλεμόνδε,** *into the fight, to the war.*

πολεύω: *move* or *live in,* inf., χ 223†.

πολέων: see πολύς.

πόληας, πόληες: see πόλις.

πολίζω (πόλις), aor. πολίσσαμεν, pass. plup. πεπόλιστο: *found* a city, *build,* Η 453 and Υ 217.

πολιήτης = πολίτης, pl., Β 806†.

πόλινδε: *to the city.*

πολιο-κρόταφος: *with hoary temples,* gray with age, Θ 518†.

πολιός: *gray, hoary;* of hair, iron, the sea, Ι 366, Α 350.

πόλις, πτόλις, ιος, πόληος, dat. πόληι, pl. πόληες, πόλιες, gen. πολίων, dat. πολίεσσι, acc. πόλιας, πόληας: *city,* the whole district and community; hence with the name in apposition (not gen.); or as a part, ἄκρη πόλις, 'acropolis,' 'citadel;' see ἄστυ.

πολίτης: *citizen,* only pl.

Πολίτης: (1) a son of Priam, Β 791, Ν 533, Ο 339, Ω 250.—(2) a companion of Odysseus, κ 224.

πολλάκι(ς): *many times, often.*

πολλός, πολλόν: see πολύς.

Πολυαιμονίδης: *son of Polyaemon,* Amopāon, Θ 276†.

πολύ-αινος (αἰνέω): *much-praised, illustrious,* epith. of Odysseus.

πολυ-ᾶιξ, ῖκος (ἀίσσω): *much-darting* or *rushing, impetuous;* κάματος, weariness 'caused by impetuosity in fighting,' Ε 811.

πολυ-ανθής, ές (ἄνθος): *much* or *luxuriantly blooming,* ξ 353†.

πολυ-άρητος (ἀράομαι): *much-prayed-to, much-desired,* ζ 280 and τ 404.

πολύ-αρνι, dat., cf. πολύρρην: *rich in lambs* or *flocks,* Β 106†.

πολυ-βενθής, ές (βένθος): *very deep;* λιμήν, Α 432. Elsewhere of the sea, and in Od.

Πόλυβος: *Polybus.*—(1) a son of Antēnor, Λ 59.—(2) an Egyptian, δ 126.—(3) an Ithacan, the father of Eurymachus, ο 519.—(4) a suitor of Penelope, χ 243, 284.—(5) a Phaeacian, θ 373.

πολυ-βότειρα, πουλυβότειρα (βόσκω): *much-* or *all-nourishing,* epith. of the earth, Ἀχαιίς, Λ 770.

πολύ-βουλος (βουλή): *full of counsel, exceeding wise,* epith. of Athēna.

πολυ-βούτης (βοῦς): *rich in cattle,* Ι 154 and 296.

πολυ-γηθής, ές (γηθέω): *much-rejoicing,* 'ever gay,' epith. of the Horae, conceived as never ceasing from the choral dance, Φ 450†.

πολυ-δαίδαλος: *highly* or *cunningly wrought,* of works of art; of men, *artistic, skilful,* Ψ 743.

πολύ-δακρυς and **πολυδάκρυος**: *of*

many tears, *tearful*, *deplorable*, epith. of war, battle, etc., Ρ 192.

πολυ-δάκρῡτος: *much wept* or *lamented*, *tearful*, γόος, Ω 620, τ 213.

Πολύδαμνα: wife of the Egyptian Thon, δ 228†.

πολυ-δειράς, άδος (δειρή): *many-ridged*, epith. of Mt. Olympus. (Il.)

πολυ-δένδρεος (δένδρον): *with many trees*, *full of trees*. (Od.)

πολύ-δεσμος: *much* or *firmly bound together*, ε 33 and 338.

Πολυδεύκης: *Polydeuces* (Pollux), son of Zeus and Leda, twin brother of Castor, Γ 237, λ 300.

πολυ-δίψιος (δίψα): *very thirsty*, *dry*, epith. of Argos, Δ 171†.

Πολυδώρη: daughter of Peleus, wife of Spercheius, and mother of Menestheus, Π 175†.

πολύ-δωρος (δῶρον): *richly dowered*.

Πολύδωρος: (1) the youngest son of Priam by Laothoe, slain by Achilles, Υ 407, 419, Φ 91, Χ 46.—(2) a Greek, Ψ 637.

Πολύειδος: see Πολύῑδος.

πολύ-ζυγος (ζυγόν): *with many rowers' benches*, Β 293†.

πολυ-ηγερής, ές (ἀγείρω): *numerously assembled*, reading of Aristarchus in Λ 564†.

πολυ-ήρατος (ἔραμαι): *greatly loved* or *desired*, *lovely*. (Od.)

πολυ-ηχής, ές: *many-toned*, nightingale, τ 521; *echoing*, *resounding*, Δ 422.

πολυ-θαρσής, ές (θάρσος): *bold*, *intrepid*.

Πολυθερσεΐδης: *son of Polytherses*, Ctesippus, χ 287†.

Πολύῑδος: (1) son of Eurydamas, slain by Diomed, Ε 148.—(2) a seer in Corinth, father of Euchēnor, Ν 663, 666.

πολυ-ϊδρείη: *much knowledge*, *shrewdness*, β 346 and ψ 77.

πολύ-ιδρις (ϝίδρις): *very knowing*, *shrewd*, *subtle*, ο 459 and ψ 82.

πολύ-ιππος: *rich in horses*, Ν 171†.

πολυ-καγκής, ές (κάγκανος): *very dry*, *parching*, Λ 642†.

πολύ-καρπος (καρπός): *fruitful*, η 122 and ω 221.

Πολυκάστη: the youngest daughter of Nestor, γ 464†.

πολυ-κερδείη: *great craft*, ω 167†.

πολυ-κερδής, ές (κέρδος): *very crafty*, *cunning*, ν 255†.

πολύ-κεστος (κεντέω): *much* or *richly embroidered*, Γ 371†.

πολυ-κηδής, ές (κῆδος): *full of sorrows*, *woful*, ι 37 and ψ 351.

πολυ-κληΐς, ῖδος (κληΐς): *with many thole-pins*, *many-oared*.

πολύ-κληρος: *of large estate*, *wealthy*, ξ 211†.

πολύ-κλητος (καλέω): *called together in large numbers*, i. e. from many a land, Δ 438 and Κ 420.

πολύ-κλυστος (κλύζω): *much* or *loudly surging*. (Od.)

πολύ-κμητος (κάμνω): *wrought with much labor*, *well wrought*, *firmly built*.

πολύ-κνημος (κνήμη): *with many glens* or *ravines*, Β 497†.

πολυ-κοιρανίη (κοίρανος): *rule* or *sovereignty of many*, Β 204†.

πολυ-κτήμων: *with much possessions*, Ε 613†.

Πολυκτορίδης: *son of Polyctor*, Pisander, σ 299†.

Πολύκτωρ: *Polyctor*.—(1) a fabled name, Ω 397.—(2) name of an ancient hero in Ithaca, ρ 207.—(3) the father of Pisander.

πολυ-λήϊος (λήϊον): *rich in harvests*, Ε 613†.

πολύ-λλιστος (λίσσομαι): *object of many prayers*, ε 445†.

Πολυμήλη: daughter of Phylas, mother of Eudōrus, Π 180†.

πολύ-μηλος: *rich in sheep* or *flocks*. (Il.)

Πολύμηλος: a Lycian, son of Argeas, slain by Patroclus, Π 417†.

πολύ-μητις: *of many devices*, *crafty*, *shrewd*, epith. of Odysseus; of Hephaestus, Φ 355.

πολυ-μηχανίη: *manifold cunning*, ψ 321†.

πολυ-μήχανος: *much contriving*, *full of device; ever ready*, epith. of Odysseus.

πολυ-μνήστη (μνάομαι): *much wooed*. (Od.)

πολύ-μῡθος: *of many words*, *fluent*, Γ 214 and β 200.

Πολυνείκης: *Polynīces*, son of Oedipus, king of Thebes, and brother of Eteocles, mover of the expedition of the Seven against Thebes, Δ 377†.

Πολύνηος: a Phaeacian, the father of Amphialus, θ 114†.

Πολύξεινος: son of Agasthenes, a chief of the Epeians, B 623†.

πολυ-παίπαλος (παιπάλη, 'fine meal'): *very artful, sly*, ο 419†.

πολυ-πάμων, ονος (πέπαμαι): *much possessing, exceeding wealthy*, Δ 433†.

πολυ-πενθής, ές: *much-mourning, deeply mournful*, I 563, ψ 15.

Πολυπημονίδης: *son of Polypēmon* ('Great Possessor' or 'Sufferer'), a feigned name, ω 305†.

πολυ-πῖδαξ, ακος: *rich in springs*. (Il.)

πολύ-πικρος: neut. pl. as adv., *very bitterly*, π 255†.

πολύ-πλαγκτος (πλάζω): *much-wandering, far-roving; ἄνεμος, driving far from the course, baffling*, Λ 308.

Πολυποίτης: a Lapith, the son of Pirithous, B 740, Z 29, M 129, 182, Ψ 836, 844.

πολύ-πτυχος (πτύσσω): *with many folds, many-furrowed*. (Il.)

πολύ-πῦρος: *abounding in wheat*.

πολύ-ρρην and **πολύρρηνος** (ϝρην, ϝάρνα): *rich in sheep*, I 154 and 296.

πολύς, πολλή, πολύ, peculiar forms, **πολλός, πολλόν, πουλύς** (also fem.), **πουλύ,** gen. πολέος (υ 25), acc. πουλύν, pl. nom. πολέες, πολεῖς, gen. πολέων (Π 655), πολλάων, πολλέων, dat. πολέσι, πολέεσσι, acc. πολέας, for comp. and sup. see πλείων, πλεῖστος: *much, many*, with numerous applications that call for more specific words in Eng., as 'long,' of time, 'wide,' 'broad,' of space, 'loud,' 'heavy,' of a noise or of rain, etc. πολλοί (Att. οἱ πολλοί), *the many, the most, the greater part*, B 483, and w. part. gen., πολλοὶ Τρώων, etc. Freq. as subst., πολλοί, πολλά, 'many men,' 'many things,' but predicative in β 58, ρ 537; often with other adjectives, πολέες τε καὶ ἐσθλοί, πολλὰ καὶ ἐσθλά, 'many fine things,' β 312. —Neut. as adv., **πολύ, πολλόν, πολλά,** *much, far, by far, very;* πολλὰ ἠρᾶτο, prayed 'earnestly,' 'fervently,' A 35; w. comp. and sup., πολὺ μᾶλλον, πολλὸν ἀμείνων, ἄριστος, so πολὺ πρίν, πολλὸν ἐπελθών, Υ 180.

πολύ-σκαρθμος (σκαίρω): *much* or *far-springing, bounding, agile*, epith. of the Amazon Myrīne, B 814†.

πολυ-σπερής, ές (σπείρω). *wide-strewn, wide-spread*, over the earth.

πολυ-στάφυλος (σταφυλή): *with many clusters, rich in grapes*, B 507 and 537.

πολύ-στονος: *much-sighing, mournful*, τ 118; *grievous*, O 451.

πολύ-τλᾶς (τλῆναι): *much-suffering* or *enduring*, epith. of Odysseus.

πολυ-τλήμων = πολύτλᾶς.

πολύ-τλητος: *having endured* or *suffered much*, λ 38†.

πολυ-τρήρων, ωνος: *abounding in doves*, B 502 and 582.

πολύ-τρητος: *pierced with many holes, porous*. (Od.)

πολύ-τροπος (τρέπω): *of many shifts, versatile*, epith. of Odysseus, α 1 and κ 330.

πολυ-φάρμακος: *skilled in drugs*, Π 28, κ 276.

Πολυφείδης: son of Mantius, grandson of Melampus, ο 249 and 252.

πολύ-φημος (φήμη): *of many songs;* ἀοιδός, χ 376; *of many voices, buzzing;* ἀγορή, β 150.

Πολύφημος: *Polyphēmus*.—(1) son of Poseidon and the nymph Thoōsa, one of the Cyclōpes, a man-eater, α 70, ι 371 ff.—(2) one of the Lapithae, A 264.

πολύ-φλοισβος (φλοῖσβος): *loud-roaring*, always πολυφλοίσβοιο θαλάσσης.

Πολυφήτης: chief of the Trojan allies from Ascania, N 791†.

Πολυφόντης: son of Autophonus, slain by Tydeus before Thebes, Δ 395†.

πολύ-φορβος (φορβή): *much-nourishing, bountiful*. (Il.)

πολύ-φρων, ονος: *very sagacious*.

πολύ-χαλκος: *rich in bronze; οὐρανός, all-brazen*, fig. epithet, E 504, γ 2.

πολύ-χρῦσος: *rich in gold*.

πολυ-ωπός (ὀπή): *with many holes, meshy*, χ 386†.

πομπεύς, ῆος: = πομπός, only pl.; πομπῆες νηῶν, δ 362.

πομπεύω (πομπεύς): *be escort, conduct, escort*, ν 422†.

πομπή (πέμπω): *sending away, dismissal, escort*.

πομπός (πέμπω): *conductor, escort;* fem., δ 826.

πονέομαι (πόνος), part. πονεύμενος,

ipf. (ἐ)πονεῖτο, πονέοντο, fut. πονησόμεθα, aor. πονήσατο, plup. πεπόνητο: *be engaged in toil, toil, labor, be busy,* περί τι, κατὰ δῶμα, ὑσμίνην, and abs., ρ 258; trans., *work upon, make with care,* Σ 380, ι 310.

πόνος: *labor, toil,* esp. of the toil of battle, Ζ 77; frequently implying suffering, grievousness, 'a grievous thing,' Β 291; hence joined with ὀιζύς, κήδεα, ἀνίη, Ν 2, Φ 525, η 192.

Ποντεύς: a Phaeacian, θ 113†.

ποντόθεν: *from the sea,* Ξ 395†.

πόντονδε: *into the sea,* ι 495 and κ 48.

Ποντόνοος: a herald of Alcinous, η 182, θ 65, ν 50, 53.

ποντο-πορεύω and **ποντοπορέω**: *traverse the sea.* (Od.)

ποντο-πόρος: 'sea-faring,' *sea-traversing.*

πόντος, gen. ποντόφιν: the deep *sea, deep;* w. specific adj., Θρηίκιος, Ἰκάριος; πόντος ἁλός, the 'briny deep' (cf. ἁλὸς ἐν πελάγεσσιν), Φ 59.

πόποι (cf. παπαί): interjection, always ὢ πόποι, *alas! alack! well-a-day!* Β 272. Usually of grief or displeasure, except in the passage cited.

πορ-, aor. ἔπορον, πόρον, part. πορών, pass. perf. πέπρωται, πεπρωμένος: *bring to pass, give, grant,* of things, both good and evil (τινί τι), and of circumstances and events, w. acc. and inf., Ι 513; pass. perf. πέπρωται, *it is decreed* by fate, *ordained, destined,* Σ 329; mostly the part. πεπρωμένος, Ο 209, Γ 309.

πόρδαλις, ιος, also πάρδαλις: *panther, leopard.*

Πορθεύς: king of Calydon, father of Oeneus, Ξ 115†.

πορθέω (πέρθω), ipf. (ἐ)πόρθεον, fut. πορθήσω: *lay waste, devastate.*

πορθμεύς, ῆος (πόρος): *ferryman,* pl., υ 187†.

πορθμός (πόρος): *strait, sound,* δ 67 and ο 29.

πόρις: see πόρτις.

πόρκης: an iron *ring,* around the shaft of a spear to hold the head firm, Ζ 320 and Θ 495. (See cut No. 4.)

πόρος (cf. πείρω): *passage-way, ford;* πόροι ἁλός, 'paths of the sea,' μ 259.

πόρπη (πείρω): *buckle, brooch,* Σ 401†. (See cut No. 97.)

πορσύνω, πορσαίνω (root πορ), ipf. πόρσυνε, fut. part. πορσανέουσα (v. l. πορσυν.): *make ready, prepare, tend;* λέχος καὶ εὐνήν, euphemistic for sharing the bed.

πόρταξ, ακος = πόρτις, Ρ 4†.

πόρτις and **πόρις,** ιος: *calf* or *heifer.*

πορφύρεος: *purple;* φᾶρος, τάπητες, αἷμα, Θ 221, Ι 200, Ρ 361; of the sea, with reference to its dark-gleaming, changeable hues, likewise of a swollen river, Α 482, Φ 326; also of the rainbow, a cloud, Ρ 547, 551. Met., θάνατος, probably with reference to the optical sensations of dissolution, Ε 83.

πορφύρω (φύρω): *boil* or *surge up,* of waves, Ξ 16; met., of mental disquiet, *be troubled, brood,* δ 427, etc.

πόσε: interrog. adv., *whether?*

Ποσειδάων: *Poseidon* (Neptūnus), son of Cronus and Rhea, brother of Zeus, Hades, etc., and husband of Amphitrīte. As god of the sea, the element assigned to him by lot (Ο 189), he sends winds and storms, moves the waters with his trident, and causes earthquakes, ἐνοσίχθων, ἐννοσίγαιος, γαιήοχος. To him, as to Hades, black bulls were sacrificed, γ 6; cf. the epithet κυανοχαίτης. Poseidon is the enemy of the Trojans in consequence of the faithlessness of Laomedon, Φ 443 ff.; and of Odysseus, because of the blinding of Polyphēmus, his son, α 20. His dwelling is in the depths of the sea near Aegae, Ν 21, ε 381; but he attends the assembly of the gods on Olympus, Θ 440, Ο 161.

Ποσιδήιος: *sacred to Poseidon,* Β 506; as subst., **Ποσιδήιον,** *temple of Poseidon,* ζ 266.

1. πόσις, ιος (πίνω): *drink.*

2. πόσις, ιος (cf. δεσπότης, potens): *husband, spouse.*

ποσσ-ῆμαρ: *how many days?* Ω 657†.

πόστος: the 'how-manyeth?' πόστον δὴ ἔτος ἐστίν, ὅτε, 'how many years is it, since, etc.?' ω 288†.

ποταμόνδε: *into* or *to the river.*

ποταμός: *river;* freq. personified as river-god, Ε 544, Ξ 245.

ποτάομαι and **ποτέομαι** (frequentative of πέτομαι), ποτῶνται, ποτέονται, perf. πεπότηται, 3 pl. πεποτήαται: *flit,* *fly;* said of the souls of the departed, λ 222.

πότε: interrog. adv., *when? at what time?*

ποτέ: enclitic indef. adv., *at some time, once, some day.*

ποτέομαι: see ποτάομαι.

πότερος: *which* (of two)? Pl., *which party?*

ποτή (πέτομαι): *flying, flight,* ε 337†.

ποτής, ῆτος: *drink.*

ποτητός (ποτάομαι): *flying;* subst. ποτητά, *birds,* μ 62†.

ποτί: see πρός. Compounds beginning with ποτι- must be looked for under προσ-.

ποτιδέγμενος: see προσδέχομαι.

ποτικέκλιται: see προσκλίνω.

ποτιπεπτηυῖα: see προσπτήσσω.

ποτιφωνήεις: see προσφωνήεις.

πότμος (πετ, πίπτω): that which befalls one, *fate, death,* always in bad sense in Homer, ἀεικέα πότμον ἐφιέναι τινί, πότμον ἀναπλῆσαι, θάνατον καὶ πότμον ἐπισπεῖν, Δ 396, Λ 263.

πότνια, voc. **πότνα** (cf. πόσις 2, δέσποινα): *mistress, queen,* θηρῶν, Artemis, Φ 470; freq. as honorable title or epith. of goddesses and women, πότνα θεά, 'mighty' goddess (cf. 'our Lady'), πότνια μήτηρ, 'revered,' 'honored,' σ 5.

ποτόν (πίνω): *drink.*

ποῦ: interrog. adv., *where? whither?*

πού: enclitic indef. adv., *somewhere, anywhere; methinks, doubtless, perhaps.*

πουλυβότειρα: see πολυβότειρα.

Πουλυδάμᾱς: *Polydamas,* a Trojan, son of Panthoüs, Ξ 449, 453, Ο 339, 518, 521, Π 535, Σ 249.

πουλύπος, ποδος: *polypus,* cuttle-fish, ε 432.

πουλύς, πουλύ: see πολύς.

πούς, ποδός, pl. dat. ποσσί, πόδεσσι, du. ποδοῖιν: *foot;* said also of the 'talons' of birds, ο 526; designating swiftness of foot, in the race, Ν 325; fig., of the base of a mountain, Υ 59; technically, νηός, *sheet,* a rope fastened to the lower corners of a sail to control it (see plate IV.), ε 260, κ 32.

Πράκτιος: a river in the Troad, north of Abȳdus, Β 835†.

Πράμνειος: οἶνος, *Pramnian* wine, of dark color and fiery quality.

πραπίδες = φρένες, *diaphragm, midriff,* Λ 579; then for *heart, mind, thoughts,* Χ 43, Σ 380, η 92.

πρασιή: *garden-bed,* ω 247 and η 127.

πρέπω, ipf. ἔπρεπε: *be conspicuous* or *distinguished,* Μ 104, θ 172, σ 2.

πρέσβα: see πρέσβυς.

πρεσβήιον (πρέσβυς): *gift of honor,* Θ 289†.

πρεσβυ-γενής: *first-born,* Λ 249†.

πρέσβυς, in Hom. only fem. **πρέσβα,** comp. πρεσβύτερος, sup. πρεσβύτατος: *aged, venerable, honored,* comp. *older,* sup. *oldest;* Ἥρη πρέσβα θεά, not with reference to age (although of course it never made any difference how old a goddess was), Ε 721; cf. δ 59.

πρήθω, aor. ἔπρησα, πρῆσε, inf. πρῆσαι: a verb combining the notions, *blow, stream, burn;* ἔπρησεν δ' ἄνεμος μέσον ἱστίον, 'swelled,' 'filled,' β 427; with ἐν, Α 481; (αἷμα) ἀνὰ στόμα καὶ κατὰ ῥῖνας | πρῆσε χανών, 'spirted,' Π 350; πυρί and πυρός, Η 429, 432, Β 415.

πρηκτήρ, ῆρος (πρήσσω): *doer;* ἔργων, Ι 433; pl., *traders,* θ 162.

πρηνής, ές (πρό, cf. p r o n u s): *forward, on the face, head-foremost,* Ζ 43, Π 310; opp. ὕπτιος, Ω 11.

πρῆξις, ιος (πρήσσω): *accomplishment, result;* οὔ τις πρῆξις ἐγίγνετο μῡρομένοισιν, 'they gained nothing' by weeping, κ 202, 568; *business, enterprise,* γ 82; κατὰ πρῆξιν, 'on business,' γ 72.

πρήσσω (πέρην), ipf. iter. πρήσσεσκον, fut. πρήξω, aor. ἔπρηξα: *fare, pass over,* ἅλα, ι 491; *complete* a journey, κέλευθον, ὁδοῖο (part. gen.), Ξ 282, Ω 264, γ 476; then in general, *do, accomplish,* ἔργον, οὔ τι, τ 324, Ω 550, Α 562.

πρίατο, defective aor.: *bought, purchased.* (Od.)

Πριαμίδης: *son of Priam.* (Il.)

Πρίαμος: *Priam,* son of Laomedon, and king of Troy. He was already an aged man at the time of the war, and took no part in the fighting, Ω 487. Homer says that Priam was the father of fifty sons, of whom his wife Hecuba bore him nineteen. Besides Hector, Paris, Helenus, and Cassandra, the following children are named: Echemmon, Chromius, Lycāon, Polītes, Gorgythion, Democoön, Deïphobus, Isus, Antiphus, Laodice.

πρὶν (πρό): (1) adv., *before, formerly, first;* πρίν μιν καὶ γῆρας ἔπεισιν, 'sooner' shall old age come upon her, A 29, Ω 551, γ 117; freq. τὸ πρίν, πολὺ πρίν, β 167.—(2) conj., *before,* with some peculiarities of construction which may be learned from the grammars; the inf. is used more freely with πρίν in Homer than in other authors. Freq. doubled in correlation, πρὶν . . πρίν, Θ 452, A 97; so πάρος . . πρίν, πρόσθεν . . πρίν, πρίν γ' ὅτε, πρίν γ' ἤ (priusquam), E 288. Without verb, πρὶν ὥρη, 'before it is time,' ο 394.

πριστός (πρίω): *sawn,* ivory, σ 196 and τ 564.

πρό: *before, forward, forth.*—I. adv., (κύματα) πρὸ μέν τ' ἄλλ', αὐτὰρ ἐπ' ἄλλα, some 'before,' others after, N 799, cf. 800; πρὸ γὰρ ἧκε, sent 'forth,' A 195; Ἰλιόθι πρό, οὐρανόθι πρό, 'before Ilium,' 'athwart the sky' (at Ilium, in the sky, 'in front'), Γ 3; of time, ἠῶθι πρό, in the morning 'early'; πρό τ' ἐόντα, 'things past'; πρό οἱ εἴπομεν, 'beforehand,' A 70, α 37; a subst. in the gen. may specify the relation of the adv., πρὸ δ' ἀρ' οὐρῆες κίον αὐτῶν (gen. of comparison), Ψ 115.—II. prep. w. gen., (1) of space, πρὸ πυλάων, πρὸ ἄνακτος, *before the gates, in the presence* of the master, Ω 734; πρὸ ὁδοῦ, well *forward* on the way, Δ 382.—(2) of time, ο 524, K 224.—(3) fig., *in behalf of, for;* μάχεσθαι, ὀλέσθαι πρὸ πόληος (pro patria mori), X 110; causal, πρὸ φόβοιο, *for,* P 667.

προ-αλής, ές (ἅλλομαι): springing forward, *sloping,* Φ 262†.

προ-βαίνω, part. προβιβάς, προβιβῶντι, -α, perf. προβέβηκα, plup. προβεβήκει: *go forward, advance,* and fig., *surpass,* τινός, Z 125; ἄστρα προβέβηκε, are 'verging low,' 'forward' toward their setting, K 252.

προ-βάλλω, aor. 2 iter. προβάλεσκε, part. προβαλόντες, mid. aor. 2 προβάλοντο, opt. προβαλοίμην: act., *throw forth,* 'tossed it over,' of the winds playing ball with Odysseus's raft, ε 331; met., ἔριδα, 'begin' strife, Λ 529; mid., *cast down before,* subjectively, A 458; met., *excel,* τινός, T 218.

πρό-βασις (προβαίνω): *live-stock,* as opp. to κειμήλια (κεῖμαι), β 75†. Cf. the foll.

πρό-βατον (προβαίνω): only pl., *cattle, droves* or *flocks,* Ξ 124 and Ψ 550.

προ-βέβουλα (βούλομαι), def. pf.: *prefer before;* τινά τινος, A 113†.

προβιβάς, προβιβῶν: see προβαίνω.

προ-βλής, ῆτος (προβάλλω): *projecting.*

προ-βλώσκω, inf. προβλωσκέμεν, aor. 2 πρόμολον, imp. πρόμολε, part. -ών, -οῦσα: *come* or *go forward* or *forth.*

προ-βοάω, part. προβοῶντε: *shout loudly* (above the rest), M 277†.

πρό-βολος (προβάλλω): *jutting rock,* μ 251†.

προ-γενέστερος: *born before, older,* comp. of προγενής.

προ-γίγνομαι, aor. 2 προγένοντο: *get on, advance,* Σ 525†.

πρό-γονος: pl., *earlier-born* lambs, 'spring lambs,' 'firstlings,' ι 221†.

προ-δαείς (root δα): aor. part., *learning beforehand,* δ 396†.

προ-δοκή (προδέχομαι): *lurking-place, ambush,* pl., Δ 107†.

πρό-δομος: *vestibule,* a portico before the house, supported by pillars (see plate III. D D, at end of volume), I 473, δ 302, cf. θ 57.

προ-εέργω (Ϝέργω): *hinder* (by standing before), w. inf., ipf., Λ 569†.

προέηκα: see προΐημι.

προ-εῖδον, subj. προΐδωσιν, part. προϊδών, mid. subj. προΐδωνται: *look forward, catch sight of* in front, mid., ν 155.

προέμεν: see προΐημι.

προ-ερέσσω, aor. προέρεσσα: *row forward.*

προ-ερύω, aor. προέρυσσεν, subj. προερύσσω: *draw forward, launch.*

πρόες: see προΐημι.

προ-έχω, προὔχω, προὔχουσιν, part. προὔχων, ipf. πρόεχε; mid. ipf. προὔχοντο: *be ahead,* Ψ 325, 453; *jut forward,* μ 11, τ 544; mid., *hold* or *have before oneself,* γ 8.

προ-ήκης, ες (ἀκή): *sharp in front, with sharp blades,* μ 205†.

προ-θέλυμνος (θέλυμνον): *with the root, roots and all*, K 15, I 541; *overlapping*, of the layers of ox-hide forming a shield, N 130.

προθέουσι: see προτίθημι.

προ-θέω, ipf. iter. προθέεσκε, subj. προθέῃσι: *run before, outstrip.*

Προθοήνωρ: son of Areïlycus, a chief of the Boeotians, B 495, Ξ 450, 471.

Πρόθοος: son of Tenthrēdon, a leader of the Magnesians, B 756, 758.

προθορών: see προθρώσκω.

Προθόων: a Trojan, slain by Teucer, Ξ 515†.

προ-θρώσκω, aor. part. προθορών: *spring forward.* (Il.)

προ-θῡμίη (πρόθῡμος): *zeal, courage*, pl., B 588†. The ῑ is due to the necessities of the rhythm.

πρό-θυρον (θύρη): *front gateway*, α 103, γ 493; front *doorway* (see plate III. *t*), θ 304, σ 10; *porch* at the entrance of the court, with pillars (see plate III. A).

προ-ϊάλλω, ipf. προΐαλλεν: *send forth.*

προ-ιάπτω, fut. προϊάψει, aor. προΐαψεν: *hurl (forth)*, Ἄϊδι, Ἀϊδωνῆι, A 3, E 190. The προ- is merely for emphasis. (Il.)

προ-ΐημι, προΐησι, 3 pl. προϊεῖσι, imp. προΐει, part. προϊεῖσα, ipf. προΐειν, -εις, -ει (-ην, -ης, -η), aor. προέηκε, προῆκε, 3 pl. πρόεσαν, imp. πρόες, -έτω, inf. προέμεν: *let go forth, send forth*, τινά, w. inf. of purpose, K 125, κ 25; so of missiles, water, 'pour,' etc., Θ 297, B 752; 'let drop,' 'let fall,' ε 316, τ 468; fig., φήμην, ἔπος, υ 105, ξ 466; κῦδός τινι, 'bestow,' Π 241.

προ-ΐκτης: *beggar, mendicant.* (Od.)

προΐξ, προικός: *gift, present;* προικός, 'for nothing,' i. e. without compensation, ν 15.

προ-ΐστημι: only aor. 1 part., προστήσᾱς, *having put forward* (in the front), w. inf., Δ 156†.

Προῖτος: *Proetus*, king of Tiryns, son of Abas, and husband of Anteia, Z 157 ff.

προ-καθ-ίζω: alight after flying forward, *settle down*, part., B 463†.

προ-καλέομαι, aor. προκαλέσσατο, imp. προκάλεσσαι, subj. προκαλέσσεται: *challenge;* χάρμῃ, μαχέσασθαι, H 218, Γ 432.

προ-καλίζομαι = προκαλέομαι.

πρό-κειμαι: *lie before*, only part.

πρό-κλυτος (κλύω): *heard of old, ancient* and *celebrated;* ἔπεα, Υ 204†.

Πρόκρις: daughter of Erechtheus, king of Athens, λ 321†.

πρό-κροσσος (κρόσσαι): *in rows, in tiers*, pl., Ξ 35†.

προ-κυλίνδομαι: *roll forward*, Ξ 18†.

προ-λέγω: only pass. perf. part., προλελεγμένοι, *chosen, picked*, N 689†.

προ-λείπω, aor. part. προλιπών, inf. προλιπεῖν, perf. προλέλοιπεν: *leave behind*, met., *forsake*, β 279.

προ-μαχίζω (πρόμαχος): *be a champion, fight in the front rank*, **Τρωσί** (among the Trojans), **τινί** (with some one), Γ 16 and Υ 376.

προ-μάχομαι: *fight before* one, Λ 217 and P 358.

πρό-μαχος: *champion, foremost fighter.*

Πρόμαχος: son of Alegēnor, a Boeotian chief, Ξ 476, 482, 503.

προ-μίγνῡμι: only pass. aor. 2 inf., προμιγῆναι, *to have intercourse with* (τινί) *before* one, I 452†.

προ-μνηστῖνοι: *one before (after) another, successively*, opp. ἅμα πάντες, φ 230 and λ 233.

προμολών: see προβλώσκω.

πρόμος (πρό): *foremost (man), foremost fighter.*

προ-νοέω, aor. προνόησαν, inf. προνοῆσαι: *think* or *devise beforehand, suspect*, ε 264, Σ 526.

Πρόνοος: a Trojan, slain by Patroclus, Π 399†.

πρόξ, προκός (cf. περκνός): *deer, roe*, ρ 295†.

προ-παροιθε(ν): *before, formerly*, of space and of time; w. gen. of place, *before, along;* ἠιόνος προπάροιθε, B 92.

πρό-πᾶς, -ᾱσα, -αν: *all* (day) *long, all* (the ships) *together*, ι 161.

προ-πέμπω, aor. προὔπεμψα: *send before* or *forth.*

προπέφανται: see προφαίνω.

προ-πίπτω, aor. part. προπεσών: *fall forward*, 'lay to,' in rowing, ι 490 and μ 194.

προ-ποδίζω: only part., *striding forward*, N 158 and 806.

προ-πρηνής, ές: *leaning forward, bent* (*forward*), Γ 218, χ 98.

προ-προ-κυλίνδομαι: *roll* (as suppliant) *before*, Διός, Χ 221; 'wander from place to place,' ρ 525.

προ-ρέω, προρέει, -έουσι, inf. -έειν, part. -έοντος: *flow forth, flow on.*

πρό-ρριζος (ῥίζα): *with the roots*, 'root and branch,' Λ 157 and Ξ 415.

πρός, προτί, ποτί: I. adv., *thereto, in addition; πρὸς δ' ἄρα πηδάλιον ποιήσατο*, 'to it,' 'for it,' ε 255; *ποτὶ δ' αὖ καὶ ἐγείρομεν ἄλλους, besides*, Κ 108; with a specifying case of a subst. in the same clause, *ποτὶ δὲ σκῆπτρον βάλε γαίῃ* (local gen.), threw it *to* ('down,' we should say) on the ground, Α 245.—II. prep., (1) w. gen., with reference to motion either *toward* or *from* some direction, (ἵκετο) *ἠὲ πρὸς ἠοίων ἢ ἑσπερίων ἀνθρώπων*, 'from,' θ 29; *προτὶ πτόλιος πέτετ' ἀεί*, 'toward,' Χ 198; as of origin, source, *ἀκούειν τι πρός τινος*, Ζ 525; hence to denote mastery, authority, *διδάσκεσθαι πρός τινος*, Λ 831; *πρὸς ἄλλης ὑφαίνειν*, 'at the command of,' Ζ 456; *πρὸς Διός εἰσι ξεῖνοι*, 'under the protection of,' ζ 207; 'in the eyes of,' 'before,' 'by,' in oaths and entreaties, Α 399, Τ 188, ν 324.—(2) w. dat., *to, at, on, besides*, κ 68.—(3) w. acc., *to, toward, at, upon*, with verbs of motion, and very freq. w. verbs of saying, so *ὀμνύναι πρός τινα*, ξ 331; of hostile action, *μάχεσθαι πρὸς Τρῶας, with, against*, Ρ 471; *πρὸς ῥόον*, up stream, Φ 303; fig., *πρὸς δαίμονα*, Ρ 98, 104.—Of time, *ποτὶ ἕσπερα*, 'towards evening,' ρ 191.

προσ-άγω, aor. 2 προσήγαγε: *bring upon*, ρ 446†.

προσ-āΐσσω, aor. part. προσāΐξāς: *spring to, dart to*, χ 337, 342, 365.

προσ-αλείφω: *anoint, apply as ointment; φάρμακόν τινι*, κ 392†.

προσ-αμύνω, aor. inf. προσαμῦναι: *ward off* from one (*τινί*), *bring help* or *aid to.* (Il.)

προσ-άπτω, προτιάπτω: *attach to, accord*, Ω 110†.

προσ-αρηρώς (ἀραρίσκω), part.: *closely fitted*, Ε 725†.

προσ-αυδάω, imp. προσαυδάτω, ipf. προσηύδων, προσηύδā, du. προσαυδήτην: *speak to, address*, abs., or w. acc., and freq. w. two accusatives, **τινὰ** *ἔπεα*, Α 201. See *αὐδάω* and *αὐδή*.

προσ-βαίνω, aor. 2 προσέβην, 3 pl. προσέβαν, mid. aor. προσεβήσετο: *go to, arrive at, step upon.*

προσ-βάλλω, mid. 2 sing. προτιβάλλεαι: *cast upon, strike; Ἠέλιος ἀρούρāς*, Η 421; mid., met., *reprove*, Ε 879.

προσ-δέρκομαι, ποτιδέρκεται, ipf. προσεδέρκετο: *look upon.*

προσ-δέχομαι, aor. part. **ποτιδέγμενος**: *expect, await, wait.*

προσ-δόρπιος, ποτιδόρπιος: *for supper*, ι 234 and 249.

προσ-ειλέω, προτιειλέω (ϝειλέω), inf. προτιειλεῖν: *press forward*, Κ 347†.

προσ-εῖπον, προτιεῖπον (ϝεῖπον), προσέειπον, opt. προτιείποι: *speak to, address, accost.*

προσ-ερεύγομαι: *belch at; προσερεύγεται πέτρην*, 'breaks foaming against the rock,' Ο 621†.

πρόσθε(ν): *in front, before, formerly*, of place and of time; (the Chimaera), *πρόσθε λέων, ὄπιθεν δὲ δράκων*, Ζ 181; *οἱ πρόσθεν*, 'the men of old,' Ι 524; as prep., w. gen., often of place, also to denote protection, like **πρό** or *ὑπέρ*, Φ 587, θ 524; local and temporal, Β 359.

πρόσ-κειμαι: *be attached to* (pass. of *προστίθημι*), ipf., Σ 379†.

προσ-κηδής, ές (κῆδος): *solicitous, affectionate*, φ 35†.

προσ-κλίνω, ποτικλίνω, ipf. προσέκλῖνε, pass. perf. **ποτικέκλιται**: *lean against*, **τινί τι**; perf. pass., *is placed* or *stands near.* (Od.)

προσ-λέγομαι, aor. 2 **προσέλεκτο**: *lie* or *recline beside*, μ 34†.

προσ-μῡθέομαι, προτιμῡθέομαι, aor. inf. προτιμῡθήσασθαι: *speak to*, λ 143†.

προσ-νίσσομαι, ποτινίσσομαι: *go* or *come in; εἴς τι*, Ι 381†.

προσ-πελάζω, aor. part. προσπελάσāς: *bring in contact with, drive upon*, ι 285†.

προσ-πίλναμαι: *draw near*, ipf., ν 95†.

προσ-πλάζω, part. προσπλάζον: *strike upon, reach to*, Μ 285 and λ 583.

προσ-πτήσσω, ποτιπτήσσω, perf. part. **ποτιπεπτηυῖαι**: *sink down towards*, **τινός**, ν 98†.

προσ-πτύσσομαι, ποτιπτύσσομαι, opt. ποτιπτυσσοίμεθα, fut. προσπτύξεται, aor. προσπτύξατο, subj. προσπτύξομαι: *fold to oneself, embrace, receive* or *greet warmly*, λ 451, θ 478, γ 22; μύθῳ, in entreaty, 'entreat,' β 77.

πρόσσοθεν: *before* him, Ψ 533†.

πρόσσω: see πρόσω.

προσ-στείχω, aor. 2 προσέστιχε: *ascend*, υ 73†.

προσ-τέρπω: ποτιτερπέτω; 'let him please,' 'entertain' thee, Ο 401†.

προσ-τίθημι, aor. 1 προσέθηκε: *place at* (the entrance), ι 305†.

προσφάσθαι: see πρόσφημι.

πρόσ-φατος: usually interpreted, *freshly slain* (φένω): according to others, *that may be addressed* (φημί), i. e. with lifelike countenance, Ω 757†.

πρόσ-φημι, ipf. (aor.) προσέφην, mid. inf. προσφάσθαι: *speak to, address.*

προσ-φυής, ές: *grown upon*, i. e. *fastened to*, τ 58†. (See cut No. 105.)

προσ-φύω, aor. 2 part. προσφύς, -ῦσα: aor. 2 intrans., *grow to, cling*, μ 433 and Ω 213.

προσ-φωνέω, ipf. προσεφώνεον: *speak to, address, accost;* in χ 69, μετεφώνεε is the better reading. See φωνέω and φωνή.

προσ-φωνήεις, ποτιφωνήεις, εσσα, εν: *capable of addressing, endued with speech*, ι 456†.

πρό(σ)σω: *forward, in the future*, Π 265, Α 343.

πρόσ-ωπον (ὤψ), pl. πρόσωπα and προσώπατα: *face, visage, countenance*, usually pl.; sing., Σ 24.

προ-τάμνω, aor. part. προταμών, mid. aor. opt. προταμοίμην: *cut before* one (forward, from the root toward the top), ψ 196; *cut up*, Ι 489; mid., *cut straight before* me, 'draw straight before me,' σ 375.

πρότερος (comp. to πρό): *fore, former;* πόδες, τ 228; usually of time, (οἱ) πρότεροι, 'men of former time,' Δ 308; τῇ προτέρῃ (sc. ἡμέρῃ), π 50; γενέῃ, 'elder,' Ο 166.

προτέρω: *forward, further.*

προ-τεύχω, pass. perf. inf. προτετύχθαι: perf. pass., *be past and done*, let 'by-gones be by-gones.' (Il.)

προτί: see πρός. For compounds with προτι-, see under προς-.

Προτιάων: a Trojan, the father of Astynous, Ο 455†.

προτιβάλλεαι, προτιειλεῖν: see προσβάλλω, προσειλέω.

προτιεῖποι: see προσεῖπον.

προ-τίθημι, 3 pl., προθέουσιν, ipf. 3 pl. πρότιθεν, aor. προὔθηκεν: *place before*, 'throw before' dogs, Ω 409; fig., 'permit,' Α 291.

προτιμῡθήσασθαι: see προσμῡθέομαι.

προτι-όσσομαι, imp. προτιόσσεο, ipf. -ετο: *look upon* or *toward*, and, with the eyes of the mind, *forbode;* 'recognize thee for what I had foreboded,' Χ 356.

πρό-τμησις (τέμνω): *parts about the navel*, Λ 424†.

πρό-τονος (τείνω): only pl., *forestays* of a ship, ropes extending from the mast to the inner portion of the bows, Α 434, β 425. (See cut under Σειρήν.)

προ-τρέπομαι (τρέπω), ipf. προτρέποντο, aor. 2 subj. προτράπηται, opt. -οίμην, inf. -έσθαι: *turn* (in flight) *to*, fig., *give oneself to*, ἄχεϊ, Ζ 336.

προ-τροπάδην: adv., *in headlong flight*, Π 304†.

προ-τύπτω, aor. προὔτυψα: *strike forward*, intrans., *press forward; ἀνὰ ῥῖνας δριμὺ μένος*, 'forced itself forward' (rose quickly in spite of him), ω 319.

προὔθηκε: see προτίθημι.

προὔπεμψε: see προπέμπω.

προὔχοντα, προυχούσῃ: see προέχω.

προ-φαίνω, ipf. προὔφαινον, mid. ipf. προυφαίνετο, pass. perf. 3 sing. προπέφανται, aor. part. προφανείς: *show forth, reveal*, and intrans., *shine forth*, ι 145; mid., *shine forth, be visible, appear;* οὐδὲ προὐφαίνετ' ἰδέσθαι, 'it was not light enough to see,' ι 143.

πρό-φασις (φημί): *pretext;* acc. as adv., *ostensibly*, Τ 262 and 302.

προ-φερής, ές, comp. **προφερέστερος,** sup. **-έστατος**: *preferred*, τινός, 'above' some one, *superior* in, τινί, φ 134; w. inf., 'better in drawing,' Κ 352.

προ-φέρω, subj. προφέρῃσι, opt. -οις, imp. -ε, part. -ων, mid. pres. προφέρονται, subj. -ηται: *bear forth* or *away, proffer*, fig., ὀνείδεα τινί, Β 251; 'display,' *μένος*, K 479; mid., *ἔριδά τινι*, 'challenge,' θ 210; 'begin' combat, Γ 7.

προ-φεύγω, aor. 2 subj. *προφύγῃ*, opt. 2 sing. *προφύγοισθα*, inf. *προφυγεῖν*, part. *-ών*: *flee away*, *escape*, abs., and w. acc.

πρό-φρασσα, fem. of *πρόφρων*: *cheerful(ly)*, *serious(ly)*, *in earnest*, κ 386.

πρό-φρων, *ονος* (*φρήν*): adj., regularly used not as attributive but as adverb, *cheerful(ly)*, *gracious(ly)*, *kind(ly)*, *zealous(ly)*, *earnest(ly)*; ironical, *πρόφρων κεν δὴ ἔπειτα Δία λιτοίμην*, 'in good earnest,' i. e. I could not do it, ξ 406; as adj., *θυμῷ πρόφρονι*, Θ 40.—Adv., **προφρονέως** (Il.).

προ-χέω, pass. ipf. *προχέοντο*: *pour forth*; met., B 465, etc. (Il.)

πρό-χνυ (*γόνυ*): (*forward*) *on the knee*, 'on her knees,' I 570; fig., *ἀπολέσθαι*, laid 'low,' 'utterly' destroyed, Φ 460.

προ-χοή (*χέω*): only pl., *out-pourings*, *mouth* of a river, *stream*, υ 65.

πρό-χοος (*χέω*): vessel for pouring, *pitcher*, *vase* (for the form see cut No. 26). Used for wine, σ 397, and for water in ablutions (see cut No. 76).

πρυλέες, dat. *πρυλέεσσι*: heavy-armed *foot-soldiers* (= *ὁπλῖται*), Λ 49, M 77, O 517, E 744.

Πρυμνεύς: a Phaeacian, θ 112†.

πρύμνη: *stern* of a ship; for *πρυμνὴ νηύς*, see *πρυμνός*.

πρύμνηθεν: *at the stern*; *λαμβάνειν*, 'by the stern-post,' O 716†.

πρυμνήσια: neut. adj. as subst., sc. *πείσματα*, *stern*-cables, by means of which the ship was made fast to the shore; *πρυμνήσια καταδῆσαι*, *ἀνάψαι*, *λῦσαι*, β 418.

πρυμνός, sup. **πρυμνότατος** (ρ 463): at the *extreme* end, usually the *lower* or *hinder* part; *βραχίων*, 'end' of the arm near the shoulder, N 532; *γλῶσσα*, 'root' of the tongue, E 292; so *κέρας*, N 705; *νηῦς πρυμνή*, at the stern, 'aft,' 'after part,' cf. *πρύμνη*, β 417; *δόρυ*, here apparently the upper end, 'by the point,' P 618; of a stone, *πρυμνὸς παχύς*, thick 'at the base,' M 446; *ὕλην πρυμνήν*, wood 'at the root,' M 149.—Neut. as subst., *πρυμνὸν θέναρος*, 'end of the palm,' just below the fingers, E 339.

πρυμν-ωρείη (*ὄρος*): *foot of a mountain*, Ξ 307†.

Πρύτανις: a Lycian, slain by Odysseus, E 678†.

πρῴην (*πρό*): *lately*, *recently*. (Il.)

πρωθ-ήβης (*πρῶτος*, *ἥβη*): *in the prime* or 'bloom' of youth.

πρῶι (*πρό*): *early*, *in the morning*; 'untimely,' v. l. for *πρῶτα*, ω 28.

πρώιζ(α), *πρωιζά*: *day before yesterday*, B 303†.

πρώιον, neut. adj. as adv., *early in the morning*, O 470†.

πρών, *πρῶνος*, pl. *πρώονες*: *foreland*, *headland*. (Il.)

Πρωρεύς: a Phaeacian, θ 113†.

πρῴρη (*πρό*): fem. adj. as subst., *prow*, μ 230†.

Πρωτεσίλᾱος: *Protesilāus*, son of Iphiclus, a leader of the Thessalians, the first Greek to tread on Trojan soil, and the first to fall, B 698, 706, O 705, N 681, Π 286.

Πρωτεύς: *Proteus*, the prophetic old man of the sea, changing himself into many shapes, δ 365, 385.

πρώτιστος, sup. to *πρῶτος*: *first of all*, *chiefest*.—Adv., **πρώτιστον**, **πρώτιστα** (*πρώτισθ'*), λ 168.

πρωτό-γονος: *first-born*, *ἄρνες*, 'firstlings.' (Il.)

πρωτο-παγής, *ές* (*πήγνῡμι*): *new-made*, E 194 and Ω 267.

πρωτο-πλόος (*πλέω*): *sailing* or *going to sea for the first time*, θ 35†.

πρῶτος (sup. from *πρό*): *first*, of position, rank, or time, opp. *ὕστατος*, B 281; *ἐν πρωτῃ ἀγορῇ*, 'front' of the assembly, T 50; *ἐνὶ πρώτῃσι θύρῃσι* (cf. *πρόθυρα*), 'at the first entrance,' α 255; *πρῶτοι* for *πρόμαχοι*, E 536, σ 379; *τὰ πρῶτα* (sc. *ἆθλα*), Ψ 275.—Adv., **πρῶτον**, **πρῶτα**, *τὸ πρῶτον*, *τὰ πρῶτα*, Δ 267, A 6; w. *ἐπειδή* (cum primum), 'as soon as.'

πρωτο-τόκος (*τίκτω*): *having borne* ('come in') *for the first time*, of a heifer, P 5†.

Πρωτώ: a Nereid, Σ 43†.

πρώονες: see *πρών*.

πταίρω, aor. 2 *ἔπταρεν*: *sneeze*, ρ 541†.

πτάμενος, **πτάτο**: see **πέτομαι**.

πτελέη: *elm*. (Il.)

Πτελεός: (1) a harbor-town in Thessaly, Β 697.—(2) in Elis, a colony of the Thessalian Pteleus, Β 594.

πτέρνη: *heel*, Χ 397†.

πτερόεις, εσσα, εν: *winged*, epith. of the feathered arrow; also of targes (λαισήια), because of the fluttering apron attached to them, Ε 453 (see cuts Nos. 73 and 79); met., ἔπεα πτερόεντα, 'winged words.'

πτερόν (πέτομαι): *feather, wing*; πτερὰ βάλλειν, 'ply,' τινάσσεσθαι, Λ 454, β 151; symbol of lightness, swiftness, Τ 386, η 36; fig., of oars, πτερὰ νηυσίν, λ 125.

πτέρυξ, υγος, pl. dat. πτερύγεσσιν: *wing, pinion*.

πτήσσω, aor. πτῆξε, perf. part. πεπτηώς: *cower, crouch*, perf.; aor. trans. in an interpolated verse, 'make to cower,' 'terrify,' Ξ 40.

πτοιέω: only pass. aor. 3 pl., ἐπτοίηθεν, *were dismayed*, χ 298†.

Πτολεμαῖος: son of Piraeus, father of Eurymedon, Δ 228†.

πτολεμίζω, πτολεμιστής, πτόλεμος: see πολεμίζω, etc.

πτολίεθρον: *town, city*, but often in a more restricted sense than πόλις, hence w. gen., Τροίης ἱερὸν πτολίεθρον, Πύλου αἰπὺ πτολίεθρον, α 2, γ 485.

πτολι-πόρθιος, πτολίπορθος (πέρθω): *sacker of cities*, epith. of gods and heroes (in the Od. only of Odysseus).

πτόλις: see πόλις.

πτόρθος: *sapling*, ζ 128†.

πτύγμα (πτύσσω): *fold*, Ε 315†.

πτυκτός (πτύσσω): *folded*, Ζ 169†.

πτύξ, πτυχός (πτύσσω): *fold, layer*, of the layers of a shield, Σ 481 (see cut No. 130); fig., of mountains, *cleft, vale, ravine*, Λ 77, Υ 22, τ 432.

πτύον, gen. πτυόφιν: *winnowing shovel* or *fan*, used to throw up grain and chaff against the wind, Ν 588†.

πτύσσω, aor. part. πτύξᾶσα, mid. ipf. ἐπτύσσοντο: *fold, fold together*; pass., 'were bent,' Ν 134.

πτύω: *spit* forth, part., Ψ 697†.

πτώξ, πτωκός (πτώσσω): *timid*, epith. of the hare, Χ 310; as subst., *hare*, Ρ 676.

πτωσκάζω, inf. -έμεν: *crouch in fear*, Δ 372†.

πτώσσω (cf. πτήσσω, πτώξ), ipf. πτῶσσον: *cower, hide*; ὑπό τινι, 'before' one, Η 129; of a beggar, 'go cringing about,' κατὰ δῆμον, ρ 227, σ 363; trans., ὄρνῖθες νέφεα, 'flee' the clouds, χ 304.

πτωχεύω (πτωχός), ipf. iter. πτωχεύεσκε, fut. part. πτωχεύσων: *be a beggar, beg*; trans., δαῖτα, ρ 11, 19.

πτωχός (πτώσσω): *beggar*-(man), ἀνήρ, φ 327, ξ 400. (Od.)

Πυγμαῖοι (πυγμή, 'Fistlings,' cf. Tom 'Thumb,' 'Thumbkin): the *Pygmies*, a fabulous race of dwarfs or manikins, Γ 6†.

πυγ-μαχίη: *boxing*, Ψ 653 and 665.

πυγ-μάχος: *boxer*, pl., θ 246†. (Cf. cut.)

102

πυγμή (πύξ, cf. pugnus): *fist*, then *boxing, boxing-match*, Ψ 669†.

πυγούσιος (πυγών): *a cubit long*; ἔνθα καὶ ἔνθα, i. e. a cubit square, κ 517 and λ 25.

πύελος: *feeding-trough*, τ 553†.

πυθέσθαι: see πυνθάνομαι.

πυθμήν, ένος: *bottom* of a vase, *trunk, butt* of a tree, Λ 635, ν 122, 372.

πύθω, fut. πύσει, pass. pres. πύθεται: *cause to rot*, pass., *rot, decay*.

Πῡθώ, Πῡθών, dat. Πῡθοῖ, acc. Πῡθώ and Πυθῶνα: *Pytho*, the most ancient name of the oracle of Apollo on Mt. Parnassus near Delphi in Phocis, Β 519, Ι 405, θ 80.

Πῡθῶδε: *to Pytho*, λ 581.

πύκα: *thickly, strongly*, Ι 588; met., *wisely, carefully*; φρονεῖν, τρέφειν, Ε 70.

πυκάζω (πύκα), opt. πυκάζοιεν, aor. πύκασα, pass. perf. part. πεπυκασμένος: *cover closely* or *thickly, wrap up*; τινὰ νεφέλῃ, Ρ 551; of a helmet, πύκασε κάρη, Κ 271; σφέας αὐτούς, 'crowd' themselves, μ 225; pass., of chariots 'overlaid' with gold, etc., Ψ 503; met., of grief, τινὰ φρένας, 'overshadow' the soul, Θ 124.

πυκι-μηδής, ές (μῆδος): *deep-counselled*, α 438†.

πυκινός, πυκνός (πύκα): *close, thick, compact*; θώρηξ, ἀσπίς, χλαῖνα, ξ 521; with reference to the particles or parts of anything, *νέφος*, *φάλαγγες*, *στίχες*; of a bed with several coverings, 'closely spread,' I 621; *πυκινὰ πτερά*, perhaps to be taken adverbially, of the movements in close succession (see below), β 151, etc.; of thick foliage, *ὄζος*, *θάμνος*, *ὕλη*; 'closely shut,' 'packed,' *θύρη*, *χηλός*, Ξ 167, ν 68; metaph., 'strong,' 'sore,' *ἄχος*, *ἄτη*, Π 599, Ω 480; *wise*, *prudent*, *sagacious*, *φρένες*, *μήδεα*, *ἔπος*, etc.—Adv., **πυκ(ι)νόν, πυκ(ι)νά, πυκινῶς,** *close*, *fast*, *rapidly*, *often*; also *deeply*, *wisely*.

Πυλαιμένης: king of the Paphlagonians, an ally of the Trojans, father of Harpalion, B 851, N 643. He is slain by Menelāus, E 576, but appears later as still living, N 658.

Πυλαῖος: son of Lethus, a chief of the Pelasgians, B 842†.

πυλ-άρτης, ᾱο: *gate-closer*, *doorkeeper* of the nether world, w. *κρατερός*, epith. of Hades, Θ 367, λ 277.

Πυλάρτης: the name of two Trojans, one overcome by Ajax, Λ 491; the other by Patroclus, Π 696.

πυλα-ωρός (root *Ϝορ*, *ὁράω*): *gatekeeper*, pl. (Il.)

πύλη: *gate*, *gates*, always pl., with reference to the two wings. Poetically *'Αΐδāο* (periphrasis for death), *οὐρανοῦ*, *'Ολύμπου*, *'Ηελίοιο*, *ὀνείρειαι*, *ὀνείρων*, δ 809, τ 562, E 646, ξ 156.

Πυληγενής: see *Πυλοιγενής*.

Πυλήνη: a town in Aetolia, B 639†.

Πύλιος: *of Pylus;* **Πύλιοι**, the *Pylians*, H 134, Λ 753, Ψ 633, ο 216.

Πυλοιγενής, ές: *born in Pylos*, *bred in Pylus*, Nestor, *ἵπποι*, B 54, Ψ 303.

Πυλόθεν: *from Pylos*, π 323†.

Πυλόνδε: *to Pylos*.

Πύλος: *Pylos*.—(1) a city in Messenian Elis, on the coast opposite the southern extremity of the island of Sphacteria; the home of Neleus and Nestor. Under the epith. 'sandy' Pylos the entire region is designated, B 77, γ 4.—(2) a city in Triphylia of Elis, south of the Alphēus, Λ 671 ff. —(3) see *πύλος*.

πύλος: *ἐν πύλῳ*, E 397†, explained by those who prefer not to read *ἐν Πύλῳ* as *in the gateway*, i. e. at the gates of Hades.

Πύλων: a Trojan, slain by Polypoetes, M 187†.

πύματος: *last*, of time or place, *ἄντυξ ἀσπίδος*, 'outermost,' Z 118, cf. Σ 608; 'root' of the nose, N 616.—Adv., **πύματον, πύματα,** joined with *ὕστατον*, *ὕστατα*, X 203, δ 685.

πυνθάνομαι, πεύθομαι, opt. 3 pl *πευθοίατο*, ipf. *πυνθανόμην*, (ἐ)*πεύθετο*, fut. *πεύσομαι*, aor. 2 (ἐ)*πυθόμην*; opt. redup. *πεπύθοιτο*, perf. *πέπυσμαι*, *πέπυσσαι*, plup. (ἐ)*πέπυστο*, du. *πεπύσθην*: *learn* by inquiry, *ascertain*, *hear tell of*; w. gen. (or *ἐκ*) of the person giving the information, also gen. of the person or thing learned about, ν 256, ξ 321; *βοῆς*, 'hear,' Z 465; freq. w. part., 'hear of all this wrangling on your part,' A 257.

πύξ (cf. *πύκα*, *πυκνός*, *πυγμή*): adv., *with the fist*, *at boxing*.

πύξινος (*πύξος*): *of box-wood*, Ω 269†.

πῦρ, *πυρός*: *fire;* pl. **πυρά**, *watch-fires*, Θ 509, 554.

πυρ-άγρη (*ἀγρέω* = *αἱρέω*): *fire-tongs*, γ 434 and Σ 477.

Πυραίχμης: a chief of the Paeonians, an ally of the Trojans, slain by Patroclus, B 848, Π 287.

πυρακτέω: only ipf. *ἐπυράκτεον*, *I brought to a glow*, ι 328†.

Πύρασος: (1) a Trojan, slain by Ajax, Λ 491.—(2) name of a town in Thessaly, B 695.

πυργηδόν: adv., *like a tower*, 'in solid masses.' (Il.)

πύργος: *tower*, *turreted wall;* fig., of Ajax, *πύργος 'Αχαιῶν*, Λ 556; his shield also is compared to a tower, H 219, Λ 485; of a 'column,' 'compact body' of troops, Δ 334.

πυργόω, aor. *πύργωσαν*: *surround with towers*, *fortify*, λ 264†.

πυρετός: *fever*, X 31†.

πυρή (*πῦρ*): *pyre*, *funeral-pile*, Ψ 110–177, 192–258, Ω 786–799. (Cf. cut No. 103, on following page.)

πῡρηφόρος: see *πῡροφόρος*.

πυρι-ήκης, ες (*ἀκή*): *fire-pointed*, *with blazing point*, ι 387†.

πυρί-καυστος (*καίω*): *charred*, N 564†.

Πύρις: a Lycian, slain by Patroclus, Π 416†.

Πυριφλεγέθων: *Pyriphlegethon*, a river of the nether world, κ 513†.

103

πυρ-καϊή (καίω): place where fire is kindled, *funeral-pile.* (Il.)

πύρνον: *wheaten loaf.* (Od.)

πῡρός: *wheat,* often pl.; mentioned only once as food for men, υ 109, but cf. *πύρνον.*

πῡρο-φόρος and **πῡρηφόρος**: *wheat-bearing,* γ 495.

πυρ-πολέω: *tend fires* (watch-fires), part., κ 30†.

πυρσός (πῦρ): *torch, beacon, signal-light,* pl., Σ 211†.

πώ: enclitic adv., always w. neg., οὔ πω, not *yet,* (n)*ever,* οὐ γάρ πω, μὴ δή πω, etc.; also like πώς, οὔ (μή) πω, 'in no wise,' 'by no means.'

πωλέομαι (frequentative of πέλομαι), πώλε(αι), part. πωλεύμενοι, ipf. πωλεύμην, -εῖτο, iter. πωλέσκετο, fut. πωλήσομαι: *frequent* a place, *go and come* to or among, *consort with.*

πῶλος: *foal.*

πῶμα, ατος: *lid, cover,* of a chest, a vase, a quiver, Π 221, β 353, Δ 116. (See the quiver of Heracles in cut.)

104

πώ-ποτε: *ever yet,* always after οὐ, referring to past time.

πῶς: interrog. adv., *how? in what way?* Also with merely exclamatory effect, κ 337. Combined, πῶς γάρ, πῶς δή, πῶς τ' ἄρα, etc.

πώς: enclitic indef. adv., *somehow, in some way;* if *in any way, perchance, perhaps;* w. neg., *by no means.*

πωτάομαι (πέτομαι), ipf. πωτῶντο: *fly,* Μ 287†.

πῶυ, εος, pl. dat. **πώεσι**: *flock,* ὀίων, μήλων.

Ρ.

Ρ. Many words beginning with ρ originally began with two consonants, esp. ϝρ or σρ (ϝρήγνῡμι, σρέω), and the quantitative (metrical) effect of the two letters has been preserved in the frequent doubling of ρ (ἔρρεον). What the initial consonant was cannot always be determined.

ῥά, ῥ': see ἄρα.

ῥάβδος: *rod, wand,* esp. the magic wand of Hermes, Circe, Athēna, Ω 343, κ 238, ν 429; of a fishing-rod, μ 251; pins, Μ 297.

ῥαδαλός: see ῥοδανός.

Ῥαδάμανθυς: *Rhadamanthys,* son of Zeus and brother of Minos, a ruler in Elysium, Μ 322, η 323, δ 564.

ῥαδινός (ϝρ.): *slender, pliant,* Ψ 583†.

ῥαθάμιγξ, ιγγος: pl., *drops;* fig., κονίης, 'particles' of dust, Ψ 502. (Il.)

ῥαίνω, aor. imp. ῥάσσατε, pass. ipf. ῥαίνοντο, perf. 3 pl. ἐρράδαται, plup. ἐρράδατο: *sprinkle, besprinkle.*

ῥαιστήρ, ῆρος (ῥαίω): *hammer,* Σ 477†.

ῥαίω, fut. inf. ῥαισέμεναι, aor. subj. ῥαίσῃ, inf. ῥαῖσαι, pass. pres. opt. ῥαίοιτο, aor. ἐρραίσθη: *shatter*, *dash* (in pieces), πρὸς οὔδεϊ, ι 459; 'wreck,' ζ 326, ε 221.

ῥάκος, εος (Ϝρ.): *ragged garment, tatters.* (Od.)

ῥαπτός: *sewed, patched*, ω 228 and 229.

ῥάπτω, ipf. ῥάπτομεν, aor. ῥάψε, inf. ῥάψαι: *sew, stitch*, or *rivet* together, M 296; met., 'devise,' 'contrive,' Σ 367, γ 118, π 379, 422.

ῥάσσατε: see ῥαίνω.

ῥαφή (ῥάπτω): *seam*, pl., χ 186†.

ῥάχις, ιος: *chine*, back-piece, cut lengthwise along the spine, I 208†.

Ῥέᾱ, Ῥείη: *Rhea*, daughter of Uranus, sister and consort of Cronus, mother of Zeus, Poseidon, Hades, Hera, Demēter, Hestia.

ῥέα, ῥεῖα: *easily; θεοὶ ῥεῖα ζώοντες*, i. e. without the effort entailed by care and trouble, ε 122.

ῥέεθρον (ῥέω): pl., *streams, stream, current; ποταμοῖο ῥέεθρα*, periphrasis for ποταμός.

ῥέζω (Ϝρ., Ϝέργον), ipf. iter. ῥέζεσκον, fut. ῥέξω, aor. ἔρεξα, ἔρρεξε, ῥέξε, subj. ῥέξομεν, pass. aor. inf. ῥεχθῆναι, part. ῥεχθείς, cf. ἔρδω: *do, work, act, μέγα ἔργον*, εὖ or κακῶς τινά, ψ 56; *οὐ κατὰ μοῖραν ἔρεξας*, ι 352; pass., ῥεχθὲν δέ τε νήπιος ἔγνω, 'a thing once done,' P 32; esp., 'do' sacrifice, 'perform,' 'offer,' 'sacrifice,' ἑκατόμβην, θαλύσια, abs. θεῷ, I 535, Θ 250.

ῥέθος, εος: pl., *limbs.* (Il.)

ῥεῖα: see ῥέα.

Ῥείη: see Ῥέᾱ.

Ῥεῖθρον: name of a harbor in Ithaca, α 186†.

ῥέπω (Ϝρ.): *sink* in the scale, used figuratively of the balances of fate, ῥέπε δ' αἴσιμον ἦμαρ Ἀχαιῶν (meaning that their fate was sealed, an expression the converse in form, but the counterpart in sense, of our 'kick the beam'), Θ 72, X 212. (Il.)

ῥερυπωμένος: see ῥυπόω.

ῥεχθείς: see ῥέζω.

ῥέω (σρέϜω), ipf. ἔρρεον, ῥέε, aor. ἐρρύην, ῥύη: *flow, stream;* met., of speech, missiles, hair, A 249, M 159, κ 393.

ῥηγμίν, ῖνος (Ϝρήγνῡμι): *surf, breakers.*

ῥήγνῡμι (Ϝρ., cf. frango), 3 pl. ῥηγνῦσι, ipf. iter. ῥήγνυσκε, fut. ῥήξω, aor. ἔρρηξα, ῥῆξε, mid. pres. imp. ῥήγνυσθε, aor. (ἐρ)ρήξαντο: *break, burst, rend* in twain, different from ἄγνῡμι. Freq. of breaking the ranks of the enemy in battle, φάλαγγας, ὅμῑλον, στίχας, Z 6, Λ 538, O 615.—Mid., *break* for oneself, Λ 90, M 90; *break* intrans., as waves, and fig., 'let break out,' 'let loose,' ἔριδα, Υ 55.

ῥῆγος, εος (Ϝρ.): *rug, blanket*, probably of wool, opp. λίνον, ν 73; often pl., mentioned as covers, cushions, for bed or chairs. (Od. and I 661, Ω 664.) (Cf. the Assyrian and Greek θρόνος with θρῆνυς attached.)

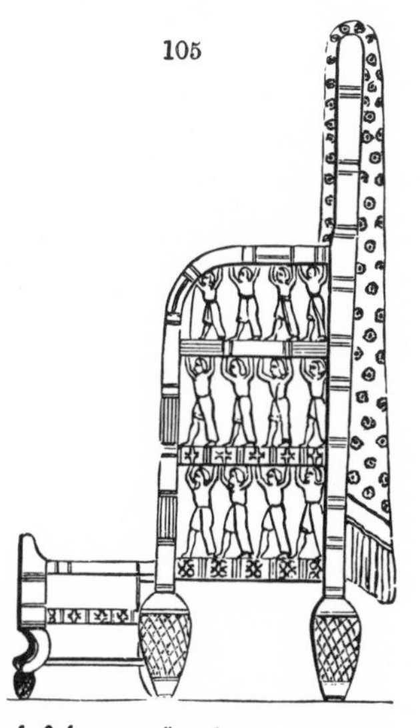
105

ῥηθείς: see εἴρω 1.

ῥηΐδιος (Att. ῥᾴδιος), comp. **ῥηΐτερος,** sup. **ῥηΐτατος** and **ῥήϊστος**: *easy;* w. dat., also foll. by inf.; pers. for impers., ῥηΐτεροι πολεμίζειν ἦσαν Ἀχαιοί, Σ 258.—Adv., **ῥηϊδίως,** sup. **ῥηΐτατα,** Δ 390, τ 577.

ῥηκτός (Ϝρήγνῡμι): *breakable, penetrable, vulnerable*, N 323†.

Ῥήνη: concubine of Oïleus, mother of Medon, B 728†.

ῥηξ-ηνορίη: *might to break* hostile ranks of *men*, ξ 217†.

ῥηξ-ήνωρ, ορος (Ϝρήγνῡμι, ἀνήρ):

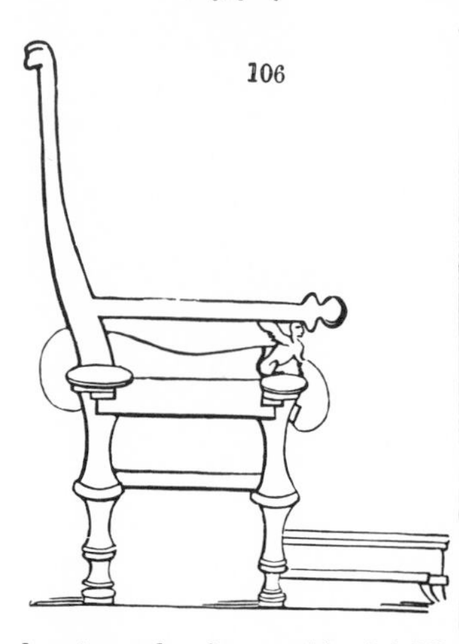

bursting ranks of *men*, epith. of Achilles.

Ῥηξήνωρ: son of Nausithous, and brother of Alcinous, η 63 and 146.

ῥῆσις, ιος (root ϝερ, εἴρω 1): *speaking, speech*, φ 291†.

Ῥῆσος: *Rhesus*, king of the Thracians, slain by Odysseus and Diomed, K 474, 519.

ῥήσσω (cf. ῥήγνῡμι): *stamp*, part., Σ 571†.

ῥητήρ, ῆρος (root ϝερ, εἴρω 1): *speaker*, I 443†.

ῥητός: *spoken, stipulated*, Φ 445†.

ῥήτρη: *stipulation, bargain*, ξ 393†.

ῥῑγεδανός (ϝρῑγέω): *horrible*, Τ 325†.

ῥῑγέω (ϝρῖγος), fut. inf. ῥῑγήσειν, aor. (ἐρ)ρίγησα, perf., w. pres. signif., ἔρρῑγα, subj. ἐρρίγῃσι, plup. ἐρρίγει: properly, to shudder with cold, but in Homer always met., *shudder* (*at*) with fear, *be horrified*, abs., also w. acc., inf., Γ 353; part., Δ 279; μή, ψ 216.

ῥίγιον (ϝρῖγος), comp.: *colder*, ρ 191; met., *more horrible, more terrible*, cf. ἄλγιον.—Sup., **ῥίγιστος,** ῥίγιστα, E 873†.

Ῥίγμος: son of Piroüs, from Thrace, an ally of the Trojans, Υ 485†.

ῥῖγος, εος (cf. frigus): *cold*, ε 472†.

ῥῑγόω, fut. inf. ῥῑγωσέμεν: *be cold*, ξ 481†.

ῥίζα: *root;* fig., of the eye, ι 390.

ῥιζόω, aor. ἐρρίζωσε, pass. perf. ἐρρίζωται: cause to take root, *plant, plant out*, pass., η 122; fig., 'fix firmly,' ν 163. (Od.)

ῥίμφα (ϝρίπτω): *swiftly*.

ῥίν: see ῥίς.

ῥῑνόν and **ῥῑνός** (ϝρ.): *skin* of men, or *hide* of animals, then *shield* of oxhide (with and without βοῶν), Δ 447, M 263; reading and sense doubtful in ε 281 (v. l. ἐρῑνόν, 'cloud'?).

ῥῑνο-τόρος (τορέω): *shield-piercing*, Φ 392†.

ῥίον: *peak, crag, headland*, γ 295.

ῥῑπή (ϝρίπτω): *impulse, flight, rush*, of a stone thrown, a spear, wind and fire, θ 192, Π 589, Φ 12.

Ῥίπη: a town in Arcadia, B 606†.

ῥῑπτάζω (frequentative of ϝρίπτω): *hurl about*, part., Ξ 257†.

ῥίπτω (ϝρ.), ipf. iter. ῥίπτασκον, fut. ῥίψω, aor. ἔρρῑψεν, ῥῖψα: *fling, hurl;* τὶ μετά τινα, 'toss into the hands of,' Γ 378.

ῥίς, ῥῑνός (ϝρ.): *nose*, pl. *nostrils*.

ῥοδανός: *waving, swaying*, Σ 576† (v. l. ῥαδαλόν).

Ῥόδιος: see Ῥόδος.

Ῥοδίος: a river in the Troad, rising in Mt. Ida, M 20†.

ῥοδο-δάκτυλος: *rosy-fingered*, epith. of Eos, goddess of the dawn.

ῥοδόεις, εσσα, εν (ϝρόδον): *rosy*, 'fragrant with roses,' Ψ 186†.

Ῥόδος: *Rhodes*, the celebrated island southwest of Asia Minor, B 654 ff., 667.—**Ῥόδιος,** *of Rhodes*, pl. Ῥόδιοι, the *Rhodians*, B 654.

ῥοή (σρέω): pl., *flood, stream, streams*.

ῥόθιος: *plashing, dashing, surging*, ε 412†.

ῥοιβδέω (ῥοῖβδος, ῥοῖζος), aor. opt. ῥοιβδήσειεν: *gulp, suck in*, μ 106†.

ῥοιζέω, aor. ῥοίζησε: *whistle*, K 502†.

ῥοῖζος (cf. ῥοῖβδος, ῥοιβδέω): *whistling, whizzing*, of arrows, Π 361; of the shepherd's call, ι 315.

ῥοιή: *pomegranate*, tree and fruit, pl., η 115 and λ 589.

ῥόος (σρέω): *flow, stream, current*.

ῥόπαλον (ϝρέπω): *club, cudgel*.

ῥοχθέω, ῥοχθεῖ, ipf. ῥόχθει: *roar*, of the waves, μ 60 and ε 402.

ῥύατο: see ῥύομαι.

ῥυδόν (σρέω): adv., *in floods*, 'enormously,' ο 426†.

ῥύη: see ῥέω.

ῥυμός (ἐρύω): *pole* of a chariot, Z 40, K 505. (Cf. cut No. 42 for the method of attaching the pole; cf. also Nos. 45, 92.)

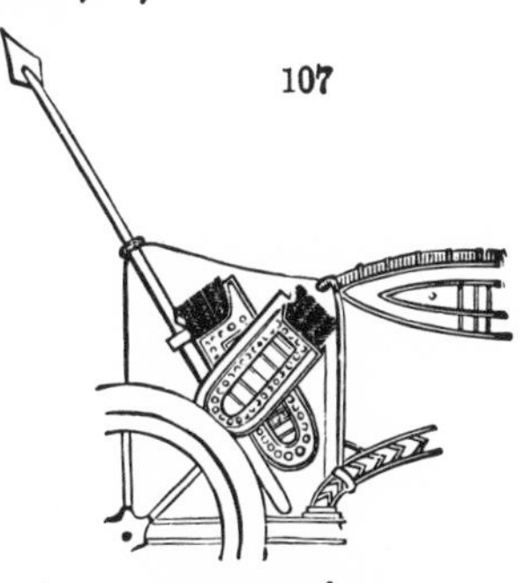

107

ῥῦομαι (ἐρύω), inf. ῥῦεσθαι and ῥῦσθαι, ipf. ῥῦετο, 3 pl. ῥῦατ(ο), iter. ῥύσκευ, aor. ῥυσάμην, (ἐρ)ρύσατο, imp. ῥῦσαι: *rescue, save; ὑπέκ, ὑπό τινος*, 'out of,' 'from,' M 107, P 645; in general, 'protect,' 'cover,' 'hide,' ζ 129, P 224, M 8; *detain*, ψ 244.

ῥυπάω, ῥυπόω, part. ῥυπόωντα: *be dirty, soiled.*

ῥύπος, pl. **ῥύπα**: *dirt*, ζ 93†.

ῥῦσαι, ῥύσατο, ῥῦσθαι: see ῥύομαι.

ῥύσιον (ἐρύω): pl., *booty* dragged away, of cattle, Λ 674†.

ῥυσίπτολις: see ἐρυσίπτολις.

ῥύσκευ: see ῥύομαι.

ῥῦσός (ἐρύω): *wrinkled*, I 503†.

ῥυστάζω (ἐρύω), ipf. iter. ῥυστάζεσκεν: *drag about, maltreat*, π 109.

ῥυστακτύς, ύος (ῥυστάζω): *dragging, maltreatment*, σ 224†.

ῥῦτήρ, ῆρος (ἐρύω): (1) *one who draws, drawer* of a bow, φ 173, σ 262.—(2) *guard*, ρ 187 and 223.—(3) *reins drawn tight, taut reins*, which in Π 475 are described as having been drawn to one side and entangled by the fall of the παρήορος.

Ῥύτιον: a town in Crete, B 648†.

ῥῦτός (ἐρύω): *dragged, hauled*, of stones too large to carry, ζ 267 and ξ 10.

ῥωγαλέος: *torn, ragged.*

ῥώξ, ῥωγός (Ϝρήγνῡμι): pl., *clefts, loop-holes* or windows in the rear wall of the μέγαρον, to light the stairway behind them, χ 143. (See cut No. 83.)

ῥώομαι (cf. r u o), ipf. (ἐρ)ρώοντο, aor. ἐρρώσαντο: *move quickly; γούνατα, κνῆμαι*, ψ 3, Σ 411; of dancing, marching in armor, horses' manes fluttering, Ω 616, ω 69, Ψ 367.

ῥωπήιον (ῥώψ): pl., *undergrowth.*

ῥωχμός (ῥώξ): *place gullied out, hollow*, Ψ 420†.

ῥώψ, ῥωπός: pl., *twigs, brushwood.*

σ' = (1) σέ.—(2) rarely **σοί**, A 170, Φ 122, cf. δῶκε δέ μ', κ 19.—(3) σά, α 356.

Σαγγάριος: *Sangarius*, a river flowing through Bithynia and Phrygia, and emptying into the Euxine, Γ 187, Π 719.

σαίνω, ipf. σαῖνον, aor. ἔσηνε: *wag* the tail, *fawn upon*, w. dat. of the tail wagged, ρ 302.

σακέσ-παλος (πάλλω): *shield-swinging*, E 126†.

σάκος, εος: the great *shield.* (See cuts Nos. 9, 16, 17.)

Σαλαμίς: *Salamis*, the island near Athens, home of Telamonian Ajax, B 557, H 199.

Σαλμωνεύς: son of Aeolus and father of Tyro, λ 236†.

σάλπιγξ, γγος: *trumpet*, Σ 219†.

σαλπίζω: only aor., σάλπιγξεν, fig., *resounded, quaked*, Φ 388†.

Σάμη: *Same*, an island near Ithaca, perhaps Cephallenia or a part of Cephallenia, ι 24, π 249.

Σάμος: (1) = Σάμη, B 634.—(2) Θρηικίη, *Samothrace*, an island off the coast of Thrace, N 12.

σανίς, ἴδος: *board, plank;* pl., esp. the wings of folding-doors, *doors; scaffolding, stage,* φ 51.

σάος: only comp., **σαώτερος,** *more safe(ly),* A 32†.

σαο-φροσύνη: *sound sense, discretion;* 'bring into ways of reason,' ψ 13.

σαό-φρων (Att. σώφρων): *sound-minded, discreet,* δ 158 and Φ 462.

σαόω (σάος), **σώω, σώζω,** subj. σόῃς, σόῃ (σόῳς, σόῳ), 3 pl. σόωσι (σάωσι, σοῶσι), imp. σάω, part. σώζων, σώοντες, ipf. σάω (σάου), iter. σώεσκον, fut. σαώσω, inf. σαωσέμεν(αι), aor. (ἐ)σάωσα, mid. fut. σαώσεαι, pass. aor. 3 pl. ἐσάωθεν, imp. σαωθήτω, inf. σαωθῆναι: *save, preserve, deliver,* mid., *oneself,* ε 490, Π 363; freq. implying motion, ἐκ πολέμου, τηλόθεν, ἐς προχοάς, ἐπὶ νῆα, γ 231, P 692, φ 309.

σαπήῃ: see σήπω.

σαρδάνιον: neut. adj. as adv., *sardonically,* of a bitter, sarcastic smile, υ 302†

σάρξ, σαρκός: *flesh,* τ 450; elsewhere pl.

Σαρπηδών: *Sarpēdon,* son of Zeus, leader of the Lycians, an ally of the Trojans, slain by Patroclus, B 876, E 633, 658, M 392, Π 464, 480 ff., Ψ 800.

Σατνιόεις: a forest stream in Mysia, Z 34, Ξ 445, Φ 87.

Σάτνιος: son of Enops, wounded by Ajax, Ξ 443†.

σαυρωτήρ, ῆρος: a *spike* at the butt-end of a spear, by means of which it could be stuck in the ground, K 153†. (See cut No. 4.)

σάφα (σαφής): *clearly, plainly, for certain.*

σάω, σαῶσαι: see σαόω.

σαώτερος: see σάος.

σβέννῡμι, aor. 1 ἔσβεσεν, σβέσαν, inf. σβέσσαι, aor. 2 ἔσβη: aor. 1, trans., *quench, extinguish,* Ψ 237; then *quell, calm, allay,* I 678, Π 621.—Aor. 2, intrans., of fire, *go out,* I 471; of wind, *go down, cease,* γ 182.

-σε = -δε, a suffix denoting motion toward, *to,* κεῖσε, πόσε, κυκλόσε, ὑψόσε, etc.

σεβάζομαι (σέβας), aor. σεβάσσατο: *stand in awe of, fear, scruple,* Z 167 and 417.

σέβας: *awe, reverence, dread;* then 'astonishment,' 'wonder,' γ 123, δ 75.

σέβομαι, σέβεσθε: *feel awe, scruple, be ashamed,* Δ 242†.

σέθεν: see σύ.

σεῖ(ο), σεῦ: see σύ.

σειρή (root σερ, εἴρω 2): *cord.*

Σειρήν, pl. Σειρῆνες, du. Σειρήνοιιν: pl., the *Sirens,* two in number, singing maidens, by their enchanting song luring mariners to destruction, μ 39 ff., 158, 167, 198, ψ 326. (The conception of the Sirens as bird-footed and three in number, as seen in the cut, is post-Homeric.)

108

σείω, ipf. σεῖον, aor. σεῖσε, part. σείσᾱσα, pass. pres. part. σειόμενος, ipf. σείετο, ἐσσείοντο, mid. aor. σείσατο: *shake, brandish;* σανίδας, of no gentle knocking, I 583; ζυγόν, of horses as they run, γ 486; pass. often, of spears, a forest, Ξ 285; mid., 'moved herself,' Θ 199.

Σέλαγος: the father of Amphīus, from Paesus, E 612†.

σέλας, αος: *brightness, light, gleam, radiance,* of fire, lightning, the eyes in anger, P 739, Θ 76, T 17.

σελήνη (cf. σέλας): *moon.*

Σεληπιάδης: *son of Selepius,* Evēnus, B 693†.

σέλῑνον: *parsley,* B 776 and ε 72.

Σελλήεις: (1) a river in Elis near Ephyra, B 659, O 531.—(2) a river in the Troad near Arisbe, B 839, M 97.

Σελλοί: the *Selli,* priests of Zeus at Dodōna, Π 234†.

Σεμέλη: *Semele,* daughter of Cadmus and mother of Dionȳsus by Zeus, Ξ 323 and 325.

σέο: see σύ.

σεῦα: see σεύω.

σεύω, aor. ἔσσευα, σεῦα, mid. ipf. ἐσσεύοντο, aor. 1 σεύατο, ἐσσεύαντο, subj. σεύωνται, aor. 2 ἔσσυο, ἔσσυτο, σύτο, pass. perf. ἔσσυμαι, part., w. pres. signif. and irreg. accent, ἐσσύμενος: I. act. and mid. aor. 1, *set a going rapidly, chase, drive, start*; of impulsion by the hand of a god, 'swung' him, Υ 325; so of chasing persons down-hill, Ζ 133; driving away animals, ξ 35, Γ 26; making a stone fly, a head roll, Ξ 413, Λ 147; starting or drawing blood, Ε 208.—II. pass. and mid., sometimes even aor. 1, set oneself a going rapidly, *rush, hasten, speed;* w. inf., σεύατο διώκειν, 'made haste' to pursue, Ρ 463, Ψ 198; met., θῡμός μοι ἔσσυται, Κ 484; esp. the part. ἐσσύμενος, *striving, eager, desirous*, w. gen., δ 733, w. inf. δ 416.

σηκάζω (σηκός), pass. aor. 3 pl. σήκασθεν: *pen up*, Θ 131†.

σηκο-κόρος (κορέω): *cleaner of pens* or *folds*, ρ 224†.

σηκός: *pen, fold.*

σῆμα, ατος: *sign, token, mark*, by means of which anything is identified, ψ 188; of the *mark* on a lot, Η 189; a *spot* or *star* on a horse, Ψ 455; mark to show the length of a throw, θ 195; a sign from heaven, *prodigy*, φ 413, Ν 244, Χ 30; a *sepulchre*, Β 814, Η 86; *characters* as a sort of pictorial writing, Ζ 168.

σημαίνω (σῆμα), ipf. σήμαινε, fut. σημανέω, aor. 1 σήμηνε, mid. aor. 1 ἐσημήνατο: *give* the *sign*, hence, *command, dictate*, Α 289; w. gen., Ξ 85; ἐπί τινι, χ 427; trans., *mark, point out*, τέρματα, Ψ 358; mid., *mark* for oneself, something of one's own, Η 175.

σημάντωρ, ορος (σημαίνω): one who gives the sign, *commander, leader*, then *driver, herder*, of horses, cattle, Θ 127, Ο 325.

σήμερον (Att. τήμερον, τῇ ἡμέρᾳ): *to-day.*

σήπω, perf. σέσηπε, pass. aor. subj. σαπήῃ: pass., and perf., *rot, decay.* (Il.)

Σήσαμος: a town in Paphlagonia, Β 853†.

Σηστός: *Sestus*, a Thracian city on the Hellespont, opposite Abȳdus, Β 836†.

σθεναρός (σθένος): *strong*, Ι 505†.

Σθενέλᾱος: son of Ithaemenes, slain by Patroclus, Π 586†.

Σθένελος: *Sthenelus.*—(1) son of Capaneus, and one of the Epigoni ('Descendants') who took Thebes, companion of Diomed, Β 564, Δ 367 ff., Ψ 511, Ι 48.—(2) son of Perseus and Andromeda, father of Eurystheus, Τ 116, 123.

σθένος, εος: *strength;* in periphrasis like βίη, ἴς, σθένος Ἰδομενῆος, i. e. the strong Idomeneus himself, Ν 248, Σ 486, Ψ 827; strength of the spirit, valor, Β 451, Ξ 151; and in general, 'power,' 'might,' 'forces' (army), Σ 274.

σίαλος: *fat hog*, with and without σῦς.

σῑγαλόεις, εσσα, εν: *shining, glistening*, of garments, rugs, reins, room and furniture, Ε 226, ζ 81, ε 86, π 449, σ 206.

σῑγάω: only imp. σίγᾱ, *hush!*

σῑγή: *silence*, only dat. as adv., *still, silently.*

σιδήρεος, σιδήρειος: *of iron; ὀρυμαγδός*, 'of iron weapons,' Ρ 424; fig., οὐρανός, κραδίη, θῡμός, 'hard,' 'unwearied,' etc., Χ 357, Ω 205, μ 280.

σίδηρος: *iron*, epithets, πολιός, αἴθων, ἰόεις, tempered to blue steel; symbol of firmness, inexorableness, τ 494; πολύκμητος, of iron tools or weapons.

Σῑδονίηθεν: *from Sidonia*, Ζ 291†.

Σῑδόνιος: *Sidonian;* as subst., δ 84, 618.—**Σῑδονίη**, *Sidonia*, the district containing the city Sidon, ν 285.

Σῑδών, ῶνος: *Sidon*, the principal city of the Phoenicians, ο 425.

Σιδών, όνος: pl., Σιδόνες, the *Sidonians*, Ψ 743.

σίζω (cf. 'sizzle'), ipf. σίζ(ε): *hiss*, ι 394†.

Σῑκανίη: *Sicania*, earlier name of Sicily, ω 307†.

Σικελός: *Sicilian*, ω 211, 366, 389; pl., the *Sicilians*, υ 383.

Σικυών: *Sicyon*, a city on the south shore of the gulf of Corinth, in the realm of Agamemnon, Β 572, Ψ 299.

Σιμόεις: *Simois.*—(1) a small river

rising in Mt. Ida, and flowing through the Trojan plain into the Scamander, Ε 774, 777, Μ 22, Δ 475, Ζ 4, Υ 52. (See plate V., at end of volume).—(2) the same personified, the god of the river, Φ 307.

Σιμοείσιος: son of the Trojan Anthemion, slain by Ajax, Δ 474 ff.

σίνομαι, ipf. iter. *σινέσκοντο*: *rob, plunder; τινί τι*, μ 114; 'harm' in a spurious verse, Ω 45.

σίντης: *ravening.* (Il.)

Σίντιες ('Plunderers'): the *Sintians*, ancient inhabitants of Lemnos, Α 594, θ 294.

Σίπυλος: *Sipylus*, a branch of the mountain range of Tmolus, near Magnesia, on the borders of Lydia, Ω 615†.

Σίσυφος (redup. from *σοφός*): *Sisyphus*, son of Aeolus, father of Glaucus, and founder of Ephyra (Corinth), renowned for craft and wiles, Ζ 153 ff. He was punished in Hades by rolling the 'resulting' stone up-hill, λ 593.

σῑτέω, mid. ipf. iter. *σῑτέσκοντο*: *feed*, mid., *eat*, ω 209†.

σῖτος: *grain, wheat, wheaten bread*, ι 9, α 139; then in general, *food*, Ω 602, Τ 306.

σῑτο-φάγος: *grain-eating, bread-eating*, ι 191†.

σιφλόω, aor. opt. *σιφλώσειεν*: *deform, ruin*, Ξ 142†.

σιωπάω, inf. *σιωπᾶν*, aor. opt. *σιωπήσειαν*, inf. *σιωπῆσαι*: *keep silence*, ρ 513 and Ψ 568.

σιωπή: *silence*, only dat. as adv., *silently, secretly*, Ξ 310. See *ἀκήν.*

σκάζω, part. du. *σκάζοντε*, mid. inf. *σκάζεσθαι*: *limp.* (Il.)

Σκαιαί: *πύλαι*, and without *πύλαι*, Γ 263; the *Scaean* Gate of Troy, the only gate of the city which Homer mentions by name. It appears to have faced the Greek camp, affording a view over the Trojan plain, Γ 145, 149, 263, Ζ 237, 307, 393, Ι 354, Λ 170, Π 712, Σ 453, Χ 6, 360.

σκαιός (cf. scaevus): *left* (hand), Α 501; *western*, γ 295.

σκαίρω: *skip*, κ 412; *ποσί*, 'with tripping feet,' Σ 572.

Σκαμάνδριος: (1) *of the Scamander; πεδίον, λειμών*, Β 465, 467.—(2) *Scamandrius*, the real name of Hector's son Astyanax, Ζ 402.—(3) a Trojan, the son of Strophius, slain by Menelāus, Ε 49.

Σκάμανδρος: *Scamander*, a river rising in Mt. Ida, called by the gods (ancient name) Xanthus, Ξ 434, Υ 74, Χ 147 ff.

Σκάνδεια: name of a harbor in the island of Cythēra, Κ 268†.

Σκάρφη: a place in Locris, near Thermopylae, Β 532†.

σκαφίς, *ίδος* (*σκάπτω*): *bowl*, pl., ι 223†.

σκεδάννῡμι, aor. (*ἐ*)*σκέδασε*, imp. *σκέδασον*: *scatter, disperse; αἷμα, shed*, Η 330.

σκέδασις, *ιος*: *scattering; σκέδασιν θεῖναι* = *σκεδάσαι*, α 116 and υ 225.

σκέλλω, aor. 1 opt. *σκήλειε*: *parch*, Ψ 191†.

σκέλος, *εος*: *πρυμνόν*, upper part of the *thigh*, Π 314†.

σκέπαρνον: *adze*, ε 237 and ι 391.

σκέπας: *shelter; ἀνέμοιο*, 'against the wind,' ζ 210. (Od.)

σκεπάω, *σκεπόωσι*: *shelter against, keep off*, ν 99†.

σκέπτομαι, imp. *σκέπτεο*, aor. *ἐσκέψατο*, part. *σκεψάμενος*: *take a view, look about; ἐς, μετά τι, αἴ κεν*, at or after something, to see whether, etc., Ρ 652; trans., *look out for*, Π 361.

σκηπάνιον = *σκῆπτρον*, Ν 59 and Ω 247.

σκηπτ-οῦχος (*σκῆπτρον, ἔχω*): *sceptre-holding, sceptred*, epithet of kings; as subst., Ξ 93.

σκῆπτρον: *staff* of a wanderer or mendicant, *sceptre* of kings, priests, heralds, judges. (See the cut, No. 109, representing Agamemnon.) When a speaker arose to address the assembly, a sceptre was put into his hands by a herald. Fig., as symbol of royal power and dignity, Β 46; see also β 37, λ 91.

σκήπτω: only mid. pres. part. *σκηπτόμενος, supporting himself, leaning on his staff;* ironically of one transfixed with a spear, Ξ 457.

σκηρίπτω, mid. inf. *-εσθαι*, part. *-όμενος*: *lean upon*, 'push against,' λ 595.

σκιάζω (*σκιή*), aor. subj. *σκιάσῃ*: *overshadow*, Φ 232†.

σκιάω (*σκιή*): only pass. ipf. *σκιόωντο, were darkened.* (Od.)

109

σκίδναμαι (= σκεδάννυμαι), imp. σκίδνασθε, inf. -ασθαι, inf. σκίδνατο, ἐσκίδναντο : intrans., *disperse*, *scatter*, *be diffused*, of persons, dust, foam of the sea, a streamlet, Π 375, Λ 308, η 130.

σκιερός : *shady*, Λ 480 and υ 278.

σκιή : *shadow*, *shade ;* also of the nether shades, ghosts of the departed, κ 495, λ 207.

σκιόεις, εσσα, εν : *affording shade*, *shady; μέγαρα*, *shadowy* halls, an epithet appropriate to a large apartment illuminated by flickering fire-lights.

σκιρτάω (cf. σκαίρω), opt. 3 pl. σκιρτῷεν : *skip*, *gambol*, *bound along*, Υ 226 and 228.

σκολιός : *crooked ;* met., 'perverse,' 'unrighteous' (opp. ἰθύντατα), Π 387†.

σκόλοψ, οπος : *stake* for impaling, *palisades*, Ο 344.

σκόπελος : *cliff*.

σκοπιάζω (σκοπιή), inf. -ἐμεν : *keep a look-out*, *watch*, *spy out*, Κ 40.

σκοπιή (σκοπός) : *look-out place* on a rock or mountain; *watch*, ἔχειν, θ 302.

σκοπός (σκέπτομαι) : *watchman*, *watch*, *look-out*, *scout*, *spy ;* also of an overseer or person in charge, Ψ 359, χ 396 ; *mark* to shoot at, *target*, χ 6 ; ἀπὸ σκοποῦ, see ἀπό.

σκότιος : *in the dark*, *in secret*, Ζ 24†.

σκοτο-μήνιος (σκότος, μήν) : *dark* from the absence of *moonlight*, *moonless*, νύξ, ξ 457†.

σκότος : *darkness*, *gloom ;* often in relation to death, Δ 461, Ε 47.

σκυδμαίνω, inf. -έμεν = σκύζομαι, Ω 592†.

σκύζομαι, imp. σκύζευ, inf. -εσθαι, part. -όμενος : *be wroth*, *incensed*, *indignant*, τινί.

σκύλαξ, ακος : *whelp*, *puppy*. (Od.)

Σκύλλη : *Scylla*, daughter of Crataeis, a monster inhabiting a sea-cave opposite Charybdis, μ 85, 108, 125, 223, 235, ψ 328.

σκύμνος : *whelp* of a lion, pl., Σ 319†.

Σκῦρος : *Scyros*. — (1) an island northwest of Chios, with a city of the same name, λ 509, Τ 326.—**Σκῦρόθεν,** *from Scyros*, Τ 332.—(2) a town in Lesser Phrygia, Ι 668.

σκῦτος, εος : *hide*, *leather*, ξ 34†.

σκῦτο-τόμος : *leather-cutter*, *leather-worker*, Η 221†.

σκύφος : rude *cup*, for drinking, ξ 112†.

σκώληξ, ηκος : *earth-worm*, Ν 654†.

σκῶλος : *pointed stake*, Ν 564†.

Σκῶλος : a place in Boeotia, Β 497†.

σκώψ, σκωπός : horned *owl*, ε 66†.

σμαραγέω, aor. subj. σμαραγήσῃ : *roar*, *thunder*, *re-echo*, of the sea, storm, meadow full of cranes. (Il.)

σμερδαλέος : *fearful*, *terrible*, to look upon, δράκων, λέων, etc.—Adv., **σμερδαλέον, σμερδαλέα,** δέδορκεν, Χ 95 ; elsewhere of sounds.

σμερδνός = σμερδαλέος, Ε 472.—Adv., **σμερδνόν,** βοᾶν, Ο 687, 732.

σμήχω, ipf. ἔσμηχε : *wipe off*, *cleanse*, ζ 226†.

σμῑκρός = μῑκρός, Ρ 757.

Σμινθεύς, voc. Σμινθεῦ : *Smintheus*, epith. of Apollo, explained by ancient commentators as meaning destroyer of field-mice (σμίνθοι). (The cut, showing a mouse at work, is reproduced from the tetradrachm of Metapontum.)

110

σμῡ́χω, aor. inf. σμῦξαι, pass. pres opt. σμῡ́χοιτο : *destroy* by fire, *consume*, *burn* down, Ι 653 and Χ 411.

σμῶδιξ, ιγγος: bloody *wale, weal*, B 267 and Ψ 716.

σόῃ: see σαόω.

σοῖο: see σός.

σόλος: mass of cast iron used as a *quoit*, Ψ 826, 839, 844.

Σόλυμοι: the *Solymi*, a Lycian tribe, Z 184, 204, ε 283.

σόος (σάος): *safe, sound*, see σῶς.

σορός: *funeral-urn*, Ψ 91†.

σός, σή, σόν, gen. σοῖο: *thy, thine*, usually without article, with art., A 185, Z 457; neut. as subst., ἐπὶ σοῖσι, 'thy possessions,' β 369; σὸς πόθος, σὴ ποθή, longing 'for thee,' T 321, λ 202.

Σούνιον: *Sunium*, the southernmost promontory of Attica, γ 278†.

σοφίη (σοφός): *skill, accomplishment*, O 412†.

σόῳς: see σαόω.

Σπάρτη: *Sparta*, the principal city of Laconia, residence of Menelāus and Helen. Epith., εὐρεῖα, **καλλιγύναιξ**, λ 460, ν 412, B 582, Δ 52, α 93, β 214, 359.—**Σπάρτηθεν,** *from Sparta*, β 327, δ 10.—**Σπάρτηνδε,** *to Sparta*, α 285.

σπάρτον (cf. σπεῖρον): pl., *ropes*, B 135†.

σπάω, aor. ἔσπασα, σπάσε, mid. aor. (ἐ)σπα(σ)σάμην, pass. aor. part. σπασθέντος: *pull* up or out, *draw* forth or away; mid., for oneself, something of one's own, β 321, κ 166, 439.

σπεῖο: see ἕπω.

σπεῖος: see σπέος.

σπεῖρον (cf. **σπάρτον, σπείρω**): any wrap, *garment, shroud, sail*, ε 318, ζ 269.

σπεῖσαι, σπείσατε: see σπένδω.

Σπειώ: a Nereid, Σ 40†.

σπένδω, subj. 2 sing. σπένδῃσθα, ipf. iter. σπένδεσκον, aor. ἔσπεισα, σπεῖσαν, iter. σπείσασκε, imp. σπεῖσον: *pour* a drink-offering, οἶνον, ὕδατι, 'with water,' *make a libation*, Διί, θεοῖς. Unmixed wine was poured upon the ground or on the altar (μ 363) before drinking. δέπαι, 'with (from) the goblet,' Ψ 196, η 137.

σπέος, σπεῖος, gen. σπείους, dat. σπῆι, pl. dat. σπέσσι and σπήεσσι: *cave, cavern, grotto*; pl., of one with many parts, π 232.

σπέρμα, ατος (σπείρω): *seed, germ*; fig., **πυρός**, ε 490†.

Σπερχειός: *Spercheius*, a river in Thessaly; as river-god the father of Menestheus, Π 174, 176, Ψ 144.

σπέρχω, mid. opt. 3 pl. σπερχοίατ(ο): *speed, drive fast*, intrans. and mid. (freq. the part.), **ἄελλαι, ἐρετμοῖς, νηῦς**, N 334, ν 22, 115.

σπέσθαι: see ἕπω.

σπεύδω, inf. σπευδέμεν, aor. **σπεῦσε**, imp. σπεύσατε, subj. σπεύσομεν, mid. fut. σπεύσομαι: *be quick, hasten*; σπεῦσε πονησάμενος τὰ ἃ ἔργα, 'hastily performed,' ι 250; 'struggle for,' **περί** τινος, P 121; trans., *hurry*, **τί, γάμον**, τ 137.

σπῆι, σπήεσσι: see σπέος.

σπιδής, ές: *broad*, Λ 754† (v. l. ἀσπιδέος).

σπιλάς, άδος: pl., *reefs*. (Od.)

σπινθήρ, ῆρος: *spark*, pl., Δ 77†.

σπλάγχνον: pl., *inwards*, the nobler parts of the animal, esp. heart, liver, and lungs. While other parts of the victim were burning on the altar, these were roasted and tasted preliminary to the sacrificial banquet, A 464, γ 9.

σπόγγος: *sponge*, Σ 414, α 111.

σποδιή: *ash-heap*, ε 488†.

σποδός: *ashes*, ι 375†.

σπονδή: *drink-offering, libation*, see σπένδω. Then a *treaty*, ratified by libations, pl., B 341 and Δ 159.

σπουδή (σπεύδω): earnest *effort*; ἀπὸ σπουδῆς, 'in earnest,' H 359; ἄτερ σπουδῆς, 'without difficulty,' φ 409; σπουδῇ, *eagerly, quickly*; also *with difficulty, hardly*, γ 297.

σταδίη: see στάδιος.

στάδιος (ἵστημι): ὑσμίνη, standing fight, *close combat*; also **ἐν** σταδίῃ alone, H 241, N 514, O 283.

στάζω, aor. στάξε, imp. στάξον: *drop, instil*, T 39, 348, 354.

στάθμη (ἵστημι): chalk *line*; **ἐπὶ** στάθμην ἰθύνειν, straighten or make true 'to the line,' phrase used of various mechanical operations, ε 245, φ 121.

σταθμός (ἵστημι): any standing-place or thing that stands, hence *stall, pen*, or *fold* for animals, also the shepherd's *lodge*, B 470, T 377, ρ 20; so *post, door-post*, Ξ 167, δ 838; *weight* for the balance, M 434.—**σταθμόνδε,** *to the stall, homeward*, ι 451.

στάμεναι: see ἵστημι.

σταμῖνες, dat. *σταμίνεσσιν*: *braces* in a boat, enabling the ribs to resist the inward pressure of the water, ε 252†. (In plate IV., however, the *σταμῖνες* are taken as the same as ribs.)

στάν: see ἵστημι.

στάξ(ε): see *στάζω*.

στᾶς: see ἵστημι.

στατός (ἵστημι): ἵππος, *stalled* horse. (Il.)

σταυρός: *stake, pale*, pl., Ω 453 and ξ 11.

σταφυλή: *bunch of grapes*.

σταφύλη: *plummet; σταφύλῃ ἐπὶ νῶτον ἐΐσαι*, matched to a hair in height (plumb-equal), B 765†.

στάχυς, υος: *ear of grain*, pl., Ψ 598†.

στέαρ, *στέᾱτος*: *hardened fat, tallow*, φ 178 and 183.

στείβω, ipf. *στεῖβον*: *tread, stamp, trample* upon, Λ 534; of washing clothes by foot-power, ζ 92.

στεῖλα: see *στέλλω*.

στειλειή (*στέλλω*): *hole* in an axhead for the helve, φ 422†.

στειλειόν (*στέλλω*): *axe-helve, handle*, ε 236†.

στεῖνος, εος (*στενός*): *close* or *confined space, narrow entrance, narrows*, M 66, Ψ 419.

στείνω (*στενός*), pass. pres. opt. *στείνοιτο*, ipf. *στείνοντο*: pass., *be narrow, too narrow, crowded, dammed, weighed down*, Φ 220, ι 445, σ 386.

στεινωπός (*στενός, ὤψ*): *narrow; ὁδός, narrow pass*, H 143; (sc. *πόντος*), *strait*, μ 234.

στείομεν: see ἵστημι.

1. στεῖρα (*στερεός*): *unfruitful, barren*. (Od.)

2. στεῖρα: fore part of the keel, *stem, cut-water*, A 482, β 428. (See cut No. 31, *e*.)

στείχω (*στίχος, στίχες*), subj. *στείχῃσι*, ipf. *ἔστειχε, στεῖχον*, aor. 2 *ἔστιχον*: *march* up or forward, *go, move;* of the sun, *climb*, λ 17.

στέλλω, opt. *στέλλοιμι*, fut. *στελέω*, aor. *στεῖλα*, mid. aor. *στείλαντο*; *put in order, arrange, make ready, equip, send off, dispatch*, mid., subjectively: *στέλλεσθε*, 'make yourselves ready,' Ψ 285; *ἱστία*, 'took in their' sails, A 433.

στέμμα, *ατος* (*στέφω*): *chaplet* or *fillet* of a priest. Chryses takes the fillet from his head and places it upon his sceptre, because he comes as a suppliant, A 14. (The cut shows the band in two positions—as extended at full length, and as wrapped around the head. In the second representation the ends should hang down by the sides of the head below the ears, A 28.)

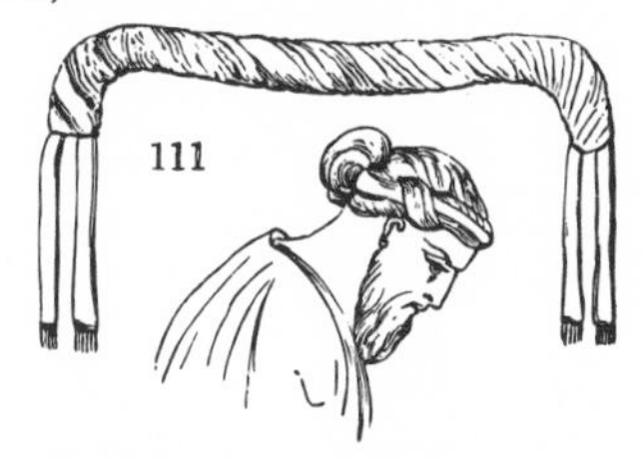

στενάχεσχ': see *στενάχω*.

στεναχίζω, mid. ipf. *στεναχίζετο*: *sigh, groan, resound* with groans, κ 454.

στενάχω (*στένω*), ipf. iter. *στενάχεσκε*, mid. ipf. *στενάχοντο*: *sigh, groan* act. and mid.; act. also trans., *lament, τινά*, T 132; fig. of torrents, and of horses, Π 391, 393.

Στέντωρ: *Stentor*, whose voice was as loud as the united cry of 50 men, E 785†.

στένω (*στενός*), ipf. *ἔστενε*: *sigh, groan*, the bursting of pent-up breath and emotion, cf. *στείνω*.—Fig. of the sea, Ψ 230.

στερεός, comp. *στερεώτερος*: *hard, stiff; λίθος, βοέη*, P 493; fig., *ἔπεα, κραδίη*, M 267, ψ 103.—Adv., **στερεῶς,** *firmly, obstinately*, Ψ 42.

στερέω, aor. inf. *στερέσαι*: *deprive; τινά τινος*, ν 262†.

στέρνον: *breast, chest*.

στεροπή (*ἀστεροπή, ἀστράπτω*): *lightning;* then the *gleam, sheen* of metals, T 363, δ 72, ξ 268.

στεροπ-ηγερέτα: (if from *ἐγείρω*) *waker of lightning*, (if from *ἀγείρω*) *gatherer of lightning, lightning-compeller*, Π 298†.

στεῦμαι, *στεῦται*, ipf. **στεῦτο**: denotes the expression of a wish by a gesture, *have the appearance, make as if*, foll. by inf., regularly the fut., once aor., 'pretends to have heard,' ρ 525; διψάων, 'stood as if thirsty,' λ 584; in general, *engage, threaten, promise,* τινί, E 832.

στεφάνη (στέφω): that which surrounds, encircles anything at the top, as if it were a *crown.* Hence (1) a woman's *head-band,* Σ 597. (See cuts Nos. 16, 40, 41.)—(2) *brim* or *visor* of a helmet, *helmet,* Λ 96, K 30, H 12. (See cuts Nos. 12, 79, 80, 81, 86, 116.)—(3) of the *edge* of a cliff, N 138.

στέφανος (στέφω): *crown, ring,* N 736†. See στεφάνη.

στεφανόω (στέφανος), pass. perf. ἐστεφάνωται, plup. -το: *put around as a crown;* the pass. is to be understood literally, but it may be paraphrased 'encircles,' 'encompasses,' etc., κ 195, Λ 36, E 739, O 153; τά τ' οὐρανὸς ἐστεφάνωται, 'with which the heaven is crowned,' Σ 485.

στέφω (cf. stipo): properly to *stuff* or *set close around, put on* as a crown, *crown* with (cf. στεφανόω), Σ 205; fig., θ 170.

στέωμεν, στῇ, στήῃ: see ἵστημι.

στῆθος, εος, στήθεσφι: *breast;* as source of voice and breath, Δ 430, I 610; pl., often fig., as seat of the heart, Ξ 140, I 256, K 95, A 189; hence of passions, emotions, reason.

στήλη (στέλλω): *pillar,* N 437; esp., *grave stone, monument* (cf. cut), Π 457, M 259.

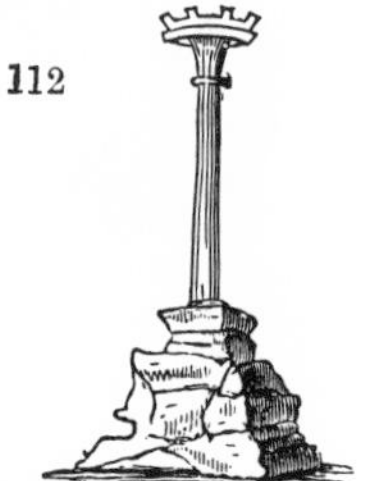

112

στήμεναι: see ἵστημι.

στηρίζω (στερεός), aor. (ἐ)στήριξα, mid. aor. inf. στηρίξασθαι, plup. ἐστήρικτο: *set* or *fix firmly,* Λ 28, Δ 443; intrans. and mid., *support oneself* or *stand firmly,* Φ 242; κακὸν κακῷ, 'was piled upon,' Π 111.

στιβαρός (στείβω), comp. στιβαρώτερος: *close-pressed, trodden firm, firm, compact, strong,* of limbs, weapons.—Adv., **στιβαρῶς,** M 454.

στίβη (στείβω): *rime, hoar-frost,* ε 467 and ρ 25.

στίλβω (cf. στεροπή): only part., *glistening, glittering;* ἐλαίῳ, Σ 596; fig., κάλλεϊ, etc., Γ 392, ζ 237.

στιλπνός: *sparkling,* Ξ 351†.

στίξ (Att. στίχος), assumed nom., gen. στιχός: *row, rank,* or *file,* of warriors, dancers, Σ 602; ἐπὶ στίχας, 'in ranks'; κατὰ στίχας, 'by ranks,' B 687, Γ 113, 326.

στιχάομαι, ipf. ἐστιχόωντο: *move in ranks, march, advance,* of soldiers, herdsmen, ships, Σ 577, B 516.

Στιχίος: an Athenian leader, slain by Hector, N 195, O 329, 331.

στόμα, ατος: *mouth;* ἀνὰ στόμα ἔχειν, διὰ στόμα ἄγεσθαι, phrases relating to utterance, B 250, Ξ 91; fig., of the *mouth* of rivers or harbors, *point* of a lance, O 389; ἠιόνος, 'opening,' 'inlet,' Ξ 36.

στόμαχος (στόμα): *throat, gullet.* (Il.)

στοναχέω (στοναχή), aor. inf. στοναχῆσαι: *sigh, lament,* Σ 124†.

στοναχή (στενάχω): *sighing, groaning,* often pl.

στοναχίζω: see στεναχίζω.

στονόεις, εσσα, εν: full of, or causing sighs and groans, *mournful, grievous,* ἀοιδή, βέλεα, Ω 721, Θ 159.

στόνος (στένω): *sighing, groaning.*

στορέννῡμι, στρώννῡμι, aor. (ἐ)στόρεσα, pass. perf. ἔστρωμαι, plup. ἔστρωτο: *spread, lay* (sternere), a bed, couch, carpet; 'lay,' 'calm,' the waves, γ 158.

Στρατίη: a town in Arcadia, B 606†.

Στρατίος: a son of Nestor, γ 413 and 439.

στρατός (στρώννῡμι), gen. στρατόφιν: *army, host,* β 30. In the Iliad στρατός is the encamped army of the Greeks before Troy, the 1186 ships, with streets throughout the camp, K 66. The tents or barracks stood parallel with the ships, and opposite the intervals between them, O 653 ff. At first the camp had no wall, the presence of Achilles rendering such defence needless, but after his withdrawal from warfare, by the advice of

Nestor (H 436–441), a massive wall was built, with gates and towers, M 118–123.

στρατόομαι, ipf. στρατόωντο: *be encamped, take the field,* 'conduct an expedition.' (Il.)

στρεπτός (στρέφω): *twisted, braided;* fig., γλῶσσα, 'voluble,' Υ 248; φρένες, θεοί, *to be turned, placable,* Ο 203, Ι 497.

στρεύγομαι (στράγγω, cf. s t r i n g o): *be exhausted* drop by drop, *be wearied out,* inf., Ο 512, μ 341.

στρεφε-δῑνέω (στρέφω, δῑνέω): only pass. aor. 3 pl., στρεφεδίνηθεν δέ οἱ ὄσσε, his eyes *whirled round and round,* everything was in a whirl before his eyes, Π 792†.

στρέφω, aor. στρέψα, iter. στρέψασκον, mid. ipf. ἐστρέφετο, fut. inf. στρέψεσθαι, pass. aor. ἐστρέφθην: *turn* around the other way (more than τρέπω), *twist;* of a chariot in battle or the race, Ψ 323; intrans, of ploughing, Σ 544, 546; mid. and pass., *turn oneself about* (to and fro), *twist,* Ω 5, Μ 42; 'twisting myself' into his wool, ι 435.

στρέψασκον: see στρέφω.

στρόμβος (στρέφω): *top,* Ξ 413†.

στρουθός: *sparrow.* (Il.)

στροφάλιγξ, λιγγος (στρέφω): *eddy, whirl,* of dust.

στροφαλίζω: *twirl, ply,* σ 315†.

Στρόφιος: the father of Scamandrius, Ε 49†.

στρόφος (στρέφω): *cord, rope.* (Od.)

στρώννῡμι: see στορέννῡμι.

στρωφάω (στρέφω), στρωφῶσι, mid. inf. στρωφᾶσθαι, ipf. στρωφᾶτο: *turn constantly;* ἠλάκατα, ζ 63, ρ 97; mid., intrans., *keep turning, tarry, dwell* (v e r s a r i), κατ' αὐτούς, fighting among them, Ν 557.

στυγερός (στυγέω): *abominable, hateful, hated.* Adv. στυγερῶς.

στυγέω, aor. 2 ἔστυγον, aor. 1 opt. στύξαιμι: *abominate, loathe, hate; κατὰ* (adv.) δ' ἔστυγον αὐτήν, 'were disgusted' at the sight of her, κ 113; aor. 1 is causative, *make hateful* or *horrible,* λ 502.

Στύμφηλος: a town in Arcadia, Β 608†.

Στύξ, Στυγός ('River of Hate'): the *Styx,* a river of the nether world, by which the gods swore their most solemn oaths, Β 755, κ 514, Θ 369, Ξ 271, Ο 37.

Στύρα, pl.: a town in Euboea, Β 539†.

στυφελίζω, aor. (ἐ)στυφέλιξα, pass. pres. part. στυφελιζομένους: *smite, knock about, thrust rudely* from, Α 581, Χ 496, ρ 234; in general, *buffet, maltreat,* σ 416; pass., π 108; 'scatter' the clouds, Λ 305.

σύ, gen. σέο, σεῦ, σεῖο, σέθεν, dat. σοί, τοί, τεΐν, acc. σέ: *thou, thee.* Most of the oblique forms are either enclitic or accented; σεῖο and σοί are never enclitic, τοί is always enclitic; in connection with αὐτός all forms retain their accent. The pron. is frequently strengthened by γέ or πέρ.

συ-βόσιον (βόσις), pl. συβόσια (συβόσεια): *herd* of swine, pl., Λ 769, ξ 101.

συ-βώτης (βόσκω), -εω: *swineherd.* (Od.)

σύγε: see σύ.

συγ-καλέω, aor. part. συγκαλέσᾱς: *call together, summon,* Β 55 and Κ 302.

συγ-κλονέω, ipf. συνεκλόνεον: *confound,* Ν 722†.

συγ-κυρέω, aor. opt. συγκύρσειαν: *hit* or *strike together,* Ψ 435†.

συγ-χέω, imp. σύγχει, ipf. σύγχει, aor. 1 συνέχευε, inf. συγχεῦαι, mid. aor. 2 σύγχυτο: *pour together, mix up,* ψάμαθον, Ο 364; mid. intrans, *get entangled,* ἡνία, Π 471; met., *confuse, confound, bring to naught,* νόον, ἰούς, κάματον, ὅρκια, Ι 612, Ο 366, 473; ἄνδρα, 'break down,' θ 139.

συκέη, συκῆ: *fig-tree.* (Od.)

σῦκον: *fig,* η 121†.

σῡλάω, ipf. (ἐ)σύλᾱ, fut. σῡλήσετε, aor. subj. σῡλήσω: *strip off* the armor from a fallen foe, *despoil,* τινά (τι), Ζ 71; in general, *take off* or *from,* Δ 105, 116.

σῡλεύω: *despoil, rob, take advantage of,* Ε 48, Ω 436.

συλ-λέγω, aor. part. συλλέξᾱς, mid. aor. συλλέξατο, fut. συλλέξομαι: *collect, gather up,* mid., for oneself.

συμ-βάλλω, ξυμβάλλω, συμβάλλετον, aor. 2 σύμβαλον, du. ξυμβλήτην, inf. -ήμεναι, mid. aor. 2 ξύμβλητο, -ηντο, subj. ξυμβλῆται, part. -ήμενος, fut. συμβλή(σ)εαι: I. act., *throw, bring,* or *put together;* of bringing men together in battle, Γ 70; rivers uniting their waters, E 774; also intrans., like mid., Π 565, Φ 578, φ 15.—II. mid., intrans., *meet, encounter*, abs. and with dat., aor. 2 very freq., Ξ 39, 27, 231, ζ 54, κ 105.

Σύμη: an island between Rhodes and Cnidus in Caria.—Adv., **Σύμηθεν,** *from Syme*, B 671.

συμ-μάρπτω, aor. part. συμμάρψᾱς: *seize* or *grasp together*, in order to break off, K 467†.

συμ-μητιάομαι, inf. -άασθαι: *take counsel together*, K 197†.

συμ-μίσγομαι: *be mingled with, flow into*, B 753.

σύμ-πᾱς, ξύμπᾱς, ᾱσα, αν: *all* (*together*).

συμ-πήγνῡμι, aor. συνέπηξε: of milk, *curdle*, E 902†.

συμ-πλαταγέω, aor. συμπλατάγησεν: χερσί, *smite* the hands *together*, Ψ 102†.

συμ-φερτός: *combined, united*, N 237†.

συμ-φέρω, mid. ipf. συμφερόμεσθα, fut. συνοισόμεθα: mid., *be borne* or *come together*, *meet* in battle, Θ 400, Λ 736. (Il.)

συμ-φράδμων (φράζω): *counselling together*, pl., *joint counsellors*, B 372†.

συμ-φράζομαι, fut. συμφράσσομαι, aor. συμφράσσατο: *take* or *share counsel with, concert plans with*, I 374, A 537; with oneself, *deliberate*, ο 202.

σύν, ξύν, the latter (older) form for metrical convenience, but more freely in compounds: *along with, together*.—I. adv., *together, at once; σὺν δὲ δύω μάρψᾱς*, ι 289 (cf. 311, 344); σὺν δὲ νεφέεσσι (dat. instr.) κάλυψεν | γαῖαν ὁμοῦ καὶ πόντον, ε 293; ἦλθε Δολίος, σὺν δ' υἱεῖς, 'along with him,' ω 387; of mingling, confusing, breaking up, σὺν δ' ἡμῖν δαῖτα ταράξῃ, A 579 (cf. Θ 86); σὺν δ' ὅρκι' ἔχευαν, Δ 269; σὺν δὲ γέροντι νόος χύτο, Ω 358.—II. prep. w. dat., *with, in company with, by the aid of; σὺν θεῷ, σὺν θεοῖσιν, σὺν Ἀθήνῃ, σὺν σοί*, ν 391; of things, *with*, denoting accompaniment and secondarily instrument, the clothing or armor one wears, the ship one sails with, Γ 29, A 179; met., of quality or characteristic, ἄκοιτιν σὺν μεγάλῃ ἀρετῇ **ἐκτήσω**, ω 193; of consequence, penalty, σὺν δὲ μεγάλῳ ἀπέτῑσαν, Δ 161. σύν sometimes follows its case, ο 410.

συν-αγείρω, ξυναγείρω, aor. ξυνάγειρα, mid. pr. part. συναγειρόμενοι, aor. 1 ξυναγείρατο, aor. 2 part. συναγρόμενος: *collect together, assemble;* mid. aor. 1, for oneself, ξ 323; aor. 2, intrans., Λ 687.

συν-άγνῡμι, ξυνάγνῡμι, aor. -έαξα, *break* or *dash to pieces, crunch up*, Λ 114.

συν-άγω, ξυνάγω, fut. -άξουσι: *lead* or *bring together, collect;* fig., ἔριδα, Ἄρηα, *join* battle, 'bring about,' 'stir up,' E 861, Π 764.

συν-αείρω, mid. aor. subj. συναείρεται: mid., *couple together* for oneself, O 680.

συν-αίνυμαι, ipf. συναίνυτο: *take together, gather up*, Φ 502†.

συν-αιρέω, aor. 2 σύνελε, part. συνελών: *take together, lay hold of at once*, υ 95; 'tore away,' Π 740.

συν-αντάω and **συνάντομαι,** part. συναντόμενος, ipf. συνήντετο, συναντέσθην, συναντήτην, aor. subj. συναντήσωνται: *meet, encounter*.

συν-δέω, ξυνδέω, aor. -έδησα: *bind together, bind fast, bind up*.

συνέδραμον: see συντρέχω.

συν-εέργω, aor. **συνεέργαθον**: *shut in* or *confine together, bind together*, ι 427, μ 424.

συν-είκοσι, ξυνεείκοσι: *twenty* (men) *together*, ξ 98†.

1. σύν-ειμι, ξύνειμι (εἰμί), fut. inf. -έσεσθαι: *be with*, 'be linked to,' η 270†.

2. σύν-ειμι, ξύνειμι (εἶμι), part. ξυνιόντες, ipf. 3 pl. ξύνισαν, du. συνίτην: *go* or *come together*, esp. in hostile ways, *meet;* περὶ ἔριδος, ἔριδι, 'in a spirit of strife,' Υ 66.

συν-ελαύνω, ξυνελαύνω, inf. ξυνελαυνέμεν, aor. συνέλασσα, subj. ξυνελάσσομεν, inf. ξυνελάσσαι: *drive* or *bring together*, booty, men in battle, Λ 677, σ 39, Υ 134; intrans., ἔριδι, X 129.

σύνελον: see συναιρέω.

συν-εοχμός (root Ϝεχ, ὀχέω): *junction*, Ξ 465†.

συν-έρῑθος: *fellow-worker*, ζ 32†.

σύν-εσις, ξύνεσις (ἵημι): *conflux*, κ 515†.

συν-εχής (ἔχω): neut. as adv., **σῡνεχές**, *continuously*, M 26; w. αἰεί, ι 74.

συν-έχω, ξυνέχω, ipf. σύνεχον: *hold together*, intrans., *meet*, Δ 133, Υ 415; an old perf. part. συνοχωκότε means *bent together over*, Β 218.

συν-ημοσύνη (ἵημι): only pl., *compacts*, Χ 261†.

συν-ήορος (ἀείρω): *joined with*, an *accompaniment to*, θ 99†.

συν-θεσίη (τίθημι): only pl., *treaty*, Β 339; *instructions*, Ε 319.

συν-θέω, fut. συνθεύσεται: *run with*, *go well*, υ 245†.

συν-ίημι, ξυνίημι, imp. ξυνίει, ipf. 3 pl. ξύνιεν, aor. ξυνέηκε, imp. ξύνες, mid. aor. ξύνετο, subj. συνώμεθα: *let go with*.—I. act., *send* or *bring together*, esp. in hostile ways, Α 8, Η 210; metaph., *mark*, *attend to*, *hear* (cf. c o n i c e r e), w. acc., sometimes gen., of person or of thing, Α 273, Β 26.—II. mid., *agree*, *covenant*, Ν 381; also like act., *mark*, δ 76.

συν-ίστημι: only perf. part. πολέμοιο συνεσταότος, *having arisen*, Ξ 96†.

συνοισόμεθα: see συμφέρω.

συν-ορίνω: only mid. part., φάλαγγες συνορῑνόμεναι, *stirring* or *beginning to move* (*together*), Δ 332†.

συν-οχή, ξυνοχή (ἔχω): pl., *meeting*, ὁδοῦ, of the forward and the home-stretch, Ψ 330†.

συνοχωκότε: see συνέχω.

συν-τίθημι, mid. aor. σύνθετο, imp. σύνθεο, σύνθεσθε: *put together*; mid., metaph. with and without θῡμῷ, *heed*, *take heed to*, *hear* (a n i m o c o m p o n e r e), abs. and w. acc., Α 76, ο 27.

σύν-τρεις: *three together*, *by threes*, ι 429†.

συν-τρέχω, aor. 2 συνέδραμον: *run* or *rush together*, Π 335 and 337.

συνώμεθα: see συνίημι.

σῦριγξ, ιγγος: any *tube*, hence (1) shepherd's *pipe*, *Pan's-pipe*, Κ 13, Σ 526.—(2) *spear-case*, Τ 387.

Συρίη: a mythical island, far in the West, beyond Ortygia, ο 403†.

συρ-ρήγνῡμι: only pass. perf., συνέρρηκται, *is broken*, fig., κακοῖσιν, θ 137†.

σῦς, συός, pl. dat. συσί, σύεσσι, acc. σύας, σῦς: *swine*, *pig*, *hog*; κάπριος, *wild boar*, and so without κάπριος, Idomeneus συῒ εἴκελος ἀλκήν, Δ 253.

σύτο: see σεύω.

συφειός, συφεός: *sty*; συφεόνδε, *to the sty*. (Od.)

συ-φορβός (φέρβω): *swineherd*; παῖς, *tending swine*. (Od. and Φ 282.)

σφάζω, aor. ἔσφαξα, σφάξε, pass. pres. part. σφαζόμενοι, perf. part. ἐσφαγμένα: *cut the throat*, *slaughter*, always of animals, esp. victims for sacrifice, Α 459, γ 449, 454, α 92. The blood was caught in a vessel made for the purpose. (See cut under ἀμνίον.)

σφαῖρα: *ball*; σφαίρῃ παίζειν, 'play at ball,' ζ 100. (Od.)

σφαιρηδόν: *like a ball*, Ν 204†.

σφάλλω (cf. f a l l o), aor. 1 σφῆλε, inf. σφῆλαι: *make to totter* or *fall*, ρ 464, Ψ 719.

σφαραγέομαι, ipf. σφαραγεῦντο: *hiss*, *be full to bursting*, ι 390, 440.

σφάς, σφέ: see σφεῖς.

σφεδανόν (cf. σφοδρός): neut. adj. as adv., *eagerly*, *impatiently*. (Il.)

σφεῖς (root σϝε, cf. s u i), gen. σφέων, σφείων, σφῶν (αὐτῶν), dat. σφίσι(ν), σφ(ίν), acc. σφέας, σφάς, σφ(έ): personal and reflexive pron. of 3d pers., *them*(*selves*). σφέ and σφί are always enclitic, σφῶν and σφείων never. σφί is probably never reflexive. Rarely of things, ι 70, κ 355.

σφέλας, αος, pl. σφέλᾱ: *footstool*, *foot-block*, σ 394 and ρ 231.

σφενδόνη: *sling*; serves in case of need as a bandage for a wound, Ν 600†. (See cut, representing an Assyrian slinger.)

113

σφέτερος (σφεῖς): poss. pron. of 3d

pers., *their;* strengthened by *αὐτός*, α 7; as subst., ἐπὶ σφέτερα, α 274.

σφηκόω (σφήξ), pass. plup. ἐσφήκωντο: compress in a wasp-like shape, *bind together*, P 52†.

Σφῆλος: son of Bucolus, of Athens, O 338.

σφῆλε: see σφάλλω.

σφήξ, σφηκός (cf. vespa): *wasp* or *hornet*, M 167 and Π 259.

σφί, σφίν: see σφεῖς.

σφοδρῶς (cf. σφεδανόν): *strongly, earnestly, eagerly*, μ 124†.

σφονδύλιος: *vertebra* of the spine, pl., *back-bone*, Υ 483†.

σφός (σφεῖς): *their;* always referring to a pl. subst., β 237, Σ 231.

σφῦρα: *hammer*, γ 434†.

σφυρόν: *ankle*.

σφω(έ), gen. and dat. **σφωίν**: dual of σφεῖς, *they two, both of them*, A 8, 338. Both forms are enclitic, and instead of them the pl. forms are freq. employed.

σφῶι, σφώ, gen. and dat. **σφῶιν, σφῷν**: dual of σύ, *ye two, you two, you both*, A 336, 574, Λ 776, 862. σφῶι and σφῶιν are never enclitic.

σφωίτερος: *of you two, of you both*, A 216†.

σχεδίη: *raft*, light *boat*, ε 234 ff. (An attempt has been made to represent the construction and parts of Odysseus's σχεδίη under ἁρμονίη: *a*, the beams forming the ἔδαφος, *h*. *b*, σταμῖνες. *c*, γόμφοι. *d*, ἁρμονίαι. *e*, ἐπηγκενίδες. *f*, ἴκρια. *g*, ἱστός.)

σχεδίην (ἔχω): fem. adj. as adv., *near at hand, in hand to hand fight*, E 830†.

Σχεδίος: (1) a Phocian, the son of Iphitus, slain by Hector, B 517, P 306.—(2) a Phocian, the son of Perimēdes, slain by Hector, O 515.

σχεδόθεν (ἔχω): *from near at hand, close by, near*, w. dat. or gen., Π 800, τ 447.

σχεδόν (ἔχω): *near, hard by;* w. dat. or gen., ι 23, ζ 125; of relationship, κ 441; of time, N 817, β 284, ζ 27.

σχεθέειν: see ἔχω.

σχεῖν, σχέμεν, σχέο: see ἔχω.

Σχερίη: *Scheria*, a fabulous country, the home of the Phaeacians, ε 34, ζ 8–263.

σχέτλιος (ἔχω), σχετλίῃ, Γ 414: properly, *holding out, enduring*, then in moral sense, *hard, hardened, perverse, cruel;* σχέτλιός εἰς, Ὀδυσεῦ, μ 279 (cf. what follows); similarly, but without serious reproach, K 164; of things in Od., ἔργα, ὕπνος, ι 295, κ 69.

σχέτο: see ἔχω.

σχίζα: *split wood;* δρυός, oaken *billet*, ξ 425.

σχίζω (cf. scindo), aor. ἔσχισεν: *cleave, split*, δ 507.

σχοίατο: see ἔχω.

σχοῖνος: *rush, rushes*, ε 463†.

Σχοῖνος: a town on a river of the same name in Boeotia, B 497†.

σχόμενος: see ἔχω.

σώεσκον, σώζων: see σοάω.

σῶκος (cf. σῶς, σώζω): *saviour*, epith. of Hermes, Υ 72†.

Σῶκος: a Trojan, the son of Hippasus, slain by Odysseus, Λ 427 f., 440 ff.

σῶμα, ατος: dead *body, corpse, carcase*.

σῶς (σάος, σόος): *safe, sound, unharmed; certain*, N 773, ε 305.

σώω: see σαόω.

T.

τ᾽ = (1) τέ.—(2) τοί (σοί), α 60, 347.—(3) τοί after μέν (μέντοι).

τᾱγός (τάσσω): *arranger, marshal, leader* (v. l. τ᾽ ἀγοί), Ψ 160†.

ταθείς, τάθη: see τείνω.

ταλα-εργός (τλῆναι, Ϝέργον): *enduring labor, patient, drudging*, epith. of mules.

Ταλαιμένης: a leader of the Maeonians, B 865†.

Ταλαϊονίδης: *son of Talaus*, Mecisteus, B 566, Ψ 678.

τάλαντον (root ταλ, τλῆναι): (1) *scale*, pl. *scales*, *balance*, M 433; esp. fig., of the golden scales in which Zeus balances the fates of men, Θ 69, Π 658, T 223.—(2) a definite (unknown) weight, *talent*, χρῡσοῖο, I 122, δ 129.

ταλα-πείριος (τλῆναι, πεῖρα): *enduring trials, much tried.* (Od.)

ταλα-πενθής, ές (πένθος): *bearing sorrow, patient in suffering*, ε 222†.

τάλαρος (root ταλ): *basket*, of wicker-work, for fruit, etc., Σ 568; of silver, for wool, δ 125.

τάλας, voc. **τάλαν** (root ταλ): *foolhardy, wretch*, σ 327 and τ 68. Cf. σχέτλιος.

ταλασί-φρων (root ταλ, φρήν): *stout-hearted;* epith. esp. of Odysseus.

ταλάσσαι: see τλῆναι.

ταλαύρῑνος (root ταλ, ϝρῑνός): lit., *enduring the ox-hide shield, tough, doughty, brave;* epith. of Ares, with πολεμιστής.—Neut. as adv., *bravely*, H 239. (Il.)

ταλά-φρων = ταλασίφρων, N 300†.

Ταλθύβιος: *Talthybius*, a herald of Agamemnon, A 320, Γ 118, Δ 192, H 276, T 196, 250, 267, Ψ 897. (Represented in the foll. cut, from a very ancient Greek relief.)

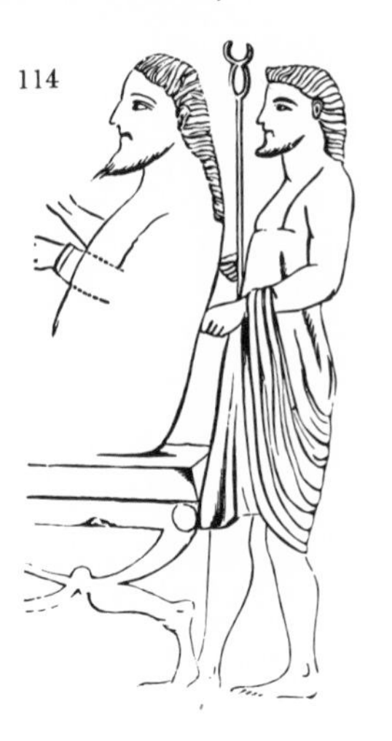

τἆλλα, τἄλλα: see ἄλλος.

τάμε, ταμέειν: see τάμνω.

ταμεσί-χρως, οος (τάμνω, χρώς): *cutting the skin, sharp-cutting.* (Il.)

ταμίη (fem. of ταμίης): *house-keeper, stewardess;* with and without γυνή, α 139, Z 390; ἀμφίπολος, π 152.

ταμίης (τάμνω): *steward, dispenser*, T 44; fig., πολέμοιο, ἀνέμων, Δ 84, κ 21.

τάμνω, τέμνω, τέμω, aor. τάμε, inf. ταμέειν, mid. aor. inf. ταμέσθαι, pass. perf. part. τετμημένον: *cut, cut* up, off, out, etc., mid. subjectively; of 'felling' or 'lopping' trees, 'hewing' beams, 'marking off' an enclosure, 'furrowing' the earth with the plough, 'cutting off' (intercepting, driving away) cattle, 'cutting' the waves in sailing, I 580, N 707, Σ 528, Φ 38, γ 175; ὅρκια, 'conclude' a treaty, see ὅρκιον.

τανα-ήκης, ες: *with long edge* or *point*, sword or spear, axe, Ψ 118.

ταναός: *long*, Π 589†.

ταναύ-πους, ποδος: *long-legged*, i. e. slender-legged, ι 464†.

τανηλεγής, gen. έος: doubtful word, epith. of θάνατος, anciently interpreted *prostrating, laying stretched out at length* (of a corpse); acc. to some moderns, from ἄλγος, *long-lamented.*

Τάνταλος: *Tantalus*, son of Zeus, and father of Pelops, a king of Sipylus, who revealed the secrets of the gods, and was punished in Hades, λ 582 ff.

τανυ- (τείνω): stem of an adj., used as a prefix, meaning *stretched out long* or *thin.*

τανύ-γλωσσος: *slender-tongued, long-tongued*, ε 66†.

τανυ-γλώχῑν, ῑνος: *with slender* (sharp) *point*, Θ 297†.

τανυ-ήκης, ες: *with thin edge* or *point, keen, tapering*, Π 768.

τανύ-πεπλος: *with trailing robes, long-robed.*

τανυ-πτέρυξ, υγος: *with wide-stretching wings*, M 237 and T 350.

τανυσί-πτερος: *broad-winged*, ε 65 and χ 468.

τανυστύς, ύος (τανύω): *stretching* or *stringing* of a bow, φ 112†. (Illustrated in cut No. 34.)

τάνυται: see τανύω.

τανύ-φλοιος: *with thin* (smooth, tender) *bark*, Π 767†.

τανύ-φυλλος: *with long* or *slender leaves*. (Od.)

τανύω, τάνῦμι (Att. τείνω), aor. (ἐ)τάνυ(σ)σα, mid. pres. τάνυται, ipf. τανύοντο, aor. part. τανυσσάμενος, pass. perf. τετάνυσται, plup. τετάνυστο, aor. 3 pl. τάνυσθεν, part. τανυσθείς: I. act., *stretch, strain, extend,* as in 'stringing' a bow, a lyre, φ 407, 409; 'holding horses to their speed' with the reins, Ψ 324; 'drawing' the shuttle to and fro in weaving, Ψ 761; and in general of 'arranging' anything long or broad, spears, spits, tables, I 213, ο 283, α 138. Metaph., ἔριδα πολέμοιο, μάχην, πόνον, ἔριδος πεῖραρ, Ξ 389, N 359.—II. pass. and mid., *be stretched* or *extended, be tight;* the cheeks 'became full' again, π 175; of mules, horses 'stretching out,' 'laying themselves out' to run, Π 375, 475, ζ 83; νῆσος τετάνυσται, 'extends,' ι 116.—Mid., subjectively, Δ 112; reflexive, ι 298.

τάπης, ητος: *rug, coverlet,* laid upon chairs or beds. (See cuts Nos. 69, 105.)

ταπρῶτα: see πρῶτος.

τάρ: see τέ and ἄρα.

ταράσσω (τραχύς), aor 'τάραξα, perf. part. τετρηχυῖα, plup. τετρήχει: *stir up, trouble, disturb, throw into confusion;* πόντον, ἵππους, δαῖτα, ε 291, Θ 86, A 579. The perf. is intrans., *be in confusion, stormy,* B 95, H 346.

ταρβέω, imp. τάρβει, ipf. τάρβει, aor. τάρβησα: *be afraid, dread,* intrans. and trans.

τάρβος, εος: *fear, dread.*

ταρβοσύνη = τάρβος, σ 342†.

Τάρνη: a city on Mt. Tmolus, the later Sardis, E 44†.

ταρπήμεναι, ταρπῆναι: see τέρπω.

ταρσός (τερσαίνω): a surface for drying, *crate,* ι 219; *flat of the foot,* Λ 377, 388.

Τάρταρος: *Tartarus,* a dark abyss, place of imprisonment of the Titans, as far below Hades as the earth is below the heavens, Θ 13, 481.

ταρφέες (τρέφω): *thick, close together, frequent.*—Neut. as adv., **ταρφέα,** *often, thickly,* M 47†.

Τάρφη: a town in Locris, B 533†.

τάρφος, εος (τρέφω): *thicket,* only dat. pl., ἐν τάρφεσιν ὕλης, E 555 and O 606

ταρχύω, fut. ταρχύσουσι, aor. subj. ταρχύσωσι: solemnly *bury.* (Il.)

ταύρειος: *of a bull, of bull-* or *ox-hide.* (Il.)

ταῦρος: *bull,* with and without βοῦς.

ταφήιος (τάφος): *for burial,* φᾶρος, *winding-sheet, shroud.* (Od.)

Τάφιοι: the *Taphians,* inhabitants of Taphos, notorious for their piracy, α 105, 181, 419, ξ 452, ο 427, π 426.

Τάφος: *Taphos,* an island between Leucadia and Acarnania, near Meganisi, α 417.

1. τάφος (θάπτω): *burial; funeral-feast,* γ 309.

2. τάφος (root θαπ, ταφών): *astonishment.* (Od.)

τάφρος (θάπτω): *ditch, trench.*

ταφών: see θαπ-.

τάχα: *quickly, soon.*

ταχέως: *quickly, speedily,* Ψ 365†.

τάχιστα: see ταχύς.

τάχος, εος: *speed.* (Il.)

ταχύ-πωλος: *with swift steeds.*

ταχύς, εῖα, ύ, comp. **θάσσων,** sup. **τάχιστος**: *quick, swift, fleet.*—Adv. comp. **θᾶσσον,** sup. **τάχιστα**: *quicker, most speedily;* ὅ ττι τάχιστα, 'with all speed,' Δ 193, ε 112; the comp. is also similarly used for emphasis, η 152, etc.

ταχυτής, ῆτος: *swiftness, speed,* Ψ 740 and ρ 315.

τέ (cf. que): enclitic conj., *and;* correl., τέ . . τέ (*both* . . *and*), also τέ . . καί, and with ἠδέ. τέ has some uses in Homer of which only traces remain in the later language. Their exact force cannot always be discerned, and the particle itself remains untranslatable. It attaches itself esp. to rel. words (seemingly as if they needed a connective), ὅς τέ, οἷός τε, ὅσος τε, ἔνθα τε, ἵνα τε, ἐπεί τε, ὥς τε, etc.; thus in Att. (with special meanings), οἷός τε, ὥστε. So τίς τε (τὶς), ἄλλα τε, γάρ τε, μέν τε, δέ τε, ἀτάρ τε, οὐδέ τε. In all these cases with or without a corresponding τέ in the connected clause, A 81, T 164. Many Latin words may be compared (for form, not necessarily for sense) with these combinations of τέ, namque, atque, quisque, etc.

Τεγέη: *Tegea,* a city in Arcadia, B 607†.

τέγεος: *roofed over*, Z 248†.

τέγος, εος: *roof, building*, λ 64, α 333. (Od.)

τεεῖο: see σύ.

τεθαλυῖα, τέθηλα: see θάλλω.

τέθηπα: see θαπ-.

τέθναθι, τεθνάμεναι, τεθνᾶσι, τεθνεώς, τεθνηώς, τεθνειώς: see θνήσκω.

τεθυωμένος: see θυόω.

τεΐν: see σύ.

τείνω (cf. tendo), aor. 1 ἔτεινα, τεῖνε, pass. perf. τέταται, plup. τέτατο, τετάσθην, aor. τάθη, pass. ταθείς: *stretch, stretch out, extend, draw tight;* of a bow, Δ 124; reins fastened tightly to the chariot rim (see cut No. 10), E 322; a sword hung by the baldric, X 307; a helmet-strap drawn under the chin, Γ 372. Metaph., λαῖλαπα, pass., νύξ, πτόλεμος, Π 365, Ρ 736, λ 19. ἵπποισι τάθη δρόμος, 'was exerted,' Ψ 375, 758. Cf. τανύω.

τεῖος: see τέως.

Τειρεσίης: *Tiresias*, the blind seer of Thebes. He alone retained his mental faculties in Hades. κ 524, 537, λ 32, 50, 89, 139, 151, 479, μ 267, ψ 251, 323.

τεῖρος, εος (cf. τέρας, ἀστήρ): pl., *constellations*, Σ 485†.

τείρω (cf. tero), ipf. ἔτειρε, τεῖρε, pass. ipf. (ἐ)τείρετο: *wear out* or *away*, only met., *weary, exhaust, distress*, of age, hunger, troubles, Δ 315, Ο 61, α 342; freq. the pass., *be worn, hard pressed, afflicted*, Z 387.

τειχεσι-πλήτης: *stormer of walls* or *cities*, E 31 and 455.

τειχίζω (τεῖχος): only mid. aor., ἐτειχίσσαντο, *built for themselves*, H 449†.

τειχιόεις, εσσα, εν: *walled, well walled, well fortified*, B 559 and 646.

τειχίον (dimin. from τεῖχος): *wall* belonging to a building, not a city or town, π 165 and 343.

τεῖχος, εος: *wall* of a city or town, then in general any *fortification, rampart;* τεῖχος ἐλαύνειν, δεῖμαι, ποιήσασθαι, M 4, H 436.

τείως: see τέως.

τέκε, τεκέειν: see τίκτω.

τεκμαίρομαι (τέκμωρ), aor. τεκμήρατο, -ντο: set an end, hence *decree, appoint, ordain*, Z 349, η 317; *portend, predict*, H 70, λ 112, μ 139.

τέκμωρ (Att. τέκμαρ): *goal, end;* Ἰλίου, 'overthrow,' H 30, I 48; then *token, pledge*, A 526.

τέκνον (τίκτω): *child;* freq. in endearing or conciliatory address, X 84, β 363. Of animals, *young.*

τέκον: see τίκτω.

τέκος, εος = τέκνον.

τεκταίνομαι (τέκτων), aor. τεκτήνατο, -αιτο: *build*, E 62; met., *contrive, devise*, K 19. (Il.)

Τεκτονίδης: *son of Tecton* ('Builder'), Polynäüs, θ 114†.

τεκτοσύνη: *art of the joiner, carpentry*, pl., ε 250†.

τέκτων, ονος (cf. τίκτω, τεύχω): *maker, builder, joiner, carpenter.*

Τέκτων: the father of Phereclus, E 59†.

τελαμών, ῶνος (root ταλ): any belt or strap to *bear* or *support* something, hence (1) *sword-belt, baldric* (see cuts Nos. 86, 109).—(2) *shield-strap*, λ 610, Ξ 404 (see cut).—(3) *thong* attached to the ankles of a dead body, to drag it away, P 290. (Cf. cut No. 16.)

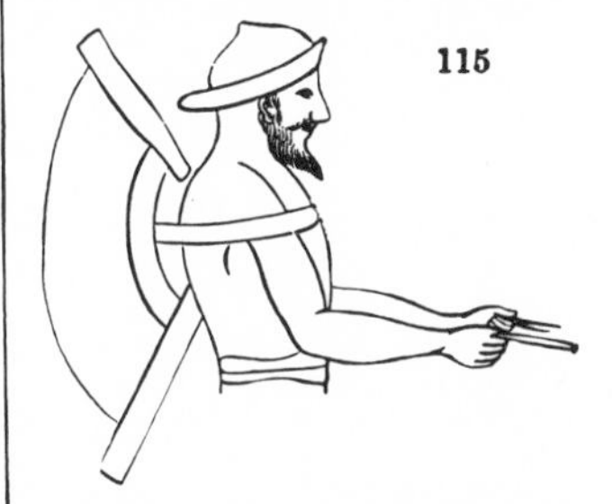

115

Τελαμών: *Telamon*, the son of Aeacus, brother of Peleus, king in Salamis, and father of Ajax and Teucer, Θ 283, N 177, P 284, 293, λ 553.

Τελαμωνιάδης: *son of Telamon*, Ajax, N 709.

Τελαμώνιος: *Telamonian*, Ajax the greater, as distinguished from Ajax son of Oïleus, so with υἱός, Λ 591. Also of Teucer, N 170, O 462.

τελέθω (τέλλω): poetic synonym of εἶναι or γίγνεσθαι, νὺξ ἤδη τελέθει, 'it is already night,' H 282; ἄρνες ἄφαρ κεραοὶ τελέθουσιν, 'become horned,' 'get horns' straightway, δ 85; παν-

τοῖοι τελέθοντες, 'assuming all sorts of shapes,' ρ 486.

τέλειος (τέλος): *perfect;* said of victims that are without spot or blemish, Α 66; the eagle is τελειότατος πετεηνῶν, because he brings the surest omen from Zeus, Θ 247, Ω 315.

τελείω: see τελέω.

τελεσ-φόρος (= φέρων τέλος): *bringing to perfection* or maturity, hence ἐνιαυτός, a *full* year. (Od. and Τ 32.)

τελευτάω, ipf. τελεύτᾱ, fut. τελευτήσω, aor. τελεύτησα, mid. fut. τελευτήσεσθαι, pass. aor. inf. τελευτηθῆναι: *complete, bring to pass, fulfil;* νοήματα, ἐέλδωρ, Σ 328, φ 200; ὅρκον, in due and solemn form, Ξ 280; pass. and fut. mid., *be fulfilled, come to pass,* Ο 74, β 171, θ 510.

τελευτή: *end, accomplishment, purpose,* Ι 625, α 249.

τελέω, τελείω, ipf. τέλεον, ἐτέλειον, fut. τελέω, τελεῖ, aor. (ἐ)τέλε(σ)σα, mid. fut., w. pass. signif., τελεῖται, inf. τελέεσθαι, -εῖσθαι, pass. perf. τετέλεσται, plup. -το, aor. (ἐ)τελέσθη: *bring to an end* or *to completion, end, complete, accomplish, fulfil;* freq. the pass., *be fulfilled, come to pass,* β 176, ε 302; τὸ καὶ τετελεσμένον ἔσται, Α 212; but τετελεσμένος also means 'to be accomplished,' 'practicable,' Ξ 196, ε 90.—*Pay, render* (τινί τι), tribute, gifts, Ι 156 f., 598, β 34.

τελήεις, εσσα, εν: 'rich in fulfilment,' *perfect,* hecatombs.

τέλος, εος (cf. τέρμα): *end* in the sense of *completion, sum, consummation, fulfilment;* μῦθον, 'sum and substance,' Π 83; perfect 'state' of affairs, ι 5; τέλος θανάτοιο, periphrasis for θάνατος (the idea concretely expressed); concrete and technical, a division of the army, *company* (Il.)

τέλοσδε = εἰς τέλος. (Il.)

τέλσον = τέρμα.

τέμενος, εος (τέμνω, cf. templum): a piece of land marked off and reserved as the *king's estate,* λ 185; or as the *sacred precinct* of a god (grove with temple), θ 363.

Τεμέση: a town celebrated for its copper mines, perhaps in Cyprus, α 184†.

τέμνω, τέμει, τεμεῖ: see τάμνω.

Τένεδος: *Tenedos,* a small island west of the Troad, Α 38, Λ 625, Ν 33, γ 159.

Τενθρηδών: a leader of the Magnesians from Thessaly, father of Prothoüs, Β 756†.

τένων, οντος (τείνω): du. and pl., *muscles.*

τέξω, τέξομαι: see τίκτω.

τέο, τεό: see τίς, τὶς.

τεοῖο: see σύ.

τεός = σός.

τέρας, ατος and αος (cf. τεῖρος, ἀστήρ): *prodigy, portent, omen,* found in some manifestation of nature, such as thunder, lightning, the rainbow. τέρας Διός, 'sent by Zeus,' Μ 209; ἀνθρώπων, 'for men,' Λ 28; of a *monster,* the Gorgon, Ε 742.

τέρετρον (τετραίνω): *auger,* ε 246 and ψ 198.

τέρην, εινα, εν (cf. τείρω): *tender, soft, delicate.*

τέρμα, ατος (cf. τέλος, terminus): *limit, goal;* the turning-post in the race, Ψ 307; a *mark* to show how far a quoit was thrown, θ 193.

τερμιόεις, εσσα, εν (τέρμις = πούς): *reaching to the feet;* according to others, *fringed, tasselled;* χιτών, ἀσπίς, τ 242, Π 803.

Τερπιάδης: *son of Terpis,* Phemius, χ 330†.

τερπι-κέραυνος: *delighting in thunder,* epith. of Zeus.

τέρπω, ipf. ἔτερπον, τέρπε, mid. fut. τέρψομαι, aor. 1 part. τερψάμενος, aor. 2 red. τεταρπόμην, subj. ταρπώμεθα, red. τεταρπώμεσθα, part. τεταρπόμενος, pass. aor. ἐτέρφθην, ἐτάρφθην, aor. 2 ἐτάρπην, 3 pl. ἔτερφθεν, τάρφθεν, τάρπησαν, subj. τραπείομεν: I. act., *delight, cheer;* τινὰ λόγοις, θῡμὸν φόρμιγγι, ἀείδων, Ο 393, Ι 189, α 107, ρ 385; ἀκαχημένον, Τ 312.—II. mid. and pass., *enjoy oneself, take pleasure in, rejoice;* τινί. Also τινός, *enjoy;* fig., γόοιο, 'have one's fill' of lamentation, Ψ 10, λ 212. The form τραπείομεν = τερφθῶμεν occurs Γ 441, Ξ 314, θ 292.

τερπωλή (τέρπω): *delight, rare sport,* σ 37†.

τερσαίνω, aor. τέρσηνε: *dry, dry up,* Π 529†.

τέρσομαι, ipf. ἐτέρσετο, τέρσοντο

aor. 2 inf. τερσῆναι, -ήμεναι: *be* or *become dry;* w. gen., δακρυόφιν, ε 152.

τερψί-μβροτος (βροτός): *delighting mortals,* μ 269 and 274.

τεσσαρά-βοιος (βοῦς): *worth four cattle,* Ψ 705†.

τεσσαράκοντα: *forty.*

τέσσαρες: *four.*

τεταγών (cf. t a n g o), defective aor. part.: *laying hold of,* A 591 and O 23.

τέταται: see τείνω.

τετάρπετο, τεταρπώμεσθα, τεταρπόμενος: see τέρπω.

τέταρτος and **τέτρατος**: *fourth.*—Adv. (τὸ)**τέταρτον,** *for the fourth time,* Π 786, X 208.

τετάσθην: see τείνω.

τετεύξεται, τετεύχεται, τετεύχετον: see τεύχω.

τετευχῆσθαι (τευχέω, τεύχεα), inf. perf. pass.: *to have armed ourselves, be armed,* χ 104†.

τέτηκα: see τήκω.

τετίημαι, τετίησθον, part. τετιημένος, also act. perf. part. **τετιηώς**: *be troubled, sad;* τετιημένος ἦτορ, τετιηότι θυμῷ, Λ 555.

τέτλαθι, τετλαίην, τετλάμεν, τετλάμεναι, τετληώς: see τλῆναι.

τετμημένος: see τάμνω.

τέτμον, τέτμῃς: see ἔτετμον.

τετρά-γυος (γύης): containing 4 γύαι, *four-acre* lot; as subst., a piece of land as large as a man can plough in a day, σ 374.

τετρα-θέλυμνος (θέλυμνον): *of four layers* (of hide), O 479 and χ 122.

τετραίνω (cf. τείρω), aor. τέτρηνε: pierce with holes, *perforate, bore.*

τετράκις: *four times,* ε 306†.

τετρά-κυκλος: *four-wheeled;* (ᾱ) ι 242.

τετράορος (ἀείρω): *yoked four abreast,* pl., ν 81†.

τετρα-πλῆ: *four-fold,* A 128†.

τέτραπτο: see τρέπω.

τέτρατος: see τέταρτος.

τετρα-φάληρος: *with four-fold crest,* κυνέη. (Il.) (See cut under αὐλῶπις.)

τετρά-φαλος: *with four-banded crest,* κυνέη. (Il.) (See cut No. 116.)

τετράφατο: see τρέπω.

τετραχθά: *in four parts.*

τέτρηνε: see τετραίνω.

τετρήχει, τετρηχυῖα: see ταράσσω.

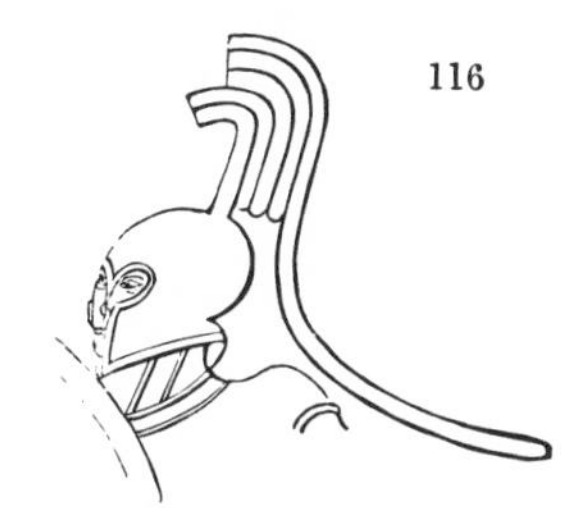

116

τετρίγει, τετρῖγυῖα: see τρίζω.

τέτροφεν: see τρέφω.

τέττα, voc.: a form of familiar address, as of a younger friend to an elder, *Father;* Diomed to Sthenelus, Δ 412†.

τέττιξ, ῑγος: *tettix* or *cicada,* an insect whose note was greatly liked by the ancients, Γ 151†.

τετυγμένα, τετυχεῖν, τετυχέσθαι, τέτυξαι, τετύχθαι: see τεύχω.

τετύχηκα: see τυγχάνω.

τεῦ, τεύ: see τίς, τὶς.

Τευθρανίδης: *son of Teuthras,* Axylus, Z 13†.

Τεύθρᾱς: (1) the father of Axylus.—(2) a Greek from Magnesia, slain by Hector, E 705.

Τεῦκρος: *Teucer,* son of Telamon and Hesione, half-brother of Ajax, the best archer before Troy, M 350, 371 f., N 170, Z 31, Θ 273, 322, O 484.

Τευταμίδης: *son of Teutamias,* Lethus, B 843†.

τεῦχος, εος: *implement* of any kind, regularly pl., *arms, armor,* also *tackling* of a ship, ο 218.

τεύχω, fut. -ξω, aor. ἔτευξα, τεῦξε, aor. 2 inf. red. τετυκεῖν, perf. part. τετευχώς, mid. fut. inf. τεύξεσθαι, aor. 2 red. τετύκοντο, opt. -οίμεθα, inf. -έσθαι, pass. perf. 2 sing. τέτυξαι, τέτυκται, 3 pl. τετεύχαται, inf. τετύχθαι, imp. τετύχθω, τετύγμην, (ἐ)τέτυξο, -το, 3 pl. (ἐ)τετεύχατο, aor. ἐτύχθη, fut. perf. τετεύξεται: I. act., *make, cause,* of all kinds of handiwork, and metaph., ἄλγεα, κήδεά τινι, A 110, α 244; so *prepare,* δεῖπνον, etc.; with two accusatives, *make, render,* A 4.—Mid., *prepare* or *have prepared* for oneself, A 467, T 208.—II. pass. (fut. mid. w. pass. signif., E 653), *be made, wrought, furnished,* or *ready,* very often the perf. and plup.; also the perf. act. in this sense, μ 423; *τετυγμένος*, 'well wrought,' Π 225, etc.; metaph., *νόος τετυγμένος*, 'sound,' υ 366.—Esp. as synonym of *εἶναι*, *γενέσθαι*, *be*, *become*, *take place*, *happen*; *οἷον ἐτύχθη*, *ποθὴ Δαναοῖσι τέτυκται*, *θαῦμ' ἐτέτυκτο* (for *ἐγένετο*, *γέγονε*, *ἔστιν*, *ἦν*), Β 320, Ρ 690, ι 190, and often.

τέφρη: *ashes*. (Il.)

τεχνάω, τεχνάομαι, aor. inf. *τεχνῆσαι* (v. l. *τεχνῆσσαι*), fut. *τεχνήσομαι*, aor. *τεχνήσατο*, opt. *-αιτο*, part. *-άμενος*: *construct with art*, *contrive*, *devise*. (Od. and Ψ 415.)

τέχνη (cf. *τίκτω*, *τεκεῖν*): *art*, *skill*, *device*, *craft*, *cunning*, δ 455, 529. (Od. and Γ 61.)

τεχνήεις, *εσσα*, *εν*: *full of art* or *skill*, *skilful*, θ 297. Contracted pl. nom. fem. *τεχνῆσσαι* (v. l. *τεχνῆσαι*, from *τεχνάω*), η 110.—Adv., **τεχνηέντως**, ε 270.

τέῳ, τέων: see *τίς*.

τέως, τείως: *so long*, Ω 658; *meanwhile*, ο 127, σ 190; *some time*, ο 231; correl. to *ἕως*, *ὄφρα*, Υ 42, Τ 189.

τῆ (cf. *τείνω*): an old imp. used in offering something, *here* (extend your hand and *take*)! *there!* Ξ 219, ε 346.

τῇ, τῆ: demonstr., *here*; rel., *where*, *as*, Μ 118, δ 565, θ 510.

τῇδε: see *ὅδε*.

τῆθος, *εος*: *oyster*, pl., Π 747†.

Τηθύς: *Tethys*, daughter of Uranus and Gaea, wife of Oceanus, and mother of the river-gods, Ξ 302. Mother of all the gods according to Ξ 201.

τηκεδών, *όνος*: *melting*, *wasting away*, *decline*, λ 201†.

τήκω, ipf. *τῆκε*, mid. ipf. *τήκετο*, perf., w. pres. signif., *τέτηκα*: act., *melt*; fig., *θυμόν*, 'consume' with grief, τ 264.—Mid. and perf., intrans., *melt*, *thaw*, τ 207; fig., *waste away*, *pine away*, Γ 176.

τῆλε: adv., *far*, *far away*; w. gen., *far from*, ρ 250, Χ 445; also with *ἀπό*, *ἐκ*, γ 313, Β 863.

τηλεδαπός: *distant*, Φ 454; *strange*, *foreign*, Χ 45.

τηλεθάων (*θάλλω*), *-θόωσα*, defective part.: *luxuriant*, *blooming*, of plants, forest, hair; *παῖδες*, Χ 423.

τηλε-κλειτός: *far-famed*, *wide-renowned*.

τηλε-κλυτός = *τηλεκλειτός*.

Τηλέμαχος: *Telemachus*, the son of Odysseus and Penelope. The name ('Afar-fighting') was given to the child because he was born as his father was about to depart for the war of Troy. Telemachus is the principal figure in the first four books of the Odyssey, and his journey in quest of tidings of his father to Pylos and Sparta, under the guidance of Athēna in the form of Mentor, has made the name of his 'mentor' proverbial. After the return of Odysseus, Telemachus assists him in taking revenge upon the suitors. He is mentioned in the Iliad only in Β 260, Δ 354.

Τήλεμος: son of Eurymus, a seer among the Cyclōpes, ι 509.

Τηλέπυλος: a town of the Laestrȳgons, κ 82, ψ 318.

τηλε-φανής, *ές* (*φαίνομαι*): *conspicuous far and wide*, ω 83†.

Τηλεφίδης: *son of Telephus*, Eurypylus, λ 519.

τηλίκος: *of such an age*, so old or so young, of the right age.

τηλόθεν: *from far* away.

τηλόθι: *far away*; w. gen., *far from*, Α 30.

τηλόσε: *to a distance*, *far away*.

τηλοτάτω: adv., sup. to *τηλοῦ*, *most distant*, η 322†.

τηλοῦ: *afar*; w. gen., *far from*.

τηλύγετος: doubtful word, *dearly beloved*. Neither the ancient nor the modern guesses as to the etymology of this word are worth recording.

τῆμος: *then*, *thereupon*, correl. to *ἦμος*.

τῆπερ = *ᾗ περ*.

Τηρείη: a mountain in Mysia, Β 829†.

Τηΰγετον: *Taygetus*, a mountain range in Laconia, extending to Cape Taenarum, ζ 103†.

τηΰσιος: *vain*, *fruitless*, *useless*, γ 316 and ο 13.

τίεσκον: see *τίω*.

τίη (*τί ἤ*): *why then? why pray? τίη δέ*; *τίη δή*; *ἀλλὰ τίη*; Ο 244, ο 326, Υ 251.

τιθαιβώσσω: *lay up honey*, ν 106†.

τίθημι, τιθέω, *τίθησθα*, *τίθησι* and *τιθεῖ*, 3 pl. *τιθεῖσι*, ipf. (*ἐ*)*τίθει*, *τίθεσαν*, fut. inf. *θησέμεναι*, aor. *ἔθηκα*, *θῆκε*, θῆκαν, ἔθεσαν, θέσαν, subj. θείω, θείῃς (θήῃς), θέωμεν, θείομεν, opt. θείην, θεῖμεν, θεῖεν, imp. θές, inf. θεῖναι, θέμεναι, mid. pres. part. τιθήμενος, fut. θήσομαι, aor. θήκατο, ἔθετο, θέτο, ἔθεσθε, θέσθε, opt. θεῖο, θεῖτο, imp. θέω, θέσθε: I. act., *put*, *place*, properly local, w. dat. of place or w. prep.; metaph., *put into one's mind*, *inspire*, *suggest*, μένος τινὶ ἐν θυμῷ, θῡμόν τινι, βουλὴν ἐν στήθεσσιν, α 321, Ω 49, Ρ 470, λ 146; similarly of 'proposing,' 'offering' prizes at games, 'depositing,' 'setting up' offerings in a temple, 'determining' the limit, end, or outcome of anything, Ψ 263, μ 347, Ψ 333, θ 465; *make*, *cause* (poetic for ποιεῖν), ὀρυμαγδὸν ἔθηκεν, ι 235; κέλευθόν τινι, Μ 399; and forming a periphrasis, σκέδασιν θεῖναι (= σκεδάσαι), α 116; Ἀχαιοῖς ἄλγε' ἔθηκεν, 'caused,' 'gave rise to' miseries for the Greeks, Α 2; so w. double acc., τινὰ ἄλοχον θεῖναι, Τ 298, ν 163.—II. mid., the above meanings subjectively applied, *put* or *place* for oneself, something of one's own, κολεῷ ἄορ, ἀμφὶ ὤμοισιν ἔντεα, κ 34, 333; met., ἐν φρεσί τι, 'take to heart,' 'consider,' δ 729; ἐλέγχεα ταῦτα τίθεσθε, 'hold,' 'deem this a disgrace to yourselves,' φ 333; *make* or *prepare* for oneself, Ι 88, Ω 402; w. two accusatives, τινὰ θέσθαι γυναῖκα, φ 72, Ι 629.

τιθήνη (θῆσθαι): *nurse*. (Il.)

τίθησθα: see τίθημι.

Τιθωνός: *Tithōnus*, a son of Laomedon, carried off by the goddess Eos, to be her spouse, Υ 237, Λ 1, ε 1.

τίκτω (root τεκ, cf. τέκτων, τέχνη), fut. τέξεις, aor. 2 ἔτεκον, τέκεν, mid. fut. inf. τέξεσθαι, aor. 2 τεκόμην: *give birth to*, *bear*, *bring forth*, also of the father, *beget*; the mid., too, is said of either parent, Β 741, 742, ω 293.

τίλλω, ipf. τίλλε, mid. ipf. τιλλέσθην, -οντο: *pluck out*, mid., one's own hair; w. acc. of the person mourned for in this way, Ω 711.

τῑμάω, ipf. ἐτίμᾱ, τίμᾱ, aor. τίμησα, subj. τῑμήσομεν, inf. τίμησον, mid. aor. (ἐ)τῑμησάμην, pass. perf. τετῑμήμεσθα, inf. -ῆσθαι: *prize*, *deem worthy* of honor, *honor*, mid. subjective.

τῑμή (τίω): *valuation*, *price*, then (1) *satisfaction*, *penalty*, *punishment*; ἄρνυσθαι, ἀποτίνειν, ἄγειν, Α 159, Γ 286, χ 57.—(2) *honor*, *dignity*, *prerogative*, of gods and kings, Ι 498, ε 535, Β 197, α 117.

τῑμήεις, εσσα, εν, and **τῑμῆς**, acc. τῑμῆντα, comp. τῑμηέστερος, sup. τῑμηέστατος: *precious*, Σ 475, λ 327; then *honored*, σ 161, Ι 605.

τίμιος: *honored*, κ 38†.

τινάσσω, ipf. ἐτίνασσον, τίνασσε, aor. ἐτίναξα, mid. ipf. τινάσσετο, aor. τιναξάσθην, pass. aor. 3 pl. τίναχθεν: *shake*, *brandish*; δοῦρε, αἰγίδα, ἀστεροπήν, mid. πτερά, 'shook their' wings, β 151; θρόνον, 'overthrow,' χ 88; ἐκ (adv.) δ' ἐτίναχθεν ὀδόντες, 'were dashed' out, Π 348; 'plucked her garment,' Γ 385.

τίνυμαι, τίνυται, -υσθον, -νται, part. τῑνύμενος = τίνομαι: *punish*, *chastise*, τινά, λώβην, ω 326.

τίνω (τίω), fut. τίσω, aor. ἔτῑσα, inf. τῖσαι, mid. fut. τίσομαι, aor. ἐτῑσάμην, τίσατο, opt. 3 pl. τῑσαίατο, inf. τίσασθαι: I. act., *pay* a debt or a penalty, *atone for*; in good sense, ζωάγρια, αἴσιμα πάντα, ἀμοιβὴν βοῶν, ε 407, θ 348, μ 382; in bad sense, τῑμήν τινι, θωήν, β 193; w. acc. of the thing atoned for, Α 42, ω 352; rarely acc. of the person atoned for, Ρ 34; 'reward,' ξ 166.—II. mid., *exact satisfaction*, *make one pay* you for something, τινά τι, τινά τινος, ο 236, Γ 366; hence *punish*.

τίπτε (= τί ποτε), τίπτ', τίφθ': *why pray?*

Τῖρυνς, υθος: *Tiryns*, an ancient city in Argolis, with Cyclopean walls, residence of Perseus and other kings of Argos, Β 559†.

τίς, τί, gen. τέο, τεῦ, pl. gen. τέων (τέων, ζ 119, ν 200): interrog. pron., *who? what?* ἐς τί, *how long?* Ε 465.—Rarely in indirect questions, Σ 192, ο 423, ρ 368.—Adv. **τί**, *why? how?*

τὶς, τὶ, gen. τεύ, τεό, dat. (οὔ) τινι, τεῷ, τώ, pl. neut. ἄσσα: indef. pron. enclitic, *some* (*any*) *one*, *some* (*any*) *thing*; *many a one*, (*every*) *one*, τ 265, Β 388, 355; appended to adjectives, it makes them less precise, ὁπποῖ' ἄσσα εἵματα, 'about what sort of clothing,' τ 218.—Adv., **τὶ**, *somewhat*, *in a degree*, but adds force to a negation, **οὔ τι**, *not at all*, *by no means*; **οὐδέ τι**, *nothing whatever*, γ 184.

τίσις, ιος (τίω): *recompense,* β 76; then *vengeance, punishment,* τινός, 'for something,' ἔκ τινος, 'at the hands of some one.'

τιταίνω (τανύω, τείνω), ipf. ἐτίταινε, aor. 1 part. τιτήνᾱς, mid. ipf. (ἐ)τιταίνετο: *stretch, draw, extend,* mid., reflexive and subjective; of drawing the bow, chariot, plough, Θ 266, Β 390; stretching out the hands, spreading a table, poising the balance, Ν 534, Θ 69, κ 354; mid., of exerting one's strength, λ 599; horses, birds, stretching themselves to run or fly, χ 23, β 149; stringing a bow for oneself, φ 259.

Τίτανος: a place (mountain or town) in Thessaly, Β 735†.

Τιταρήσιος: a river (later Eurōpus) of Thessaly, rising in Mt. Olympus and a branch of the Peneius, Β 751†.

Τιτῆνες: the *Titans,* sons of Uranus and Gaea. Under the lead of Cronus they took possession of heaven, but were cast down by him into Tartarus. Finally Zeus, aided by Gaea, overpowered Cronus and shut him up with the other Titans, Ε 898, Ξ 279.

τίτος (τίνω): *paid for, avenged;* τίτα ἔργα, 'works of vengeance,' Ω 213 (v. l. ἄντιτα).

τιτρώσκω: see **τρώω.**

Τιτυός: *Tityus,* a giant, the son of Gaea, punished in Hades, λ 576-580, η 324.

τιτύσκομαι (root τυκ, τυχεῖν), ipf. τιτύσκετο: (1) lit., try to hit, hence *aim;* ἄντα, 'straight before one,' φ 48; τινός, 'at something'; met., of purpose, design, φρεσί, Ν 558, θ 556.—(2) try to get, hence *make ready, prepare;* πῦρ, ἵππους ὑπ' ὄχεσφι, 'couple,' 'put to,' Θ 41.

τίφθ': see τίπτε.

τίω, inf. τῑέμεν, ipf. **τῖον,** ἔτιε, iter. τῑεσκον, fut. τίσω, aor. ἔτῑσα, mid. ipf. iter. τιέσκετο, pass. perf. part. τετῑμένος: *value, estimate,* then *esteem, prize, honor.*

τλήμων, ονος (τλῆναι): *enduring, patient,* Ε 670; then *bold, impudent,* Φ 430. Cf. σχέτλιος.

τλῆναι (root ταλ), aor. 2 inf., ind. ἔτλην, τλῆ, τλῆμεν, ἔτλαν, opt. τλαίην, imp. τλῆθι, τλήτω, τλῆτε, aor. 1 ἐτάλασσα, subj. ταλάσσῃς, fut. τλήσομαι, perf., w. pres. signif., **τέτληκα,** 1 pl. **τέτλαμεν,** imp. **τέτλαθι, -άτω,** opt. **τετλαίη,** inf. τετλάμεν(αι), part. **τετληώς, -υῖα**: *endure, suffer, bear up under, submit to,* τί, Σ 433; so the part. as adj., τετληότι θυμῷ, with *steadfast* soul; and with part., ε 362, υ 311; with inf., *bring oneself* to do something (by overcoming any kind of a scruple), *dare, venture, have the heart* or *the hardihood* to do it, Ρ 166.

Τληπόλεμος: (1) a son of Hercules and Astyoche, who as a fugitive found safety in Rhodes, and became king there, Β 653, 657, 661, Ε 628, 631, 632, 648, 656, 660, 668.—(2) a Lycian, son of Damastor, slain by Patroclus, Π 416.

τλητός (τλῆναι): *enduring,* Ω 49†.

τμήγω (τέμνω): *cut;* only pass., aor. 3 pl. τμάγεν, fig., 'they separated,' 'dispersed,' Λ 146, Π 374.

τμήδην (τέμνω): adv., *so as to cut* or *graze,* Η 262†.

Τμῶλος: *Tmolus,* a mountain in Lydia, near Sardis, Β 866, Υ 385.

τόθι: *there,* ο 239†.

τοί: pronoun. See (1) ὁ.—(2) σύ.

τοί: enclitic particle of asseveration, *certainly, you may be sure, I assure you, let me tell you;* τοί has been called the 'gnomic' particle from the frequency of its occurrence in the statement of general truths or maxims, *κιχάνει τοι βραδὺς ὠκύν,* 'the race is not always to the swift,' θ 329, β 276, Β 298, etc. Sometimes it is impossible to decide whether this particle or the ethical dat. (τοί = σοί) is meant, and probably the two were originally identical.

τοίγαρ: *so then, accordingly,* always at the beginning of the clause.

τοῖος: *of such a kind, such* (talis), answering to οἷος, Σ 105, α 257; to ὁποῖος, φ 421; to ὅς, β 286; to ὅπως, π 208; with inf., *capable, able;* with adjs., *so really, so very, just,* α 209, cf. λ 135, β 286.—Adv., **τοῖον,** *so, so very.*

τοιόσδε, -ήδε, -όνδε: *such,* like **τοῖος,** but properly deictic, i. e. said with reference to something present or near, that can be pointed out, 'such as that there,' Φ 509, ο 330. Sometimes implying 'so good,' 'so fine,' 'so bad,' etc., Β 120, Γ 157, υ 206; w. inf., Ζ 463.

τοιοῦτος, τοιαύτη, τοιοῦτο(ν): *of such a kind, such*, like τοῖος, but a stronger demonstrative; 'so excellent,' B 372, Π 847; 'so heinous' things, Ψ 494, χ 315.

τοίσδε(σ)σι: see ὅδε.

τοῖχος: *wall* of a house or court; *sides* of a ship, μ 420, O 382.

τοκάς, ἄδος (τίκτω): σύες, *having just littered*, ξ 16†.

τοκεύς, ῆος: pl., *parents; ancestors*, δ 596, η 54.

τόκος: *bringing forth, delivery; offspring, young*, O 141, ο 175.

τολμάω (root ταλ), ipf. τόλμων, ἐτόλμᾱς, fut. τολμήσω, aor. τόλμησα: *endure, bear*, with part., ω 162; with inf., ω 261; *be bold, dare*, E 670, Θ 424.

τολμήεις, εσσα, εν: *enduring, steadfast, daring*, ρ 284, K 205.

τολυπεύω, fut. -εύσω, aor. τολύπευσα: wind up as a ball (τολύπη), hence *contrive*, δόλους, τ 137, cf. ὑφαίνω. Also *achieve, finish*, ω 95, Ω 7.

τομή (τέμνω): end left after cutting, *stump, stock*, A 235†.

τοξάζομαι (τόξον), opt. 3 pl. τοξαζοίατο, fut. τοξάσσεται, aor. opt. τοξάσσαιτο: *shoot with the bow*; τινός, 'at something,' θ 218.

τοξευτής: *bowman, archer*, pl., Ψ 850†.

τοξεύω = τοξάζομαι, Ψ 855†.

τόξον (root τυκ, τυχεῖν), pl. τόξα: *bow*, freq. the pl. for the sing., as the weapon was made of two horns joined by a centre-piece, see Δ 105–111. The bow was strung by slipping the loop at one end of the string (νευρή) over the curved tip (κορώνη) at the end of the bow, see cut No. 34. For the way of shooting, see cuts Nos. 63, 89, 90, 104; and for the bow-case, Nos. 24, 124. The archer was regarded as an inferior sort of warrior, Λ 385.—For the art, *archery*, B 718, cf. 827.

τοξοσύνη: *archery*, N 314†.

τοξότης: *archer*, Λ 385†.

τοξο-φόρος: *bow-bearing*, Φ 483†.

τόπριν: see πρίν.

τοπρόσθεν: see πρόσθεν.

τοπρῶτον: see πρῶτον.

τορέω (cf. τείρω, τετραίνω), aor. 2 ἔτορε: *bore, pierce*, Λ 236†.

τορνόω, mid. aor. τορνώσαντο, subj. τορνώσεται: *round off*, mid., for oneself.

τό(σ)σος: *so great, so much*, pl., *so many*.—Adv., **τό(σ)σον, τόσα,** *so much, so very*.

το(σ)σόσδε, -ήδε, -όνδε = τόσος, but properly deictic, referring to something present or near.—Adv., **το(σ)σόνδε.**

το(σ)σοῦτος, -αύτη, -οῦτον = τόσος, but a stronger demonstrative.—Adv., **το(σ)σοῦτον.**

τοσσάκι, τοσσάχ': *so many times, so often*; answering to ὁσσάκι, Φ 268.

τόσσος, τοσσοῦτον: see τόσος, τοσοῦτος.

τότε: *at that time, then*; freq. in apodosis, in phrases, καὶ τότε δή, ῥα, ἔπειτα.

τοτέ: *sometimes*; τοτὲ μὲν . . τοτὲ δέ, 'now . . then,' ω 447 f.; standing alone, *at another time, anon*, Λ 63.

τοῦ: see (1) ὁ.—(2) τίς.—(3) τὶς.

τοὔνεκα = τοῦ ἕνεκα, *therefore*.

τοὔνομα = τὸ ὄνομα.

τόφρα: *so long*, answering to ὄφρα, also to ἕως, ὅτε, πρίν, εὖτε. With δέ, Δ 221. *Up to the time* (when), A 509. *Meanwhile*, N 83, μ 166.

τράγος: *he-goat*, pl., ι 239†.

τράπεζα (τετράπεδya, 'four-foot,' cf. τρίπος): *table*; ξενίη, 'hospitable board,' ξ 158. Guests as a rule, though not always, had each his own table, α 111.

τραπεζεύς, ῆος: *belonging to the table*; κύνες, 'table-dogs,' i. e. fed from the table, cf. 'lap-dog.'

τραπείομεν: see τέρπω.

τραπέω (τρέπω): *tread, press*, η 125†.

τραφέμεν, τράφεν: see τρέφω.

τραφερός (τρέφω): *solid, firm*; as subst., ἐπὶ τραφερήν τε καὶ ὑγρήν, cf. 'terra firma,' Ξ 308 and υ 98.

τρεῖς: *three*.

τρέμω (cf. tremo): *tremble*.

τρέπω, fut. τρέψω, aor. ἔτρεψα, τρέψα, aor. 2 ἔτραπον, τράπον, mid. aor. 1 part. τρεψάμενος, aor. 2 (ἐ)τραπόμην, pass. perf. τέτραμμαι, imp. τετράφθω, part. τετραμμένος, plup. 3 pl. τετράφαθ', aor. inf. τραφθῆναι: *turn*, so as to alter the direction more or less.—I. act., *turn, direct*; τὶ ἔς τι, πρός, παρά, κατά, ἀνά τι, etc., pass., Ξ 403; of guiding or leading one to a place, δ 294, ι 315; turning missiles aside, horses to flight, E 187, Θ 157, and without ἵππους, Π 657; esp., of turning, 'routing' an enemy, O 261; metaph., νόον, θῡμόν, E 676.—With πάλιν, *turn* about or around, ὄσσε, 'avert' the eyes, N 3; ἵππους, Θ 432; met., φρένας τινός, Z 61.—II. mid., intrans., *turn* oneself, with direction specified by preposition or adv., as above; metaph., τραπέσθαι ἐπὶ ἔργα, Γ 422, α 422; of motion to and fro (versari), τραφθῆναι ἀν' Ἑλλάδα, 'wander up and down' through Hellas, ο 80; met., *change*, τρέπεται χρώς, N 279; τράπετο νοός, φρήν, κραδίη τέτραπτο, P 546, K 45, δ 260.

τρέφω, aor. 1 ἔθρεψα, aor. 2 ἔτραφον, ἔτραφ' (τράφ'), du. ἐτραφέτην, inf. τραφέμεν, perf. τέτροφε, mid. aor. 1 opt. θρέψαιο, pass. aor. 2, 3 pl., τράφεν: trans., *make big* or *thick*, *make to grow* by feeding, *nourish*, *bring up*, *rear*, *tend;* of curdling milk, ι 246; among the trans. forms the aor. 1 mid. (causative) is to be included, τ 368; said of plants, P 53; so fig., ὕλη τρέφει ἄγρια, χθὼν φάρμακα, Λ 741.—Intrans. (pass., with aor. 2 and perf. act.), *thicken*, *congeal*, *grow big*, *wax*, *grow up;* περὶ χροὶ τέτροφεν ἅλμη, 'encrusted,' ψ 237; τράφεν ἠδ' ἐγένοντο, were born and *bred*, A 251.

τρέχω, aor. 1 iter. θρέξασκον, aor. 2 ἔδραμον, δράμε: *run;* fig., of the auger, ι 386.

τρέω, τρεῖ, inf. τρεῖν, ipf. τρέε, aor. ἔτρε(σ)σα: turn to flee, *flee* in terror, *be afraid*, *fear*. (Il.)

τρήρων, ωνος (τρέω): *timid*, epith. of the dove.

τρητός (τιτράω): *bored*, *pierced* with holes, *perforated.* Mooring stones had a hole through them to receive the cable, bedsteads were perforated for the bed-cord.

Τρηχίς, ῖνος: *Trachis*, a town in Thessaly near Thermopylae, B 682†.

Τρῆχος: an Aetolian, slain by Hector, E 706†.

τρηχύς, εῖα, ύ: *rough*, *rugged:* λίθος, ἀκτή, ἀταρπός, ξ 1; also of places, esp. Ithaca, ι 27.

τρίαινα (τρεῖς): the *trident* (three-forked harpoon), weapon of Poseidon, the symbol of his power, M 27, δ 506.

τρίβω (cf. τείρω), inf. τρῑβέμεναι, aor. ἔτρῑψα, inf. τρῖψαι: *rub*, hence *thresh* corn (by treading out with oxen, see cut), Υ 496; μοχλὸν ἐν ὀφθαλμῷ,

'plunge' we should say (cf. 'rubbed in'), ι 333; pass. and fig., *wear oneself out*, Ψ 735.

τρί-γληνος (γλήνη): with three eyeballs, of ear-rings *with three drops* or *pearls*, Ξ 183 and σ 297. (See cut, from an ancient Greek coin.)

τρι-γλώχῑν, ῖνος (γλωχίν, γλῶσσα): *three-barbed*, arrow, E 393 and Λ 507.

τρί-ετες (Ϝέτος): *three years long.* (Od.)

τρίζω (cf. strideo, strix), part. τρίζουσαι, perf. part., w. pres. signif., τετρῑγυῖα, τετρῑγῶτες, plup. τετρίγει: of birds, *twitter*, B 314; of bats, ghosts, *squeak*, *gibber*, ω 5, 7, 9; of wrestlers' backs, *crack*, Ψ 714.

τριήκοντα: *thirty.*

τριηκόσιοι: *three hundred.*

Τρί(κ)κη: a city in Thessaly, on the Peneius, B 729, Δ 202.

τρί-λλιστος (λίσσομαι): *thrice-earnestly prayed for*, Θ 488†.

τρί-πλαξ, ακος: *threefold*, Σ 480†.

τρι-πλῇ: *threefold*, *thrice over*, A 128†.

τρί-πολος (πολέω): *thrice turned*, i. e. *thrice ploughed.*

τρί-πος, οδος: *tripod.* In Homer usually a three-footed kettle for warming water, Ψ 702. Also used to mix wine in, as an ornament, and as a prize in games, Σ 373, Ψ 264. (The cut is from an ancient relief, representing a Delphic tripod, which was a favorite subject of representation.)

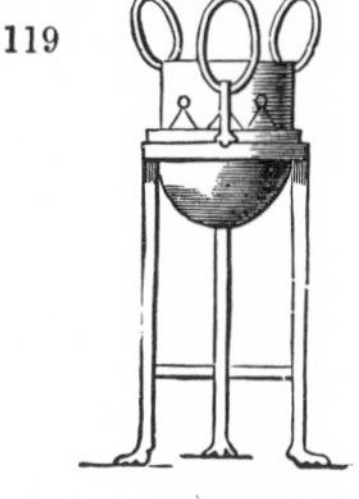
119

τρί-πτυχος (πτύσσω): *triple, of three layers*, τρυφάλεια, Λ 353†.

τρίς: *thrice.*

τρισ-καί-δεκα: *thirteen.*

τρισ-και-δέκατος: *thirteenth.*

τρι-στοιχί: *in three rows*, Κ 473†.

τρί-στοιχος: *in three rows*, μ 91†.

τρισ-χίλιοι: *three thousand*, Υ 221†.

τρίτατος: *third.*

Τρῑτογένεια: 'Trito-born,' *Tritogenīa*, epith. of Athēna, also alone as name, Θ 39, Χ 183, Δ 515, γ 378. The significance of the first part of the word is unknown.

τρίχες: see θρίξ.

τριχθά: *in three parts.*

Τροιζήν, ῆνος: *Troezen*, a town in Argolis, near the shore of the Saronic gulf, Β 561†.

Τροίζηνος: son of Ceas, father of Euphēmus, Β 847†.

Τροίη: (1) the *Troad*, or the district of which Troy was the principal city, Β 162.—(2) *Troy*, otherwise called Ilium, Α 129.

Τροίηθε(ν): *from Troy.*

Τροίηνδε: *to Troy.*

τρομέω, mid. opt. 3 pl. τρομεοίατο: *tremble* with fear, *quake*, φρένες, Ο 627; so the mid., Κ 10; trans., *fear, dread*, π 446.

τρόμος: *trembling, tremor, shudder*, ω 49; then *fear, terror.*

τροπέω (τρέπω): *turn about*, Σ 224†.

τροπή: pl., ἠελίοιο, *turning-places* (cf. 'tropics'), where the sun daily turns back his steeds, indicating the extreme west, ο 404†.

τρόπις, ιος: *keel.* (Od.) (See cut under δρύοχος.)

τροπός: pl., *thongs* or *straps*, by means of which oars were loosely attached to the thole-pins (κληῖδες), δ 782 and θ 53. (See cut No. 32, *d.* A later different arrangement is seen in the following cut, and in No. 38.)

120

τρίτος: *third; τὸ τρίτον, in the third place, for the third time*, Γ 225.

τρίχα (τρίς): *threefold, in three parts;* τρίχα νυκτὸς ἔην, 'a third of the night remained,' ''twas in the third watch,' μ 312. (Od.)

τριχάϊκες: doubtful word, epith. of Δωριέες, *with waving* or *flowing plume* (θρίξ, ἀΐσσω ?), τ 177†.

τροφέοντο: see τροφόεις.

τρόφις, τρόφι (τρέφω): *big, huge;* κῦμα, Λ 307†.

τροφόεις, εσσα, εν: *big, swollen;* κύματα τροφόεντα (v. l. τροφέοντο, 'were swelling'), γ 290†.

τροφός: *nurse.* (Od.)

τροχάω: only part., ἅμα τροχόωντα, *running* about after me, ο 451†.

τροχός (τρέχω): *wheel; potter's* wheel, Σ 600; a round cake of wax or tallow, μ 173, φ 178.

τρυγάω, 3 pl. **τρυγόωσιν,** opt. **τρυγόῳεν**: *gather* harvest or vintage.

τρύζω (cf. **τρυγών,** 'turtle-dove'): *coo,* fig., *gossip,* 'din into one's ears,' I 311†.

τρῠ́πανον: *auger, drill,* of the carpenter, turned by a bow and string, ι 385†. (The cut is from an ancient Egyptian representation.)

121

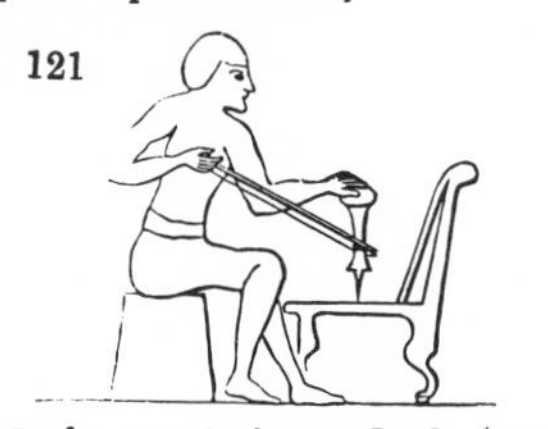

τρῡπάω, opt. 3 sing. **τρῡπῷ**: *bore,* ι 384†.

τρυφάλεια: *helmet.* (See the cut.)

122

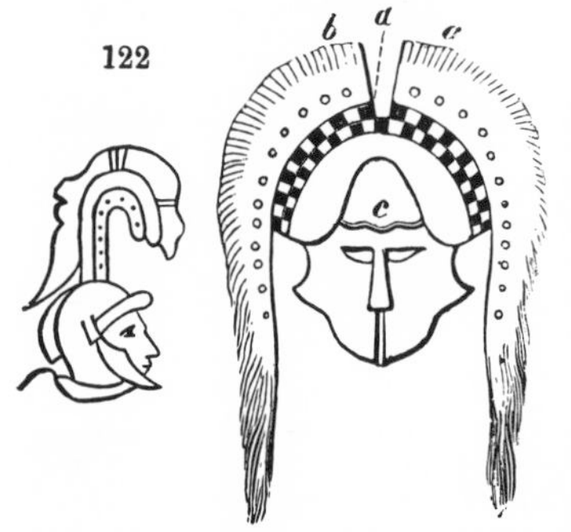

τρύφος, εος (θρύπτω): *fragment,* δ 508†.

τρῡ́χω (τρύω), fut. part. **τρύξοντα**: *wear out, exhaust, consume, impoverish;* οἶκον, α 248; pass., α 288, κ 177.

Τρῳαί, Τρωάς: see Τρῳός.

τρώγω: *gnaw, crop, browse upon,* ζ 90†.

Τρῶες: the *Trojans,* inhabitants of the Troad.

Τρωιάς: see Τρώιος.

Τρωικός: *Trojan;* Τρωικὸν πεδίον, 'the Trojan plain,' between Ilium and the sea.

Τρώιλος: *Troïlus,* son of Priam and Hecuba, Ω 257†.

Τρώιος: (1) *of Tros,* belonging to Tros, the son of Erichthonius, Ε 222, Ψ 378.—(2) *Trojan,* belonging to the Trojans, Ν 262.—Fem., **Τρωιάς,** άδος, ληίς, γυναῖκες, ν 263, Ι 139; and as subst., without γυναῖκες, Σ 122.

τρώκτης: *deceiver, knave,* ξ 289 and ο 415.

Τρῳός: (1) *of Tros,* belonging to Tros, the son of Erichthonius, Ψ 291.—(2) *Trojan,* belonging to the Trojans, Ε 461.—Subst., **Τρῳαί, Τρῳάδες,** *Trojan women,* Γ 384, Ζ 442.

τρωπάω (τρέπω), part. **τρωπῶσα,** mid. ipf. **τρωπῶντο,** iter. **τρωπάσκετο**: act., *change* frequently, *vary,* τ 521; mid., intrans., *turn* oneself.

Τρώς: *Tros.*—(1) son of Erichthonius, father of Ilus, Assaracus, and Ganymēdes, Ε 265 ff., Υ 230 ff.—(2) son of Alastor, slain by Achilles, Υ 463.

τρωτός: *vulnerable,* Φ 568†.

τρωχάω (τρέχω), ipf. **τρώχων**: *run.*

τρώω, τρώει, aor. subj. **τρώσῃ, -ητε,** mid. fut. inf. **τρώσεσθαι**: *wound;* fut. mid. w. pass. signif., Μ 66; fig. (like βλάπτω), φ 293.

τυγχάνω, fut. **τεύξομαι,** aor. 2 **ἔτυχον, τύχον,** subj. **τύχωμι,** aor. 1 (ἐ)**τύχησα,** perf. part. **τετυχηκώς**: (1) *hit* the mark, w. gen., Π 609, etc.; freq. the part. **τυχών, τυχήσᾱς** and βάλλω, **οὐτάω, νύσσω** (where the acc. is to be construed not w. the part. but w. the verb), Δ 106, Ε 582; so fig. w. part. of another verb, *be successful* in doing something, *succeed;* **οὐκ ἐτύχησεν ἐλίξᾱς,** Ψ 466; abs. (without part.), Θ 430; then, *come upon, chance upon,* hence *get, gain, obtain,* φ 13, Ε 587, ο 158.—(2) *happen* to be there, *be by chance, happen;* often nearly equiv. to εἶναι, Ρ 748, κ 88; often w. part. which in Eng. becomes the principal verb, **τύχησε γὰρ ἐρχομένη νηῦς,** 'was by chance about to sail,' ξ 334; impers., *fall to one's share,* Λ 684.

Τῡδεΐδης: *son of Tydeus,* Diomēdes, Ε 1, 281, Ξ 380.

Τῡδεύς: *Tydeus,* son of Oeneus, king of Calydon in Aetolia, and father of Diomed, Ε 813, 163, Ζ 96. While a fugitive at Argos he married the daughter of Adrastus, and joined Polynīces in the expedition of the Seven against Thebes, Δ 376 ff.

τυκτός (τεύχω): well *made*, well *wrought*; τυκτὸν κακόν, 'a born plague,' E 831.

τύμβος: funeral *mound, tomb, grave*. The mound was raised over the urn containing the ashes of the deceased.

τυμβο-χοέω (χέω), aor. inf. τυμβοχοῆσ(αι): *heap up a funeral mound*, Φ 323. The elision is exceptional, hence the v. l. τυμβοχόης, 'of a mound.'

τυμβοχόη: see the foregoing.

Τυνδάρεος: *Tyndareüs*, of Sparta, husband of Leda, and father of Clytaemnestra, Castor, and Pollux, ω 199, λ 298 ff.

τύνη = σύ.

τυπή: *blow, stroke*, pl., E 887†.

τύπτω, aor. τύψα, pass. perf. part. τετυμμένος, aor. 2 ἐτύπην: *strike, hit*, esp. in hand-to-hand encounter, hence opp. to βάλλειν, Λ 191, N 288, O 495; met., τὸν ἄχος κατά φρένα τύψε βαθεῖαν, 'struck deep into his soul,' T 125; pass., N 782, Ω 421; of rowers, ἅλα τύπτον ἐρετμοῖς, ι 104; 'trod in' his (Ajax's) footsteps, Ψ 754; λαίλαπι, 'lashing' with the tempest, Λ 306.

τῡρός: *cheese*.

Τῡρώ: *Tyro*, daughter of Salmōneus, and mother of Pelias and Neleus by Poseidon, β 120, λ 235.

τυτθός: *little, small*, of persons with reference to age, Z 222, X 480, α 435; of things, τυτθὰ διατμῆξαι, κεάσσαι, into small pieces, 'small,' μ 174, 388. —Adv., **τυτθόν**, *little, a little*; φθέγγεσθαι, 'low,' Ω 170; temporal, T 335.

τυφλός: *blind*, Z 139†.

Τυφωεύς, έος: *Typhōeus*, a monster, originally symbolical of the volcanic agencies of nature, B 782 f.

τυχήσᾱς: see τυγχάνω.

Τυχίος: a Boeotian from Hyle, the maker (τεύχω) of Ajax's shield, H 220†.

τῷ, τῶ: dat. of τό, *then, therefore*.

τώς = ὥς, οὕτως, *thus*.

Υ.

Ὑάδες (ὕω): the *Hyades*, seven stars in the head of the Bull, whose rising marks the beginning of the rainy season, Σ 486†.

ὑακίνθινος: *hyacinthine*; ἄνθος, ζ 231 and ψ 158.

ὑάκινθος: *hyacinth*, Ξ 348†. An entirely different flower from our hyacinth, perhaps the larkspur.

Ὑάμπολις: a town in Phocis, on the Cephissus, B 521†.

ὑββάλλειν: see ὑποβάλλω.

ὑβρίζω: *be insolent* or *arrogant*; trans., *insult, outrage*; w. cognate acc., λώβην, 'perpetrate wantonly,' υ 170.

ὕβρις, ιος (cf. ὑπέρ): *insolence, arrogance*, wanton *violence*. (Od. and A 203, 214.)

ὑβριστής: *overbearing, insolent*, wantonly *violent* person. (Od. and N 633.)

ὑγιής, ές: *healthful, sound, salutary, wholesome*, Θ 524†.

ὑγρός: *liquid, wet, moist*; ὕδωρ, ἔλαιον, γάλα, κέλευθα 'watery ways,' i. e. the sea, γ 71; ἄνεμοι ὑγρὸν ἀέντες, blowing 'rainy,' ε 478. As subst., **ὑγρή**, 'the waters,' opp. τραφερή, Ξ 308.

ὑδατο-τρεφής, ές: *water-fed, growing by the water*, ρ 208†.

Ὕδη: a town on Mt. Tmolus in Lydia, perhaps the later Sardis, Υ 385†.

ὑδραίνω, mid. aor. part. ὑδρηναμένη: mid., *wash oneself, bathe*. (Od.)

ὑδρεύω: *draw water*, mid., for one self. (Od.)

ὑδρηλός: *watery, well-watered*, ι 133†.

ὕδρος: *water-snake*, B 723†.

ὕδωρ, ατος: *water*; pl., ν 109;

prov., ὕδωρ καὶ γαῖα γένοισθε, as we say 'become dust and ashes,' Η 99.

ὑετός (ὕω): *shower*, Μ 133†.

υἱός, gen. υἱοῦ, υἷος, υἱέος, dat. υἱῷ, υἷι, υἱέι, acc. υἱόν, υἷα, υἱέα, du. υἷε, pl. υἷες, υἱέες, dat. υἱοῖσι, υἱάσι, acc. υἷας, υἱέας, υἱεῖς: *son;* freq. υἷες Ἀχαιῶν for Ἀχαιοί. The diphthong is sometimes shortened in υἱός, υἱόν, υἱέ, λ 270, 478, Δ 473.

υἱωνός: *grandson.*

ὑλαγμός: *barking, howling*, Φ 575†.

Ὑλακίδης: *son of Hylacus* or *Hylax*, a name assumed by Odysseus, ξ 204.

ὑλακόμωρος: *loud-barking*, ξ 29 and π 4.

ὑλακτέω, ipf. ὑλάκτεον, ὑλάκτει: *bark, bay;* κραδίη, 'growled with wrath,' υ 13, 16.

ὑλάω, ὑλάομαι: *bark, bay, bark at*, π 5. (Od.)

ὕλη (cf. s i l v a): *wood, forest;* also of cut wood, firewood, Ψ 50, ι 234. In general of brush, stuff, raw material, ε 257.

Ὕλη: *Hyle*, a town in Boeotia, Ε 708, Η 221, Β 500.

ὑλήεις, εσσα, εν: *woody, wooded;* also as two endings, α 246, π 123.

Ὕλλος: a branch of the river Hermus in Lydia, Υ 392†.

ὑλο-τόμος (τέμνω): *wood-cutting*, axe, Ψ 114; as subst., pl., *wood-cutters, woodmen*, Ψ 123.

ὑμεῖς, ὑμέων, ὑμείων, dat. ὑμῖν, encl. ὕμῖν, or ὕμιν, also **ὔμμες,** dat. ὔμμ(ιν), acc. ὔμμε: *ye, you*, pl. of σύ.

ὑμέναιος: *wedding-song, bridal-song*, Σ 493†.

ὑμέτερος: *your, yours;* w. gen. in apposition, **αὐτῶν, ἑκάστου,** β 138, Ρ 226.

ὔμμε, ὔμμες, ὔμμιν: see ὑμεῖς.

ὕμνος: *strain, melody*, θ 429†.

ὑμός=ὑμέτερος. Forms: ὑμή, ὑμῆς, ὑμήν, ὑμά, Ν 815, Ε 489, ι 284, α 375.

ὑπ-άγω, ipf. ὕπαγον: *lead under;* ἵππους ζυγόν, i. e. *yoke*, and without ζυγόν, ζ 63; *lead out from under, withdraw*, **τινὰ ἐκ βελέων,** Λ 163.

ὑπαί: see ὑπό.

ὕπαιθα: *out from under, sidewise*, Ο 520; τινός, *sidewise away, at one's side*, Σ 421.

ὑπ-ᾱΐσσω, fut. ὑπᾱΐξει, aor. part. **ὑπᾱΐξᾱς**: *dart* or *spring up under* or *out from under*, Φ 126, Β 310.

ὑπ-ακούω, aor. ὑπάκουσε, inf. ὑπακοῦσαι: *hearken* or *give ear to*, hence *reply*, δ 283, κ 83.

ὑπ-αλεύομαι, aor. part. ὑπαλευάμενος: *avoid, evade*, ο 275†.

ὑπ-άλυξις: *escape*, Χ 270 and ψ 287.

ὑπ-αλύσκω, aor. ὑπάλυξα: *avoid, evade, escape from.*

ὑπ-αντιάω, aor. part. ὑπαντιάσᾱς: *come to meet*, i. e. to meet the enemy and defend the man, Ζ 17†.

ὕπαρ: *reality*, real appearance as opp. to a dream, τ 547 and υ 90.

ὑπ-άρχω, aor. subj. ὑπάρξῃ: *begin, make a beginning*, ω 286.

ὑπ-ασπίδιος: *under the shield;* adv., ὑπασπίδια, 'under shelter of the shield.' (Il.)

ὕπατος: *highest, supremest, most high* or *exalted*, usually as epith. of Zeus; also ἐν πυρῇ **ὑπάτῃ,** 'on the top' of the pyre, Ψ 165.

ὑπέᾱσι: see ὕπειμι.

ὑπέδδεισαν: see ὑποδείδω.

ὑπέδεκτο: see ὑποδέχομαι.

ὑπεθερμάνθη: see ὑποθερμαίνω.

ὑπ-είκω, ὑποείκω (ϝείκω), fut. ὑποείξω, aor. 1 ὑπόειξε, subj. **ὑποείξομεν,** mid. fut. ὑπείξομαι and **ὑποείξομαι**: *retire, withdraw from* (τινός), *yield, make way for* (τινί); w. both gen. and dat., **τῷ** δ' ἕδρης ὑπόειξεν, π 42; w. acc., χεῖράς τινος, 'before one's hands,' Ο 227.

ὕπ-ειμι, 3 pl. ὑπέᾱσι, ipf. **ὑπῆσαν,** *be under;* πολλῇσι, 'many had sucking foals,' Λ 681.

ὑπείρ, ὑπειρέχω, ὑπείροχος: see ὑπέρ, ὑπερ-.

Ὑπείροχος: a Trojan, slain by Odysseus, Λ 335†.

Ὑπειροχίδης: *son of Hypirochus*, Itymoneus, Λ 673†.

Ὑπείρων: a Trojan, slain by Diomed, Ε 144†.

ὑπ-έκ, ὑπέξ: *out from under.*

ὑπ-εκ-προ-θέω: *run on before, outrun*, Ι 506.

ὑπ-εκ-προ-λύω: only aor., **ὑπεκπροέλῡσαν,** *loosed from under* the yoke (wagon), ζ 88†.

ὑπ-εκ-προ-ρέω: *flow forth from* the depth below, ζ 87†.

ὑπ-εκ-προ-φεύγω, aor. 2 -φύγοιμι, part. -φυγών: *escape by furtive flight.*

ὑπ-εκ-σαόω, aor. ὑπεξεσάωσε: *save from under, rescue*, Ψ 292†.

ὑπ-εκ-φέρω, ipf. ὑπεξέφερον and ὑπέκφερον: *bear out from under, carry away;* apparently intrans., 'bear forward,' γ 496.

ὑπ-εκ-φεύγω, aor. 2 ὑπεξέφυγον and ὑπέκφυγον, opt. -οι, inf. -έειν: *escape* or *come safely forth from*, w. acc.

ὑπεμνήμῡκε: see ὑπημύω.

ὑπ-ένερθε(ν): *beneath, below, underneath;* opp. καθύπερθεν, κ 353; w. gen., Β 150, γ 172; 'in the nether world,' Γ 278.

ὑπέξ: see ὑπέκ.

ὑπ-εξ-άγω, aor. 2 opt. ὑπεξαγάγοι: *bring safely forth, rescue*, bring safe home, σ 147†.

ὑπ-εξ-αλέομαι, aor. inf. ὑπεξαλέασθαι: *avoid, shun*, Ο 180†.

ὑπ-εξ-ανα-δύω: only aor. 2 part., ὑπεξαναδύς, *emerging from under* the sea, Ν 352†.

ὑπέρ, ὑπείρ (cf. super): *over*, prep. w. gen. and acc., accented ὕπερ when it follows its case.—(1) w. gen., local, *over, above, beyond, across;* ὑπὲρ οὐδοῦ βῆναι, ρ 575; ὑπὲρ κεφαλῆς στῆναί τινι, Β 20; τηλοῦ ὑπὲρ πόντου, ν 257. Metaph., *for, in defence of*, Α 444, Η 449; w. verbs of entreaty, *by, for the sake of* (per), γουνάζεσθαι ὑπὲρ τοκέων, ὑπὲρ ψῡχῆς καὶ γούνων, Ο 660, ο 261; then like περί, *concerning* (de), Ζ 524.—(2) w. acc., local, *over, beyond*, ἀλαλῆσθαι ὑπεὶρ ἅλα, γ 74; 'along the surface' of the hand, Ε 339. Metaph., *beyond, transcending, against*, ὑπὲρ αἶσαν, μοῖραν, θεόν, Ρ 327, α 34.

ὑπερ-ᾱής, ές (ἄημι): *blowing excessively* or *strongly*, Λ 297†.

ὑπερ-άλλομαι, aor. ὑπερᾶλτο, part. ὑπεράλμενον: *leap* or *spring over*, w. gen. or acc. (Il.)

ὑπερ-βαίνω, aor. 2 ὑπέρβη, 3 pl. ὑπέρβασαν, subj. ὑπερβήῃ: *step over, overstep, transgress.*

ὑπερ-βάλλω, ὑπειρβάλλω, aor. 2 ὑπειρέβαλον, ὑπέρβαλε: *cast beyond;* σήματα, 'beyond the marks,' Ψ 843; ἄκρον, 'over the crest of the hill,' λ 597; rarely w. gen., Ψ 847. Fig., *excel*, τινὰ δουρί, in throwing the spear, Ψ 637.

ὑπέρβασαν: see ὑπερβαίνω.

ὑπερ-βασίη: *transgression, violence.*

ὑπερβήῃ: see ὑπερβαίνω.

ὑπέρ-βιος (βίη): *violent, lawless, insolent, wanton;* not in bad sense, θῡμός, 'abrupt,' ο 212.—Adv., **ὑπέρβιον**, *insolently.*

ὑπερ-δεής, ές, acc. ὑπερδέᾱ (for -δεέα): having *very scanty* forces, Ρ 330†.

Ὑπέρεια: *Hyperīa.*—(1) a spring in Pelasgian Argos, Ζ 457, Β 734.—(2) the former abode of the Phaeacians, near the island of the Cyclōpes, before they removed to Scheria, ζ 4.

ὑπ-ερείπω: only aor. 2 ὑπήριπε, *sank under* him, Ψ 691†.

ὑπ-ερέπτω: *eat away;* 'was washing away' the sand 'under' his feet, Φ 271†.

ὑπερ-έχω, ὑπειρέχω, aor. 2 ὑπερέσχε, ὑπερέσχεθε, subj. ὑπέρσχῃ: trans., *hold over* or *above;* τινός τι, Β 426; for protection, χεῖράς τινι or τινός, Δ 249, Ι 420; intrans., *overtop*, Γ 210; of the sun and stars, *rise*, Λ 735, ν 93.

ὑπέρη (ὑπέρ): pl., *braces*, attached to the yards of a ship, by means of which the sails were shifted, ε 260†. (See cut No. 37.)

ὑπερ-ηνορέων, οντος (ἀνήρ): part. as adjective, *overbearing, overweening, haughty;* epith. esp. of the suitors of Penelope. (Od. and Δ 176, Ν 258.)

Ὑπερήνωρ: son of Panthoüs, slain by Menelāus, Ξ 516, Ρ 24.

Ὑπερησίη: a town in Achaea, Β 573, ο 254.

ὑπερηφανέων, οντος: part. as adj., *exulting over, arrogant*, Λ 694†.

ὕπερθε(ν): *from above, above.*

ὑπερ-θρώσκω, fut. ὑπερθορέονται, aor. 2 ὑπέρθορον, inf. -έειν: *spring over.* (Il.)

ὑπέρ-θῡμος: *high-spirited, high-hearted.*

ὑπερ-θύριον (θύρη): *lintel* of a door, opp. οὐδός, η 90†.

ὑπερ ίημι, fut. ὑπερήσει: *throw beyond* (this mark), θ 198†.

ὑπερ-ικταίνομαι: doubtful word, only ipf., πόδες δ' ὑπερικταίνοντο, *stumbled from haste*, ψ 3†.

Ὑπερῑονίδης and **Ὑπερίων**: *son of Hyperīon* and *Hyperīon*, epithets of

Helios, with and without Ἠέλιος, μ 133, 176, α 24, Τ 398.

ὑπερ-κατα-βαίνω, aor. 2 3 pl. ὑπερκατέβησαν: *go down over, surmount.* (Il.)

ὑπερ-κύδαντας, acc. pl.: *of high renown,* Δ 66, 71.

ὑπερ-μενέων, οντος (μένος): part. as adj., *haughty,* τ 62†.

ὑπερ-μενής, ές (μένος): *high-spirited, exalted.*

ὑπέρ-μορον: *beyond,* i. e. *against fate,* adj. as adv., usually written separately ὑπὲρ μόρον.—Pl., **ὑπέρμορα,** with the same adverbial force, Β 155.

ὑπερ-οπλίη: *presumption, arrogance,* pl., Α 205†. The ῑ is a necessity of the rhythm.

ὑπερ-οπλίζομαι, aor. opt. -σσαιτο: *vanquish by force of arms;* according to others, *presumptuously blame,* ρ 268†.

ὑπέρ-οπλος: *arrogant;* neut. as adv., *arrogantly,* Ο 185 and Ρ 170.

ὑπέρ-οχος, ὑπείροχος: *eminent.* (Il.)

ὑπερ-πέτομαι, aor. ὑπέρπτατο: *fly over, fly past* (the marks), θ 192.

ὑπερράγη: see ὑπορρήγνῡμι.

ὑπέρσχῃ: see ὑπερέχω.

ὑπέρτατος (sup. from ὑπέρ): *highest, on the top, aloft,* Μ 381 and Ψ 451.

ὑπερτερίη: *upper part, awning, wagon-cover,* ζ 70†.

ὑπέρτερος (comp. from ὑπέρ): *higher;* then *superior, better, more excellent; outer* (flesh), γ 65.

ὑπερ-φίαλος (root φυ, φύω): strictly *overgrown,* then *mighty,* Ε 881; in bad sense, *overbearing, arrogant, insolent.*—Adv., **ὑπερφιάλως,** *excessively, insolently,* Ν 293, δ 663.

ὑπ-έρχομαι, aor. 2 ὑπήλυθε, ὑπήλθετε, subj. ὑπέλθῃ: *go under, enter,* w. acc.; fig., Τρῶας τρόμος ὑπήλυθε γυῖα, 'seized,' Η 215.

ὑπ-ερωέω: only aor., ὑπερώησαν, *started back.* (Il.)

ὑπερ-ῴη: *palate,* Χ 495†.

ὑπερωιόθεν: *from the upper chamber.*

ὑπερ-ώϊον, ὑπερῷον: *upper chamber, upper apartments,* often pl. in both forms. The ὑπερώιον was over the women's apartment, and was occupied by women of the family, not by servants, Β 514, ρ 101.

ὑπέστην: see ὑφίστημι.

ὑπ-έχω, aor. ὑπέσχεθε, part. ὑποσχών: *hold under,* Η 188 ('held out' his hand); θήλεας ἵππους, 'putting them to' the horses of Tros, Ε 269.

ὑπ-ημύω: only perf., ὑπεμνήμῡκε, *is* utterly (πάντα) *bowed down,* Χ 491†.

ὑπήνεικα: see ὑποφέρω.

ὑπ-ηνήτης (ὑπήνη, under part of the face): *with a beard;* πρῶτον, 'getting his first beard,' κ 279 and Ω 348.

ὑπ-ηοῖος (ἠώς): *toward morning,* adj. for adv.

ὑπ-ίσχομαι (ἔχω), ipf. ὑπίσχεο, aor. 2 ὑπέσχεο, -ετο, subj. ὑπόσχωμαι, imp. ὑπόσχεο, inf. -σχέσθαι, part. -σχόμενος: *take upon oneself, undertake, promise,* τινί τι, and w. inf., regularly the fut. (exc., pres. inf. explanatory of subst., Κ 40); also 'betroth,' 'vow,' Ν 376, δ 6, Ζ 93, Ψ 209.

ὕπνος: *sleep;* epithets, ἡδύς, νήδυμος, λῡσιμελής, πανδαμάτωρ, χάλκεος, fig. of death, Λ 241.—Personified, **Ὕπνος,** *Sleep,* the brother of Death, Ξ 231 ff.

ὑπνόω: only part., ὑπνώοντας, *sleeping, slumbering.*

ὑπό, ὑπαί (cf. sub): *under.*—I. adv., *underneath, below, beneath,* of motion or rest, ὑπὸ δὲ θρῆνυν ποσὶν ('for the feet') ἥσει, Ξ 240; ὑπὸ δὲ θρῆνυς ποσὶν ἦεν, α 131; χεῦεν ὕπο ῥῶπας, π 47; often to indicate the position of parts of the body (in 'plastic' style as if one were looking at a picture up and down), ὑπὸ γούνατ' ἔλῡσεν (the knees 'beneath him'), ὑπὸ δ' ἔτρεμε γυῖα, Κ 390; sometimes causal, *thereunder, thereby,* θ 380, Θ 4; thus to denote accompaniment in music, λίνον δ' ὑπὸ καλὸν ἄειδεν (*to* it, the harp), Σ 570, φ 411.—II. prep., (1) w. gen., of position or motion; *under,* out or forth *from under;* ὑπ' ἀνθερεῶνος ἑλεῖν, κρήδεμνον ὑπὸ στέρνοιο τανύσσαι, ε 346, and thus often w. verbs of hitting; ῥέει κρήνη ὑπὸ σπείους, 'from beneath,' ι 141; then of agency, influence, *by, through, in consequence of;* δαμῆναι, θνήσκειν ὑπό τινος ('at the hands of'), φεύγειν ὑπό τινος ('before'), Σ 149; ὑπ' ἀνάγκης ('from necessity,' 'perforce'), *ὑπὸ δείους* ('for'), *ὑπὸ φρῑκὸς* Βορέω, Ψ 692. —(2) w. dat., of position, *under*, and w. verbs of motion when the resulting position of rest is chiefly in mind, *πίπτειν, τιθέναι τι ὑπό τινι*, χ 449, Π 378; instrumental or causal, *under* (not 'by' as w. the gen., but rather denoting *subjection*), *ὑπὸ χερσί τινος θανέειν, ὀλέσαι ψῡχήν, γήραι ὕπο ἀρημένος*, λ 136; of power, mastery, *δέδμητο λᾱὸς ὑπ' αὐτῷ*, γ 305, Ω 636; and of accompanying circumstances, *ὑπὸ πομπῇ* ('under the guidance'), *πνοιῇ ὕπο* ('with the breeze'), δ 402. —(3) w. acc., of motion (or extension), *under*, but often where the idea of motion is quite faint, *ζώειν ὑπ' αὐγᾱς ἠελίοιο*, thinking of the *duration* of life, ο 349, Ε 267; of time, *during*, Π 202, Χ 102.

ὑπο-βάλλω, inf. *ὑββάλλειν*: *throw* or *lay underneath; interrupt*, Τ 80.

ὑπο-βλήδην: *interrupting*, Α 292†.

ὑπό-βρυχα: adj. as adv., *under water*, ε 319†.

ὑπο-δάμνημι: only mid., *ὑποδάμνασαι*, *thou subjectest thyself*, γ 214 and π 95.

ὑποδέγμενος: see *ὑποδέχομαι*.

ὑπο-δείδω, aor. *ὑπόδδεισαν, ὑποδείσατε*, part. *ὑποδδείσᾱς*, perf. *ὑποδείδια*, plup. *ὑπεδείδισαν*: *be afraid before, shrink under, fear*, abs., and w. acc.

ὑπο-δεξίη (*δέχομαι*): *hospitable welcome*, Ι 73†. The ῑ is a necessity of the rhythm.

ὑπο-δέχομαι, fut. *ὑποδέξομαι*, aor. 1 *ὑπεδέξατο*, aor. 2 *ὑπέδεξο, -έδεκτο*, inf. *ὑποδέχθαι*, part. *ὑποδέγμενος*: *receive*, esp. of friendly, hospitable welcome, *πρόφρων, οἴκῳ*, π 70; also with a thing as subject, *κοῖτος, πῆμα*, ξ 275; *βίᾱς*, receive silently, submit to, *endure*, ν 310; *undertake, promise*, Η 93, β 387.

ὑπό-δημα, *ατος* (*δέω*, 'bind'): pl., *sandals*.

ὑπο-δμώς: *under-servant, underling*, δ 386†.

ὑπόδρα: look *sternly, darkly, grimly*.

ὑπο-δράω, *-δρώωσι*; *work* as servant *under, wait upon*, ο 333†.

ὑπο-δρηστήρ, *ῆρος* (*δράω*): *underworker, attendant*, ο 330†.

ὑπο-δύομαι, fut. *ὑποδῡ́σεαι*, aor. *ὑπεδύσετο*, aor. 2 *ὑπέδῡ*, part. *ὑποδῦσα, -δύντε*: *plunge* or *dive under* the water, δ 435, Σ 145; abs., *go under* to carry, take on one's shoulders, Θ 332, Ρ 717; fig., *πᾶσιν γόος*, grief 'penetrated' all, κ 398; w. gen., *emerge from, escape from*, ζ 127, υ 53.

ὑπόεικε: see *ὑπείκω*.

ὑπο-ζεύγνῡμι, fut. *ὑποζεύξω*: *put under the yoke, harness*, ο 81†.

ὑπο-θερμαίνω: only aor. pass., *ὑποθερμάνθη*, *was warmed*, Π 333 and Υ 476.

Ὑποθῆβαι: a town in Boeotia, Β 505†.

ὑπο-θημοσύνη (*τίθημι*): *suggestion, counsels*, pl., Ο 412 and π 233.

ὑπο-θωρήσσω: only mid. ipf., *ὑπεθωρήσσοντο*, *were arming themselves*, Σ 513†.

ὑποκῑνήσαντος: v. l. for *ὕπο κῑνήσαντος*.

ὑπο-κλίνω: only pass. aor., *ὑπεκλίνθη*, *he lay down*, ε 463†.

ὑπο-κλονέω: only mid., *ὑποκλονέεσθαι*, *to crowd themselves together in flight before* Achilles, Φ 556†.

ὑπο-κλοπέομαι: *conceal oneself under* something, opt., χ 382†.

ὑπο-κρίνομαι, aor. opt. *-κρίναιτο*, imp. *ὑπόκρῑναι*, inf. *-κρίνασθαι*: *answer* (*τινί*); *interpret*, *ὄνειρον*, and abs., τ 535, 555, Μ 228, cf. Ε 150.

ὑπο-κρύπτω: only pass. aor., *ὑπεκρύφθη*, *was hidden*, Ο 626†.

ὑπό-κυκλος: *with wheels beneath, wheeled*, δ 131†.

ὑπο-κύομαι, aor. part. *ὑποκῡσαμένη*: *become pregnant, conceive.*

ὑπο-λείπω, mid. fut. *ὑπολείψομαι*: *leave over*, mid., *remain.*

ὑπο-λευκαίνομαι: *grow white below, whiten*, Ε 502†.

ὑπ-ολίζων, *ονος* (comp. from *ὀλίγος*): *somewhat smaller, on a smaller scale*, Σ 519†. Also written as two words.

ὑπο-λύω, aor. *ὑπέλῡσα*, mid. aor. 1 *ὑπελῡ́σαο*, aor. 2 *ὑπέλυντο*: act., *loose from under, undo*, ι 463; fig., *γυῖα, μένος*, *make to sink* or *fail, paralyze* (slay), Ο 581, Ζ 27; aor. 2 mid., as pass., Π 341; mid., aor. 1, *secretly set free*, Α 401.

ὑπο-μένω, aor. *ὑπέμεινα*, inf. *ὑπομεῖναι*: *remain, wait, sustain, withstand.*

ὑπο-μιμνήσκω, fut. part. *ὑπομνή-*

σουσα, aor. ὑπέμνησε: *remind, put in mind of.* (Od.)

ὑπο-μνάομαι, ipf. ὑπεμνάασθε: *woo* or *court unlawfully,* χ 38†.

ὑπο-νήιος: lying *under Mt. Neium,* γ 81†.

ὑπο-πεπτηῶτες: see ὑποπτήσσω.

ὑπο-περκάζω (περκνός): *begin to grow dark* or *turn,* of grapes, η 126†.

ὑπο-πλάκιος: situated *under Mt. Placus, Hypoplacian* Thebe, Z 397†.

ὑπο-πτήσσω: only perf. part., ὑποπεπτηῶτες, *having crouched down* timidly *under* and hidden themselves amid the leaves, πετάλοις, B 312†.

ὑπ-όρνῡμι: only aor. 2, τοῖον ὑπώρορε Μοῦσα, in so moving strains *did* the Muse *begin,* ω 62†.

ὑπο-ρρήγνῡμι (ϝρήγνῡμι), pass. aor. ὑπερράγη: pass., *burst forth* (under the clouds), αἰθήρ, Π 300 and Θ 558.

ὑπό-ρρηνος (ϝρήν): *having a lamb under her,* κ 216†.

ὑπο-σσείω: *whirl around* (laying hold) *below,* ι 385†.

ὑποσταίη: see ὑφίστημι.

ὑπο-σταχύομαι (στάχυς): fig., *wax gradually like ears of corn, increase,* υ 212†.

ὑπο-στεναχίζω: *groan under;* τινί, B 781†.

ὑπο-στορέννῡμι, aor. inf. ὑποστορέσαι: *spread out under;* δέμνιά τινι, υ 139†.

ὑπο-στρέφω, aor. subj. ὑποστρέψωσι, opt. -ειας, mid. fut. inf. -ψεσθαι, pass. aor. part. ὑποστρεφθείς: *turn about, turn* in flight, trans. and intr., E 581, Λ 446; mid. and pass., intr., *turn, return,* σ 23.

ὑποσχεθεῖν: see ὑπέχω.

ὑποσχέσθαι: see ὑπίσχομαι.

ὑπο-σχεσίη = ὑπόσχεσις, pl., N 369†.

ὑπό-σχεσις, ιος (ὑπίσχομαι): *promise.*

ὑπο-ταρβέω: only aor. part., ὑποταρβήσαντες, *shrinking before* them, P 533†.

ὑπο-ταρτάριος: dwelling *below in Tartarus,* the Titans, Ξ 279†.

ὑπο-τίθημι, mid. fut. ὑποθήσομαι, aor. 2 ὑπεθέμην, inf. ὑποθέσθαι: *place under,* mid., fig., *suggest, counsel;* τινί (τι), εὖ, πυκινῶς, δ 163, β 194, Φ 293.

ὑπο-τρέχω: only aor. 2 ὑπέδραμε, *ran under* (the menacing arm and weapon), Φ 68 and κ 323.

ὑπο-τρέω, aor. ὑπέτρεσα, inf. ὑποτρέσαι: *take to flight, flee before* one, P 587.

ὑπο-τρομέω, ipf. iter. ὑποτρομέεσκον: *tremble before.*

ὑπό-τροπος (τρέπω): *returning, back again.*

ὑπ-ουράνιος (οὐρανός): *under the heaven,* 'far and wide under the whole heaven,' ι 264.

ὑπο-φαίνω, aor. 1 ὑπέφηνε: *bring into view from under;* θρῆνυν τραπέζης, ρ 409†.

ὑπο-φέρω: only aor., ὑπήνεικαν, *bore* me *away,* E 885†.

ὑπο-φεύγω: *flee before, escape by flight,* X 200†.

ὑπο-φήτης (φημί): *declarer, interpreter* of the divine will, pl., Π 235†.

ὑπο-φθάνω, aor. 2 part. ὑποφθάς, mid. aor. 2 part. ὑποφθάμενος: *be* or *get beforehand, anticipate.*

ὑπο-χείριος (χείρ): *under the hand,* 'under my hands,' ο 448†.

ὑπο-χέω, aor. 1 ὑπέχευα: *pour, spread,* or *strew underneath.*

ὑπο-χωρέω, ipf. ὑπεχώρει, aor. ὑπεχώρησαν: *retire before* one, *retreat.* (Il.)

ὑπ-όψιος (ὄψις): *despised;* ἄλλων, 'by the rest,' Γ 42†.

ὕπτιος (ὑπό, cf. supinus): *back, backward, on his back;* opp. πρηνής, Λ 179.

ὑπ-ώπιον (ὤψ): pl., *face, countenance,* M 463†.

ὑπ-ώρεια (ὄρος), fem. adj. as subst.: *foot of a mountain, skirts of a mountain range,* pl., Υ 218†.

ὑπώρορε: see ὑπόρνῡμι.

ὑπ-ωρόφιος (ὀροφή): *under the* same *roof,* i. e. table-companions, pl., I 640†.

Ὑρίη: *Hyria,* a town in Boeotia on the Eurīpus, B 496†.

Ὑρμίνη: a port in northern Elis, B 616†.

Ὑρτακίδης: *son of Hyrtacus,* Asius, B 837 ff., M 96, 110, 163.

Ὕρτακος: a Trojan, the husband of Arisbe, N 759 and 771.

Ὕρτιος: son of Gyrtius, a Mysian, slain by Ajax, Ξ 511†.

ὗς, ὑός (σῦς), acc. ὗν, pl. dat. ὕεσσι: *swine, pig,* sow or boar. ὗς or σῦς according to metrical convenience, but the latter is more common than the former.

ὑσμίνη: *battle, conflict, combat; κρατερὴ ὑσμίνη, ὑσμίνη δηιότητος*, B 40, Υ 245.—**ὑσμίνηνδε**, *into the battle.*

ὑστάτιος, adv. **ὑστάτιον** = the following.

ὕστατος: *last, hindmost.* — Adv., **ὕστατον.**

ὕστερος: *after, later; γένει*, i. e. *younger*, Γ 215.—Adv., **ὕστερον, ὕστερα**, *later, afterward, hereafter*, π 319; ἐς ὕστερον, μ 126.

ὑφαίνω, ὑφάω, ὑφόωσιν, ipf. iter. ὑφαίνεσκον, aor. 1 ὕφηνα: *weave*, ἱστόν, 'at the loom.' (The Greek loom stood upright, like the Roman loom represented in the cut, or like the Egyptian

123

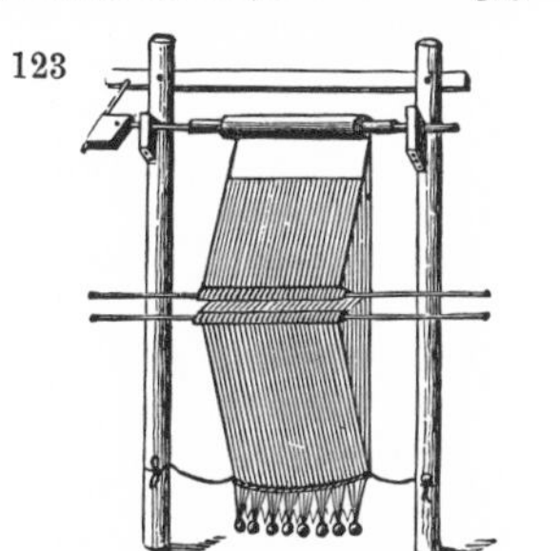

loom in cut No. 59.) Fig., *devise, contrive*, as we say 'spin,' δόλον, **μῆτιν**, ι 422, δ 678.

ὑφαντός: *woven*, ν 136 and π 231.

ὕφασμα: something woven, *web*, pl., γ 274†.

ὑφάω: see ὑφαίνω.

ὑφ-έλκω: only ipf., ὕφελκε, *sought to drag away* by laying hold *below* at the feet, ποδοῖιν, Ξ 477†.

ὑφ-ηνίοχος: *charioteer* as subject (ὑπό) or subordinate to the warrior in the chariot, Z 19†.

ὑφ-ίημι, aor. 2 part. ὑφέντες: *let under* or *down, lower*, A 434†.

ὑφ-ίστημι, aor. 2 ὑπέστην, 3 pl. **ὑπέσταν**, imp. ὑποστήτω, part. **-στάς**: aor. 2, intrans., *take upon oneself, undertake, promise*, Φ 273, I 445; *place oneself lower, submit*, τινί, I 160.

ὑ-φορβός (ὗς, φέρβω): *swineherd*; with ἄνέρες, ξ 410. (Od.)

ὑφόωσι: see ὑφαίνω.

ὑψ-αγόρης: *high-talking, big talker, boaster.* (Od.)

ὑψ-ερεφής, ές (ἐρέφω), **ὑψηρεφής**: *high-roofed.*

ὑψηλός (ὕψος): *high, lofty, high-lying.*

Ὑψήνωρ: (1) a Trojan, the son of Dolopion, slain by Eurypylus, E 76.—(2) a Greek, the son of Hippasus, slain by Deiphobus, N 411.

ὑψηρεφές: see ὑψερεφής.

ὑψ-ηχής, ές (ἦχος): *high-neighing*, with head raised on high, E 772 and Ψ 27.

ὕψι: *on high, up, aloft; ὁρμίζειν*, 'on the high sea,' in deep water, Ξ 77.

ὑψι-βρεμέτης (βρέμω): *thundering aloft, high-thundering.*

ὑψί-ζυγος: on the high rower's bench, high at the helm, *high-throned, high-ruling.* (Il.)

ὑψι-κάρηνος: *with lofty head* or *peak*, M 132†.

ὑψί-κερως (κέρας): *with lofty antlers*, κ 158†.

ὑψί-κομος (κόμη): *with lofty foliage.*

ὑψι-πετήεις = ὑψιπέτης.

ὑψι-πέτηλος (πέταλον): *with lofty leaves* or *foliage.*

ὑψι-πέτης (πέτομαι): *high-flying.*

Ὑψιπύλη: *Hypsipyle*, wife of Jason, H 469†.

ὑψί-πυλος (πύλη): *high-gated.*

ὑψόθεν: *from on high, aloft.*

ὑψόθι: *high, on high, aloft.*

ὑψ-όροφος (ὀροφή): *with lofty covering, high-roofed.*

ὑψόσε: *upward, aloft.*

ὑψοῦ: *aloft, on high;* of moving a ship 'far out' in the roadstead, δ 785.

ὕω, ipf. ὗε, pass. part. ὑόμενος: *rain;* subj. Ζεύς, 'sent rain;' pass., 'beaten by rain,' 'drenched with rain,' ζ 131.

Φ.

φάανθεν: see *φαίνω*.

φαάντατος, sup. (root *φαϝ*): *most brilliant*, ν 93†.

φάγον: see *ἔδω*, *ἐσθίω*.

φάε: see *φαίνω*.

φάεα: see *φάος*.

Φαέθουσα: daughter of Helius and Neaera, μ 132†.

φαέθων, *οντος* (root *φαϝ*), part. as adj., *beaming, radiant*.

Φαέθων: name of a steed of Eos, ψ 246.

φαεινός (root *φαϝ*), comp. *φαεινότερος*: *bright, brilliant, radiant*.

φαείνω, parallel form of *φαίνω*, the aor. pass. *φαάνθη*, 3 pl. *φάανθεν* being referable to either pres.: *shine, give light*.

φαεσί-μβροτος (*βροτός*): *bringing light to mortals, shining for mortals*, epith. of the sun and of Eos, κ 138, Ω 785.

Φαίαξ: see *Φαίηκες*.

φαιδιμόεις = *φαίδιμος*.

φαίδιμος: *shining;* only fig., 'stately,' *γυῖα, ὦμος*, λ 128; of persons, *illustrious*.

Φαίδιμος: king of the Sidonians, δ 617, ο 117.

Φαίδρη: *Phaedra*, wife of Theseus, λ 321†.

Φαίηκες: the *Phaeacians*, a fabulous people related to the gods, dwelling in Scheria, where they lived a life of ease, averse to war and devoted to sea-faring. The ships in which they escort guests to their homes, however distant, are themselves possessed of intelligence to find the way. The names of nearly all the Phaeacians mentioned are significant of the love of ships, not excepting that of Nausicaa (*ναῦς*), the most charming of them all, ε 34, ζ 4, θ 244 ff.

φαινέσκετο, φαινομένηφι(ν): see *φαίνω*.

Φαῖνοψ: son of Asius from Abȳdus, the father of Xanthus and Thoön, P 583, E 152.

φαίνω, φάω (root *φαϝ*), ipf. *φάε*, *φαῖνε*, aor. *ἔφηνα*, mid. ipf. iter. *φαινέσκετο*, fut. *πεφήσεται*, inf. *φανεῖσθαι*, pass. aor. 2 (*ἐ*)*φάνην*, 3 pl. *φάνεν*, iter. *φάνεσκεν*, subj. *φάνῃ, φανήῃ*, inf. *φανῆναι, -ήμεναι*, aor. 1 (may be referred to *φαείνω*) *φαάνθην*, 3 pl. *φάανθεν*, perf. 3 sing. *πέφανται*, part. *πεφασμένος*: I. act., trans., *bring to light, make to appear, show*, *τέρας, ὁδόν τινι*, B 324, μ 334; met., *show, reveal, exhibit, express*, *νοήματα, ἀοιδήν, ἀεικείᾱς*, Σ 295, υ 309; intrans., *shine, give light*, η 102, τ 25.—II. mid. and pass., *come to light, be visible, appear, shine*, Θ 561; w. part. (yet not purely supplementary), δ 361, ω 448; w. inf., λ 336, ξ 355, ο 25.

Φαῖστος: son of Borus, from Tarne in Maeonia, slain by Idomeneus, E 43†.

Φαιστός: a city in Crete, near Gortȳna, B 648, γ 296.

φαλαγγηδόν: *by phalanxes, in companies, in columns*.

φάλαγξ, *αγγος*: *phalanx, line of battle, column*.

φάλαρ(α): burnished *plates* of metal, rising above the helmet, Π 106†.

φαληριάω: only part., *φαληριόωντα*, *brightly shining, gleaming*, N 799†.

Φάλκης: a Trojan, slain by Antilochus, N 791, Ξ 513.

φάλος: (1) the metal *ridge* or *crest* of the helmet, extending from back to front, with a socket to hold the plume (see cut No. 122).—(2) in narrower signification, the rounded *boss*, projecting *forepiece*, in which the *φάλος* terminated, Z 9, N 132.

φάν: see *φημί*.

φάνεν, φάνεσκε, φανήμεναι: see *φαίνω*.

124

φάος (*φάϝος*), **φόως,** dat. *φάει*, pl. *φάεα*: *light; φόωσδε, to the light;* pl., fig., *eyes*, π 15; also fig. as typical of deliverance, victory, Z 6, Σ 102, π 23.

φαρέτρη (*φέρω*): *quiver*. (Cf. the cut, and Nos. 89, 90, 104.)

Φᾶρις: a town in Laconia, south of Amyclae, B 582†.

φάρμακον: *herb, drug;* as medicinal remedy, or esp. as magic drug, poisonous drug, draught, or potion, κ 392, X 94, α 261, β 329.

φαρμάσσω: apply a φάρμακον, of metal, *temper;* part., ι 393†.

φᾶρος, εος: large piece of cloth, a *shroud*, Σ 353; *mantle, cloak*, for both men and women, ε 230.

Φάρος: *Pharus*, a small island at the mouth of the Nile, δ 355†.

φάρυγξ, gen. φάρυγος: *throat.* (Od.)

φάσγανον: *sword.*

φάσθαι: see φημί.

φάσκω (φημί), ipf. ἔφασκον: *declare, promise, think*, cf. φημί.

φασσο-φόνος (φάσσα, φένω): *dove-slayer*, the ἴρηξ, 'pigeon-hawk,' O 238†.

φάτις, ιος (φημί): *report, reputation;* w. obj. gen., 'tidings' (of the slaughter) of the suitors, ψ 362.

φάτνη (πατέομαι): *crib, manger.*

Φαυσιάδης: *son of Phausius*, Apisāon, Λ 578.

Φεαί: see Φειά.

φέβομαι, ipf. (ἐ)φέβοντο: *flee, flee from.* (Il.)

Φειά, Φεαί: a town in northern Elis, on the river Jardanus, H 135, ο 297.

Φείδᾱς ('Sparer'): a leader of the Athenians, N 691†.

Φείδιππος: son of Thessalus, B 678†.

φείδομαι, aor. φείσατο, aor. 2 red. opt. πεφιδοίμην, inf. πεφιδέσθαι, fut. πεφιδήσεται: *spare*, w. gen.

φειδώ: *sparing, thrift;* 'one must not fail' in the case of the dead, etc.

φειδωλή: *sparing, grudging use*, X 244†.

Φείδων: *Phidon*, king of the Thesprotians, ξ 316, τ 287.

φεν- and **φα-** (cf. φόνος), **φένω,** roots and assumed pres. for the foll. forms, red. aor. 2 ἔπεφνον, πέφνε, subj. πέφνῃ, inf. πεφνέμεν, part. πεφνόντα, pass. perf. πέφατ(αι), inf. πεφάσθαι, fut. πεφήσεαι, πεφήσεται: *kill, slay;* of a natural death, only λ 135; fig., ἐκ δ' αἰὼν πέφαται, 'extinguished,' T 27.

Φένεος: a town in Arcadia, B 605†.

Φεραί: *Pherae*, a city in Thessaly, on Lake Boebēis, the residence of Admētus and Alcestis, and of Eumēlus, B 711, δ 798.

Φέρεκλος: son of Harmonides, builder of the ship in which Paris carried away Helen, slain by Meriones, E 59†.

Φέρης: son of Cretheus and Tyro, father of Admētus, λ 259†.

φέριστος = φέρτατος, used esp. in the vocative.

Φέρουσα: a Nereid, Σ 43†.

φέρτατος: one of the superlatives to ἀγαθός, *best, bravest*, etc.

φέρτερος: one of the comparatives to ἀγαθός, *better, braver*, etc.

φέρτε: see φέρω.

φέρτρον (φέρω): *litter, bier* for the dead, Σ 236†.

φέρω, subj. φέρῃσι, imp. φέρτε, inf. φερέμεν, ipf. iter. φέρεσκον, fut. οἴσω, inf. οἰσέμεν, aor. 2 imp. οἶσε, -έτω, -ετε, inf. οἰσέμεν(αι), aor. 1 ἤνεικα, ἔνεικα, opt. ἐνείκαι, inf. ἐνεῖκαι, part. ἐνείκᾱς, also aor. 2 opt. ἐνείκοι, inf. ἐνεικέμεν, mid. fut. οἴσομαι, aor. 1 ἠνείκαντο: I. act., *bear, carry, bring, convey*, in the ordinary ways not needing illustration; more special uses, of the earth yielding fruits, of rendering homage or offerings, bearing tidings, of winds sweeping, driving, scattering things, δ 229, O 175, κ 48; fig., 'endure,' σ 135; 'spread wide,' γ 204; ἦρα φέρειν (see ἦρα), **κακόν, πῆμά τινι,** φέρειν καὶ ἄγειν (agere ferre), 'plunder,' E 484. The part. φέρων is often added to verbs by way of amplification, so the inf. φέρειν (φέρεσθαι), cf. 'to keep,' α 127, Ψ 513.—II. pass., *be borne* (ferri), either intentionally, *rush, charge*, O 743, υ 172; or involuntarily, *be swept, hurried along*, A 592.—III. mid., *carry off* for oneself, *bear away*, esp. of prizes, victory, **τὰ πρῶτα, κράτος**, Ψ 275, N 486.

φεύγω, inf. φευγέμεν(αι), ipf. iter. φεύγεσκεν, fut. φεύξομαι, aor. 2 ἔφυγον, φύγον, subj. φύγῃ(σι), inf. φυγέειν, perf. opt. **πεφεύγοι,** part. πεφυγότες, πεφυζότες, mid. perf. part. πεφυγμένος: *flee, flee from, escape;* esp. flee one's country, go into exile, ἵκετο **φεύγων,** came as fugitive, π 424; often trans., **θάλασσαν,** θάνατον, Λ 362; fig., with a thing as subj., Θ 137, Δ 350; mid., *πεφυγμένος*, usually w. acc.; *ἀέθλων*, 'escaped' from toils, *α* 18.

φῆ: see *φημί*.

φή = *ὡς*, *as*, *just as*, *like*, Β 144, Ξ 499.

Φηγεύς: son of Dares, priest of Hephaestus in Troy, slain by Diomed, Ε 11, 15.

φήγινος: *of oak-wood*, *oaken*, Ε 838†.

φηγός (cf. fagus): a sort of *oak* with edible acorns. An ancient tree of this species was one of the landmarks on the Trojan plain, Η 22, Ι 354. (Il.)

φήμη: ominous or prophetic *utterance*, *voice*, *omen*, *υ* 100, *β* 35.

φημί (cf. fari), 2 sing. *φῄς* not enclitic like the other forms of the pres. ind., *φησί*, *φαμέν*, *φατέ*, *φᾶσ(ίν)*, subj. *φῇ(σιν)*, *φήῃ*, opt. *φαίην*, *φαῖμεν*, part. *φάς*, ipf. *ἔφην*, *φῆν*, *ἔφησθα*, *φῆσθα*, *φῆς*, *ἔφαμεν*, *φάμεν*, *ἔφαν*, *φάν*, fut. *φήσει*, mid. pres. imp. *φάο*, *φάσθω*, inf. *φάσθαι*, part. *φάμενος*, ipf. *ἐφάμην*, *φάτο* (for *πεφασμένος* see *φαίνω*): *say*, *declare*, mostly of subjective statement, to express opinion, hence reg. const. w. acc. and inf. The ipf. and the pres. inf. have aoristic signification. No distinction between act. and mid. is to be sought. Often simply *think*, *believe*, Β 37, *α* 391; *ὅ γ' ἀνὴρ ὅν φημι*, whom 'I mean,' Ε 184; *οὔ φημι* (nego), *ο* 213.

Φήμιος: *Phemius*, son of Terpis, a bard in Ithaca, *α* 154, 337, *ρ* 263, *χ* 331.

φῆμις, ιος: *rumor*, *common talk*; *δήμου*, 'public opinion,' *ξ* 239, cf. *π* 75; also to designate the place of discussion, assembly, *ο* 468.

φῆν: see *φημί*.

φήναι: see *φαίνω*.

φήνη: *sea-eagle*, *osprey*, *γ* 372 and *π* 217.

φήρ, *φηρός* (= *θήρ*), pl. dat. *φηρσίν*: *wild beast*, then *monster*, as the Centaurs, Α 268, Β 743.

Φηραί, Φηρή: a town in Messenia, in Homer's time belonging to the Laconian territory, Ε 543, Ι 151, 293, *γ* 488, *ο* 186.

Φηρητιάδης: *son* (*grandson*) *of Pheres*, Eumēlus, Β 763 and Ψ 376.

φῄς, φῆς, φῇσθα, φῆσθα: see *φημί*.

φθάν: see *φθάνω*.

φθάνω, fut. *φθήσονται*, aor. 2 *ἔφθην*, *φθῆ*, 3 pl. *φθάν*, subj. *φθῶ*, *φθῇ(σιν)*, *φθέωμεν*, *φθέωσιν*, opt. *φθαίη*, mid. aor. 2 part. *φθάμενος*: *be* or *get before*, *anticipate*, Φ 262; w. part. the verb appears as an adv. in Eng., *φθῆ σε τέλος θανάτοιο κιχημένον*, death overtook thee 'sooner,' 'first,' Λ 451, *χ* 91; foll. by *πρίν*, Π 322.

φθέγγομαι, fut. *φθέγξομαι*, aor. *ἐφθεγξάμην*, subj. *φθέγξομαι*: *utter a sound*, *speak out*, cf. *φθογγή*, *φθόγγος*. Since the verb merely designates the effect upon the ear, it may be joined with a more specific word, *ἐφθέγγοντο καλεῦντες*, called *aloud*, *κ* 229, Φ 192, 341; *φθεγγομένου . . κάρη κονίῃσιν ἐμίχθη*, while the voice still *sounded*, Κ 457, *χ* 329.

φθείρω, *φθείρουσι*, pass. *φθείρεσθε*: *destroy*, *ruin*; pass., 'ruin seize ye,' Φ 128.

Φθειρῶν, Φθερῶν: *ὄρος*, name of a mountain in Caria, Β 868.

φθέωμεν, φθέωσιν: see *φθάνω*.

φθῇ, φθήῃ, φθῇσιν: see *φθάνω*.

Φθίη, dat. *Φθίηφι*: *Phthia*.—(1) the chief city of the Myrmidons in Thessaly, on the Spercheius, residence of Peleus and Achilles, Β 683.—(2) the region about the city, with Hellas forming the realm of Achilles, Ι 395, *λ* 496.—**Φθίηνδε**, *to Phthia*.

φθίμενος: see *φθίνω*.

φθινύθω, ipf. *φθίνυθον*, iter. *φθινύθεσκε*: *waste away*, *perish*, *die*; as a sort of imprecation, 'to go to perdition,' Β 346; trans., *waste*, *consume*, *οἶκον*, *οἶνον*, *κῆρ*, 'whose grief breaks my heart,' *κ* 485.

φθίνω, φθίω, fut. *φθίσω*, aor. 3 pl. *φθῖσαν*, inf. *φθῖσαι*, mid. fut. *φθίσομαι*, aor. 2 *ἔφθιτο*, subj. *φθίεται*, *φθιόμεσθα*, opt. *φθίμην*, *φθῖτ(ο)*, inf. *φθίσθαι*, part. *φθίμενος*, pass. perf. *ἔφθιται*, plup. *ἐφθίμην*, 3 pl. *ἐφθίαθ'*, aor. 3 pl. *ἔφθιθεν*: trans., fut. and aor. act., *consume*, *destroy*, *kill*, Π 461, *υ* 67, *π* 428; intrans. and mid., *waste* or *dwindle away*, *wane*, *perish*, *die*; *μηνῶν φθῖνόντων* (as the months 'waned'), *φθίμενος*, 'deceased,' *λ* 558.

Φθῖος: *Phthian*, inhabitant of Phthia, pl., Ν 686, 693, 699.

φθισ-ήνωρ, ορος: *man-consuming*. (Il.)

φθισί-μβροτος (βροτός): *consuming mortals*, 'life-destroying.'

φθογγή = φθόγγος.

φθόγγος (φθέγγομαι): *voice*, merely as audible sound; φθόγγῳ ἐπερχόμεναι, 'with talking,' making themselves heard, σ 198.

φθονέω (φθόνος): *grudge, deny, refuse*, τινί τινος, ζ 68; w. inf., λ 381, τ 348; acc. and inf., α 346, σ 16.

-φι(ν): a vestige of several old case-endings, appended to the stem-vowel of the various declensions, (1st decl.) -ηφι, -ῆφι (but ἐσχαρόφι), (2d decl.) -όφι, (3d decl.) -έσφι (but ναῦφι); of persons only in two words, θεόφι, αὐτόφι. The form produced by the suffix may stand for a gen. (ablative), or a dative (instrumental, locative), with or without prepositions.

φιάλη: wide, flaring *bowl, saucer*, or *urn*, Ψ 243.

φῖλαι, φίλατο: see φιλέω.

φιλέω, φιλέει, φιλεῖ, inf. φιλήμεναι, part. φιλεῦντας, ipf. (ἐ)φίλει, iter. φιλέεσκε, fut. inf. φιλησέμεν, aor. (ἐ)φίλησα, mid. fut., w. pass. signif., φιλήσεαι, aor. (ἐ)φίλατο, imp. φῖλαι, pass. aor. 3 pl. φίληθεν: *love, hold dear*, mid., Υ 304; also *entertain, welcome* as guest, ε 135.

φιλ-ήρετμος (ἐρετμός): *fond of the oar, oar-loving*. (Od.)

Φιλητορίδης: *son of Philētor*, Demūchus, Υ 457†.

Φιλοίτιος: *Philoetius*, the faithful herdsman of Odysseus, υ 185, 254, φ 240, 388, χ 268, 286.

φιλο-κέρτομος: *fond of jeering* or *mocking, contemptuous*, χ 287†.

φιλο-κτεανώτατος (κτέανον), sup.: *most greedy of* other men's *possessions*, Α 122†.

Φιλοκτήτης: *Philoctētes*, son of Poeas, from Meliboea in Thessaly. A famous archer, he possessed the bow and arrows of Heracles, without which Troy could not be taken. On the way to Troy he was bitten by a serpent in the island of Chryse, near Lemnos, and the Greeks left him behind sick in Lemnos, Β 718, 725, γ 190, θ 219.

φιλο-μμειδής (σμειδιάω): *laughter-loving*, epith. of Aphrodīte.

Φιλομηλείδης: a king in Lesbos, who challenged all strangers to wrestle with him, δ 343 and ρ 134.

φιλό-ξεινος: *loving guests* or *guest-friends, hospitable*. (Od.)

φιλο-παίγμων, ονος (παίζω): *fond of play, merry*, ψ 134†.

φιλο-πτόλεμος: *fond of war, war-loving*. (Il.)

φίλος, comp. **φιλίων** and **φίλτερος**, sup. **φίλτατος**, voc. at the beginning of the verse φῖλε: *own, dear*, but it must not be supposed that the first meaning has not begun everywhere in Homer to pass into the stage of the latter, hence neither Eng. word represents its force in many instances, φίλα εἵματα, φίλος αἰών, and of parts of the body, φίλαι χεῖρες, etc. Pl. φίλοι, *dear ones, friends*, one's *own*, δ 475. Neut., φίλον, φίλα, *pleasing, acceptable*; φίλον ἔπλετο θυμῷ, αἰεί τοι τὰ κάκ' ἐστὶ φίλα φρεσὶ μαντεύεσθαι, you *like* to, Α 107; φίλα φρονεῖν, εἰδέναι τινί, be *kindly* disposed, Δ 219, γ 277.

φιλότης, ητος: *love, friendship*; φιλότητα τιθέναι, τάμνειν, μετ' ἀμφοτέροισι βάλλειν, Δ 83, Γ 73, Δ 16; also for a pledge of friendship, hospitable *entertainment*, ο 537, 55; of sexual love, in various oft-recurring phrases.

φιλοτήσιος: *of love*, λ 246†.

φιλο-φροσύνη (φρήν): *kindliness, friendly temper*, Ι 256†.

φιλο-ψευδής: *friend of lies, false*, Μ 164†.

φίλτατος, φίλτερος: see φίλος.

φίλως: *gladly*, Δ 347, τ 461.

-φιν: see φι.

φιτρός: *trunk, block, log*, pl. (Il. and μ 11.)

φλεγέθω, pass. opt. 3 pl. φλεγεθοίατο: parallel form of **φλέγω**, *blaze, glow*; trans., *burn up, consume*, Ρ 738, Ψ 197. (Il.)

φλέγμα, ατος (φλέγω): *flame, blaze*, Φ 337†.

Φλέγυαι and **Φλέγυες**: a robber tribe in Thessaly, Ν 302†.

φλέγω: *burn, singe, consume*; pass., *blaze*, Φ 365.

φλέψ, φλεβός: *vein*, the main artery in, Ν 546†.

φλιή: *door-post*, pl., ρ 221†.

φλόγεος (φλόξ): *flaming, gleaming*, Ε 745 and Θ 389.

φλοιός: *bark*, Α 237†.

φλοῖσβος: *roar* of waves, applied also to the roar of battle. (Il.)

φλόξ, φλογός (φλέγω): *flame, blaze.* (Il. and ω 71.)

φλύω: *foam* or *boil* up, Φ 361†.

φοβέω, aor. (ἐ)φόβησα, mid. pres. part. φοβεύμενος, fut. φοβήσομαι, pass. aor. 3 pl. (ἐ)φόβηθεν, perf. part. πεφοβημένος, plup. 3 pl. πεφοβήατο: act., *put to flight*, τινά, Λ 173; δουρί, Υ 187; mid. and pass., *flee, be put to flight*, ὑπό τινος or ὑπό τινι, Θ 149, Ο 637; τινά, Χ 250.

φόβος: *flight* in consequence of fear, and once *fear*, Λ 544; **φόβονδε,** *to flight*.—Personified, **Φόβος,** son and attendant of Ares, Δ 440, Λ 37, Ν 299, Ο 119.

Φοῖβος: *Phoebus*, epithet of Apollo, probably as god of light, with or without Ἀπόλλων.

φοινήεις, εσσα, εν (φόνος): *blood-red*, δράκων, Μ 202 and 220.

Φοίνῑκες: the *Phoenicians*, inhabitants of Phoenicia, their chief city Sidon. They appear in Homer as traders, skilful in navigation, famous alike for artistic skill and for piracy, Ψ 744, ν 272, ξ 288, ο 415, 419, 473.

φοινῑκόεις, εσσα, εν (-όεσσαι, pronounce -οῦσσαι): *purple, red.*

φοινῑκο-πάρῃος (παρειά): *purple* or *red-cheeked*, epith. of painted ships (cf. μιλτοπάρῃος), λ 124 and ψ 271.

Φοῖνιξ: *Phoenix.*—(1) the father of Eurōpa, Ξ 321.—(2) son of Amyntor, aged friend and adviser of Achilles. He tells the story of his life, Ι 434 ff.

φοῖνιξ, ῖκος: I. subst., (1) *purple*, the invention of which was ascribed to the Phoenicians.—(2) *date-palm*, ζ 163†.—II. adj., *purple, red.*

φοίνιος (φόνος): *(blood) red*, Σ 97†.

Φοίνισσα: γυνή, *Phoenician* woman.

φοινός = φοίνιος, Π 159†.

φοιτάω, φοιτᾷ, part. φοιτῶντε, ipf. (ἐ)φοίτᾱ, du. φοιτήτην, aor. part. φοιτήσᾱσα: frequentative verb, *go, go* or *hurry* to and fro, *roam* up and down, ἔνθα καὶ ἔνθα, πάντοσε, πάντῃ, Β 779, Μ 266; of birds flying the air, β 182.

φολκός: *bow-legged*, Β 217†.

φονεύς, ῆος: *slayer, murderer, homicide.*

φονή: *massacre, murder*, pl., 'rending,' Ο 633.

φόνος (φένω): *bloodshed, murder*, also for *blood*, Ω 610; and poetically for the instrument of death, the lance, φ 24; φόνος αἵματος, 'reeking blood,' of mangled beasts, Π 162.

φοξός: *sharp-pointed*, of a head low in front, sharp behind, a sugar-loaf head, Β 219†.

Φόρβᾱς: (1) king of Lesbos, father of Diomēdes, Ι 665.—(2) a wealthy Trojan, father of Ilioneus, Ξ 490.

φορβή (φέρβω, cf. herba): *forage, fodder*, Ε 202 and Λ 562.

φορεύς, ῆος: *carrier*, of grapes in the wine-harvest, *vintager*, Σ 566†.

φορέω (φέρω), φορέει, subj. φορέῃσι, opt. φοροίη, inf. φορέειν, φορῆναι, φορήμεναι, ipf. (ἐ)φόρεον, iter. φορέεσκον, aor. φόρησεν, mid. ipf. φορέοντο: *bear* or *carry* habitually or repeatedly, ὕδωρ, μέθυ, κ 358, ι 10; hence *wear*, Δ 137, etc.; fig., ἀγλαΐᾱς, 'display,' ρ 245.

φορήμεναι, φορῆναι: see φορέω.

Φόρκῡνος: λιμήν, harbor or inlet *of Phorcys*, in Ithaca, ν 96†.

Φόρκυς, ῡνος and υος: *Phorcys.*—(1) old man of the sea, father of Thoōsa, α 72, ν 96, 345.—(2) a Phrygian, the son of Phaenops, slain by Ajax, Β 862, Ρ 218, 312, 318.

φόρμιγξ, ιγγος: *phorminx*, a kind of *lute* or *lyre*. The cross-piece (bridge) was called ζυγόν, the pegs κόλλοπες. Played not only by the professional bard, and by Apollo, Ω 63, but exceptionally also by heroes, Ι 186. In form substantially like the κίθαρις represented in the cut.

125

φορμίζω: *touch* or *play the phorminx* (*lyre, lute*), Σ 605; said also of one playing the κίθαρις, α 155.

φορτίς, ίδος (φόρτος): νηῦς, *ship of burden*, ε 250 and ι 323. (See cut.)

126

φόρτος (φέρω): *freight, cargo*, θ 163 and ξ 296.

φορύνω (φύρω): only pass. ipf. φορύνετο, *was defiled*, χ 21†.

φορύσσω (parallel form of φορύνω), aor. part. φορύξᾱς: *defile*, σ 336†.

φόως, φόωσδε: see φάος.

φραδής, ές (φράζω): *prudent, clear*, νόος, Ω 354†.

φράδμων, ονος (φράζω): *observing*, Π 638†.

φράζω, aor. φράσε, aor. 2 red. (ἐ)πέφραδον, imp. πέφραδε, opt. πεφράδοι, inf. -δέειν, -δέμεν, mid. pres. imp. φράζεο, φράζευ, inf. φράζεσθαι, fut. φρά(σ)σομαι, aor. (ἐ)φρα(σ)σάμην, imp. φράσαι, subj. φράσσεται, pass. aor. ἐφράσθην: *point out, show, indicate;* w. inf., ἐπέφραδε χερσὶν ἑλέσθαι, *showed* the blind bard how to take down the lyre with his hands (i. e. guided his hands), θ 68; so ὁδόν, σήματα, μῦθον, 'make known,' α 273; mid., point out to oneself, *consider, ponder, bethink oneself*, foll. by clause w. εἰ, ὡς, ὅπως, μή, Δ 411; *devise, plan, decree* (of Zeus), βουλήν, μῆτιν, κακά τινι, β 367: *perceive, note*, w. acc.; w. part., K 339; inf., λ 624; 'look to,' χ 129.

φράσσω (cf. farcio), aor. φράξε, part. φράξαντες, mid. aor. φράξαντο, pass. aor. part. φραχθέντες: *fence* or *hedge around;* ἐπάλξεις ῥῑνοῖσι βοῶν, the wall with shields, M 263; σχεδίην ῥίπεσσι, 'caulked' it (in the cracks between the planks), ε 256; mid., νῆας ἕρκεϊ, 'their' ships, O 566.

φρεῖαρ, ατος: *well*, pl., Φ 197†.

φρήν, φρενός, pl. φρένες: (1) pl., *midriff, diaphragm*, K 10, Π 481, ι 301. Since the word physically designates the parts enclosing the heart, φρήν, φρένες comes to mean secondarily:—(2) *mind, thoughts*, etc. φρεσὶ νοεῖν, κατὰ φρένα εἰδέναι, μετὰ φρεσὶ βάλλεσθαι, ἐνὶ φρεσὶ γνῶναι, etc. φρένες ἐσθλαί, a good *understanding;* φρένας βλάπτειν τινί, O 724; of the will, Διὸς ἐτράπετο φρήν, K 45; feelings, φρένα τέρπετο, A 474.

φρήτρη (φράτηρ, cf. frater), dat. φρήτρηφιν: *clan*. (Il.)

φρίξ, φρῑκός (φρίσσω): *ruffling* of water caused by wind, *ripple*.

φρίσσω, aor. ἔφριξεν, part. φρίξᾱς, perf. πεφρίκᾱσι, part. -υῖαι: grow rough, *bristle*, as the fields with grain, the battle-field with spears, Ψ 599, N 339; the wild boar as to his back or crest, λοφιήν, νῶτον, τ 446, N 473; *shudder, shudder at* (cf. 'goose-flesh'), Λ 383, Ω 775.

φρονέω (φρήν), subj. φρονέῃσι: use the mind, *have living thoughts, live*, X 59; *have in mind*, hence *consider, think, intend;* ἄριστοι μάχεσθαί τε φρονέειν τε, intellectual activity opp. to physical prowess, Z 79; to express opinion, foll. by inf., Γ 98; sentiment, habit of mind, πυκινὰ φρονέειν (intelligence), ἶσόν τινι φρονέειν, ἀμφίς, εὖ, κακῶς, be 'well' or 'ill-disposed,' η 74, σ 168.

Φρόνιος: father of Noëmon, β 386 and δ 630.

φρόνις, ιος (φρήν): *knowledge, counsel;* much 'information,' δ 258.

Φρόντις, ιδος: wife of Panthoüs, mother of Euphorbus and Polydamas, P 40†.

Φρόντις, ιος: son of Onētor, pilot of Menelāus, γ 282†.

Φρύγες: the *Phrygians*, inhabitants of Phrygia, B 862, Γ 185, K 431.

Φρυγίη: *Phrygia*, a district in Asia Minor, lying partly on the Hellespont, partly on the river Sangarius, Ω 545, Γ 401, Π 719, Σ 291. (Greek art is indebted to the Phrygian costume for the pointed cap, which is an attribute of skilled artisans like Hephaestus, and of shrewd wanderers like Odysseus. The cut, from a Greek relief, represents a Phrygian archer.)

127

φῦ: see φύω.

φύγαδ(ε): *to flight*. (Il.)

φυγή: *flight*, χ 306 and κ 117.

φυγο-πτόλεμος: *battle-fleeing, cowardly*, ξ 213†.

φύζα (root φυγ, φυγή): *panic* (flight).

φυζακινός: *shy, timid*, N 102†.

φυή (φύω): *growth, form, physique;*

joined with δέμας, μέγεθος, εἶδος, A 115, B 58, ζ 16.

φῡκιόεις, εσσα, εν: *full of sea-weed, weedy,* Ψ 693†.

φῦκος, εος: *sea-weed, sea-grass,* I 7†.

φυκτός (φεύγω): *to be escaped;* neut. pl. impers., οὐκέτι φυκτὰ πέλονται, 'there is no escape more,' Π 128, θ 299.

φυλακή (φυλάσσω): *watch, guard;* φυλακὰς ἔχειν, 'keep guard,' I 1; 'outposts,' K 416.

Φυλάκη: a town in Phthiōtis, on the northern slope of Mt. Othrys, in the domain of Protesilāüs, λ 290, ο 236, B 695, 700, N 696, O 335.

Φῡλακίδης: *son of Phylacus,* Iphiclus, B 705, N 698.

φύλακος = φύλαξ, pl., Ω 566†.

Φύλακος: (1) father of Iphiclus, ο 231.—(2) a Trojan, slain by Leitus, Z 35†.

φυλακτήρ, ῆρος, = φύλαξ, pl. (Il.)

φύλαξ, ακος: *guard, watchman.*

Φύλᾱς: the father of Polymēle, king of Thesprotian Ephyra, Π 181 and 191.

φυλάσσω, inf. φυλασσέμεναι, fut. -ξω, aor. φύλαξεν, pass. and mid. perf. part. πεφυλαγμένος: I. act., *watch, keep watch,* abs., νύκτα, 'all night,' ε 466, χ 195; trans., *watch over, guard,* K 417; pass., K 309; *watch for,* B 251, δ 670; fig., 'treasure up,' 'keep' faith, Π 30, Γ 280.—II. mid., *watch* for oneself, K 188; πεφυλαγμένος εἶναι, 'be on thy guard,' Ψ 343.

Φῡλείδης: *son of Phyleus,* Meges, E 72, O 519, 528, Π 313.

Φῡλεύς: son of Augēas of Elis, banished by his father, because when appointed arbiter in the dispute between Augēas and Heracles he decided in favor of the latter, B 628, K 110, 175, O 530, Ψ 637.

φυλίη: *wild olive-tree,* ε 477†.

φύλλον: *leaf;* φύλλων γενεή, Z 146.

Φῡλομέδουσα: wife of Arithoüs, H 10†.

φῦλον (φύω): *race, people,* in the widest sense, θεῶν, E 441; usually pl., *tribes, host,* etc., γυναικῶν, ἀοιδῶν, γ 282, θ 481; of animals, ἄγρια φῦλα, T 30. In narrow sense, *tribe, class, clan, family,* B 362.

φύλοπις, ιδος, acc. -ιν, -ιδα, λ 314; *combat, din of battle;* usual epith., αἰνή, also ἀργαλέη, κρατέρη, π 268; πολέμοιο, N 635.

Φῡλώ: name of a maid of Helen, δ 125 and 133.

φύξηλις: *cowardly,* P 143†.

φύξιμος: neut., φύξιμον, chance *of escape,* ε 359†.

φύξις (φεύγω): *flight.* (Il.)

φῡρω, aor. ἔφυρσα, subj. φύρσω, pass. perf. part. πεφυρμένος: *wet, moisten.*

φῦσα, pl. φῦσαι: *bellows.* (Σ)

φῡσάω, part. φῡσῶντες, ipf. ἐφύσων: *blow,* Σ 470 and Ψ 218.

φῡσιάω: only part., φυσιόωντες, *panting,* Δ 227 and Π 506.

φῡσί-ζοος (φύω, ζωή): *producing life, life-giving,* αἶα. (Il. and λ 301.)

φύσις, ιος (φύω): natural characteristic, *quality, property,* κ 303†.

φῡταλιή (φυτόν): *plantation; vineyard* or *orchard,* Z 195. (Il.)

φυτεύω, ipf. φύτευεν, aor. ἐφύτευσαν, subj. φυτεύσω, inf. -εῦσαι: *plant;* fig., *devise, plan,* β 165, δ 668, O 134.

φυτόν (φύω): *plant, tree;* collective, 'plants,' ω 227, 242.

φύω, ipf. φύεν, fut. φῦσει, aor. 1 ἔφῡσε, aor. 2 ἔφῡν, φῦ, part. φύντες, perf. πέφῡκα, 3 pl. -ασι (not -ᾶσι), πεφύᾱσι, subj. πεφύκῃ, part. πεφυῖα, πεφυῶτας, πεφῡκότας, plup. πεφύκει, mid. φύονται, ipf. φύοντο: I. trans., pres. (exc. once), fut., and aor. 1 act., *make to grow, produce;* φύλλα, τρίχας, A 235, κ 393.—II. intrans., mid., perf., and aor. 2 act., *grow;* phrases, ὀδὰξ ἐν χείλεσι φύντες, 'biting their lips'; ἐν δ' ἄρα οἱ φῦ χειρί, 'grasped,' 'pressed' his hand; the pres. act. is once used intransitively, Z 149.

Φωκεῖς: the *Phocians,* inhabitants of Phocis, B 517, 525, O 516, P 307.

φώκη: *seal.* (Od.)

φωνέω (φωνή), aor. (ἐ)φώνησε, part. φωνήσᾱς: *raise the voice, speak aloud, speak,* see φωνή. Often joined to another verb of saying, either as participle, or as parallel tense, A 201, δ 370.

φωνή: *voice,* properly with reference to its quality, whereby one individual may be distinguished from another. Transferred to animals, συῶν, βοῶν, κ 239, μ 396, τ 521.

φωριαμός: *chest*, *coffer*, *box*, pl., Ω 228 and ο 104.

φῶς· see φάος.

φώς, φωτός: *man*, *wight*; like ἀνήρ, but not so much a mark of distinction; freq. in apposition to a name, Δ 194. ἀλλότριος φώς, 'somebody else.'

Χ.

χάδε, χαδέειν: see χανδάνω.

χάζομαι, subj. χαζώμε(σ)θ(α), imp. χάζεο, ipf. (ἐ)χάζετ(ο), -οντ(ο), fut. χάσσονται, aor. χάσσατ(ο), inf. -ασθαι, part. -άμενος, aor. red. part. **κεκαδών**, mid. **κεκάδοντο**: *give way*, *fall back*, *retire* before some one, ἄψ, ὀπίσω, and w. ὑπό, Δ 497; φράζεο καὶ χάζεο, 'bethink and shrink,'' Ε 440; then with gen., *give over*, *rest from*, μάχης, δουρός, Ο 426, Λ 539. Here belongs the causative κεκαδών, *depriving*, Λ 334, φ 153, 170, unless this form should be referred to κήδω.

χαίνω or **χάσκω** (root χα, cf. h i s c o), aor. 2 opt. **χάνοι**, part. **χανών**, perf. part. **κεχηνότα**: *gape*, *yawn*; 'may the earth engulf me,' Δ 182, etc.; perf. part., 'with open mouth,' aor., **πρὸς κῦμα χανών**, 'opening my mouth' to the wave, i. e. swallowing the water, μ 350.

χαίρω (cf. g r a t u s), ipf. χαῖρον, ἔχαιρε, χαῖρε, iter. χαίρεσκεν, fut. inf. χαιρήσειν, aor. ἐχάρη, -ημεν, -ησαν, χάρη, opt. χαρείη, part. χαρέντες, perf. part. κεχαρηότα, also red. fut. inf. κεχαρησέμεν, mid. fut. **κεχαρήσεται**, aor. 2 κεχάροντο, opt. -οιτο, 3 pl. -οίατο, aor. 1 χήρατο: *be glad*, *be joyful*, *rejoice*; (ἐν) θυμῷ, νόῳ, φρεσί and φρένα, also χαίρει μοι ἦτορ, κῆρ, Ψ 647, δ 260; w. dat. of the thing rejoiced at, **νίκῃ**, ὄρνῑθι, φήμῃ, Κ 277, β 35; freq. w. part. and dat., **τῷ** χαῖρον νοστήσαντι, 'at his return,' τ 463; also w. part. agreeing with the subj., Γ 76; οὐ χαιρήσεις, 'thou wilt be sorry,' 'rue it,' Υ 363, β 249; **χαῖρε**, *hail* or *farewell*, α 123, ν 59.

χαίτη: flowing *hair*; of horses, *mane*, sing. and pl.

χάλαζα: *hail*. (Il.)

χαλεπαίνω (χαλεπός), ipf. χαλέπαινε, aor. subj. χαλεπήνῃ, inf. -ῆναι be hard, severe, *rage*, of wind and storm, Ξ 399; freq. of persons, *be vexed*, *angry*, τινί, π 114, Ξ 256, Υ 133.

χαλεπός, comp. χαλεπώτερος: *hard*, *difficult*, *dangerous*, ἄεθλος; λιμήν, 'hard to approach,' λ 622, τ 189; personal const. w. inf., χαλεπή τοι ἐγὼ μένος ἀντιφέρεσθαι, Φ 482; χαλεποὶ θεοὶ ἐναργεῖς φαίνεσθαι, 'it is dangerous when gods appear, etc.', Υ 131; oftener the impers. const. Of things, *harsh*, *grievous*, *severe*; γῆρας, μόχθος, ὀνείδη, ἔπεα, Ψ 489; of persons, *stern*, *angry*, τινί, ρ 388.

χαλέπτω (χαλεπός): *be hard upon*; τινά, δ 423†.

χαλεπῶς: *with difficulty*. (Il.)

χαλῑνός: *bit* (of a bridle), Τ 393†.

χαλι-φρονέω (χαλίφρων): only part. as adj., *thoughtless*, *indiscreet*, ψ 13†.

χαλι-φροσύνη: *thoughtlessness*, π 310†.

χαλί-φρων, ον (χαλάω): *slack-minded*, *thoughtless*, δ 371 and τ 530.

χαλκεο-θώρηξ, ηκος: *with breastplate of bronze*; *bronze-cuirassed*, Δ 448 and Θ 62.

χάλκεος and **χάλκειος**: *of copper* or *bronze*, *brazen*; fig., ὄψ, ἦτορ, ὕπνος (of death), Λ 241.

χαλκεό-φωνος: *with brazen voice*, epith. of Stentor, Ε 785†.

χαλκεύς, ῆος: *coppersmith*, *worker in bronze*; with ἀνήρ, ι 391, Δ 187; of a worker in metals, goldsmith, ι 391, γ 432.

χαλκεύω: only ipf., χάλκευον, *I wrought*, Σ 400†.

χαλκεών, ῶνος: *forge*, θ 273†.

χαλκήιος: *of a smith*; δόμος, *smithy*. (Od.)

χαλκ-ήρης, ες (ἀραρίσκω): *fitted with bronze, brazen-shod.*

χαλκίς, ιδος = κύμινδις, Ξ 291†.

Χαλκίς: *Chalcis.*—(1) a town in Euboea on the Eurīpus, B 537.—(2) in Aetolia, at the mouth of the Evē-nus, ο 295.

χαλκο-βαρής, ές: *heavy with bronze, of ponderous bronze.* —Fem., **χαλκο-βάρεια**, Λ 96, χ 259.

χαλκο-βατής, ές (βαίνω): *with brazen floor* or *threshold.*

χαλκο-γλώχῖν, ῖνος: *with bronze point*, X 225†.

χαλκο-κνήμῖς, ῖδος: *with greaves of bronze*, H 41†.

χαλκο-κορυστής (κορύσσω): *in bronze armor, brazen-clad.* (Il.)

χαλκο-πάρῃος: *with cheeks* (side-pieces) *of bronze*, helmet.

χαλκό-πος, -πουν, gen. -ποδος: *with hoofs of bronze, brazen-hoofed*, Θ 41 and N 23.

χαλκός: *copper* or *bronze* (an alloy of copper and tin; brass, which is made of copper and zinc, was unknown to the ancients), α 184. The word stands often for things made of bronze, knife, axe, weapons and armor in general. Epithets, αἶθοψ, νῶροψ, ἀτειρής, and others appropriate to the things severally designated.

χαλκό-τυπος (τύπτω): *inflicted with brazen weapons*, T 25†.

χαλκο-χίτων, ωνος: *brazen-clad.*

Χαλκωδοντιάδης: *son of Chalcōdon*, king of the Abantes in Euboea, Elephēnor, B 541†.

Χάλκων: a Myrmidon, the father of Bathycles, Π 595†.

χαμάδις (χαμαί): *to the ground.*

χαμᾶζε (χαμαί): *to the ground, down; to* or *into the earth*, Θ 134, φ 136.

χαμαί (loc. form χαμά, cf. h u m i): *on the ground, to the ground.*

χαμαι-ευνής (εὐνή): pl., *making their beds on the ground*, Π 235†.

χαμαι-ευνάς, άδος = the foregoing, σύες, 'grovelling,' κ 243 and ξ 15.

χανδάνω (root χαδ, cf. pre-h e n d o), ipf. ἐχάνδανον, χάνδανε, fut. χείσεται, aor. 2 ἔχαδε, χάδε, inf. -έειν, perf. part. κεχανδότα, plup. κεχάνδει: *hold, contain*, of the capacity of vessels, etc., Ψ 742, ρ 344, δ 96; fig., of capacity of shouting, ὅσον κεφαλὴ χάδε φωτός, as loud as a man's 'head holds,' as loud as human voice is capable of shouting, Λ 462; fig., also Δ 24, Θ 461.

χανδόν (χαίνω): lit., 'with open mouth,' *greedily*, φ 294†.

χάνοι: see χαίνω.

χαράδρη (χαράσσω): *gully, ravine, mountain torrent*, Δ 454 and Π 390.

χαρείη, χάρη: see χαίρω.

χαρίεις, εσσα, εν (χάρις), comp. **χαριέστερος**, sup. **χαριέστατος**: *full of grace, graceful, charming, winsome*; neut. pl. as subst., 'winning gifts,' θ 167.

χαρίζομαι (χάρις), aor. opt. χαρίσαιτο, inf. -ασθαι, pass. perf. part. κεχαρισμένος, plup. κεχάριστο: *show favor, gratify*, τινί, very often the part., Δ 71, κ 43; τινὶ ψευδέσι, 'court favor by lies,' ξ 387; w. acc., 'bestow graciously' or 'abundantly,' Λ 134; also with partitive gen., esp. παρεόντων, 'giving freely of her store,' α 140; perf. and plup. as pass., *be dear* or *pleasing*; κεχαρισμένος ἦλθεν, was *welcome*, β 54; κεχαρισμένα θεῖναι, like χαρίσασθαι, Ω 661.

χάρις, ιτος (χαίρω, cf. g r a t i a): *quality of pleasing, grace, charm, charms*, pl., ζ 237; then *favor, thanks, gratitude*; φέρειν τινι, 'confer,' E 211; ἀρέσθαι, 'earn'; δοῦναι, ἴδμεναι, 'thank,' 'be grateful,' Ξ 235.—Acc. as adv., **χάριν**, *for the sake of*, τινός, i. e. to please him, O 744.

Χάρις: the foregoing personified, as wife of Hephaestus, Σ 382.—Pl., **Χάριτες**, the *Graces*, handmaids of Aphrodīte, E 338, Ξ 267, P 51, ζ 18, σ 194.

χάρμα, ατος (χαίρω): concr., *a thing of joy*, Ξ 325; esp., γίγνεσθαί τινι, be a source of malignant joy,' Γ 51, Z 82.

χάρμη (cf. χαίρω): *joy of battle, desire for the fray, eagerness for combat.*

χαρ-οπός: *with glaring eyes*, λ 611†.

Χάροπος: king of Syme, father of Nireus, B 672†.

Χάροψ: son of Hippasus, brother of Socus, Λ 426†.

Χάρυβδις: *Charybdis*, the whirlpool opposite Scylla, μ 104, 113, 235, ψ 327.

χάσκω: see χαίνω.

χατέω (cf. χάσκω): *have need of, desire, beg, demand.*

χατίζω = χατέω.

χειή (χάσκω): *hole*, Χ 93 and 95.

χεῖλος, εος: *lip;* for phrases, see φύω, γελάω, prov., Χ 495; in general, *rim, border*, Μ 52; cf. δ 132, ο 116.

χεῖμα, ατος: *winter, cold.* (Od.)

χειμά-ρροος (σρέω), **χειμάρρους**, **χείμαρρος**: *flooded* with winter snow, *winter-flowing.*

χειμέριος (χεῖμα): *wintry;* ὕδωρ, 'snow-water,' Ψ 420.

χειμών, ῶνος: *storm, tempest, rain, rainy weather.*

χείρ, χειρός, besides the usual forms also dat. χερί, pl. dat. χείρεσσι and χείρεσι (Υ 468): *hand*, as flat hand or fist, μ 174; including the *arm*, Ζ 81, α 238; often the pl., esp. fig. as typical of strength, violence, etc., joined with μένος, βίη, δύναμις, Ζ 502, Μ 135, υ 237; χερσίν τε ποσίν τε καὶ σθένει, Υ 360; χεῖρα ἐπιφέρειν τινί, χεῖρας ἐφιέναι, ἰάλλειν, χερσὶν ἀρήγειν, χεῖρα ὑπερέχειν τινί, in defence, Δ 249; (εἰς) χεῖρας ἱκέσθαι, 'fall into the power,' Κ 448.

χειρίς, ῖδος: pl., probably loose or false *sleeves*, bound over the hands instead of gloves, ω 230†.

χειρότερος = χείρων, Υ 436 and Ο 513.

χείρων, ονος (comp. to χέρης): *inferior, worse.*

Χείρων: *Chiron*, the centaur, skilled in the arts of healing and prophecy, the instructor of Asclepius and Achilles, δικαιότατος Κενταύρων, Λ 832, Δ 219, Π 143, Τ 390.

χείσομαι: see χανδάνω.

χελῑδών, ονος: *swallow*, φ 411 and χ 240.

χέραδος, εος: *gravel, pebbles*, Φ 319†.

χέρειον: see χερείων.

χερειότερος = χερείων. (Il.)

χερείων, ον (χέρης): *inferior, worse;* τὰ χερείονα, 'the worse' part, Α 576; οὔ τι χέρειον, ''t is not ill,' ρ 176.

χέρης (χείρ, i. e. under one's hand), dat. χέρηι, acc. χέρηα, pl. χέρηες, neut. χέρεια: *low, humble, weak, mean, poor*, the positive to χείρων, χερείων, χειρότερος, χερειότερος. With gen. it has the force of a comp., Δ 400, ξ 176.

χερμάδιον: *stone*, of a size suitable to be thrown by hand.

χερνῆτις: *living by hand labor*, a woman who spins for daily hire, Μ 433†.

χέρ-νιβον (χείρ, νίπτω): *wash-basin*, Ω 304†.

χερ-νίπτομαι: only aor., χερνίψαντο, *washed their hands*, Α 449†.

χέρ-νιψ, ιβος: *water for washing the hands.* (Od.)

Χερσιδάμᾱς: a son of Priam, Λ 423†.

χέρσονδε: *to* or *on the dry land*, Φ 238†.

χέρσος: dry *land, shore.*

χεῦαι, χεῦαν, χεῦε: see χέω.

χεῦμα, ατος (χέω): that which is poured, *casting*, Ψ 561†.

χέω (χέϝω, root χυ), ipf. χέον, χέε(ν), aor. 1 (Att.) ἔχεεν, ἔχεαν, also ἔχευα, χεῦα, subj. χεύω, χεύομεν, mid. pres. inf. χεῖσθαι, ipf. χεόμην, aor. 1 (ἐ)χεύατο, aor. 2 ἔχυτο, part. χυμένη, pass. perf. 3 pl. κέχυνται, plup. κέχυτο, aor. opt. χυθείη: I. act., *pour, shed*, not of liquids only, but freq. of dry things, leaves strewn, let fall, earth heaped up, etc., χυτὴν ἐπὶ γαῖαν ἔχευαν, so τύμβον, σῆμα, α 291, Ψ 256; still more naturally said of mist, cloud, darkness, Ρ 270, Υ 321; then fig., ὕπνον, κάλλος, φωνήν, η 286, ψ 156, τ 521.—II. pass. and aor. 2 mid., *be poured, shed*, or *strewn, pour, flow*, with the same freedom of application as act., ἀήρ, χιών, κόπρος, ι 330; of persons pouring forth in numbers, pressing around one, Π 267, κ 415; ἀμφ' αὐτῷ χυμένη, i. e. embracing him, Τ 284; so once aor. 1, Η 63.—III. mid., aor. 1, but not aor. 2, *pour* for oneself, or in any way subjectively, κ 518; χεύατο κὰκ κεφαλῆς, on 'his' head, Σ 24; βέλεα χέοντο, 'their' missiles, Θ 159; ἀμφὶ υἱὸν ἐχεύατο πήχεε, 'threw her' arms about him, Ε 314.

χηλός (χαίνω): *chest, coffer.*

χἠμεῖς = καὶ ἡμεῖς, Β 238.

χήν, χηνός: *goose.*

χηραμός (χαίνω): *hole* or *crevice* in a rock, Φ 495†.

χήρατο: see χαίρω.

χηρεύω (χήρη): *be deprived of, without;* ἀνδρῶν, ι 124†.

χήρη: *bereaved, widowed;* w. gen., Ζ 408.

χηρόω (χῆρος, χήρη), aor. χήρωσας: *bereave, make desolate.* (Il.)

χηρωστής: pl., surviving *relatives, heirs* of one who dies childless, E 158†.

χῆτος, εος (χατέω): *lack.*

χθαμαλός (χαμαί), comp. -ώτερος, sup. -ώτατος: *low-lying, low.*

χθιζός (χθές): *of yesterday, yesterday*, usually as adv., A 424.—Neut. as adv., **χθιζόν, χθιζά.** *χθιζά τε καὶ πρώϊζα*, phrase meaning 'but a day or two since,' B 303.

χθών, χθονός: *earth, ground; land, region*, ν 352.

χίλιοι, χίλια: a *thousand.* (Il.)

χίμαιρα: *she-goat*, Z 181†.

Χίμαιρα: the *Chimaera*, a monster sent as a plague upon Lydia, but slain by Bellerophon, described Z 179–182. (The cut is from an Etruscan bronze figure of large size in the museum at Florence.)

128

Χίος: *Chios*, island on the Ionian coast of Asia Minor, γ 170, 172.

χιτών, ῶνος: *tunic.* The χιτών was like a shirt, but without sleeves, woollen, and white. It was worn by both men and women, next the body, and confined by a girdle, ξ 72. (See the cut, representing Achilles—clothed in the χίτών—taking leave of Peleus. Cf. also No. 55). There were also long tunics, see ἑλκεχίτων. Of soldiers, *coat-of-mail, cuirass*, B 416, Λ 100 (cf. cuts Nos. 12, 17, 79, 86). λάινος, 'tunic of stone,' fig., of death by stoning, Γ 57.

χιών, όνος: *snow.*

χλαῖνα: *cloak, mantle*, consisting of a piece of coarse, shaggy woollen cloth, worn double or single, διπλῆ, δίπλαξ, ἁπλοΐς, and freq. of a purple color, X 493, ξ 460, 478, 480, 488, 500, 504, 516, 520, 529. It also served as a blanket in sleeping, υ 4, 95, γ 349, δ 50.

χλούνης: doubtful word, epith. of

129

the wild-boar, according to the ancients, *making its bed in the grass* (ἐν χλόῃ εὐνὴν ἔχων), I 539†.

χλωρηΐς (χλωρός): *pale green, olive green*, epith. of the nightingale as dwelling in the fresh foliage, τ 518†.

Χλῶρις: *Chloris*, daughter of Amphīon, king in Orchomenus, the wife of Neleus, and mother of Nestor, Chromius, Periclymenus, and Pero, λ 281†.

χλωρός (χλόη): *greenish yellow* or *yellowish green*, as honey; δέος, *pale* fear, H 479, λ 43, O 4; then *fresh, verdant*, ι 379, 320.

χνόος (κνάω, κόνις): *foam; ἁλός*, ζ 226†.

χόανος (χέω): *melting-pit*, pl., Σ 470†.

χοή (χέω): *libation, drink-offering*, esp. in sacrifices for the dead, κ 518 and λ 26.

χοῖνιξ, ικος: *measure* (for grain) = a soldier's daily ration, about one quart; ἅπτεσθαι χοίνικός τινος, 'to eat of one's bread,' τ 28†.

χοίρεος: *of a pig, of swine; κρέα, pork*, ξ 81†.

χοῖρος: young *pig, porker*, ξ 73†.

χολάς, άδος: pl., *bowels, intestines*, Δ 526 and Φ 181.

χόλος (cf. fel): *gall*, Π 203; then, *wrath*, of animals, *rage*, X 94.

χολόω, fut. inf. χολωσέμεν, aor. ἐχόλωσα, mid. χολοῦμαι, χολώσομαι, κεχολώσομαι, aor. (ἐ)χολωσάμην, pass. perf. κεχόλωται, inf. -ῶσθαι, part. -ωμένος, plup. κεχόλωσο, -ωτο, 3 pl. **-ώατο,** aor. ἐχολώθην: act., *enrage, anger;* mid. and pass., *be wroth, angry, incensed,* θῡμῷ, **ἐνὶ** φρεσί, κηρόθι, φρένα, ἦτορ, and **τινί,** 'at' or 'with' one; w. causal gen., also **ἐκ, εἵνεκα,** etc., **I** 523, **N** 203, **P** 710.

χολωτός: *angry, wrathful.*

χορδή: *string* of gut, φ 407†.

χοροι-τυπίη (χορός, τύπτω): *choral dance,* pl., Ω 261†.

χορός: *dancing-place,* Σ 590, μ 318; then *dance,* Π 180.

χόρτος (cf. h o r t u s): *enclosure,* **Λ** 774 and **Ω** 640.

χραισμέω (χρήσιμος), aor. 2 ἔχραισμε, χραῖσμε, subj. χραίσμῃ(σι), -ωσι, inf. -εῖν, fut. χραισμήσω, inf. -σέμεν, aor. 1 χραίσμησε, inf. -ῆσαι: *be useful* to one in something (τινί τι), **H** 144; hence *avail, help, ward off* something, abs., and w. acc. (τί), **A** 566, 589. Always with negative.

χράομαι, part. χρεώμενος, perf. part. κεχρημένος, plup. κέχρητο: *have use* or *need of;* 'according to his need,' Ψ 834; **κεχρημένος,** 'desiring,' **T** 262; as adj., 'needy,' ρ 347; plup., φρεσὶ γὰρ κέχρητ' ἀγαθῇσιν, 'had,' γ 266.

χραύω, aor. subj. χραύσῃ: *scratch, graze,* wound slightly, **E** 138†.

1. χράω (χράϝω, cf. χραύω), ipf. (or aor. 2) ἔχραε, ἐχράετε: *fall foul of, assail, handle roughly,* **τινί,** ε 396, κ 64; w. acc., and inf. of purpose, **Φ** 369, φ 69.

2. χράω, χρείω, part. χρείων, mid. fut. part. χρησόμενος: act., *deliver an oracle,* θ 79; mid., *have an oracle delivered* to oneself, ***consult the oracle,*** θ 81, λ 165, κ 492.

χρεῖος: see χρέος.

χρείων: see χράω 2.

χρειώ: see χρεώ.

χρείως: v. l. for χρεῖος, see χρέος.

χρεμετίζω: *neigh, whinny,* **M** 51†.

χρέος, χρεῖος (χράομαι): (1) *want, need,* then *affair, business,* α 409, β 45; Τειρεσίαο κατὰ χρέος, for *want* of T., i. e. to consult him, λ 479.—(2) what one must pay, *debt,* ὀφείλειν **τινί, ὀφέλλεταί μοι, Λ** 688, 686.

χρεώ, χρεῷ, **Λ** 606, **χρειώ** (χρή): *want, need, necessity;* χρειοῖ ἀναγκαίῃ, **Θ** 57; **ἐστί, γίγνεται** (cf. o p u s e s t), w. gen. of thing and acc. of person, also freq. ἵκει, ἱκάνει, ἱκάνεται, ζ 136; χρέω without ἐστί or ἱκάνει, like **χρή,** τίπτε δέ σε χρεῷ; α 225.

χρεώμενος: see χράομαι.

χρή (act. of χράομαι): impers., *there is need,* w. acc. of person and gen. of thing, α 124; then, one *must, ought, should,* w. acc. and inf. (either or both), οὐδέ τί σε χρή, 'it behooves thee not,' τ 500, etc.

χρηΐζω (χράομαι): *need,* **τινός.**

χρῆμα, ατος (χράομαι): what one has use or need of, pl., ***possessions,*** *property.* (Od.)

χρίμπτω: only pass. aor. part., χριμφθείς, πέλας, *approaching* very near, κ 516†.

χρίω, ipf. χρῖον, aor. ἔχρῖσα, χρῖσε, mid. fut. χρίσομαι: *smear* with oil, *anoint;* mid., oneself, or something of one's own, ἰοὺς **φαρμάκῳ,** α 262.

χροιή (cf. χρώς): skin or surface of the *body,* Ξ 164†.

χρόμαδος: *grinding* sound, Ψ 688†.

Χρόμιος: *Chromius.*—(1) a son of Priam, **E** 160.—(2) a son of Neleus, λ 286, Δ 295.—(3) a Lycian, **E** 677.—(4) a Trojan, **Θ** 275.—(5) a chief of the Mysians, **P** 218, 494, 534.

Χρόμις = Χρόμιος (5), **B** 858.

χρόνιος: *after a long time,* ρ 112†.

χρόνος: *time.*

χροός, χροΐ, χρόα: see χρώς.

χρῡσ-άμπυξ, υκος: ***with frontlet of gold.*** (Il.)

χρῡσ-άορος (ἄορ): ***with sword of gold,*** epith. of Apollo, **E 509** and **O** 256.

χρῡ́σεος, χρῡ́σειος: *of gold, golden,* adorned with gold, δ 14 (see cut No. 2). Of color, ἔθειραι, **νέφεα, Θ** 42, **N** 523. The word is esp. applied to things worn or used by the gods. χρῡσέῃ, χρῡσέῳ, etc., pronounced with synizesis.

Χρῡ́ση: *Chryse,* a port in the Troad, with a temple of Apollo, **A 37, 100,** 390, 431, 451.

Χρῡσηΐς: *daughter of Chryses, Chryseïs,* **A 111,** 143, 182, 310, 369, 439. Her proper name was Astynome.

χρῡσ-ηλάκατος (ἠλακατή): ***with*** *golden arrow,* Artemis, δ 122.

χρῡσ-ήνιος (ἡνία): *with golden **reins*** or *bridle,* **Z** 205 and θ 285.

Χρύσης: *Chryses*, priest of Apollo at Chryse, A 11, 370, 442, 450.

Χρῡσόθεμις: *Chrysothemis*, daughter of Agamemnon and Clytaemnestra, I 145 and 287.

χρῡσό-θρονος: *golden-throned.*

χρῡσο-πέδῑλος: *golden-sandalled.*

χρῡσό-πτερος: *with wings of gold*, Θ 398 and Λ 185.

χρυσό-ρραπις: *with wand of gold*, Hermes.

χρῡσός: *gold;* collectively for utensils of gold, ο 207.

χρῡσο-χόος (*χέω*): *goldsmith*, γ 425†.

χρώς, *χρωτός* and *χροός*, dat. *χροΐ*, acc. *χρῶτα* and *χρόα*: properly surface, esp. of the body, *skin, body* with reference to the skin; then *color, complexion*, *τρέπεται*, 'changes,' of turning pale with fear, N 279, φ 412.

χυμένη, χύντο: see *χέω.*

χύσις (*χέω*): *pouring, heap.* (Od.)

χυτλόω, mid. aor. opt. *χυτλώσαιτο*: mid., *bathe and anoint oneself*, ζ 80†.

χυτός (*χέω*): *poured, heaped up.*

χωλεύω: *be lame, limp.* (Il.)

χωλός: *lame, halt.*

χώομαι (*χέω*), imp. *χώεο*, ipf. *χώετο*, aor. (ἐ)*χώσατο*, subj. *χώσεται*, part. *-άμενος*: *be agitated, troubled, angered;* *κῆρ*, (*κατὰ*) *θῡμόν*, *φρεσίν*, and w. dat. of the person, A 80, I 555; causal gen. of thing or person, A 429.

χωρέω (*χῶρος*), fut. *χωρήσουσι*, aor. (ἐ)*χώρησα*: properly, make space or room; *give place, make way, withdraw;* *τινί*, 'before' one, N 324; *τινός*, 'from' something, M 406.

χώρη: *space, place;* pl., *regions, countries*, θ 573.

χωρίς: *separately, apart, by oneself.*

χῶρος: a *space, place;* more concrete than *χώρη*. *Spot, region*, ξ 2.

Ψ.

ψάμαθος: *sand, sands;* to designate the strand, or the sand-hills of the shore, δ 426; as simile for a countless multitude, B 800.

ψάμμος: *sand*, μ 243†.

ψάρ, ψήρ, pl. gen. *ψαρῶν*, acc. *ψῆρας*: *starling*, or *meadow lark*, P 755 and Π 583.

ψαύω (*ψάϝω*), ipf. *ψαῦον*, aor. *ἔψαυσα*: *touch* lightly, *graze; τινος*, Ψ 519, 806.

ψεδνός (*ψάω*): rubbed off, *thin, sparse*, B 219†.

ψευδ-άγγελος: *reporting lies, false messenger*, O 159†.

ψευδής, *ές*: *false;* as subst., *liar*, Δ 235†.

ψεῦδος, *εος*: *falsehood, lie;* of fiction, τ 203.

ψεύδομαι, imp. *ψεύδεο*, fut. *ψεύσομαι*, aor. part. *ψευσάμενος*: *speak falsely, lie, deceive; ψεύσομαι ἦ ἔτυμον ἐρέω*, 'shall (do) I deceive myself, or?' K 534.

ψευστέω, fut. *ψευστήσεις*: *be a liar*, 'deceive oneself,' T 107†.

ψεύστης: *liar, deceiver*, pl., Ω 261†.

ψηλαφάω, part. *-φόων*: *feel about, grope*, ι 416†.

ψῆρας: see *ψάρ.*

ψηφίς, *ῖδος*: *pebble*, pl., Φ 260†.

ψιάς, *άδος*: *drop*, pl., Π 459†.

ψῑλός (*ψάω*): worn smooth and *bare; νῆα*, 'dismantled,' without sides, μ 421.

ψολόεις, *εσσα, εν* (*ψόλος*, 'smoke'): *smouldering, sulphurous*, ψ 330 and ω 539.

Ψυρίη: *Psyria*, a small island between Lesbos and Chios, γ 171†.

ψῡχή (*ψύχω*): properly, breath of life, *life, soul, spirit; τὸν ἔλιπε ψῡχή*, of one falling in a faint, E 696; of life itself, *ψῡχῆς ὄλεθρος*, X 325; *περὶ ψῡχῆς μάχεσθαι*, χ 245; of animals, ξ 426; *ψῡχὰς ὀλέσαντες*, N 763. Also of the disembodied spirits, souls of the departed in the nether world, *ψῡχὴ καὶ εἴδωλον*, Ψ 104, cf. ω 14; opp. to the body or the man himself, A 3.

For the supposed condition of the souls in Hades, see λ 153, 232 ff., 476.

ψῦχος, εος (ψύχω): *cold, coolness,* κ 555†.

ψῡχρός: *cold.*

ψύχω, aor. 1 ψύξᾱσα: *blow, breathe,* Υ 440†.

ψωμός (ψάω): *morsel, gobbet,* pl., ι 374†.

Ω.

ὦ: ***O,*** interjection used w. voc.; placed between adj. and subst., δ 206. With synizesis, ρ 375.

ὤ: *Oh!* interjection expressive of feeling, ὤ μοι, ὤ πόποι, etc.

Ὠγυγίη: *Ogygia,* a fabulous island, the residence of Calypso, α 85, ζ 172, η 244, 254, μ 448, ψ 333.

ὧδε (adv. from ὅδε): *so, thus, in this way,* referring either to what follows or to what precedes, Α 181, Η 34; correl. to ὡς, Γ 300, Ζ 477; like αὔτως, ὧδε θέεις ἀκίχητα διώκων, 'just as you do,' i. e. in vain, Ρ 75, Υ 12; *just, as you see,* α 182, β 28 (according to Aristarchus ὧδε never means *hither* in Homer); *to such a degree,* Μ 346.

ᾤδεε: see οἰδέω.

ὠδίνω: writhe with pain, *be in pain, travail,* Λ 269.

ὠδίς, ῖνος: pl., *pains of labor, travail,* Λ 271†.

ὠδύσαο, ὠδύσατο: see ὀδύσσομαι.

ὠθέω, ὠθεῖ, ipf. ὦθει, iter. ὤθεσκε, aor. ὦσα, ἔωσε (Π 410), iter. ὤσασκε, mid. aor. ὠσάμην: *thrust, push, shove;* mid., thrust oneself, i. e. 'press forward,' Π 592; *force, drive,* from or for oneself, Ε 691, Θ 295; w. gen., τείχεος, 'from' the wall, Μ 420.

ὠΐετο, ὠΐσθην: see ὀΐω.

ὦκ(α) (adv. from ὠκύς): *quickly.*

Ὠκαλέη: a village in Boeotia near Haliartus, Β 501†.

Ὠκεανός: *Oceanus,* distinguished from the sea (θάλασσα, πόντος, ἅλς) as a mighty *stream* (ποταμός, Σ 607, Υ 7; ῥόος Ὠκεανοῖο, Π 151; cf. Milton's 'ocean stream') encircling the whole Earth, Σ 607. The constellations (excepting the Great Bear, which in Greek latitudes does not dip below the horizon) are conceived as sinking below Oceanus and emerging from it on the other side of the Earth, as they set and rise. Beyond Ocean is the entrance to the nether world, and Elysium is on its hither bank, κ 508, δ 568. (In the cut, which represents a

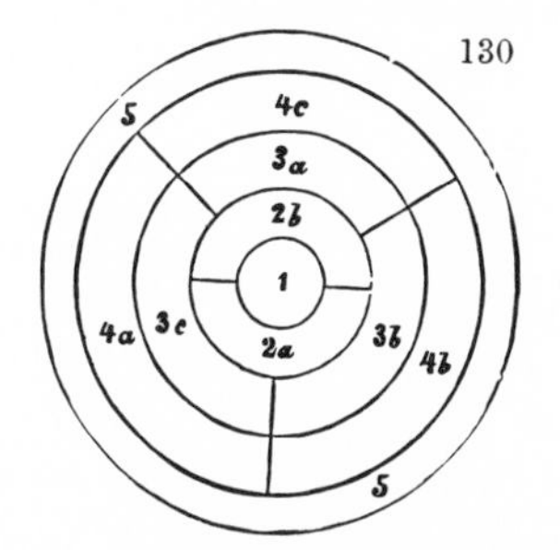

130

design of the shield of Achilles, the outer rim [5] indicates the stream of Ocean.) — Personified, **Ὠκεανός,** husband of Tethys, father of all streams and fountains, and, indeed, of all the gods, δ 568, κ 139, Ξ 311, 201.

ὤκιστος: see ὠκύς.

ᾤκτειρα: see οἰκτείρω.

ὠκύαλος: *swift-sailing.*

Ὠκύαλος: a Phaeacian, θ 111†.

ὠκύ-μορος, sup. -ρώτατος: *quickly-dying,* doomed to a speedy death, *swift-fated,* Σ 95, Α 417; ἰοί, *swift-slaying,* χ 75.

ὠκυ-πέτης (πέτομαι): *swift-flying,* Ν 24 and Θ 42.

ὠκύ-πορος: *swift-sailing, fast-going.*

ὠκύ-πος, ποδος: *swift-footed,* horses.

ὠκύ-πτερος (πτερόν): *swift-winged,* Ν 62†.

ὠκύ-ροος: *swift-flowing*, Ε 598 and Η 133.

ὠκύς, ὠκεῖα and ὠκέα, ὠκύ (cf. ocior), sup. **ὤκιστος, ὠκύτατος** (θ 331): *swift, fleet*, often πόδας ὠκύς, 'swift-footed.' Of things, βέλος, ὀιστός, ὄλεθρος, Χ 325. Predicatively as adv., μ 374, Ψ 880.—Sup. neut. pl. as adv., ὤκιστα, χ 77, 133.

Ὠλενίη πέτρη: *Olenian* rock, a peak of Mt. Scollis, on the borders of Elis, Β 617, Λ 757.

Ὤλενος: a town in Aetolia, on Mt. Aracynthus, Β 639†.

ὠλεσί-καρπος: *losing* their *fruit*, of the willow which drops its fruit before ripening, κ 510†.

(**ὦλξ**), acc. **ὦλκα** (Ϝέλκω): *furrow*, Ν 707 and σ 375.

ὠμ-ηστής (ὠμός, ἔδω): *eating raw flesh*, of animals; hence, *cruel, savage*, of men, Ω 207.

ὠμο-γέρων (ὠμός, cf. cruda senectus): *fresh, vigorous old man*, Ψ 791†.

ὠμο-θετέω, aor. ὠμοθέτησαν, mid. ipf. ὠμοθετεῖτο: *place* (as offering to the gods) *raw pieces* of flesh upon the μηρία wrapped in the caul, *consecrate flesh*, Α 461; mid., *have flesh consecrated*, ξ 427.

ὦμος: *shoulder*.

ὠμός: *raw, uncooked*, opp. ὀπταλέος, μ 396; prov., ὠμὸν βεβρώθειν τινά, 'eat alive,' of intense hate, Δ 35; ὠμά, adverbial, devour 'raw,' Ψ 21; fig., 'premature' old age, ο 357.

ὠμο-φάγος: *eating raw flesh*. (Il.)

ᾤμωξα: see οἰμώζω.

ὤνατο: see ὄνομαι.

ὠνήμην, ὤνησα: see ὀνίνημι.

ὠνητός (ὠνέομαι): *bought*, 'slave-mother,' ξ 202†.

ὦνος (Ϝῶνος, cf. venum): *purchase-money*; ἐπείγετε ὦνον ὁδαίων, 'hurry forward the delivery of the goods given in exchange for your freight,' i. e. the return freight, ο 445.

ὠνοσάμην: see ὄνομαι.

ᾠνοχόει: see οἰνοχοέω.

ᾦξε: see οἴγνῡμι.

ὤρεσσιν: see ὄαρ.

ὤρετο: see ὄρνῡμι.

ὥρη: *season*, esp. the spring, Β 468, ι 51; and in pl., *seasons* of the year, κ 469, β 107; Διὸς ὧραι, ω 394; then the fitting, right *time* (like καιρός), δόρποιο, ὕπνου, γάμου, ο 126; with inf., εὕδειν, λ 373; πρὶν ὥρη ('before 't is time'), ἐν ὥρῃ, εἰς ὥρᾱς, ι 135.—Personified, **Ὧραι**, the *Hours* (Horae), door-keepers of Olympus and goddesses of the seasons, Ε 749 ff., Θ 393, 433.

Ὠρείθυια: a Nereid, Σ 48†.

ὥριος (ὥρη): ὥρια πάντα, all things *in their season*, ι 131†.

ὥριστος = ὁ ἄριστος.

Ὠρίων: *Orīon*, the mighty hunter, beloved of Eos, ε 121. Slain by Artemis, he continues to follow the chase in the nether world, λ 572, 310, Σ 486. He appears even in Homer as a constellation, Σ 488, ε 274.

ὤρορε: see ὄρνῡμι.

Ὦρος: a Greek, slain by Hector, Λ 303†.

ὦρσε, ὦρτο, ὠρώρει: see ὄρνῡμι.

1. ὡς: prep. w. acc., only with personal obj., *to*; ὡς τὸν ὁμοῖον, ρ 218†.

2. ὡς (*γως*): I. adv., *as, how*; answering to τώς, ὥς (ὣς), οὕτω, τόσσον, ξ 44; 'so surely as,' Θ 541; often ὡς ὅτε, ὡς εἰ, and used with single words as well as with clauses. Exclamatory, *how!* π 364, ω 194.—II. conj., (1) temporal, *as, when*, always of a fact, with ind., Ψ 871.—(2) explanatory (like ὅτι), *that*, γ 346; and causal, *because* (= ὅτι οὕτως), Δ 157, β 233, ρ 243.—(3) final, *that, in order that.*—(4) idiomatically used in the expression of a wish, like utinam, Σ 107, Γ 428.

1. ὥς: by anastrophe for ὡς 2, when it follows its subst. In such cases the preceding short syllable is usually lengthened, ὄρνῑθες γώς (end of verse).

2. ὥς (ὣς after οὐδ' and καί): *thus, so, in this way*; often καὶ ὥς, 'even thus' (οὐδ' ὥς, 'not even thus'), i. e. *nevertheless* (*not*).

ὡσεί (ὡς εἰ): *as if, as though*, never separated by an intervening word, ι 314; w. part., Ε 374; also without a verb, *as, like*, η 36.

ὥσπερ (ὥς περ): *just as, even as*; often separated by an intervening word, ὡς ἔσεταί περ, Α 211.

ὥστε (ὥς τε): *as, just as*, with or without verb. Only twice used to express result as in Attic, *so that*, Ι 42, ρ 21.

ὠτειλή: *wound.*

Ὦτος: *Otus.*—(1) a giant, son of Poseidon and Iphimedīa, λ 308, Ε 385.—(2) of Cyllēne, a chief of the Epeians, Ο 518.

ὠτώεις, εσσα, εν (οὖς): *with ears* or *handles*, Ψ 264 and 513.

ὡὐτός: = ὁ αὐτός, Ε 396†.

ὤφελλον, ὤφελες: see ὀφείλω.

ὠχράω: only aor. part., ὠχρήσαντα, *having become pale*, λ 529.

ὦχρος: *paleness, pallor*, Γ 35†.

ὤψ: only acc., εἰς ὦπα, *in the face* ('in the eye'), full in the face, ἰδέσθαι, χ 405; *in face, in person*, ἔοικεν, Γ 158.

Ὦψ: *Ops*, son of Pisēnor, father of Euryclēa, α 429, β 347, υ 148.

PLATE I.

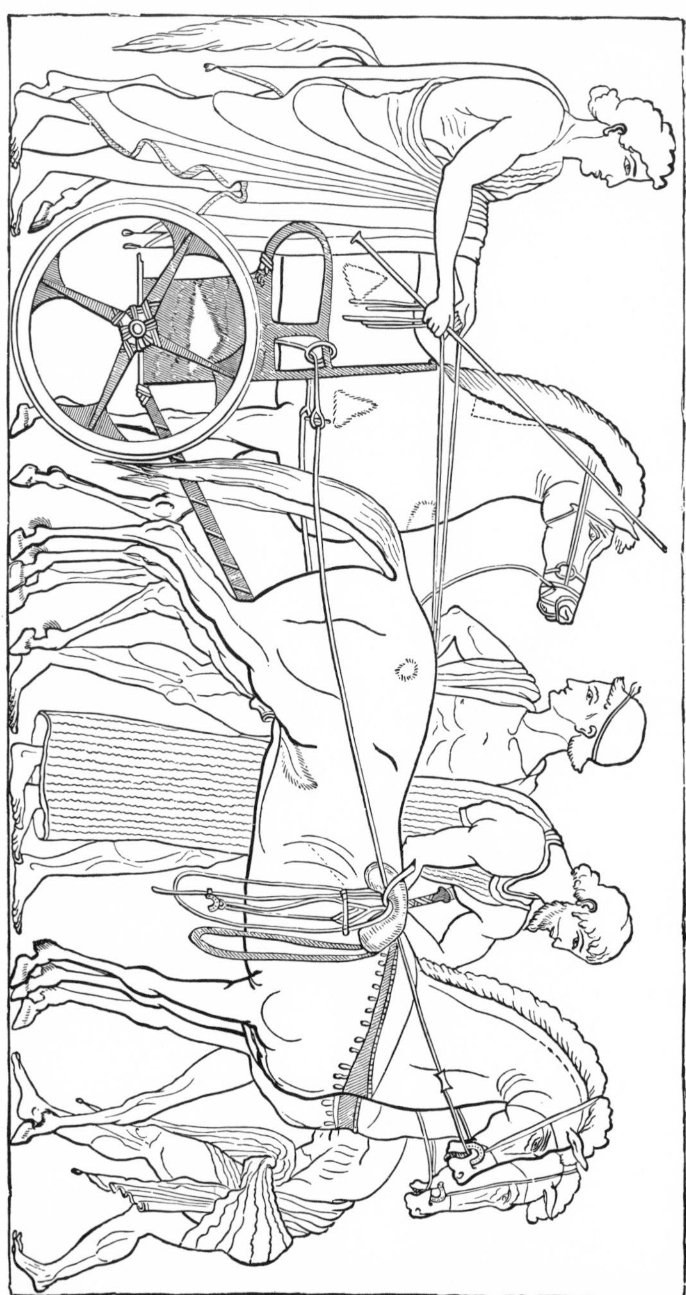

PLATE II.

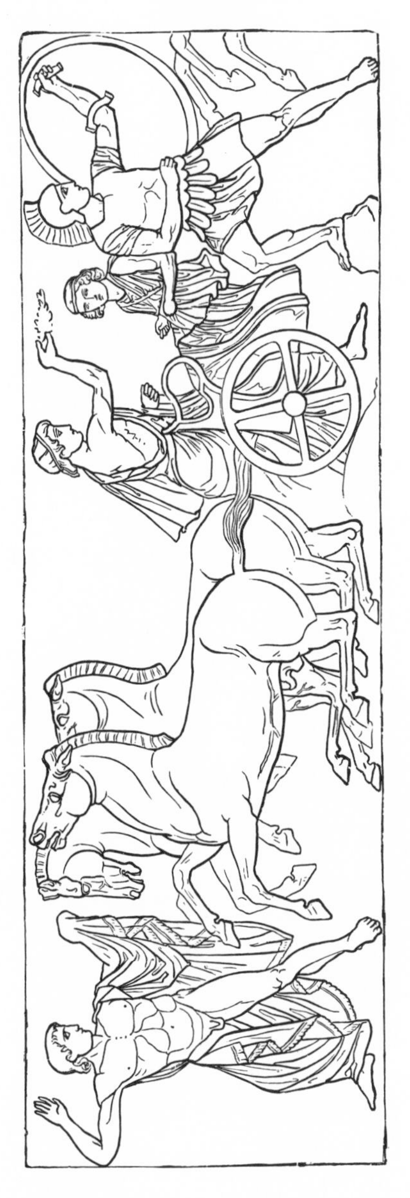

PLATE III.

House of Odysseus.

(After L. Gerlach.)

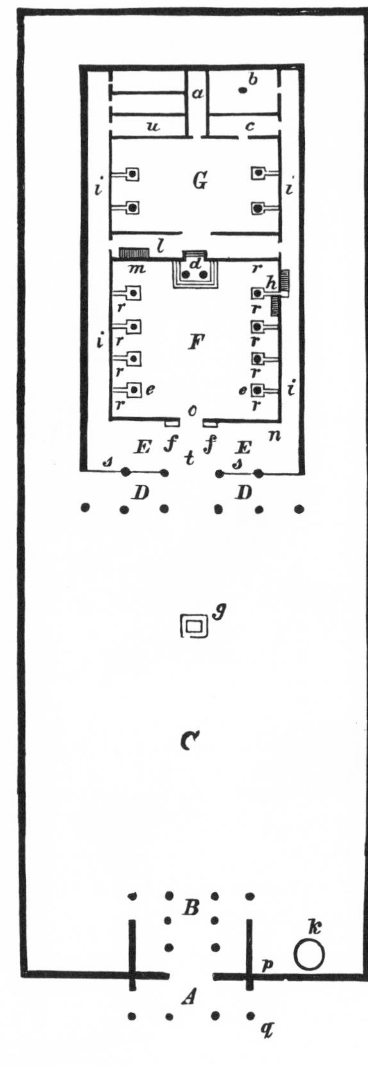

A πρόθυρον.

B αὐλῆς αἴθουσα, δ 678, π 342.

C αὐλή, δ 625.

D αἴθουσα.

E E πρόδομος, ο 5, υ 1.

F μέγαρον.

G Women's apartment; overhead the ὑπερώιον.

a Treasure-chamber.

b Chamber of Odysseus and Penelope.

c Chamber of Eurykleia, β 348.

d Seats of the king and queen.

e e Post of Odysseus as beggar.

f f ξεστοὶ λίθοι.

g Ζεὺς ἑρκεῖος.

h ὀρσοθύρη.

i λαύρη.

k θόλος.

l κλῖμαξ.

m ῥῶγες.

n στόμα λαύρης, } χ 137.

o αὐλῆς καλὰ θύρετρα, } χ 137.

p cf. χ 450 sq.

q ρ 297.

r καλαὶ μεσόδμαι, τ 37, υ 354.

s s Wicket barriers.

t πρόθυρον, σ 10, 33, 102.

u Sleeping-apartment of Odysseus, ψ 190.

PLATE IV.

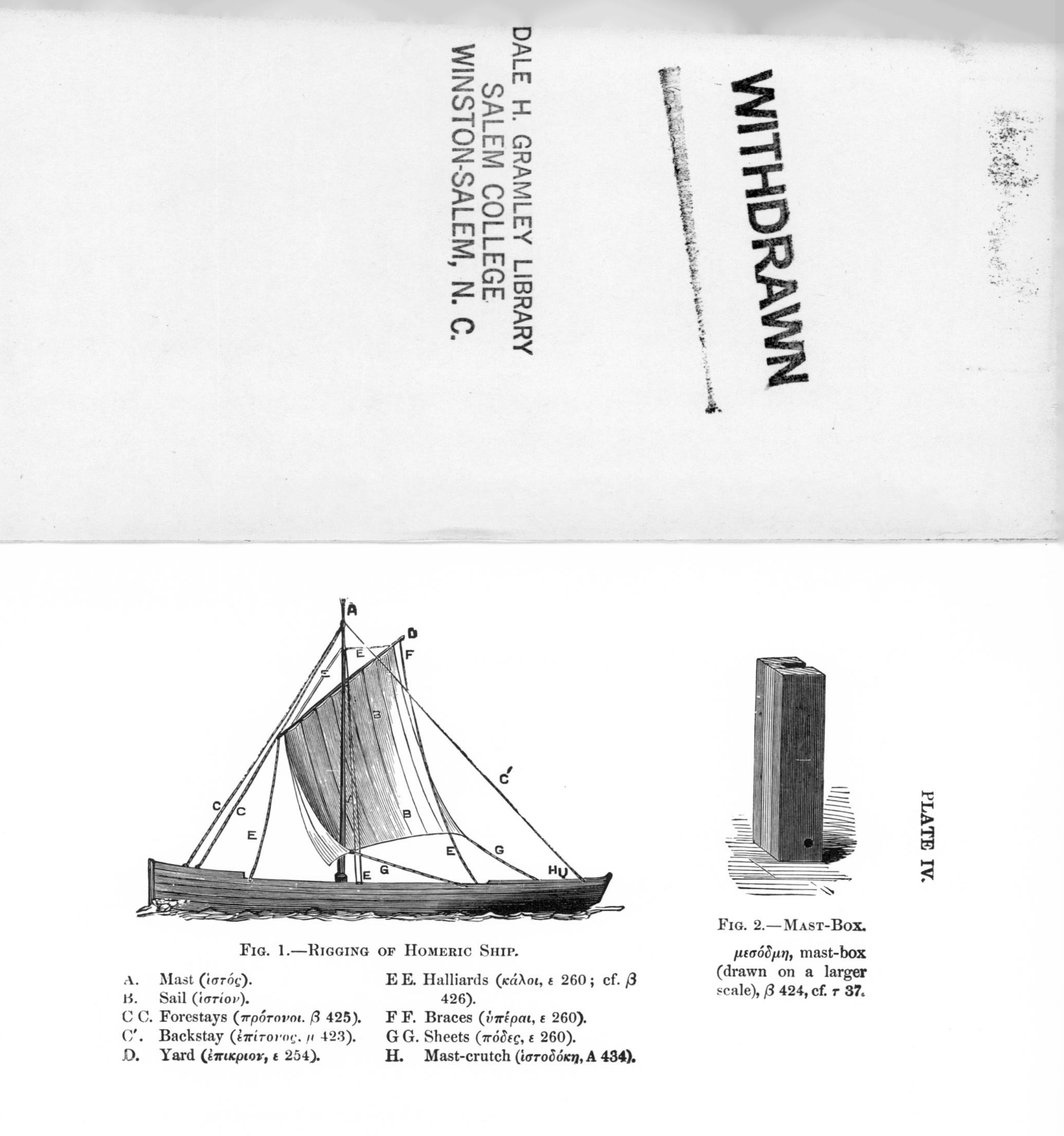

FIG. 1.—RIGGING OF HOMERIC SHIP.

A. Mast (ἱστός).
B. Sail (ἱστίον).
C C. Forestays (πρότονοι. β 425).
C′. Backstay (ἐπίτονος, μ 423).
D. Yard (ἐπικριον, ε 254).
E E. Halliards (κάλοι, ε 260; cf. β 426).
F F. Braces (ὑπέραι, ε 260).
G G. Sheets (πόδες, ε 260).
H. Mast-crutch (ἱστοδόκη, A 434).

FIG. 2.—MAST-BOX.

μεσόδμη, mast-box (drawn on a larger scale), β 424, cf. τ 37.

PLATE V.

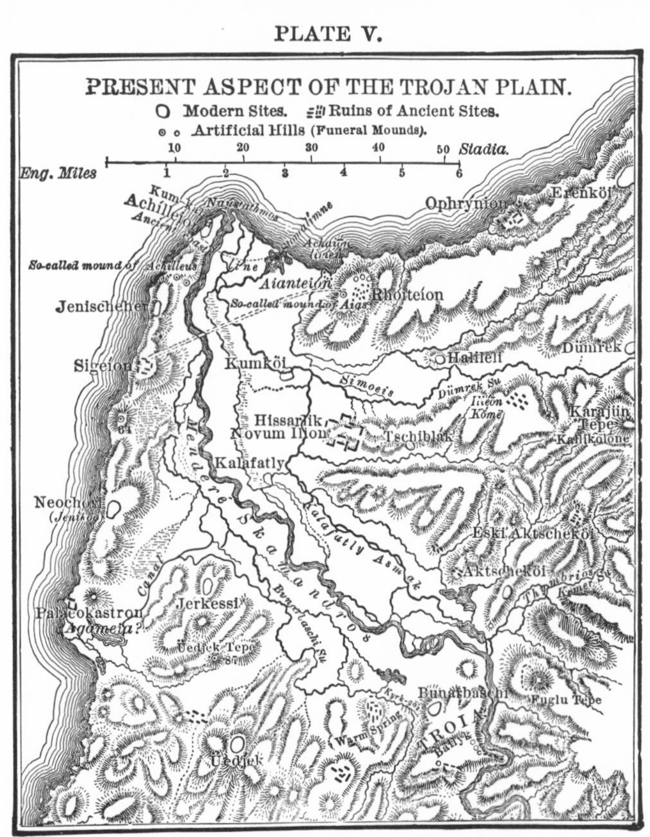

The prevalent opinion of antiquity located Homer's Troy on the hill *Hissarlik*, about three miles south of the Hellespont. The only important dissent from this view, among the ancients, was on the part of Demetrios of Skepsis, who was followed by Strabo, and who located Ilios at Ἰλιέων κώμη, some three miles east of Hissarlik, in the valley of the Simoeis.

Toward the close of the last century, the French traveller Le Chevalier visited the Troad, and boldly declared that he had identified the site of the ancient city on the height *Ballyk*, behind the village *Bunarbaschi*. Le Chevalier's view was announced with great positiveness, and has been generally received by modern scholars, e. g., Welcker, E. Curtius, Stark, Tozer, and the geographers Spratt, Kiepert, and Field-Marshal Von Moltke. In 1864 the Austrian Consul in Syra, Von Hahn, an eager partisan of Le Chevalier's theory, undertook excavations at *Ballyk*, which were prosecuted for several months, but without success.

The results of Schliemann's recent excavations at *Hissarlik* are familiar to all, and his discoveries go far to establish the fact that upon the hill *Hissarlik* the metropolis of the Trojan Plain, in prehistoric as well as in more recent times, must have stood. Among those who have advocated the claims of this site may be mentioned Gladstone, Grote, Eckenbrecker, Keller, Christ, Steitz, Büchner, and the writer of the article *Ilium* in Smith's Dictionary of Ancient Geography.